THIRD

— THE OLD —
TESTAMENT
MADE EASIER

PART FOUR
JEREMIAH 13 THROUGH MALACHI 4

THIRD EDITION

— The OLD —
Testament
MADE EASIER

PART FOUR
JEREMIAH 13 THROUGH MALACHI 4

David J. Ridges

CFI, AN IMPRINT OF

CEDAR FORT
Publishing & Media

SPRINGVILLE, UTAH

ISBN: 978-1-4621-4272-9

Published by CFI, an imprint of Cedar Fort, Inc.
2373 W. 700 S., Springville, UT 84663
Distributed by Cedar Fort, Inc., www.cedarfort.com

Library of Congress Control Number: 2021939516

Cover design by Shawnda T. Craig
Cover design © 2021 Cedar Fort, Inc.

Printed in the United States of America

10 9 8 7 6 5 4 3 2 1

Printed on acid-free paper

Dedication

To my wife, my eternal companion, Janette,
who has supported and helped me every step
of the way. We are just getting started, here
during mortality, on our eternal journey together.

Books by David J. Ridges

The Gospel Study Series

- *Your Study of The Book of Isaiah Made Easier, Second Edition*

- *The New Testament Made Easier, Second Edition, Part 1*

- *The New Testament Made Easier, Second Edition, Part 2*

- *Your Study of The Book of Mormon Made Easier, Part 1*

- *Your Study of The Book of Mormon Made Easier, Part 2*

- *Your Study of The Book of Mormon Made Easier, Part 3*

- *Book of Mormon Made Easier, Family Deluxe Edition, Volumes 1 and 2*

- *Your Study of The Doctrine and Covenants Made Easier, Second Edition, Part 1*

- *Your Study of The Doctrine and Covenants Made Easier, Second Edition, Part 2*

- *Your Study of The Doctrine and Covenants Made Easier, Second Edition, Part 3*

- *The Old Testament Made Easier, Third Edition, Part 1*

- *The Old Testament Made Easier—Selections from the Old Testament, Third Edition, Part 2*

- *The Old Testament Made Easier—Selections from the Old Testament, Third Edition, Part 3*

- *The Old Testament Made Easier—Selections from the Old Testament, Third Edition, Part 4*

- *Your Study of the Pearl of Great Price Made Easier*

- *Your Study of Jeremiah Made Easier*

- *Your Study of The Book of Revelation Made Easier, Second Edition*

Our Savior, Jesus Christ: His Life and Mission to Cleanse and Heal

Mormon Beliefs and Doctrines Made Easier

The Proclamation on the Family: The Word of the Lord on More than 30 Current Issues

Using the Signs of the Times to Strengthen Your Testimony

Doctrinal Details of the Plan of Salvation: From Premortality to Exaltation

CONTENTS

FOREWORD

The Old Testament is a most valuable book of scripture. It is the source of many favorite Bible stories many of us heard when we were growing up, such as Adam and Eve in the Garden of Eden, Noah and the Flood, David and Goliath, Ruth, Daniel in the lions' den, and many more. However, far beyond these precious stories that remain in our hearts, the Old Testament is a rich source of gospel doctrines and teachings of the plan of salvation. It teaches the Creation, the Fall, and the Atonement of Christ in many ways and with rich illustrations, including in the law of Moses and daily worship and ritual. It teaches the mercy and willingness to forgive over and over, of Jehovah, the premortal Jesus Christ. It teaches and illustrates time and again what kinds of thinking and actions we need to avoid if we desire to remain firmly on the covenant path. And it teaches how to repent and return to Christ, whose arms of mercy are extended all the day long (Isaiah 65:2), inviting us to repent.

This study guide is designed to help you enjoy learning from the Old Testament. It is designed to help beginners as well as seasoned experts in scripture study. The format is simple. I provide brief commentary within the verses, in brackets with italics, as well as between the verses in a different font. I define many, many scriptural words and phrases right within the verses so that you naturally learn the vocabulary of the scriptures as you go along. In effect, you learn a new language—the language of the scriptures. This will help as you read and study the other "standard works" (the other scriptures) used by the Church. I also use the books of Moses and Abraham and the JST (the Joseph Smith Translation of the Bible), inserting them where they belong.

THIRD EDITION

This third edition has been expanded to four volumes in order to include verse-by-verse study of many more Old Testament books than previous editions. It includes most of the scripture reading blocks referenced in "Come, Follow Me" for Old Testament.

By the way, I almost always use "we" rather than "I," even though I am the one commenting. The reason is simple. My parents taught me from a young age to avoid "I" trouble (talking about myself too much).

—David J. Ridges

THE USE OF THE JST
(JOSEPH SMITH TRANSLATION OF THE BIBLE)
IN STUDY GUIDES BY DAVID J. RIDGES

Be aware that some of the JST references I use in my study guides are not found in the footnotes or in the JST section at the back of our Latter-day Saint version of the King James Bible (the one we use in the English-speaking part of the Church). The reason for this, as explained to me some years ago while writing curriculum materials for the Church, is simply that there is not enough room, for practical purposes, to include all of the JST additions and changes. As you can imagine, as was likewise explained to me, there were difficult decisions that had to be made by the Scriptures Committee and Church leaders as to which JST contributions were included and which were not.

The Joseph Smith Translation of the Bible in its entirety can generally be found in Latter-day Saint bookstores or ordered through them. It was originally published under the auspices of the Reorganized Church of Jesus Christ of Latter Day Saints in Independence, Missouri. The version of the JST that I prefer to use is a parallel column version entitled Joseph Smith's "New Translation" of the Bible, published by Herald Publishing House, Independence, Missouri, in 1970. This parallel column version compares the King James Bible with the JST side by side and includes only the verses that have changes, additions, or deletions made by the Prophet Joseph Smith.

By the way, some members of the Church have wondered whether we can trust the JST since it was published by a breakaway faction from our Church who retained the original manuscripts after the martyrdom of the Prophet Joseph Smith. They worry that some changes to the Prophet's original manuscript might have been made to support doctrinal differences between the RLDS Church (the Reorganized Church of Jesus Christ of Latter Day Saints) and us. This is not the case. Many years ago, Robert J. Matthews of the Brigham Young University Religion Department was teaching a summer school class I attended. He told us that he was given permission by leaders of the RLDS Church to come to their Independence, Missouri, headquarters to see their publication of the JST. Brother Matthews was thus, through his own laborious and exacting study, able to verify that they had been meticulously true to the Prophet's original work.

JEREMIAH

JEREMIAH 13

Selection: all verses

Have you noticed by now that the same basic messages are being repeated over and over in these chapters of Jeremiah? One of the benefits of studying some chapters in considerable detail is that it prepares you to understand the basic messages in other chapters, even though you may not understand all the details.

One of my friends recently observed that although he did not understand everything he was listening to in Isaiah (on a portable recorder while walking), he discovered that he understood far more than he anticipated, just by paying attention to the main messages and words of the Lord and thinking how they might apply to him and the world today. This approach can be of great help to all of us as we study the writings of Old Testament prophets.

In this chapter, Israel and Judah are compared to a linen girdle or sash (verse 1) which is hidden or buried in a crevice of some rocks and later dug up (verse 7). Through this treatment, it becomes useless. We don't know if what the Lord commanded Jeremiah to do here, with respect to the linen sash, is literal, or if it is symbolic, a type of parable. Either way, the lesson is the same: Israel and Judah have become so marred by "hiding" from the Lord that they have basically become of no use as the covenant people.

1 THUS saith the LORD unto me [*Jeremiah*], **Go and get thee a linen girdle, and put it upon thy loins** [*put it around your waist*], and put it not in water.

2 **So I got a girdle** according to the word of the LORD, **and put *it* on my loins.**

3 And the word of the LORD came unto me the second time, saying,

4 **Take the girdle** that thou hast got, which *is* upon thy loins, **and arise, go to Euphrates, and hide it there in a hole of the rock.**

It may be that "Euphrates," in verse 4, above, symbolizes Babylon, since a river by that name flows through that country. If so, this could symbolize the Babylonian captivity of Judah, which is just around the corner at this time in the history of the Jews.

5 **So I went, and hid it by Euphrates,** as the LORD commanded me.

6 And it came to pass **after many days,** that **the LORD said** unto me, Arise, **go to Euphrates, and take the girdle from thence,** which I commanded thee to hide there.

7 Then **I went to Euphrates, and digged, and took the girdle from the place where I had hid it:** and, **behold, the girdle was marred, it**

was profitable for nothing [*it was ruined, good for nothing*].

8 Then the word of the LORD came unto me, saying,

The meaning of verses 1–7 is given in the next verses.

9 Thus saith the LORD, **After this manner will I mar the pride of Judah, and the great pride of Jerusalem**.

10 **This evil people**, which refuse to hear my words, which walk in the imagination of their heart [*pridefulness, stubbornness*], and walk after other gods, to serve them, and to worship them, **shall even be as this girdle, which is good for nothing**.

In verse 11, next, the Lord explains the symbolism. Just as a sash or girdle is wrapped around a man's waist, so also the house of Israel was invited to be the Lord's covenant people, and to "stick to Him" tightly, just as a girdle sticks tightly to the person wearing it. But when a girdle rots (see heading to this chapter in your Bible), it is of no use. Israel (the northern ten tribes in this context) and Judah (the tribes of Judah and Benjamin) could have been a glorious people, a credit to the Lord and to themselves, but they refused.

11 For **as the girdle cleaveth to the loins of a man, so have I caused to cleave unto me the whole house of Israel and the whole house of Judah**, saith the LORD; that they might be unto me for a people, and for a

name, and for a praise, and for a glory: **but they would not hear**.

Verses 12–14, next, basically say that these people will become drunk with wickedness, in other words, out of control with wickedness, and will be destroyed.

12 ¶ Therefore thou shalt speak unto them this word; Thus saith the LORD God of Israel, Every bottle [*symbolic of every person in Jerusalem and the other cities of Judah*] shall be filled with wine: and they shall say unto thee, Do we not certainly know that every bottle shall be filled with wine?

13 Then shalt thou say unto them, Thus saith the LORD, Behold, **I will fill all the inhabitants of this land, even the kings that sit upon David's throne, and the priests** [*false priests*]**, and the prophets** [*false prophets*]**, and all the inhabitants of Jerusalem, with drunkenness**.

14 **And I will dash them one against another**, even the fathers and the sons together, saith the LORD: I will not pity, nor spare, nor have mercy, but **destroy them**.

Next, the Lord issues yet another invitation to these people to repent, before it is too late and destruction comes upon them.

15 ¶ **Hear ye**, and give ear; **be not proud**: for the LORD hath spoken.

16 **Give glory to the LORD your God**, before he cause darkness, and before your feet stumble upon the

dark mountains, and, while ye look for light, he turn it into the shadow of death, *and* make *it* gross darkness.

17 **But if ye will not hear** it, **my soul shall weep** in secret places **for** *your* **pride**; and **mine eye shall weep sore, and run down with tears, because the LORD's flock is carried away captive.**

18 Say unto the king and to the queen, **Humble yourselves**, sit down: for your principalities shall come down, *even* the crown of your glory [*if you don't repent*].

19 The cities of the south shall be shut up, and none shall open *them:* **Judah shall be carried away captive all of it**, it shall be wholly carried away captive.

20 Lift up your eyes, and behold them [*the Babylonian armies*] that come from the north: where *is* the flock *that* was given thee, thy beautiful flock?

Verse 21, next, in effect asks the question "What will you have to say for yourselves, how will you explain your foolishness in ignoring the call from the Lord to repent, when all that is prophesied happens to you?"

21 **What wilt thou say when he shall punish thee?** for thou hast taught them *to be* captains, *and* as chief over thee: shall not sorrows take thee, as a woman in travail? [*In other words, unless you repent, the coming sorrows and destructions are as sure as the labor of a woman who is expecting a child.*]

22 ¶ And **if thou say in thine heart, Wherefore come these things upon me** [*why am I being punished*]? **For the** [*the answer is because of the*] **greatness of thine iniquity** are thy skirts discovered, *and* thy heels made bare [*you will be ravished and reduced to bondage*].

23 **Can the Ethiopian change his skin, or the leopard his spots?** *then* **may ye also do good, that are accustomed to do evil** [*in effect, if the impossible can happen, then people like you can do good who are completely caught up in wickedness*].

Next, we see another direct prophecy of the scattering of the Jews.

24 **Therefore** [*because of the above-mentioned wickedness*] **will I scatter them** as the stubble that passeth away by the wind of the wilderness.

25 **This** *is* **thy lot** [*this is what you have coming*], the portion of thy measures from me, saith the LORD; **because thou hast forgotten me, and trusted in falsehood.**

26 Therefore will **I discover thy skirts upon thy face** [*I will pull your skirts up over your face*], **that thy shame may appear** [*in effect, your protection, your false façade will be taken off and your sins will be exposed for all to see*].

Verse 27, next, contains a very brief summary of the sins of Judah, which will lead to Babylonian captivity. They are already spiritually in bondage to the devil.

27 I have seen thine **adulteries**, and thy **neighings** [*chasing after other men's wives—see Jeremiah 5:8*], the **lewdness** of thy **whoredom**, *and* thine **abominations on the hills** [*symbolic of idol worship*] in the fields. **Woe unto thee, O Jerusalem!** wilt thou not be made clean? **when** *shall it* once *be* [*when will the day finally come*]?

JEREMIAH 14

Selection: all verses

This chapter deals with a devastating drought that will come to the Jerusalem area. Verses 1–6 describe how serious the drought will be and the famine that will ensue.

1 THE word of the LORD that came to Jeremiah **concerning the dearth** [*famine*].

2 **Judah mourneth**, and the gates thereof languish [*are wasting away*]; they are black [*dejected, discouraged*] unto the ground; and the cry of Jerusalem is gone up [*their desperate cry is heard everywhere*].

3 And their nobles have sent their little ones to the waters: they came to the pits [*wells*], *and* **found no water**; they returned with their **vessels empty**; they were ashamed [*dismayed*] and confounded [*in deep despair*], and covered their heads.

4 Because **the ground is chapt** [*cracked, parched*], for there was **no rain** in the earth, the plowmen were ashamed [*dismayed, desperate to know what to do*], they covered their heads.

5 Yea, **the hind** [*deer*] also **calved** [*had its baby*] in the field, **and forsook** *it* [*deserted its newborn fawn*], because there was **no grass**.

6 And the wild asses did stand in the high places, they snuffed up the wind [*pant*] like dragons [*jackals; wild dogs*]; their eyes did fail, because *there was* **no grass**.

In the next several verses, Jeremiah prays for his people, but is told that the Lord cannot answer his prayers because of the wickedness of Judah. In verse 7, it appears that Jeremiah humbly includes himself with his people.

7 ¶ **O LORD, though our iniquities testify against us, do thou** *it* [*please turn Thy wrath aside*] **for thy name's sake** [*for the sake of Your reputation as a merciful God*]: **for our backslidings are many; we have sinned against thee.**

8 O the **hope of Israel** [*another name for the Savior*], the **saviour thereof in time of trouble**, why shouldest thou be as a stranger in the land [*must You be far from us in our time of need*], and as a wayfaring [*traveling*] man *that* turneth aside to tarry for a night?

9 **Why shouldest thou be** as a man astonied [*astonished, paralyzed with surprise, unable to act*], **as a mighty man** *that* **cannot save** [*why can't You show your power for us*]? yet thou, O LORD, *art* in the midst of us, and

we are called by thy name; **leave us not.**

Next, the Lord answers the questions raised above and explains why He cannot help them while they are wicked with no intent to repent.

10 ¶ Thus saith the LORD unto this people, **Thus have they loved to wander** [*in sin*]**, they have not refrained their feet** [*they have not stopped wandering in the paths of sin*]**, therefore the LORD doth not accept them;** he will now remember their iniquity, and visit [*punish*] their sins.

11 **Then said the LORD** unto me [*Jeremiah*]**, Pray not for this people** for *their* good.

12 When they fast, **I will not hear their cry;** and when they offer burnt offering and an oblation, **I will not accept them:** but **I will consume them** by the sword, and by the famine, and by the pestilence.

13 ¶ Then said I, Ah, Lord GOD! behold, **the prophets** [*the false prophets among the Jews*] **say unto them, Ye shall not see the sword, neither shall ye have famine;** but I will give you assured peace in this place [*in effect, the false prophets have told the people that sin is not really sin and that there can be peace in wickedness*].

Sometimes we think of false prophets, such as those in verse 13, above, as being various religious leaders gone astray. But we would do well to think of political leaders,

media idols, philosophers, teachers, in fact any who lead us away from the teachings of the gospel of Jesus Christ, as being false prophets also.

In verse 14, next, the Savior delivers a stern rebuke against such false prophets.

14 Then the LORD said unto me, **The prophets prophesy lies in my name** [*in other words, there are many who teach falsehoods in the name of God*]**: I sent them not,** neither have I commanded them, neither spake unto them: **they prophesy unto you a false vision** and divination, and a thing of nought, **and the deceit of their heart** [*they teach the wicked thoughts and intents of their own hearts as the word of God*].

15 **Therefore thus saith the LORD concerning the prophets that prophesy in my name, and I sent them not** [*in other words, concerning false prophets*]**,** yet they say, Sword and famine shall not be in this land; **By sword and famine shall those prophets be consumed.**

16 **And the people to whom they prophesy shall be cast out in the streets of Jerusalem because of the famine and the sword;** and they shall have none to bury them, them, their wives, nor their sons, nor their daughters: **for I will pour their wickedness upon them.**

In verses 17–18, we see that the Lord weeps when His people become wicked.

17 ¶ Therefore thou shalt say this word unto them; **Let mine eyes run down with tears night and day,** and let them not cease: **for the virgin daughter of my people** [*Jerusalem*] **is broken with a great breach** [*is conquered*], with a very grievous blow.

18 If I go forth into the field, then **behold the slain** with the sword! and if I enter into the city, then **behold them that are sick with famine!** yea, both the prophet and the priest [*false prophets and priests*] go about into a land that they know not [*will be taken captive into a foreign land*].

Next, Jeremiah asks heartrending questions. He has the ability to love the wicked even though he has been told that they will be destroyed because of their rejecting the Lord.

19 **Hast thou utterly rejected Judah?** hath thy soul lothed [*loathed*] Zion? why hast thou smitten us, and *there is* no healing for us? we looked for peace, and *there is* no good; and for the time of healing, and behold trouble!

20 **We acknowledge, O LORD, our wickedness,** *and* the iniquity of our fathers: for **we have sinned against thee.**

21 **Do not abhor** *us,* for thy name's sake, do not disgrace the throne of thy glory: remember, break not thy covenant with us.

22 **Are there** *any* **among the vanities** [*false gods*] **of the Gentiles that can cause rain?** or can the heavens give showers? *art* **not thou he, O LORD our God?** therefore we will wait upon thee: for thou hast made all these *things.*

JEREMIAH 15

Selection: all verses

This chapter gives more prophetic detail about the destruction and scattering of the Jews in Jeremiah's day. Because of their intentional rebellion, there is no stopping the coming famine and captivity.

First, in verse 1, the Lord tells Jeremiah that even if the great prophets Moses and Samuel asked Him to stop the coming destruction upon Judah, it would not happen. We are seeing the law of justice in action. One of the lessons we are taught here is that mercy cannot "rob justice" (see Alma 42:25).

Major Message

Mercy cannot rob justice

1 THEN said the LORD unto me, **Though Moses and Samuel stood before me,** *yet* **my mind** *could* **not** *be* **toward this people** [*in other words, He could not bless them*]: cast *them* out of my sight, and let them go forth [*they will be scattered*].

As mentioned several times already in this study guide, the "manner of speaking and prophesying among the Jews" is to repeat things many times for emphasis and to use words skillfully to paint pictures in our minds and create deep emotion in our hearts. We see this again in the next several verses.

2 And it shall come to pass, **if they say unto thee, Whither shall we go forth** [*if they ask you, "Where are we going"*]? then thou shalt **tell them**, Thus saith the LORD; Such as *are* for death, **to death**; and such as *are* for the sword, **to the sword**; and such as *are* for the famine, **to the famine**; and such as *are* for the captivity, **to the captivity**.

3 And I will appoint over them four kinds, saith the LORD: **the sword to slay**, and **the dogs to tear**, and **the fowls** [*carrion birds, such as vultures*] **of the heaven, and the beasts** of the earth, **to devour and destroy**.

4 And I will cause them to be **removed into all kingdoms of the earth** [*scattered to all nations of the earth*], because of Manasseh [*a very wicked king of Judah*] the son of Hezekiah king of Judah, for *that* which he did in Jerusalem.

5 For **who shall have pity upon thee, O Jerusalem?** or who shall bemoan thee? or who shall go aside to ask how thou doest?

6 **Thou hast forsaken me, saith the LORD**, thou art gone backward [*have gone away from the Lord*]: therefore will I stretch out my hand against thee, and destroy thee; **I am weary with repenting** [*since the Lord has no need to repent, this phrase is saying, in effect, I am tired of "relenting" and giving you chance after chance to repent; it doesn't do a bit of good*].

7 And **I will fan them with a fan** in the gates of the land [*I will scatter them, as a fan scatters chaff from wheat*]; I will bereave *them* of children [*they will lose their children*], **I will destroy my people, *since* they return not from their ways** [*since they refuse to repent*].

8 **Their widows are increased** to me above the sand of the seas [*there will be more widows than you can count*]: I have brought upon them against the mother of the young men **a spoiler at noonday** [*the enemy armies will be so powerful that they don't have to sneak up on you, rather, they can approach in broad daylight*]: I have caused *him* to fall upon it suddenly, and terrors upon the city.

9 She that hath borne seven languisheth [*grows weak*]: she hath given up the ghost [*has died*]; her sun is gone down while *it was* yet day [*all her hopes are suddenly dashed to pieces*]: she hath been ashamed and confounded [*confused and stopped*]: and the residue of them [*those who don't die of the famine*] will I deliver to the sword before their enemies, saith the LORD.

Next, Jeremiah laments the fact that he was born to be such a focal point of contention to the wicked. Even though he has lived righteously, everyone hates him.

10 ¶ **Woe is me**, my mother, that thou hast borne me **a man of strife and**

a man of contention to the whole earth! I have neither lent on usury, nor men have lent to me on usury [*in effect, I have faithfully kept the laws of God*]; *yet* **every one of them** [*the wicked*] **doth curse me.**

Verse 11, next, could have several fulfillments. It could refer to Jeremiah, or it could be a prophecy that many of the Jews who are captured and carried away will be treated such that they survive. It could also be a prophecy about the return of the Jews from Babylonian captivity, or all of the above.

If it refers to Jeremiah, then it can remind us of the words of the Lord to Joseph Smith when he was in Liberty Jail (D&C 121 and 122). He will eventually be delivered from his enemies. This can be literal on earth or literal in eternity.

If it refers to the Jews and their eventual return, then it prophesies that their captors will eventually take pity on them and allow them to return.

11 The LORD said, **Verily it shall be well with thy remnant**; verily I will cause the enemy to entreat thee *well* in the time of evil and in the time of affliction.

12 Shall iron break the northern iron and the steel?

The Martin Luther German Bible roughly translates verse 12, above, as saying, "Don't you know that such iron exists that can break iron and brass from the north?" Perhaps

this could mean, in effect, that the Lord has power over the strong "iron hand" of nations (including Babylon who came from the north) who hold the Jews captive, and He can cause their captors to treat them well and eventually let them go free.

Verse 13, next, seems to refer to the Jews and be yet another reminder as to why many of them are to be slaughtered and the remainder carried away into captivity at this point of their history.

13 Thy substance and thy treasures will I give to the spoil without price, and *that* **for all thy sins**, even in all thy borders [*the whole nation of Judah is riddled with wickedness*].

Verse 14, next, tells Jeremiah that he too will be carried away captive into a foreign country. He was eventually taken by a group of Jews to Egypt as they escaped the conquerors of Jerusalem, and then, according to tradition, stoned to death by them. (See Bible Dictionary under "Jeremiah." It appears that Jeremiah is being reminded that the righteous also suffer when the wicked rule and incur the wrath of God [*compare with D&C 98:9*].)

14 And **I will make** *thee* **to pass with thine enemies into a land** *which* **thou knowest not**: for a fire is kindled in mine anger, *which* shall burn upon you.

Verse 15, next, reminds us of the words of the Prophet Joseph Smith in Liberty Jail, as he pled with the Lord. He said:

D&C 121:5

5 Let thine anger be kindled against our enemies; and, in the fury of thine heart, with thy sword **avenge us of our wrongs**.

15 ¶ O LORD, thou knowest: remember me, and visit [*bless*] me, and **revenge me of my persecutors**; take me not away in thy longsuffering: know that for thy sake I have suffered rebuke.

16 **Thy words were found** [*were given to me*], **and I did eat them** [*internalized them, made them a part of me*]; and **thy word was unto me the joy and rejoicing of mine heart**: for I am called by thy name, O LORD God of hosts.

17 **I sat not in the assembly of the mockers, nor rejoiced** [*I did not join in wickedness and take pleasure in it with the wicked*]; **I sat alone** because of thy hand: for thou hast filled me with indignation [*against sin and wickedness*].

18 **Why is my pain perpetual, and my wound incurable**, *which* refuseth to be healed? wilt thou be altogether unto me as a liar, *and as* waters *that* fail [*perhaps meaning, in effect, "Are You not going to keep Your word? Why aren't Your promises of peace and protection and help fulfilled?"*]? [*Perhaps similar to Joseph Smith's pleading—see Doctrine and Covenants 121:1–6.*]

The Lord responds to Jeremiah's pleading.

19 ¶ Therefore thus saith the LORD, If thou return, then will I bring thee again, *and* **thou shalt stand before me**: and if thou take forth the precious from the vile, **thou shalt be as my mouth**: let them return unto thee; but return not thou unto them [*perhaps meaning for Jeremiah to stand firm, and if the people want the word of the Lord, let them come to him*].

The Lord's word to Jeremiah, in verses 20–21, next, seems to be that of being saved spiritually rather than physically. Spiritual salvation is the only thing that counts in the perspective of eternity.

20 And I will make thee unto this people a fenced brasen wall [*a fortified wall of brass or bronze*]: and **they shall fight against thee, but they shall not prevail against thee**: for I *am* with thee to save thee and to deliver thee, saith the LORD.

21 And **I will deliver thee out of the hand of the wicked, and I will redeem thee out of the hand of the terrible**.

JEREMIAH 16

Selection: all verses

This chapter contains a prophecy that is quite often referred to in our lessons and talks on missionary work in the last days. It is verse 16. We will say more about it when we get there.

Verse 2, if taken literally, would mean that Jeremiah was told not to marry. As we proceed, we will take the viewpoint that this was symbolic, rather than literal. One possible message is that Jerusalem has become so polluted with wickedness that it is no longer a safe place to attempt to raise children. Another possible message is that the coming enemy armies from Babylon will show no mercy to the inhabitants, including children.

1 THE word of the LORD came also unto me, saying,

2 **Thou shalt not take thee a wife, neither shalt thou have sons or daughters in this place.**

We will quote from the *Old Testament Student Manual* for help with verse 2, above (**bold** added for emphasis):

"Jeremiah's day was a sad one for Judah. To symbolize that truth, the Lord told his prophet three things that he was not to do:

"1. He was not to marry or father children (see Jeremiah 16:2). So universal was the calamity bearing down upon the people that God did not want children to suffer its outrage. **This commandment,** however, like the one to Hosea (see Hosea 10), who was commanded to take a wife of whoredoms, **was probably not a literal one; rather, it probably was allegorical, that is, Jeremiah was not to expect that his people would marry themselves to the covenant again, nor was he to expect to get spiritual children (converts) from his ministry.**

"2. He was not to lament those in Judah who died by the sword or famine (see Jeremiah 16:5), since they brought these judgments upon themselves.

"3. He was not to feast or eat with friends in Jerusalem (see verse 8), since feasting was a sign of celebration and eating together a symbol of fellowship.

"In addition, Jeremiah was commanded to explain very clearly to the people the reasons for his actions as well as the reasons for their coming punishment" (Old Testament Student Manual, page 241).

3 For thus saith the LORD **concerning the sons and concerning the daughters that are born in this place,** and concerning their mothers that bare them, and concerning their fathers that begat them in this land;

4 **They shall die of grievous deaths;** they shall not be lamented; **neither shall they be buried;** *but* they shall be as dung upon the face of the earth: and they shall be **consumed by the sword,** and by **famine;** and their carcases shall be **meat for the fowls of heaven, and for the beasts of the earth.**

Verse 5, next, is another reminder that if people do not repent, the law of mercy cannot take over from the law of justice.

5 For thus saith the LORD, Enter not into the house of mourning, neither go to lament nor bemoan them: for **I have taken away my peace from this people, saith the LORD,** *even* **lovingkindness and mercies.**

6 Both **the great** [*the famous and prominent in their society*] **and the small shall die in this land:** they

shall **not be buried** [*implying a terrible slaughter*], neither shall *men* lament for them, **nor cut themselves, nor make themselves bald for them** [*signs of deep mourning and grief in their culture*]:

Verses 6 and 7, here, seem to indicate that everyone will be in such distress because of their own circumstances that they will not take time nor have inclination to mourn for others being ravished by the famines and conquering enemy armies.

7 Neither shall *men* tear *themselves* for them in mourning, to comfort them for the dead [*no one will comfort those who mourn*]; neither shall *men* give them the cup of consolation to drink for their father or for their mother.

8 Thou shalt not also go into the house of feasting, to sit with them to eat and to drink.

In verse 9, next, Jeremiah is told that these terrible devastations will come upon the Jews in his lifetime.

9 For thus saith the LORD of hosts, the God of Israel; Behold, I will cause to cease out of this place in your eyes, and **in your days**, the voice of mirth, and the voice of gladness, the voice of the bridegroom, and the voice of the bride.

Verse 10, next, warns Jeremiah that the wicked people against whom he preaches will act as if they are righteous and do not deserve such warnings and condemnation.

10 ¶ And it shall come to pass, when thou shalt shew this people all these words, and they shall say unto thee, **Wherefore** [*why*] **hath the LORD pronounced all this great evil against us?** or **what** *is* **our iniquity** [*what have we done wrong*]? or what *is* our sin that we have committed against the LORD our God?

11 **Then shalt thou say** unto them, **Because your fathers** [*parents; ancestors*] **have forsaken me**, saith the LORD, and have walked after other gods, and have served them, and have worshipped them, and have forsaken me, **and have not kept my law**;

12 **And ye have done worse than your fathers**; for, behold, ye walk every one after the imagination of his evil heart, that they may not hearken unto me:

13 **Therefore will I cast you out of this land** into a land that ye know not, *neither* ye nor your fathers; and there shall ye serve other gods day and night; where I will not shew you favour [*I will not be able to bless you with the choicest gospel blessings*].

Next, we see a major prophecy concerning the gathering of Israel in the last days. The prophecy includes the fact that the deliverance of the children of Israel from Egypt, by the Lord, will no longer be the most spectacular event spoken of among the people. Rather, the gathering of Israel from all nations will become the focus of effort and conversation.

Major Prophecy

The Lord will gather scattered Israel in the last days.

14 ¶ Therefore, behold, **the days come, saith the LORD, that it shall no more be said, The LORD liveth, that brought up the children of Israel out of the land of Egypt;**

15 **But, The LORD liveth, that brought up the children of Israel** from the land of the north, and **from all the lands whither he had driven them**: and I will bring them again into their land that I gave unto their fathers.

Notice the order of the missionary work in the last days, as given in verse 16, next. First, large numbers of converts will come into the Church, in various nations. This is represented by "fishers" who fish with nets and catch large numbers with them. These mass conversions are followed by missionaries who are depicted as "hunters" who search the once-fertile mission field for anyone else who will join the Church.

16 ¶ Behold, **I will send for many fishers**, saith the LORD, and **they shall fish them**; and **after will I send for many hunters**, and they shall hunt them [*converts*] **from every mountain**, and from every **hill**, and out of the **holes of the rocks**.

One example of "fishers," in verse 16, above, might be Wilford Woodruff and other early missionaries who baptized thousands of converts in England in the early days of the Church. Another example could be the missionary work in South America in our day, where tens of thousands of converts are being baptized. Yet other examples might be found in any one of several countries or areas, including Africa, where initial missionary efforts have resulted in abundant baptisms in our day.

Now, though, in some areas of the world, convert baptisms are very few in number. The missionaries serving in such areas might be considered to be the "hunters," prophesied of by Jeremiah, who search everywhere for just a few who are willing to be taught the gospel.

Next, the topic turns to the fact that the Lord sees all, including the supposedly "secret" doings of the wicked.

17 For **mine eyes** *are* **upon all their ways: they are not hid from my face**, neither is their iniquity hid from mine eyes.

18 **And first** [*before the great latter-day gathering*] **I will recompense** [*punish*] **their iniquity** and their sin double; because they have defiled my land [*polluted it with wickedness*], they have filled mine inheritance with the carcases of their detestable and abominable things [*such as idol worship*].

Next, in verse 19, we see a prophecy that Gentiles from all nations will join the Church also in the last days.

19 O LORD, my strength, and my fortress, and my refuge in the day of affliction, **the Gentiles shall come unto thee from the ends of the earth**, and **shall say, Surely our fathers have inherited lies, vanity, and** *things* **wherein** *there is* **no profit** [*these converts will discard the false traditions and beliefs of their parents and ancestors in order to join the Church*].

Verse 20, next, is yet another reminder that it is completely ridiculous to make idols with one's own hands, and then worship them.

20 **Shall a man make gods unto himself, and they** *are* **no gods?**

The Lord says, in verse 21, next, that through the coming punishments, the wicked will know once and for all that there is just one true God.

21 Therefore, behold, **I will this once cause them to know**, I will cause them to know mine hand and my might; and they shall know **that my name** *is* **The LORD** [*that I am the only true God, in other words, that their idols are not gods*].

JEREMIAH 17

Selection: all verses

This chapter continues emphasizing the sins that will lead to the destruction of Jerusalem and the cities of Judah as a nation in Jeremiah's day. Among other things, we are shown comparison and contrast between the lives of the wicked and the righteous.

First, in verse 1, we are told that they are hardened sinners, and that the deepest desire of their hearts is to be wicked.

1 **THE sin of Judah** *is* **written with a pen of iron,** *and* **with the point of a diamond** [*the fact that they are deeply wicked is irrefutable*]: *it is* **graven upon the table of their heart** [*the innermost desire of their heart is to be wicked*], and **upon the horns of your altars** [*their religions are dedicated to wickedness, rather than protection and blessings from the Lord*];

The "horns of the altar," mentioned in verse 1, above, served as a place of protection and refuge for anyone who was being pursued by another. If they could get to the altar, and grab hold of one of the horns built on the four corners of it, they were safe from their enemy (see 1 Kings 1:50).

2 Whilst their children remember their altars and their groves by the green trees upon the high hills [*the children have been led astray by their idol-worshiping parents*].

Verse 3, next, says, in effect, that everything the people of Judah treasure in their wicked hearts will be given to their enemies.

3 O my mountain in the field, **I will give thy substance** *and* **all thy treasures to the spoil** [*to your enemies*], *and* thy high places for sin, throughout all thy borders.

4 And **thou,** even thyself, **shalt discontinue from thine heritage that I gave thee** [*you will be taken from the Holy Land*]; and **I will cause thee to serve thine enemies in the land which thou knowest not:** for ye have kindled a fire in mine anger, *which* shall burn for ever.

5 ¶ Thus saith the LORD; **Cursed** *be* **the man that trusteth in man, and maketh flesh his arm, and whose heart departeth from the LORD.**

6 For **he shall be like the heath** [*juniper tree—see footnote 6a in your Bible*] **in the desert,** and shall not see when good cometh; but **shall inhabit the parched places in the wilderness,** *in* a salt land and not inhabited.

The "wilderness," spoken of in verse 6, above, is obviously literal, representing their trials in the land of Babylon. But it can also be symbolic of their apostasy, living in a "spiritual wilderness" without the gospel of Jesus Christ.

Verses 7–8, next, are a beautiful representation of the blessings of living the true gospel, in contrast to the devastations of apostasy depicted above.

7 **Blessed** *is* **the man that trusteth in the LORD, and whose hope the LORD is.**

8 **For he shall be as a tree planted by the waters, and** *that* **spreadeth out her roots by the river, and shall not see when heat cometh, but her leaf shall be green; and**

shall not be careful in the year of drought, neither shall cease from yielding fruit.

Verse 9, next, is a reminder of how devastating a heart that is filled with wicked desires can be. A question is asked and an answer is given.

Question

9 ¶ The heart *is* deceitful above all *things,* and desperately wicked: **who can know it** [*who can tell what is in it*]?

Answer

10 I the LORD search the heart, *I* try the reins [*the innermost thoughts and feelings*], even to give every man according to his ways, *and* according to the fruit of his doings.

11 As the partridge sitteth *on eggs,* and hatcheth *them* not; *so* he that getteth riches, and not by right [*dishonestly*], shall leave them in the midst of his days, and at his end shall be a fool.

Next, Jeremiah praises the Lord.

12 ¶ **A glorious high throne from the beginning** *is* **the place of our sanctuary** [*the Lord is above all and is the only safe refuge*].

13 O LORD, the hope of Israel, **all that forsake thee shall be ashamed** [*will come up empty; will be disappointed, put to shame*], *and* they that depart from me shall be written in the earth, **because they have forsaken the LORD, the fountain of living waters.**

14 Heal me, O LORD, and I shall be healed; save me, and I shall be saved: for thou *art* my praise.

In verses 15–18, next, Jeremiah stands firm and faithful before the Lord, and prays for protection from his enemies.

15 ¶ Behold, **they** [*Jeremiah's enemies*] **say unto me, Where** *is* **the word of the LORD** [*where are all the destructions you have prophesied*]? **let it come now.**

16 As for me, **I have not hastened from** *being* **a pastor** to follow thee [*I have been faithful to my calling*]: neither have I desired the woeful day [*the coming destruction*]; **thou knowest: that which came out of my lips was** *right* **before thee.**

17 **Be not a terror unto me: thou** *art* **my hope in the day of evil.**

18 **Let them be confounded that persecute me, but let not me be confounded:** let them be dismayed, but let not me be dismayed: bring upon them the day of evil, and destroy them with double destruction.

Next, in verses 19–22, we are reminded of the importance of keeping the Sabbath holy.

Major Message

Keep the Sabbath Day holy.

19 ¶ Thus said the LORD unto me; **Go and stand in the gate** [*entrance*] of the children of the people, whereby the kings of Judah come in, and by the which they go out, and in **all the gates of Jerusalem** [*in other words, chose locations where everyone can hear your message*];

20 And say unto them, **Hear ye the word of the LORD**, ye kings of Judah, and all Judah, and **all the inhabitants of Jerusalem**, that enter in by these gates:

21 Thus saith the LORD; Take heed to yourselves, and **bear no burden on the sabbath day**, nor bring *it* in by the gates of Jerusalem;

22 Neither carry forth a burden out of your houses on the sabbath day, **neither do ye any work, but hallow ye the sabbath day**, as I commanded your fathers.

The reaction of the people to Jeremiah's message about the Sabbath is given in verse 23, next.

23 **But they obeyed not**, neither inclined their ear [*wouldn't listen*], but made their neck stiff [*they were full of pride, not humble enough to be taught*], that they might not hear, nor receive instruction.

Verses 24–26 explain the great blessings which could have come to these people, had they listened and repented.

24 And it shall come to pass, **if ye diligently hearken unto me, saith the LORD**, to bring in no burden through the gates of this city on the sabbath day, but **hallow the sabbath day, to do no work therein**;

25 Then shall there enter into the gates of this city kings and princes sitting upon the throne of David, riding in chariots and on horses, they, and their princes, the men of Judah, and the inhabitants of Jerusalem: and **this city shall remain for ever** [*in other words, great prosperity, protection and peace will be yours*].

26 **And they shall come** from the cities of Judah, and from the places about Jerusalem, and from the land of Benjamin, and from the plain, and from the mountains, and from the south, **bringing burnt offerings, and sacrifices, and meat offerings, and incense, and bringing sacrifices of praise, unto the house of the LORD.**

27 **But if ye will not hearken unto me to hallow the sabbath day,** and not to bear a burden, even entering in at the gates of Jerusalem on the sabbath day; **then will I kindle a fire in the gates thereof, and it shall devour the palaces of Jerusalem, and it shall not be quenched.**

Did you see the message in the above verses about the importance of keeping the Sabbath day holy? Among other things, when individuals and nations keep the Sabbath holy, it serves to remind them of God and the importance of keeping His commandments in their daily living. When people forget the Sabbath, they tend to forget God.

JEREMIAH 18

Selection: all verses

A problem comes up in this chapter where the King James version (the Bible we use for English-speaking areas of the Church) has the Lord repenting in verses 8 and 10. The Lord does not repent since He does not sin. As you will see, when you come to these two verses, the JST makes corrections in both instances.

This chapter starts out by using the symbolism of a potter creating a pot from clay on a potter's wheel. While the clay is pliable, he can form it according to his plans. He can even start over with the clay, if necessary. This symbolizes what the Lord (the Potter) desires to do with His people (the clay). He desires to mold and shape them to become His people.

Jeremiah is told to go to the potter's house in his neighborhood where this message and lesson from the Lord can be demonstrated.

1 **THE word which came to Jeremiah from the LORD,** saying,

2 Arise, and **go down to the potter's house, and there I will cause thee to hear my words.**

3 Then I went down to the potter's house, and, behold, he wrought a work on the wheels [*the potter was making a clay pot on a potter's wheel*].

4 And **the vessel that he made of clay was marred** [*damaged; was not shaping according to plan*] in the hand of the potter: **so he made it again** another vessel [*so he started over*

with it and made another pot with it], as seemed good to the potter to make *it.*

Next, the Lord explains the symbolism of the potter throwing (making) a pot.

5 **Then the word of the LORD came to me**, saying,

6 O house of Israel [*the twelve tribes of Israel; the Lord's covenant people*], cannot I do with you as this potter? saith the LORD. Behold, **as the clay** *is* **in the potter's hand, so** *are* **ye in mine hand**, O house of Israel.

Next, the Lord explains that He, as the Potter, will do whatever it takes to shape and form His covenant people, even if it means destroying them in order to start over with them. If they will then use their agency to repent (see verse 8), He will be enabled to form them into a covenant people, in other words, a people whom He can bless with exaltation.

7 *At what* instant [*NIV: "if at any time"*] **I shall speak concerning a nation**, and concerning a kingdom, to pluck up, and to pull down, and **to destroy** *it* [*like a potter as he starts over with a failed pot by kneading it back into lump of clay*]*;*

As mentioned in the background to this chapter, the idea that the Lord "repents" on occasions is not correct. We will first read verse 8, next, and will then use the JST to correct the translation.

(By the way, someone asked me recently where I get these JST quotes from, since they are not all in the footnotes or in the back of our Latter-day Saint Bible. The answer is that there is not room in our Latter-day Saint Bible to include all the JST corrections. You can see all of them in Joseph Smith's "New Translation" of the Bible, published by Herald Publishing House, Independence, Missouri. I use the 1970 edition. Most Latter-day Saint bookstores have it or can get it for you.)

8 If that nation, against whom I have pronounced, turn from their evil, **I will repent** of the evil that I thought to do unto them.

JST Jeremiah 18:8

8 If that nation, against whom I have pronounced, turn from their evil, **I will withhold the evil** that I thought to do unto them.

9 **And** *at what* **instant** [*whenever*] **I shall speak concerning a nation**, and concerning a kingdom, **to build and to plant** *it;*

10 If it do evil in my sight, that it obey not my voice, then **I will repent of the good**, wherewith I said I would benefit them.

JST Jeremiah 18:10

10 If it do evil in my sight, that it obey not my voice, then **I will withhold the good**, wherewith I said I would benefit them.

Next, in verse 11, the Lord instructs Jeremiah to once again invite these wicked people to repent.

Major Message

Even when it may appear that it is far too late to repent, there can still be hope.

11 ¶ Now therefore **go to, speak to the men of Judah, and to the inhabitants of Jerusalem**, saying, Thus saith the LORD; Behold, I frame evil against you, and devise a device against you [*your destruction looms before you*]: **return ye now every one from his evil way, and make your ways and your doings good** [*please repent*].

As we look at the phrase "there is no hope" in the context of verse 12, next, we understand that the people are not saying that there is no hope for them. Rather, they are saying, in effect, "Don't get your hopes up. There is no reason for us to repent. We like wickedness and we want to continue the way we are going."

12 And they said, There is no hope: but **we will walk after our own devices, and we will every one do the imagination of his evil heart**.

The basic question in verses 13–14, next, is "Have you ever heard of such a thing as a people leaving a God who has power to bless them?" Even the heathen are wiser than that!

13 Therefore thus saith the LORD; Ask ye now among the heathen, **who hath heard such things: the virgin of Israel** [*Jerusalem*] **hath done a very horrible thing**.

14 Will *a man* leave the snow of Lebanon *which cometh* from the rock of the field? *or* shall the cold flowing waters that come from another place be forsaken?

JST Jeremiah 18:14

14 Will you not leave the snow of the fields of Lebanon; shall not the cold flowing waters that come from another place from the rock, be forsaken?

It may be that verse 14, above, in the context of verse 13, is saying, in effect, "Would you not be better off not to leave a sure thing, like the God of Israel?"

The Lord goes on to describe the "horrible thing" mentioned in verse 13.

15 Because **my people hath forgotten me**, they have **burned incense to vanity** [*idols*], and **they** [*their false gods and idols*] **have caused them to stumble in their ways** *from* the ancient paths, to walk in paths, *in* a way not cast up [*in a path which has not been graded and maintained*];

16 **To make their land desolate** [*their choices are setting up their land for destruction*], *and* a perpetual hissing; every one that passeth thereby shall be astonished, and wag his head [*there will be much negative and derisive gossip in the future about what happened to Judah and Jerusalem*].

17 **I will scatter them** as with an east wind [*symbolic of rapid and terrible*

devastation] before the enemy: I will shew them the back, and not the face [*the Lord will turn His back to them*], in the day of their calamity.

The people don't like what Jeremiah is saying, so they plot to discredit him (verse 18). Verse 23 indicates that they plotted to kill him.

18 ¶ Then said they, **Come, and let us devise devices against Jeremiah**; for the law shall not perish from the priest, nor counsel from the wise, nor the word from the prophet [*the things he is prophesying will not come to pass*]. **Come, and let us smite him with the tongue**, and let us not give heed to any of his words.

Next, Jeremiah petitions the Lord for help and protection against his enemies. He asks that the Lord's punishments be upon them.

19 **Give heed to me**, O LORD, **and hearken to the voice of them that contend with me** [*be sure to hear the threats my enemies are giving out against me*].

20 Shall evil be recompensed for good? for **they have digged a pit for my soul**. Remember that **I stood before thee to speak good for them, *and* to turn away thy wrath from them** [*I have tried to save them*].

Verse 21, next, can serve to remind us of the application of the law of justice. It may also reflect the Lord's law of self-defense, as described in D&C 98.

21 Therefore deliver up their children to the famine, and pour out their *blood* by the force of the sword; and let their wives be bereaved of their children, and *be* widows; and let their men be put to death; *let* their young men *be* slain by the sword in battle.

22 Let a cry be heard from their houses, when thou shalt bring a troop suddenly upon them: for **they have digged a pit to take me, and hid snares for my feet**.

23 Yet, LORD, **thou knowest all their counsel against me to slay *me:*** forgive not their iniquity, neither blot out their sin from thy sight, but **let them be overthrown before thee; deal *thus* with them in the time of thine anger**.

As mentioned in our note before verse 21, above, D&C 98 may shed some light on verses 21–23, above. Jeremiah's life has been in danger and his enemies have tried to stop him a number of times by now. It may be that the "one, two, three" of D&C 98:23–27 have, in effect, been fulfilled, and he is now seeking to stop them, according to the law of self-defense that the Lord gave to the ancient prophets (D&C 98:32). We will quote some relevant verses from the Doctrine and Covenants, using bold for emphasis:

D&C 98:23–35

23 Now, I speak unto you concerning your families—**if men will smite you, or your families, once**, and ye bear it

patiently and revile not against them, neither seek revenge, ye shall be rewarded;

24 But if ye bear it not patiently, it shall be accounted unto you as being meted out as a just measure unto you.

25 And again, if your enemy shall smite you **the second time**, and you revile not against your enemy, and bear it patiently, your reward shall be an hundred fold.

26 And again, if he shall smite you **the third time**, and ye bear it patiently, your reward shall be doubled unto you four–fold;

27 And these three testimonies shall stand against your enemy if he repent not, and shall not be blotted out.

28 And now, verily I say unto you, if that enemy shall escape my vengeance, that he be not brought into judgment before me, then ye shall **see to it that ye warn him in my name**, that he come no more upon you, neither upon your family, even your children's children unto the third and fourth generation.

29 And then, **if he shall come upon you or your children**, or your children's children unto the third and fourth generation, **I have delivered thine enemy into thine hands**;

30 And then if thou wilt spare him, thou shalt be rewarded for thy righteousness; and also thy children and thy children's children unto the third and fourth generation.

31 Nevertheless, thine enemy is in thine hands; and if thou rewardest

him according to his works thou art justified; **if he has sought thy life, and thy life is endangered by him, thine enemy is in thine hands and thou art justified.**

32 Behold, **this is the law I gave unto my servant Nephi, and thy fathers, Joseph, and Jacob, and Isaac, and Abraham, and all mine ancient prophets and apostles.**

33 And again, this is the law that I gave unto mine ancients, that they should not go out unto battle against any nation, kindred, tongue, or people, save I, the Lord, commanded them.

34 And if any nation, tongue, or people should proclaim war against them, they should first lift a standard of peace unto that people, nation, or tongue;

35 And **if that people did not accept the offering of peace, neither the second nor the third time, they should bring these testimonies before the Lord;**

JEREMIAH 19

Selection: all verses

In this chapter, we see that the inhabitants of Jerusalem and the cities of Judah had arrived at the point where they were sacrificing their own children to idols. Such sacrifice is the ultimate blasphemy against the voluntary sacrifice of the Son of God for our sins.

Again, as in the case of the potter and the potter's wheel (chapter 18), Jeremiah is requested by the Lord to go to a certain place to obtain this message.

This time, he is asked to pick up a clay jar and go to the "valley of the son of Hinnom" (verse 2), and await the word of the Lord. This valley was just south of Jerusalem and was the site of human sacrifices (see Bible Dictionary under "Topheth.") These sacrifices included their own children (verse 5). The breaking (verse 10) of the clay jar (mentioned in verse 1) is symbolic of the destruction of Jerusalem.

1 THUS saith the LORD, **Go and get a potter's earthen bottle** [*a clay jar*], and *take* of the ancients of the people, and of the ancients of the priests [*take some of the city elders and old priests with you*];

2 And **go forth unto the valley of the son of Hinnom,** which *is* by the entry of the east gate, and proclaim there the words that I shall tell thee,

3 **And say,** Hear ye the word of the LORD, O kings of Judah, and inhabitants of Jerusalem; **Thus saith the LORD** of hosts, the God of Israel; Behold, **I will bring evil upon this place,** the which whosoever heareth, his ears shall tingle [*whoever hears about it will hardly believe their ears*].

4 **Because they have forsaken me, and have estranged this place** [*have desecrated this place; made it no longer a "Holy Land"*], and **have burned incense in it unto other gods** [*worshiped idols*], whom neither they nor their fathers have known, nor the kings of Judah, and **have filled this place with the blood of innocents** [*have offered human sacrifices, including children*];

5 They have built also the high places of Baal [*they have built altars to Baal*], to **burn their sons with fire** *for* **burnt offerings unto Baal,** which I commanded not, nor spake *it,* neither came *it* into my mind:

> Verses 6–9 are yet another prophecy concerning the coming destruction of Jerusalem and the surrounding area.

6 **Therefore** [*because of gross wickedness*], behold, **the days come,** saith the LORD, **that this place shall no more be called** Tophet, nor **The valley of the son of Hinnom, but The valley of slaughter.**

7 And **I will make void the counsel of Judah and Jerusalem in this place** [*they will no longer have political clout*]; and **I will cause them to fall by the sword** before their enemies, and by the hands of them that seek their lives: **and their carcases will I give to be meat for the fowls of the heaven, and for the beasts of the earth**.

8 And **I will make this city desolate,** and an hissing [*an object of scorn and gossip*]; every one that passeth thereby shall be astonished and hiss [*deride them*] because of all the plagues thereof.

> Next, in verse 9, we see a frightful prophecy of cannibalism during the coming siege of Jerusalem.

9 And **I will cause them to eat the flesh of their sons and the flesh of their daughters, and they**

shall eat every one the flesh of his friend in the siege and straitness [*dire circumstances*], wherewith their enemies, and they that seek their lives, shall straiten them.

The above prediction of hunger and cannibalism was fulfilled during the siege of Jerusalem by Nebuchadnezzar, king of Babylon. We read of it in Lamentations:

Lamentations 4:8–10

8 Their visage is blacker than a coal; they are not known in the streets: their skin cleaveth to their bones; it is withered, it is become like a stick.

9 They that be slain with the sword are better than they that be slain with hunger: for these pine away, stricken through for want of the fruits of the field.

10 The hands of the pitiful women have sodden [*boiled, cooked*] their own children: they were their meat [*food*] in the destruction of the daughter of my people [*during the destruction of Jerusalem*].

Next, Jeremiah is instructed to break the clay jar (representing the people of Judah) that he was instructed (in verse 1) to take with him to the site of human sacrifices.

10 **Then shalt thou break the bottle** [*symbolic of the "breaking" of Jerusalem and the scattering of the Jews in pieces—see verse 11*] **in the sight of the men** [*the city elders and leaders— see verse 1*] that go with thee,

11 And shalt **say unto them, Thus saith the LORD of hosts; Even so will I break this people and this city, as** *one* **breaketh a potter's vessel**, that cannot be made whole again: and they shall bury *them* in Tophet [*a spot in the Valley of Hinnon—see verse 2*], till *there be* no place to bury [*in other words, there will be a great slaughter of the Jews in that valley*].

12 **Thus will I do unto this place, saith the LORD,** and to the inhabitants thereof, and *even* make this city as Tophet [*a place of great slaughter*]:

There is symbolism in the phrase "make this city as Tophet" in verse 12, above. As noted above, Tophet was a place in the valley, south of Jerusalem, where human sacrifice was practiced, including the sacrifice of children to the fire god Molech. (See Bible Dictionary under "Molech.") Therefore, to make Jerusalem like Tophet means that the wicked will be sacrificed to their wickedness, just like they wickedly sacrificed others to their false gods.

13 And **the houses of Jerusalem,** and the houses [*palaces*] of the kings of Judah, **shall be defiled as the place of Tophet**, because of all the houses upon whose roofs they have burned incense unto all the host of heaven [*all the false gods and idols imaginable*], and have poured out drink offerings unto other gods.

14 **Then came Jeremiah from Tophet**, whither the LORD had sent him to

prophesy; **and he stood in the court of the LORD's house** [*the outer court-yard of the Jerusalem Temple*]; **and said to all the people,**

15 Thus saith the LORD of hosts, the God of Israel; **Behold, I will bring** upon this city and upon all her towns **all the evil that I have pronounced** [*prophesied*] against it, **because they have hardened their necks** [*refused to humble themselves*]**, that they might not hear my words.**

JEREMIAH 20

Selection: all verses

In this chapter, Pashur, the senior officer or chief overseer of the temple in Jerusalem, vents his anger against Jeremiah because of the things he is teaching and prophesying about the wickedness of the Jews and their leaders (see, for example, Jeremiah 19:14–15). He beats Jeremiah (verse 2) and has him placed in the stocks.

1 NOW **Pashur** the son of Immer the priest, who *was* also **chief governor in the house of the LORD, heard that Jeremiah prophesied these things.**

2 **Then Pashur smote Jeremiah** the prophet, **and put him in the stocks** that *were* in the high gate of Benjamin, which *was* by the house of the LORD.

We will quote from the Old Testament Student Manual for a description of being "put in the stocks." We will add bold for emphasis.

"Jeremiah 19:14–15 records Jeremiah's standing in the court of the temple, again reminding the people of the troubles that lay ahead because of their wickedness. When Pashur, the chief overseer of the temple, heard of the incident, he had Jeremiah beaten and placed in stocks. Stocks were an instrument of torture by which the body was forced into an unnatural position, much as the wooden stocks of medieval times confined certain parts of the body, such as the arms, legs, or head, by means of wooden beams that locked the parts of the body into place" (Old Testament Student Manual, page 245).

In verse 3, next, Jeremiah, under the direction of the Lord, uses the common technique (in their culture) of changing a person's name as a means of confirming a change in status, either good or bad. In this case, it is bad. "Pashur" means "free." But watch what the change of names denotes for Pashur's future, at the end of the verse.

3 And it came to pass **on the morrow** [*the next day*], that **Pashur brought forth Jeremiah out of the stocks.** Then said Jeremiah unto him, **The LORD hath not called thy name Pashur, but Magor-missabib** [*"terror all around"—see footnote 3a in your Bible*].

4 For thus saith the LORD, **Behold, I will make thee a terror to thyself, and to all thy friends**: and **they shall fall by the sword** of their enemies, and **thine eyes shall behold** *it* [*you will see this prophecy fulfilled*]:

and **I will give all Judah into the hand of the king of Babylon, and he shall carry them captive into Babylon, and shall slay them with the sword.**

5 **Moreover** [*in addition*] **I will deliver all the strength of this city**, and all the labours thereof, and **all the precious things** thereof, and **all the treasures** of the kings of Judah will I give **into the hand of their enemies**, which shall spoil them, and take them, and carry them to Babylon.

6 **And thou, Pashur, and all that dwell in thine house shall go into captivity**: and thou shalt come **to Babylon, and there thou shalt die**, and shalt be buried there, thou, and all thy friends, to whom thou hast prophesied lies.

The scene in verse 6, above, reminds us of Abinadi in King Noah's court (Mosiah 17:16–18).

The word, "deceived," in verse 7, next, can be a problem. We will read it and then get some help on the matter.

7 ¶ O LORD, thou hast **deceived** me, and I was deceived: thou art stronger than I, and hast prevailed: I am in derision daily, every one mocketh me.

"The great stress the prophetic calling caused Jeremiah is particularly discernible in Jeremiah 20:7–8, 14–18. The Hebrew word translated in verse 7 as "deceived" means literally "enticed" or "persuaded." The

power that persuaded the prophet to continue to preach God's word at such great personal cost was 'as a burning fire shut up in [*his*] bones' (verse 9). It could not be stayed. Verses 14–18 reflect Jeremiah's despair over the lonely ministry he was given" (Old Testament Student Manual, page 245).

We will now repeat verse 7, above, and incorporate the helps given in the student manual. We catch a glimpse of Jeremiah's personality.

Jeremiah 20:7 (repeated)

¶ O LORD, thou hast deceived me [*persuaded me to serve as a prophet*], and I was deceived [*and I have been successfully persuaded*]: thou art stronger than I, and hast prevailed [*You win*]: I am in derision daily, every one mocketh me [*this is a most difficult calling*].

8 **For since I spake, I cried out, I cried violence and spoil** [*ever since I began to prophesy, I have had to say much about violence and devastation*]; **because the word of the LORD was made a reproach unto me, and a derision, daily** [*and it has caused me to be mocked and brought much personal pain*].

We continue to see insights into Jeremiah's personality. He is without guile and rather straightforward with the Lord. Next, he confesses that he considered not delivering the messages, but his burning testimony compelled him to be faithful to his calling as a prophet.

9 Then I said, I will not make mention of him, nor speak any more in his name [*I said to myself, "I will not do any more prophesying for the Lord"*]. But *his word* was in mine heart as a burning fire shut up in my bones, and I was weary with forbearing, and I could not *stay* [*I just could not hold back any more*].

Jeremiah continues, sharing his frustrations and confirming his absolute commitment to be true to the Lord. According to the first part of verse 10, next, it appears that there were many attempts to discredit Jeremiah through slander against his name. People were constantly watching to catch him in any kind of slip up.

10 ¶ For **I heard the defaming** [*slander*] **of many**, fear on every side [*paranoia everywhere*]. Report, *say they*, and we will report it. **All my familiars** [*close acquaintances*] **watched for my halting** [*watched, hoping to see me slip up*], *saying*, **Peradventure he will be enticed** [*perhaps he will compromise his standards*], **and we shall prevail against him, and we shall take our revenge on him**.

11 But **the LORD** *is* **with me** as a mighty terrible one [*NIV: "like a mighty warrior"*]: **therefore my persecutors shall stumble, and they shall not prevail**: they shall be greatly ashamed [*disgraced*]; for **they shall not prosper**: *their* everlasting confusion shall never be forgotten.

Again, we see Jeremiah plead with the Lord for help against his enemies, much the same as Joseph Smith did as recorded in D&C 121:2–5.

12 But, O LORD of hosts, that triest [*tests*] the righteous, *and* seest the reins and the heart [*and sees the innermost feelings and desires of the heart*], **let me see thy vengeance on them: for unto thee have I opened my cause**.

Next, Jeremiah reaffirms his faith that the Lord has power to deliver him from the wicked.

13 Sing unto the LORD, praise ye the LORD: for **he hath delivered the soul of the poor** [*those in need*] **from the hand of evildoers**.

This seems to be a low point in Jeremiah's life (understatement). We feel his discouragement and frustration in verses 14–18.

14 ¶ **Cursed** *be* **the day wherein I was born**: let not the day wherein my mother bare me be blessed.

15 **Cursed** *be* **the man who brought tidings to my father, saying, A man child is born unto thee**; making him very glad.

16 And let that man be as the cities which the LORD overthrew, and repented not: and **let him hear the cry in the morning, and the shouting at noontide** [*in other words, in effect, if the man who told my father that I was born could just hear what I hear*]

everyday, he would be sorry he even announced my birth];

17 Because he slew me not from the womb; **or that my mother might have been my grave, and her womb** *to be* **always great** *with me* [*if I could just not have been born; if my mother could have remained pregnant with me forever*].

18 **Wherefore came I forth out of the womb** [*why did I have to be born*] to see labour and sorrow, that my days should be consumed with shame [*perhaps meaning "that my life should be spent as a social outcast"*]?

JEREMIAH 21

Selection: all verses

As mentioned in the introduction to the Book of Jeremiah, in this study guide, Jeremiah served during the reigns of five different kings of Judah. The last king was Zedekiah. He was the wicked king who ruled when Lehi and his family left Jerusalem in 600 BC (see 1 Nephi 1:4).

In this chapter, wicked King Zedekiah (who was twenty-one years old when he began his reign and reigned for eleven years until the Babylonians took him prisoner) sends a servant to Jeremiah to see what the Lord has to say about the coming Babylonian armies.

1 **THE word** which came unto Jeremiah **from the LORD, when king Zedekiah sent unto him Pashur** [*not the same man as the "Pashur" in chapter 20, verse 1*] the son of Melchiah,

and Zephaniah the son of Maaseiah the priest, **saying,**

2 **Enquire, I pray thee, of the LORD for us; for Nebuchadrezzar king of Babylon maketh war against us**; if so be that the LORD will deal with us according to all his wondrous works, that he may go up from us [*in other words, is there a possibility that the Lord will cause Nebuchadnezzar and his armies to go away without attacking Jerusalem?*].

Perhaps you noticed a technical detail in verse 2, above. We usually refer to this powerful Babylonian king as "Nebuchadnezzar" (see, for example, Daniel 3:1–3), but in verse 2, it is spelled "Nebuchadrezzar" (with an "r" instead of an "n"). The spelling used in verse 2 is a Hebrew variation of the spelling.

Jeremiah's answer to the question of protection from the Lord, for this wicked king and his wicked people, is given in verses 3–14, next.

3 ¶ **Then said Jeremiah unto them** [*the messengers sent by king Zedekiah, of Jerusalem*], Thus shall ye say to Zedekiah:

4 **Thus saith the LORD God of Israel; Behold, I will turn back** [*make ineffective*] **the weapons of war that** *are* **in your hands**, wherewith ye fight against the king of Babylon, and *against* the Chaldeans [*another name for the Babylonians, in this context*], which besiege you without [*outside of*] the walls, and I will assemble them into the midst of this city [*I will*

bring your enemies right into the middle of Jerusalem].

5 And **I** [the Lord] **myself will fight against you** with an outstretched hand and with a strong arm, even in anger, and in fury, and in great wrath.

6 And **I will smite the inhabitants of this city**, both man and beast: they shall die of a great pestilence.

7 And afterward, saith the LORD, **I will deliver Zedekiah king of Judah, and his servants, and the people**, and such as are left in this city from the pestilence, from the sword, and from the famine, **into the hand of Nebuchadrezzar king of Babylon**, and into the hand of their enemies, and into the hand of those that seek their life: and he shall smite them with the edge of the sword; **he shall not spare them, neither have pity, nor have mercy**.

In fulfillment of the above prophecy, King Zedekiah was captured by Nebuchadnezzar's armies, his sons (except for Mulek—see Helaman 6:10) were killed before his eyes, and then his eyes were put out and he was carried as a trophy of war to Babylon (see Jeremiah 52:8–11).

Next, the Lord instructs Jeremiah to tell the inhabitants of Jerusalem how they can avoid being killed by the invading armies.

8 ¶ And **unto this people thou shalt say**, Thus saith the LORD; Behold, **I set before you the way of life, and the way of death** [you can either live or die in the coming siege].

9 **He that abideth** [remains] **in this city** [Jerusalem] **shall die by the sword, and by the famine, and by the pestilence**: but he that goeth out [leaves the city], and falleth [surrenders] **to the Chaldeans** [Babylonian armies] that besiege you, he **shall live**, and **his life shall be unto him for a prey** [in other words, you will be taken captive and put in bondage—that's the condition under which you will remain alive].

10 For **I have set my face against this city for** [because of their] **evil**, and not for good, saith the LORD: **it shall be given into the hand of the king of Babylon, and he shall burn it with fire**.

Next, in verses 11–14, the Lord tells the royal family as well as the people that there is one way they can yet be preserved as a nation. It is if they will repent and turn to righteousness.

11 ¶ And **touching** [concerning] **the house of the king of Judah** [the royal family], say, Hear ye the word of the LORD;

12 O house of David, thus saith the LORD; **Execute judgment** [be fair and righteous] in the morning, and **deliver him that is spoiled out of the hand of the oppressor** [conduct the business of the kingdom with integrity], lest my fury go out like fire, and burn that none can quench it, because of the evil of your doings.

13 **Behold, I am against thee**, O inhabitant of the valley, and rock of

the plain, saith the LORD; **which say**, Who shall come down against us [*who can conquer us*]? or who shall enter into our habitations [*what enemies could possibly come into our land*]?

14 But I will punish you according to the fruit of your doings [*according to your wicked deeds], saith the LORD: and I will kindle a fire in the forest thereof [in other words, the Lord will burn their trees; trees are often symbolic of people, in Old Testament symbolism*], and it shall devour all things round about it.

JEREMIAH 22

Selection: all verses

In this chapter, Jeremiah is given yet another uncomfortable task. He is to go to the palace of the king and deliver a prophecy.

Verses 1–9 are a general invitation to the kings of Judah to repent and do right, and a warning about the ultimate consequences of their wickedness if they choose to continue doing evil.

1 THUS saith the LORD; **Go down to the house** [*palace*] **of the king of Judah, and speak there this word,**

2 And say, **Hear the word of the LORD, O king of Judah**, that sittest upon the throne of David [*who occupies the office of king, once held by King David*], **thou, and thy servants, and thy people** that enter in by these gates:

3 Thus saith the LORD; **Execute ye judgment and righteousness** [*be fair and exercise righteousness in your reign as king*], and **deliver the spoiled out of the hand of the oppressor** [*redeem the oppressed*]: and **do no wrong**, do no violence to the stranger [*foreigners*], the fatherless [*orphans*], nor the widow, neither shed innocent blood in this place.

4 For **if ye do this thing** indeed, then shall there enter in by the gates of this house kings sitting upon the throne of David, riding in chariots and on horses, he, and his servants, and his people [*in other words, if you do what is right, the nation of Judah will continue and will thrive*].

5 **But if ye will not** hear these words, I swear by myself, saith the LORD, that **this house shall become a desolation** [*the royal family will be destroyed, along with its subjects*].

For verse 6, next, it is helpful to know that "Gilead" had the richest soil in Israel, and "Lebanon" had the highest mountain and the finest trees in the surrounding area. Remember that trees often represent people in Old Testament symbolism. The message seems to be that Israel was planted in the best gospel soil (the promised land) and its people (the covenant people) were to be the very best "trees." The Lord knows their potential, and the stewardship of the kings of Judah was to foster righteousness and loyalty to God among their citizens.

6 For thus saith the LORD unto the king's house of Judah; **Thou *art***

Gilead unto me, *and* the head of Lebanon [*you have the potential to be the very best*]: *yet* surely [*if you don't repent*] I will make thee a wilderness [*I will cut down all your "trees"*], *and* cities *which* are not inhabited.

7 And I will prepare destroyers against thee, every one with his weapons: and they shall cut down thy choice cedars [*your people*], and cast *them* into the fire.

8 And many nations shall pass by this city [*travelers from many nations will see the ruins of Jerusalem*], and they shall say every man to his neighbour, Wherefore hath the LORD done thus unto this great city [*what did they do to deserve such destruction*]?

9 Then they shall answer, Because they have forsaken the covenant of the LORD their God, and worshipped other gods, and served them.

Verses 10–12, next, are a very specific prophecy, directed to Jehoahaz, who succeeded his righteous father, King Josiah. Josiah reigned from about 641 BC to 610 BC, when he died of a wound received in the Battle of Megiddo. His wicked son, Jehoahaz became the next king of Judah, and ruled for just three months. People were mourning King Josiah's death at the time of this prophecy.

10 ¶ Weep ye not for the dead [*King Josiah*], neither bemoan him: *but* weep sore for him [*Jehoahaz*] that goeth away: for he shall return no more, nor see his native country.

After just three months as king, Jehoahaz was captured and taken away to Egypt where he died.

11 For thus saith the LORD touching Shallum [*Jehoahaz*] the son of Josiah king of Judah, which reigned instead of [*in the place of*] Josiah his father, which went forth out of this place; He shall not return thither any more [*will never return to Jerusalem*]:

12 But he shall die in the place [*Egypt*] whither they have led him captive, and shall see this land no more.

In verses 13–19, next, Jeremiah rebukes Jehoiakim, also a son of righteous King Josiah, for his tyranny and self-centeredness as king. He ruled from about 609 BC to 598 BC.

13 ¶ Woe unto him [*Jehoiakim—see verse 18*] that buildeth his house by unrighteousness, and his chambers by wrong; *that* useth his neighbour's service without wages, and giveth him not for his work;

14 That saith, I will build me a wide house [*a large palace*] and large chambers, and cutteth him out windows; and *it is* cieled [*paneled*] with cedar, and painted with vermilion [*bright red to red orange*].

15 Shalt thou reign, because thou closest *thyself* in cedar? did not thy father [*righteous King Josiah*] eat and drink, and do judgment and justice, *and* then *it was* well with him?

16 **He judged the cause of the poor and needy** [*he was a righteous judge over his people*]; then *it was* well *with him: was* **not this to know me** [*isn't this what the gospel is all about*]? saith the LORD.

17 **But thine eyes and thine heart** *are* **not but for thy covetousness** [*you are self-centered and greedy*], and for **to shed innocent blood** [*you are a murderer*], and for **oppression**, and for **violence**, to do *it*.

18 **Therefore thus saith the LORD concerning Jehoiakim** the son of Josiah king of Judah; **They shall not lament for him**, *saying,* Ah my brother! or, Ah sister! they shall not lament for him, *saying,* Ah lord! or, Ah his glory!

19 **He shall be buried with the burial of an ass** [*a phrase in Jeremiah's day which meant to be dumped in an open field without burial*], **drawn and cast forth beyond the gates of Jerusalem** [*when he dies his carcass will be treated like that of a dead donkey, dragged outside the city and dumped*].

The Jewish historian, Josephus, recorded that Nebuchadnezzar killed Jehoiakim and commanded that he be thrown out without a burial. (See Antiquities of the Jews, 10.6.3.)

Lebanon and Bashan, in verse 20, next, are a prophetic description of the route of the captives of Judah as they were taken to Babylon.

20 ¶ **Go up to Lebanon, and cry**; and **lift up thy voice in Bashan, and cry from the passages** [*as you pass through that country*]: **for all thy lovers** [*false gods with whom you have committed spiritual adultery*] **are destroyed.**

21 **I spake unto thee in thy prosperity;** *but* **thou saidst, I will not hear** [*I invited you to repent when you were prosperous, but you refused*]. This *hath been* thy manner from thy youth, that thou obeyedst not my voice [*you have been this way for a long time*].

22 **The wind** [*the hot, dry east wind, symbolic of destruction*] **shall eat up all thy pastors** [*your wicked leaders*], **and thy lovers** [*false gods; also, sexual immorality was rampant among the Jews at this time in their history*] **shall go into captivity**: surely then shalt thou be ashamed and confounded for all thy wickedness.

Verse 23, next, can best be understood if you know that the cedars of Lebanon were often used as symbols of prideful people, in the vocabulary of the day. Here they represent the proud, rebellious leaders of Judah.

23 **O inhabitant of Lebanon** [*Judah's proud, haughty leaders*], **that makest thy nest in the cedars** [*whose lives are filled with pride*], **how gracious shalt thou be when pangs** [*the pains of Babylonian captivity*] **come upon thee**, the pain as of a woman in travail [*which are as unavoidable now for you as the pains of a woman in labor*]!

Next, Jeremiah turns his attention to Jehoiachin, another wicked king of Judah, whose wicked reign lasted only a few months. He and his mother will be carried captive into Babylon (verses 26–27) and none of his posterity will ever sit on the throne of King David (verses 28–30).

24 *As* I live, saith the LORD, though [*even if*] Coniah [*Jehoiachin*] the son of Jehoiakim king of Judah were the signet [*the signet ring*] upon my right hand, yet would I pluck thee thence [*I would take you off and throw you to Babylon*];

25 And I will give thee into the hand of them that seek thy life, and into the hand *of them* whose face thou fearest, even into the hand of Nebuchadrezzar [*another spelling of "Nebuchadnezzar"—see Jeremiah 27:8*] king of Babylon, and into the hand of the Chaldeans [*the Babylonians*].

26 And I will cast thee out, and thy mother that bare thee, into another country [*Babylon*], where ye were not born; and there shall ye die.

27 But to the land whereunto they desire to return [*Jerusalem and the land of Judah*], thither [*there*] shall they not return.

Next, as a technique for emphasizing what has already been said, several questions are asked by Jeremiah about Jehoiachin (Coniah).

28 *Is* this man Coniah a despised broken idol [*is he like a despicable broken idol*]? *is he* a vessel wherein *is* no pleasure [*is he an empty vessel*]? Wherefore [*why*] are they cast out [*of Jerusalem*], he and his seed [*his posterity*], and are cast into a land which they know not?

29 O earth, earth, earth [*everyone listen up*], hear the word of the LORD.

30 Thus saith the LORD, Write ye this man childless [*consider this man to be childless, as far as ever having a son who will rule as king in Jerusalem*], a man *that* shall not prosper in his days: for no man of his seed shall prosper, sitting upon the throne of David, and ruling any more in Judah.

JEREMIAH 23

Selection: all verses

For us, probably the most significant thing about this chapter is that it contains a marvelous prophecy of the gathering of Israel in the last days (verses 3–8). We are part of the fulfillment of that prophecy. The most important aspect of the "gathering" for each of God's children is to be converted to the gospel of Jesus Christ, to be baptized, and then to remain faithful to all covenants made in the Church. In other words, the top priority of the "gathering of Israel" is to "gather" each one of us to Christ, if we are willing.

The rest of the chapter lists and describes the terrible sins of the Jewish religious leaders, including false priests and false prophets of Jeremiah's day.

Jeremiah begins with a powerful denunciation of the wicked religious leaders of his day. This rebuke can apply to any, including political leaders, media personalities, and individuals, who lead people away from the Lord at anytime.

1 **WOE be unto the pastors** [*false religious leaders*] **that destroy and scatter the sheep** [*Israel*] of my pasture! saith the LORD.

2 Therefore thus saith the LORD God of Israel against the pastors that feed my people; **Ye have scattered my flock, and driven them away**, and have not visited [*taken good care of*] them: behold, **I will visit upon you the evil of your doings** [*you will be punished for the evil you have done*], saith the LORD.

Next, in verse 3, we see a great prophecy concerning the gathering of Israel in the last days.

3 And **I will gather the remnant of my flock** [*Israel*] **out of all countries whither I have driven them**, and will bring them again to their folds [*various lands*]; and they shall be fruitful and increase.

4 And **I will set up shepherds** [*righteous religious leaders*] **over them which shall feed them**: and they shall fear no more, nor be dismayed, neither shall they be lacking [*because they will have the true gospel of Jesus Christ*], saith the LORD.

Elder Bruce R. McConkie explained the gathering, spoken of in the above verses. He taught:

"The gathering of Israel consists of receiving the truth, gaining again a true knowledge of the Redeemer, and coming back into the true fold of the Good Shepherd. In the language of the Book of Mormon, it consists of being 'restored to the true church and fold of God,' and then being 'gathered' and 'established' in various 'lands of promise.'" (2 Ne. 9:2; "Come: Let Israel Build Zion," Ensign, May 1977, p. 117)

President Spencer W. Kimball also instructed us on this important topic.

"He (the Lord) said through Nephi, 'The house of Israel (sooner or later will) be scattered upon all the face of the earth.' (1 Nephi 22:3) And now He says, 'I will gather the remnant of my flock out of all countries whither I have driven them.' (Jeremiah 23:3)

"The gathering of Israel is now in progress. Hundreds of thousands of people have been baptized into the Church. Millions more will join the Church. And this is the way that we will gather Israel. The English people will gather in England. The Japanese people will gather in the Orient. The Brazilian people will gather in Brazil. So that important element of the world history is already being accomplished.

"It is to be done by missionary work. It is your responsibility to attend to this missionary work." (In Conference Report, Sao Paulo Brazil Area Conference, Feb.–Mar. 1975, p. 73)

Verses 5–6, next, prophesy of the millennial reign of the Savior (see footnote 5d in your Bible).

5 ¶ Behold, the days come, saith the LORD, that I will raise unto David a righteous Branch [*Christ*],

and **a King shall reign and prosper** [*Jesus Christ will rule during the
Millennium as King of kings and Lord
of lords"—see Revelation 117:14*], **and
shall execute judgment and justice in the earth**.

6 **In his days Judah shall be saved,
and Israel shall dwell safely**: and
this *is* his name whereby he shall
be called, THE LORD OUR RIGH-
TEOUSNESS.

Verses 7–8, next, prophesy more
about the gathering of Israel in the
last days, leading up to the Millennium. At that time, the much-talked-
about event will no longer be the
miraculous deliverance of the children of Israel from Egypt. Rather,
the "buzz" will be about missionary
work and the exciting gathering of
Israel in all nations and lands.

7 Therefore, behold, **the days come,
saith the LORD, that they shall no
more say, The LORD liveth, which
brought up the children of Israel
out of the land of Egypt**;

8 **But, The LORD liveth**, which
brought up and **which led the seed
of the house of Israel** [*the descendants of scattered Israel*] out of the
north country, and **from all countries whither I had driven them;
and they shall dwell in their own
land**.

From here to the end of the chapter, the main message is the terrible
damage done by dishonest and
wicked leaders of false religions
among the Jews of Jeremiah's day.

9 ¶ **Mine heart within me is broken because of the** [*false*] **prophets**; all my bones shake; I am like a
drunken man, and like a man whom
wine hath overcome, because of the
LORD, and because of the words of
his holiness [*perhaps meaning that
Jeremiah is heartbroken and almost out
of his mind because of what he knows
about the true gospel in contrast to what
the false prophets among the Jews are
teaching*].

10 For **the land is full of adulterers**;
for because of swearing [*because of
the curse of the Lord*] **the land mourneth**; the pleasant places of the
wilderness are dried up, and **their
course is evil, and their force** *is*
not right [*their influence leads people
astray*].

11 **For both** [*false*] **prophet and**
[*false*] **priest are profane** [*are not
religious themselves—see footnote 11c
in your Bible*]; yea, **in my house** [*in
the temple in Jerusalem*] **have I found
their wickedness**, saith the LORD.

12 Wherefore [*therefore*] **their way**
[*their evil course in life*] **shall be unto
them as slippery ways** [*will become
treacherous*] in the darkness [*spiritual
darkness*]: **they shall** be driven on,
and **fall therein**: for I will bring evil
upon them, *even* **the year of their
visitation** [*the time when the Lord's
punishment catches up with them*],
saith the LORD.

By now you are probably quite used
to seeing repetition as a means of
driving home a particular point or

message in Jeremiah's writing. We will see much of this repetition for emphasis in the next several verses.

The reason we bring this up is that occasionally students of the Old Testament will begin to wonder if perhaps they are missing something as they read such repetitions. They have already caught the message and wonder if maybe the prophet isn't saying something else instead of repeating and they are missing it. They are not.

Verse 13, next appears to refer specifically to the false prophets among the northern ten tribes (who were led away captive by Assyria about 722 BC) who led Israel away from the worship of Jehovah into the worship of Baal.

13 And **I have seen folly** [*wickedness*] in **the prophets of Samaria** [*the former capital of the ten tribes (Israel)*]; **they prophesied in Baal, and caused my people Israel to err.**

14 I have seen also in the [*false*] **prophets of Jerusalem** an horrible thing: they **commit adultery**, and **walk in lies**: they strengthen also the hands of evildoers [*they support wickedness*], that none doth return from his wickedness: **they are all of them unto me as Sodom, and the inhabitants thereof as Gomorrah** [*they have become just like the residents of Sodom and Gomorrah*].

15 **Therefore thus saith the LORD** of hosts **concerning the** [*false*] **prophets**; Behold, **I will feed them with wormwood** [*a terribly*

bitter herb—see Bible Dictionary under "Wormwood"], **and make them drink the water of gall** [*in other words, these false prophets will have a bitter fate*]: for from the prophets of Jerusalem is profaneness [*lack of being truly religious*] gone forth into all the land.

Next, we see a warning to avoid heeding the words of false prophets. Remember, "false prophets" can be anyone, including religious leaders, politicians, media personalities, philosophers, atheists, gang leaders, and friends whose influence tends to lead people away from God.

16 Thus saith the LORD of hosts, **Hearken not unto the words of the** [*false*] **prophets that prophesy unto you**: they make you vain [*they make you miss the truth*]: they speak a vision of their own heart [*they teach their own beliefs*], *and* not out of the mouth of the LORD.

17 **They say** still **unto them that despise me**, The LORD hath said, **Ye shall have peace**; and they say unto every one that walketh after the imagination of his own heart, No evil shall come upon you [*in other words, they teach that you can have peace in wickedness*].

18 For **who** [*which of these false prophets*] **hath stood in the counsel of the LORD, and hath perceived and heard his word?** who hath marked his word [*in his heart and daily life*], and heard *it* [*in other words, which of these false prophets and teachers has*

embraced the true gospel and is attempting to live it].

19 Behold, **a whirlwind** of [*destruction from*] the LORD is gone forth in fury, even a grievous whirlwind: it **shall fall grievously upon the head of the wicked.**

20 **The anger of the LORD shall not return** [*turn away*], **until he have executed, and till he have performed the thoughts of his heart** [*until the prophesied destruction takes place*]: in the latter days [*NIV: "in days to come"*] ye shall consider [*understand*] it perfectly.

21 **I have not sent these** [*false*] **prophets**, yet they ran [*took over quickly*]: I have not spoken to them, yet they prophesied.

22 But **if they had stood in my counsel** [*if they had understood and followed My counsel*], and had caused my people to hear my words, **then they should have turned them from their evil way**, and from the evil of their doings.

23 *Am* I a God at hand, saith the LORD, and not a God afar off [*perhaps meaning "Am I not a God who knows all things, near and far—see verse 24*]?

24 **Can any hide himself** in secret places **that I shall not see him?** saith the LORD. **Do not I fill heaven and earth?** saith the LORD.

25 **I have heard what the** [*false*] **prophets said, that prophesy lies in** **my name**, saying, I have dreamed, I have dreamed [*the false prophets claim to have had dreams from God*].

26 **How long shall *this* be in the heart of the prophets that prophesy lies?** yea, *they are* prophets of the deceit of their own heart [*they teach according to the deceitfulness in their own hearts*];

27 **Which think to cause my people to forget my name** by their dreams which they tell every man to his neighbour, as their fathers [*ancestors*] have forgotten my name for [*because of*] Baal.

28 **The** [*true*] **prophet that hath a dream, let him tell a dream**; and **he** [*true prophets, such as Jeremiah and Lehi*] **that hath my word, let him speak my word faithfully**. What *is* the chaff to the wheat [*what is the word of false prophets compared to the true word of God*]? saith the LORD.

The power of the true word of God to burn out false doctrines and destroy the false philosophies of men is described in verse 29, next. We often see this power of the word described in scriptures as a two-edged sword, able to cut in all directions through falsehood and deception.

29 *Is* **not my word like as a fire?** saith the LORD; and **like a hammer** *that* **breaketh the rock in pieces?**

30 Therefore, behold, **I *am* against the prophets**, saith the LORD, **that steal my words every one from his neighbour** [*in other words, against the false prophets who borrow lies and*

falsehoods from one another to teach their followers].

31 Behold, **I** *am* **against the** [*false*] **prophets**, saith the LORD, **that use their tongues, and say, He saith** [*who claim to be teaching the will of God*].

32 Behold, **I** *am* **against them that prophesy false dreams**, saith the LORD, and do tell [*preach*] **them**, and **cause my people to err by their lies**, and **by their lightness** [*failure to take the true words of God seriously*]; yet **I sent them not**, nor commanded them: therefore they shall not profit this people at all, saith the LORD.

> The word, "burden," as used in the context of the next verses, basically means "prophesy," especially "message of doom." Thus, the Lord is telling Jeremiah what to say when people sarcastically come up to him and ask him what the next message of doom for them from God is.

33 ¶ And when this people, or the [*false*] prophet, or a [*false*] priest, shall ask thee, saying, **What** *is* **the burden of the LORD? thou shalt then say** unto them, What burden? **I will even forsake you, saith the LORD**.

34 And *as for* the prophet, and the priest, and the people, that shall say, The burden of the LORD, **I will even punish that man and his house**.

> Next, in verse 35, Jeremiah is instructed to tell the wicked to spread the word that the Lord will forsake them (verse 33) because of their willful failure to repent.

35 **Thus shall ye say every one to his neighbour**, and every one to his brother, What hath the LORD answered [*what was the Lord's answer to our question [verse 33]*]? and, What hath the LORD spoken?

36 **And the burden of the LORD shall ye mention no more: for every man's word shall be his burden** [*you don't need to talk about the fact that the Lord has forsaken you, because you yourselves are your own worst enemies*]; for **ye have perverted** [*twisted and corrupted*] **the words of the living God**, of the LORD of hosts our God.

37 **Thus shalt thou say to the** [*false*] **prophet**, What hath the LORD answered thee? and, **What hath the LORD spoken** [*what has the Lord revealed to you*]?

38 But **since ye say, The burden of the LORD; therefore thus saith the LORD** [*since you claim to speak for the Lord*]; Because ye say this word, The burden of the LORD, and I have sent unto you, saying, **Ye shall not say, The burden of the LORD**;

39 **Therefore**, behold, I, even I, will utterly forget you, and **I will forsake you, and the city** that I gave you and your fathers, *and cast you* out of my presence:

> The phrase "I will utterly forget you," in verse 39, above, does not mean that the Lord actually forgets the wicked. Of course, His memory is perfect. It means that He will withdraw His blessings from them and will bring punishments upon them.

40 And **I will bring an everlasting reproach upon you** [*you will be looked down upon by other nations*], and a perpetual shame, which shall not be forgotten.

JEREMIAH 24

Selection: all verses

Ultimately, as pro-phesied by Jeremiah, the Jews were taken captive into Babylon (sometimes referred to in these scriptures as "Chaldea"). After about seventy years, a remnant of them was allowed to return to Jerusalem to rebuild it.

In this chapter, Jeremiah has a vision of "two baskets of figs" (verse 1), one good and one bad (verse 2). The good figs represent the remnant of the Jews who will be brought back to Jerusalem by the Lord (verses 5–6) after seventy years.

The bad figs represent wicked King Zedekiah and the evil leaders of the Jews as well as many of their people (verses 8–10).

Jeremiah's vision in verse 1 shows the actual captivity of Jerusalem and the carrying of the captives into Babylon (roughly the location of modern Iraq). This is an interactive vision, where Jeremiah is asked questions and gives answers (starting with verse 3). In a way, it reminds us of Nephi's vision, beginning with 1 Nephi, chapter 11, where he is asked many questions as to what he sees in his vision.

1 **THE LORD shewed me**, and, behold, **two baskets of figs** *were* set before the temple of the LORD,

after that **Nebuchadrezzar king of Babylon had carried away captive** Jeconiah the son of Jehoiakim king of Judah, and the princes [*leaders*] of Judah, with the carpenters and smiths [*in other words, with the skilled craftsmen*], from Jerusalem, **and had brought them to Babylon**.

2 **One basket *had* very good figs**, *even* like the figs *that are* first ripe: **and the other basket *had* very naughty figs**, which could not be eaten, they were so bad.

3 Then said the LORD unto me, **What seest thou, Jeremiah?** And I said, Figs; the good figs, very good; and the evil, very evil, that cannot be eaten, they are so evil.

Next, the Lord explains the meaning of the two baskets of figs. One thing we learn from this vision is that there were some good people among the Jews who were taken captive. It was not just the wicked that suffered because of the corrupt leaders who were among the people at this time.

4 ¶ Again **the word of the LORD came unto me, saying,**

5 Thus saith the LORD, the God of Israel; **Like these good figs, so will I acknowledge them that are carried away captive of Judah**, whom I have sent out of this place into the land of the Chaldeans **for *their* good**.

6 For I will set mine eyes upon them **for good**, and **I will bring them again to this land** [*Jerusalem and the surrounding territory of Judah*]: **and**

I will build them [*they will rebuild Jerusalem and the surrounding country*], and not pull *them* down; and **I will plant them, and not pluck** *them* up.

7 And **I will give them an heart to know me, that I** *am* **the LORD**: and **they shall be my people**, and I will be their God: for **they shall return unto me with their whole heart.**

8 ¶ And as **the evil figs**, which cannot be eaten, they are so evil; surely thus saith the LORD, So will I give **Zedekiah the king of Judah, and his princes, and the residue of Jerusalem**, that remain in this land [*who are left behind*], and them that dwell in the land of Egypt:

9 And **I will deliver them to be removed** [*scattered*] **into all the kingdoms of the earth** for *their* hurt, **to be** a reproach and a proverb, a taunt and a curse [*to be looked down upon and disparaged*], **in all places whither I shall drive them.**

10 And **I will send the sword**, the **famine**, and the **pestilence**, among them, **till they be consumed from off the land** [*the Holy Land*] that I gave unto them and to their fathers [*ancestors; the children of Israel whom Joshua led into the promised land*].

JEREMIAH 25

Selection: all verses

In this chapter, we learn that the captives of Judah will serve in Babylon for seventy years (verse 11). At the end of that time, Babylon will be conquered and will serve other kings and nations (verses 12–14). The Lord also has Jeremiah prophesy against all wicked nations, warning them that all who are wicked and do not repent will eventually be punished by the Lord (verses 15–29).

The last part of the chapter "prophetically leaps forward to the time of the battle of Armageddon" in the last days (see Old Testament Student Manual, page 246).

In verse 1, Jeremiah identifies the time of this prophecy as about 605 BC. Be aware that almost all dates given in Old Testament chronology are approximations. Thus, you will see slight variations in dates given for specific events, depending on the sources used.

The first part of this prophecy is directed at the people of Judah.

1 **THE word that came to Jeremiah concerning all the people of Judah in the fourth year of Jehoiakim** [*about 605 BC*] the son of Josiah king of Judah, that *was* **the first year of Nebuchadrezzar king of Babylon**;

2 The which Jeremiah the prophet spake **unto all the people of Judah, and to all the inhabitants of Jerusalem**, saying,

In verse 3, next, Jeremiah tells us when he was first called to be a prophet. Remember, as stated above, dates vary a bit, depending on the sources. Thus, we often see anywhere from 628 to 626 BC given for the beginning of Jeremiah's service as a prophet.

3 **From the thirteenth year of Josiah** [*about 628 BC—see chronology
chart in Bible Dictionary*] the son of
Amon king of Judah, even **unto this
day**, that *is* the three and twentieth
year [*the twenty-third year that I have
been serving as a prophet*], **the word
of the LORD hath come unto me,
and I have spoken unto you**, rising
early and speaking; **but ye have not
hearkened**.

Next, in verse 4, Jeremiah informs
us that the Lord sent many prophets
to the people of Judah, including Jerusalem, at this time in history. This
is confirmed in the Book of Mormon.
We read (bold added for emphasis):

1 Nephi 1:4

4 For it came to pass in the com-
mencement of the first year of the
reign of Zedekiah, king of Judah,
(my father, Lehi, having dwelt at Jerusalem in all his days); and **in that
same year there came many prophets**, prophesying unto the people that
they must repent, or the great city Jerusalem must be destroyed.

Included in these "many prophets"
were Jeremiah, Lehi, Nahum, Habakkuk, Zephaniah, and perhaps
Ezekiel.

4 And **the LORD hath sent unto
you all his servants the prophets**,
rising early and sending *them* [*sending them way ahead of your pending
destruction*]; **but ye have not hearkened, nor inclined your ear to
hear**.

5 **They** [*the true prophets*] **said, Turn
ye again now every one from his**
evil way, and from the evil of your
doings [*in other words, repent*], and
dwell in the land that the LORD
hath given unto you and to your fathers for ever and ever:

6 And **go not after other gods** to
serve them, and to worship them,
and provoke me not to anger with
the works of your hands [*idols*]; and I
will do you no hurt.

7 Yet **ye have not hearkened unto
me, saith the LORD**; that ye might
provoke me to anger with the works
of your hands [*including idols*] to your
own hurt [*you are damaging yourselves*].

8 ¶ **Therefore** thus saith the LORD
of hosts; **Because ye have not heard
my words**,

In verse 9, next, we see an illustra-
tion of something Mormon taught.
He said:

Mormon 4:5

5 But, behold, the judgments of God
will overtake the wicked; and **it is
by the wicked that the wicked are
punished**; for it is the wicked that
stir up the hearts of the children of
men unto bloodshed.

This principle applies to Nebuchadnezzar (spelled "Nebuchadrezzar"
here), the wicked king whom the
Lord uses to punish the wicked people of Judah.

9 Behold, **I will send and take all
the families of the north** [*in other
words, I will bring hordes of enemies
upon you, and they will come in from*

the north], saith the LORD, **and Nebuchadrezzar the king of Babylon**, my servant [*the instrument of destruction which the Lord will use against Judah*], **and will bring them against this land, and against the inhabitants thereof**, and against all these nations round about [*the Babylonians will conquer and devastate many surrounding nations also*], **and will utterly destroy them, and make them an astonishment** [*objects of startled horror*], **and an hissing** [*objects of scorn*], and perpetual **desolations** [*leave in ruins*].

10 **Moreover** [*in addition*] **I will take from them** the voice of **mirth** [*lighthearted pleasantness*], and the voice of **gladness** [*happiness*], the voice of the **bridegroom**, and the voice of the **bride**, the sound of the **millstones** [*grinding grain; in other words, economic well-being*], and the **light of the candle** [*pleasant evenings*].

11 And **this whole land shall be a desolation**, *and* an astonishment; and **these nations shall serve the king of Babylon seventy years**.

Next, Jeremiah tells us what will happen when the seventy years of captivity and servitude are over.

12 ¶ And it shall come to pass, **when seventy years are accomplished** [*are over*], *that* **I will punish the king of Babylon, and that nation**, saith the LORD, **for their iniquity** [*for their wickedness*], and the land of the Chaldeans [*another name for Babylonia, sometimes used to refer to*

southeastern Babylon, where Abraham came from—see Abraham 1:1], and will make it perpetual desolations.

Verse 12, above, is rather important because it clears up any confusion about the phrase "the king of Babylon, my servant," reminding us that "servant," in this context, means an instrument used by the Lord to accomplish His purposes.

13 And **I will bring upon that land all my words which I have pronounced against it,** *even* all that is written in this book, **which Jeremiah hath prophesied against all the nations**.

14 For many nations and great kings shall serve themselves of them also: and **I will recompense** [*punish*] **them according to their deeds**, and according to the works of their own hands [*all the wicked will eventually be punished (unless they repent when given ample opportunity to do so)*].

The "cup of fury" is commonly used imagery to represent the anger of the Lord, in other words, the law of justice as it descends upon the unrepentant wicked. We see this imagery next, in verses 15–17, as the Lord tells Jeremiah to give the wicked nations what they have asked for.

15 ¶ For **thus saith the LORD God of Israel unto me** [*Jeremiah*]; **Take the wine cup of this fury at my hand, and cause all the nations, to whom I send thee** [*to whom you are called to prophesy*], **to drink it** [*in effect, "give them the punishments they*

have asked for from Me and have them drink them in"].

16 And **they shall drink** [*the Lord's punishments will come upon them*], **and be moved** [*will stagger*], **and be mad** [*will be out of their mind with anguish*], **because of the sword** [*symbolic of destruction*] that I will send among them.

Next, Jeremiah testifies that he has obeyed the Lord and carried out His instructions. He is a witness against the wickedness of the people to whom he preaches.

17 **Then took I the cup at the LORD's hand** [*the cup of fury (the punishments of the Lord upon the wicked)*], **and made all the nations to drink, unto whom the LORD had sent me**:

As indicated in our note at the beginning of verse 18, next, "to wit" means "namely." In other words, Jeremiah is now going to list several of the nations implicated in his prophecy of punishment and destruction. He starts out by naming Jerusalem, and then goes on to name several other nations and peoples who will eventually drink the "fury" of the Lord.

18 *To wit* [*namely—see footnote 18a in your Bible*], **Jerusalem**, and **the cities of Judah**, and **the kings** thereof, and **the princes** [*political and religious leaders*] thereof, to make them a desolation, an astonishment, an hissing, and a curse; as *it is* this day;

As pointed out previously, "princes" is a word that generally means

"leaders." You will see this use of the word quite often in your Old Testament study.

19 Pharaoh king of **Egypt**, and his servants, and his princes, and all his people;

20 And all the mingled people, and all the kings of the land of **Uz**, and all the kings of the land of the **Philistines**, and **Ashkelon**, and **Azzah**, and **Ekron**, and the remnant of **Ashdod**,

21 **Edom**, and **Moab**, and the **children of Ammon**,

22 And all the kings of **Tyrus** [*NIV: "Tyre"*], and all the kings of **Zidon**, and the kings of the **isles** [*other nations*] which *are* beyond the sea,

23 **Dedan**, and **Tema**, and **Buz**, and all *that are* **in the utmost corners**,

24 And all the kings of **Arabia**, and all the kings of **the mingled people** [*foreigners*] **that dwell in the desert**,

25 And all the kings of **Zimri**, and all the kings of **Elam**, and all the kings of the **Medes**,

26 And **all the kings of the north**, far and near, one with another, and **all the kingdoms of the world**, which *are* **upon the face of the earth**: and the king of **Sheshach** [*NIV: "Babylon"—see also Jeremiah 51:41*] shall drink after them [*NIV: "will drink it too"*].

No doubt you noticed that Jeremiah did not leave out any of the wicked anywhere. The message is clear: It is impossible for the wicked, who chose not to repent when given ample opportunity to do so, to escape the punishments of God.

Next, the fact that all have agency to choose is emphasized. Just like a person can choose to get drunk and throw up (verse 27), so also can nations and people choose to get drunk, or out of control with wickedness, where they lurch and stagger from one form of evil to another, until they fall and are destroyed.

27 Therefore thou shalt say unto them, Thus saith the LORD of hosts, the God of Israel; **Drink ye, and be drunken** [*symbolic of wickedness; in other words, you have agency to choose to be out of control with wickedness*], and **spue** [*NIV: "vomit"*], and **fall,** and **rise no more**, because of the sword [*destruction*] which I will send among you.

Verse 28, next, reminds us that it is impossible for the unrepentant wicked to avoid the law of justice.

28 And it shall be, **if they refuse to take the cup at thine hand to drink** [*if they think they can stop the punishments of God*], then shalt thou **say unto them**, Thus saith the LORD of hosts; **Ye shall certainly drink.**

29 For, lo, **I begin to bring evil on the city which is called by my name** [*I am beginning even now to punish the inhabitants of Jerusalem*], and **should ye be utterly unpunished?**

Ye shall not be unpunished: for I will call for a sword upon all the inhabitants of the earth [*none of the wicked anywhere will ultimately escape their punishment*], saith the LORD of hosts.

As mentioned in the background to this chapter in this study guide, the final verses here seem to point to the last days and eventually to the Battle of Armageddon. Evil and wickedness will spread throughout the earth, and nations will gather in a concerted effort against the work of the Lord and His people.

30 **Therefore prophesy thou against them** [*the wicked*] **all these words**, and say unto them, **The LORD shall roar** [*everyone will hear it; "roar" can also symbolize the destructive power of a lion when it falls upon its prey, as mentioned in verse 38, below*] from on high, and **utter his voice** from his holy habitation; he shall mightily roar upon his habitation; he shall give a shout, as they that tread *the grapes,* **against all the inhabitants of the earth**.

The imagery in the phrase "tread the grapes" in verse 30, above, can symbolize the destruction of the wicked. This symbolism is also used to represent the destruction of the wicked at the time of the Second Coming. The red on the Savior's clothing symbolizes the blood of the wicked as they are destroyed at His coming. We will quote from the Doctrine and Covenants:

Doctrine & Covenants 133:48–51

48 And **the Lord shall be red in his apparel**, and his garments **like him that treadeth in the wine-vat**.

49 And so great shall be the glory of his presence that the sun shall hide his face in shame, and the moon shall withhold its light, and the stars shall be hurled from their places.

50 And his voice shall be heard: I have trodden the wine–press alone, and have brought judgment upon all people; and none were with me;

51 And **I have trampled them** [*the wicked*] **in my fury**, and I did tread upon them in mine anger, and **their blood have I sprinkled upon my garments, and stained all my raiment** [*the blood of the wicked is symbolically spattered upon the Savior's clothing, dying it red*]; for this was the day of vengeance which was in my heart [*this was the execution of the law of justice, which is in His heart as a vital part of the Plan of Salvation*].

31 **A noise shall come** *even* **to the ends of the earth**; for the LORD hath a controversy with the nations, he will **plead** with all flesh [*in effect, "He will bring all people to His court of law*]; **he will give them** *that are* **wicked to the sword**, saith the LORD.

32 Thus saith the LORD of hosts, Behold, **evil shall go forth from nation to nation**, and a great whirlwind shall be raised up from the coasts of the earth.

33 And **the slain of the LORD** [*the wicked who are destroyed*] **shall be at that day from** *one* **end of the earth even unto the** *other* end of the earth: they shall not be lamented, neither gathered, nor buried; they shall be dung upon the ground.

Next, Jeremiah targets the wicked leaders throughout the earth who lead the people astray.

34 ¶ **Howl, ye shepherds**, and cry; and **wallow yourselves** *in the ashes* [*a sign of great anguish and mourning in the culture of Jeremiah's day*], ye principal [*leaders*] of the flock: for **the days of your slaughter and of your dispersions are accomplished** [*the time for you to be punished has arrived*]; and ye shall fall like a pleasant vessel [*you will be shattered like fine pottery*].

35 And **the shepherds shall have no way to flee**, nor the principal of the flock to escape [*there is no escaping the Lord's punishments for you*].

As you have no doubt noticed, Jeremiah is definitely using the technique of repetition for emphasis here.

36 A voice of **the cry of the shepherds** [*the anguish of the evil leaders*], and an **howling of the principal** [*leaders*] of the flock, *shall be heard:* **for the LORD hath spoiled their pasture.**

37 And **the peaceable habitations** [*the pleasant living conditions*] **are cut down because of the fierce anger of the LORD**.

38 **He** [*the Lord*] **hath forsaken his covert, as the lion** [*He has come out of hiding like a lion*]: for **their land is desolate** because of the fierceness of the oppressor, and because of his fierce anger.

JEREMIAH 26

Selection: all verses

It is helpful to understand that the book of Jeremiah is not all arranged in chronological order. For example, chapter 25 fits in the fourth year of the reign of King Jehoiakim (see Jeremiah 25:1), whereas chapter 26 fits chronologically in the first year of his reign as king (see verse 1, next).

The JST makes important changes to seven verses in this chapter (verses 3, 5, 6, 13, 18, 19, and 20). We will include the JST text for each of these verses as we go along.

You have seen several prophecies about the destruction of Jerusalem so far in Jeremiah, and this chapter contains that same message. After he delivers this prophecy, Jeremiah will be arrested (verse 8) and tried in court for his life. The scene reminds us of Abinadi the prophet, arrested and tried in wicked King Noah's court because of the things he prophesied against the king and the people (Mosiah 12:9).

1 **IN the beginning of the reign of Jehoiakim** [*about 609 BC*] the son of Josiah king of Judah **came this word from the LORD** [*to Jeremiah*], saying,

2 Thus saith the LORD; Stand in the court of the LORD's house [*the outer courtyard of the temple in Jerusalem*], and **speak unto all the cities of Judah**, which come to worship in the LORD's house, **all the words that I command thee to speak unto them; diminish not a word** [*don't leave out a thing*]:

Verse 3, next, contains an invitation to the people to repent. And the JST makes an important correction, showing that it is the people who need to repent, not the Lord.

3 **If so be they will hearken, and turn every man from his evil way** [*if they will repent*], that I may repent me of the evil, which I purpose to do unto them because of the evil of their doings.

JST Jeremiah 26:3

3 If so be they will hearken, and turn every man from his evil way, **and repent, I will turn away the evil** which I purpose to do unto them because of the evil of their doings.

4 And thou shalt say unto them, Thus saith the LORD; **If ye will not hearken to me, to walk in my law**, which I have set before you,

5 **To hearken to the words of my servants the prophets, whom I sent** unto you, both rising up early, and sending *them,* **but ye have not hearkened**;

JST Jeremiah 26:5

5 To hearken to the words of my servants, the prophets, whom I sent unto you, **commanding them to rise up early**, and sending them;

In order to understand the comparison between the temple in Jerusalem and Shiloh, in verse 6, next, it helps to know that Shiloh (about twenty miles northeast of Jerusalem) was the final resting place for the tabernacle after the children of Israel settled in the promised land. Due to the eventual wickedness of the Israelites, the Lord allowed the Philistines to desecrate the tabernacle and destroy it. So also will the Lord allow the Babylonians to destroy the Jerusalem Temple and ravish Jerusalem.

6 Then will I make this house [*the temple in Jerusalem*] **like Shiloh, and will make this city a curse** to all the nations of the earth.

The JST adds an important phrase to verse 6, above.

JST Jeremiah 26:6

6 Then will I make this house like Shiloh, and will make this city a curse to all the nations of the earth; **for ye have not hearkened unto my servants the prophets**.

7 So the priests and the prophets and all the people heard Jeremiah speaking these words in the house of the LORD.

8 ¶ Now it came to pass, **when Jeremiah had made an end of speaking** all that the LORD had commanded *him* to speak unto all the people, that **the priests and the [***false***] prophets and all the people took him [***arrested him***], saying, Thou shalt surely die**.

9 **Why hast thou prophesied** in the name of the LORD, **saying, This house shall be like Shiloh, and this city shall be desolate without an inhabitant?** And all the people were gathered against Jeremiah in the house of the LORD.

Next, beginning with verse 10, we see that a court was convened to try Jeremiah. The trial was held near the temple in a public place where large crowds could watch the proceedings.

10 ¶ **When the princes [*leaders*]** of Judah **heard these things, then they came** up from the king's house unto the house of the LORD, **and sat down in the entry of the new gate of the LORD's** *house*.

11 Then spake the priests and the prophets unto the princes and to all the people, saying, **This man** *is* **worthy to die; for he hath prophesied against this city, as ye have heard with your ears**.

12 ¶ **Then spake Jeremiah** unto all the princes and to all the people, saying, **The LORD sent me to prophesy against this house and against this city all the words that ye have heard**.

13 Therefore now **amend your ways and your doings [***in other***

words, repent], and obey the voice of the LORD your God; and the LORD will repent [*see JST changes, next*] him of the evil that he hath pronounced against you.

JST Jeremiah 26:13

13 Therefore now, amend your ways and your doings, and **obey the voice of the Lord your God, and repent, and the Lord will turn away the evil that he hath pronounced against you.**

14 **As for me**, behold, I *am* in your hand: **do with me as seemeth good and meet** [*appropriate*] **unto** you.

15 **But** know ye for certain, that **if ye put me to death**, ye shall surely bring innocent blood upon yourselves, and upon this city, and upon the inhabitants thereof: for of a truth the LORD hath sent me unto you to speak all these words in your ears [*compare with Abinadi's words in Mosiah 17:9–10*].

Next, we see that controversy arose concerning what to do with Jeremiah.

16 ¶ **Then said the princes and all the people** unto the [*false*] priests and to the [*false*] prophets; **This man** *is* **not worthy to die**: for he hath spoken to us in the name of the LORD our God.

17 Then rose up **certain of the elders** [*older, wiser men*] of the land, and **spake to all the assembly** of the people, saying,

18 **Micah** the Morasthite **prophesied** [*see Micah, chapter 1*] in the days

of Hezekiah king of Judah, and spake to all the people of Judah, saying, Thus saith the LORD of hosts; **Zion shall be plowed** *like* **a field, and Jerusalem shall become heaps**, and the mountain of **the house** [*Temple*] as the high places of **a forest**.

JST Jeremiah 26:18

18 Micah the Morasthite prophesied in the days of Hezekiah king of Judah, and spake to all the people of Judah, saying, Thus saith the Lord of hosts; Zion shall be ploughed like a field, and Jerusalem shall become heaps, and the mountain of the house **of the Lord** as the high places of a forest.

19 **Did Hezekiah king of Judah and all Judah put him at all to death** [*did they even come close to putting Micah to death for what he prophesied*]? did he not fear the LORD, and besought the LORD, and the LORD repented him of the evil which he had pronounced against them? Thus might we procure great evil against our souls [*we could lose our souls if we execute Jeremiah*].

JST Jeremiah 26:19

19 Did Hezekiah, king of Judah, and all Judah put him at all to death? Did he not fear the Lord and beseech the Lord and repent? **and the Lord turned away the evil** which he had pronounced against them. **Thus by putting Jeremiah to death** we might procure great evil against our souls.

Next, in verses 20–24, we catch a glimpse of how wicked King

Jehoiakim was and thus understand that Jeremiah's life was indeed in danger. In these verses, a case from the past is brought up at Jeremiah's trial, detailing what had happened to Urijah, one of the Lord's prophets who had previously prophesied against the King and his wicked people.

20 And **there was also a man** that prophesied in the name of the LORD, **Urijah** the son of Shemaiah of Kirjath-jearim, **who prophesied against this city** and against this land according to all the words of Jeremiah [*just like Jeremiah has done*]:

You will see many changes made here by the Prophet Joseph Smith.

JST Jeremiah 26:20

20 But there was a man among the priests, rose up and said, that, Urijah the son of Shemaiah of Kirjath-jearim, prophesied in the name of the Lord, who also prophesied against this city, and against this land, according to all the words of Jeremiah;

21 **And when Jehoiakim the king, with all his mighty men, and all the princes, heard his words, the king sought to put him to death**: **but** when **Urijah** heard it, he was afraid, and **fled**, and went **into Egypt**;

22 **And Jehoiakim the king sent men into Egypt,** *namely,* Elnathan the son of Achbor, and *certain* men with him into Egypt.

23 **And they fetched forth Urijah out of Egypt, and brought him**

unto Jehoiakim the king; who slew him with the sword [*King Jehoiakim personally killed Urijah*], and cast his dead body into the graves of the common people.

The implication in verse 24, next, is that the officials of the court tried to turn Jeremiah over to the people to take him and kill him. But a man by the name of Ahikam protected him and saved his life. We will probably have to wait until we pass through the veil to get the rest of this story.

24 **Nevertheless** the hand of **Ahikam** the son of Shaphan **was with Jeremiah, that they should not give him into the hand of the people to put him to death.**

JEREMIAH 27

Selection: all verses

In this chapter, we see clearly that Judah is not the only nation that will be conquered by the coming armies of King Nebuchadnezzar of Babylon. We saw this same basic message in chapter 25.

As the Lord sends Jeremiah to deliver this message, He instructs him to use visual aids to help get the message across.

There appears to be a contradiction within the chapter as to when this prophecy was given. Verse 1 indicates that it came at the beginning of Jehoiakim's reign, but verses 3 and 12 suggest that it was given during King Zedekiah's reign several years later. We will quote from the Old Testament Student Manual for some helpful background.

"Ambassadors from several neighboring countries had come to Zedekiah with the proposal that unitedly they could defeat Babylon. Jeremiah was instructed to take bonds and yokes and wear them to symbolize that it was the Lord's will that they submit to their would-be conquerors. The message that they not try to change the decrees of God was also given by Jeremiah. Their lands were assigned to Babylon until that country ripened in iniquity and reaped its own reward. A specific promise to Judah was given in verse 11 that submission was their only hope of retaining their lands" (Old Testament Student Manual, page 247).

1 IN the beginning of the reign of Jehoiakim the son of Josiah [*should say "Zedekiah the son of Josiah"—see verse 3; also NIV, Jeremiah 27:1; this is probably an error made by a scribe somewhere along the way*] king of Judah came this **word unto Jeremiah from the LORD, saying,**

Can you imagine how unpopular Jeremiah's message of surrender was, which he gives in the next verses? He would be viewed as a coward and as a traitor.

2 Thus saith the LORD to me; **Make thee bonds and yokes, and put them upon thy neck** [*in other words, the Lord says for you to prepare to surrender*],

3 **And send them to the king of Edom,** and to the king of **Moab,** and to the king of the **Ammonites,** and to the king of **Tyrus** [*Tyre*], and to the king of **Zidon,** by the hand of the messengers [*the ambassadors*] which come to Jerusalem unto Zedekiah king of Judah;

4 And **command them to say unto their masters, Thus saith the LORD** of hosts, the God of Israel; Thus shall ye say unto your masters;

5 **I have made the earth,** the man and the beast that *are* upon the ground, by my great power and by my outstretched arm, **and have given it unto whom it seemed meet** [*good, appropriate*] unto me.

6 And **now have I given all these lands into the hand of Nebuchadnezzar the king of Babylon,** my servant [*an instrument temporarily in the hands of the Lord through whom to accomplish His purposes*]; and the beasts of the field have I given him also to serve him.

7 **And all** [*these*] **nations shall serve him, and his son, and his son's son, until the very time of his land** [*JST "of their end"*] **come**: and then many nations [*JST "and after that many nations"*] and great kings shall serve themselves of him [*will conquer him and be served by him*].

8 And it shall come to pass, *that* **the nation and kingdom which will not serve** the same **Nebuchadnezzar** the **king of Babylon,** and **that will not put their neck under the yoke of the king of Babylon** [*those who will not surrender to him*], **that nation will I punish,** saith the LORD, with the sword, and with the famine,

and with the pestilence, until I have consumed them by his hand.

When we combine verse 9, next, with verse 14, below, we come up with one scriptural definition of the term "false prophets."

9 Therefore **hearken not ye to your** [*false*] **prophets**, nor to your **diviners** [*fortune tellers who predict the future*], nor to your **dreamers**, nor to your **enchanters**, nor to your **sorcerers**, **which speak** unto you, **saying, Ye shall not serve the king of Babylon** [*who prophesy to you, saying that you will not come into bondage to Babylon*]:

10 For they **prophesy a lie unto you**, to remove you far from your land; and that I should drive you out, and ye should perish.

11 **But the nations that bring their neck under the yoke of** [*voluntarily surrender to*] **the king of Babylon**, and serve him, those **will I let remain still in their own land, saith the LORD; and they shall till it, and dwell therein**.

Next, in verses 12–15, Jeremiah tells us that he personally delivered this message of surrender to King Zedekiah.

12 ¶ **I spake also to Zedekiah** king of Judah according to all these words, **saying, Bring your necks under the yoke of the king of Babylon, and serve him and his people, and live**.

13 **Why will ye die**, thou and thy people, by the sword, by the famine, and by the pestilence, **as the LORD hath spoken against the nation that will not serve the king of Babylon?**

14 Therefore **hearken not unto the words of the** [*false*] **prophets** [*such as those described in verse 9, above*] **that speak** unto you, **saying, Ye shall not serve** [*you will not come into bondage to*] **the king of Babylon**: for they prophesy **a lie** unto you.

15 For **I have not sent them**, saith the LORD [*in other words, they are false prophets*], yet **they prophesy a lie in my name**; that I might drive you out, and that ye might perish, ye, and the prophets that prophesy unto you.

Next, Jeremiah reports that he has also delivered this same message to the false priests and to the people.

16 **Also I spake to the priests and to all this people, saying**, Thus saith the LORD; **Hearken not to the words of your** [*false*] **prophets** that prophesy unto you, saying, Behold, the vessels of the LORD's house shall now shortly be brought again from Babylon: **for they prophesy a lie unto you**.

Apparently, according to verse 16, above, some of the false prophets had told the people that the furnishings and adornments of the temple in Jerusalem would be taken to

Babylon but would be returned to Jerusalem shortly thereafter.

17 **Hearken not unto them; serve** [*surrender to*] **the king of Babylon, and live**: wherefore should this city be laid waste?

Next, Jeremiah issues a challenge to the people to test their false prophets as to whether or not they are sent from God.

18 But **if they *be* prophets**, and if the word of the LORD be with them, **let them now make intercession to the LORD of hosts** [*let them use their influence with the true God*], **that the vessels** [*the treasures*] which are left in the house of the LORD, and *in* the house of the king of Judah, and at Jerusalem, **go not to Babylon**.

Perhaps you sensed from the above verses that some of the Jews have already been taken to Babylon by this time. This is indeed the case. The conquest came in waves. For example, Daniel was taken to Babylon with many others in about 606 BC (see verse 20, below). The temple had not yet been completely looted, as indicated in verses 19–20, next.

19 ¶ For thus saith the LORD of hosts concerning the **pillars** [*of brass—see 2 Kings 25:13*], and concerning the **sea** [*the brass basin*], and concerning the **bases** [*stands*], and concerning the **residue of the vessels** [*furnishings, etc.*] that **remain in this city** [*Jerusalem*],

20 **Which Nebuchadnezzar king of Babylon took not, when he** **carried away captive Jeconiah** the son of Jehoiakim king of Judah from Jerusalem to Babylon, **and all the nobles of Judah and Jerusalem**;

We get a bit more information about the above-indicated wave of conquest from Daniel, which took place about 606 BC, including a definition of "the nobles of Judah" (verse 20, above).

Daniel 1:1–6

1 IN the third year of the reign of Jehoiakim king of Judah came Nebuchadnezzar king of Babylon unto Jerusalem, and besieged it.

2 And the Lord gave Jehoiakim king of Judah into his hand, with **part of the vessels of the house of God**: which he carried into the land of Shinar [*Babylon*] to the house of his god; and he brought the vessels into the treasure house of his god.

3 ¶ And the king spake unto Ashpenaz the master of his eunuchs, that he should **bring *certain* of the children of Israel, and of the king's seed, and of the princes**;

4 Children **in whom *was* no blemish, but well favoured, and skilful in all wisdom, and cunning in knowledge, and understanding science, and such as *had* ability in them** to stand in the king's palace, and **whom they might teach the learning and the tongue of the Chaldeans**.

5 And the king appointed them a daily provision of the king's meat, and of the wine which he drank: so nourishing them three years, that at the end thereof they might stand before the king.

6 Now **among these were** of the children of Judah, **Daniel, Hananiah, Mishael, and Azariah** [*Shadrach, Meshach, and Abednego—see Daniel 3:12*]:

21 Yea, **thus saith the LORD of hosts, the God of Israel, concerning the vessels that remain** *in* the house of the LORD, and *in* the house of the king of Judah and of Jerusalem;

22 **They shall be carried to Babylon, and there shall they be until the day that I visit them** [*bring the Jews back to Jerusalem, in about seventy years*], saith the LORD; then will I bring them up, and restore them to this place [*treasures will be brought back to Jerusalem*].

JEREMIAH 28

Selection: all verses

In this chapter we see Hananiah, a false prophet, go head-to-head with Jeremiah. It gets rather dramatic as Hananiah breaks the yoke (symbolic of slavery and forced labor—see Jeremiah 27:2) off of Jeremiah's neck and shoulders. In so doing, Hananiah emphasized his prophecy that those of Judah who had already been taken to Babylon would be back within two years, rather than in seventy years, as Jeremiah had prophesied (see Jeremiah 25:11).

Hananiah chooses a very public place to make his claim and challenge Jeremiah (verse 1). Let's see what happens.

1 AND it came to pass the same year, **in the beginning of the reign of Zedekiah** king of Judah, in the fourth year, *and* in the fifth month, *that* **Hananiah** the son of Azur the prophet, which *was* of Gibeon, **spake unto me** [*Jeremiah*] in the house of the LORD, **in the presence of the priests and of all the people**, saying,

2 **Thus speaketh the LORD** of hosts, the God of Israel, saying, **I have broken the yoke of the king of Babylon.**

3 **Within two full years** will I bring again into this place **all the vessels** of the LORD's house, **that Nebuchadnezzar king of Babylon took away from this place**, and carried them to Babylon:

4 And **I will bring again to this place** Jeconiah the son of Jehoiakim king of Judah, **with all the captives of Judah, that went into Babylon**, saith the LORD: for **I will break the yoke** [*power*] **of the king of Babylon.**

Imagine the exited anticipation among the onlookers as Jeremiah responded to Hananiah's challenge.

5 ¶ **Then the prophet Jeremiah said unto the** [*false*] **prophet Hananiah** in the presence of the priests, and in the presence of all the people that stood in the house of the LORD,

6 Even the prophet **Jeremiah said, Amen: the LORD do so: the LORD**

perform thy words which thou hast prophesied, to bring again the vessels of the LORD's house, and all that is carried away captive, from Babylon into this place.

Did Jeremiah's response, above, catch you a little off guard? It might appear that he is giving in and agreeing with Hananiah, in front of the crowds of people. But he is not. The following quote helps us understand what is going on:

"In verse 6, Jeremiah's 'Amen, the Lord do so,' is sarcastic, a challenge to see whose prophecies would be fulfilled. Moses taught that one test of a true prophet is whether his words come to pass (see Deuteronomy 18:22). Jeremiah had prophesied destruction and captivity; Hananiah, return and restoration. Jeremiah's response was simply that the prophet whose words come to pass is the one chosen by the Lord (see verse 9)" (Old Testament Student Manual, page 247).

7 Nevertheless **hear thou now this word that I** [*Jeremiah*] **speak** in thine ears, and in the ears of all the people;

Next, Jeremiah points out that many true prophets of old have prophesied misery and destruction against wicked nations.

8 The **prophets** that have been before me and before thee **of old prophesied both against many countries, and against great kingdoms**, of war, and of evil, and of pestilence.

As mentioned above, the test of a true prophet is whether or not his prophecies come true. Jeremiah points this out, next, in verse 9.

9 The prophet which prophesieth of peace, **when the word of the prophet shall come to pass**, *then* shall the prophet be known, that **the LORD hath truly sent him**.

Not yet satisfied, Hananiah next removes the wooden yoke, which Jeremiah is wearing around his neck (to symbolize the coming Babylonian captivity of the Jews and other nations), and breaks it in front of the crowd.

10 ¶ **Then Hananiah the prophet took the yoke from off the prophet Jeremiah's neck, and brake it.**

11 **And Hananiah spake** in the presence of all the people, saying, **Thus saith the LORD; Even so will I break the yoke of Nebuchadnezzar** king of Babylon from the neck of all nations **within the space of two full years**. And the prophet **Jeremiah went his way**.

12 ¶ **Then the word of the LORD came unto Jeremiah** *the prophet,* after that Hananiah the prophet had broken the yoke from off the neck of the prophet Jeremiah, **saying,**

13 **Go and tell Hananiah**, saying, Thus saith the LORD; **Thou hast broken the yokes of wood; but thou shalt make for them** [*in their place*] **yokes of iron** [*in other words, the yokes of wood will be replaced with yokes of iron*].

14 For **thus saith the LORD** of hosts, the God of Israel; **I have put a yoke of iron** [*symbolizing something they cannot get away from*] **upon the neck of all these nations** [*some of whom are mentioned in Jeremiah 27:3*], **that they may serve Nebuchadnezzar** king of Babylon; **and they shall serve him** [*the emphasis is on "shall" as the Lord bears His own witness that this prophecy will come true*]: and I have given him the beasts of the field also.

15 ¶ **Then said the prophet Jeremiah unto Hananiah** the [*false*] prophet, Hear now, Hananiah; **The LORD hath not sent thee** [*you are not a true prophet*]; but **thou makest this people to trust in a lie.**

16 **Therefore** thus saith the LORD; Behold, I will cast thee from off the face of the earth: **this year thou shalt die**, because thou hast taught rebellion against the LORD.

17 **So Hananiah the [*false*] prophet died the same year in the seventh month**.

JEREMIAH 29

Selection: all verses

This chapter contains the words of a letter (see verse 1) that Jeremiah sent to the captives who had already been taken to Babylon (see note following Jeremiah 27:18 in this study guide), attempting to counteract the words of false prophets among the Jews there. He tells them not to fight against their captivity, rather to build homes, plant gardens, marry, raise families, support the Babylonians, pray for the Babylonians, and, in short, to prepare for many years in Babylon. The following quote sets the stage for understanding this chapter:

"As in Jerusalem, so too in Babylon the predictions of the false prophets fostered a lively hope that the domination of Nebuchadnezzar would not last long, and that the return of the exiles to their fatherland would soon come about. The spirit of discontent thus excited must have exercised an injurious influence on the fortunes of the captives, and could not fail to frustrate the aim which the chastisement inflicted by God was designed to work out, namely, the moral advancement of the people. Therefore Jeremiah makes use of an opportunity furnished by an embassy (ambassador) sent by King Zedekiah to Babel, to address a letter to the exiles, exhorting them to yield with submission to the lot God had assigned to them. He counsels them to prepare, by establishing their households there, for a long sojourn in Babel (Babylon), and to seek the welfare of that country as the necessary condition of their own. They must not let themselves be deceived by the false prophets' idle promises of a speedy return, since God will not bring them back and fulfil His glorious promises till after seventy years have passed (verses 4–14)" (C. F. Keil and F. Delitzsch, Commentary on the Old Testament, 8:1:408–9).

1 NOW **these** *are* **the words of the letter that Jeremiah the prophet sent from Jerusalem** unto the residue of the elders which were carried away captives, and to the priests, and to the prophets, and **to all the**

people whom Nebuchadnezzar had carried away captive from Jerusalem to Babylon [*in the first wave or two of captives already taken to Babylon*];

Verse 1, above, will continue after a rather long "parentheses" (verse 2) and then yet another implied "parentheses" (verse 3). The last word of verse 3 continues, in effect, the substance of verse 1.

Verse 2, next, points out the common practice of first taking captives who were highly educated and capable of learning new languages and customs, skilled craftsmen, and so forth, in the initial waves of conquering a foreign country. This usually included those of the royal family, leaving a puppet king behind. In other words, they first carried off into captivity those who could make a significant contribution to the Babylonian economy.

2 (After that Jeconiah the king, and the queen, and the eunuchs, the princes of Judah and Jerusalem, and the carpenters, and the smiths, were departed from Jerusalem;)

3 By the hand of Elasah the son of Shaphan, and Gemariah the son of Hilkiah, (whom Zedekiah king of Judah sent unto Babylon to Nebuchadnezzar king of Babylon) **saying,**

4 **Thus saith the LORD** of hosts, the God of Israel, **unto all that are carried away captives**, whom I have caused to be carried away **from Jerusalem unto Babylon;**

5 **Build ye houses** [*prepare for many years (seventy years—see verse 10) in Babylonian captivity*], and dwell *in them;* and **plant gardens**, and eat the fruit of them;

6 **Take ye wives,** and **beget sons and daughters;** and **take wives for your sons,** and **give your daughters to husbands,** that they may bear sons and daughters; **that ye may be increased there** [*in Babylon*], and not diminished [*so that you do not die out as a people in captivity*].

7 And **seek the peace of the city** [*do things that contribute to the well-being of Babylon*] whither I have caused you to be carried away captives, and pray unto the LORD for it: **for in the peace thereof shall ye have peace** [*if the Babylonians have peace, you will have peace*].

Next, Jeremiah warns the captives not to listen to the false doctrines and messages of false prophets among them. By the way, there were also true prophets among the captives, such as Daniel (see Daniel 1:1–6) and Ezekiel (see Ezekiel 1:1–3).

8 ¶ For thus saith the LORD of hosts, the God of Israel; **Let not your** [*false*] **prophets and your diviners** [*soothsayers, fortune tellers, and the like*], **that *be* in the midst of you, deceive you,** neither hearken to your dreams which ye cause to be dreamed [*perhaps meaning don't give credibility to dreams which you dream in which you see yourselves free and back in Jerusalem*].

9 **For they** [*the false prophets among you*] **prophesy falsely unto you in my name: I have not sent them**, saith the LORD.

10 ¶ For thus saith the LORD, That **after seventy years** be accomplished at Babylon I will visit [*bless you*] **you**, and perform my good word toward you, **in causing you to return to this place** [*Jerusalem*].

Verses 11–14, next, contain very tender and encouraging words of prophecy to the Jews who find themselves in Babylonian captivity at this time. They describe what will happen to the Jews after the seventy years in captivity.

11 For **I know the thoughts that I think toward you**, saith the LORD, **thoughts of peace, and not of evil**, to give you an expected end [*freedom in Jerusalem again*].

12 **Then shall ye call upon me**, and ye shall go and pray unto me, **and I will hearken unto you**.

13 **And ye shall seek me, and find me,** when ye shall search for me **with all your heart**.

14 **And I will be found of you** [*and I will be available for you to find*], saith the LORD: and I will turn away your captivity, and **I will gather you** from all the nations, and from all the places whither I have driven you, saith the LORD; and **I will bring you again into the place** [*Jerusalem and Judah*] whence I caused you to be carried away captive.

The prophets referred to in verse 15, next, are false prophets. Jeremiah counsels the captives about such deceivers and warns them not to follow them. Verses 15–19 prophetically inform the captives what is yet to happen to those Jews who are still at home in Jerusalem and Judah.

15 ¶ **Because ye have said** [*claimed*], **The LORD hath raised us up prophets in Babylon** [*who are preaching lies to them, telling them that they will soon rejoin their friends and relatives back in Jerusalem*];

16 *Know* **that thus saith the LORD of** [*concerning*] **the king** that sitteth upon the throne of David [*the puppet king in Jerusalem*], **and of** [*about*] **all the people that dwelleth in this city**, *and* **of** [*about*] **your brethren that are not gone forth with you into captivity**;

17 Thus saith the LORD of hosts; Behold, **I will send upon them the sword**, the **famine**, and the **pestilence**, and will make them like vile figs [*that one throws away*], that cannot be eaten, they are so evil.

18 And **I will persecute them with the sword**, with the **famine**, and with the **pestilence**, and will deliver them to be **removed** [*scattered*] **to all the kingdoms of the earth**, to be a curse, and an astonishment, and an hissing, and a reproach [*to be disparaged and spoken of with contempt*], **among all the nations whither I have driven them**:

Verse 19, next, makes it sound like the Lord rises up early (which might falsely imply that, as a glorified, resurrected being, He still needs sleep). The JST straightens this out for us.

19 **Because they have not hearkened to my words**, saith the LORD, which I sent unto them by my servants the prophets, **rising up early and sending** *them;* but ye would not hear, saith the LORD.

JST Jeremiah 29:19

19 Because they have not hearkened to my words, saith the Lord, which I sent unto them by my servants the prophets, **commanding them to rise early, and sending them**; but ye would not hear, saith the Lord.

Next, Jeremiah warns specifically of two false prophets among the captives, one by the name of Ahab and one by the name of Zedekiah (both in verse 21).

20 ¶ **Hear** ye therefore the word of the LORD, **all ye of the captivity** [*all of you in Babylonian captivity*], whom I have sent from Jerusalem to Babylon:

21 **Thus saith the LORD** of hosts, the God of Israel [*in other words, Jehovah, the premortal Jesus Christ*], **of** [*about*] **Ahab** the son of Kolaiah, **and of** [*about*] **Zedekiah** the son of Maaseiah, **which prophesy a lie unto you in my name**; Behold, **I will deliver them into the hand of Nebuchadrezzar** [*usually spelled "Nebuchadnezzar"*] king of Babylon;

and **he shall slay them before your eyes**;

Not only will these two false prophets among the Jews in Babylon be killed by the King of Babylon, but they will become the brunt of a saying which will become a popular way to wish death upon enemies.

22 **And of them** [*from what happens to them*] **shall be taken up a curse** [*a saying*] **by all the captivity of Judah which** *are* **in Babylon** [*among all the captive Jews in Babylon*], saying, **The LORD make thee like Zedekiah and like Ahab**, whom the king of Babylon roasted in the fire;

23 **Because they** [*Ahab and Zedekiah*] **have committed villany** [*vile deeds—see footnote 23a in your Bible*] in Israel [*among the Lord's people*], and **have committed adultery** with their neighbours' wives, and **have spoken lying words in my name**, which I have not commanded them; even I know, and *am* a witness, saith the LORD.

Beginning with verse 24, next, Jeremiah responds (in his letter) to a man named Shemaiah, a man among the captives in Babylon, who has attempted to stir up trouble for Jeremiah by writing letters against him to people in Jerusalem. One letter, sent to a priest named Zephaniah in Jerusalem (verse 25) asks why he has done nothing to stop Jeremiah from prophesying. Among other things, Shemaiah suggests that Jeremiah be put in prison and in the stocks (verses 26–27).

The Lord has instructed Jeremiah as to what to say to Shemaiah in this letter.

24 ¶ *Thus* shalt thou also speak to Shemaiah the Nehelamite, saying,

25 Thus speaketh the LORD of hosts, the God of Israel, saying, **Because thou hast sent letters** in thy name **unto all the people that** *are* **at Jerusalem, and to Zephaniah** the son of Maaseiah **the priest, and to all the priests, saying,**

26 **The LORD hath made thee priest** in the stead of [*in place of*] Jehoiada the priest, **that ye should be officers** in the house of the LORD [*in other words, you are supposed to have authority and be in charge*], **for every man** *that is* **mad, and maketh himself a prophet, that thou shouldest put him in prison, and in the stocks.**

27 Now therefore **why hast thou not reproved Jeremiah** of Anathoth, **which maketh himself a prophet** to you [*who has set himself up as a false prophet*]?

Next, Shemaiah complains to Zephaniah that Jeremiah has prophesied a long period of captivity for the Jews in Babylon, and instructed them to settle down as if permanent there. (This is in stark contrast to the false prophets' prophecies of a brief, no longer than two year period of captivity.)

28 For therefore **he** [*Jeremiah*] **sent unto us** *in* **Babylon, saying, This** *captivity is* **long**: build ye houses, and dwell *in them;* and plant gardens, and eat the fruit of them.

29 And **Zephaniah the priest read this letter in the ears of Jeremiah the prophet.**

30 ¶ **Then came the word of the LORD unto Jeremiah, saying,**

31 **Send to all them of the captivity** [*write to all the Jews in Babylonian captivity*], **saying, Thus saith the LORD concerning Shemaiah** the Nehelamite; **Because** that **Shemaiah hath prophesied unto you, and I sent him not, and he caused you to trust in a lie** [*his own false prophecies*]:

32 **Therefore** thus saith the LORD; Behold, **I will punish Shemaiah the Nehelamite, and his seed**: he shall not have a man to dwell among this people; neither shall he behold [*live to see*] the good that I will do for my people, saith the LORD; **because he hath taught rebellion against the LORD** [*in other words, none of his posterity will return with the Jews in seventy years (about 537 BC—see chronology chart in Bible Dictionary), when Cyrus the Persian decrees that they can return and take the temple treasures back with them to Jerusalem*].

JEREMIAH 30

Selection: all verses

We will quote from the Old Testament Student Manual for background for chapters 30–33.

"The prophet Jeremiah lived through one of the most troubled periods of history in the ancient Near East. He witnessed the fall of a great empire (Assyria) and the rising of another (Babylon). In the midst of this turmoil the kingdom of Judah was ruled by five kings, four of them deplorable. Jeremiah declared God's message for forty years, warning of coming disaster and appealing in vain to the nation to turn back to God.

"During Manasseh's long reign (687–642 BC), which was just before Jeremiah's time, Judah remained Assyria's vassal. This situation brought a resurgence of idolatry, in this case a mixture of belief in the Mesopotamian astrological gods and belief in the Canaanite fertility deities. As has been discussed, a great reformation was conducted by Josiah when the book of the law was discovered in the temple and its contents were made known to the people. Aside from this brief period of reform, Judah became increasingly insensitive to spiritual things during Jeremiah's time.

"The Lord showed Jeremiah a vision of the future that put the calamities he had witnessed into a perspective of hope. Like other prophets of his time (Isaiah, Ezekiel, Hosea, Amos, Micah, and Zechariah), Jeremiah was shown that scattered Israel would one day be gathered, that Judah would return to the lands of her possession, and that eventually all of Israel would become great. These visions and prophecies were recorded by Jeremiah and for centuries have provided hope to a nation of suffering people. They hold a very important place in the latter-day work of restoration" (Old Testament Student Manual, page 253).

Remember that "Israel," in an overall sense, refers to the Lord's covenant people, descendants of Abraham through Jacob (whose name was changed to Israel—see Genesis 32:28). It includes all who will make and keep covenants with the Lord, which will ultimately lead to exaltation in the highest degree of the celestial kingdom.

After Solomon's reign as King of Israel, the kingdom split into two nations, Judah and Israel. The tribes of Judah and Benjamin became known as Judah, and the northern ten tribes became known as Israel. The northern ten tribes became known as the lost ten tribes, after Assyria captured and carried them away, in about 722 BC. Judah is being carried away into Babylonian captivity in waves, during Jeremiah's lifetime.

One of the great prophecies of the latter days is that Israel will be gathered and that the Lord will once again have a righteous covenant people. Jeremiah prophesied of this great gathering in many places, including these next three chapters.

In verses 1–2, next, Jeremiah is instructed by the Savior to record these prophecies of the future gathering of Judah and Israel.

1 THE word that came to Jeremiah from the LORD, saying,

2 Thus speaketh the LORD God of Israel, saying, **Write thee all the words that I have spoken unto thee in a book.**

3 For, lo, **the days come**, saith the LORD, **that I will bring again** the

captivity of [*out of captivity*] **my people Israel and Judah**, saith the LORD: and I will cause them to return **to the land that I gave to their fathers**, and they shall possess it.

We understand verse 3, above, to refer both to the return of the captives after seventy years in Babylon and to the gathering of Israel in the last days (see heading to chapter 30 in your Bible). But the main emphasis in this chapter is on the restoration of the gospel and the gathering of Israel in the last days.

4 ¶ And **these** *are* **the words that the LORD spake concerning Israel and concerning Judah**.

Verses 5–7 seem to set the emotional stage for the latter-day gathering of Israel. They serve as reminders of the extreme agony and distress Israel and Judah have gone through throughout the centuries, because of their rebellion against their God.

5 For thus saith the LORD; **We have heard a voice of trembling, of fear, and not of peace**.

The picture "painted" by Jeremiah's words in verse 6, next, is, in effect, a scene in which strong men are trembling in agony, as if they were in childbirth labor. The message is that Israel and Judah have gone through terrible agony to get their attention and prepare them for redemption.

6 **Ask ye now, and see whether a man doth travail with child** [*have you ever heard of a man having labor pains*]? **Wherefore** [*why then*] **do I see every man with his hands on**

his loins, as a woman in travail [*NIV: "with his hands on his stomach like a woman in labor"*], **and all faces are turned into paleness?**

7 Alas! for that day *is* great [*the punishments and pains of the past*], so that none *is* like it: it *is* even the time of Jacob's trouble [*Jacob (Israel) has gone through terrible pain*]; **but he shall be saved out of it** [*Israel will be gathered and saved in the last days*].

The major message that now follows is that the gospel of Jesus Christ has power to redeem us out of the worst of conditions and spiritual bondage.

8 For it shall come to pass **in that day** [*in the last days*], saith the LORD of hosts, *that* **I will break his yoke from off thy neck, and will burst thy bonds**, and strangers shall no more serve themselves of him [*Israel will no more be in bondage (including the terrible bondage of sin—see footnote 8a in your Bible)*]:

9 **But they shall serve the LORD their God, and David their king** [*Christ—see heading to this chapter in your Bible*], whom I will raise up unto them.

10 ¶ **Therefore fear thou not**, O my servant Jacob, saith the LORD; neither be dismayed, O Israel: for, lo, **I will save thee** from afar, and thy seed from the land of their captivity; and **Jacob** [*Israel*] **shall return**, and shall be in rest, and be quiet [*live in peace*], and none shall make *him* afraid.

11 **For I** *am* **with thee**, saith the LORD, to save thee: though I make a full end of all nations whither **I have scattered thee, yet will I not make a full end of thee** [*you will not be destroyed completely*]: but I will correct [*discipline*] thee in measure, and will not leave thee altogether unpunished.

Without the help of the JST, verses 12, 13, and 15, next, would be completely negative. Whereas, with the JST, we see that there is still hope for these people.

12 For thus saith the LORD, **Thy bruise** *is* **incurable**, *and* **thy wound** *is* **grievous**.

JST Jeremiah 30:12

12 For thus saith the Lord, **Thy bruise is not incurable, although thy wounds are grievous**.

13 *There is* **none** to plead thy cause, that thou mayest be bound up: **thou hast no healing medicines**.

JST Jeremiah 30:13

13 **Is there none** to plead thy cause, that thou mayest be bound up? **Hast thou no healing medicines?**

14 **All thy lovers** [*false gods, idols*] **have forgotten thee; they seek thee not** [*they are not coming to help you out of trouble*]; for I have wounded thee with the wound of an enemy [*in effect, "I have punished you because you are an enemy of righteousness"*], with the chastisement of a cruel one, for [*because of*] the multitude of thine **iniquity**; *because* thy sins

were increased [*you just keep getting more wicked*].

JST Jeremiah 30:14

14 **Have all thy lovers forgotten thee, do they not seek thee?** For I have wounded thee with the wound of an enemy, with the chastisement of a cruel one, for the multitude of thine **iniquities**; because thy sins **are** increased.

Next, in verse 15, the Lord again repeats the reason He has had to bring such calamities upon these people.

15 Why criest thou for [*because of*] thine affliction? **thy sorrow** *is* **incurable** for the multitude of thine iniquity: *because* thy sins **were** increased, I have done these things unto thee.

JST Jeremiah 30:15

15 Why criest thou for thine affliction? **Is thy sorrow incurable?** It was for the multitude of thine iniquities, and because thy sins **are** increased I have done these things unto thee.

16 **Therefore** all they that devour thee shall be devoured [*the wicked who conquer you will themselves be conquered*]; and all thine adversaries, every one of them, shall go into captivity [*for example, the Medes and the Persians eventually conquered the Babylonians*]; and they that spoil thee shall be a spoil [*shall become a prey to their own enemies*], and all that prey upon thee will I give for a prey.

JST Jeremiah 30:16

16 But all they that devour thee shall be devoured; and all thine adversaries, every one of them, shall go into captivity; and they that spoil thee shall be a spoil, and all that prey upon thee will I give for a prey.

It is interesting to note that all the foreign kingdoms in ancient times who conquered and persecuted the Jews have ceased to exist, but the Jews themselves still exist as a distinct people today.

Verse 17, next, prophesies that Israel will eventually be restored as the people of the Lord, and that their spiritual wounds will be healed.

17 For **I will restore health unto thee, and I will heal thee of thy wounds**, saith the LORD; because they called thee an Outcast, *saying,* This *is* Zion, whom no man seeketh after.

In verses 18–22, next, we see a prophecy of the conversion and restoration of Israel in the last days, including the establishment of their own political kingdoms. Remember, "Israel," in this context, is a collective term for all of the Lord's covenant people, including the Jews.

18 ¶ Thus saith the LORD; Behold, **I will bring again** [*restore*] **the captivity of Jacob's tents** [*the things lost during Israel's captivity*], and have mercy on his dwellingplaces; and the city shall be builded upon her own heap [*on the same site*], and the palace shall remain after the manner thereof.

19 And **out of them** [*the devastated cities and ruins*] **shall proceed thanksgiving and the voice of them that make merry**: and I will multiply them, and they shall not be few; **I will also glorify them, and they shall not be small** [*insignificant in world politics and influence*].

20 Their children also shall be as aforetime, and their congregation shall be established before me, and **I will punish all that oppress them**.

21 And **their nobles** [*governors, political leaders*] **shall be of themselves, and their governor shall proceed from the midst of them** [*in other words, they will no longer be governed and ruled over by foreigners, rather, will produce their own political leaders*]; and I will cause him to draw near, and **he shall approach unto m**e: for who is this that engaged his heart to approach unto me? saith the LORD.

22 And **ye shall be my people, and I will be your God**.

Verses 23–24, next, serve as a reminder that the punishments of God will continue to be poured out upon the wicked.

23 Behold, **the whirlwind of the LORD** goeth forth with fury, a continuing whirlwind: it **shall fall with pain upon the head of the wicked**.

24 **The fierce anger of the LORD shall not return** [*will not be pulled back*], until he have done *it,* and until he have performed the intents of his heart: **in the latter days ye**

shall consider it [*fully understand it—see footnote 24b in your Bible*].

JEREMIAH 31

Selection: all verses

This chapter continues with the theme of the gathering and restoration of Israel in the last days—see heading in your Bible.

Remember, the most important eternal aspect of the gathering of Israel is that each of us be gathered spiritually to the gospel of Jesus Christ. The physical gathering of Israel to various places, including stakes of Zion (D&C 109:39) is part of the plan which enables people to be gathered to Christ.

As we study this chapter, we will see the restoration of the gospel in the latter days, the role that Ephraim plays in the latter-day gathering, the renewal of the covenant with Israel, including Judah (verse 31), and the eventual coming of the Millennium (verse 34).

In verse 1, Jeremiah begins with the Restoration of the gospel to scattered Israel in the last days.

1 **AT the same time** [*referring to the "latter days," mentioned at the very end of chapter 30*], saith the LORD, **will I be the God of all the families of Israel, and they shall be my people.**

Verse 2, next, speaks of the future as if it has already taken place. This is a common form of prophesying among Old Testament prophets.

2 Thus saith the LORD, **The people** *which were* **left of the sword** [*the remnant who survived the destruction*

and captivity] **found grace** [*the favor of the Lord*] in the wilderness [*after they had been in apostasy*]; *even* **Israel**, when I went to cause him to rest [*when I restored the gospel to them*].

3 The LORD hath appeared of old [*in times past*] unto me [*Israel*], *saying,* Yea, I have loved thee with an everlasting love: therefore with lovingkindness have I drawn thee [*nourished and brought you forward*].

4 **Again I will build thee** [*beginning with the Restoration through Joseph Smith*], and **thou shalt be built**, O virgin of Israel [*the Lord's covenant people*]: thou shalt again be adorned with thy tabrets, and shalt go forth in the dances of them that make merry.

5 **Thou shalt yet plant vines upon the mountains of Samaria** [*you will be restored to your lands*]: the planters shall plant, and shall eat *them* as common things.

We will quote from the Old Testament Student Manual as background for verses 6–9, next:

"The watchmen mentioned in verse 6 are the righteous prophets of the latter days (see also Ezekiel 3:16–21). In the last dispensation they shall cry to all people to join together in proper worship of the Lord (see D&C 1:1–2). Verse 8 speaks of gathered Israel coming from the north country (see D&C 110:11; 133:26) and from the coasts (ends) of the earth.

"Elder LeGrand Richards said of this gathering: ' "I will bring them . . . a great company shall return thither." This was something the Lord was going to do. Note that Jeremiah does not say that they will return hither, or to the place where this prediction was made, but thither, or to a distant place. He understood that Joseph was to be given a new land in the "utmost bound of the everlasting hills" ' (See Genesis 49:22–26; Deuteronomy 33:13–17.)" (Israel! Do You Know? pp. 177–78).

"Verse 9 refers to Israel returning with weeping. They will weep because they will realize that the sufferings they have endured throughout the centuries came about because they rejected the Lord Jesus Christ, who shall lead them in the last days (see Jeremiah 50:4; Zechariah 12:10)" (Old Testament Student Manual, pages 254–55).

6 For **there shall be a day,** *that* **the watchmen** [*righteous latter-day prophets*] upon the mount Ephraim **shall cry**, Arise ye, and **let us go up to Zion unto the LORD our God**.

7 For thus saith the LORD; Sing with gladness for Jacob [*Israel*], and shout among the chief of the nations: publish ye, praise ye, **and say, O LORD, save thy people, the remnant of Israel**.

8 Behold, **I will bring them from the north country** [*when Israel (the lost ten tribes) were captured in about 722 BC, the Assyrians took them to the north*], **and gather them from the coasts of the earth**, *and* with them the blind and the lame, the woman with child and her that travaileth with child

together: **a great company shall return** thither.

The role of the birthright son in ancient times included the responsibility to take care of the rest of his father's children. We see this role for Ephraim, in verse 9, next.

9 They shall come with weeping, and with supplications will I lead them: I will cause them to walk by the rivers of waters in a straight way, wherein they shall not stumble: for **I am a father to Israel, and Ephraim** *is* **my firstborn** [*has the birthright and thus the first responsibility to shepherd the rest of the tribes to the safety of the gospel*].

The word, "isles," as used in the Old Testament, generally means continents and peoples throughout the earth, other than the Near East.

10 ¶ **Hear the word of the LORD**, O ye nations, and **declare** *it* **in the isles** [*continents*] **afar off** [*preach the gospel throughout the world*], and say, He that scattered Israel will gather him, and keep him, as a shepherd *doth* his flock.

11 For **the LORD hath redeemed Jacob** [*through the Restoration, the Lord will have redeemed Israel*], **and ransomed him from the hand of** *him that was* **stronger than he** [*and rescued him from his enemies*].

Note the beautiful descriptive language of Jeremiah as he describes the blessings of the Restoration and the blessings that come to people who allow the Lord to take care of them.

12 Therefore they shall come [*will be gathered*] and **sing** in the height of Zion, and shall **flow together to the goodness of the LORD**, for wheat, and for wine, and for oil, and for the young of the flock and of the herd: **and their soul shall be as a watered garden; and they shall not sorrow any more at all**.

13 **Then shall the virgin** [*the faithful saints of Zion*] **rejoice** in the dance, both young men and old together: **for I will turn their mourning into joy, and will comfort them, and make them rejoice from their sorrow**.

14 **And I will satiate** [*completely satisfy*] **the soul of the priests** [*Church leaders*] **with fatness** [*the very best*], **and my people shall be satisfied** [*filled*] **with my goodness**, saith the LORD.

Next, we see the stage set emotionally for us to truly appreciate what it will mean for Israel to finally be gathered.

15 ¶ Thus saith the LORD; **A voice was heard in Ramah** [*a place in southern Israel, associated with Rachel's tomb, where the captives were gathered before being taken to Babylon—see BD, under "Ramah"*], **lamentation, *and* bitter weeping; Rahel** [*Rachel, the mother of Joseph, hence the grandmother of Ephraim*] **weeping for her children** refused to be comforted for her children, because they

were not [*the descendants of Rachel, symbolically representing Israel, were carried away captive, both literally by enemies and figuratively by Satan into spiritual bondage*].

Verses 16–17, next, say, in effect, "Cheer up! Look at the future and see the glorious restoration of the gospel and the gathering of Israel to the Lord in the last days."

16 Thus saith the LORD; **Refrain thy voice from weeping, and thine eyes from tears**: for thy work shall be rewarded, saith the LORD; and **they shall come again from the land of the enemy**.

17 And **there is hope** in thine end, saith the LORD, that **thy children shall come again** to their own border.

Using repetition, Jeremiah again drives home the point that Ephraim (another name for Israel or the northern ten tribes, with headquarters in Samaria before the Assyrians carried them away in 722 BC) has mourned his wickedness and apostasy and will repent in the last days.

18 ¶ **I** [*the Lord*] **have surely heard Ephraim bemoaning himself *thus;* Thou hast chastised me**, and I was chastised, as a bullock unaccustomed *to the yoke* [*the "yoke" of bondage settled me down and brought me under control*]: **turn thou me, and I shall be turned** [*please guide me now and I will follow*]; **for thou *art* the LORD my God**.

19 Surely after that I was turned, **I repented; and after that I was instructed**, I smote upon *my* thigh [*I mourned because of my past wickedness*]: I was ashamed, yea, even confounded, because I did bear the reproach of my youth [*I had to live with the disgrace of my past wickedness*].

Next, the Lord assures Ephraim (Israel, in this context) that he can indeed repent and be gathered back to the Lord. The Lord will once again take delight in blessing him.

20 *Is* **Ephraim my dear son?** *is he* **a pleasant child** [*can he still be blessed*]**?** for since I spake against him [*punished him in times past*], **I do earnestly remember him still**: therefore **my bowels** [*My deepest feelings*] **are troubled for him** [*sympathize with him*]**; I will surely have mercy upon him**, saith the LORD.

Next, the Lord encourages Israel to do everything in his power to turn around (from apostasy) and return home to God. Highway signs are used to symbolize his finding the right direction to return home.

21 Set thee up waymarks [*roadsigns*], make thee high heaps [*rocks pointing the direction to return to God*]: **set thine heart toward the highway** [*turn your heart to Me*], *even* the way *which* thou wentest: **turn again** [*turn around from the apostate direction you've been going*], O virgin of Israel, turn again to these thy cities [*return home*].

The "paragraph" mark (backward "P") at the beginning of verse 22 in your Bible (if it is a King James version) signals the change to a new topic. In this case, the Lord, having told them how wonderful it will be for them in the future, now asks Israel how long they are going to continue wandering in sin. Then, speaking of the future again, He tells them that a new experience (for them) will be available at that time, namely, "A woman shall compass a man" (end of verse 22).

22 ¶ **How long wilt thou go about, O thou backsliding** [*apostate*] **daughter?** for the LORD hath created a new thing in the earth, **A woman shall compass a man** [*see note, next*].

The last phrase of verse 22, above, needs explaining. As you know, in the covenant relationship between Israel and the Lord, Israel is often referred to as the "bride" or wife, and the Lord (Jesus Christ or Jehovah) is referred to symbolically as the "bridegroom" or husband. The tender and intimate relationship between the husband and wife are symbolic of the closeness that should exist between the Lord and His people. We generally think of the Lord nourishing His people, but in the phrase above, the implication is that, in the last days, Israel will nourish the Lord and be tender toward Him. This can remind us that the Savior and our Father in Heaven both have joy when we are righteous.

We will use a quote to further explain this:

"In the verse (Jeremiah 31:22) now before us (the Hebrew word which is translated as 'compass'), signifies to encompass with love and care, to surround lovingly and carefully,—the natural and fitting dealing on the part of the stronger to the weak and those who need assistance. And the new thing that God creates consists in this, that the woman, the weaker nature that needs help, will lovingly and solicitously surround the man, the stronger. Herein is expressed a new relation of Israel to the Lord, a reference to a new covenant which the Lord, ver. 31ff., will conclude with His people, and in which He deals so condescendingly toward them that they can lovingly embrace Him. This is the substance of the Messianic meaning in the words" (Keil and Delitzsch, Commentary, 8:2:30).

23 Thus saith the LORD of hosts, the God of Israel; **As yet** [*sometime in the future*] **they shall use this speech** [*phrase; saying*] **in the land of Judah and in the cities thereof,** when I shall bring again their captivity [*NIV: "When I bring them back from captivity"*]; **The LORD bless thee, O habitation of justice, *and* mountain of holiness** [*in other words, there will be peace and righteousness*] .

24 And there shall dwell in Judah itself, and in all the cities thereof together, husbandmen [*farmers*], and they *that* go forth with flocks.

Again, in verse 25, next, a future time of peace is spoken of prophetically as if it had already come to pass.

25 For I have satiated [*satisfied*] the weary soul, and I have replenished [*renewed*] every sorrowful soul.

26 Upon this I awaked, and beheld; and my sleep was sweet unto me [*this is a sweet dream of the future which will someday be fulfilled*].

In verses 27–28, next, we see yet another form of the prophecy concerning the gathering and restoration of Israel and Judah in the last days.

27 ¶ Behold, **the days come**, saith the LORD, **that I will sow** [*plant*] **the house of Israel and the house of Judah with** the seed of **man, and with** the seed of **beast** [*whereas, in the past, Israel and Judah have been killed, reduced in population, and scattered, in the last days they will multiply and prosper*].

28 **And it shall come to pass, *that* like as I have watched over them, to pluck up**, and to **break down**, and to **throw down**, and to **destroy**, and to **afflict** [*just as I supervised their past punishments*]; **so will I watch over them, to build, and to plant**, saith the LORD.

Verse 29, next, is apparently a Jewish proverb in common use in Jeremiah's day, which says, in effect, that children are negatively affected by the sins of their parents.

29 In those days [*in the last days*] they shall say no more [*the false doctrine will no longer be taught among the*

Lord's people], The fathers have eaten a sour grape, and the children's teeth are set on edge [*the children are cursed by the sins of their parents*].

Verse 30, next, says that when the gospel is restored, in the last days, the true doctrine will be taught, namely that we are accountable for our own transgressions, not for the sins of others.

30 But **every one shall die for his own iniquity**: every man that eateth the sour grape, his teeth shall be set on edge.

When you read verse 30, above, did you think of the second Article of Faith? We will quote it here:

Article of Faith 2

2 We believe that men will be punished for their own sins, and not for Adam's transgression.

We learn more about the latter-day gathering of Israel and Judah and the important role of covenants associated with it beginning with verse 31, next.

31 ¶ **Behold, the days come, saith the LORD, that I will make a new covenant with** the house of **Israel, and with** the house of **Judah**:

32 **Not according to** [*not like*] **the covenant that I made with their fathers** [*ancestors—the children of Israel*] **in the day *that* I took them by the hand to bring them out of the land of Egypt**; which my covenant they brake, although I was an hus-

band unto them [*even though I took good care of them*], saith the LORD:

The covenant, or Law of Moses that the Lord gave the wayward children of Israel, included many laws and details that demanded strict obedience to detail. In verse 33, next, the Lord reveals that in the last days the covenants He will make with His people will require deep conversion and the heartfelt desire to live gospel principles, rather than the step-by-step demands of old.

33 **But this *shall be* the covenant that I will make with the house of Israel**; After those days, saith the LORD, **I will put my law in their inward parts, and write it in their hearts**; and will be their God, and they shall be my people.

The peaceful and glorious conditions mentioned in verse 33, above, lead into verse 34, next, which alludes to the Millennium (see footnote 34a in your Bible).

34 And **they shall teach no more every man his neighbour, and every man his brother,** saying, Know the LORD: **for they shall all know me** [*during the Millennium*], from the least of them unto the greatest of them, saith the LORD; for I will forgive their iniquity, and I will remember their sin no more.

Verse 35, next, says, in effect, "Thus saith the Lord, the Creator of heaven and earth."

35 ¶ Thus saith the LORD, which giveth the sun for a light by day, *and*

the ordinances [*orbits—see footnote 35c in your Bible*] of the moon and of the stars for a light by night, which divideth the sea when the waves thereof roar; The LORD of hosts *is* his name:

36 **If those ordinances** [*the ordinances contained in the covenant spoken of in verse 33, above*] **depart from before me**, saith the LORD, *then* **the seed of Israel also shall cease from being a nation before me for ever**.

> We will quote from the Old Testament Student Manual to further explain verse 36, above:

> "The Lord, who has worked so long and hard to establish his righteous people, said that if those saving and exalting priesthood ordinances cease to exist, then Israel also will cease to exist—forever. This statement surely indicates the importance of ordinances in the Lord's plan" (Old Testament Student Manual, page 256).

37 Thus saith the LORD; **If heaven above can be measured** [*which it cannot be by man*], and the foundations of the earth searched out beneath, **I will also cast off all the seed of Israel** for [*because of*] all that they have done, saith the LORD [*in other words, He will not reject Israel forever but will restore them through the use of covenants in the last days*].

> In verses 38–40, next, we see a prophecy that Jerusalem will become one of two cities (Old Jerusalem, in the Holy Land, and New Jerusalem,

in Independence, Missouri) during the Millennium that will serve as headquarters for the Savior as He rules and reigns during the one thousand years. You can read a bit about these two cities in Ether 13:3–11.

38 ¶ Behold, **the days come, saith the LORD, that the city** [*Jerusalem*] **shall be built to the LORD** from the tower of Hananeel unto the gate of the corner.

39 And the measuring line shall yet go forth over against it upon the hill Gareb, and shall compass about to Goath.

40 And the whole valley of the dead bodies, and of the ashes, and all the fields unto the brook of Kidron, unto the corner of the horse gate toward the east, *shall be* **holy unto the LORD; it shall not be plucked up, nor thrown down any more for ever**.

JEREMIAH 32

Selection: all verses

At this point in history, about 588 BC, wicked King Zedekiah has put Jeremiah in prison. The king is displeased with his prophecies about the impending Babylonian captivity of Jerusalem and the prophecy that the king will also be captured and will be taken to Babylon (verses 2–5). Daniel, along with Shadrach, Meshach, and Abednego (Daniel 3:12) have already been taken captive to Babylon with the first group of Jewish intellectuals and craftsmen in about 606 BC. Lehi and his family left Jerusalem in 600 BC. Ezekiel was taken to Babylon with another group of captives in about 598 BC. He will serve as a prophet to the Jews in captivity for about twenty-two years, from 592–570 BC (see Bible Dictionary under "Ezekiel"). The final wave of Babylonian attacks and resulting captivity will soon take place.

It is the tenth year of the eleven-year reign of Zedekiah (see verse 1 coupled with Jeremiah 52:1), which puts the date of this chapter at about 588 BC. Zedekiah is now about thirty-one years old, and Jeremiah has been serving as a prophet to the Jews for about thirty years.

As the heading to this chapter in your Bible states, Jeremiah will be instructed by the Lord to purchase some property as a means of symbolizing and prophesying that scattered Israel (including the Jews who are soon to be scattered) will be gathered by the Lord back to their land. The final gathering of Israel in the last days will be accomplished by means of covenants with the Lord, such as baptism and the covenants that follow among the faithful.

In verses 1–5, King Zedekiah has Jeremiah brought to him from prison and asks him why he has been so negative in his prophecies about the king and his kingdom.

1 THE word that came to Jeremiah from the LORD **in the tenth year** [*the tenth year of the reign*] **of Zedekiah** king of Judah, which *was* the eighteenth year of Nebuchadrezzar [*king of Babylon*].

2 For then the king [*Nebuchadnezzar (another biblical name for Nebuchadrezzar)*] of Babylon's army besieged Jerusalem: and **Jeremiah** the prophet **was shut up in** the court of the **prison,** which *was* in the king of Judah's house [*this prison was located in the king's palace*].

3 For **Zedekiah** king of Judah **had shut him up** [*put him in prison*], **saying, Wherefore** [*why*] **dost thou prophesy, and say, Thus saith the LORD, Behold, I will give this city** [*Jerusalem*] **into the hand of the king of Babylon**, and he shall take it;

4 **And Zedekiah** king of Judah **shall not escape** out of the hand of the Chaldeans [*another name for Babylonians*], but shall surely be delivered into the hand of the king of Babylon, and shall speak with him mouth to mouth, and his eyes shall behold his eyes;

5 **And he shall lead Zedekiah to Babylon**, and there shall he be until I visit him, saith the LORD: though ye fight with the Chaldeans, ye shall not prosper [*will not win*].

Next, beginning with verse 6, Jeremiah records that, at this point, the Lord told him to buy some property in Anathoth (Jeremiah's home town, about three miles north of Jerusalem). This purchase was to prophetically symbolize the return of Israel.

6 ¶ **And Jeremiah said, The word of the LORD came unto me, saying,**

7 **Behold, Hanameel** [*Jeremiah's cousin*] the son of Shallum thine uncle **shall come unto thee, saying,**

Buy thee my field that *is* in Anathoth: for the right of redemption *is* thine to buy *it* [*you have the legal right to buy it before anyone else is given the option to purchase it*].

8 So Hanameel mine uncle's son came to me in the court of the prison according to the word of the LORD, and said unto me, Buy my field, I pray thee, that *is* in Anathoth, which *is* in the country of Benjamin: for the right of inheritance *is* thine, and the redemption *is* thine [*symbolic of the prophetic fact that Israel would someday be redeemed by the Savior*]; buy *it* for thyself. Then I knew that this *was* the word of the LORD.

9 And I bought the field of Hanameel my uncle's son, that *was* in Anathoth, and weighed him the money, *even* seventeen shekels [*NIV: about seven ounces*] of silver.

10 And I subscribed the evidence, and sealed *it* [*I signed and sealed the deed*], and took witnesses, and weighed *him* the money in the balances [*paid the bill*].

11 So I took the evidence of the purchase, *both* that which was sealed *according* to the law and custom, and that which was open:

12 And I gave the evidence of the purchase unto Baruch [*Jeremiah's personal scribe*] the son of Neriah, the son of Maaseiah, in the sight of Hanameel mine uncle's *son,* and in the presence of the witnesses that

subscribed the book [*deed—see footnote 12b in your Bible*] of the purchase, before [*in the presence of*] all the Jews that sat in the court of the prison.

13 ¶ And I charged Baruch before them, saying,

14 Thus saith the LORD of hosts, the God of Israel; Take these evidences [*paper, documents*], this evidence of the purchase, both which is sealed, and this evidence which is open; and put them in an earthen vessel [*a clay jar*], that they may continue [*be preserved*] many days.

The prophetic symbolism of this transaction is explained in verse 15, next.

15 For thus saith the LORD of hosts, the God of Israel; Houses and fields and vineyards shall be possessed again in this land [*Israel, including the Jews, will return to their own lands*].

16 ¶ Now when I had delivered the evidence of the purchase unto Baruch the son of Neriah, I prayed unto the LORD, saying,

The words of Jeremiah's prayer are given in verses 17–25, next.

17 Ah Lord GOD! behold, thou hast made the heaven and the earth by thy great power and stretched out arm, *and* there is nothing too hard for thee:

18 Thou shewest lovingkindness unto thousands, and recompensest the iniquity of the fathers into the

bosom of their children after them: the Great, the Mighty God, the LORD of hosts, *is* his name,

19 **Great in counsel**, and **mighty in work**: for **thine eyes** *are* **open upon all** the ways of the sons of men: **to give every one according to his ways**, and according to the fruit of his doings [*the law of the harvest*]:

20 Which **hast set signs and wonders in the land of Egypt** [*redeemed Israelites from Egyptian bondage; symbolic of being redeemed from the bondage of sin*], *even* unto this day, and in Israel, and among *other* men; and hast made thee a name, as at this day;

21 And **hast brought forth thy people Israel out of the land of Egypt** with signs, and with wonders [*miracles*], and with a strong hand, and with a stretched out arm, and with great terror;

22 **And hast given them this land** [*Palestine*], which thou didst swear [*covenant, promise*] to their fathers [*ancestors*] to give them, a land flowing with milk and honey [*a land of prosperity; symbolic of heaven*];

23 **And they came in, and possessed it; but they obeyed not thy voice**, neither walked in thy law; they have done nothing of all that thou commandedst them to do: **therefore thou hast caused all this evil** [*the Babylonian armies*] **to come upon them**:

24 **Behold the mounts** [*the mounds of dirt around Jerusalem, used by the Babylonians in the siege*], **they are come unto the city to take it**; and the city is given into the hand of the Chaldeans [*Babylonians*], that fight against it, because of the sword, and of the famine, and of the pestilence: **and what thou hast spoken** [*the prophecies of Jerusalem's downfall*] **is come to pass**; and, behold, thou seest *it*.

25 **And thou hast said unto me** [*Jeremiah*], O Lord GOD, **Buy thee the field for money, and take witnesses**; for the city is given into the hand of the Chaldeans.

Beginning with verse 26, the Lord answers Jeremiah's prayer.

26 ¶ **Then came the word of the LORD unto Jeremiah, saying**,

27 Behold, I *am* the LORD, the God of all flesh: is there any thing too hard for me?

28 Therefore thus saith the LORD; Behold, **I will give this city** [*Jerusalem*] **into the hand of the Chaldeans**, and into the hand of Nebuchadrezzar king of Babylon, and he shall take it:

29 **And the Chaldeans** [*Babylonians*], that fight against this city, **shall come and set fire on this city**, and burn it with the houses, upon whose roofs they [*the Jews*] have offered incense unto Baal [*idol worship*], and poured out drink offerings

unto other gods, to provoke me to anger.

30 **For the children of Israel** [*the northern ten tribes, who were taken captive by Assyria in about 722 BC*] **and the children of Judah** [*the Jews*] **have only done evil before me from their youth**: for the children of Israel have only provoked me to anger with the work of their hands [*such as idols*], saith the LORD.

31 **For this city** [*Jerusalem*] **hath been** to me *as* **a provocation of mine anger** and of my fury **from the day that they built it even unto this day**; that I should remove it from before my face,

32 **Because of all the evil of the children of Israel and of the children of Judah**, which they have done to provoke me to anger, they, their kings, their princes, their priests, and their [*false*] prophets, and the men of Judah, and the inhabitants of Jerusalem.

33 And **they have turned unto me the back, and not the face** [*they have rebelled against the Lord, and gone away from Him*]: though I taught them, rising up early and teaching them [*having My prophets teach and warn them constantly*], yet **they have not hearkened to receive instruction**.

34 But **they set their abominations in the house**, which is called by my name, **to defile it** [*they set up idols to worship in the temple in Jerusalem*].

35 **And they built the high places** [*worship sites*] **of Baal**, which *are* in the valley of the son of Hinnom [*south and west of Jerusalem where idol worship included human sacrifices*], **to cause their sons and their daughters to pass through** *the fire* **unto Molech** [*Baal worship included idol worship, sexual immorality, and human sacrifice, including babies*]; which I commanded them not, neither came it into my mind, that they should do this abomination, to cause Judah to sin.

36 ¶ And **now therefore thus saith the LORD, the God of Israel, concerning this city** [*Jerusalem*], **whereof ye say** [*about which Jeremiah has prophesied*], **It shall be delivered into the hand of the king of Baby-lon** by the sword, and by the famine, and by the pestilence;

> Verses 37–41, next, contain the marvelous prophecy of the gathering of Israel in the last days.

37 Behold, **I will gather them out of all countries, whither I have driven them** in mine anger, and in my fury, and in great wrath; and **I will bring them again unto this place, and I will cause them to dwell safely**:

38 **And they shall be my people, and I will be their God**:

39 And **I will give them one heart, and one way** [*they will be united in following the gospel of Jesus Christ*], **that they may fear** [*respect and honor*] **me for ever, for the good of them**

[*to their great benefit*], **and of their children after them**:

> Next, in verses 40–41, we see the great value of making and keeping covenants with God.

40 And **I will make an everlasting covenant with them**, that I will not turn away from them, to do them good; but I will put my fear in their hearts, **that they shall not depart from me**.

41 Yea, **I will rejoice over them to do them good**, and **I will plant them in this land assuredly with my whole heart and with my whole soul**.

> The return of Israel to the various lands of their inheritance in the last days is symbolic of the return of Israel to the Lord, which, as stated above, is accomplished through making and keeping covenants with Him.

42 For thus saith the LORD; **Like as I have brought all this great evil upon this people, so will I bring upon them all the good that I have promised them**.

> The symbolism involved in having Jeremiah purchase land in his hometown is again explained in verses 43–44, next.

43 And **fields shall be bought in this land**, whereof ye say, *It is* desolate without man or beast; it is given into the hand of the Chaldeans.

> Next, in verse 44, the Lord again explains the prophetic symbolism

of having Jeremiah purchase land, having witnesses and proper documents to close the deal. It is prophesying the fact that the day will come in the future that the Jews will be gathered back to the Holy Land and be again able to buy land.

44 Men shall buy fields for money, and subscribe evidences, and seal *them,* and take witnesses in the land of Benjamin, and in the places about Jerusalem, and in the cities of Judah, and in the cities of the mountains, and in the cities of the valley, and in the cities of the south: **for I will cause their captivity to return** [*in the future, I will cause Israel to be gathered and return*], saith the LORD.

JEREMIAH 33

Selection: all verses

This chapter continues the prophetic theme of the gathering of Israel, including the Jews, in the last days. The most important aspect of the gathering is the gathering of people to Christ, regardless of what land they live in.

This prophecy was given to Jeremiah while he was in the king's personal prison in the palace.

1 MOREOVER **the word of the LORD came unto Jeremiah the second time, while he was yet shut up in the court of the prison**, saying,

2 **Thus saith the LORD** the maker thereof [*the Creator of the earth*], the LORD that formed it, to establish it; the LORD *is* his name;

3 **Call unto me, and I will answer thee, and shew thee great and mighty things**, which thou knowest not.

4 For thus saith the LORD, the God of Israel, **concerning** the houses of **this city** [*Jerusalem*], **and** concerning **the houses of the kings of Judah**, which are thrown down by the mounts [*the mounds of dirt used in laying siege to a city*], and by the sword;

Next, in verse 5, the Lord tells Jeremiah that any attempts by the Jews to successfully defeat the Babylonian armies who have laid siege to Jerusalem will be unsuccessful because of the wickedness of the people of Judah. In their rebellion against God, they plan to defeat the Babylonians without His help, but in reality, they are coming to fill the trenches dug by the enemy armies around Jerusalem with their own dead bodies.

5 **They** [*the people of Judah and Jerusalem*] **come to fight with the Chaldeans** [*Babylonians*], **but** *it is* **to fill them with the dead bodies of men**, whom I have slain in mine anger and in my fury, and for [*because of*] all whose wickedness I have hid my face from this city.

Next, beginning with verse 6, the Lord speaks of the restoration of the gospel and the gathering of Israel, including the Jews in the last days. You have likely noticed that when Old Testament prophets speak and prophesy, they often jump directly from their day to the future without particularly announcing that they

are doing so. We have an example of this in these verses.

6 Behold, **I will bring it health and cure, and I will cure them**, and will reveal unto them the abundance of peace and truth [*found in the true gospel of Jesus Christ*].

7 And **I will cause the captivity of Judah and the captivity of Israel to return** [*I will restore Judah and Israel*], and will build them, as at the first.

8 And **I will cleanse them from all their iniquity**, whereby they have sinned against me; and **I will pardon all their iniquities**, whereby they have sinned, and whereby they have transgressed against me.

9 ¶ **And it** [*Israel, the Lord's covenant people*] **shall be to me a name of joy**, a praise and **an honour before all the nations of the earth, which shall hear all the good that I do unto them**: and they shall fear and tremble [*have respect and admiration for the Lord*] for all the goodness and for all the prosperity that I procure unto it.

10 **Thus saith the LORD; Again there shall be heard in this place, which ye say** [*which Jeremiah has prophesied under the direction of the Lord*] *shall be* **desolate** without man and without beast, *even* in the cities of Judah, and in the streets of Jerusalem, that are desolate, without man, and without inhabitant, and without beast,

11 **The voice of joy, and the voice of gladness**, the voice of the bridegroom, and the voice of the bride, the voice of them that shall say, Praise the LORD of hosts: for the LORD *is* good; for his mercy *endureth* for ever: *and* of them that shall bring the sacrifice of praise into the house of the LORD. **For I will cause to return the captivity of the land, as at the first, saith the LORD**.

12 Thus saith the LORD of hosts; **Again in this place**, which is desolate without man and without beast, and in all the cities thereof, **shall be an habitation of shepherds causing *their* flocks to lie down** [*once again, the Holy Land will be inhabited in righteousness by the Lord's covenant people*].

13 In the cities of the mountains, in the cities of the vale, and in the cities of the south, and **in the land of Benjamin, and in the places about Jerusalem, and in the cities of Judah**, shall the flocks pass again under the hands of him that telleth *them,* saith the LORD.

14 Behold, **the days come**, saith the LORD, **that I will perform that good thing which I have promised unto the house of Israel and to the house of Judah**.

Verses 15–16, next, remind us again that the source of the peace and prosperity spoken of above is the Savior.

15 ¶ **In those days, and at that time, will I cause the Branch of righteousness** [*Jesus Christ—see heading to this chapter in your Bible*] **to grow up unto David**; and **he shall execute judgment and righteousness in the land** [*in the earth—see footnote 15d in your Bible*].

16 **In those days shall Judah be saved, and Jerusalem shall dwell safely**: and this *is the name* wherewith she shall be called, The LORD our righteousness.

We will quote from the Old Testament Student Manual for additional clarification of verses 15–16, above:

"'The Branch of righteousness to grow up unto David' who will 'execute judgment and righteousness in the land' (verse 15) is Jesus Christ (see Isaiah 11:1; Jeremiah 23:5–6). When this millennial event occurs, the Jews will dwell safely in Jerusalem.

"The last part of verse 16 is not a particularly good translation since it implies that Jerusalem herself shall be called 'the Lord our righteousness.' According to Adam Clarke it should read: 'And this one who shall call to her is the Lord our Justification,' that is, Jesus Christ himself, the Branch of David (The Holy Bible . . . with a Commentary and Critical Notes, 4:344)" (Old Testament Student Manual, page 257).

17 ¶ For thus saith the LORD; **David shall never want** [*lack*] **a man to sit upon the throne of the house of Israel** [*when this time comes, there will be no lack of leadership for Israel*];

18 **Neither shall the priests the Levites want** [*lack*] **a man** before me to offer burnt offerings, and to kindle meat offerings, and **to do sacrifice continually** [*there will be no lack of authorized priesthood holders to carry on the work of salvation among the covenant people of the Lord*].

19 ¶ **And the word of the LORD came unto Jeremiah, saying,**

Next, in verses 20–22, the Lord says, in effect, that just as sure as day and night come and go, His promise to restore and redeem Israel someday in the future will be fulfilled.

20 Thus saith the LORD; **If ye can break my covenant of the day, and my covenant of the night** [*if you can stop the coming of day and night*], and that there should not be day and night in their season;

21 *Then* **may also my covenant** [*given in verses 17–18, above*] **be broken** with David my servant, that he should not have a son to reign upon his throne; and with the Levites the priests, my ministers.

22 **As the host of heaven cannot be numbered, neither the sand of the sea measured: so will I multiply the seed of David** [*faithful members of the Lord's covenant people*] **my servant**, and the Levites that minister unto me [*innumerable hosts of Israel will yet be converted and gathered to the Father through Christ—compare with D&C 76:67*].

23 **Moreover** [*in addition*] **the word of the LORD came to Jeremiah, saying,**

24 **Considerest thou not** [*don't pay any attention to*] **what this people** [*the apostate Jews*] **have spoken, saying, The two families** [*Israel and Judah*] **which the LORD hath chosen, he hath even cast them off?** thus they have despised my people, that they should be no more a nation before them.

In verses 25–26, next, the Lord says, yet again, in effect, that just as sure as He is the Creator, He will keep His promise to restore Israel and Judah when the proper time arrives. He uses the opposite to emphasize the positive.

25 Thus saith the LORD; **If my covenant** *be* **not with day and night, and if** **I have not appointed the ordinances of heaven and earth** [*if I have not created the heaven and earth*];

26 **Then will I cast away the seed of Jacob** [*Israel*], **and David** [*symbolic of Judah*] my servant, *so* that I will not take *any* of his seed *to be* rulers over the seed of Abraham, Isaac, and Jacob: **for I will cause their captivity to return** [*I will cause them to return from captivity*], **and have mercy on them.**

JEREMIAH 34

Selection: all verses

In this chapter, Jeremiah foretells the captivity of Zedekiah, king of

Jerusalem. As you have no doubt noticed thus far in your study of Jeremiah, the prophecy of the destruction of Jerusalem and the scattering and subsequent gathering of the Jews is often repeated in Jeremiah's writings.

In chapter 32, verses 4–5, we saw the prophecy that Zedekiah would be captured and taken to Babylon. Here, in chapter 34, we see it again. Chapter 52, verses 1–11, will tell of the fulfillment of this prophecy including the fact that Zedekiah was forced to watch as his sons were killed, then his eyes were put out and he was taken prisoner to Babylon.

It is a bit interesting, from an academic standpoint, to note that here in verse 1, "Nebuchadnezzar" is spelled in the way that we normally think of it (not that many people worry a whole lot about how to spell it), rather than "Nebuchadrezzar," as was the case earlier in Jeremiah (example: 24:1).

1 **THE word which came unto Jeremiah from the LORD, when Nebuchadnezzar king of Babylon**, and all his army, and all the kingdoms of the earth of his dominion [*every nation under Nebuchadnezzar's subjection*], and all the people, **fought against Jerusalem, and against all the cities thereof, saying,**

2 Thus saith the LORD, the God of Israel; **Go and speak to Zedekiah king of Judah, and tell him, Thus saith the LORD**; Behold, **I will give this city** [*Jerusalem*] **into the hand of the king of Babylon, and he shall burn it with fire**:

3 **And thou shalt not escape** out of his hand, but shalt surely be taken, and delivered into his hand; and thine eyes shall behold the eyes of the king of Babylon, and he shall speak with thee mouth to mouth, **and thou shalt go to Babylon**.

4 Yet hear the word of the LORD, O Zedekiah king of Judah; Thus saith the LORD of thee, **Thou shalt not die by the sword**:

5 *But* **thou shalt die in peace: and with the burnings of thy fathers** [*people will light funeral fires in honor of you, like they did for previous kings of Judah*], the former kings which were before thee, so shall they burn *odours* for thee; **and they will lament thee**, *saying,* Ah lord [*in effect, hail to the king*]! for I have pronounced the word [*I, the Lord, have said it*], saith the LORD.

6 **Then Jeremiah the prophet spake all these words unto Zedekiah** king of Judah in Jerusalem,

7 **When the king of Babylon's army fought against Jerusalem, and against all the cities of Judah that were left**, against Lachish, and against Azekah: for these defenced cities remained of the cities of Judah.

The deceptiveness and dishonesty of King Zedekiah and his corrupt people is illustrated in verses 8–11, next. It is helpful to remember that the possession of slaves, including servants who had been put in bondage for a period of time to pay off personal or family debts, was a common part of the culture in this society at the time.

It appears that Zedekiah, for whatever reason, had proclaimed that all Hebrews who were in bondage to other Hebrews should be set free. After the people had carried out the king's orders, they simply turned around and put the freed Jews back into bondage.

8 ¶ *This is* **the word that came unto Jeremiah from the LORD, after** that the **king Zedekiah had made a covenant with all the people which** *were* **at Jerusalem, to proclaim liberty unto them;**

9 **That every man should let his manservant, and** every man his **maidservant,** *being* an **Hebrew or** an **Hebrewess, go free;** that none should serve himself of them, *to wit* [*namely; for example*], of a Jew his brother.

10 Now when **all the princes, and all the people, which had entered into the covenant,** heard that every one should let his manservant, and every one his maidservant, go free, that none should serve themselves of them any more, then they **obeyed, and let** *them* **go.**

11 **But afterward they turned, and caused the servants and the handmaids, whom they had let go free, to return, and brought them into subjection for servants and for handmaids.**

Next, Jeremiah is told by the Lord to tell these Jews that they are hypocrites.

12 ¶ **Therefore the word of the LORD came to Jeremiah** from the LORD, saying,

13 Thus saith the LORD, the God of Israel; **I made a covenant with your fathers in the day that I brought them forth out of the land of Egypt,** out of the house of bondmen [*when I set them free from Egyptian bondage*], **saying,**

14 **At the end of seven years let ye go every man his brother** an Hebrew, which hath been sold unto thee; and when he hath served thee six years, thou shalt let him go free from thee: **but your fathers** [*ancestors*] **hearkened not unto me, neither inclined their ear** [*refused to listen to Me*].

15 **And ye were now turned** [*had reversed your position on holding slaves*], **and had done right in my sight,** in proclaiming liberty every man to his neighbour; and ye had made a covenant before me in the house which is called by my name [*in the temple at Jerusalem*]:

16 **But ye turned and polluted my name** [*violated your covenant*], and caused every man his servant, and every man his handmaid, whom ye had set at liberty at their pleasure, to return, **and brought them into subjection,** to be unto you for servants and for handmaids.

Verse 17, next, contains a very impactful message.

Major Message

When we set ourselves "free" from covenants we have made with the Lord, He is obligated by the law of justice to set us "free" from His blessings and protection.

17 **Therefore** thus saith the LORD; **Ye have not hearkened unto** [*obeyed*] **me**, in proclaiming liberty, every one to his brother, and every man to his neighbour: **behold, I proclaim a liberty for you**, saith the LORD, **to the sword**, to the **pestilence**, and to the **famine**; and I will make you to be **removed** [*scattered*] **into all the kingdoms of the earth**.

18 **And I will give the men that have transgressed my covenant**, which have not performed the words of the covenant which they had made before me, when they cut the calf in twain, and passed between the parts thereof [*a reference to a type of ritual associated with making covenants in the culture of the Jews at the time—compare with Genesis 15:8–10, 17*],

19 The princes of Judah, and the princes of Jerusalem, the eunuchs, and the priests, and all the people of the land, which passed between the parts of the calf [*who made a covenant and did not keep it—see note at end of verse 18, above*];

20 **I will even give them into the hand of their enemies**, and into the hand of them that seek their life: and

their dead bodies shall be for meat [*food*] unto the fowls of the heaven, and to the beasts of the earth.

21 **And Zedekiah king of Judah and his princes will I give into the hand of their enemies**, and into the hand of them that seek their life, and into the hand of **the king of Babylon's army**, which are gone up from you [*who have temporarily gone away from you to do battle with an army which has come up from Egypt—see Jeremiah 37:5–10*].

22 **Behold, I will** command, saith the LORD, and **cause them to return** [*after temporarily leaving to defeat the Egyptians*] **to this city** [*Jerusalem*]; **and they shall fight against it, and take it, and burn it** with fire: and I will make the cities of Judah a desolation without an inhabitant.

JEREMIAH 35

Selection: all verses

According to verse 1, the date of this chapter would be somewhere between 609 BC and 598 BC (see dates for Jehoiakim's reign on the chronology chart at the back of your Bible).

Some Bible scholars believe that the Rechabites, spoken of here, were descendants of Jethro, father-in-law to Moses. They are mentioned in 2 Kings 2:15, and were also known as Kenites (1 Chronicles 2:55). It is believed that they came into the Holy Land along with the children of Israel. They existed at various times in both the Northern Kingdom (Israel) and the Southern Kingdom (Judah).

The ancestors of these Rechabites had made a covenant long ago not to drink wine or other strong drink, and they were still faithful to that covenant, as shown in this chapter. The Lord holds them up as an example of people who keep their promises (as opposed to the Jews at this time in history), and, as you will see in this chapter, they are blessed because of this integrity.

1 **THE word which came unto Jeremiah** from the LORD **in the days of Jehoiakim** the son of Josiah **king of Judah** [*from 609–598 BC*], **saying,**

2 **Go unto** the house of **the Rechabites, and speak unto them, and bring them into the house of the LORD**, into one of the chambers, **and give them wine to drink.**

3 **Then I took** Jaazaniah the son of Jeremiah, the son of Habaziniah, and his brethren, and all his sons, and **the whole house of the Rechabites;**

4 **And I brought them into the house of the LORD** [*the temple in Jerusalem*], into the chamber of the sons of Hanan, the son of Igdaliah, a man of God, which *was* by the chamber of the princes, which *was* above the chamber of Maaseiah the son of Shallum, the keeper of the door:

Next, Jeremiah puts these Rechabites to the test, as instructed by the Lord, to see if they will keep their covenant not to drink wine or strong drink.

5 **And I set before the sons** [*descendants*] **of the house of the Rechabites pots full of wine, and cups, and I said unto them, Drink ye wine.**

6 **But they said, We will drink no wine**: for Jonadab the son of Rechab **our father** [*ancestor*] **commanded us, saying, Ye shall drink no wine**, *neither* ye, nor your sons for ever:

7 Neither shall ye build house [*they had also covenanted to live in tents*], nor sow seed, nor plant vineyard, nor have *any:* but all your days ye shall dwell in tents; that ye may live many days in the land where ye *be* strangers.

8 **Thus have we obeyed the voice of Jonadab the son of Rechab our father** in all that he hath charged us, **to drink no wine all our days, we, our wives, our sons, nor our daughters;**

9 Nor to build houses for us to dwell in: neither have we vineyard, nor field, nor seed:

10 **But we have dwelt in tents, and have obeyed, and done according to all that Jonadab our father commanded us.**

Next, in verse 11, these Rechabites explain why they are currently living in the city of Jerusalem instead of in their tents elsewhere.

11 **But** it came to pass, **when Nebuchadrezzar king of Babylon came** up into the land [*in earlier waves of siege and attack*], that **we said,**

Come, and let us go to Jerusalem for fear of the army of the Chaldeans [*Babylonians*], and for fear of the army of the Syrians: **so we dwell at Jerusalem**.

12 ¶ **Then came the word of the LORD unto Jeremiah, saying,**

13 Thus saith the LORD of hosts, the God of Israel; **Go and tell the men of Judah and the inhabitants of Jerusalem, Will ye not receive instruction to hearken to my words? saith the LORD.** [*In other words, can't you be like the Rechabites and keep your word?*]

14 **The words of Jonadab** the son of Rechab, that he commanded his sons not to drink wine, **are performed**; for **unto this day they drink none, but obey their father's commandment**: notwithstanding I have spoken unto you, rising early and speaking [*having My prophets teach and preach to you from early each day—see verse 15*]; **but ye hearkened not unto me.**

Next, in verse 15, the Lord reminds the wicked people of Judah that He has sent many prophets (see 1 Nephi 1:4) to invite them to repent.

A very important message, repeated yet again by the Lord at this point in Jeremiah's teaching, is that in spite of their gross and repeated wickedness, these people are still invited to repent. They can still successfully return to the Lord. This is a most comforting testimony of the power of the Atonement of Jesus Christ to cleanse and heal all of us, if we will.

15 **I have sent also unto you all my** servants the **prophets**, rising up early [*and they have risen up early*] and **sending *them*, saying, Return ye now every man from his evil way, and amend your doings**, and go not after other gods [*idols*] to serve them, and ye shall dwell in the land which I have given to you and to your fathers: **but ye have not inclined your ear, nor hearkened unto me.**

16 **Because the sons of Jonadab** the son of Rechab [*the Rechabites*] **have performed the commandment of their father**, which he commanded them; **but this people** [*Judah*] **hath not hearkened unto me:**

17 **Therefore thus saith the LORD** God of hosts, the God of Israel; Behold, **I will bring upon Judah and upon all the inhabitants of Jerusalem all the evil that I have pronounced against them**: because I have spoken unto them, but they have not heard; and I have called unto them, but they have not answered.

18 ¶ **And Jeremiah said unto** the house of **the Rechabites, Thus saith the LORD** of hosts, the God of Israel; **Because ye have obeyed the commandment of Jonadab** your father, and kept all his precepts, and done according unto all that he hath commanded you:

19 **Therefore** thus saith the LORD of hosts, the God of Israel; **Jonadab the son of Rechab shall not want a man to stand before me for ever**

[*in other words, the Rechabites will be protected and preserved*].

JEREMIAH 36

Selection: all verses

Baruch, Jeremiah's faithful scribe, had painstakingly written down the prophecies of Jeremiah so far, in order to have a written record of the words of the Lord given through him. After Baruch had read them in the temple at Jerusalem, King Jehoiakim ordered the writings of Jeremiah to be burned. He reaps the reward of his tyranny.

Afterward, Jeremiah dictates the prophecies again, and adds many additional revelations and teachings. This could remind us of the destruction by mobs of the original compilation of revelations through the Prophet Joseph Smith, known as the Book of Commandments, published in 1833. As the revelations were assembled again for publication, many more were added and it was named the Doctrine and Covenants, published in 1835. It can also remind us of the loss of the 116 manuscript pages by Martin Harris, which were replaced by the translation of the small plates of Nephi, which contained more spiritual matters (see Doctrine & Covenants 10:30, 38–45).

As we proceed, we will remind you again that the chapters in Jeremiah are not necessarily compiled in chronological order.

1 AND it came to pass **in the fourth year of Jehoiakim** [*about 605 BC*] the son of Josiah king of Judah, *that* **this word came unto Jeremiah from the LORD, saying,**

2 **Take thee a roll of a book** [*NIV: "a scroll"*], **and write therein all the words that I have spoken unto thee against Israel, and against Judah, and against all the nations**, from the day I spake unto thee, from the days of Josiah, even unto this day [*over the last twenty-three years, since the time you were called (in about 628 BC) up to the present time (about 605 BC)*].

3 **It may be that the house of Judah** [*the Jews*] **will hear all the evil** [*the punishments*] **which I purpose to do unto them; that they may return every man from his evil way** [*repent*]**; that I may forgive their iniquity and their sin**.

4 **Then Jeremiah called Baruch** [*Jeremiah's scribe*] the son of Neriah: **and Baruch wrote from the mouth of Jeremiah** [*as Jeremiah dictated*] **all the words of the LORD**, which he had spoken unto him, upon a roll of a book.

5 **And Jeremiah commanded Baruch, saying, I** *am* **shut up** [*I am under arrest—see footnote 5a in your Bible*]**; I cannot go into the house of the LORD** [*the temple in Jerusalem*]:

6 **Therefore go thou, and read in the roll** [*scroll*], which thou hast written from my mouth, **the words of the LORD in the ears of the people in the LORD's house** upon the fasting day [*a special day set aside for fasting and reading the scriptures together—see verse 9; also see Nehemiah 9:1–3*]: and **also thou shalt read them in the ears of all Judah that come out of**

their cities [*who gather to the Jerusalem Temple from surrounding cities*].

7 **It may be they will present their supplication before the LORD** [*ask the Lord for forgiveness*], **and** will **return** [*repent*] every one from his evil way: for great *is* the anger and the fury that the LORD hath pronounced against this people.

8 **And Baruch** the son of Neriah **did according to all that Jeremiah the prophet commanded him**, reading in the book the words of the LORD in the LORD's house.

9 And it came to pass **in the fifth year** [*about 604 BC*] **of Jehoiakim** the son of Josiah king of Judah, in the ninth month, *that* **they proclaimed a fast** before the LORD **to all the people in Jerusalem**, **and to all the people** that came from the cities **of Judah** unto Jerusalem.

10 **Then read Baruch in the book the words of Jeremiah in the house of the LORD**, in the chamber of Gemariah the son of Shaphan the scribe, in the higher court, **at the entry of the new gate of the LORD's house, in the ears of all the people.**

11 ¶ **When Michaiah** the son of Gemariah, the son of Shaphan, **had heard** out of the book all the words of the LORD,

12 **Then he went down into the king's house** [*to the palace*], into the scribe's chamber: **and, lo, all the princes** [*leaders of the Jews*] **sat there**, *even* Elishama the scribe, and

Delaiah the son of Shemaiah, and Elnathan the son of Achbor, and Gemariah the son of Shaphan, and Zedekiah the son of Hananiah, and all the princes.

13 **Then Michaiah declared unto them all the words that he had heard**, when Baruch read the book in the ears of the people.

Next, in verses 14–15, the princes (usually means "government leaders") send for Baruch and ask him to come to them and read Jeremiah's words to them.

14 **Therefore all the princes sent Jehudi** the son of Nethaniah, the son of Shelemiah, the son of Cushi, **unto Baruch, saying, Take in thine hand the roll** [*scroll*] **wherein thou hast read in the ears of the people, and come.** So Baruch the son of Neriah took the roll in his hand, and came unto them.

15 **And they said unto him, Sit down now, and read it in our ears**. So Baruch read *it* in their ears.

16 Now it came to pass, **when they had heard all the words, they were afraid** both one and other, **and said unto Baruch, We will surely tell the king of all these words.**

17 **And they asked Baruch**, saying, Tell us now, **How didst thou write all these words at his mouth** [*how did you end up writing all this; did he dictate it to you*]?

18 Then **Baruch answered** them, **He pronounced all these words**

unto me with his mouth [*he dictated them to me*], and I wrote *them* with ink in the book [*scroll*].

19 **Then said the princes** unto Baruch, **Go, hide thee, thou and Jeremiah**; and let no man know where ye be.

20 ¶ **And they went in to the king** into the court, but they laid up the roll [*put the scroll*] in the chamber of Elishama the scribe, **and told all the words in the ears of the king**.

21 **So the king sent Jehudi to fetch the roll**: and he took it out of Elishama the scribe's chamber. **And Jehudi read it in the ears of the king**, and in the ears of all the princes which stood beside the king.

22 Now **the king sat in the winterhouse** [*the winter apartment*] in the ninth month: **and *there was a fire on the hearth** [*in the fireplace*] burning before him.

Next, in verses 23–25, we see that the king became angry after hearing just three or four pages of the scroll, and cut it up with a knife and threw it into the fire, despite the objections from some of his men.

23 And it came to pass, *that* **when Jehudi had read three or four leaves, he** [*the king*] **cut it with the penknife, and cast *it* into the fire** that *was* on the hearth, **until all the roll was consumed** in the fire that *was* on the hearth.

24 Yet they were not afraid, nor rent their garments, *neither* the king, nor

any of his servants that heard all these words [*they were not afraid of the prophecies of Jeremiah*].

25 Nevertheless **Elnathan** and **Delaiah and Gemariah had made intercession to** [*had tried to intervene with*] **the king that he would not burn the roll: but he would not hear them**.

Next, in verse 26, the king commands that Baruch and Jeremiah be arrested, but the Lord hides them. It will be interesting someday to get the rest of this story.

26 **But the king commanded** Jerahmeel the son of Hammelech, and Seraiah the son of Azriel, and Shelemiah the son of Abdeel, **to take Baruch** the scribe **and Jeremiah the prophet: but the LORD hid them**.

Next, in verses 27–32, the Lord commands Jeremiah to dictate the same words to Baruch to write again plus add many more words from the Lord.

27 ¶ **Then the word of the LORD came to Jeremiah**, after that the king had burned the roll, and the words which Baruch wrote at the mouth of Jeremiah, **saying,**

28 **Take thee again another roll, and write in it all the former words that were in the first roll, which Jehoiakim** the king of Judah hath **burned**.

29 **And thou shalt say to Jehoiakim** king of Judah, Thus saith the LORD; Thou hast burned this roll,

saying, Why hast thou written therein, saying, The king of Babylon shall certainly come and destroy this land, and shall cause to cease from thence man and beast?

30 **Therefore thus saith the LORD of Jehoiakim king of Judah; He shall have none to sit upon the throne of David** [*he shall have no posterity to take his place on the throne when he dies*]: **and his dead body shall be cast out in the day to the heat, and in the night to the frost** [*he will be despised and won't even get a burial*].

31 **And I will punish him and his seed and his servants for their iniquity**; and I will bring upon them, and upon the inhabitants of Jerusalem, and upon the men of Judah, all the evil that I have pronounced against them; but they hearkened not.

32 ¶ **Then took Jeremiah another roll, and gave it to Baruch the scribe, the son of Neriah; who wrote therein from the mouth of Jeremiah all the words of the book which Jehoiakim king of Judah had burned in the fire: and there were added besides unto them many like words.**

JEREMIAH 37

Selection: all verses

This chapter begins at the start of Zedekiah's wicked reign over the kingdom of Judah, about 598 BC. He is twenty-one years old (see 52:1) and will rule as king for eleven years.

The Babylonians have already begun the process of defeating the cities of Judah and Jerusalem. Daniel and others have already been taken captive to Babylon. Lehi and his family fled from the Jerusalem area in 600 BC and are likely still in the wilderness, journeying toward the ocean where Nephi will be commanded to build a ship.

Egyptian armies are coming up from Egypt to engage the Babylonian armies in battle, which will cause Nebuchadnezzar, king of Babylon to pull his armies away from Jerusalem temporarily in order to engage and defeat the Egyptians.

As we begin the chapter, we are given a brief description of King Zedekiah and his people.

1 AND **king Zedekiah** the son of Josiah **reigned instead of** [*in the place of*] **Coniah** the son of Jehoiakim, whom Nebuchadrezzar king of Babylon made king in the land of Judah.

2 **But neither he, nor his servants, nor the people of the land, did hearken unto the words of the LORD**, which he spake by the prophet Jeremiah.

Next, wicked King Zedekiah sends word to Jeremiah requesting him to pray for him and his people. The king has not yet arrested Jeremiah and put him in prison.

3 **And Zedekiah the king sent** Jehucal the son of Shelemiah and Zephaniah the son of Maaseiah the

priest **to the prophet Jeremiah, saying, Pray now unto the LORD our God for us**.

4 **Now Jeremiah came in and went out among the people** [*he was still free to come and go as he pleased*]: **for they had not put him into prison**.

At this point in history, the Babylonian armies had already laid siege to Jerusalem. As you can see in verse 5, next, Egyptian armies had been sent up from Egypt by Pharaoh to engage the Babylonians in battle. It will prove to be merely a temporary distraction for Nebuchadnezzar's powerful Babylonian forces.

5 **Then Pharaoh's army was come forth out of Egypt**: and **when the Chaldeans** [*Babylonians*] that besieged Jerusalem **heard** tidings of them, **they departed from Jerusalem**.

The prophecy that Jeremiah now gives King Zedekiah is not well received by him and his people.

6 ¶ **Then came the word of the LORD unto the prophet Jeremiah, saying,**

7 Thus saith the LORD, the God of Israel; **Thus shall ye say to the king** of Judah [*Zedekiah*], that sent you unto me to enquire of me; **Behold, Pharaoh's army, which is come forth to help you, shall return to Egypt into their own land**.

8 **And the Chaldeans shall come again, and fight against this city** [*Jerusalem*], and take it, and burn it with fire.

Remember that false prophets among the Jews at this time have repeatedly prophesied that the King of Babylon and his armies would not destroy Jerusalem—see verse 19. This made Jeremiah look bad as he prophesied the opposite.

9 Thus saith the LORD; **Deceive not yourselves, saying, The Chaldeans shall surely depart from us: for they shall not depart**.

As you can see by what the Lord says in verse 10, next, the Jews do not have any chance at all of defeating the Babylonians, when they focus again on the siege of Jerusalem after coming back from defeating the Egyptians.

10 **For though** [*even if*] ye had smitten the whole army of the Chaldeans** [*the Babylonians*] that fight against you, **and there remained** *but* **wounded men among them,** *yet* **should they rise up** every man in his tent, **and burn this city with fire**.

Next, beginning with verse 11, we are told what happened to Jeremiah during the temporary lull in the siege while the Chaldeans (Babylonian army) left to deal with the Egyptians.

11 ¶ And it came to pass, **that when the army of the Chaldeans was broken up from Jerusalem for fear of Pharaoh's army,**

12 Then **Jeremiah went** forth out of Jerusalem **to go into the land**

of Benjamin [*in other words, as Jeremiah started to leave Jerusalem*], to separate himself thence in the midst of the people.

13 And **when he was in the gate of Benjamin** [*in other words, just as he was leaving Jerusalem*], **a captain** of the ward [*an officer in the king's army*] was there, whose name *was* Irijah, the son of Shelemiah, the son of Hananiah; and he **took** [*arrested*] **Jeremiah the prophet, saying** [*accusing him, saying*]**, Thou fallest away to the Chaldeans** [*you are deserting to the Babylonians*].

14 **Then said Jeremiah,** *It is* **false; I fall not away to the Chaldeans**. But he [*the officer*] hearkened not to him: **so Irijah took Jeremiah, and brought him to the princes** [*the leaders of the Jews*].

15 Wherefore **the princes were wroth with Jeremiah, and smote him, and put him in prison** in the house of Jonathan the scribe: for they had made that the prison.

16 ¶ **When Jeremiah was entered into the dungeon**, and into the cabins, **and Jeremiah had remained there many days**;

Next, King Zedekiah secretly sends for Jeremiah and asks what the Lord has to say. He doesn't want anyone to know that he is asking such a question.

17 **Then Zedekiah the king sent, and took him out** [*of the dungeon*]: **and** the king **asked him secretly** in his house, and said, **Is there** *any* **word from the LORD?** And **Jeremiah said, There is**: for, said he, **thou shalt be delivered into the hand of the king of Babylon.**

18 **Moreover** Jeremiah said unto king Zedekiah, **What have I offended against thee, or against thy servants, or against this people, that ye have put me in prison?**

19 **Where** *are* **now your** [*false*] **prophets** which prophesied unto you, saying, The king of Babylon shall not come against you, nor against this land?

20 **Therefore hear now**, I pray thee, O my lord the king: **let my supplication**, I pray thee, **be accepted before thee; that thou cause me not to return to the house of Jonathan the scribe, lest I die there**.

In response to Jeremiah's urgent request (verse 20, above) not to go back to the terrible conditions in the dungeon, Zedekiah has him put in the palace prison. As you can see, in verse 21, next, conditions of famine were already getting severe because of the Babylonian siege of Jerusalem.

21 **Then Zedekiah the king commanded that they should commit Jeremiah into the court of the prison** [*a prison in the palace*]**, and that they should give him daily a piece of bread** out of the bakers' street, **until all the bread in the city were spent.** Thus Jeremiah remained in the court of the prison.

JEREMIAH 38

Selection: all verses

This chapter continues the account of Jeremiah's imprisonment, which started in chapter 37. Our hearts go out to him as he is put in a miserable dungeon, where he sinks in the mud. A kindly Ethiopian, in the service of the king, is gentle with Jeremiah as he pulls him out of the mire, giving the prophet rags to put under his shoulders to pad the ropes used to pull him out so that they won't cut him (verses 11–13). It is apparently a dungeon that is accessed only by a hole in the ceiling. Prisoners are dropped in and must be hauled out with ropes.

As we begin reading this chapter, we soon discover that some influential government leaders are angry at what Jeremiah has prophesied concerning the destruction of Jerusalem by the Babylonians. They feel that his prophecies are demoralizing the Jewish soldiers assigned to protect Jerusalem and do battle against the Babylonians. They are particularly angry about Jeremiah's counsel from the Lord to them that they should surrender the city to Nebuchadnezzar's forces—see background to chapter 27 in this study guide. See also verse 2 here in chapter 38.

1 **THEN Shephatiah** the son of Mattan, **and Gedaliah** the son of Pashur, **and Jucal** the son of Shelemiah, **and Pashur** the son of Malchiah, **heard the words that Jeremiah had spoken unto all the people, saying,**

2 **Thus saith the LORD, He that remaineth in this city shall die by the** sword, by the famine, and by the pestilence: but he that goeth forth [*surrenders*] **to the Chaldeans shall live**; for he shall have his life for a prey, and shall live.

3 Thus saith the LORD, **This city shall surely be given into the hand of the king of Babylon's army, which shall take it.**

4 **Therefore the princes** [*government leaders, rulers—see footnote 4a in your Bible*] **said unto the king, We beseech thee, let this man** [*Jeremiah*] **be put to death**: for thus he weakeneth the hands of the men of war [*soldiers and defenders*] that remain in this city, and the hands of all the people, in speaking such words unto them: **for this man seeketh not the welfare of this people, but the hurt** [*Jeremiah is trying to undermine and hurt our people*].

> Next, in verse 5, we see the cowardly nature of King Zedekiah as he meekly claims he can do nothing to stop these men if they want to harm Jeremiah.

5 Then Zedekiah the king said, **Behold, he** *is* **in your hand: for the king** *is* not *he that* **can do** *any* **thing against you.**

6 **Then took they Jeremiah, and cast him into the dungeon of Malchiah** the son of Hammelech, that *was* in the court of the prison: **and they let down Jeremiah with cords** [*ropes*]. **And in the dungeon** *there was* no water, but mire: so Jeremiah sunk in the mire.

7 ¶ Now when Ebed-melech the Ethiopian, one of the eunuchs which was in the king's house [*one of the king's servants*], **heard that they had put Jeremiah in the dungeon**; the king then sitting in the gate of Benjamin [*the king was conducting business in an area set aside for that purpose in a city gate*];

8 **Ebed-melech** went forth out of the king's house, and **spake to the king, saying,**

9 **My lord the king, these men have done evil in all that they have done to Jeremiah the prophet**, whom they have cast into the dungeon; **and he is like to die for hunger in the place where he is**: for *there is* no more bread in the city [*the famine as a result of the Babylonian siege was getting very severe*].

10 **Then the king commanded Ebed-melech** the Ethiopian, saying, Take from hence thirty men with thee, and **take up Jeremiah the prophet out of the dungeon, before he die.**

11 **So Ebed-melech took the men with him**, and went into the house of the king under the treasury, **and took** thence old cast clouts [*threadbare, worn out clothes*] and **old rotten rags, and let them down by cords into the dungeon to Jeremiah.**

12 **And** Ebed-melech the Ethiopian **said unto Jeremiah, Put now** *these* **old cast clouts** [*discarded clothes*] **and rotten rags under thine**

armholes [*armpits*] **under the cords** [*to pad the ropes*]. **And Jeremiah did so.**

13 **So they drew up Jeremiah with cords, and took him up out of the dungeon**: and Jeremiah remained in the court of the prison [*stayed in another prison in the palace*].

Beginning with verse 14, next, we watch as Zedekiah again calls for Jeremiah to be brought from prison in order to speak with him. He asks, in effect, that Jeremiah tell him exactly what the Lord has told him about the fate of Jerusalem and her king, and to withhold no information. You will see that this makes Jeremiah a bit nervous.

14 ¶ **Then Zedekiah the king sent, and took Jeremiah the prophet unto him** into the third entry that *is* in the house of the LORD: **and the king said unto Jeremiah, I will ask thee a thing; hide nothing from me**.

15 **Then Jeremiah said** unto Zedekiah, **If I declare** *it* **unto thee, wilt thou not surely put me to death?** and if I give thee counsel, wilt thou not hearken unto me [*and if I give you advice, isn't it true that you won't listen to me*]?

16 **So Zedekiah the king sware** [*promised*] **secretly unto Jeremiah**, saying, As the LORD liveth [*the strongest oath in Jewish culture of that day*], that made us this soul [*who gave us life*], **I will not put thee to death, neither will I give thee into**

the hand of these men that seek thy life.

17 **Then said Jeremiah unto Zedekiah,** Thus saith the LORD, the God of hosts, the God of Israel; **If thou wilt assuredly go forth** [*surrender*] **unto the king of Babylon's princes** [*army commanders*]**, then thy soul shall live, and this city shall not be burned** with fire; **and thou shalt live, and thine house** [*your wives and children also—see verse 23*]:

18 **But if thou wilt not go forth to the king of Babylon's princes,** then shall this city be given into the hand of the Chaldeans, and they shall burn it with fire, and thou shalt not escape out of their hand.

19 **And Zedekiah** the king **said unto Jeremiah, I am afraid of the Jews that are fallen to the Chaldeans** [*who have already deserted to the Babylonians—see footnote 19a in your Bible*]**, lest they deliver me into their hand** [*lest the Babylonians turn me over to them*]**, and they mock** [*abuse, mistreat*] **me.**

20 **But Jeremiah said, They shall not deliver** *thee* [*hand you over to the Jews who have surrendered*]. Obey, I beseech thee, the voice of the LORD, which I speak unto thee: so it shall be well unto thee, and thy soul shall live.

21 **But if thou refuse to go forth** [*surrender*]**, this** *is* **the word that the LORD** hath shewed me:

In order to understand verse 22, next, it is helpful to know that one of the worst insults in Jewish culture of the day was to be mocked in public by women. Jeremiah warns Zedekiah that this is exactly what will happen to him if he does not follow the Lord's counsel and surrender to the invading army.

22 And, **behold, all the women that are left in the king of Judah's house** [*in other words, in the palace*] **shall be brought forth to the king of Babylon's princes** [*generals and leaders*]**, and those** *women* **shall say** [*mock you, saying*]**, Thy friends** [*German Bible: your trusted advisers*] **have set thee on** [*have misled you; i.e., you are gullible*]**, and have prevailed against thee** [*have overruled you, the king*]**: thy feet are sunk in the mire** [*they have led you into a trap*]**,** *and* **they are turned away back** [*your friends have deserted you*].

23 So **they shall bring out all thy wives and thy children to the Chaldeans** [*this indeed happened; and all of his sons (except Mulek) were killed before his eyes—see 52:10*]: and **thou shalt not escape** out of their hand, **but shalt be taken by the hand of the king of Babylon**: and **thou shalt cause this city to be burned with fire** [*it will be your fault that Jerusalem is burned*].

Next, King Zedekiah tells Jeremiah that under penalty of death he is not to tell anyone about their secret conversation.

24 ¶ Then said Zedekiah unto Jeremiah, **Let no man know of these words, and thou shalt not die**.

25 **But if the princes hear that I have talked with thee, and they come unto thee**, and say unto thee, Declare unto us now what thou hast said unto the king, hide it not from us, and we will not put thee to death; also what the king said unto thee:

26 **Then thou shalt say** unto them, I presented my supplication before the king, that he would not cause me to return to Jonathan's house [*which had been made into a prison—see 37:15*], to die there.

27 **Then came all the princes unto Jeremiah, and asked him**: and he told them according to all these words that the king had commanded. So they left off speaking with him; for the matter was not perceived [*they did not find out what Jeremiah and Zedekiah had discussed*].

Verse 28, next, informs us that Jeremiah was kept in the royal palace prison until Jerusalem was captured.

28 **So Jeremiah abode in the court of the prison until the day that Jerusalem was taken**: and he was *there* when Jerusalem was taken.

JEREMIAH 39

Selection: all verses

This chapter is an account of the fall of Jerusalem, about 587 BC (see "Capture of Jerusalem" on the chronology chart in the Bible Dictionary at the back of your Latter-day Saint Bible).

1 **IN the ninth year of Zedekiah** king of Judah, in the tenth month, **came Nebuchadrezzar king of Babylon and all his army against Jerusalem, and they besieged it** [*laid siege to it*].

2 *And* **in the eleventh year of Zedekiah, in the fourth month, the ninth** *day* of the month, **the city was broken up** [*the Babylonian soldiers broke through the city wall*].

3 **And all the princes** [*military leaders*] **of the king of Babylon came in**, and sat in the middle gate, *even* Nergal-sharezer, Samgar-nebo, Sarsechim, Rab-saris, Nergal-sharezer, Rab-mag, with all the residue of the princes [*other military leaders*] of the king of Babylon.

Next we are told that King Zedekiah and some of his people made a futile attempt to escape and were captured near Jericho.

4 ¶ And it came to pass, *that* **when Zedekiah the king of Judah saw them**, and all the men of war, then **they fled, and went forth out of the city by night**, by the way of the king's garden, by the gate betwixt the two walls: and he went out the way of the plain.

5 **But the Chaldeans' army pursued after them, and overtook Zedekiah in the plains of Jericho: and** when they had taken him, they

brought him up to Nebuchadnezzar king of Babylon to Riblah [*in northern Syria*] in the land of Hamath, where he gave judgment upon him [*where he sentenced him*].

6 Then the king of Babylon slew the sons of Zedekiah in Riblah before his eyes: also the king of Babylon slew all the nobles of Judah.

We know from the Book of Mormon that one of Zedekiah's sons, Mulek, escaped, and was brought by the Lord to America. We will include two references from the Book of Mormon here:

Helaman 6:10

10 Now the land south was called Lehi and the land north was called Mulek, which was after the son of Zedekiah; for **the Lord did bring Mulek into the land north**, and Lehi into the land south.

Helaman 8:21

21 And now will you dispute that Jerusalem was destroyed? **Will ye say that the sons of Zedekiah were not slain, all except it were Mulek?** Yea, and do ye not behold that the seed of Zedekiah are with us, and they were driven out of the land of Jerusalem? But behold, this is not all—

7 Moreover **he put out Zedekiah's eyes, and bound him with chains, to carry him to Babylon**.

8 ¶ And the Chaldeans burned the king's house [*the palace in Jerusalem*]**, and the houses of the people,** with fire, and brake down the walls of Jerusalem.

Some groups of Jewish prisoners had already been taken to Babylon in earlier waves of the Babylonian conquest. Included in those groups of prisoners were Daniel and Ezekiel. Next, in verses 9–10, we see that many of the remaining Jews were taken to Babylon. However, many of the poor were left in the land of Judah and given land to farm.

9 Then Nebuzar-adan the captain of the guard [*NIV: commander of the imperial guard*] **carried away captive into Babylon the remnant** of the people that remained in the city, and those that fell away, that fell to him [*who had deserted to the Babylonians—see footnote 9a in your Bible*], with the rest of the people that remained.

10 But Nebuzar-adan the captain of the guard **left of the poor** of the people, which had nothing, **in the land of Judah, and gave them vineyards and fields** at the same time.

Next, in verses 11–14, we see that King Nebuchadnezzar commanded that Jeremiah be set free from the prison he was in and be treated well.

11 ¶ Now Nebuchadrezzar king of Babylon **gave charge concerning Jeremiah** to Nebuzar-adan the captain of the guard, saying,

12 **Take him, and look well to him, and do him no harm; but do unto him even as he shall say unto thee.**

13 So Nebuzar-adan the captain of the guard sent, and Nebushasban, Rab-saris, and Nergal-sharezer, Rab-mag, and all the king of Babylon's princes;

14 Even **they sent, and took Jeremiah out of the court of the prison**, and committed him unto Gedaliah the son of Ahikam the son of Shaphan, **that he should carry him home**: so he dwelt among the people.

> Next, in verses 15–18, we find that before Jeremiah was set free, he had prophesied concerning the kind Ethiopian servant who threw him rags with which to pad his armpits with when he was pulled from the dungeon—see Jeremiah 38:7–13.

15 ¶ **Now the word of the LORD came unto Jeremiah, while he was shut up in the court of the prison, saying**,

16 **Go and speak to Ebed-melech the Ethiopian**, saying, Thus saith the LORD of hosts, the God of Israel; **Behold, I will bring my words upon this city for evil** [all that has been prophesied concerning the destruction of Jerusalem will take place, because of wickedness], and not for good; and they shall be *accomplished* in that day before thee.

17 **But I will deliver thee** [the kind Ethiopian servant] **in that day, saith the LORD: and thou shalt not be given into the hand of the men of whom thou** *art* **afraid**.

18 For **I will surely deliver thee, and thou shalt not fall by the** sword, **but thy life shall be for a prey unto thee** [your life will be preserved]: **because thou hast put thy trust in me, saith the LORD**.

JEREMIAH 40

Selection: all verses

After the fall of Jerusalem to the Babylonians, in about 587 BC, King Nebuchadnezzar's soldiers captured King Zedekiah, as detailed in chapter 39, verses 4–7. He then appointed a Jew named Gedaliah to serve as the governor over the remaining Jews who were left behind in Judah. It was Gedaliah's father, Ahikam, who had saved Jeremiah's life about twenty-two years earlier (see Jeremiah 26:24).

Jeremiah had been taken to Ramah, about five miles north of Jerusalem, in chains, with the other prisoners, but was set free by order of King Nebuchadnezzar of Babylon to Nebuzaradan, his captain of the guard (verse 1). (By the way, there were two towns called Ramah that were significant in Old Testament times. One was about twenty miles northwest of Jerusalem, and the other, mentioned here in verse 1, was about five miles north of Jerusalem.) After having been set free at Ramah, Jeremiah was allowed to choose whether to accompany the Jews being taken to Babylon or remain in Judah. In either case, he was to be treated well, by order of the king of Babylon. He stayed in Judah.

1 **THE word that came to Jeremiah from the LORD, after** that **Nebuzar-adan** the captain of the guard **had let him go** [set him free] **from Ramah**, when he had taken him being bound

in chains among all that were carried away captive of Jerusalem and Judah, which were carried [*which were about to be carried*] away captive unto Babylon.

2 **And the captain of the guard took Jeremiah, and said** unto him, The LORD thy God hath pronounced this evil upon this place.

3 Now the LORD hath brought *it,* and done according as he hath said: because ye have sinned against the LORD, and have not obeyed his voice, therefore this thing is come upon you.

4 And now, **behold, I loose thee this day from the chains** which *were* upon thine hand. **If it seem good unto thee to come with me into Babylon, come**; and I will look well unto thee: **but if it seem ill unto thee to come with me** into Babylon, forbear [*don't come*]: **behold, all the land *is* before thee: whither it seemeth good and convenient for thee to go, thither go** [*you may live wherever you desire in Judah*].

5 Now while he [*Jeremiah*] was not yet gone back [*before Jeremiah turned to go back*], *he* [*Nebuzar-adan*] *said,* **Go back** also **to Gedaliah** the son of Ahikam [*who had saved Jeremiah's life about twenty-two years ago*] the son of Shaphan, **whom the king of Babylon hath made governor** over the cities of Judah, **and dwell with him among the people: or go wheresoever it seemeth convenient unto thee to go.** So the captain of the guard gave him victuals [*a food allowance—see footnote 5b in your Bible*] and a reward, and let him go.

6 **Then went Jeremiah unto Gedaliah** the son of Ahikam to Mizpah; and dwelt with him among the people that were left in the land.

Next, in verses 7–11, we see that many Jews who had fled to open country to escape the Babylonians, or to neighboring nations, came back when things settled down and Gedaliah had been made governor.

7 ¶ **Now when all the captains of the forces** [*Jewish army*] **which *were* in the fields** [*who had fled to open country*], *even* they **and their men, heard that the king of Babylon had made Gedaliah** the son of Ahikam **governor** in the land, and had committed unto him [*had put him in charge of*] men, and women, and children, and of the poor of the land, of them that were not carried away captive to Babylon;

8 **Then they came to Gedaliah to Mizpah** [*about ten miles north of Jerusalem*], even Ishmael the son of Nethaniah, and Johanan and Jonathan the sons of Kareah, and Seraiah the son of Tanhumeth, and the sons of Ephai the Netophathite, and Jezaniah the son of a Maachathite, **they and their men**.

Next, Governor Gedaliah assures these men that they will be safe if they submit to the Babylonian rule.

9 **And Gedaliah** the son of Ahikam the son of Shaphan **sware unto them**

and to their men, saying, **Fear not to serve the Chaldeans** [*the Babylonians*]: **dwell in the land, and serve the king of Babylon, and it shall be well with you.**

10 **As for me, behold, I will dwell at Mizpah to serve the Chaldeans,** which will come unto us: **but ye, gather ye wine, and summer fruits, and oil,** and put *them* in your vessels, **and dwell in your cities that ye have taken** [*in other words, settle down to farming in the cities you have occupied*].

11 **Likewise when all the Jews** [*other Jews who had fled to neighboring countries*] that *were* **in Moab,** and **among the Ammonites,** and **in Edom, and** that *were* **in all the countries, heard that the king of Babylon had left a remnant of Judah, and that he had set over them Gedaliah** the son of Ahikam the son of Shaphan;

12 Even **all the Jews returned** out of all places whither they were driven, and came to the land of Judah, to Gedaliah, unto Mizpah, **and gathered wine and summer fruits very much** [*and gathered an abundant harvest*].

Next, Governor Gedaliah is warned about a plot by the Ammonite king to assassinate him. The Ammonite nation was located east of the Jordan River, north of Jerusalem.

13 ¶ Moreover **Johanan** the son of Kareah, **and all the captains** of the forces that *were* in the fields, **came to Gedaliah to Mizpah,**

14 **And said** unto him, **Dost thou certainly know that Baalis the king of the Ammonites hath sent Ishmael the son of Nethaniah to slay thee? But Gedaliah** the son of Ahikam **believed them not.**

15 **Then Johanan** the son of Kareah **spake to Gedaliah** in Mizpah **secretly, saying, Let me go, I pray thee, and I will slay Ishmael** the son of Nethaniah, and no man shall know *it:* **wherefore should he slay thee** [*why should he be allowed to assassinate you*], that all the Jews which are gathered unto thee should be scattered, and the remnant in Judah perish?

16 **But Gedaliah** the son of Ahikam **said** unto Johanan the son of Kareah, **Thou shalt not do this thing: for thou speakest falsely of Ishmael** [*you are falsely accusing Ishmael*].

JEREMIAH 41

Selection: all verses

The assassination plot discussed in chapter 40 is carried out in this chapter. Jeremiah's friend, Gedaliah, who has been appointed governor of the remaining Jews in the land of Judah, by the king of Babylon, is murdered. As you found out near the end of chapter 40, Gedaliah was warned by friends about Ishmael's plot, but refused to believe that he would do such a thing to him.

As verse 1 indicates, Ishmael was a member of the Jewish royal family. He plotted with other former government leaders of the Jews to go visit Gedaliah at his headquarters at Mizpah, about ten miles north of Jerusalem, and kill him.

1 NOW it came to pass in the seventh month, *that* **Ishmael** the son of Nethaniah the son of Elishama, **of the seed royal, and the princes of the king** [*who was of royal blood and who had been one of King Zedekiah's officers in his government*], even **ten men with him, came unto Gedaliah** the son of Ahikam to Mizpah; **and** there **they did eat bread together in Mizpah.**

2 **Then** arose **Ishmael** the son of Nethaniah, **and the ten men that were with him,** and **smote Gedaliah** the son of Ahikam the son of Shaphan with the sword, **and slew him,** whom the king of Babylon had made governor over the land.

Next, in verse 3, we see that Ishmael and his men not only killed Governor Gedaliah and the Jews who were with him, but they also killed the Babylonian soldiers there, so that it took a couple of days before anyone found out about the assassination and slaughter.

3 **Ishmael also slew all the Jews that were with** him, *even* with **Gedaliah,** at Mizpah, **and the Chaldeans** that were found there, *and* **the men of war** [*NIV as well as the Babylonian soldiers who were there*].

Apparently, Gedaliah's stronghold was sufficiently isolated from the rest of Mizpah that no one immediately noticed the slaughter.

4 And it came to pass **the second day** after he had slain Gedaliah, and **no man knew** *it,*

5 That **there came certain from Shechem, from Shiloh, and from Samaria** [*cities in the Holy Land*], *even* **fourscore men** [*eighty men*], having their beards shaven, and their clothes rent, and having cut themselves [*physical signs in that culture that they had made a vow, in this case to bring offerings to the temple no matter what*], **with offerings and incense** in their hand, **to bring** *them* **to the house of the LORD** [*on their way to the temple in Jerusalem*].

Next, Ishmael and his henchmen set up an ambush for these Jews who were going to Jerusalem.

6 **And Ishmael** the son of Nethaniah **went forth from Mizpah to meet them, weeping all along** as he went: and it came to pass, **as he met them, he said** unto them, **Come to Gedaliah the son of Ahikam.**

7 **And** it was *so,* **when they came into the midst of the city,** that **Ishmael** the son of Nethaniah **slew them,** *and cast them* into the midst of the pit, **he, and the men that** *were* **with him.**

Next, ten of the men who were ambushed persuade Ishmael not to kill them, in return for supplies of food.

8 But **ten men** were found among them that **said unto Ishmael, Slay**

us not: for we have treasures in the field, of wheat, and of barley, and of oil, and of honey. So he forbare, and slew them not among their brethren.

9 Now the pit wherein Ishmael had cast all the dead bodies of the men, whom he had slain because of Gedaliah, *was* it which Asa the king had made for fear of Baasha king of Israel: *and* Ishmael the son of Nethaniah filled it with *them that were* slain.

10 **Then Ishmael carried away captive all the residue** [*the rest*] **of the people that** *were* **in Mizpah,** *even* [*including*] **the king's daughters, and all the people that remained in Mizpah,** whom Nebuzar-adan the captain of the guard had committed to Gedaliah the son of Ahikam: and **Ishmael the son of Nethaniah carried them away captive, and departed to go** [*intending to go*] **over to the Ammonites** [*an area east of the Jordan River and north of Jerusalem*].

11 ¶ **But when Johanan** the son of Kareah, **and all the captains of the forces that** *were* **with him, heard of all the evil that Ishmael** the son of Nethaniah **had done,**

12 Then **they took all the men, and went to fight with Ishmael** the son of Nethaniah, and found him by the great waters that *are* in Gibeon [*some pools of water, a bit northwest of Jerusalem*].

Imagine the relief of the prisoners taken by Ishmael and his accomplices when they saw Johanan and the Jewish soldiers that were with him coming to rescue them!

13 Now it came to pass, *that* **when all the people which** *were* **with Ishmael saw Johanan** the son of Kareah, **and all the captains of the forces that** *were* **with him, then they were glad.**

14 **So all the people that Ishmael had carried away captive** from Mizpah **cast about** [*turned around*] **and returned,** and went unto Johanan the son of Kareah.

15 **But Ishmael** the son of Nethaniah **escaped from Johanan with eight men, and went to the Ammonites.**

Next, we see that Johanan and his men and the people with them were afraid of retaliation from the Babylonians, and so they decided to go to Egypt for safety.

16 **Then took Johanan** the son of Kareah, **and all the captains** of the forces that *were* with him, **all the remnant of the people whom he had recovered** [*rescued*] from Ishmael the son of Nethaniah, from Mizpah, after *that* he had slain Gedaliah the son of Ahikam, *even* mighty men of war, and the women, and the children, and the eunuchs, whom he had brought again from Gibeon:

17 **And they departed, and dwelt** in the habitation of Chimham, which

is **by Beth-lehem, to go to enter into Egypt,**

18 Because of the Chaldeans: **for they were afraid** of them, **because Ishmael** the son of Nethaniah **had slain Gedaliah** the son of Ahikam, **whom the king of Babylon made governor in the land.**

JEREMIAH 42

Selection: all verses

This chapter is a continuation of the account in chapters 40–41. At the end of chapter 41, you saw Johanan and his soldiers, along with the Jews they had rescued from Ishmael, gather near Bethlehem, preparing to attempt an escape to Egypt.

They decided to go visit Jeremiah and ask for counsel from the Lord concerning their plans. Let's see what happens.

1 **THEN** all **the captains** of the forces [*the military officers*], **and Johanan** the son of Kareah, and Jezaniah the son of Hoshaiah, **and all the people** [*in Johanan's group*] from the least even unto the greatest, **came near** [*went and found Jeremiah*],

2 **And said unto Jeremiah** the prophet, Let, we beseech thee, our supplication be accepted before thee, and **pray for us unto the LORD thy God,** *even* **for all this remnant**; (for we are left *but* a few of many, as thine eyes do behold us [*we are a*

small enough group that you can see all of us before your eyes]:)

3 **That the LORD thy God may shew us** the way wherein we may walk, and **the thing that we may do.**

4 **Then Jeremiah** the prophet **said** unto them, I have heard *you;* behold, **I will pray unto the LORD** your God according to your words; **and** it shall come to pass, *that* **whatsoever thing the LORD shall answer you, I will declare** *it* **unto you; I will keep nothing back** from you.

Next, these refugees promise faithfully that they will follow the Lord's counsel exactly, no matter what He says.

5 **Then they said to Jeremiah,** The LORD be a true and faithful witness between us, **if we do not even according to all things** for the which the LORD thy God shall send thee to us.

6 **Whether** *it be* **good, or whether** *it be* **evil, we will obey the voice of the LORD** our God, to whom we send thee; that it may be well with us, when we obey the voice of the LORD our God.

7 ¶ And it came to pass **after ten days, that the word of the LORD came unto Jeremiah.**

8 **Then called he Johanan** the son of Kareah, **and all the captains** of the forces which *were* with him, **and all the people** from the least even to the greatest,

9 And said unto them, Thus saith the LORD, the God of Israel, unto whom ye sent me to present your supplication before him;

Next, Jeremiah gives these men the answer from the Lord per their request (in verses 1 and 2). We will need the JST to clarify correct doctrine regarding the last phrase of verse 10.

By the way, some have wondered why JST changes such as the one following verse 10 are not found in the footnotes in our Latter-day Saint English edition of the Bible or at the back of it. The answer is that there was not enough room in our Bible to include them all. I use Joseph Smith's "New Translation" of the Bible, printed by Herald Publishing House, Independence, Missouri, 1970, which contains all of the Prophet's changes to the Bible as the source for these additional JST changes. It has been shown by Latter-day Saint scholars to be reliable and true to the Prophet's original work on the Bible. Most Latter-day Saint bookstores either carry books that have all of the JST changes to the Bible or can get it for you if you ask them to.

10 If ye will still abide in this land [if you will stay here in Judah], then will I build you, and not pull *you* down, and I will plant you, and not pluck *you* up [in other words, you will prosper if you stay in Judah in subjection to the Babylonians]: for I repent me of the evil that I have done unto you.

JST Jeremiah 42:10

10 If you will still abide in this land, then will I build you, and not pull down; I will plant you, and not pluck up; **and I will turn away the evil that I have done unto you.**

11 **Be not afraid of the king of Babylon,** of whom ye are afraid; be not afraid of him, saith the LORD: **for I** *am* **with you to save you, and to deliver you from his hand.**

12 **And I will shew mercies unto you, that he may have mercy upon you,** and cause you to return to your own land.

13 ¶ **But if ye say, We will not dwell in this land, neither obey the voice of the LORD** your God,

14 **Saying, No; but we will go into the land of Egypt,** where we shall see no war, nor hear the sound of the trumpet [the signal to battle for armies], nor have hunger of bread; and there will we dwell:

15 And now therefore hear the word of the LORD, ye remnant of Judah; **Thus saith the LORD** of hosts, the God of Israel; **If ye** wholly set your faces to **enter into Egypt, and go to sojourn** [remain] **there;**

16 **Then it shall come to pass,** *that* **the sword,** which ye feared, shall overtake you there in the land of Egypt, **and the famine,** whereof ye were afraid, **shall follow close after you there in Egypt; and there ye shall die.**

17 So shall it be with all the men that set their faces to go into Egypt to sojourn there; **they shall die by the sword**, by the **famine**, and by the **pestilence** [*disease, plagues, disasters, and so forth*]: and **none of them shall remain or escape** from the evil that I will bring upon them.

18 For **thus saith the LORD** of hosts, the God of Israel; **As mine anger and my fury hath been poured forth upon the inhabitants of Jerusalem; so shall my fury be poured forth upon you, when ye shall enter into Egypt**: **and ye shall be an execration** [*people will curse and swear at you*], and **an astonishment** [*horror*], and **a curse**, and **a reproach** [*people will look down on you*]; **and ye shall see this place no more** [*you will never come back to Jerusalem and the land of Judah*].

19 ¶ **The LORD hath said** concerning you, O ye remnant of Judah [*fragment of the Jews*]; **Go ye not into Egypt**: know certainly that I have admonished you this day [*consider yourselves fairly warned*].

Next, Jeremiah warns these people, who were not being honest with themselves when they asked Jeremiah to get the word of the Lord to them, that they have made a fatal mistake by planning to ignore the Lord's counsel.

20 **For ye dissembled in your hearts** [*you were not sincere in your request for counsel from the Lord*], **when ye sent me unto the LORD** your God, saying, Pray for us unto the LORD our God; and according unto all that the LORD our God shall say, so declare unto us, and we will do *it.*

21 **And** *now* **I have this day declared** *it* **to you; but ye have not obeyed the voice of the LORD** your God, nor any *thing* for the which he hath sent me unto you.

22 **Now therefore know certainly that ye shall die by the sword, by the famine, and by the pestilence, in the place whither ye desire to go** [*Egypt*] *and* to sojourn [*live*].

JEREMIAH 43

Selection: all verses

This chapter is a continuation of the tense situation described at the end of chapter 42. In the end, Jeremiah and his faithful scribe, Baruch, will be kidnapped and taken by these rebels to Egypt.

1 And it came to pass, *that* **when Jeremiah had made an end of speaking unto all the people all the words of the LORD** their God [*as recorded in chapter 42*], for which the LORD their God had sent him to them, *even* all these words,

2 **Then spake Azariah** the son of Hoshaiah, **and Johanan** the son of Kareah, **and all the proud men**, saying unto **Jeremiah, Thou speakest falsely** [*you are lying*]: the LORD our God hath not sent thee to say, Go not into Egypt to sojourn there:

Next, these rebellious men claim that Jeremiah's faithful scribe, Baruch, has prejudiced him against them and induced Jeremiah to give them a false revelation that will lead to their deaths or captivity.

3 **But Baruch** the son of Neriah **setteth thee on against us,** for to deliver us into the hand of the Chaldeans, that they might put us to death, and carry us away captives into Babylon.

4 **So Johanan** the son of Kareah, **and all the captains of the forces, and all the people, obeyed not the voice of the LORD**, to dwell in the land of Judah.

Next, we see that these rebels not only reject Jeremiah's words, but they kidnap Jeremiah and Baruch, and take them to Egypt with them.

5 **But Johanan** the son of Kareah, **and all the captains** of the forces, **took all the remnant of Judah**, that were returned from all nations, whither they had been driven, to dwell in the land of Judah;

6 *Even* men, and women, and children, and the king's daughters, and **every person that Nebuzar-adan the captain of the guard had left with Gedaliah** [*the Jewish governor who was assassinated by Jewish rebels led by Ishmael—see chapter 41*] the son of Ahikam the son of Shaphan, **and Jeremiah the prophet, and Baruch** the son of Neriah.

7 **So they came into the land of Egypt**: for they obeyed not the voice of the LORD: thus came they *even* **to Tahpanhes** [*in Egypt, in the land of Goshen, where Joseph, his brothers, father and their families settled*].

Next, the Lord uses drama as He has Jeremiah prophesy that the Babylonians will attack and overcome Egypt.

8 ¶ **Then came the word of the LORD unto Jeremiah in Tahpanhes, saying,**

9 **Take great stones in thine hand, and hide them** in the clay in the brickkiln, which *is* **at the entry of Pharaoh's house in Tahpanhes, in the sight of the men of Judah**;

10 **And say unto them, Thus saith the LORD** of hosts, the God of Israel; Behold, **I will send** and take **Nebuchadrezzar the king of Babylon**, my servant [*the tool of the Lord to "hammer" Egypt*], **and will set his throne upon these stones** that I have hid; **and he shall spread his royal pavilion over them**.

11 **And when he cometh, he shall smite the land of Egypt**, *and deliver* such *as are* for death to death; and such *as are* for captivity to captivity; and such *as are* for the sword to the sword.

12 And **I will kindle a fire in the houses of the gods of Egypt; and he shall burn them, and carry them away captives**: and he shall array himself with the land of Egypt, as a shepherd putteth on his garment;

and he shall go forth from thence in peace.

13 **He shall break also the images of Beth-shemesh, that** *is* **in the land of Egypt; and the houses of the gods of the Egyptians shall he burn with fire**.

JEREMIAH 44

Selection: all verses

Jeremiah and Baruch, his scribe, have now been taken captive into Egypt by a group of Jewish rebels, who believe they will find peace and safety from the Babylonians in Egypt. They won't. They have rebelled against the clear counsel of the Lord to them to stay in Judah (chapters 42–43). Jeremiah will prophesy that the group will all be destroyed, except for a small remnant.

1 **THE word that came to Jeremiah concerning all the Jews which dwell in the land of Egypt**, which dwell at Migdol [*in northern Egypt*], and at Tahpanhes [*in the eastern part of the Nile Delta*], and at Noph [*Memphis, capital of ancient Egypt, not far south of modern Cairo*], and in the country of Pathros [*upper Egypt*], saying,

2 **Thus saith the LORD** of hosts, the God of Israel; **Ye have seen all the evil that I have brought upon Jerusalem, and upon all the cities of Judah**; and, behold, this day they *are* a desolation, and no man dwelleth therein,

3 **Because of their wickedness** which they have committed to provoke me to anger, **in that they went to burn incense,** *and* **to serve other gods** [*worshiping false gods, including idol worship*], whom they knew not, *neither* they, ye, nor your fathers.

The JST helps us with verse 4, next.

4 Howbeit **I sent unto you all my servants the prophets**, rising early and sending *them,* **saying, Oh, do not this abominable thing that I hate**.

JST Jeremiah 44:4

4 Howbeit I sent unto you all my servants the prophets, **commanding them to rise early**, and sending them, saying, Oh, do not this abominable thing that I hate.

5 **But they hearkened not**, nor inclined their ear to turn from their wickedness, to burn no incense unto other gods.

6 **Wherefore my fury and mine anger** [*the law of justice*] **was poured forth, and was kindled in the cities of Judah and in the streets of Jerusalem**; and they are wasted *and* desolate, as at this day.

Next, having reviewed the recent destruction of the Jews in the land of Judah, the Lord asks this rebellious colony of Jews in Egypt why they can't learn a lesson from what happened to their fellow Jews in the Holy Land. In effect, He asks them why they would want to get themselves likewise cut off from mortality.

7 **Therefore now thus saith the LORD**, the God of hosts, the God of Israel; **Wherefore** [*why*] **commit ye** *this* **great evil against your souls** [*against yourselves*], to cut off from you man and woman, child and suckling, out of Judah, to leave you none to remain;

8 **In that ye provoke me unto wrath with the works of your hands, burning incense unto** [*worshiping*] **other gods in the land of Egypt**, whither ye be gone to dwell, **that ye might cut yourselves off**, and that ye might be a curse and a reproach among all the nations of the earth?

> Sometimes we tend to think mainly in terms of wicked men when it comes to the destruction of nations. However, as shown in verse 9, next, wicked women likewise play a major role in the downfall of nations. In fact, as described in Isaiah 3:16–26, when Satan succeeds in luring women as well as men into the paths of sin and evil, a nation and people are doomed. They are "ripe in iniquity."

9 **Have ye forgotten the wickedness of your fathers** [*ancestors*], **and** the wickedness of **the kings of Judah**, and the wickedness of **their wives**, and **your** own **wickedness, and the wickedness of your wives**, which they have committed in the land of Judah, and in the streets of Jerusalem?

10 **They are not humbled** *even* **unto this day**, neither have they feared, nor walked in my law, nor in my statutes, that I set before you and before your fathers [*those who were not slaughtered by the Babylonians still have not repented*].

11 ¶ **Therefore** thus saith the LORD of hosts, the God of Israel; Behold, **I will set my face against you for evil** [*because of wickedness*], and to cut off all Judah.

12 **And I will take the remnant of Judah** [*the group of rebel Jews*], **that have set their faces to go into the land of Egypt** to sojourn there, **and they shall all be consumed**, *and* fall in the land of Egypt; they shall *even* be consumed **by the sword** *and* **by** the **famine**: they shall die, from the least even unto the greatest, by the sword and by the famine: and they shall be an execration [*people will curse you and swear at you*], *and* an astonishment [*horror*], and a curse, and a reproach [*people will look down on you*].

13 For **I will punish them that dwell in the land of Egypt, as I have punished Jerusalem**, by the sword, by the famine, and by the pestilence:

14 **So that none of the remnant of Judah, which are gone into the land of Egypt to sojourn there, shall escape or remain**, that they should return into the land of Judah, to the which they have a desire to return to dwell there: for **none shall return but such as shall escape** [*there will be a few Jews who will survive*].

Next, these rebellious people blatantly reject the word of the Lord, knowing full well that they are guilty as stated. We see that the women were just as wicked as their husbands.

15 ¶ **Then all the men which knew that their wives had burned incense unto other gods, and all the women** that stood by, a great multitude, **even all the people** [*the Jews in this group*] that dwelt in the land of Egypt, in Pathros [*upper Egypt*], **answered Jeremiah, saying,**

16 *As for* the word that thou hast spoken unto us in the name of the LORD, **we will not hearken unto thee.**

Next, these rebels proudly boast that they will go on doing what they have been doing.

17 **But we will certainly do whatsoever thing goeth forth out of our own mouth** [*we will do whatever we want*], **to burn incense unto the queen of heaven** [*a heathen female god*], and to pour out drink offerings unto her, **as we have done, we, and our fathers, our kings, and our princes, in the cities of Judah, and in the streets of Jerusalem**: for *then* had we plenty of victuals [*food*], and were well, and saw no evil [*in other words, we prospered under the false gods we were worshiping in the land of Judah*].

18 **But since we left off to burn incense to the queen of heaven** [*when we quit worshiping that female god*], and to pour out drink offerings unto

her, **we have wanted** [*lacked*] **all** *things,* and have been consumed by the sword and by the famine.

19 **And when we** [*the women in the group are speaking now*] **burned incense to the queen of heaven,** and poured out drink offerings unto her, **did we make her cakes to worship her, and pour out drink offerings unto her, without our men?**

20 ¶ **Then Jeremiah said unto all the people,** to the men, and to the women, and to all the people which had given him *that* answer, saying,

21 **The incense that ye burned in the cities of Judah** [*as you worshiped your idols*], and in the streets of Jerusalem, ye, and your fathers, your kings, and your princes, and the people of the land, did not the LORD remember them, and came it *not* into his mind?

22 **So that the LORD could no longer bear, because of the evil of your doings,** *and* **because of the abominations which ye have committed**; therefore **is your land** [*Judah, including Jerusalem*] **a desolation**, and an astonishment, and a curse, without an inhabitant, as at this day.

23 **Because ye have burned incense** [*worshiped idols*], and **because ye have sinned against the LORD,** and have not obeyed the voice of the LORD, nor walked in his law, nor in his statutes, nor in his testimonies; **therefore this evil is happened unto you,** as at this day.

24 **Moreover Jeremiah said unto all the people, and to all the women**, Hear the word of the LORD, all Judah that *are* in the land of Egypt:

25 **Thus saith the LORD** of hosts, the God of Israel, saying; **Ye and your wives have both spoken with your mouths, and fulfilled with your hand, saying, We will surely perform our vows that we have vowed, to burn incense to the queen of heaven**, and to pour out drink offerings unto her: ye will surely accomplish your vows, and surely perform your vows.

26 **Therefore hear ye the word of the LORD, all Judah that** [*all of you Jews who*] **dwell in the land of Egypt**; Behold, I have sworn by my great name, saith the LORD, that **my name shall no more be named in the mouth of any man of Judah in all the land of Egypt, saying, The Lord GOD liveth** [*in other words, apostasy will be complete among the Jews who fled to Egypt at this time*].

27 **Behold, I will watch over them for evil, and not for good** [*punishments instead of blessings will come upon them*]: and all the men of Judah that *are* in the land of Egypt shall be consumed by the sword and by the famine, until there be an end of them.

28 **Yet a small number that escape the sword shall return out of the land of Egypt into the land of Judah, and all the remnant of Judah**, that are gone into the land of Egypt to sojourn there, **shall know whose words shall stand, mine, or theirs** [*in other words, these proud and haughty people will find out who is right, them or God*].

Verses 29–30, next, contain the last words of Jeremiah that we are aware of. It is a prophecy foretelling the death of Pharaoh in Egypt. He was killed during a rebellion in his own kingdom about 570 BC.

29 ¶ **And this** *shall be* **a sign unto you, saith the LORD, that I will punish you in this place**, that ye may know that my words shall surely stand against you for evil:

30 Thus saith the LORD; Behold, **I will give Pharaoh-hophra king of Egypt into the hand of his enemies**, and into the hand of them that seek his life; as I gave Zedekiah king of Judah into the hand of Nebuchadrezzar king of Babylon, his enemy, and that sought his life.

NOTE

The remaining chapters in the Book of Jeremiah, except for chapter 52, are a compilation of prophecies given by Jeremiah. They appear to be added by someone as a sort of appendix to the main book, chapters 1–44. They are not given in chronological order and consist of chapter 45, which is a promise to Baruch, Jeremiah's faithful scribe; chapters 46–51, which are prophecies against several surrounding wicked nations; and chapter 52, a review of the conquest of Jerusalem and Judah by King Nebuchadnezzar in about 587 BC in which Zedekiah was taken captive.

JEREMIAH 45

Selection: all verses

Baruch served faithfully as Jeremiah's scribe throughout his ministry. The last we hear of him is in Egypt, where he continued to serve with Jeremiah. The prophecy and blessing for him, given in this chapter, was given about 605 BC.

1 **THE word that Jeremiah the prophet spake unto Baruch** the son of Neriah, when he had written these words in a book at the mouth of Jeremiah, in the fourth year of Jehoiakim the son of Josiah king of Judah, saying,

2 **Thus saith the LORD, the God of Israel, unto thee, O Baruch**;

In verse 3, next, we are given to understand that it was a rough life for Baruch, as he faithfully remained loyal to Jeremiah through thick and thin.

3 **Thou** [*Baruch*] **didst say, Woe is me now!** for **the LORD hath added grief to my sorrow** [*it has been one thing after another*]; **I fainted in my sighing** [*I am constantly worn out and groaning under my burdens*], and **I find no rest.**

4 ¶ **Thus shalt thou** [*Jeremiah*] **say unto him** [*Baruch*], **The LORD saith thus; Behold,** *that* **which I have built will I break down, and that which I have planted I will pluck up, even this whole land.**

5 And **seekest thou great things for thyself? seek** *them* **not** [*don't set your heart on great things of the*

world]: for, behold, I will bring evil upon all flesh [*mortality has its share of troubles*], saith the LORD: **but thy life will I give unto thee for a prey** [*your life will be preserved*] **in all places whither thou goest.**

JEREMIAH 46

Selection: all verses

This chapter is a prophecy against Egypt, foretelling that the Egyptian army will be conquered by Babylon. It also contains a prophecy about the scattering and gathering of Israel (verses 27–28). As mentioned in the note before Jeremiah, chapter 45 in this study guide, this chapter is not in chronological sequence.

Verses 1–26 foretell the Babylonian conquest of Egypt in about 605 BC. The Egyptian army had marched as far north as Carchemish (on the border between modern-day Turkey and Syria), and, as explained in verse 2, Pharaoh-necho (the king or Pharaoh of Egypt at the time) was defeated there by the Babylonians.

Jeremiah is a master at using lively language to describe his visions. For example, you will feel the Egyptians' optimistic rallying call to prepare for battle (verses 3–4) and then the sudden devastation among them as they realize defeat (verse 5).

1 **THE word of the LORD** which came to Jeremiah the prophet **against the Gentiles;**

2 **Against Egypt**, against the army of Pharaoh-necho king of Egypt, **which was by the river Euphrates in**

Carchemish, which Nebuchadrezzar king of Babylon smote in the fourth year of Jehoiakim the son of Josiah king of Judah.

A vivid, prophetic description of the battle is seen in the next verses.

3 **Order ye the buckler and shield, and draw near to battle**.

4 **Harness the horses**; and get up, ye horsemen, and stand forth with *your* helmets; furbish the spears, *and* **put on the brigandines** [*armor*].

5 **Wherefore** [*why*] **have I seen them dismayed *and* turned away back** [*why are they retreating*]? and their mighty ones are beaten down, and are fled apace, and look not back: *for* fear *was* round about, saith the LORD.

6 Let not the swift flee away, nor the mighty man escape; **they shall stumble, and fall toward the north by the river Euphrates**.

7 [*Question*] **Who *is* this *that* cometh up as a flood**, whose waters are moved as the rivers [*what nation is behind this flood of soldiers*]?

8 [*Answer*] **Egypt** riseth up like a flood, and *his* waters are moved like the rivers; **and he saith, I will go up, *and* will cover the earth; I will destroy the city and the inhabitants thereof** [*Egypt plans to conquer the whole known world*].

Verse 9, next, shows us that the Egyptians had allies with them as

they went north to "conquer the world."

9 Come up, ye horses; and rage, ye chariots; and **let the mighty men come forth**; the **Ethiopians** and the **Libyans**, that handle the shield; and the **Lydians**, that handle *and* bend the bow.

10 For this *is* the day of the Lord GOD of hosts, a day of vengeance, that he may avenge him of his adversaries: and **the sword shall devour**, and it shall be satiate and made drunk with their blood: **for the Lord GOD of hosts hath a sacrifice in the north country by the river Euphrates** [*Egypt will become a sacrifice to the Babylonians, along the Euphrates River*].

11 Go up into Gilead, and take balm, O virgin, the daughter of Egypt: **in vain shalt thou use many medicines** [*try different strategies to win the battle*]; *for* thou shalt not be cured [*you will be defeated, no matter what*].

Next, Jeremiah prophetically describes the shame to be felt by the Egyptians when their mighty army is defeated.

12 **The nations have heard of thy shame**, and thy cry hath filled the land: for the mighty man hath stumbled against the mighty, *and* they are fallen both together.

13 ¶ **The word that the LORD spake to Jeremiah** the prophet, **how Nebuchadrezzar king of Babylon**

should come *and* **smite the land of Egypt**.

Several Egyptian cities are mentioned in verses 14–15, next, as Jeremiah describes the future destruction in Egypt by the Babylonians under King Nebuchadnezzar.

14 Declare ye in Egypt, and publish in **Migdol**, and publish in **Noph** and in **Tahpanhes**: say ye, Stand fast, and prepare thee; for **the sword shall devour round about thee**.

15 **Why are thy valiant** *men* **swept away?** they stood not, **because the LORD did drive them**.

16 **He made many to fall**, yea, one fell upon another: and they said, Arise, and let us go again to our own people, and to the land of our nativity, from the oppressing sword.

17 **They did cry there, Pharaoh king of Egypt** *is but* **a noise** [*does not have any power against the Babylonians*]; he hath passed the time appointed.

18 *As* **I live, saith the King** [*Jehovah*], whose name *is* the LORD of hosts, **Surely as Tabor** [*Mt. Tabor, just southwest of the Sea of Galilee*] *is* **among the mountains, and as Carmel by the sea** [*Mt. Carmel, by the Mediterranean Sea*], *so* **shall he come**.

19 **O thou daughter dwelling in Egypt** [*O you inhabitants of Egypt*], furnish thyself to go into captivity [*prepare yourselves for captivity*]: for

Noph [*the capital of ancient Egypt, not far south of modern-day Cairo*] shall be waste and desolate without an inhabitant.

20 **Egypt** *is like* **a very fair heifer** [*a vulnerable young cow, that has not yet had a calf*], *but* **destruction cometh**; it cometh **out of the north** [*the direction from which the Babylonian army will come*].

21 Also **her hired men** [*the trained soldiers who intend to protect Egypt*] *are* **in the midst of her like fatted bullocks** [*ready to be sacrificed*]; **for they also are turned back,** *and* **are fled away together** [*will be forced to retreat and flee*]: they did not stand [*they will not stand their ground*], because the day of their calamity was come upon them, *and* the time of their visitation [*punishment for wickedness*].

22 **The voice thereof shall go like a serpent** [*they will be like a hissing snake as it retreats from danger*]; for **they** [*the Babylonians*] **shall march with an army, and come against her** [*Egypt*] **with axes, as hewers of wood** [*the Babylonians will chop down the Egyptians like an army of lumberjacks chopping down a forest*].

23 **They shall cut down her forest**, saith the LORD, **though it cannot be searched** [*even though the "forest" of Egyptians seems very dense*]; **because they** [*the Babylonian armies*] **are more than the grasshoppers, and** *are* **innumerable**.

24 The daughter of [*people of*] **Egypt shall be confounded** [*confused; stopped*]; **she shall be delivered into the hand of the people of the north** [*the Babylonians*].

25 **The LORD** of hosts, the God of Israel, **saith**; Behold, **I will punish the multitude of No** [*Thebes, the capital city of upper Egypt*], **and Pharaoh, and Egypt, with their gods,** and their kings; even Pharaoh, and *all* them that trust in him [*the Egyptians considered their Pharaoh to be a god and worshiped him as such*]:

26 **And I will deliver them into the hand of those that seek their lives** [*in other words, their enemies*], and **into the hand of Nebuchadrezzar king of Babylon**, and into hand of his servants: and afterward it shall be inhabited, as in the days of old, saith the LORD.

The last two verses are a prophecy about the scattering and gathering of Israel.

27 ¶ **But fear not** thou, O my servant [*the Lord's covenant people*] **Jacob** [*Israel*], and **be not dismayed** [*discouraged*], O **Israel** [*Jacob*]: for, behold, **I will save thee from afar off** [*I will gather you from far away*], and thy seed from the land of their captivity; and **Jacob shall return**, and **be in rest** and at ease, and **none shall make** *him* **afraid** [*this will be fulfilled in the last days and into the Millennium*].

28 **Fear thou not**, O Jacob my servant, saith the LORD: for **I** *am* **with thee**; for **I will make a full end of**
all the nations [*when the Millennium comes—see D&C 87:6*] whither I have driven thee: **but I will not make a full end of thee, but correct** [*discipline*] **thee in measure** [*appropriately*]; **yet will I not leave thee wholly unpunished** [*you still need some correction and discipline in order to fill your role as the Lord's covenant people*].

JEREMIAH 47

Selection: all verses

This chapter is a prophecy against the Philistines, a wicked nation at the time, located to the west of Jerusalem, down on the coast of the Mediterranean Sea.

1 **THE word of the LORD that came to Jeremiah** the prophet **against the Philistines**, before that Pharaoh smote Gaza.

2 Thus saith the LORD; **Behold, waters rise up out of the north, and shall be an overflowing flood** [*in other words, a "flood" of enemy soldiers is coming from the north, a reference to the army of Babylon*], **and shall overflow the land** [*you will be flooded, overrun with Babylonians*], and all that is therein; the city, and them that dwell therein: then the men shall cry, and **all the inhabitants of the land shall howl**.

Next, Jeremiah describes the sounds of war and battle, which will be heard when the Babylonians attack the Philistines.

3 At the noise of the **stamping of the hoofs of his strong** *horses,* at the

rushing of his **chariots**, *and at* the **rumbling of** his **wheels**, the fathers shall not look back to *their* children for feebleness of hands [*NIV Fathers will not turn to help their children; their hands will hang limp*];

4 **Because of the day that cometh to spoil all the Philistines**, *and* to cut off from Tyrus and Zidon every helper [*ally*] that remaineth: for **the LORD will spoil** [*will cause the defeat of*] **the Philistines**, the remnant of the country of Caphtor.

5 **Baldness** [*humiliation, captivity— conquering nations often shaved their captives bald, for purposes of humiliation and identification*] **is come upon Gaza**; **Ashkelon** [*Gaza and Ashkelon were cities in southern Philistia*] **is cut off** *with* the remnant of their valley: **how long wilt thou cut thyself** [*how long will you keep bringing destruction upon yourselves through wicked living*]?

> With great dramatic skill, Jeremiah poses a question in verse 6 and then gives the answer in verse 7. The "sword of the Lord" could be considered to be the law of justice, which cannot be sheathed until the unrepentant wicked are punished by justice. You may wish to read Alma 42 for a refresher course on the laws of mercy and justice.

6 **O thou sword of the LORD, how long** *will it be* **ere thou be quiet?** put up thyself into thy scabbard, rest, and be still.

7 **How can it be quiet, seeing the LORD hath given it a charge against Ashkelon** [*a charge or mission against the Philistines*], and against the sea shore [*the Philistines, many of whom lived along the coast of the Mediterranean Sea*]? **there hath he appointed it** [*the sword of justice still has work to do there*].

JEREMIAH 48

Selection: all verses

This chapter contains a prophecy of destruction against Moab. You might wish to read Isaiah, chapters 15–16, as well as Ezekiel 25:8–11, for similar prophecies against this nation. Moab was a country immediately east of the Dead Sea. In fact, as recorded in the Book of Ruth, Naomi had been living in Moab because of the famine in the Holy Land (see Ruth 1:1–2) and returned to Bethlehem to live when the famine was over. Her daughter-in-law, Ruth, came with her.

The citizens of Moab were known for their materialism and contempt for Jehovah, the God of Israel. They were engulfed in idol worship, with its associated sexual immorality and debauchery.

The Babylonians conquered the land of Moab and took many of its people into captivity. The country never regained its status as an independent nation. The last verse of this chapter contains a message of hope for the people of that area and seems to say that they will receive the gospel of Jesus Christ in the last days.

As is often the case, Jeremiah specifies many cities and landmarks in Moab as he prophesies about it. Remember,

Jeremiah is speaking of the future as if it had already taken place. He will use many words and phrases, along with much repetition to get his message across.

1 **AGAINST Moab thus saith the LORD** of hosts, the God of Israel; Woe unto Nebo [*a mountainous area in northern Moab, east of the Jordan River*]! for **it is spoiled** [*ruined*]: Kiriathaim [*a city in central Moab*] is **confounded** *and* taken: Misgab is confounded and **dismayed**.

2 *There shall be* **no more praise of Moab** [*Moab will cease to exist as a nation*]: in Heshbon [*a city to the northeast of Mt. Nebo, which originally was part of the country of Moab but eventually belonged to the Amorites and then to the Israelite tribes of Reuben and Gad*] they have devised evil against it; come, and **let us cut it off from** *being* **a nation**. Also **thou shalt be cut down**, O Madmen; **the sword shall pursue thee**.

3 A voice of **crying** *shall be* from Horonaim, **spoiling** and **great destruction**.

4 **Moab is destroyed**; her little ones have caused a cry to be heard.

5 For in the going up of Luhith **continual weeping** shall go up; for in the going down of Horonaim the enemies have heard a cry of **destruction**.

6 **Flee, save your lives**, and be like the heath [*juniper tree—see Jeremiah 17:6, footnote a in your Bible*] in the wilderness.

Next, in verse 7, we see that materialism was a major cause of Moab's destruction. The worship of false gods was likewise a major cause of their demise.

7 ¶ For **because thou hast trusted in thy works and in thy treasures, thou shalt also be taken**: and **Chemosh** [*the god of the Moabites; Solomon introduced the worship of Chemosh at Jerusalem—see 1 Kings 11:7*] **shall go forth into captivity *with* his priests and his princes together** [*in other words, Chemosh, your false god, with all his false priests and servants will not protect you from destruction*].

8 And **the spoiler shall come upon every city**, and no city shall escape: the valley also shall perish, and the plain shall be destroyed, as the LORD hath spoken.

9 **Give wings unto Moab, that it may flee and get away** [*in order to escape this destruction, you would have to sprout wings and fly away*]: for the cities thereof shall be desolate, without any to dwell therein.

10 **Cursed** *be* **he that doeth the work of the LORD deceitfully** [*with hypocrisy*], and cursed *be* he that keepeth back his sword from blood.

Next, in effect, Jeremiah says that Moab has had it so good for so long that they are not able to face reality or change their thinking and attitudes.

11 ¶ **Moab hath been at ease from his youth,** and he hath settled on his lees [*has relaxed his guard against danger—see footnote 11a in your Bible*], and hath not been emptied from vessel to vessel, neither hath he gone into captivity: **therefore his taste** [*for wickedness*] **remained in him, and his scent is not changed.**

12 **Therefore, behold, the days come, saith the LORD, that I will send unto him wanderers** [*enemies*], **that** shall cause him to wander, and **shall empty his vessels** [*enemies will tip you over and empty you out—compare with footnote 12a in your Bible*], **and break their bottles.**

13 And **Moab shall be ashamed of Chemosh** [*embarrassed, put to shame, by the inability of Chemosh, their false god, to save them*], **as the house of Israel** [*the northern ten tribes*] **was ashamed of Beth-el** [*a formerly sacred site selected by Jeroboam for setting up golden calf worship in place of worshiping God—see 1 Kings 12:28–29*] **their confidence** [*in which the Israelites had trusted*].

14 ¶ **How say ye, We** *are* **mighty and strong men for the war** [*how can you say you are powerful and strong and can defend yourselves just fine*]?

15 **Moab is** [*will be*] **spoiled,** and gone up *out of* her cities, and his chosen young men are gone down to the slaughter, **saith the King** [*the true God*], whose name *is* the LORD of hosts.

16 **The calamity of Moab** *is* **near** to come, and **his affliction hasteth fast** [*is rapidly approaching*].

17 All ye that are about him, **bemoan him**; and all ye that know his name, **say, How is the strong staff broken,** *and* **the beautiful rod** [*be startled at what will happen to a once-strong nation*]!

18 **Thou daughter that dost inhabit Dibon** [*you people of Dibon—a town in central Moab*], **come down from** *thy* **glory, and sit in thirst**; for the spoiler of Moab [*the coming Babylonian armies; they would be at least one fulfillment of this prophecy*] shall come upon thee, *and* he shall destroy thy strong holds.

19 **O inhabitant of Aroer** [*a town south of Dibon, in central Moab*], stand by the way, and espy [*watch*]; ask him that fleeth, and her that escapeth, *and* **say, What is done** [*prepare to ask what is going on*]?

20 **Moab is confounded** [*brought to a halt*]; for it is **broken down: howl and cry**; tell ye it in Arnon [*a river that formed the border between the Moabites and the Amorites to the north*], that Moab is spoiled,

21 And **judgment is come** upon the plain country; upon Holon, and upon Jahazah, and upon Mephaath,

22 And upon Dibon, and upon Nebo, and upon Beth-diblathaim,

23 And upon Kiriathaim, and upon Beth-gamul, and upon Beth-meon,

24 And upon Kerioth, and upon Bozrah, and **upon all the cities of the land of Moab**, far or near.

25 **The horn** [*power*] **of Moab is cut off, and his arm** [*power*] **is broken**, saith the LORD.

26 ¶ **Make ye him drunken** [*in your mind's eye, picture him drunk*]: for he magnified *himself* [*exhibited pride*] against the LORD: **Moab** also **shall wallow in his vomit**, and he also shall be in derision [*will be mocked by others*].

27 **For was not Israel a derision unto thee** [*didn't you make fun of Israel, the Lord's people, and claim that their God, Jehovah, was not as powerful as your god, therefore you rebelled against Israel—see 2 Kings 3:5*]? was he found among thieves? for since thou spakest of him [*every time you ridiculed Israel*], thou skippedst for joy.

Jeremiah is a master at using imagery with which the people were familiar to illustrate his message. As he continues this rather lively and frightening prophecy of coming doom to Moab, he warns the inhabitants of that country to get out while they can.

28 O ye that dwell in Moab, **leave the cities**, and **dwell in the rock** [*hide among the boulders*], and **be like the dove** *that* **maketh her nest in the sides of the hole's mouth** [*find caves to live in*].

Next, in verse 29, we are reminded that the Moabites were afflicted by the sin of pride, just as is the case with many today.

29 **We have heard the pride of Moab**, (he is exceeding proud) his **loftiness**, and his **arrogancy**, and his **pride**, and the **haughtiness of his heart**.

30 **I know his wrath** [*anger at righteousness*], saith the LORD; **but** *it* **shall** not *be* so [*but it will not do him any good*]; **his lies shall not so effect** *it* [*his false beliefs and boasts against Jehovah will not turn back his destruction*].

31 **Therefore will I howl for Moab, and I will cry out for all Moab**; *mine heart* **shall mourn** for the men of Kir-heres.

32 O vine of Sibmah, **I will weep for thee** with the weeping of Jazer [*an Amorite town east of the Jordan River, which was conquered by the Israelites as they entered the promised land*]: thy plants are gone over the sea, they reach *even* to the sea of Jazer: the spoiler [*enemy*] is fallen upon thy summer fruits and upon thy vintage.

33 And **joy and gladness is taken** from the plentiful field, and **from the land of Moab**; and I have caused wine to fail [*become nonexistent*] from the winepresses: none shall tread with shouting; *their* shouting *shall be* no shouting.

Next, in verse 34, Jeremiah uses specific geography in Moab to illustrate the prophetic message that Moab will be devastated from north to south and east to west, in other words, completely.

34 From the cry of Heshbon [*in the far northeast of Moab*] *even* unto El-ealeh [*a bit farther northeast*], *and even* unto Jahaz [*in the northeast*], have they uttered their voice, from Zoar [*in the far southwest*] *even* unto Horonaim [*in south central Moab*], *as* an heifer of three years old [*symbolic of being in the prime of life; in other words, prosperous and haughty Moab will be destroyed in the prime of life*]: for **the waters also of Nimrim** [*a major source of water in far west central Moab*] **shall be desolate**.

35 **Moreover I will cause to cease in Moab**, saith the LORD, **him that offereth in the high places** [*locations used for idol worship*], **and him that burneth incense to his gods** [*idol worshipers will be destroyed*].

36 **Therefore mine heart shall sound for Moab like pipes** [*like sad music played on a flute*], and mine heart shall sound like pipes for the men of Kir-heres [*Kir-hareseth, the capital city, located in south central Moab*]: because **the riches** *that* **he hath gotten are perished**.

Verse 37, next, describes symbolically as well as literally the fate of captives and slaves.

37 For every head *shall be* **bald**, and every **beard clipped**: upon all the hands *shall be* **cuttings** [*perhaps a reference to having marks cut into their hands which identify them as prisoners*], and upon the loins **sackcloth**.

38 *There shall be* **lamentation** generally [*everywhere*] upon all the housetops of Moab, and in the streets thereof: for I have broken Moab like a vessel wherein *is* no pleasure [*NIV: like a jar that no one wants*], saith the LORD.

39 **They shall howl,** *saying,* How is it broken down! how hath Moab turned the back with shame! so shall Moab be a derision and a dismaying [*a topic of gossip and a source of horror*] to all them about him.

40 For thus saith **the LORD**; Behold, he **shall fly as an eagle, and shall spread his wings over Moab** [*destruction is coming to Moab*].

41 Kerioth is taken, and the strong holds are surprised, and **the mighty men's hearts in Moab at that day shall be as the heart of a woman in her pangs** [*in labor*].

42 And **Moab shall be destroyed** from *being* a people [*as a nation*], **because he hath magnified** *himself* **against the LORD.**

43 **Fear, and the pit, and the snare,** *shall be* **upon thee**, O inhabitant of Moab, saith the LORD.

Note how Jeremiah emphasizes that the wicked in Moab cannot escape from the Lord, in verse 44, next. The imagery is that of a hunted animal, running away in fear, who escapes from one trap only to be caught in another.

44 **He that fleeth from the fear shall fall into the pit; and he that**

getteth up out of the pit shall be taken in the snare: for I will bring upon it, *even* upon Moab, the year of their visitation [*when the time for punishment is right*], saith the LORD.

Remember, as mentioned previously, Jeremiah is speaking prophetically of the future as if it has already taken place. This is illustrated in the first phrase of verse 45, next.

45 They that fled stood under the shadow of Heshbon because of the force [*those who try to flee from Moab will be helpless*]: but a fire shall come forth out of Heshbon, and **a flame** from the midst of Sihon, and **shall devour** the corner of **Moab**, and the crown of the head of the tumultuous ones [*the noisy boasters*].

46 **Woe be unto thee, O Moab! the people of Chemosh perisheth** [*the people who worship Chemosh will perish*]: for **thy sons are taken captives, and thy daughters captives**.

As mentioned in the background to this chapter in this study guide, verse 47, next, is the one bright spot in this message of doom to Moab. It is a reminder that all people will be given a completely fair chance, before final Judgment Day, to understand and then accept or reject the gospel of Jesus Christ. The great missionary work in the last days, the marvelous missionary work now being done in spirit prison, and the temple work done during the Millennium, will afford this opportunity to everyone. No one will be missed.

47 ¶ **Yet will I bring again the captivity of Moab** [*the people of Moab*

will have their opportunity to come unto Christ] **in the latter days**, saith the LORD. Thus far *is* the judgment of Moab.

JEREMIAH 49

Selection: all verses

This chapter contains prophecies of judgment and destruction directed at several different nations and peoples, the Ammonites (verses 1–6), Edom (verses 7–22), Damascus (verses 23–27), Kedar and Hazor (verses 28–33), and Elam (verses 34–39). Many Bible scholars believe that this set of prophecies was given after the downfall of Jerusalem.

All people have a certain degree of accountability to choose right and avoid wrong. Every person in the nations to whom this chapter was directed had the light of Christ (see John 1:9), which is a conscience and much more, a constant influence persuading each person born on earth to choose right and avoid wrong. Without this understanding, we might think it not fair for such stinging prophecies of doom and punishment to be directed at them. With this understanding, the reality of accountability for all people beyond age eight looms large.

Thus, one of the major messages we can derive from each of these prophecies directed at heathen nations is the fact that all people should do right and treat each other well. They have the conscience necessary to do so and are accountable to God when they go against it. We will take just another moment before we start this chapter and read a quote from the Bible Dictionary describing the light of

Christ. We will add bold for teaching purposes.

Bible Dictionary: Light of Christ

"The light of Christ is just what the words imply: **enlightenment, knowledge, and an uplifting, ennobling, persevering influence that comes upon mankind because of Jesus Christ**. For instance, Christ is 'the true light that lighteth every man that cometh into the world' (D&C 93:2; John 1:9) . . . 'the light that quickeneth' man's understanding (see D&C 88:6–13, 41). In this manner, the light of Christ is related to man's conscience and tells him right from wrong (cf. Moro. 7:12–19)."

Keeping in mind that because of the light of Christ all people are accountable for their actions to a much higher degree than their actions might indicate, we will now proceed with this chapter. The prophecy against the Ammonites is given in verses 1–6. They lived east of Jerusalem, several miles east of the Jordan River. This area was originally given to the tribe of Gad when the children of Israel entered the Holy Land. However, the Ammonites (descendants of Lot) maintained a strong presence and at the time of Jeremiah's prophecy here, they were essentially their own nation.

1 **CONCERNING the Ammonites**, thus saith the LORD; Hath Israel no sons? hath he no heir? why *then* doth their king inherit Gad, and his people dwell in his cities?

2 Therefore, behold, the days come, saith the LORD, that **I will cause an alarm of war to be heard in Rabbah** [*the capital city*] **of the Ammonites**; and it shall be a desolate heap [*it will be destroyed*], and her daughters [*her people*] shall be burned with fire: then shall Israel be heir unto them that were his heirs, saith the LORD.

3 Howl, O Heshbon, for Ai is **spoiled**: cry, ye daughters of Rabbah, gird you [*dress yourselves*] with **sackcloth** [*a sign of mourning in their culture*]; **lament**, and run to and fro by the hedges; for **their king shall go into captivity, *and* his priests and his princes** together.

4 Wherefore gloriest thou in the valleys, thy flowing valley, O **backsliding daughter** [*apostate people*]? that trusted in her treasures [*materialism*], *saying*, Who shall come unto me [*who could possibly defeat us*]?

5 Behold, **I will bring a fear upon thee, saith the Lord** GOD of hosts, from all those that be about thee [*from surrounding nations*]; and ye shall be driven out every man right forth; and none shall gather up him that wandereth.

Verse 6, next, is the Lord's promise that the Ammonites would return again to their land. One probable fulfillment of this promise was when Cyrus the Persian, who defeated Babylon in about 538 BC, decreed that these people could return to their homeland. That decree also applied to the Jews who were allowed to return to Jerusalem.

6 And **afterward I will bring again the captivity of** [*I will overturn the captivity of*] **the children of Ammon**, saith the LORD.

7 ¶ **Concerning Edom** [*a mountainous country south of the Dead Sea where the descendants of Esau settled*], thus saith the LORD of hosts; *Is* **wisdom no more** in Teman [*doesn't anyone in Edom have common sense any more*]? **is counsel perished** from the prudent? is their **wisdom vanished**?

8 Flee ye, turn back, dwell deep, O inhabitants of Dedan; for I will bring the **calamity** of Esau upon him, the time *that* I will visit [*punish*] him.

Next, a comparison is made between harvesting, where there are always a few grapes left, and the complete destruction of Edom (Esau).

9 **If grapegatherers come to thee, would they not leave** *some* **gleaning grapes?** if thieves by night, they will destroy till they have enough [*they don't take everything*].

10 **But I have made Esau bare** [*I will completely destroy Edom as a nation*], I have uncovered his secret places [*his hiding places*], and he shall not be able to hide himself: his seed is spoiled, and his brethren, and his neighbours, and **he** *is* **not**.

11 Leave thy fatherless children, I will preserve *them* alive; and let thy widows trust in me [*the Lord will take care of the orphans and widows*].

12 For thus saith the LORD; Behold, **they whose judgment** *was* **not to drink of the cup** [*those who thought to avoid punishment*] **have assuredly drunken** [*have been punished*]; and *art* thou he *that* shall altogether go unpunished? **thou shalt not go unpunished**, but thou shalt surely drink *of it* [*the bitter cup of paying for their wickedness*].

13 For I have sworn by myself, saith the LORD, that **Bozrah** [*a city in Edom, about eighty miles south of modern-day Amman in Jordan*] **shall become a desolation**, a **reproach**, a **waste**, and a **curse**; and all the cities thereof shall be perpetual wastes;

14 I have heard a rumour from the LORD, and an ambassador is sent unto the heathen, *saying,* Gather ye together, and come against her, and rise up to the battle.

15 For, lo, **I will make thee small among the heathen,** *and* **despised among men**.

16 Thy terribleness [*your fierceness*] hath deceived thee [*has given you a false sense of security*], *and* **the pride of thine heart**, O thou that dwellest in the clefts of the rock, that holdest the height of the hill: **though thou shouldest make thy nest as high as the eagle, I will bring thee down** from thence, saith the LORD.

17 Also **Edom shall be a desolation** [*NIV: will become an object of horror*]: every one that goeth by it shall be astonished [*appalled, shocked*], and

shall hiss at [gossip, deride] all the plagues thereof.

18 **As in the overthrow of Sodom and Gomorrah** and the neighbour *cities* thereof, saith the LORD, **no man shall abide there**, neither shall a son of man dwell in it.

19 **Behold, he** [the Lord] **shall come up like a lion** from the swelling [the thickets of the floodplain] of Jordan **against the habitation of the strong** [against Edom]: but I [the Lord] will suddenly make him run away from her [the inhabitants of Edom will be driven out of their land in an instant]: and who *is* a chosen *man, that* I may appoint over her? for who *is* like me? and who will appoint me the time? and who *is* that shepherd that will stand before me [in other words, who would dare try to prevent the Lord from carrying out this prophecy]?

20 **Therefore hear the counsel of the LORD**, that he hath taken **against Edom**; and his purposes, that he hath purposed against the inhabitants of Teman [part of Edom]: Surely the least of the flock shall draw them out: **surely he shall make their habitations desolate** with them.

21 The earth is moved at the noise of their fall, at the cry the noise thereof was heard in the Red sea [in effect, the whole earth will be startled by what happens to once-proud Edom].

22 **Behold, he** [the Lord; could also refer to Nebuchadnezzar and his Babylonian armies] **shall come up and fly as the eagle, and spread his wings over Bozrah** [a large city in Edom]: and at that day shall the heart of the mighty men of Edom be as the heart of a woman in her pangs [in labor; in other words, desperate for relief from the pain].

23 ¶ **Concerning Damascus** [Syria]. Hamath [a city in Syria] is **confounded**, and Arpad: for they have heard **evil tidings**: they are **fainthearted**; *there is* **sorrow** on the sea; it cannot be quiet.

24 Damascus is waxed **feeble** [has grown weak], *and* turneth herself to flee, and **fear** hath seized on *her:* **anguish** and **sorrows** have taken her, as a woman in travail [in labor].

25 How is **the city of praise not left**, the city of my joy!

26 Therefore **her young men shall fall** in her streets, and **all the men of war shall be cut off** in that day, saith the LORD of hosts.

27 And **I will kindle a fire in the wall of Damascus**, and it shall consume the palaces of Ben-hadad.

28 ¶ **Concerning Kedar** [Arabia], **and** concerning the kingdoms of **Hazor** [in Arabia; this is not the city by the same name in Palestine], which **Nebuchadrezzar king of Babylon shall smite**, thus saith the LORD; Arise ye, go up to Kedar, and **spoil** [ruin] the men of the east.

29 Their tents and their flocks shall they take away: they shall take to themselves their curtains, and all their vessels, and their camels; and they shall cry unto them, **Fear** *is* **on every side**.

30 ¶ **Flee**, get you far off, **dwell deep** [*hide in deep caves*], O ye inhabitants of Hazor, saith the LORD; **for Nebuchadrezzar king of Babylon hath taken counsel against you, and hath conceived a purpose against you**.

> Verse 31, next, appears to be symbolic instruction to Nebuchadnezzar, king of Babylon, to attack the Arabians, who are wealthy and at ease, living in tents rather than in cities with walls and gates.

31 **Arise, get you** [*Nebuchadnezzar*] **up unto the wealthy nation** [*the inhabitants of Arabia*], that dwelleth without care, saith the LORD, which have neither gates nor bars, *which* dwell alone.

32 And **their camels shall be a booty** [*will provide wealth for the Babylonian conquerors*], and the multitude of their cattle a spoil [*more wealth for you*]: and I will scatter into all winds them *that are* in the utmost corners; and I will bring their **calamity from all sides** thereof, saith the LORD.

33 And Hazor shall be a dwelling for dragons [*jackals, wild dogs; symbolically representing lonely and desolate ruins inhabited by wild animals that avoid areas inhabited by humans*], *and* a desolation [*in ruins*] for ever: there shall no man abide there, nor *any* son of man dwell in it.

34 ¶ **The word of the LORD** that came to Jeremiah the prophet **against Elam** [*located east of Babylon, in what is southwest Iran today*] in the beginning of the reign of Zedekiah king of Judah [*about 598 BC*], saying,

35 Thus saith the LORD of hosts; Behold, **I will break the bow of Elam** [*I will disarm them*], the chief of their might.

36 And **upon Elam will I bring the four winds** [*destruction*] from the four quarters of heaven, **and will scatter them** toward all those winds; and **there shall be no nation whither the outcasts of Elam shall not come** [*they will be scattered into all the world*].

37 For I will cause Elam to be **dismayed** before their enemies, and before them that seek their life: and **I will bring evil** [*calamity, disaster—see footnote 37a in your Bible*] **upon them**, *even* **my fierce anger**, saith the LORD; and I will send **the sword** after them, till I have consumed them:

38 And **I will** set my throne in Elam, and will **destroy** from thence **the king and the princes**, saith the LORD.

39 ¶ But it shall come to pass **in the latter days**, *that* **I will bring again the captivity of Elam** [*I will restore them and they will have an opportunity*

to be converted and set free from the captivity of sin], saith the LORD.

We will quote from the Old Testament Student Manual regarding the phrase "I will bring again the captivity of Elam," in verse 39, above:

"Verse 39 speaks of the Lord's bringing again the captivity of Elam in the latter days. Again, it is supposed that this passage means their conversion, as with the Moabites" (Old testament Student Manual, page 258).

JEREMIAH 50

Selection: all verses

From Jeremiah 50:1 through 51:58, we have a prophecy against Babylon. Interspersed within this prophecy is a prophecy about the scattering and gathering of Israel.

Keep in mind that "Babylon" is often used in the scriptures as well as in the teachings of modern prophets and Apostles to mean both the literal ancient city of Babylon, and also extreme wickedness, the kingdom of the devil, and so forth.

Literally, Babylon was a huge city, whose walls were fifty-six miles in length, 335 feet high, and 85 feet wide (see Bible Dictionary under "Babylon"). It was a center of military power and wickedness and seemed invincible.

Symbolically, Babylon represents Satan's kingdom, with all its worldly wickedness. It, too, can seem invincible, but it is not. Just as ancient Babylon was defeated suddenly by Cyrus the Persian, in about 538 BC, so also will Satan's kingdom be defeated suddenly

at the Second Coming. He will be let loose again at the end of the Millennium for "a little season" (D&C 88:111) and will ultimately be defeated completely and, with his evil followers, "be cast away into their own place" forever (D&C 88:112–15).

In this chapter you will see many examples of the kind of repetition used by Jeremiah, Isaiah, and others of the Old Testament prophets to drive home a point. The prophet makes a statement and then says it again, then again, then again, and again, using a bit different wording or using different examples to illustrate the message. We will point out much of this "manner of prophesying among the Jews (2 Nephi 25:1) as we go along. Be aware that the terms "Babylonians" and "Chaldeans" are used interchangeably by Jeremiah. Technically, the Chaldeans lived in the southeast portion of Babylon.

1 THE word that the LORD spake against Babylon *and* **against the land of the Chaldeans** [*Babylonians*] **by Jeremiah the prophet.**

As you have no doubt noticed, one of Jeremiah's favorite techniques in prophesying is to speak of the future as if it has already taken place. Here, he uses this approach to prophesying as he foretells the future downfall and destruction of Babylon.

2 Declare ye [*spread the news*] among the nations, and publish, and set up a standard; publish, *and* conceal not: say, **Babylon is taken, Bel** [*the chief god of Babylon*] **is confounded** [*is powerless to stop it*], **Merodach** [*the name of a Babylonian god, perhaps another name for Bel*] **is**

broken in pieces; her idols are confounded, **her images are broken in pieces**.

3 For **out of the north there cometh up a nation against her**, which shall make her land desolate, and none shall dwell therein: they shall remove, they shall depart, both man and beast.

Verses 4–8, next, contain a prophecy about the gathering of Israel and Judah.

4 ¶ In those days, and in that time, saith the LORD, the children of Israel shall come, they and the children of Judah together, going and weeping: they shall go, and seek the LORD their God.

5 They shall ask the way to Zion with their faces thitherward [*with intense, internal desire to come to Zion*], **saying,** Come, and let us join ourselves to the LORD in a perpetual covenant *that* shall not be forgotten.

6 My people hath been lost sheep: their shepherds [*their false prophets and false priests, teachers, political leaders and so forth*] have caused them to go astray, they have turned them away *on* the mountains [*have used idol worship carried out in high places in the mountains to turn them away from Jehovah*]: they have gone from mountain to hill [*from idol to idol, shrine to shrine*], they have forgotten their restingplace.

7 All that found them have devoured them [*they have been easy prey to their*

enemies]: and their adversaries [*enemies*] said, We offend not [*we are not doing anything wrong in brutalizing Israel and Judah*], because they have sinned against the LORD, the habitation of justice, even the LORD, the hope of their fathers.

The message in verse 8, next, seems to be to get out of Babylon before it is conquered (verse 9). Symbolically, we must flee Babylon, Satan's kingdom, before we are destroyed with it.

8 **Remove** [*flee*] **out of the midst of Babylon**, and go forth out of the land of the Chaldeans [*a repetition of the first phrase*], **and be as the he goats before the flocks** [*lead the way as they flee*].

9 ¶ **For, lo, I will raise and cause to come up against Babylon an assembly** [*alliance*] **of great nations** from the north country: and they shall set themselves in array against her; from thence **she shall be taken**: their arrows *shall be* as of a mighty expert man; none shall return in vain.

The alliance of nations, spoken of in verse 9, above, is described in the following quote:

"The army of Cyrus was composed of Medes, Persians, Armenians, Caducians, Sacae, &c. Though all these did not come from the north; yet they were arranged under the Medes, who did come from the north, in reference to Babylon" (Clarke's Commentary, 4:383).

10 **And Chaldea shall be a spoil** [*Babylon will be left in ruins*]: **all that spoil her shall be satisfied**, saith the LORD.

11 **Because ye were glad, because ye rejoiced, O ye destroyers of mine heritage**, because ye are grown fat as the heifer at grass, and bellow as bulls;

12 **Your mother shall be sore confounded; she that bare you shall be ashamed**: behold, the hindermost of the nations *shall be* a wilderness, a dry land, and a desert.

In verse 13, next, Jeremiah prophesies that the ruins of Babylon will never be inhabited again nor built upon. Such is still the case today.

13 **Because of the wrath of the LORD it shall not be inhabited, but it shall be wholly desolate**: every one that goeth by Babylon shall be astonished, and hiss at all her plagues.

14 **Put yourselves in array** [*lay siege*] **against Babylon round about**: all ye that bend the bow, shoot at her, **spare no arrows: for she hath sinned against the LORD**.

15 **Shout against her round about**: she hath given her hand: **her foundations are fallen, her walls are thrown down**: for it *is* the vengeance of the LORD: **take vengeance upon her; as she hath done, do unto her**.

16 **Cut off the sower** [*farmer*] from Babylon, **and him that handleth the sickle in the time of harvest**: for fear of the oppressing sword they shall turn every one to his people, and **they shall flee every one to his own land** [*foreigners who have been living in Babylon because of the available protection and prosperity will flee away*].

Verses 17–20 contain another prophecy about the scattering and gathering of Israel.

Do you find it interesting that the prophecies about Babylon and those about Israel are going along simultaneously, interwoven with each other? Could it be that there is symbolism here, pointing out that the kingdom of Satan will exist at the same time as the kingdom of God, throughout the earth's history? "It must needs be that there is an opposition in all things" (2 Nephi 2:11) is a principle illustrated effectively here.

17 ¶ **Israel** [*referring here to both the lost ten tribes and the kingdom of Judah*] **is a scattered** sheep; the lions have driven *him* away: **first the king of Assyria hath devoured him** [*the northern ten tribes*]; **and last this Nebuchadrezzar king of Babylon hath broken his** [*Judah's*] **bones**.

18 **Therefore thus saith the** LORD of hosts, the God of Israel; Behold, **I will punish the king of Babylon and his land, as I have punished the king of Assyria** [*both kings can be symbolic of Satan*].

The gathering and restoration of Israel is prophesied in verse 19, next.

19 And **I will bring Israel again to his habitation**, and he shall feed on Carmel and Bashan, and his soul shall be satisfied upon mount Ephraim and Gilead.

The doctrine of repentance and forgiveness is taught in verse 20, next. Being gathered unto Christ is the ultimate meaning of the "gathering of Israel."

20 **In those days, and in that time**, saith the LORD, **the iniquity of Israel shall be sought for** [*looked for*], **and *there shall be* none**; and the sins of Judah, and they shall not be found: **for I will pardon them whom I reserve** [*the Lord will forgive the righteous remnant of Israel whom He spares*].

This prophecy returns once again to the destruction of Babylon.

21 ¶ **Go up against the land of Merathaim** [*"double rebellion;" apparently a symbolical name for Babylon*], *even* against it, **and against the inhabitants of Pekod** [*a place in Babylonia, perhaps meaning "punishment"*]: **waste and utterly destroy after them**, saith the LORD, and do according to all that I have commanded thee.

22 **A sound of battle *is* in the land, and of great destruction.**

23 **How is the hammer** [*Babylon*] **of the whole earth cut asunder and broken** [*how incredible it is that the "hammer" that pounded all other nations is now broken*]! **how is Babylon** become a desolation among the nations!

24 **I have laid a snare for thee, and thou art also taken, O Babylon**, and thou wast not aware [*it caught you by surprise*]: **thou art found, and also caught, because thou hast striven against the LORD**.

25 **The LORD hath opened his armoury, and hath brought forth the weapons of his indignation**: for this *is* the work of the Lord GOD of hosts **in the land of the Chaldeans**.

26 **Come against her** from the utmost border, **open her storehouses**: cast her up as heaps [*throw her in piles, like grain*], and **destroy her utterly: let nothing of her be left**.

27 Slay all her bullocks [*young bulls*]; let them go down to the slaughter: woe unto them! for **their day is come, the time of their visitation** [*punishment*].

28 The voice of them that flee and escape out of the land of Babylon, to **declare in Zion the vengeance of the LORD our God**, the vengeance of his temple.

In verse 29, next, we see at least two doctrines. One is that the unrepentant wicked will not escape the punishments of God. Another is that pride is the root cause of all sin.

29 **Call together the archers against Babylon**: all ye that bend the bow, camp against it round about; **let none thereof escape: recompense her according to her**

work; according to all that she hath done, do unto her: **for she hath been proud against the LORD, against the Holy One of Israel**.

30 **Therefore shall her young men fall in the streets, and all her men of war shall be cut off** in that day, saith the LORD.

31 **Behold, I** *am* **against thee,** *O thou* **most proud**, saith the Lord GOD of hosts: for thy day is come, the time *that* I will visit [*punish*] thee.

32 And **the most proud shall stumble and fall**, and none shall raise him up: and I will kindle a fire in his cities, and it shall devour all round about him.

One of the major messages found in verses 33–34, next, is that the Savior has the power to redeem us from the bondage of sin. Satan does not want to let anyone escape from him, but he cannot prevent the Savior from setting us free if we repent.

33 ¶ Thus saith the LORD of hosts; **The children of Israel** [*the northern ten tribes who became the "lost ten tribes"*] **and the children of Judah** [*the Jews*] *were* **oppressed** together: and all that took them captives held them fast; they refused to let them go.

34 **Their Redeemer** *is* **strong**; the LORD of hosts [*Jehovah, Jesus Christ*] *is* his name: **he shall throughly plead their cause, that he may give rest to the land** [*symbolic of the righteous*], **and disquiet**

the inhabitants of Babylon [*while at the same time being a source of unrest for the wicked*].

Now, back again to the punishment of the wicked in Babylon.

35 ¶ **A sword** *is* **upon the Chaldeans**, saith the LORD, and **upon the inhabitants of Babylon**, and upon her princes, and upon her wise *men*.

36 A sword *is* upon the **liars** [*NIV: "false prophets"*]; and they shall dote [*will become viewed as fools*]: a sword *is* upon her mighty men; and **they shall be dismayed**.

In Old Testament symbolism, horses and chariots are used to symbolize military might.

37 **A sword** [*destruction*] *is* **upon their horses, and upon their chariots**, and **upon all the mingled people** [*foreigners*] that *are* in the midst of her [*outsiders who have chosen to live in Babylon*]; and they shall become as women [*a phrase meaning "weak" in the culture of the day*]: **a sword** *is* **upon her treasures; and they shall be robbed**.

38 **A drought** *is* **upon her** waters; and they shall be dried up: **for it** *is* **the land of graven images**, and they are mad upon *their* idols.

Whenever Jeremiah wants us to get the idea that a city will be destroyed completely and abandoned, he paints a picture with words depicting the ruins with lonely creatures and wild animals that live away from humans.

39 Therefore **the wild beasts of the desert with the wild beasts of the islands shall dwell** *there* [*in the ruins of Babylon*]**, and the owls shall dwell therein**: and **it shall be no more inhabited for ever**; neither shall it be dwelt in from generation to generation.

40 **As God overthrew Sodom and Gomorrah and the neighbour** *cities* **thereof, saith the LORD;** *so* **shall no man abide there**, neither shall any son of man dwell therein.

The prophecy again reminds us how the ancient wicked nation of Babylon was to be destroyed.

41 Behold, **a people shall come from the north, and a great nation, and many kings** [*a great alliance against Babylon*] shall be raised up from the coasts of the earth.

42 They shall hold the bow and the lance: **they** *are* **cruel, and will not shew mercy**: their voice shall roar like the sea, and **they shall ride upon horses**, *every one* put in array, like a man **to the battle, against thee, O daughter** [*inhabitants*] **of Babylon**.

43 **The king of Babylon hath heard** the report of them, **and his hands waxed feeble: anguish took hold of him**, *and* pangs as of a woman in travail [*labor; in other words, he can't get out of it now*].

44 **Behold, he** [*the Lord, ultimately; can also refer to the alliance of nations who will conquer Babylon*] **shall come up like a lion** from the swelling of Jordan [*from the thickets on the Jordan River floodplain*] **unto the habitation of the strong** [*to Babylon*]: but I will make them suddenly run away from her: and who *is* a chosen *man, that* I may appoint over her? for who *is* like me? and who will appoint me the time? **and who** *is* **that shepherd that will stand before me** [*in other words, whom could Babylon call upon to successfully protect her from the wrath of the Lord*]?

45 **Therefore hear ye the counsel** [*the plan*] **of the LORD**, that he hath taken **against Babylon**; and his purposes, that he hath purposed against the land of the Chaldeans: Surely the least of the flock shall draw them out: **surely he shall make** *their* **habitation desolate** with them.

46 At the noise of the taking of Babylon the earth is moved, and the cry is heard among the nations [*when Babylon falls, it will startle those who have enjoyed living in it*].

JEREMIAH 51

Selection: all verses

This chapter is a continuation of the prophecy about the downfall of Babylon, contained in chapter 50. The material in chapters 50–51 was written down in the days of Zedekiah, king of Judah, and sent to Babylon (see verses 59–64). You may wish to read

Revelation, chapters 17–18, which prophesy the fall of Babylon, along with this chapter of Jeremiah.

As explained in the background notes for chapter 50, "Babylon" can have dual meaning: (1) the literal ancient city of Babylon, and (2) wickedness; Satan's kingdom. Also keep in mind that "Israel" can mean the literal descendants of Abraham, Isaac, and Jacob (whose name was changed to Israel—see Genesis 32:28), but can also mean any who choose to accept the gospel, be baptized, and keep the commandments. Those who desire to be part of the Lord's covenant people, Israel, are commanded to flee from Babylon (verse 6).

As in other prophecies of Jeremiah, this one will make much use of symbolism and repetition. It will deal with events all the way from the literal fall of ancient Babylon (also referred to as Chaldea) to the fall of Satan's kingdom at the time of the Second Coming of the Savior.

Each time you see the word "Babylon" in this prophecy, you may wish to think of a major message as being that the Lord has power over Satan and thus will ultimately destroy his kingdom and cast him out into his "own place" (D&C 88:114). Another major message is that we must flee Babylon, in other words, wickedness, in order to be on the Lord's side when Babylon is a thing of the past.

Yet a third message to keep in mind comes from the fact that not all people who choose to live in "Babylon" know anything about the true gospel and thus have no chance at all to live it. One of the truths of the gospel is that the Lord is completely fair. Thus, before the day of final judgment, everyone, whether in this life, the postmortal spirit world mission field, or during the Millennium, will have a completely fair chance to hear, understand, accept, or reject the pure gospel of Jesus Christ.

Also, keep in mind that since everyone born into this world has the Light of Christ (John 1:9), everyone over age eight has a degree of accountability, and so those who choose to live the lifestyle found in "Babylon," despite the pricks of conscience that accompany such choices (especially initially), can rightly be taken down with the fall of Babylon. God will be the final judge as to gospel opportunities that still remain for them after their demise with the destruction of Satan's kingdom.

We will now proceed with the Lord's great prophecy through His humble prophet, Jeremiah, concerning the guaranteed fall of Babylon.

1 THUS saith the LORD; Behold, I will raise up against Babylon, and against them that dwell in the midst of them that rise up against me, a destroying wind [the "east wind" which is symbolic of destruction];

2 And will send unto Babylon fanners [foreign enemies], that shall fan her [scatter her—see footnote 2a in your Bible], and shall empty her land: for in the day of trouble they shall be against her round about.

3 Against him that bendeth [strings his bow in preparation to defend Babylon] let the archer [in the foreign armies] bend his bow [prepare for battle], and against him that lifteth himself up in his brigandine [canvas

or leather body armor, sometimes with metal strips in it]: and **spare ye not her** [Babylon's] **young men; destroy ye utterly all her host**.

4 Thus **the slain shall fall in the land of the Chaldeans** [Babylon], and *they that are* thrust through in her streets.

Next, in verses 5–6, we see that the Lord will yet gather Israel and that they will be gathered to Him as they flee from the ways of Babylon.

5 **For Israel** *hath* not *been* **forsaken, nor Judah of his God**, of the LORD of hosts; though their land was filled with sin [even though they were once involved in wickedness] against the Holy One of Israel.

6 **Flee out of the midst of Babylon, and deliver every man his soul** [and thus save your souls]: **be not cut off in her iniquity**; for this *is* the time of the LORD's vengeance; **he will render unto her a recompence** [those in Babylon will face God's punishments as they take the consequences of their sins].

The symbolism of the "golden cup" mentioned in verse 7, next, is likely the same as that found in the Book of Revelation, chapter 17. If so, it represents having one's "cup" or life full of gross wickedness. We will quote from Revelation and then go on to verse 7, here, in Jeremiah.

Revelation 17:4

4 And the woman [symbolic of Babylon; Satan's kingdom] was arrayed in purple and scarlet colour, and decked with gold and precious stones and pearls, **having a golden cup in her hand full of abominations and filthiness** of her fornication [wickedness; breaking of God's laws and commandments; counterfeits of the true gospel]:

7 **Babylon** *hath been* **a golden cup** in the LORD's hand [allowed by the Lord to exist during the mortal years of the earth's existence—compare with 2 Nephi 2:11, which says "for it must needs be, that there is an opposition in all things], **that made all the earth drunken: the nations have drunken of her wine** [have participated in her wickedness]**; therefore the nations are mad** [out of their mind with wickedness].

8 **Babylon is suddenly fallen** and destroyed: howl for her; take balm for her pain, if so be she may be healed.

9 **We would have healed Babylon** [if she had repented], **but she is not healed**: forsake her, and let us go every one into his own country: for her judgment reacheth unto heaven, and is lifted up *even* to the skies.

We will include a quote that verifies the interpretation of the first part of verse 9, above:

"God would have healed them, as he would all his children, before their destruction, but sometimes, like Babylon, they resist turning to the Lord and therefore are not healed" (Old Testament Student Manual, page 258).

Verse 10, next, depicts those who do repent, flee Babylon, and become part of righteous Israel.

10 The LORD hath brought forth our righteousness [*in effect, the Atonement of Christ has enabled us to become righteous*]: come, and let us declare in Zion the work of the LORD our God [*let's spread the word of God*].

Next, Jeremiah specifically prophesies that the Medes (an empire located east of Babylon, led by Cyrus the Persian) will defeat ancient Babylon. They did, in about 538 BC.

As you will notice, one aspect of "the manner of prophesying among the Jews," spoken of by Nephi (2 Nephi 25:1), is nicely illustrated here. Rather than simply saying that the Medes will prepare for war against Babylon, as most in our modern culture prefer and do, the "manner of prophesying" used by ancient prophets consisted of elaborate and detailed descriptions, conjuring up pictures in the minds and imaginations of the readers of a variety of activities associated with preparing for war against Babylon. In effect, Jeremiah paints dramatic pictures in our minds and involves our emotions as he tells us what will happen.

11 Make bright the arrows; gather the shields [*prepare for battle*]: the LORD hath raised up the spirit of the kings of **the Medes**: for his device *is* **against Babylon, to destroy it**; because it *is* the vengeance of the LORD, the vengeance of his temple.

12 Set up the standard upon [*lift up a banner against*] the walls of Babylon,

make the watch strong [*strengthen the guard*], set up the watchmen, **prepare the ambushes**: for the LORD hath both devised and done that which he spake **against the inhabitants of Babylon**.

13 **O thou that dwellest upon many waters** [*symbolic of Satan's kingdom— see 1 Nephi 14:11, Revelation 17:1, D&C 61 heading*], abundant in treasures, **thine end is come**, *and* the measure of thy covetousness.

14 **The LORD** of hosts **hath sworn by himself** [*has covenanted in His own name; the strongest oath or promise available in ancient Jewish culture*], *saying*, **Surely I will fill thee with men**, as with caterpillers [*enemy armies will break into your city; they will be everywhere, like an invasion of caterpillars*]; **and they shall lift up a shout against thee**.

Next, in verses 15–16, Jeremiah testifies that Jehovah, the Creator of earth and heaven, has the power to carry out this prophecy against Babylon.

15 **He** [*the Lord*] **hath made the earth by his power**, he hath established the world by his wisdom, and hath stretched out the heaven by his understanding.

16 **When he uttereth** *his* **voice** [*when He commands*], *there is* a multitude of waters in the heavens; and he causeth the vapours to ascend from the ends of the earth: he maketh lightnings with rain, and bringeth forth the wind out of his treasures [*in*

other words, all things obeyed His voice as He created the earth].

Having reminded the people of the power of Jehovah, Jeremiah now points out that idols and other false gods have absolutely no power, in verses 17–18, next.

17 **Every man is brutish by** *his* **knowledge** [*every idol worshiper is like a brute animal, completely without common sense and doesn't know what he is doing*]; **every founder** [*black-smith who pours molten metal to form graven images*] **is confounded** by the graven image: for **his molten image** *is* **falsehood, and** *there is* **no breath in them.**

18 **They** *are* **vanity, the work of errors**: in the time of their visitation they shall perish [*when idol worshipers are destroyed, their powerless idols will perish with them*].

19 **The portion of Jacob** [*the benefit available to Israel from the true God*] *is* **not like them** [*is not like that from idols to their worshipers*]; **for he** [*the Lord*] *is* **the former** [*creator*] **of all things**: and *Israel is* **the rod** [*power*] **of his inheritance** [*Israel is the covenant people of the Lord through whom the power of salvation is taken to the whole earth—see Abraham 2:9–11*]: the LORD of hosts *is* his name.

In verses 20–23, next, we see that Israel, the Lord's covenant people, are the tool in the hand of the Lord through which the Church and kingdom of God will be taken to the whole earth (see Daniel 2:34,

44–45). The true gospel of Jesus Christ has the power to cut through falsehood and error and defeat Satan's power and grasp upon the wicked, if they choose to repent.

20 **Thou** [*Israel*] *art* **my** [*the Lord's*] **battle axe** *and* **weapons of war: for with thee will I break in pieces the nations, and with thee will I destroy kingdoms;**

Remember that horses and chariots were used symbolically in Jeremiah's day to represent military might. You might think of verse 21, next, as referring to Satan's armies, the host of wicked mortals who follow his lead in their lives.

21 **And with thee will I break in pieces** the **horse** and his **rider**; and with thee will I break in pieces the **chariot** and his **rider** [*in other words, the enemy armies, or armies of the wicked*];

22 **With thee also will I break in pieces man and woman**; and with thee will I break in pieces **old and young**; and with thee will I break in pieces the young man and the maid [*in other words, all who oppose righteousness*];

23 **I will also break in pieces with thee** [*Israel*] **the shepherd** [*the false prophet and other misguided leaders*] **and his flock** [*followers*]; and with thee will I break in pieces the husbandman [*farmer*] and his yoke of oxen; and with thee will I break in pieces captains and rulers [*military and political leaders*].

One very important aspect of the message in verses 20–23, above, is the fact that goodness and righteousness will ultimately triumph over evil on earth.

24 **And I will render** [*pay back*] **unto Babylon and to all the inhabitants of Chaldea** [*another term for Babylon*] **all their evil** that they have done in Zion in your sight, saith the LORD.

The "destroying mountain" in verses 25–26, next, seems to be a reference to Babylon, both literally the ancient city and also, symbolically Satan's kingdom. See Revelation 8:8

25 Behold, **I** *am* **against thee, O destroying mountain** [*Babylon*], **saith the LORD, which destroyest all the earth**: and **I will stretch out mine hand upon thee, and roll thee down from the rocks, and will make thee a burnt mountain** [*compare with Revelation 8:8*].

26 And they shall not take of thee a stone for a corner, nor a stone for foundations; but **thou shalt be desolate for ever, saith the LORD** [*Babylon is still ruins today, and Satan and his evil followers will be cast into outer darkness, at the end of the Millennium—see Doctrine & Covenants 88:114*].

The next several verses continue to repeat much that has been said in the previous verses. As already pointed out, this type of repetition is typical in Jeremiah's culture. In some verses, he speaks prophetically of the future as though it had already happened.

27 Set ye up a standard in the land, blow the trumpet among the nations, **prepare the nations against her** [*Babylon*], call together against her the kingdoms of Ararat, Minni, and Ashchenaz; appoint a captain against her; cause the horses to come up as the rough caterpillers.

28 **Prepare against her the nations with the kings of the Medes**, the captains thereof, and all the rulers thereof, and all the land of his dominion.

29 And the land shall tremble and sorrow: for **every purpose of the LORD shall be performed against Babylon, to make the land of Babylon a desolation without an inhabitant**.

30 **The mighty men of Babylon have forborn to fight** [*have stopped fighting*], they **have remained in** *their* **holds: their might hath failed**; they became as women: **they** [*Babylon's enemies*] **have burned her dwellingplaces; her bars are broken**.

31 **One post** [*messenger*] **shall run to meet another**, and one messenger to meet another, **to shew the king of Babylon that his city is taken at** *one* **end** [*captured completely—see footnote 31d in your Bible*],

32 And that **the passages** [*NIV: "river crossings"*] **are stopped, and the reeds** [*marshlands*] **they have burned with fire**, and **the men of**

war are affrighted [*Babylon's soldiers are terrified*].

33 For **thus saith the LORD** of hosts, the God of Israel; **The daughter of Babylon** [*in other words, Babylon*] *is* **like a threshingfloor,** *it is* **time to thresh her**: yet a little while, and the time of her harvest shall come.

Symbolically, verses 34–35, next, have Israel saying that he has been beaten around badly by Satan's kingdom for thousands of years, and now (in the last days and at the Second Coming of Christ), all of Babylon's wickedness will catch up with her.

34 Nebuchadrezzar the king of **Babylon hath devoured me** [*Israel, Judah*], he hath **crushed me**, he hath **made me an empty vessel**, he hath **swallowed me up like a dragon**, he hath **filled his belly with my delicates**, he hath **cast me out**.

35 **The violence done to me and to my flesh** *be* **upon Babylon**, shall the inhabitant of Zion say; and my blood upon the inhabitants of Chaldea, shall Jerusalem say.

In verses 36–37, next, Jeremiah teaches us that it is the power of the Lord through which we are redeemed from Satan and the forces of evil.

36 **Therefore thus saith the LORD; Behold, I will plead thy cause** [*through the Atonement—see D&C 45:3–5*], and take vengeance for thee; and I will dry up her sea, and

make her springs dry [*I will destroy Babylon*].

37 And **Babylon shall become heaps** [*ruins*], a dwellingplace for dragons [*jackals*], an astonishment [*an object of surprise and horror*], and an hissing [*scorn*], without an inhabitant.

Next, beginning with verse 38, Jeremiah prophetically depicts Babylon at its prime, when its inhabitants are feeling powerful and invincible in their wickedness.

38 **They shall roar together like lions: they shall yell as lions' whelps** [*cubs*].

39 In their heat I will make their feasts, and I will make them drunken, that they may rejoice [*they will keep right on partying and living riotously*], and sleep a perpetual sleep, and not wake, saith the LORD.

40 **I will bring them down like lambs to the slaughter, like rams** with he goats.

41 **How is Sheshach** [*another name for Babylon*] **taken** [*how quickly it falls*]! and **how** is the praise of the whole earth **surprised!** how is Babylon become **an astonishment among the nations!**

The imagery in verse 42, next, takes advantage of the fact that Babylon is built in a desert. Just as it would seem impossible to believe that a tidal wave would destroy Babylon, so also it seems impossible to many that such a large kingdom as that of the devil could be destroyed suddenly. It is not impossible for the Lord. Babylon was destroyed. Satan's kingdom will be destroyed.

42 The sea is come up upon Babylon: she is covered with the multitude of the waves thereof.

43 Her cities are a desolation, a dry land, and a wilderness, **a land wherein no man dwelleth**, neither doth *any* son of man pass thereby.

44 And **I will punish Bel** [*the main false god of Babylon*] **in Babylon**, and I will bring forth out of his mouth that which he hath swallowed up: and the nations shall not flow together any more unto him [*people will no longer gather to Babylon to participate in wickedness*]: yea, **the wall of Babylon shall fall.**

45 **My people** [*Those who wish to be part of righteous Israel*], **go ye out of the midst of her, and deliver ye every man his soul** [*save your souls*] from the fierce anger of the LORD.

After reading Revelation 18:9–10, quoted next, verses 46–49 of Jeremiah, which follow, appear to include the fall of spiritual Babylon in the last days.

Revelation 18:9–10

9 And the kings [*powerful, wicked leaders*] of the earth, who have committed fornication [*who have been extremely wicked*] and lived deliciously [*riotously*] with her [*the "whore," Satan's kingdom, Babylon*], shall bewail her [*mourn losing her*], and lament for her [*instead of repenting*], when they shall see the smoke of her burning [*the wicked will be devastated by the destruction of their lifestyle*],

10 Standing afar off for the fear of her torment, saying, Alas, alas, that great city Babylon, that mighty city! for in one hour is thy judgment come [*the Second Coming will change things quickly; they can't believe how fast she was destroyed!*].

46 And [*flee from Babylon—verse 45, above*] **lest your heart faint** [*lest you be sorry when Babylon falls*], **and ye fear for the rumour** [*the news that Babylon has fallen*] that shall be heard in the land; a rumour shall both come *one* year, and after that in *another* year *shall come* a rumour, and violence in the land, ruler against ruler.

47 **Therefore, behold, the days come, that I will do judgment upon the graven images of Babylon**: and **her whole land shall be confounded** [*in confusion; startled; perplexed*], and all her slain shall fall in the midst of her.

48 **Then the heaven and the earth, and all that *is* therein, shall sing for Babylon** [*will rejoice because Babylon is gone*]: for the spoilers shall come unto her from the north, saith the LORD.

49 As Babylon *hath caused* the slain of Israel to fall, so at **Babylon shall fall** the slain of all the earth [*the wicked of the earth*].

50 **Ye that have escaped the sword** [*you who still have the opportunity to repent*], go away, stand not still: **remember the LORD** afar off, **and let Jerusalem come into your mind.**

51 **We** [*Israel*] **are confounded, because** we have heard reproach: shame hath covered our faces: for **strangers are come into the sanctuaries of the LORD's house** [*because of our wickedness, our temple has been defiled*].

Now, back to the destruction of Babylon.

52 Wherefore, behold, **the days come, saith the LORD, that I will do judgment upon her graven images**: and through all her land the wounded shall groan.

No matter how strong and powerful Satan's kingdom seems to get, the Lord can and will destroy it. Jeremiah continues using prophetic repetition to emphasize the details of this prophecy against Babylon.

53 Though [*even if*] **Babylon should mount up to heaven** [*as was attempted by the builders of the Tower of Babel*], **and though she should fortify the height of her strength,** *yet* **from me shall spoilers come unto her,** saith the LORD.

54 A sound of **a cry** *cometh* **from Babylon**, and great destruction from the land of the Chaldeans:

55 **Because the LORD hath spoiled** [*ruined, destroyed*] **Babylon**, and destroyed out of her the great voice; when her waves do roar like great waters, a noise of their voice is uttered:

56 Because the spoiler is come upon her, *even* upon Babylon, and **her mighty men are taken, every one of their bows is broken: for the LORD God of recompences shall surely requite** [*repay in full, in other words, the law of the harvest*].

Since we know that the Lord does not make people wicked, we need to interpret verse 57, next, as saying that He will allow them their agency to choose wickedness. The idea is that Babylon is filled with people who are through and through wicked.

57 And I will make drunk her princes, and her wise *men,* her captains, and her rulers, and her mighty men: and **they shall sleep a perpetual sleep, and not wake** [*they will be destroyed*], saith the King, whose name *is* the LORD of hosts.

58 Thus saith the LORD of hosts; **The broad walls of Babylon shall be utterly broken, and her high gates shall be burned with fire** [*perhaps symbolic of the burning of the wicked at the time of the Second Coming*]; and the people shall labour in vain, and the folk in the fire, and they shall be weary.

Verses 59–64, next, provide a historical note informing us that Jeremiah wrote down the prophecy contained in chapters 50–51 and sent them to Babylon with Seraiah, who accompanied King Zedekiah, king of Judah, when he traveled to Babylon on political business about 594 BC. Seraiah was instructed to read the prophecy after he arrived in Babylon and then to tie a rock to the scroll and throw it into the Euphrates River. You will see the purpose behind this act as you read verse 64.

59 ¶ **The word which Jeremiah** the prophet **commanded Seraiah** the son of Neriah, the son of Maaseiah, **when he went with Zedekiah** the king of Judah **into Babylon** in the fourth year of his reign [*he reigned for eleven years—see Jeremiah 52:1*]. And *this* Seraiah *was* a quiet prince [*German Bible: Seraiah was the officer in charge of all details for the trip*].

60 So **Jeremiah wrote** in a book [*on a scroll*] **all the evil that should come upon Babylon,** *even* **all these words** [*chapters 50–51*] **that are written against Babylon**.

61 And **Jeremiah said to Seraiah, When thou comest to Babylon**, and shalt see, and shalt **read all these words;**

62 **Then shalt thou say**, O LORD, thou hast spoken against this place [*Babylon*], to cut it off, that none shall remain in it, neither man nor beast, but that it shall be desolate for ever.

63 **And** it shall be, **when thou hast made an end of reading this book** [*this scroll*], *that* thou shalt **bind a stone to it, and cast it into the midst of Eu- phrates** [*the Euphrates River*]:

64 **And** thou shalt **say, Thus shall Babylon sink, and shall not rise** from the evil that I [*the Lord*] will bring upon her: and they shall be weary. **Thus far** *are* **the words of Jeremiah** [*NIV The words of Jeremiah end here*].

We see similar action by an angel in the vision of John as described in Revelation. It, too, depicts the final destruction of Babylon.

Revelation 18:21

21 And a mighty angel took up a stone like a great millstone, and cast *it* into the sea, saying, **Thus with violence shall that great city Baby- lon be thrown down, and shall be found no more at all.**

JEREMIAH 52

Selection: all verses

Bible scholars don't really know who added this chapter on to the end of Jeremiah's writings, which end with the last verse of chapter 51 (see note at the end of 51:64 in this study guide). Jeremiah 52 is pretty much a repeat of the material in 2 Kings 24:18 through 25:21. It is also quite similar to parts of Jeremiah 39.

In this chapter, we are given a sum- mary of events at the time Jerusalem fell to the Babylonian army of King Ne- buchadnezzar. The prophecies given by Jeremiah concerning the fall of Je- rusalem were fulfilled at this time. As stated previously, Jeremiah is one of the few prophets who have seen many of their prophecies fulfilled in their own lifetime. It begins with a brief history of

King Zedekiah of Judah, who is mentioned by Nephi in 1 Nephi 1:4. As you will see, he was twenty-one years old when he became king.

1 ZEDEKIAH *was* one and twenty years old when he began to reign [*in about 598 BC*], and he reigned eleven years in Jerusalem. And his mother's name *was* Hamutal the daughter of Jeremiah of Libnah.

2 And he did *that which was* evil in the eyes of the LORD, according to all that Jehoiakim had done [*he was wicked just like the king who preceded him*].

3 For through the anger of the LORD it came to pass in Jerusalem and Judah, till he had cast them out from his presence, that Zedekiah rebelled against the king of Babylon [*not a wise political move*].

4 ¶ And it came to pass in the ninth year of his [*Zedekiah's*] reign, in the tenth month, in the tenth *day* of the month, *that* Nebuchadrezzar king of Babylon came, he and all his army, against Jerusalem, and pitched against it [*and laid siege to it*], and built forts against it round about.

5 So the city was besieged unto the eleventh year of king Zedekiah.

By the time we get to verse 6, the Babylonian armies have had Jerusalem under siege for about eighteen months. Consequently, the Jews there are suffering from severe lack of food

6 And in the fourth month, in the ninth *day* of the month, the famine was sore [*severe*] in the city, so that there was no bread for the people of the land.

7 Then the city was broken up [*the Babylonian soldiers broke into Jerusalem*], and all the men of war fled [*including Zedekiah*], and went forth out of the city by night by the way of the gate between the two walls, which *was* by the king's garden; (now the Chaldeans *were* by the city round about:) and they went by the way of the plain.

8 ¶ But the army of the Chaldeans pursued after the king, and overtook Zedekiah in the plains of Jericho; and all his army was scattered from him.

9 Then they took the king, and carried him up unto the king of Babylon to Riblah [*about two hundred miles north of Jerusalem*] in the land of Hamath [*in Syria*]; where he gave judgment upon him [*where he sentenced Zedekiah*].

10 And the king of Babylon slew the sons of Zedekiah before his eyes: he slew also all the princes of Judah in Riblah.

We know that one of the sons of Zedekiah was not killed. We know from the Book of Mormon that his son, Mulek, escaped, and was brought by the Lord to America. We will include two references from the Book of Mormon here:

Helaman 6:10

10 Now the land south was called Lehi and the land north was called Mulek, which was after the son of Zedekiah; for **the Lord did bring Mulek into the land north**, and Lehi into the land south.

Helaman 8:21

21 And now will you dispute that Jerusalem was destroyed? **Will ye say that the sons of Zedekiah were not slain, all except it were Mulek?** Yea, and do ye not behold that the seed of Zedekiah are with us, and they were driven out of the land of Jerusalem? But behold, this is not all—

11 **Then he put out the eyes of Zedekiah**; and the king of Babylon **bound him in chains, and carried him to Babylon, and put him in prison till the day of his death.**

12 ¶ **Now in the fifth month, in the tenth** *day* **of the month** [*about a month after the fall of Jerusalem*], which *was* the nineteenth year of Nebuchadrezzar king of Babylon, **came Nebuzar-adan, captain of the guard,** *which* **served the king of Babylon, into Jerusalem,**

13 **And burned the house of the LORD** [*the temple in Jerusalem*], **and the king's house** [*the palace*]; **and all the houses of Jerusalem, and all the houses of the great** *men,* **burned he with fire:**

14 **And** all the army of the Chaldeans [*Babylonians*], that *were* with

the captain of the guard, **brake down all the walls of Jerusalem** round about [*symbolizing that they had completely conquered the city*].

15 **Then Nebuzar-adan** the captain of the guard [*one of King Nebuchadnezzar's chief military officers*] **carried away captive** *certain* **of the poor of the people**, and the residue of the people that remained in the city, and those that fell away, that fell to the king of Babylon, and the rest of the multitude.

16 **But Nebuzar-adan** the captain of the guard **left** *certain* **of the poor of the land for vinedressers and for husbandmen** [*to farm the area around Jerusalem*].

Next, in verses 17–23, the Babylonians gather up the things of value from the temple in Jerusalem and take them to Babylon.

17 Also **the pillars of brass** that *were* in the house of the LORD, and the bases, and the **brasen sea** that *was* in the house of the LORD, the Chaldeans brake, **and carried all the brass of them to Babylon.**

18 The **caldrons** also, and the **shovels**, and the **snuffers**, and the **bowls**, and the **spoons**, and all the **vessels of brass** wherewith they ministered, took they away.

19 And the **basons**, and the **firepans**, and the **bowls**, and the **caldrons**, and the **candlesticks**, and the **spoons**, and the **cups**; *that* which *was* of **gold** *in* gold [*NIV: "made of pure gold"*], and

that which *was* of **silver** *in* silver, took the captain of the guard away.

20 The **two pillars**, **one sea** [*large font*], and **twelve brasen bulls** that *were* under the bases, which king Solomon had made in the house of the LORD: the brass of all these vessels was without weight [*too much to weigh*].

21 And *concerning* the pillars, the height of one pillar *was* eighteen cubits [*about twenty-seven feet*]; and a fillet of twelve cubits did compass it; and the thickness thereof *was* four fingers: *it was* hollow.

22 And a chapiter of brass *was* upon it; and the height of one chapiter *was* five cubits, with network and pomegranates [*decorations made of brass*] upon the chapiters round about, all *of* brass. The second pillar also and the pomegranates *were* like unto these.

23 And there were ninety and six pomegranates [*made of brass*] on a side; *and* all the pomegranates upon the network *were* an hundred round about.

Next, in verses 24–27, King Nebuchadnezzar's chief military officer in Judah rounds up several dignitaries of the Jews who had been close associates of King Zedekiah and takes them about two hundred miles north to Riblah, where Nebuchadnezzar executes them.

24 ¶ And **the captain of the guard took** Seraiah [*apparently not the same person as in Jeremiah 51:59*] the chief priest, and **Zephaniah** the second priest, and **the three keepers of the door**:

25 He took also out of the city **an eunuch** [*an officer—see footnote 25a in your Bible*], which had the charge of the men of war; and **seven men of them that were near the king's person** [*who had been close associates and advisors of King Zedekiah*], which were found in the city; and **the principal scribe** of the host, who mustered the people [*drafted people for military duty*] of the land; **and threescore** [*sixty*] **men** of the people of the land, **that were found in the midst of the city**.

26 **So Nebuzar-adan the captain of the guard took them, and brought them to the king of Babylon** to Riblah.

27 **And the king of Babylon smote them, and put them to death** in Riblah in the land of Hamath. **Thus Judah was carried away captive out of his own land** [*as prophesied*].

Verses 28–30, next, inform us that Nebuchadnezzar (often spelled "Nebuchadrezzar," as seen in verse 28) carried a total of forty-six hundred Jews into captivity (see verse 30) over the next several years. He had already taken many others, including Daniel and Ezekiel, in earlier waves of conquest against the Jews in Jerusalem and Judah.

28 **This** *is* **the people whom Nebuchadrezzar carried away captive**: in the seventh year **three thousand Jews and three and twenty**:

29 In the eighteenth year of Nebu-chadrezzar he carried away cap-tive from Jerusalem **eight hundred thirty and two persons**:

30 In the three and twentieth year of Nebuchadrezzar Nebuzar-adan the captain of the guard carried away captive of the Jews **seven hundred forty and five** persons: **all the per-sons** *were* **four thousand and six hundred**.

Verses 31–34, next, are a sort of appendix, containing a very brief history of Jehoiachin, who had been king of Judah for just a few months (about 598 BC) before he and his court were taken into exile to Baby-lon and imprisoned. King Zedekiah followed him as king. When Nebu-chadnezzar died, his successor, Evil-merodach, freed Jehoiachin af-ter thirty-seven years in prison and gave him good treatment in Babylon for the rest of his life.

31 ¶ And it came to pass **in the seven and thirtieth year of the captivity of Jehoiachin king of Judah**, in the twelfth month, in the five and twen-tieth *day* of the month, *that* **Evil-merodach king of Babylon** in the *first* year of his reign lifted up the head of Jehoiachin king of Judah [*re-leased him from prison*], and **brought him forth out of prison**,

32 **And spake kindly unto him**, and set his throne [*gave him a sta-tus*] above the throne of the kings that *were* with him in Babylon [*other kings, probably from other nations that had also been conquered by Babylon*],

33 **And changed his prison gar-ments: and he did continually eat bread before him** [*he ate at the king's table*] **all the days of his life**.

34 **And *for* his diet, there was a continual diet given him of the king of Babylon, every day a por-tion until the day of his death**, all the days of his life.

LAMENTATIONS

To lament is to go into deep sorrow and morning because of a great loss. Thus, the Book of Lamentations is Jer-emiah's expression of deep loss and mourning over what happened to his people, Israel (Judah especially), who were taken into captivity and scattered.

If you have studied Jeremiah in this study guide, you will be quite familiar with the language of Jeremiah and will likely do well in understanding Lamen-tations. For example, you will be famil-iar with the fact that Jeremiah uses viv-id images and drama to express what he has seen in vision and received by direct revelation from the Lord.

LAMENTATIONS 1

Selection: all verses

Because of space limitations in this study guide, we will just do one chapter of Lamentations, chapter 1, in which Jeremiah laments and sorrows over what happened to Jerusalem. He has seen in vision the future destruction of Jerusalem by the Babylonians, the final scenes of which took place in about 587 BC. Thus, he will speak of the future as if it had already taken place.

1 **How doth the city** [*Jerusalem*] **sit solitary, *that was* full of people!** *how* is she become as a widow! she *that was* great among the nations, *and* princess among the provinces, *how* is she become tributary [*a servant to another nation*]!

2 **She weepeth sore in the night**, and her tears *are* on her cheeks: **among all her lovers** [*false gods, idols, priorities that take the place of God*] **she hath none to comfort *her*:** all her friends have dealt treacherously with her, they are become her enemies.

3 **Judah is gone into captivity** because of affliction, and because of great servitude: **she dwelleth among the heathen**, she findeth no rest: all her persecutors overtook her between the straits.

4 **The ways of Zion** [*the roads leading to Jerusalem*] **do mourn, because none come to the solemn feasts**: all her gates are desolate: her priests sigh, her virgins are afflicted, and she *is* in bitterness.

5 Her adversaries are the chief, **her enemies prosper; for the LORD hath afflicted her for** [*because of*] **the multitude of her transgressions**: her children are gone into captivity before the enemy.

6 **And from the daughter of Zion** [*another name for Jerusalem*] **all her beauty is departed**: her princes are become like harts [*deer*] *that* find no pasture, and they are gone without strength before the pursuer.

7 Jerusalem remembered in the days of her affliction and of her miseries all her pleasant things that she had in the days of old, when her people fell into the hand of the enemy, and none did help her: the adversaries saw her, *and* did mock at her sabbaths.

8 **Jerusalem hath grievously sinned; therefore she is removed**: all that honoured her despise her, because they have seen her nakedness: yea, she sigheth, and turneth backward.

9 **Her filthiness *is* in her skirts** [*her filthiness clings to her like mud clings to clothing*]; **she remembereth not her last end** [*she did not think ahead and consider the final consequences of sin*]; **therefore she came down wonderfully** [*astonishingly*]: she had no comforter. O LORD, behold my affliction: for the enemy hath magnified *himself*.

10 **The adversary hath spread out his hand upon all her pleasant things**: for she hath seen *that* the heathen entered into her sanctuary, whom thou didst command *that* they should not enter into thy congregation.

11 **All her people sigh, they seek bread** [*they are hungry*]; they have

given their pleasant things for meat [*food*] to relieve the soul [*to keep their bodies alive*]: see, O LORD, and consider; for **I am become vile** [*have become despised*].

In verses 12–22, Jeremiah depicts Judah (the Jews at this time in history) as a person, mourning what has become of her.

12 ¶ *Is it* **nothing to you, all ye that pass by** [*why don't you feel sorry for me*]? **Behold** [*look*], **and see if there be any sorrow like unto my sorrow,** which is done unto me, **wherewith the LORD hath afflicted** *me* **in the day of his fierce anger.**

13 **From above hath he sent fire into my bones**, and it prevaileth against them: **he hath spread a net for my feet** [*put me in captivity*], he hath turned me back: he hath made me desolate *and* faint all the day.

14 The yoke of my transgressions is bound by his hand: they **are wreathed** [*woven together*]**, and come up upon my neck**: he hath made my strength to fall, **the Lord hath delivered me into** *their* **hands** [*the Babylonians*], *from whom* I am not able to rise up [*escape*].

15 **The Lord hath trodden under foot all my mighty** *men* in the midst of me: he hath called an assembly against me to crush my young men: the Lord hath trodden the virgin, the daughter of Judah, *as* in a winepress [*my people have been crushed like grapes*].

16 **For these** *things* **I weep**; mine eye, mine eye runneth down with water, because the comforter [*the Lord*] that should relieve my soul is far from me: my children are desolate, because the enemy prevailed.

17 **Zion spreadeth forth her hands** [*in a plea for help*], *and there is* **none to comfort her**: the LORD hath commanded concerning Jacob [*wicked Israel*], *that* his adversaries *should be* round about him: Jerusalem is as a menstruous woman [*rejected, shunned*] among them.

18 ¶ **The LORD is righteous** [*the Lord is in the right as He punishes me*]; **for I have rebelled against his commandment**: hear, I pray you, all people, and behold my sorrow: my virgins and my young men are gone into captivity.

19 **I called for my lovers** [*I called upon my false gods*]**, *but* they deceived me**: my priests and mine elders gave up the ghost [*died*] in the city, while they sought their meat to relieve their souls [*while they searched for food to save themselves from starving to death*].

20 **Behold, O LORD; for I** *am* **in distress**: my bowels are troubled [*I am deeply troubled*]; mine heart is turned within me [*my heart is tormented*]; for **I have grievously rebelled**: abroad the sword bereaveth, at home *there is* as death [*I'm in trouble abroad and at home*].

21 **They have heard that I sigh:** *there is* **none to comfort me: all mine enemies have heard of my trouble; they are glad that thou hast done** *it:* thou wilt bring the day *that* thou hast called, and they shall be like unto me [*the day will come that they too will be punished by Thee, and then they will be like me*].

22 **Let all their wickedness come before thee**; and **do unto them, as thou hast done unto me** for all my transgressions: for my sighs *are* many, and my heart *is* faint.

LAMENTATIONS 3

You can feel Jeremiah's deep emotion and sorrow as you read this chapter. I will not add bold font nor commentary. I think you will be surprised at how much you understand because of your study of Jeremiah in this guide.

1 I *AM* the man *that* hath seen affliction by the rod of his wrath.

2 He hath led me, and brought *me into* darkness, but not *into* light.

3 Surely against me is he turned; he turneth his hand *against me* all the day.

4 My flesh and my skin hath he made old; he hath broken my bones.

5 He hath builded against me, and compassed *me* with gall and travail.

6 He hath set me in dark places, as *they that be* dead of old.

7 He hath hedged me about, that I cannot get out: he hath made my chain heavy.

8 Also when I cry and shout, he shutteth out my prayer.

9 He hath inclosed my ways with hewn stone, he hath made my paths crooked.

10 He *was* unto me *as* a bear lying in wait, *and as* a lion in secret places.

11 He hath turned aside my ways, and pulled me in pieces: he hath made me desolate.

12 He hath bent his bow, and set me as a mark for the arrow.

13 He hath caused the arrows of his quiver to enter into my reins.

14 I was a derision to all my people; *and* their song all the day.

15 He hath filled me with bitterness, he hath made me drunken with wormwood.

16 He hath also broken my teeth with gravel stones, he hath covered me with ashes.

17 And thou hast removed my soul far off from peace: I forgat prosperity.

18 And I said, My strength and my hope is perished from the LORD:

19 Remembering mine affliction and my misery, the wormwood and the gall.

20 My soul hath *them* still in remembrance, and is humbled in me.

21 This I recall to my mind, therefore have I hope.

22 ¶ *It is of* the LORD's mercies that we are not consumed, because his compassions fail not.

23 *They are* new every morning: great *is* thy faithfulness.

24 The LORD *is* my portion, saith my soul; therefore will I hope in him.

25 The LORD *is* good unto them that wait for him, to the soul *that* seeketh him.

26 *It is* good that *a man* should both hope and quietly wait for the salvation of the LORD.

27 *It is* good for a man that he bear the yoke in his youth.

28 He sitteth alone and keepeth silence, because he hath borne *it* upon him.

29 He putteth his mouth in the dust; if so be there may be hope.

30 He giveth *his* cheek to him that smiteth him: he is filled full with reproach.

31 For the Lord will not cast off for ever:

32 But though he cause grief, yet will he have compassion according to the multitude of his mercies.

33 For he doth not afflict willingly nor grieve the children of men.

34 To crush under his feet all the prisoners of the earth,

35 To turn aside the right of a man before the face of the most High,

36 To subvert a man in his cause, the Lord approveth not.

37 ¶ Who *is* he *that* saith, and it cometh to pass, *when* the Lord commandeth *it* not?

38 Out of the mouth of the most High proceedeth not evil and good?

39 Wherefore doth a living man complain, a man for the punishment of his sins?

40 Let us search and try our ways, and turn again to the LORD.

41 Let us lift up our heart with *our* hands unto God in the heavens.

42 We have transgressed and have rebelled: thou hast not pardoned.

43 Thou hast covered with anger, and persecuted us: thou hast slain, thou hast not pitied.

44 Thou hast covered thyself with a cloud, that *our* prayer should not pass through.

45 Thou hast made us *as* the offscouring and refuse in the midst of the people.

46 All our enemies have opened their mouths against us.

47 Fear and a snare is come upon us, desolation and destruction.

48 Mine eye runneth down with rivers of water for the destruction of the daughter of my people.

49 Mine eye trickleth down, and ceaseth not, without any intermission,

50 Till the LORD look down, and behold from heaven.

51 Mine eye affecteth mine heart because of all the daughters of my city.

52 Mine enemies chased me sore, like a bird, without cause.

53 They have cut off my life in the dungeon, and cast a stone upon me.

54 Waters flowed over mine head; *then* I said, I am cut off.

55 ¶ I called upon thy name, O LORD, out of the low dungeon.

56 Thou hast heard my voice: hide not thine ear at my breathing, at my cry.

57 Thou drewest near in the day *that* I called upon thee: thou saidst, Fear not.

58 O Lord, thou hast pleaded the causes of my soul; thou hast redeemed my life.

59 O LORD, thou hast seen my wrong: judge thou my cause.

60 Thou hast seen all their vengeance *and* all their imaginations against me.

61 Thou hast heard their reproach, O LORD, *and* all their imaginations against me;

62 The lips of those that rose up against me, and their device against me all the day.

63 Behold their sitting down, and their rising up; I *am* their musick.

64 ¶ Render unto them a recompence, O LORD, according to the work of their hands.

65 Give them sorrow of heart, thy curse unto them.

66 Persecute and destroy them in anger from under the heavens of the LORD.

EZEKIEL

Ezekiel (his name means "God is strong" or "God strengthens") lived at the same time as Jeremiah and Daniel. In other words, they were contemporaries, but all three served as prophets in different geographical areas. Jeremiah lived in Jerusalem. Daniel had been taken captive with other Jews into Babylon and was serving in King Nebuchadnezzar's court there. Ezekiel had likewise been taken captive by the Babylonian armies and served among the Jewish exiles in Babylon. Most biblical scholars agree that it was somewhere around

601–597 BC that King Nebuchadnezzar of Babylon (the Iraq area today) took ten thousand of Jerusalem's best and exiled them to Babylon and that Ezekiel, likely a rather young man at the time, was among this group of exiles. Daniel was in an earlier group of exiles, likely about 605 BC and probably a teenager at the time, and was taken to the king's court in Babylon to be raised and trained there. Jeremiah was one of the Lord's prophets in Jerusalem at the time Lehi and his family fled the Jerusalem area in 600 BC. We will use 2 Kings in the Old Testament to learn about the political situation at this time in the Jerusalem area (otherwise commonly known as the kingdom of Judah or the "Southern Kingdom,") when King Nebuchadnezzar of Babylon sent his armies to attack Jerusalem and the surrounding area. Let's look at these verses in Second Kings now:

2 Kings 24:10–18

10 ¶ At that time **the servants of Nebuchadnezzar king of Babylon came up against Jerusalem**, and the city was besieged [*surrounded and cut it off from outside support*].

11 And Nebuchadnezzar king of Babylon came against the city, and **his servants** [*armies*] **did besiege it.**

12 And **Jehoiachin the king of Judah** [*the wicked, 18–year-old king of Judah in Jerusalem who lasted only three months before he was captured by Nebuchadnezzar and taken to Babylon and replaced by his uncle, Zedekiah, who was 21 years old and treated the Prophet Jeremiah with disrespect and cruelty*] went out

to the king of Babylon, **he, and his mother, and his servants, and his princes, and his officers**: and the **king of Babylon took him** [*Jehoiachin*] **in the eighth year of his** [*Nebuchadnezzar's*] **reign.**

13 **And he** [*the King of Babylon*] **carried out thence** [*from there*] **all the treasures of the house of the Lord** [*the temple in Jerusalem*], **and the treasures of the king's house**, and cut in pieces all the vessels of gold which Solomon king of Israel had made in the temple of the Lord, as the Lord had said.

Next, in verses 14–16, we are told that Nebuchadnezzar also took the most capable and educated Jews, including skilled craftsmen, metal workers, etc., captive back to Babylon. It is likely that this group included young Ezekiel. Daniel, also relatively young, had been taken captive in an earlier wave of Jewish exiles to Babylon.

14 **And he** [*the King of Babylon*] **carried away all Jerusalem** [*not "all," rather, all the best, most highly skilled and educated*], and **all the princes, and all the mighty men of valour, even ten thousand captives, and all the craftsmen and smiths**: none remained, **save** [*except*] **the poorest sort of the people of the land.**

15 And **he carried away Jehoiachin** [*the young King of Judah spoken of in verse 12*] **to Babylon, and the king's mother, and the king's wives, and his officers, and the mighty of the land**, those carried he into captivity from Jerusalem to Babylon.

16 And all **the men of might**, even seven thousand, **and craftsmen and smiths** a thousand, **all that were strong and apt for war**, even them the king of Babylon brought captive to Babylon.

17 ¶ And **the king of Babylon made Mattaniah** his father's brother **king in his stead** [*in place of Jehoiachin*], and **changed his name to Zedekiah**.

18 **Zedekiah was twenty and one years old** when he began to reign, and he reigned eleven years in Jerusalem [*he was king of Judah in Jerusalem when Lehi and his family fled the Jerusalem area in 600 BC*]. And his mother's name was Hamutal, the daughter of Jeremiah of Libnah.

Probably the best-known scriptural passage in Ezekiel among the Latter-day Saints is Ezekiel 37:15–20, dealing with the stick of Judah and the stick of Joseph (the Bible and the Book of Mormon) and prophesying that in the last days, the two books would come together. They have literally come together in many ways, including when the Saints carry their scriptures to church and elsewhere. Perhaps the best-known passage among Christians in general might be Ezekiel's vision of the valley of dry bones, in chapter 37:1–14, symbolizing both the resurrection and the restoration of Israel to the promised land.

We will now begin our study of all the verses in Ezekiel.

EZEKIEL 1

Selection: all verses

According to many Bible scholars, a likely date for the beginning of Ezekiel's ministry to the Jewish captives in Babylon [*see verse one*] is around 595 BC. At that point, he had probably been a Jewish captive in Babylon for about three years, along with thousands of other Jews. The vision he mentions in verse one could very well be his call to be a prophet.

1 NOW it came to pass in the thirtieth year, in the fourth *month,* in the fifth *day* of the month, as I *was* **among the captives** by the river of Chebar [*possibly the Euphrates River or a canal that connected the Tigris and Euphrates rivers, not far from their confluence*], *that* **the heavens were opened, and I saw visions of God**.

2 In the fifth *day* of the month, which *was* the fifth year of king Jehoiachin's captivity,

3 **The word of the LORD came expressly unto Ezekiel** the priest, the son of Buzi [*his father was a priest, therefore Ezekiel was of the priestly lineage*], **in the land of the Chaldeans** [*part of Babylon*] by the river Chebar; and **the hand of the LORD was there upon him**.

Next, in verses 4–28, Ezekiel attempts to describe a glorious heavenly vision within the limits of mortal vocabulary. While there is much we don't understand, there are some things we do. I will use bold to "highlight" them. You may well see other symbolism indicative of heavenly visions.

4 ¶ And I looked, and, behold, a **whirlwind** [*a whirlwind represented the presence of the Lord to Job; see Job 38:1*] came out of the north, a great

cloud, and a **fire** [*often associated with seeing heavenly beings*] infolding itself, and **a brightness** [*often a part of heavenly visions*] *was* about it, and out of the midst thereof as the colour of **amber** [*color symbolism often associated with seeing the Lord; see D&C 110:2*], out of the midst of the fire.

5 Also out of the midst thereof *came* the likeness of four living creatures. And this *was* their appearance; they had the likeness of a man.

6 And every one had four faces, and every one had four **wings** [*associated with the ability to move and act in the work of the Lord; see D&C77:4*].

7 And their feet *were* straight feet; and the sole of their feet *was* like the sole of a calf's foot: and they sparkled like the colour of burnished **brass** [*a color often associated with the Lord; see Revelation 1:14*].

8 And *they had* the hands of a man under their wings on their four sides; and they four had their faces and their wings.

9 Their wings *were* joined one to another; they turned not when they went; they went every one straight forward.

10 As for the likeness of their faces, they four had the face of a man, and the face of a lion, on the right side: and they four had the face of an ox on the left side; they four also had the face of an eagle.

11 Thus *were* their faces: and their wings *were* stretched upward; two *wings* of every one *were* joined one to another, and two covered their bodies.

12 And they went every one straight forward: whither the spirit was to go, they went; *and* they turned not when they went.

13 As for the likeness of the living creatures, their appearance *was* like **burning coals of fire** [*associated with the Atonement of Christ and being cleansed by fire and the Holy Ghost; see Isaiah 6:6–7, 2 Nephi 16:6–7*], *and* like the appearance of lamps: it went up and down among the living creatures; and the fire was bright, and out of the fire went forth lightning.

14 And the living creatures ran and returned as the appearance of a flash of lightning.

15 ¶ Now as I beheld the living creatures, behold one wheel upon the earth by the living creatures, with his four faces.

16 The appearance of the wheels and their work *was* like unto the colour of a **beryl** [*deep green gem stone, emerald, symbolic of the beauty of God's throne; see Revelation 4;3*]: and they four had one likeness: and their appearance and their work *was* as it were a wheel in the middle of a wheel.

17 When they went, they went upon their four sides: *and* they turned not when they went.

18 As for their rings, they were so high that they were dreadful; and their rings *were* **full of eyes** [*eyes can represent being full of light and knowledge from God; see D&C 77:4*] round about them four.

19 And when the living creatures went, the wheels went by them: and when the living creatures were lifted up from the earth, the wheels were lifted up.

20 Whithersoever the spirit was to go, they went, thither *was their* spirit to go; and the wheels were lifted up over against them: for the spirit of the living creature *was* in the wheels.

21 When those went, *these* went; and when those stood, *these* stood; and when those were lifted up from the earth, the wheels were lifted up over against them: for the spirit of the living creature *was* in the wheels.

> The word "terrible," in verse 22, next, is translated as "awesome" in some modern translations of the Bible. See, for example Ezekiel 1:22 in the Holy Bible, New International Version, Zondervan Publishing House, Grand Rapids, Michigan, 1984.

22 And the likeness of the firmament [*heavens*] upon the heads of the living creature *was* as the colour of **the terrible crystal** [*could tie in symbolically with the "sea of glass" representing the earth in its celestial state, spoken of in D&C 77:1, Revelation 4:6, and D&C 130:9*], stretched forth over their heads above.

23 And under the firmament *were* their wings straight, the one toward the other: every one had two, which covered on this side, and every one had two, which covered on that side, their bodies.

24 And when they went, I heard the noise of their wings, **like the noise of great waters, as the voice of the Almighty** [*similar to "his voice was as the sound of the rushing of great waters, even the voice of Jehovah" in D&C 110:3*], the voice of speech, as the noise of an host: when they stood, they let down their wings.

25 And **there was a voice from the firmament** [*the heavens*] that *was* over their heads, when they stood, *and* had let down their wings.

> Next, in verses 26–28, Ezekiel sees God upon His throne in heaven in indescribable glory. Note that Ezekiel uses terms such as "likeness of" and "appearance of" which is a reverential and very careful approach to referring to Deity, in other words God. This reflects the culture among the Jews of being extremely careful not to even come close to taking the name of God in vain (Exodus 20:7.)

26 ¶ And **above the firmament** that *was* over their heads *was* **the likeness of a throne**, as the appearance of a sapphire stone: and upon the likeness of the throne *was* **the likeness as the appearance of a man** above **upon it**.

27 And I saw as the colour of **amber**, as the appearance of **fire** round

about within it, from the appearance of his loins even upward, and from the appearance of his loins even downward, I saw as it were the appearance of **fire**, and it had **brightness** round about.

28 As the appearance of the **bow** [rainbow, symbolic of the glory, power and authority of God: see Revelation 4:3] that is in the cloud in the day of rain, so *was* the appearance of the **brightness** round about. This *was* the appearance of the likeness of **the glory of the LORD**. And when I saw *it,* **I fell upon my face** [symbolic of complete humility and respect before God in Jewish culture], and **I heard a voice** of one that spake [the voice of the Lord; we presume, based on the scriptures and on modern revelation that this was the premortal Jesus Christ in His role as the Jehovah of the Old Testament].

EZEKIEL 2

Selection: all verses

Ezekiel received his call, in chapter one, to serve as a prophet to the Israelites in Babylonian captivity. Here, in chapter two, the Lord tells him what his message to these rebellious Israelites is to be. It is interesting to note that these captives were the same people to whom the Prophet Jeremiah, back in Jerusalem had been preaching and warning that their wickedness would result in destruction and captivity. They didn't listen and now we would hope that their captivity in Babylon

would humble them such that they would listen to Ezekiel, however, as we continue to read, it doesn't seem to be the case. They have not repented.

1 AND **he** [the Lord] **said unto me** [Ezekiel], **Son of man, stand upon thy feet, and I will speak unto thee**.

Did you notice the phrase "Son of man" in verse 1? Perhaps you are aware that the phrase "Son of Man" refers to the Savior in several places in the scriptures. For example, "Son of Man of Holiness," in Moses 6:57, is the more complete phrase and means "Son of Heavenly Father." "Son of man," as used here in Ezekiel, refers to Ezekiel, and simply means "human" see footnote 1 a in your scriptures. Most of the time it is rendered "son of man."

Next, in verse 2, we see that the Holy Ghost is there to help Ezekiel understand and fulfill his mission, similar to how He helps us in our various callings, responsibilities, and opportunities.

2 And **the spirit entered into me** when he spake unto me, and set me upon my feet, that **I heard him** that spake unto me.

3 And **he said** unto me, Son of man, **I send thee to the children of Israel, to a rebellious nation that hath rebelled against me**: they and their fathers [ancestors] have transgressed against me, *even* **unto this very day** [they still haven't humbled themselves and repented].

Next, Jehovah, the premortal Jesus Christ, explains what kind of people

Ezekiel has been called to serve as a prophet.

4 For ***they are*** **impudent children** [*disrespectful, not showing due respect to their superiors, including God in this case*] **and stiffhearted** [*stubborn, stiffnecked*]. **I do send thee unto them**; and **thou shalt say unto them, Thus saith the Lord GOD** [*you will be speaking for Me*].

5 And **they**, whether they will hear, or whether they will forbear [*refuse*], (for they *are* a rebellious house,) yet **shall know that there hath been a prophet among them**.

Next, in verses 6–7, the premortal Savior gives Ezekiel tender and very important counsel concerning his difficult mission.

6 ¶ And thou, son of man, **be not afraid of them, neither be afraid of their words**, though briers and thorns *be* with thee, and thou dost dwell among scorpions [*these rebellious Israelites can be very hard on prophets*]: **be not afraid of their words, nor be dismayed at their looks**, though they *be* a rebellious house.

7 And **thou shalt speak my words unto them, whether they will hear, or whether they will forbear** [*refuse to hear*]: for they *are* most rebellious.

8 **But thou, son of man**, hear what I say unto thee; **Be not thou rebellious like that rebellious house: open thy mouth, and eat that I**

give thee [*accept and internalize the mission I give to you*].

Next, Ezekiel is shown a vision in which he sees a hand reaching out to him with a book or scroll declaring much misery, mourning and trouble for these still rebellious captive Israelites in Babylon.

9 ¶ And when **I looked, behold, an hand** *was* **sent unto me**; and, lo, **a roll of a book** *was* **therein**;

10 And **he spread it before me** [*showed it to me*]; and it *was* written within and without: and ***there was*** **written therein lamentations, and mourning, and woe**.

EZEKIEL 3

Selection: all verses

In this chapter, Ezekiel is made a "watchman on the tower," so to speak, to Israel. In other words, a prophet who is, as it were, on a high tower where he can see things as they are, including dangers that are coming. His responsibility is that of watching out for God's children. Thus, Ezekiel is made a watchman for Israel.

1 MOREOVER **he said unto me**, Son of man, eat that thou findest; **eat this roll** [*scroll; accept this mission*], and **go speak unto the house of Israel**.

2 **So I opened my mouth** [*I started preaching*], and **he caused me to eat that roll** [*He helped me accept and carry out my mission*].

3 And he said unto me, Son of man, cause thy belly to eat, and fill thy bowels with this roll that I give thee. **Then did I eat** *it;* **and it was in my mouth as honey for sweetness.**

Verse 3, above, can remind us of the Apostle, John, in the Book of Revelation. We will quote some relevant verses that help us understand Ezekiel, with some commentary from my study guide for the New Testament.

REVELATION 10

1 And **I saw another mighty angel** [*this appears to be the seventh of the angels in 8:2; if so, it might be Adam, the "seventh angel" in D&C 88:106, 110, 112*] come down from heaven, clothed with a cloud: and a rainbow was upon his head, and his face was as it were the sun, and his feet as pillars of fire [*quite a description of Michael or Adam, if he is the seventh angel spoken of here*]:

2 And **he had in his hand a little book** [*a mission for John; see verses 8–10, also D&C 77:14*] open: and he set his right foot upon the sea, and his left foot on the earth [*D&C 88:110; i.e., this angel has a large jurisdiction*],

9 And **I went unto the angel, and said unto him, Give me the little book** [*i.e., I accept the mission*]. And he said unto me, **Take it, and eat it up** [*i.e., "internalize" it, make it a part of you*]; and **it shall make thy belly bitter, but it shall be in thy mouth sweet as honey** [*being a servant of*

God to the people has both bitter and sweet aspects].

10 **And I took the little book out of the angel's hand, and ate it up** [*"internalized it"; made it a part of me*]; **and it was in my mouth sweet as honey**: and as soon as I had eaten it, my belly was bitter [*working with stubborn, unrepentant people can sometimes cause indigestion indeed!*].

Now, back to Ezekiel.

4 ¶ **And he said unto me**, Son of man, **go,** get thee **unto the house of Israel, and speak with my words unto them**.

Next, in verses 5–7, Ezekiel is reminded that he is not being sent to foreign people who speak a foreign language, rather to his own people, Israel, who should understand his teaching, but willfully chose not to.

5 For **thou** *art* **not sent to a people of a strange speech** and of an hard language, *but* **to the house of Israel**;

6 Not to many people of a strange speech and of an hard language, whose words thou canst not understand. **Surely, had I sent thee to them** [*non-Israelites, to a foreign people in a foreign country whose language you don't understand*], **they would have hearkened unto thee.**

7 **But the house of Israel will not hearken unto thee;** for **they will not hearken unto me**: for all the house of Israel *are* impudent and hardhearted.

Next, in verses 8–9, the Lord fortifies Ezekiel to be able to handle rejection.

8 Behold, **I have made thy face strong against their faces** [*as they jeer him and reject him*], and **thy forehead strong** [*strong-willed*] **against their foreheads** [*their thickheadedness*].

9 **As an adamant** [*diamond*] harder than flint have I made thy forehead: **fear them not, neither be dismayed at their looks**, though they *be* a rebellious house.

> The counsel Jehovah gives to Ezekiel next, in verse 10, certainly can apply to each of us as we hear His word through His prophets today. The heart is considered to be the center of feeling and loyalty, the primary force for how we act and behave.

10 Moreover [*in addition*] he said unto me, Son of man, **all my words that I shall speak unto thee receive in thine heart**, and hear with thine ears.

11 And go, get thee to them of the captivity, unto the children of thy people, and speak unto them, and tell them, Thus saith the Lord GOD; **whether they will hear, or whether they will forbear** [*refuse to hear and obey*].

> At this point, Ezekiel's first vision ends (starting in chapter 1 and ending here), and in verses 12–14, the Spirit carries him away from the presence of the Lord. As he is taken from the Divine Presence, he hears things behind him that remind him of the glorious vision he has just seen.

12 **Then the spirit took me up**, and I heard behind me a voice of a great rushing [*similar to D&C 110:3*], *saying,* Blessed *be* the glory of the LORD from his place.

13 *I heard* also the noise of the wings of the living creatures that touched one another, and the noise of the wheels over against them, and a noise of a great rushing.

14 **So the spirit lifted me up, and took me away**, and **I went in bitterness** [*perhaps indicative of sadness and disappointment at being taken out of the Lord's presence*], in the heat of my spirit; but the hand of the LORD was strong upon me.

> Next, starting with verse 15, Ezekiel is taken to where many of the captives are living and prepared for his second vision in which some instruction is repeated and some additional instruction is given this newly-called prophet (verses 16–21. "Tel-abib" in verse 15, next, is the same word as the city of "Tel Aviv" in modern Israel today, and means "Spring Hill."

15 ¶ **Then I came to them of the captivity at Tel-abib, that dwelt by the river of Chebar**, and **I sat where they sat, and remained there astonished among them seven days**.

16 And it came to pass at the end of seven days, that **the word of the LORD came unto me, saying,**

17 Son of man [*Ezekiel*], **I have made thee a watchman unto the house of Israel**: therefore hear the word at my mouth, and **give them warning from me**.

Verses 18–21, next, give Ezekiel, as well as those of us who are accountable, strong warning to carry out our responsibilities to teach and preach the gospel as best we can. If we don't, then we are held accountable for the people's sins. If we do, they are responsible for their own sins. This is strong doctrine and no doubt Ezekiel was overwhelmed with his calling to preach to wicked Israel at this time (similar to Isaiah's reaction to his call, see Isaiah 6:5) so the Lord gave it to him straight in these next verses.

18 When I say unto the wicked, Thou shalt surely die [*spiritually; you are in danger of losing your salvation*]; **and thou givest him not warning, nor speakest to warn the wicked from his wicked way, to save his life**; *salvation*]; the same wicked *man* shall die in his iniquity; but **his blood will I require at thine hand**.

19 **Yet if thou warn the wicked**, and he turn not from his wickedness, nor from his wicked way, he shall die in his iniquity; but **thou hast delivered thy soul** [*you will be free from his sins*].

20 Again, When a righteous *man* doth turn from his righteousness, and commit iniquity, and I lay a stumblingblock before him, he shall die: **because thou hast not given him warning**, he shall die in his sin,

and his righteousness which he hath done shall not be remembered; but **his blood will I require at thine hand** [*you will be held accountable for his sins*].

21 **Nevertheless if thou warn the righteous** *man,* that the righteous sin not, and he doth not sin, he shall surely live, because he is warned; also **thou hast delivered thy soul**.

Ezekiel's third vision is given in verses 22–27, next.

22 ¶ And the hand of the LORD was there upon me; and he said unto me, **Arise, go forth into the plain** [*an uninhabited place*]**, and I will there talk with thee**.

23 Then **I arose, and went forth into the plain**: and, behold, **the glory of the LORD stood there**, as the glory which I saw by the river of Chebar [*possibly the Euphrates River or a canal between the Tigris and Euphrates; some scholars suggest that much of what Ezekiel saw in his first vision was repeated in this third vision—see Rasmussen, p 585*]: and I fell on my face.

24 Then **the spirit entered into me**, and set me upon my feet, and spake with me, **and said unto me, Go, shut thyself within thine house**.

In verses 25–26, next, Jehovah instructs Ezekiel not to even try to preach to his fellow-countrymen in exile, for the time being, until He tells him to.

25 But thou, O son of man, behold, they shall put bands upon thee [*they will "bind" you by not listening to you*], and shall bind thee with them [*probably symbolically*], and **thou shalt not go out among them**:

26 And **I will make thy tongue cleave to the roof of thy mouth, that thou shalt be dumb** [*I will not let you preach to them for now*], and shalt not be to them a reprover: **for they** *are* **a rebellious house**.

27 **But when I speak with thee** [*but when I tell you to preach to them*], **I will open thy mouth**, and thou shalt say unto them, Thus saith the Lord GOD; He that heareth, let him hear; and he that forbeareth [*refuses to hear*], let him forbear [*you have your agency*]: for they *are* a rebellious house [*these captive Israelites in Babylon are still rebelling against the Lord*].

EZEKIEL 4

Selection: all verses

In this chapter, Ezekiel is instructed by the Lord to use several different symbols or visual aids (called "types and shadows") to prophesy and teach these Jewish exiles in Babylon that those left behind in Jerusalem will yet be attacked by Nebuchadnezzar's Babylonian armies. This will be the third siege and taking of captives against Jerusalem by this foreign king and his soldiers and will take place about 587–586 BC, about ten years from Ezekiel's call to be a prophet (as found in chapters 1 and 2.) Remember that Daniel was taken

in the first siege against Jerusalem by King Nebuchadnezzar (about 605 BC) and that Ezekiel was taken in the second siege (according to Bible scholars about as early as 601 BC or as late as 597 BC). Remember, Lehi and his family fled from Jerusalem in 600 BC. Lehi served as a prophet in Jerusalem along with Jeremiah.

This third siege was the worst of all. Watch the imagery and symbolism now in this chapter and the next, as Ezekiel teaches his fellow exiles in Babylon, among other things, what will yet happen to Jerusalem and the kingdom of Judah because of the ongoing rebelliousness of those inhabitants against the Lord. Verses 1–3 symbolize the siege against Jerusalem.

1 THOU also, son of man [*referring to Ezekiel*], **take thee a tile** [*a clay tablet*], and lay it before thee, and **pourtray upon it the city,** *even* **Jerusalem** [*make a small portrayal of the city of Jerusalem*]:

2 And **lay siege against it**, and build a fort against it, and cast a mount against it; **set the camp also against it** [*make a model of the enemy armies surrounding it*], and set *battering* rams against it round about.

3 Moreover **take** thou unto thee **an iron pan, and set it** *for* **a wall of iron between thee and the city** [*use an iron pan to represent the wall erected around Jerusalem by the Babylonian armies and the impenetrable wall of enemy soldiers surrounding Jerusalem*]: and set thy face against it, and

it shall be besieged [*the basic prophecy*], and thou shalt lay siege against it. This *shall be* a sign to the house of Israel [*these symbols are a prophecy of what is coming to the wicked and rebellious Israelites in the Jerusalem area*].

Have you noticed that, even though it is the "Jews" in the Jerusalem area and the southern kingdom of Judah who have been taken captive and are about to be taken captive, they are often being referred to as "The House of Israel" as in verse 3, above? Keep in mind that in the nation of Judah, which included Jerusalem as its headquarters, there were many Israelites from all twelve tribes of Israel, including many especially from the tribe of Benjamin. Thus, these are "Israelites" and so are we.

Obviously, we don't know quite how Ezekiel carried out the instructions given in verses 4–8, next, but we can conclude that it represents the 390 years (verse 5) of Israel's rebellion against God from the time the northern kingdom (the northern ten tribes) divided from the southern kingdom (Judah and Benjamin)—see 1 Kings 12, up to the Babylonian captivity.

The forty years of the rebellion of the Jews are symbolically depicted in verse 6. The severe limits imposed upon the captives are depicted symbolically in verse 8. This can depict the spiritual limits and "captivity" imposed upon us if we chose to rebel against God and live in wickedness.

4 **Lie thou also upon thy left side, and lay the iniquity of the house of Israel upon it**: *according* to the number of the days that thou shalt lie upon it thou shalt bear their iniquity.

5 For I have laid upon thee the years of their iniquity, according to the number of the days, **three hundred and ninety days**: so shalt thou bear the iniquity of the house of Israel.

6 And when thou hast accomplished them, lie again on thy right side, and thou shalt bear **the iniquity of the house of Judah forty days**: I have appointed thee each day for a year.

7 Therefore thou shalt set thy face toward the siege of Jerusalem, and thine arm *shall be* uncovered, and thou shalt prophesy against it.

8 And, behold, **I will lay bands upon thee, and thou shalt not turn thee from one side to another**, till thou hast ended the days of thy siege.

The next object lesson Ezekiel is to prepare to teach his rebellious people demonstrates the miserable conditions, including lack of desirable food and adequate drinkable water, under which they will suffer during their captivity. He is to prepare a small meal of about a half pound of mixed grain bread and about a quart of water per day for a period of time, symbolizing poor living conditions in captivity. Overall, this symbolizes the penalty people pay for not living the gospel, which, if lived faithfully, enables God to bless us with prosperity and well-being.

9 ¶ Take thou also unto thee **wheat**, and **barley**, and **beans**, and **lentiles**, and **millet**, and **fitches** [*spelt, a type of wheat*], and put them in one vessel, and **make thee bread thereof**, *according* to the number of the days that thou shalt lie upon thy side, **three hundred and ninety days shalt thou eat thereof**.

10 And **thy meat** [*food*] which thou shalt eat *shall be* **by weight** [*during famine and lack of adequate food, rations are imposed*], twenty shekels a day: from time to time shalt thou eat it.

11 **Thou shalt drink also water by measure** [*good water will be rationed too*], the sixth part of an hin [*slightly more than a pint*]: from time to time shalt thou drink.

12 And thou shalt eat it [*the bread you make*] *as* barley cakes, and **thou shalt bake it with dung that cometh out of man** [*having to use human waste as fuel for their cooking fires was extremely repulsive and made the bread defiled—see verse 13—in Jewish culture*], in their sight.

13 And the LORD said, Even thus shall the children of Israel eat their **defiled bread** among the Gentiles, whither I will drive them [*wherever the Lord chooses to scatter them because of their rebellion against Him*].

Having been given the above instructions to bake the bread with fire made by burning human waste, Ezekiel gently objects, reminding the Lord that he has strictly obeyed the dietary and other laws of the Jews (see Leviticus, chapter 11) and has never polluted himself.

14 **Then said I, Ah Lord GOD!** behold, my soul hath not been polluted [*I have faithfully kept the laws given by Moses regarding what to eat and what not to eat—see Leviticus 11*]: for from my youth up even till now have I not eaten of that which dieth of itself, or is torn in pieces; neither came there abominable flesh into my mouth.

Kindly, in verse 15, the Lord gives Ezekiel permission to use cow dung (manure) for his cooking fire rather than human dung.

15 Then he said unto me, Lo, **I have given thee cow's dung for man's dung**, and thou shalt **prepare** [*bake*] **thy bread therewith**.

Next, in verses 16 and 17, Jehovah tells Ezekiel that the Jews back in Jerusalem are likewise going to have a terrible famine because of their wickedness.

16 Moreover he said unto me, Son of man, behold, **I will break the staff of bread in Jerusalem** [*I will cause a famine in Jerusalem*]: and **they shall eat bread by weight, and with care**; and **they shall drink water by measure**, and with **astonishment** [*they will be surprised and startled that this is happening to them*]:

17 **That they may want** [*lack*] **bread and water**, and be astonied one with another, and **consume away for their iniquity** [*they will be astonished

at their terrible famine and will experience horrible destruction because of
their wickedness].

EZEKIEL 5

Selection: all verses

We get a good clue as to what this
chapter is about by reading verse 12
first. In it you can see the major prophecy here that one third of the Jews
would die because of famine and pestilence, one third would be killed by their
attackers, and one third would be scattered throughout the world.

Symbolically, starting with verse 1, in
the Jewish culture, a man's hair and
beard represented his dignity, worth,
and stature among men. Shaving a
captive's hair and beard were an extreme insult and symbolized conquest
and humiliation. Perhaps you remember that the soldiers who tormented
Christ before His crucifixion "plucked
off the hair" of His cheeks (pulled His
beard out—see 2 Nephi 7:6.) Conquering armies often shaved both men and
women bald to signify that they were
slaves—see 2 Nephi 13:24.)

Thus, the symbolism of Ezekiel's acts,
starting in verse 1, prophetically represent what is going to happen to these
intentionally rebellious covenant people who had once been the prosperous and protected people of the Lord.
Ezekiel's hair represented the people
of Judah, especially the city of Jerusalem, before their destruction and captivity.

1 AND thou, son of man [Ezekiel],
take thee a sharp knife, **take thee
a barber's razor** [symbolic of the
Babylonians], **and cause** it **to pass
upon thine head and upon thy
beard** [shave off all your hair and
beard]: then take thee balances to
weight, and **divide the** *hair* [divide it
up into three piles].

Verse two symbolizes various ways
in which the rebellious Jews still in
Jerusalem as well as those already
in captivity will be punished and destroyed for their wickedness.

2 Thou shalt **burn with fire a third
part in the midst of the city** [Jeru-
salem], when the days of the siege
are fulfilled: and thou shalt **take a
third part,** *and* **smite about it with
a knife**: and **a third part thou shalt
scatter in the wind**; and I will draw
out a sword after them [destruction
and devastation will also follow them in
captivity].

3 Thou shalt also **take** thereof **a few**
[hairs] in number, **and bind them
in thy skirts** [symbolic of those who
were not killed during the attacks on Jerusalem, rather, survived as captives in
Babylon] .

4 **Then take of them** [the survivors
mentioned in verse 3] **again, and cast
them into the midst of the fire, and
burn them in the fire** [symbolic of
being destroyed after all, thinking that
they had escaped destruction. Can also
be symbolic that some of them will repent and be cleansed by fire and the
Holy Ghost]; *for* **thereof shall a fire
come forth into all the house of Israel** [all the house of Israel is in trouble
unless they repent].

In verses 5 through 11, next, we see what the Jews in Jerusalem and the surrounding area have done that has torn them away from the protection and blessings of the Lord.

First, in verse 5, Jehovah explains that Jerusalem was set up originally to be an example of righteousness to the nations around it.

5 ¶ Thus saith the Lord GOD; **This** *is* **Jerusalem: I have set it in the midst of the nations and countries** *that are* round about her.

Next, the Premortal Christ explains what the apostate Jews did to His laws, commandments, and ordinances given them through Moses.

6 And **she** [*Jerusalem*] **hath changed my judgments** [*laws and commandments*] **into wickedness** more than the nations, and **my statutes** [*laws, commandments, ordinances*] **more than the countries that** *are* **round about her** [*they became more wicked that the wicked nations around them*]: for **they have refused my judgments and my statutes, they have not walked in them**.

7 **Therefore thus saith the Lord GOD**; **Because ye multiplied more** [*sinned more*] **than the nations that** *are* **round about you,** *and* have not walked in my statutes, neither have kept my judgments, **neither have done according to the judgments of the nations that** *are* **round about you** [*haven't even lived up to the standards of the nations around you, to*

whom you were to be an example—verse 5];

8 **Therefore thus saith the Lord GOD**; Behold, I, even **I,** *am* **against thee**, and **will execute judgments** in the midst of thee [*will punish you*] in the sight of the nations.

9 And **I will do in thee that which I have not done** [*you will be punished worse than ever before*], and whereunto I will not do any more the like, **because of all thine abominations** [*extreme wickedness*].

Next, in verse 10, Ezekiel prophesies that things will get so bad in Jerusalem, during coming sieges, that cannibalism will be resorted to by her inhabitants. Moses prophesied this kind of depravity among wicked Israelites in Leviticus 26:29. Some such cannibalism was reported among the Jews during the Roman siege of Jerusalem around A.D. 70.

10 Therefore the **fathers shall eat the sons** in the midst of thee, and the **sons shall eat their fathers**; and I will execute judgments in thee, and the whole remnant of thee will I scatter into all the winds [*scattered Israel*].

11 Wherefore, *as* I live, saith the Lord GOD; Surely, **because thou hast defiled my sanctuary with all thy detestable things, and with all thine abominations**, therefore will I also diminish *thee;* neither shall mine eye spare, neither will I have any pity.

12 ¶ A third part of thee shall die with the pestilence, and with famine shall they be consumed in the midst of thee: and **a third part shall fall by the sword** round about thee and **I will scatter a third part into all the winds**, and I will draw out a sword after them [*see verse 2*].

13 Thus shall mine anger be accomplished, and **I will cause my fury to rest upon them**, and I will be comforted [*perhaps meaning that the law of justice is a vital part of the plan of salvation and provides resolution to such situations as this extreme wickedness and intentional rebellion*]: and **they shall know that I the LORD have spoken** *it* in my zeal, when I have accomplished my fury in them.

Next, in verses 14–15, the Lord tells these apostate Jews that they will be mocked and despised by other nations.

14 Moreover **I will make thee** waste, and **a reproach among the nations** that *are* round about thee, in the sight of all that pass by.

15 So it [*Jerusalem; the Jews*] **shall be a reproach and a taunt, an instruction and an astonishment unto the nations that** *are* **round about thee**, when I shall execute judgments in thee in anger and in fury and in furious rebukes. I the LORD have spoken *it*.

16 When I shall send upon them the evil arrows of famine, which shall be for *their* destruction, *and* which I will send to destroy you: and **I will** increase the famine upon you, and will break your staff of bread:

17 **So will I send upon you famine and evil beasts**, and they shall bereave thee; and **pestilence and blood shall pass through thee**; and **I will bring the sword upon thee**. I the LORD have spoken *it*.

EZEKIEL 6

Selection: all verses

Ezekiel's vision of wickedness in Jerusalem continues in this chapter. You will notice that the term, "Israel," is now used, starting in verse 2, indicating that the Jews are not the only members of the Lord's covenant people, Israel, who are now wicked. The ten tribes of Israel, or the "northern kingdom," preceded the Jews in becoming sufficiently wicked to be taken away and were taken captive by the Assyrians about 120 years ago (722–721 BC) at this point of history, because of their apostasy and wickedness.

Based on the evidence in chapters 6 through 9, we conclude that all of Israel was guilty of infidelity to God, through idol worship and other forms of wickedness. This would include remnants of the lost ten tribes left behind by the Assyrians as well as the Jews and remnants of other tribes of Israel living among them.

The "mountains of Israel" in verse 2 and going forward could easily refer to the "high places" and groves and other locations selected and set up for idol worship, often in the mountains. It could also refer to the high and mighty, haughty and rebellious leaders of the Jews in Jerusalem.

1 **AND the word of the LORD came unto me** [*Ezekiel*], **saying,**

2 Son of man, **set thy face toward the mountains of Israel, and prophesy against them,**

3 **And say, Ye mountains of Israel, hear the word of the Lord GOD**; Thus saith the Lord GOD to the mountains, and to the hills, to the rivers, and to the valleys; Behold, I, *even* **I, will bring a sword upon you, and I will destroy your high places**.

4 And **your altars shall be desolate, and your images** [*idols*] **shall be broken**: and I will cast down your slain *men* before your idols.

Perhaps you are aware that human sacrifice, including sacrificing children, was part of the idol worship practiced by Israel at this time. Thus, in verse 5, next, Ezekiel prophesies that the bones of these apostate children of Israel will be scattered among the bones of those they sacrificed to their abominable idols as they are slaughtered by the coming enemy armies.

5 And **I will lay the dead carcases of the children of Israel before their idols; and I will scatter your bones round about your altars**.

6 In **all your dwellingplaces the cities shall be laid waste**, and **the high places shall be desolate; that your altars may be laid waste and**

made desolate, and **your idols** may be **broken** and cease, and **your images** [*idols*] may be **cut down**, and **your works** may be **abolished**.

7 And **the slain shall fall in the midst of you**, and ye shall know that I *am* the LORD.

An encouraging note is found in verses 8–10, next, namely that there will be a remnant of Israel spared and scattered, and that, in the future, they will return to God and be gathered back in to covenant Israel. We are seeing and participating in this marvelous and powerful last days' gathering of Israel now.

8 ¶ **Yet will I leave a remnant**, that ye may have *some* that **shall escape** the sword among the nations, **when ye shall be scattered through the countries**.

9 And **they** that escape of you **shall remember me** [*repent and return to God*] among the nations whither they shall be carried captives, **because I am broken** [*grieved*] **with their whorish heart** [*their idol worship; their infidelity to God*], which hath departed from me, and with their eyes, which go a whoring after their idols: and **they shall lothe themselves** [*have "godly sorrow" (2 Corinthians 7:10), will truly repent*] **for the evils which they have committed** in all their abominations.

10 And **they shall know that I *am* the LORD**, *and that* **I have not said in vain** that I would do this evil unto

them [*that their suffering for their sins would bring them back to me*].

Finally, in verses 11–14, there is a review of Israel's guilt.

11 ¶ Thus saith the Lord GOD; Smite with thine hand, and stamp with thy foot, and say, Alas **for all the evil abominations of the house of Israel!** for **they shall fall by the sword**, by the **famine**, and by the **pestilence**.

12 **He that is far off** [*far away from Jerusalem in captivity*] **shall die of the pestilence**; and **he that is near shall fall by the sword**; and **he that remaineth and is besieged shall die by the famine**: thus will I accomplish my fury upon them.

13 **Then shall ye know that I** *am* **the LORD, when their slain** *men* **shall be among their idols round about their altars**, upon every high hill, in all the tops of the mountains, and under every green tree [*groves of trees maintained and cultivated for idol worship sites*], and under every thick oak, the place where they did offer sweet savour to all their idols.

14 **So will I stretch out my hand upon them, and make the land desolate**, yea, more desolate than the wilderness toward Diblath [*we don't know where this was*], in all their habitations: and they shall know that I *am* the LORD.

EZEKIEL 7

Selection: all verses

This chapter continues Ezekiel's prophecies of coming punishments to wicked Israel.

1 **MOREOVER** [*in addition*] **the word of the LORD came unto me** [*Ezekikel*]**, saying,**

2 Also, thou son of man [*Ezekiel*], **thus saith the Lord GOD unto the land of Israel**; An end, **the end is come** [*your time is up*] upon the four corners [*all*] of the land.

Have you noticed that it is typical for these Old Testament prophets such as Ezekiel and Isaiah to repeat things for extra emphasis? An example is "the end is come" in verse 2, above, repeated in verses 3 and 6. An example of Isaiah's repetition for teaching emphasis is found in Isaiah 8:9, where Isaiah warns the rebellious people of his day not to make alliances with other countries for protection. Rather, they should repent and turn to God for protection.

Isaiah 8:9

Associate yourselves [*make treaties*], O ye people, and ye shall be **broken in pieces**; and give ear, all ye of far countries: gird yourselves, and ye shall be **broken in pieces**; gird yourselves, and ye shall be **broken in pieces**.

Also, you will see that the Lord says basically the same thing, "I will punish you," many different ways all the way through verses 3–15.

3 Now *is* the end *come* upon thee, and **I will send mine anger upon thee**, and **will judge thee** according to thy ways, and **will recompense** [*pay back*] **upon thee all thine abominations** [*what you sow in wickedness will come back to punish you; the "law of the harvest"*].

4 And **mine eye shall not spare thee, neither will I have pity**: but **I will recompense thy ways upon thee**, and **thine abominations** [*extreme wickedness*] **shall be in the midst of thee** [*will come back to punish you*]: and ye shall know that I *am* the LORD.

5 Thus saith the Lord GOD; An evil, **an only evil** [*an unheard-of disaster*], behold, is come.

6 An **end is come**, the **end is come**: it watcheth for thee; behold, **it is come**.

7 The morning is come unto thee, O thou that dwellest in the land: **the time is come**, the day of **trouble** *is* **near**, and not the sounding again of the mountains [*not the sound of celebrating, rather, the sound of numerous enemy armies reverberating on the mountains of Jerusalem; the impending destruction of Jerusalem*].

8 Now will **I shortly pour out my fury upon thee**, and **accomplish mine anger upon thee**: and **I will judge** [*punish*] **thee according to thy ways**, and will **recompense thee for all thine abominations**.

9 And **mine eye shall not spare, neither will I have pity**: I will **recompense thee according to thy ways and thine abominations** *that* are in the midst of thee; and ye shall know that **I** *am* **the LORD that smiteth**.

10 Behold **the day**, behold, it **is come**: the **morning is gone** forth; the rod hath blossomed, **pride hath budded** [*you are full of crippling, evil pride*].

Verse 11, next, shows how widespread the destruction of rebellious Israel will be.

11 **Violence is risen up into a rod of wickedness** [*"rod" can symbolize punishment; you are being punished by your own wickedness*]: **none of them** *shall remain*, nor of their multitude, nor of any of theirs: **neither** *shall there be* **wailing for them** [*none will be left to mourn for them*].

12 **The time is come, the day draweth near**: let not the buyer rejoice, nor the seller mourn [*commerce, buying and selling, will be destroyed*]: for **wrath** *is* **upon all the multitude** thereof.

13 For **the seller shall not return to that which is sold** [*perhaps implying that even the buying and selling in the temple—see John 2:13–16—will cease*], although they were yet alive: for the vision *is* touching **the whole multitude** thereof, *which* **shall not return**; neither shall any **strengthen himself in the iniquity of his life** [*wickedness will no longer pay off temporarily*].

14 **They have blown the trumpet,** even to make all ready [*to go to battle against the invading armies*]; **but none goeth to the battle**: for my wrath *is* upon all the multitude thereof.

In verse 15, next, Ezekiel prophesies that none will escape the devastations and destruction.

15 **The sword** *is* **without** [*outside the city*], **and the pestilence and the famine within** [*inside the city*]: he that *is* in the field shall die with the sword; and he that *is* in the city, famine and pestilence shall devour him.

Verse 16 informs us that the few who do escape will be like helpless doves, mourning for their sins.

16 ¶ But **they that escape** of them shall escape, and **shall be on the mountains like doves** of the valleys, all of them **mourning, every one for his iniquity** [*sins*].

17 All hands shall be **feeble**, and all knees shall be **weak** *as* water.

18 **They shall also gird** [*dress themselves*] **with sackcloth** [*coarse fabric like burlap, symbolic in Jewish culture of extreme mourning*], and **horror shall cover them**; and **shame** *shall be* **upon all faces**, and **baldness upon all their heads** [*the Babylonians routinely shaved the heads of the people they conquered for purposes of humiliation, identification, and sanitation*].

In verse 19, Ezekiel prophesies that invading armies would loot the rich treasures of Jerusalem, including the treasures of the temple.

19 They shall cast their **silver** in the streets, and their **gold** shall be removed: their silver and their gold shall not be able to deliver them [*they won't be able to buy their freedom*] in the day of the wrath of the LORD: they shall not satisfy their souls, neither fill their bowels: because it is **the stumblingblock of their iniquity** [*their wickedness has become their big stumblingblock*].

20 ¶ **As for the beauty of his ornament** [*the temple in Jerusalem*], **he set it in majesty** [*it was once majestic and accepted by the Lord*]: **but they** [*the Jews*] **made the images of their abominations** [*idols*] *and* **of their detestable things therein** [*the Jews had polluted and defiled the temple*]: therefore have I [*the Lord*] set it far from them.

21 And **I will give it** [*the temple*] **into the hands of the strangers** [*foreigners, Gentiles; the conquering armies*] for a prey, and to the wicked of the earth for a spoil; **and they shall pollute it.**

22 **My face will I turn also from them** [*I will not help the Jews*], and **they** [*the conquerors*] **shall pollute** [*defile*] **my secret** *place:* for the robbers shall enter into it [*the temple*], and defile it.

Finally, in verses 23–27, a chain seems to symbolize and summarize the series of related devastations that will befall rebellious Israel as foretold in the previous verses and chapters.

23 ¶ **Make a chain:** for **the land is full of bloody crimes**, and **the city** [*Jerusalem*] **is full of violence**.

24 Wherefore [*this is why*] **I will bring the worst of the heathen** [*foreigners*], and **they shall possess their houses:** I will also make **the pomp of the strong to cease**; and **their holy places shall be defiled.**

25 **Destruction cometh**; and **they shall seek peace, and** *there shall be none*.

26 **Mischief** shall come **upon mischief**, and **rumour** shall be **upon rumour**; then shall they seek a **vision of the prophet**; but the **law** shall perish from the priest, and **counsel from the ancients** [*the word of God through prophets, authorized priests and true wisdom from the elders will no longer be available to rebellious Israel*].

27 **The king shall mourn**, and **the prince** [*leader*] **shall be clothed with desolation** [*will be ineffective*], and the hands of **the people** of the land **shall be troubled: I will do unto them** after their way, and **according to their deserts** will I judge them [*they will reap what they have sown*]; and **they shall know that I** *am* **the LORD.**

EZEKIEL 8

Selection: all verses

In chapter 8, Ezekiel sees a vision of the wickedness and evil practices of the Jews in Jerusalem, including idol worship in the temple. This vision came a year and two months after his first vision and call to be a prophet (see Ezekiel 1:1.) Verse 3 tells us that the Spirit transported him to the temple in Jerusalem where he could see for himself the abominable and evil practices of the Jews there. He will see firsthand the idol worship in the temple as well as throughout the whole land.

1 AND it came to pass in the sixth year, in the sixth *month,* in the fifth *day* of the month, *as* **I sat in mine house** [*in Babylon*], and the elders of Judah sat before me, that **the hand of the Lord GOD fell there upon me**.

Verse 2 tells us that in this vision, Ezekiel saw the same being whom he had seen in his first vision (Ezekiel 1:26–27.)

2 **Then I beheld, and lo a likeness** as the appearance of fire: from the appearance of his loins even downward, fire; and from his loins even upward, as the appearance of brightness, as the colour of amber.

3 And he put forth the form of an hand, and took me by a lock of mine head; and **the spirit lifted me up between the earth and the heaven, and brought me in the visions of God to Jerusalem**, to the door of the inner gate that looketh toward the north; **where**

was the seat of the image of jealousy [*an idol which provoked the jealously or anger of the Lord*], which provoketh to jealousy.

4 And, behold, **the glory of the God of Israel** *was* **there**, according to [*just like*] the vision that I saw in the plain [*Ezekiel 3:22*].

5 ¶ **Then said he** [*the Lord*] unto me, Son of man, lift up thine eyes now the way toward the north [*look toward the north*]. So I lifted up mine eyes the way toward the north, and behold northward at the gate of the altar **this image of jealousy** [*this idol that provoked the Lord*] in the entry.

6 **He said** furthermore unto me, **Son of man, seest thou what they do?** *even* **the great abominations that the house of Israel committeth here, that I should go far off from my sanctuary** [*that drive Me far from My temple*]? but turn thee yet again, *and* **thou shalt see greater** [*even worse*] **abominations**.

Next, in verses 7–12, Jehovah shows Ezekiel seventy Jewish leaders (verse 11; likely the Sanhedrin or supreme council of the Jews) engaged in wicked practices in dark, secret places where they think God cannot see them (see verse 12).

7 ¶ And **he brought me to the door of the court**; and when I looked, behold a hole in the wall.

8 Then said he unto me, Son of man, dig now in the wall: and when I had digged in the wall, **behold a door**.

9 And **he said unto me, Go in, and behold** [*see*] **the wicked abominations that they do here**.

10 **So I went in and saw**; and behold every form of creeping things, and abominable beasts, and all the idols of the house of Israel, pourtrayed upon the wall round about [*forbidden things to the Jews, symbolizing the wide range of evil in which these Jewish leaders were involved*].

11 And there stood before them [*the things mentioned in verse 10*] **seventy men of the ancients** [*leaders, priests*] **of the house of Israel**, and in the midst of them stood Jaazaniah [*perhaps the leader of these wicked Jewish priests*] the son of Shaphan, **with every man his censer in his hand; and a thick cloud of incense went up** [*symbolic of their worshipping these forbidden images*].

12 **Then said he** [*the Lord*] unto me [*Ezekiel*], Son of man, **hast thou seen what the ancients of the house of Israel do in the dark,**

every man in the chambers of his imagery? for **they say, The LORD seeth us not**; the LORD hath forsaken the earth.

Imagine Ezekiel's astonishment and terrible disappointment already, and then the Lord tells him verse 13!

13 ¶ He said also unto me, **Turn thee yet again,** *and* **thou shalt see greater abominations** that they do.

14 Then he brought me to the door of the gate of the LORD's house which *was* toward the north; and, behold, **there sat women weeping for Tammuz** [*a form of worshipping this idol representing nature and springtime, which had been imported from Babylon and Phonecia—see J. R. Dummelow, A Commentary on the Holy Bible, pp 497–498*].

15 ¶ Then said he unto me, **Hast thou seen** *this,* **O son of man?** turn thee yet again, *and* **thou shalt see greater abominations than these**.

Next, Ezekiel will see even more of blatant idol worship, namely, sun worship. Notice that these apostate Jews worshiped the sun with their backs toward the temple, depicting their utter rejection of Jehovah.

16 And **he brought me into the inner court of the LORD's house**, and, behold, at the door of the temple of the LORD, between

the porch and the altar [*where, during more righteous times, priests offered prayers with their faces toward the temple*], *were* **about five and twenty men, with their backs toward the temple of the LORD, and their faces toward the east; and they worshipped the sun** toward the east.

17 ¶ Then he said unto me, **Hast thou seen** *this,* **O son of man? Is it a light thing** [*is not this a most serious matter*] to the house of Judah that they commit the abominations which they commit here? for **they have filled the land with violence,** and **have returned to provoke me to anger**: and, **lo, they put the branch to their nose** [*likely meaning that, among other abominations, they were worshipping the sun; sun-worshippers held bunches of twigs from certain trees to their mouths to prevent their breath from contaminating the sun (Dummelow, p. 498)*].

18 **Therefore** [*this is why*] **will I also deal in fury**: mine eye shall not spare, neither will I have pity: and **though they cry in mine ears with a loud voice,** *yet* **will I not hear them**.

EZEKIEL 9

Selection: all verses

The vision continues with preparations for the destruction of the wicked (verses 1–2) and the withdrawing of the Lord from the temple and apostate Israel (verse 3.) However, there is a bit of a bright spot in this chapter, namely that we discover that there are a few righteous Jews among the overwhelming number of wicked and that they will be spared. In this part of the vision, Ezekiel sees these righteous ones marked for protection against the coming destruction (verse 4.)

1 HE cried also in mine ears with a loud voice, saying, **Cause them that have charge over the city to draw near, even every man** *with* **his destroying weapon in his hand** [*perhaps a symbolic depiction of destroying angels; the actual destruction will come within five years from Nebuchadnezzar's army*].

2 And, behold, **six men** [*symbolizing destroying angels*] **came from the way of the higher gate, which lieth toward the north** [*part of the temple compound*], and **every man a slaughter weapon** [*weapon of death*] **in his hand**; and **one man among them** *was* **clothed with linen** [*"linen" symbolizes righteousness in Revelation 19:8*], **with a writer's inkhorn by his side** [*with a writing kit by his side*]: and they went in, and stood beside the brazen altar [*the brass altar in the inner courtyard, just outside the temple*].

3 And **the glory of the God of Israel was gone up** [*withdrawn*] from the cherub, whereupon he was, to the threshold of the house [*the temple*]. **And he** [*the Lord*] **called to the man clothed with linen**, which *had* the writer's inkhorn by his side;

4 **And the LORD said** unto him, **Go** through the midst of the city, **through the midst of Jerusalem, and set a mark upon the foreheads of the men that sigh and that cry for all the abominations that be done** [*the righteous who mourn and weep because of all the wickedness that is being done*] in the midst thereof.

It is helpful to know that in biblical symbolism, "forehead" represents loyalty. For example, in Revelation 13:16–17, the "mark of the beast" in their foreheads symbolizes loyalty to Satan. Thus, the foreheads of the men in verse 4, above, represent loyalty to God.

5 ¶ And **to the others** [*the destroying angels*] **he said** in mine hearing, **Go ye after him** [*follow him*] through the city, **and smite** [*destroy all who have not been marked to be spared*]: **let not your eye spare, neither have ye pity**:

The slaying of little children, in verse 6, next, is likely similar to the deaths of all except Noah's family in the Flood. If only the wicked parents were killed, who would be left to raise and take care of the children? We know that, ultimately, little children are "saved in the celestial kingdom of heaven" (D&C 137:10.)

6 Slay utterly old *and* **young, both maids, and little children, and women**: **but come not near any man upon whom** *is* **the mark**; and **begin at my sanctuary** [*the temple*]. **Then they began at the ancient men** [*the wicked, apostate, Jewish leaders*] **which** *were* **before the house** [*the temple*].

To better understand verse 7, next, it helps to know that touching a human corpse made a person ritually unclean in Jewish culture (Haggai 2:13.) In other words, it defiled the person, who would have to submit to ritual cleansing in order to become clean again. With this in mind, you can see how filling the temple and temple grounds with dead bodies would be a shocking defilement in the eyes of the Jews.

7 And he said unto them [*the destroying angels*], **Defile the house** [*temple*], and **fill the courts** [*the temple grounds*] **with the slain**: go ye forth. And they went forth, and slew in the city.

Ezekiel is overwhelmed with what he is seeing, as shown in verse 8.

8 ¶ And it came to pass, while they were slaying them, and **I was left, that I fell upon my face, and cried, and said, Ah Lord GOD! wilt thou destroy all the residue**

of Israel in thy pouring out of thy fury upon Jerusalem?

In verses 9–10, Jehovah answers Ezekiel's anguished cry, reminding him that these wicked members of the house of Israel have asked for this by their rebellious actions. We would refer to this as the law of justice in action.

9 Then said he [*the Lord*] **unto me, The iniquity of the house of Israel and Judah** *is* **exceeding great**, and **the land is full of blood**, and **the city full of perverseness** [*deliberately deviating from what is good*]: for **they say, The LORD hath forsaken the earth** [*the Lord is not around anymore*], and **the LORD seeth not** [*we are successfully hiding from Him*].

10 And as for me also, mine eye shall not spare, neither will I have pity, *but* **I will recompense their way** [*pay them back for their wickedness*] **upon their head**.

Finally, in verse 11, the servant of the Lord, dressed in linen (verse 2), charged with placing a mark on the foreheads of the righteous, reports in that his mission is completed.

11 And, behold, the man clothed with linen, which *had* **the inkhorn by his side, reported** the matter, saying, **I have done as thou hast commanded me.**

EZEKIEL 10

Selection: all verses

Verse 18 summarizes what is mainly happening in this chapter of the vision, namely, that the glory of the Lord is withdrawing from the once-holy and glorious temple, which has been defiled by the Jews and the whole house of Israel. The temple was once filled with the glory of the Lord (1 Kings 8:10–11.)

The vision given in this chapter is very similar to the first vision given to Ezekiel in chapter 1. You will see many elements that are the same.

We see "cherubim" many times in this chapter. "Cherubim" are apparently an order or rank of angels who serve the Lord in various assignments. We don't know anything more about them, yet. (See Mormon Doctrine, pp 124–125.)

By way of a bit of trivia, "cherubim" is the plural in Hebrew for this class or order of angelic servants of the Lord— "cherub" is the single form in Hebrew. But, as you can see, the translators of our King James version of the English Bible used "cherubims" for the plural.

It may be helpful to know that there were two carved cherubim overlaid with gold positioned on either side of the lid of the Ark of the Covenant in the Holy of Holies of Solomon's Temple. The next several verses appear to be referring to them, thus representing the once-holy temple as the Spirit of the Lord withdraws from it.

In verses 1–7, we see the cherubim instructed to take fiery coals and scatter them over Jerusalem, representing destruction from heaven upon the wicked city.

1 THEN **I looked, and, behold, in the firmament that was above the head of the cherubims** [*in the heavens above the Holy of Holies in the temple*] **there appeared** over them as it were a sapphire stone, as the appearance of the likeness of **a throne**.

2 **And he** [*the Lord*] **spake unto the man clothed with linen**, and said, Go in between the wheels, *even* under the cherub, and **fill thine hand with coals of fire** [*symbolic of destruction from heaven*] from between the cherubims, and **scatter** *them* **over the city**. And he went in in my sight [*as I watched, he did it*].

3 Now **the cherubims stood on the right side of the house** [*the south side of the temple*], when the man went in; and the cloud filled the inner court.

In verse 4, Ezekiel sees the glory of the Lord as it prepares to leave the defiled temple.

4 Then **the glory of the LORD went up** from the cherub, *and stood* over the threshold of the **house** [*the temple*]; and **the house was filled with the cloud** [*symbolizing the presence of God*], and the court was **full of the brightness of the LORD's glory**.

5 And **the sound of the cherubims' wings** was heard *even* to the outer court, **as the voice of the Almighty God when he speaketh** [*can be compared to the "rushing" sound of the Lord's voice in D&C 110:3*].

6 And it came to pass, *that* **when he** [*Jehovah*] **had commanded** the man clothed with linen, **saying, Take fire from between the wheels, from between the cherubims** [*symbolic of fire sent from heaven to destroy the wicked*]; then he went in, and stood beside the wheels.

Perhaps you are noticing that cherubim are very actively involved in this vision in carrying out the will of the Lord. It will be interesting someday to find out more about them.

7 And *one* **cherub stretched forth his hand** from between the cherubims **unto the fire** that *was* between the cherubims, and **took** *thereof* [*took fiery coals*]*,* **and put** *it* **into the hands of** *him that was* **clothed with linen: who took** *it,* **and went out** [*to carry out the destruction of Jerusalem*].

8 ¶ And **there appeared** in the cherubims **the form of a man's hand under their wings** [*remember that "wings" are symbolic of power to move about and act in the service of God—see D&C 77:4*].

In verses 9–22, we see much repetition from Ezekiel's first vision, in chapter 1. We will **bold** the words and phrases that emphasize that the Spirit of the Lord is withdrawing from Jerusalem and the house of Israel in preparation for the coming terrible destruction by the Babylonian armies.

9 And when I looked, behold the four wheels by the cherubims, one wheel by one cherub, and another wheel by another cherub: and the appearance of the wheels *was* as the colour of a beryl stone.

10 And *as for* their appearances, they four had one likeness, as if a wheel had been in the midst of a wheel.

11 When they went, they went upon their four sides; they turned not as they went, but to the place whither the head looked they followed it; they turned not as they went.

12 And their whole body, and their backs, and their hands, and their wings, and the wheels, *were* full of eyes round about, *even* the wheels that they four had.

13 As for the wheels, it was cried unto them in my hearing, O wheel.

14 And every one had four faces: the first face *was* the face of a cherub, and the second face *was*

the face of a man, and the third the face of a lion, and the fourth the face of an eagle.

15 And **the cherubims were lifted up**. This *is* the living creature that I saw by the river of Chebar [*during his first vision—see verses 18 and 22, also Ezekiel 1:1*].

16 And when the cherubims went, the wheels went by them: and when the cherubims lifted up their wings **to mount up from the earth**, the same wheels also turned not from beside them.

17 When they stood, *these* stood; and when **they were lifted up, *these* lifted up themselves *also*:** for the spirit of the living creature *was* in them.

18 Then **the glory of the LORD departed from off the threshold of the house** [*the temple*], and stood over the cherubims.

19 And **the cherubims** lifted up their wings, and **mounted up from the earth** in my sight [*as I watched*]: when they went out, the wheels also *were* beside them, and *every one* stood at the door of the east gate of the LORD's house; and the glory of the God of Israel *was* over them above.

20 This *is* the living creature that I saw under the God of Israel by the river of Chebar; and I knew that they *were* the cherubims.

21 Every one had four faces apiece, and every one four wings; and the likeness of the hands of a man *was* under their wings.

22 And the likeness of their faces *was* the same faces which I saw by the river of Chebar, their appearances and themselves: they went every one straight forward.

EZEKIEL 11

Selection: all verses

As you will see, this chapter has many things going on as Ezekiel's vision comes to a close. First, in verses 1–3, the Spirit takes Ezekiel to the east gate of the Temple and shows him 25 Jewish leaders who have been leading the inhabitants of Jerusalem astray.

1 MOREOVER **the spirit lifted me up, and brought me unto the east gate of the LORD's house**, which looketh eastward: **and behold** at the door of the gate **five and twenty men**; among whom I saw Jaazaniah the son of Azur, and Pelatiah the son of Benaiah, princes [*leaders*] of the people.

2 Then said he unto me, Son of man, **these *are* the men that devise mischief** [*who are causing trou-*

ble], **and give wicked counsel in this city**:

Verse 3 tells us that these wicked leaders are telling the people to ignore the prophets such as Jeremiah, Lehi, Nahum, Habakkuk, and Zephaniah who have warned them to repent or be destroyed.

As you know, two groups of Jews have already been taken captive to Babylon (see heading to Ezekiel in this study guide) and the Jews yet remaining behind in Jerusalem are being given false counsel by their leaders that they are relatively secure in Jerusalem and will not also be destroyed and taken captive. This is contrary to the warnings of their true prophets.

3 **Which say,** *It is* **not near** [*destruction is not coming*]; let us build houses [*don't worry, keep living as usual*]: **this** *city is* **the caldron, and we** *be* **the flesh** [*a reference to cooking meat in a pot; the pot protects the meat from the fire, which would destroy it; in other words, Jerusalem will protect us, despite what the prophets have said and are saying; see verse 11 for more on this*].

4 ¶ **Therefore** prophesy against them, **prophesy, O son of man** [*Ezekiel*].

In verses 5–12, next, Ezekiel is told to prophesy against the false and deceptive counsel of the Jewish leaders.

5 And the **Spirit of the LORD fell upon me, and said unto me, Speak**; Thus saith the LORD; **Thus have ye said, O house of Israel** [*the things in the above verses are what you have been thinking and saying against the true prophets*]: for **I know the things that come into your mind,** *every one of* **them** [*the Lord knows what you are thinking*].

Verse 6, next, explains that the false counsel of the Jewish leaders will make things worse and more people will die as a result.

6 **Ye have multiplied your slain** in this city, and ye have filled the streets thereof with the slain.

7 Therefore thus saith the Lord GOD; Your slain whom ye have laid in the midst of it, they *are* the flesh, and this *city is* the caldron: but **I will bring you forth out of the midst of it** [*you will be taken captive away from Jerusalem*].

8 Ye have feared the sword; and **I will bring a sword upon you, saith the Lord GOD.**

9 And **I will bring you out of the midst thereof** [*Jerusalem*], **and deliver you into the hands of strangers** [*foreigners; the Babylonians*], and will execute judgments [*punishments*] among you.

10 **Ye shall fall by the sword**; I will judge you in the border of Israel; and **ye shall know that I** *am* **the LORD.**

11 **This** *city* **shall not be your caldron, neither shall ye be the flesh in the midst thereof**; *but* I will judge you in the border of Israel:

12 And **ye shall know that I** *am* **the LORD**: **for ye have not walked in my statutes, neither executed my judgments** [*you have not kept my commandments*], **but have done after the manners of the heathen that** *are* **round about you** [*you have adopted pagan worship from the countries around you*].

In verse 13, we feel the anguish that has come over Ezekiel as he continues to witness in vision the terrible destruction of his people. Remember, as was the case with Nephi when he was taken by the Spirit "into an exceedingly high mountain" (1 Nephi 11:1), the Spirit has taken Ezekiel from Babylon to Jerusalem where he is seeing these things first hand.

At the end of verse 13, Ezekiel cries out and asks if Jehovah is going to destroy all of Israel!

13 ¶ **And it came to pass, when** I prophesied, that **Pelatiah** the son of Benaiah [*the wicked Jewish leader mentioned in verse 1*] **died. Then fell I down upon my face**

[*a demonstration of extreme anguish and concern in Jewish culture*], **and** cried with a loud voice, and said, **Ah Lord GOD! wilt thou make a full end of the remnant of Israel?**

Ezekiel's pained question above opens the way for the Lord's answer and a lesson on the eventual last days' gathering of Israel, which is taking place at an accelerated pace right now in our day.

14 Again **the word of the LORD came unto me, saying,**

First, a brief reminder as to why these things are happening to them and a short lesson in agency and accountability.

15 Son of man, **thy brethren,** *even* thy brethren, **the men of thy kindred** [*your people*], **and all the house of Israel wholly,** *are* they unto whom **the inhabitants of Jerusalem have said, Get you far from the LORD** [*your people have followed their leaders in abandoning Jehovah*]: unto us is this land given in possession [*this is our land and nobody is going to take us away from it*].

Starting with verse 16, we see that the Lord still will help His people as much as He can and will ultimately gather Israel.

16 Therefore say, Thus saith the Lord GOD: **Although I have cast them far off among the hea-**

then, and although I have scattered them among the countries, **yet will I be to them as a little sanctuary** in the countries where they shall come [*I will still help them in the countries to which I have scattered them*].

17 Therefore say, Thus saith the Lord GOD; **I will even gather you from the people, and assemble you out of the countries where ye have been scattered**, and **I will give you the land of Israel** [*The day will come that the Jews will return to Jerusalem and the Holy Land*].

Verses 18–20 foretell of a time, yet future, when the Jews, as a people, will turn to Christ, accept the true gospel, and make gospel covenants with Him and live righteously.

18 And **they shall come thither** [*home to Jerusalem*], and **they shall take away all the detestable things** thereof and all the **abominations thereof from thence** [*they will remove all the idols and wicked practices they were involved with formerly*].

19 And **I will give them one heart** [*compare with Moses 7:18*], and **I will put a new spirit within you** [*this happens when we get the Gift of the Holy Ghost and follow it*]; and **I will take the stony heart** [*their unreceptive hearts*] **out of their flesh**, and will give them an heart of

flesh [*a heart that is receptive to truth and righteousness*]:

20 **That they may walk in my statutes** [*laws*], **and keep mine ordinances**, and do them: and **they shall be my people, and I will be their God.**

Just a word to those who refuse to repent and continue going their evil ways.

21 But *as for them* whose heart walketh after the heart of their detestable things and their abominations, **I will recompense their way** [*pay back their evil deeds; punish*] **upon their own heads**, saith the Lord GOD.

In verses 22–23, next, Ezekiel watches the Lord's glory leave the temple and Jerusalem and settle on the Mount of Olives, a prominent hill just east of Jerusalem.

22 ¶ **Then did the cherubims lift up their wings**, and the wheels beside them; and **the glory of the God of Israel** *was* **over them above.**

23 And **the glory of the LORD went up from the midst of the city, and stood upon the mountain which** *is* **on the east side of the city** [*the Mount of Olives*].

Finally, in verses 24–25, the Spirit takes Ezekiel back to his place in

Babylon where he tells his fellow-captives what he saw in his visions.

24 ¶ Afterwards **the spirit took me up, and brought me** in a vision by the Spirit of God **into Chaldea** [*Babylon*], **to them of the captivity** [*the Jewish exiles in Babylonian captivity*]. So **the vision** that I had seen **went up from me** [*the vision closed*].

25 **Then I spake unto them of the captivity all the things that the LORD had shewed me.**

EZEKIEL 12

Selection: all verses

In this chapter, Ezekiel, himself, becomes a visual aid (a sign—see verse 11,) for his fellow captives in Babylon, demonstrating and prophesying the coming capture and exile of the rebellious Jews still in Jerusalem as well as the capture and carrying away into Babylon of their wicked King Zedekiah, king of Judah.

1 **THE word of the LORD also came unto me, saying,**

2 Son of man [*Ezekiel*], **thou dwellest in the midst of a rebellious house** [*the house of Israel, including the Jews in exile in Babylon and those still living in Jerusalem*], **which have eyes to see, and see not** [*they are spiritually blind*]; **they have ears to hear, and hear not** [*they are spiritu-*

ally deaf, refuse to hear God]: for **they** *are* **a rebellious house.**

Next, in verses 3–7, the Lord tells Ezekiel what he should do to demonstrate this prophecy.

3 Therefore, thou son of man, **prepare** thee **stuff for removing** [*gather your things as if you were being taken into exile, representing what is going to happen to the Jews still in Jerusalem*], and **remove by day in their sight** [*let your fellow captives in Babylon see what you are doing*]; and thou shalt **remove from thy place to another place in their sight**: it may be they will consider [*you just might get their attention*], though they *be* a rebellious house.

Notice the typical repetition in verse 4.

4 Then shalt thou **bring forth thy stuff by day in their sight, as stuff for removing**: and thou shalt go forth at even [*evening time*] **in their sight**, as they that go forth into captivity [*symbolizing people going into captivity*].

5 **Dig thou through the wall** [*dig a hole in the wall*] **in their sight**, and **carry out thereby** [*take your stuff through the hole in the wall*].

6 In their sight [*as the people watch*] shalt thou **bear** *it* **upon** *thy* **shoulders** [*put your pack with your stuff on your shoulders*], *and* **carry** *it* **forth**

in the twilight [*in the evening*]: **thou shalt cover thy face, that thou see not the ground**: for **I have set thee** *for* **a sign** unto the house of Israel.

The phrase "cover thy face, that thou see not the ground," in verse 6, above, turns this prophecy into a dual prophecy. Namely, as mentioned above, it is prophesying the captivity of the Jews still in Jerusalem (they will be taken captive into Babylon, as seen in vision by Lehi (1 Nephi 10:3, 2 Nephi 1–4), but now it is also prophesying that King Zedekiah will be captured by Nebuchadnezzar's army and will be blinded (after he is forced to watch the killing of all his sons but Mulek—2 Kings 25:7). Thus, being blind, he will not see the "ground" of Babylon when he is taken there as a prisoner.

Next, Ezekiel does what he was commanded to do.

7 And **I did so as I was commanded**: I **brought forth my stuff by day, as stuff for captivity**, and in the even **I digged through the wall** with mine hand; **I brought** *it* **forth in the twilight,** *and* **I bare** *it* **upon** *my* **shoulder in their sight.**

8 ¶ And **in the morning came the word of the LORD unto me,** saying,

Next, just as the Lord said would happen, Ezekiel's fellow exiles were very curious about Ezekiel's strange behaviors and had asked him for an explanation.

9 Son of man, hath not the house of Israel, the rebellious house, said unto thee, **What doest thou?**

10 **Say** thou **unto them,** Thus saith the Lord GOD; **This burden** [*prophecy of gloom and doom*] *concerneth* [*has to do with*] **the prince** [*King Zedekiah*] **in Jerusalem, and all the house of Israel** that *are* **among them** [*the Jews in Jerusalem*].

11 Say, **I** *am* **your sign: like as I have done, so shall it be done unto them** [*what I did is a sign of what is going to happen to them*]: **they shall remove** [*leave Jerusalem*] *and* **go into captivity**.

12 And **the prince** [*King Zedekiah*] that *is* among them **shall bear upon** *his* **shoulder in the twilight** [*will take his stuff and escape from Jerusalem in the evening*], **and shall go forth: they shall dig through the wall to carry out thereby: he shall cover his face, that he see not the ground with** *his* **eyes** [*he will be captured and blinded and will, thus, not see Babylon when he gets there*].

As prophesied in verse 12, above, and verse 13, below, in 597 BC, King Nebuchadnezzar of Babylon besieged and captured Jerusalem. Zedekiah with some of his fighting men fled by night through the Dung Gate in the wall of Jerusalem and toward the Jordan River. However, they were soon captured in the plains of Jericho by the Babylonians. He was blinded, and taken in chains as a prisoner to Babylon.

13 **My net also will I spread upon him**, and he shall be taken in my snare: and **I will bring him to Babylon** *to* the land of the Chaldeans [*citizens of part of Babylon*]; **yet shall he not see it** [*because his eyes will have been put out by his captors*], though **he shall die there** [*he will spend the rest of his life in Babylon*].

14 And **I will scatter toward every wind** [*the scattering of Israel*] **all that** *are* **about him to** help him, and all his bands; and I will draw out the sword after them [*great destructions will accompany the scattering of Israel*].

15 And **they shall know that I** *am* **the LORD, when I shall scatter them among the nations, and disperse them in the countries**.

In verse 16, next, the Lord prophesies that a remnant of Israel will remain. During their long dispersion among all nations, they have intermingled and multiplied. Thus, the blood of Israel is in most of the inhabitants of the earth, today, and we are following our prophetic leadership now in the last days' gathering of Israel, on both sides of the veil.

16 But **I will leave a few** men of them from the sword, from the famine, and from the pestilence; that they may declare all their abominations among the heathen whither they come; and they shall know that I *am* the LORD.

In verses 17–25, next, we see that the Jews living now in captivity in Babylon are deriding and mocking all the prophecies that have been given about the captivity and carrying away to Babylon of their fellow Jews in Jerusalem. These Jews in exile have even developed a saying (the "proverb" mentioned in verse 22,) namely, in effect, "the days keep coming and going and none of the prophecies and visions about the destruction and captivity of those still in Jerusalem have happened. So, it is obvious that they are false prophecies."

The Lord has something to say about this and will have Ezekiel act it out in front of his fellow exiles, starting with verse 18. In effect, the message is that the Jews in Jerusalem had better start eating their meals with fear and great anxiety in anticipation of the fulfillment of these prophecies. Ezekiel is instructed to mimic this anxiety.

17 ¶ Moreover **the word of the LORD came to me, saying,**

18 Son of man, **eat thy bread with quaking**, and **drink thy**

water with trembling and with carefulness [*anxiety*];

19 And **say unto the** people of the land, Thus saith the Lord GOD of the **inhabitants of Jerusalem, *and* of the land of Israel**; They shall **eat their bread with carefulness, and drink their water with astonishment**, that **her land** may be **desolate** from all that is therein, **because of the violence** [*murders, robberies, and combined wickedness*] **of all them that dwell therein.**

20 And **the cities that are inhabited shall be laid waste, and the land shall be desolate**; and **ye shall know that I *am* the LORD.**

21 ¶ And the word of the LORD came unto me, saying,

22 Son of man, **what *is* that proverb** [*saying*] ***that* ye have in the land of Israel**, saying, **The days are prolonged, and every vision faileth** [*none of the prophecies about us are coming to pass*]?

23 **Tell them** therefore, Thus saith the Lord GOD; **I will make this proverb to cease** [*I will put an end to this saying*]**, and they shall no more use it as a proverb in Israel; but say unto them, The days are at hand** [*the prophecies are about to be fulfilled*]**, and the effect of every vision** [*every vision will be fulfilled*].

Next, in verse 24, the Lord says He will put an end to the false visions and false counsel given by false prophets and false priests. These apostate leaders have told the people that the prophecies of Jerusalem's downfall by Jeremiah, Lehi, and other prophets are false and to ignore them.

24 For **there shall be no more any vain** [*false*] **vision nor flattering divination** [*saying what people want to hear*] within the house of Israel.

25 For **I *am* the LORD**: I will speak, and **the word that I shall speak shall come to pass**; it shall be no more prolonged [*time is running out*]: for **in your days**, O rebellious house, **will I say the word, and will perform it**, saith the Lord GOD.

26 ¶ **Again the word of the LORD came to me, saying,**

27 Son of man, behold, ***they of* the house of Israel** [*these wicked, rebellious Israelites*] **say, The vision that he seeth *is* for many days *to come*** [*these prophecies are for far in the future*]**, and he prophesieth of the times *that are* far off** [*far off in the future, so don't worry about them*].

Finally, the Lord tells Ezekiel to tell these people that the Lord says that He will no longer put off fulfilling these prophecies of destruction and captivity for the remaining Jews in Jerusalem and the surrounding area.

28 Therefore say unto them, Thus saith the Lord GOD; **There shall none of my words be prolonged any more**, but the word which I have spoken shall be done [*fulfilled*], saith the Lord GOD.

EZEKIEL 13

Selection: all verses

The heading to chapter 13 in your copy of the Latter-day Saint English-speaking Bible pretty much sums up the contents of this chapter. It reads:

"Ezekiel reproves false prophets, both male and female, who speak lies and to whom God hath not spoken."

Did you notice that there can be both male and female false prophets? "Prophets" don't necessarily have to be dressed in long robes and look like prophets. They can be anyone in society who teaches, advises, counsels, demonstrates, etc., anything that leads others to leave the covenant path and ignore or go against the words of true prophets.

This chapter has much the same message as Jeremiah 23:9–40.

1 AND **the word of the LORD came unto me, saying,**

2 Son of man [*Ezekiel*], **prophesy against the prophets** [*false prophets*] **of Israel** that prophesy, and say thou unto them **that**

prophesy out of their own hearts [*who teach their own ideas as true*], Hear ye the word of the LORD;

3 Thus saith the Lord GOD; **Woe unto the foolish prophets, that follow their own spirit, and have seen nothing** [*who teach their own beliefs and have had no visions from God*]!

4 O Israel, **thy prophets are like the foxes in the deserts** [*running to and fro to protect themselves; they are predators, preying upon the rebellious people of Israel*].

Next, Ezekiel exposes these false prophets as not having any intentions to protect the people and lead them to the Lord nor to prepare them to fight the battle against their enemies, including sin and evil as well as the coming Babylonian army.

5 **Ye have not gone up into the gaps** [*you have not gone up to the breaks in the wall to repair them*], **neither made up the hedge** [*fixed the broken places in the wall*] **for the house of Israel to stand in the battle in the day of the LORD** [*in the coming days of trial*].

6 They have seen vanity and lying divination, **saying, The LORD saith** [*they tell the people that they speak for the Lord*]: and **the LORD hath not sent them** [*but they do not represent the Lord*]: and **they have made *others* to hope** [*they*

have falsely preached peace and that Babylon will not successfully attack them] **that they would confirm the word** [they say that their words will be fulfilled].

In verses 7–9, next, the Lord, through Ezekiel, very clearly exposes these false prophets as liars and deceivers.

7 **Have ye not seen a vain vision**, and **have ye not spoken a lying divination**, whereas **ye say, The LORD saith** it [you claim to speak for the Lord]; albeit **I have not spoken** [however, I didn't speak to you]?

8 **Therefore thus saith the Lord GOD**; **Because ye have spoken vanity** [false words], **and seen lies** [visions that contain lies and deception], therefore, behold, **I** am **against you, saith the Lord GOD**.

The "lies" given in visions in verse 8, above, lead us to believe that Satan has been giving these false prophets visions containing lies by which he successfully deceives the people.

Verse 9, next, contains several ways in which the Lord says, in effect, that these Israelites will no longer be His people.

9 And mine hand [punishments] shall be upon the prophets that see vanity, and that divine lies: **they shall not be in the assembly of my people, neither shall they be written in the writing** [on the records] **of the house of Israel, neither shall they enter into the land of Israel** [can be symbolic of entering heaven, i.e., "the promised land"]; and ye shall know that I am the Lord GOD.

In verses 10–16, next, the Lord explains why they will no longer be His people. (Of course, repentance is still available, but these people don't seem to be interested in it.)

10 ¶ **Because**, even because **they** [the false prophets] **have seduced** [led astray] **my people, saying, Peace; and** there was **no peace** [these false prophets told the people that the future held peace for them, whereas, Jeremiah and other true prophets warned of death and destruction, captivity and exile, if they did not repent]; and one built up a wall, and, lo, others daubed it with untempered morter:

The "untempered morter" at the end of verse 10, above, and in verses 11–15, next, illustrates how ineffectively these false prophets are preparing these foolish people for the coming depredations and troubles. Their counsel is like repairing the walls of Jerusalem with thin mortar without lime in it. It won't do the job. It won't last.

11 **Say unto them which daub** it [apply morter to the wall] with untempered morter, that **it shall fall** [it won't do the job]: there shall be an overflowing shower; and ye, O great hailstones, shall fall; and

a stormy wind shall rend *it* [*tear it apart*].

12 Lo, **when the wall is fallen, shall it not be said unto you, Where** *is* **the daubing where-with ye have daubed** *it?*

13 Therefore **thus saith the Lord GOD; I will even rend** *it* with a stormy wind in my fury; and there shall be an overflowing shower in mine anger, and great hailstones in *my* fury to consume *it.*

14 **So will I break down the wall that ye have daubed with un-tempered** *morter,* **and bring it down to the ground**, so that the foundation thereof shall be dis-covered, and it shall fall, and **ye shall be consumed in the midst thereof**: and ye shall know that I *am* the LORD.

15 **Thus will I accomplish my wrath upon the wall, and upon them that have daubed it** with untempered *morter,* and will say unto you, **The wall** *is* no *more,* **neither they** [*the false prophets*] **that daubed it;**

16 *To wit* [*in other words*]**, the** [*false*] **prophets of Israel** which proph-esy concerning Jerusalem, and **which see visions of peace for her, and** *there is* **no peace**, saith the Lord GOD.

Next, Jehovah commands Ezekiel to prophesy against the women of Israel who claim to be prophetesses and workers in sorcery and the oc-cult and, like the men mentioned in the previous verses, are leading the people away from the messages and words of God's true prophets.

17 ¶ Likewise, thou son of man, **set thy face against** [*prophesy against*] **the daughters of thy peo-ple, which prophesy out of their own heart**; and **prophesy thou against them,**

"Pillows, "armholes," and "ker-chiefs," in verse 18, next, seem to refer to so-called "magic charms" used by the sorceresses and false prophetesses among these apos-tate Israelites as they drew attention to themselves and led people away from Jehovah.

18 **And say**, Thus saith the Lord GOD; **Woe to the** *women* **that** sew pillows [*bands*] to all arm-holes, and make kerchiefs upon the head of every stature **to hunt souls! Will ye hunt the souls of my people, and will ye save the souls alive** *that come* **unto you?**

19 And **will ye pollute me among my people** for handfuls of barley and for pieces of bread, to slay the souls that should not die, and to save the souls alive that should not live, **by your lying to my people that hear** *your* **lies?**

20 Wherefore thus saith the Lord GOD; Behold, **I am against your pillows, wherewith ye there hunt the souls** to make *them* fly, and I will tear them from your arms, and will let the souls go, *even* the souls that ye hunt to make *them* fly.

21 **Your kerchiefs also will I tear, and deliver my people out of your hand**, and they shall be no more in your hand to be hunted; and ye shall know that I *am* the LORD.

22 **Because with lies ye have made the heart of the righteous sad,** whom I have not made sad; **and strengthened the hands of the wicked, that he should not return from his wicked way** [*making him not want to repent*], **by promising him life** [*by promising him salvation if he follows you*]:

23 **Therefore ye shall see no more vanity, nor divine divinations: for I will deliver my people out of your hand**: and ye shall know that I *am* the LORD.

EZEKIEL 14

Selection: all verses

In this chapter, some of the leaders of the Jews in exile come to meet with Ezekiel. These apostate elders were involved with idol worship and getting guidance from mystics and dark sources rather than from the Lord. In verses 3–5, they are severely rebuked by the Lord.

Then, in verses 6–11, the whole house of Israel, including the Jews, is invited to repent and told why they need to repent.

In verses 12–21, the Lord emphasizes how wicked these people are by telling them that even if Noah, Daniel, and Job were to call them to repentance, they would not listen.

Finally, in verses 22–23, Ezekiel prophesies that despite the dire destruction that the Lord is going to pour out upon these wicked and deserving members of the house of Israel, there will be a remnant left, and this fact will be a comfort to those who will not remain.

1 **THEN came certain of the elders of Israel unto me, and sat before me.**

2 And **the word of the LORD came unto me, saying,**

3 Son of man [*Ezekiel*], **these men have set up their idols in their heart** [*these leaders of the Jews in exile are idol worshipers*], and **put the stumblingblock of their iniquity before their face** [*and show them why the Lord is not listening to them, namely, their wickedness has become their self-imposed stumblingblock between them and the Lord*]: **should I be enquired of at all by them** [*should I, the Lord, let them talk to me at all*]?

In verse 4, the Lord basically says that He is going to answer these wicked leaders Himself, with their extreme wickedness in mind, who have come to the Prophet.

4 Therefore **speak unto them,** and say unto them, **Thus saith the Lord GOD; Every man of the house of Israel that** setteth up his idols in his heart, and putteth the stumblingblock of his iniquity before his face, and **cometh to the prophet** [*Ezekiel*]; **I the LORD will answer him that cometh according to the multitude of his idols;**

5 **That I may take the house of Israel in their own heart** [*their own evil hearts will trap them*], **because they are all estranged** [*separated*] **from me through their idols.**

> Next, in verses 6–11, the Lord invites them to repent, even though they are so far gone spiritually. And, He points out their sins and what they need to repent of.

6 ¶ Therefore say unto the house of Israel, Thus saith the Lord GOD; **Repent, and turn** *yourselves* **from your idols; and turn away your faces from all your abominations** [*sins and extreme wickedness, rebellion against God*].

7 **For every one of the house of Israel, or of the stranger that sojourneth** [*foreigners who live among the Jews*] **in Israel,** which separateth himself from me, and setteth up his idols in his heart, and putteth the stumblingblock of his iniquity before his face, and cometh to a prophet to enquire of him concerning me; **I the LORD will answer him by myself**:

Have you noticed how often the Lord uses the word "heart" in these verses? "Heart" generally refers to the center of feelings and loyalty, the main determiner of actions and behavior, as used in the scriptures.

Also, have you noticed that Ezekiel uses the terms "Jews" and "Israel" or "house of Israel" pretty much interchangeably? If you don't realize this, it might lead you to try to figure out what the difference is, and that would probably be an unsuccessful use of your time and energy.

8 **And I will set my face against** [*oppose*] **that man, and will make him a sign and a proverb** [*cause him to be mocked and despised by others*], and **I will cut him off from the midst of my people**; and **ye shall know that I** *am* **LORD.**

> We really need the help of the JST (Joseph Smith Translation of the Bible) for verse 9, next. Read it first, and then see what the JST does as we quote it after verse 9.

9 And if the prophet be deceived when he hath spoken a thing, **I the LORD have deceived that prophet**, and I will stretch out my hand upon him, and will destroy him from the midst of my people Israel.

JST Ezekiel 14:9

And if the prophet be deceived when he hath spoken a thing, **I the Lord have not deceived that prophet**; therefore I will stretch out my hand upon him, and will destroy him from the midst of my people Israel.

This is a reminder that the Lord will not let our Prophet lead us astray.

10 And **they shall bear the punishment of their iniquity: the punishment of the prophet** [*if he were to attempt to lead the people astray*] **shall be even as the punishment of him** [*the wicked Jewish Elders in verse 1*] **that seeketh *unto him;***

In verse 11, next, the Lord gives a brief, very clear statement on what repentance can do for us.

11 **That the house of Israel may go no more astray from me**, neither be polluted any more with all their transgressions; **but that they may be my people, and I may be their God**, saith the Lord GOD.

In verses 12–21, we see just how wicked these apostate Israelites have become.

12 ¶ **The word of the LORD came again to me, saying,**

13 Son of man, **when the land sinneth against me by trespassing grievously, then will I stretch out mine hand upon it**, and **will break the staff of the bread** [*stop the supply of food*] thereof, and **will send famine** upon it, and **will cut off man and beast** from it [*will kill men and animals*]:

14 **Though these three men, Noah, Daniel, and Job, were in it, they should deliver *but* their own souls by their righteousness** [*even if Noah, Daniel, and Job were among these*

people, they would be the only ones saved*], saith the Lord GOD.

15 ¶ **If I cause noisome** [*wild*] **beasts to pass through the land, and they spoil** [*ruin, devastate*] **it**, so that it be desolate, that no man may pass through because of the beasts:

16 *Though* **these three men** [*Noah, Daniel, and Job*] *were* **in it**, *as* I live, saith the Lord GOD, they shall deliver neither sons nor daughters; **they only shall be delivered**, but the land shall be desolate.

17 ¶ **Or** *if* **I bring a sword upon that land** [*if I bring enemies armies*], and say, Sword, go through the land; so that I cut off man and beast from it:

18 **Though these three men** *were* **in it**, *as* I live, saith the Lord GOD, they shall deliver neither sons nor daughters, but **they only shall be delivered** [*saved*] themselves.

Notice, as previously mentioned, we are seeing a lot of repetition for emphasis, which is typical of Old Testament prophets such as Isaiah, Ezekiel and others.

19 ¶ **Or** *if* **I send a pestilence** [*disease, natural disasters, etc.*] into that land, and pour out my fury upon it in blood, to cut off from it man and beast:

20 **Though Noah, Daniel, and Job,** *were* **in it**, *as* I live, saith the Lord GOD, **they shall deliver** [*save*] **neither son nor daughter** [*the children*

of these wicked Israelites]; **they shall** *but* **deliver their own souls by their righteousness.**

21 For thus saith the Lord GOD; How much more **when I send my four sore** [*devastating*] **judgments** [*punishments*] upon Jerusalem, the **sword**, and the **famine**, and the **noisome beast**, and the **pestilence**, to cut off from it man and beast?

22 ¶ **Yet, behold, therein shall be left a remnant** [*some survivors*] that shall be brought forth, *both* sons and daughters: behold, they shall come forth unto you, and **ye shall see their way and their doings**: and ye shall be comforted concerning the evil that I have brought upon Jerusalem, *even* concerning all that I have brought upon it.

23 And **they shall comfort you**, when ye see their ways and their doings: and **ye shall know that I have not done without cause all that I have done in it** [*you will know that I, the Lord, am justified in what I did to wicked and rebellious Israel*], saith the Lord GOD.

EZEKIEL 15

Selection: all verses

In this chapter, Jerusalem is compared to a useless grape vine in the Lord's vineyard. It was set up by the Lord to produce good grapes (righteous, covenant people) but is not doing it. Thus, it is now useless, good for nothing but to be cast in the fire and burned. Isaiah used a similar parable of a vineyard in

Isaiah 5:1–25. Parts of Jacob, chapter 5, have similar elements, where non-productive branches are pruned off of the olive trees and cast into the fire.

In verses 2–5, the Lord points out that non-productive grape vine is basically useless as wood, except as firewood and, in fact, not very good for that.

1 AND **the word of the LORD came unto me, saying,**

2 Son of man, **What is the vine tree more than any tree,** *or than* **a branch which is among the trees of the forest** [*what good is old grape vine wood*]?

3 **Shall wood be taken thereof to do any work** [*can it be used for any practical purpose*]? **or will** *men* **take a pin of it to hang any vessel thereon** [*can you even use it to hang a pan on*]?

4 Behold, **it is cast into the fire for fuel**; the fire devoureth both the ends of it, and the midst of it is burned. **Is it meet for** *any* **work** [*is it good for anything*]?

5 Behold, **when it was whole** [*before it was burned*], **it was meet for no work** [*it was good for nothing*]: how much less shall it be meet yet for *any* work, when the fire hath devoured it, and it is burned?

In verses 6–8, next, the Lord prophesies that His non-productive covenant people, like useless grape vines, will be destroyed and burned. This can even foreshadow the burning of the wicked at the second coming of Christ.

6 ¶ Therefore thus saith the Lord GOD; **As the vine tree among the trees of the forest** [*just like useless, non-productive grape vines*], **which I have given to the fire for fuel, so will I give the inhabitants of Jerusalem**.

7 And **I will set my face against them; they shall go out from** [*escape from*] **one fire, and *another* fire shall devour them** [*they can't escape from the punishments of God*]; **and ye shall know that I *am* the LORD, when I set my face against them** [*punish them*].

8 And **I will make the land desolate**, because they have committed a trespass [*broken the commandments*], saith the Lord GOD.

EZEKIEL 16

Selection: all verses

Chapter 16 contains a scathing rebuke of the people of Jerusalem and Judah who were participating in wide-spread idol worship, rampant sexual immorality and the sacrificing of children to their gods, including a fire god.

You will see that the description of these vile sins is quite detailed and leaves little to the imagination.

It is helpful to know that there is also much symbolism in what Ezekiel teaches here. For example, the relationship of Jehovah with Israel is compared to a covenant marriage, where Jehovah is the groom and Israel is the bride. Lit-eral adultery, sexual promiscuity, and idol worship among these people symbolically represents "stepping out on God," in other words, infidelity to the Lord, breaking the covenants of marriage where Jehovah is the husband and Judah the wife.

Symbolically, in this sense, when we make covenants with the Lord, such as baptism and temple covenants, He is the groom or husband and we are the bride or the wife. Revelation 21:2 contains such symbolism. We will include the heading to this chapter in our Bible, which succinctly describes the message from the Lord to the inhabitants of Jerusalem and the surrounding area.

"Jerusalem has become as a harlot [*prostitute*]*, reveling in her idols and worshipping false gods—She has partaken of all the sins of Egypt and the nations round about, and is rejected—Yet in the last days the Lord will again establish his covenant with her."*

You will see much of repetition for emphasis and clarification throughout chapter 16. Remember, as mentioned previously, repetition is commonly used by ancient prophets as a teaching tool.

1 **AGAIN the word of the LORD came unto me** [*Ezekiel*]**, saying,**

2 Son of man, **cause Jerusalem to know her abominations** [*clearly point out the people's sins to them*],

> Literally, the Jews, the Israelites, descend from Abraham, through Isaac, Jacob and Jacob's twelve sons. Thus, they are God's covenant people.

Symbolically, in verse 3, their spiritual origins are no longer from God, rather from the surrounding heathen nations, in other words, they have adopted pagan worship practices that go along with their idol worship.

3 And say, Thus saith the Lord GOD unto Jerusalem; **Thy birth and thy nativity** *is* **of the land of Canaan** [*your spiritual origins now come from surrounding heathen practices; you now pray to and worship idols rather than Jehovah*]; **thy father** *was* **an Amorite** [*a Canaanitish tribe; in other words, your spiritual father is no longer Jehovah*], and **thy mother an Hittite** [*a Canaanitish tribe; you have abandoned your spiritual heritage as the covenant people of the Lord*].

4 And *as for* **thy nativity** [*your birth*], **in the day thou wast born thy navel was not cut** [*symbolically, your umbilical cord was not cut so that you are still receiving "nourishment" from your heathen worship rather than from God*], **neither wast thou washed in water** [*cleansed from corruption; can be a reference to baptism*] to supple *thee;* **thou wast not salted** at all [*rubbed with salt, according to Jewish cultural practices of cleansing from corruption*], **nor swaddled** at all [*not wrapped in swaddling clothes, rather left naked and exposed to the wickedness of surrounding pagan cultures*].

5 **None eye pitied thee, to do any of these unto thee** [*the practices mentioned in verse 4, above*], **to have compassion upon thee**; but thou

wast cast out in the open field, to the lothing of thy person, in the day that thou wast born [*having abandoned the Lord, you have left yourselves exposed to all the evils and wiles of the devil and his followers*].

Starting with verse 6 and going through verse 14, the Lord uses an allegory to show how He took Israel as He found her and tenderly cleansed her from her spiritually corrupted birth and raised her to be a faithful bride, so to speak, as His covenant people.

6 ¶ And **when I passed by thee, and saw thee polluted** in thine own blood, I said unto thee *when thou wast* in thy blood, **Live** [*come unto Me and live the covenant life*]; yea, I said unto thee *when thou wast* in thy blood, **Live**.

7 **I have caused thee to multiply** as the bud [*plant*] of the field, and **thou hast increased and waxen** [*grown*] **great**, and thou art come to excellent ornaments: *thy* **breasts are fashioned, and thine hair is grown** [*you have grown up and matured*], **whereas thou** *wast* **naked and bare** [*before I, the Lord, took you and nurtured you*].

8 Now when I passed by thee, and looked upon thee, behold, **thy time** *was* **the time of love** [*you had grown up and it was time for you to be My covenant wife*]; and **I spread my skirt** [*robe*] **over thee** [*took you in as My bride; we see this with Ruth and Boaz in Ruth 3:9*], and **covered thy nakedness** [*protected you*]: yea, **I sware**

unto thee [*made a covenant*], **and entered into a covenant with thee**, saith the Lord GOD, **and thou becamest mine** [*I became your God and you became My people*].

9 **Then washed I thee with water** [*symbolic of baptism, being cleansed from sin*]; yea, **I throughly washed away thy blood** [*sins*] from thee, **and I anointed thee with oil** [*preparation for coming blessings, opportunities, and responsibilities as God's covenant people*].

> Verses 10–14 can symbolize the wonderful blessings and spiritual prosperity of the righteous who strive to stay on the covenant path.

10 **I clothed thee** also with broidered work, and shod thee with badgers' skin, and I girded thee about with fine linen [*can be symbolic of righteousness—see Revelation 19:8*], and I covered thee with silk.

11 **I decked thee** also with ornaments, and I put bracelets upon thy hands, and a chain on thy neck.

12 And **I put** a jewel on thy forehead, and earrings in thine ears, and a beautiful crown upon thine head.

13 **Thus wast thou decked** with gold and silver; and thy raiment *was* of fine linen, and silk, and broidered work; **thou didst eat fine flour, and honey, and oil**: and thou wast exceeding beautiful, and **thou didst prosper into a kingdom**.

14 And **thy renown went forth** [*you became famous*] among the heathen for thy beauty: for it *was* perfect through my comeliness [*splendor*], which I had put upon thee, saith the Lord GOD.

> From verse 15 through verse 59, we watch with sadness, even abhorrence, as the "covenant wife" (the Lords' covenant people, Jerusalem, Judah, Israel), becomes prideful and lusts after the other gods, idols, sexual immorality, perversions, passions, and corrupt practices of the heathens around them, thus deserting Jehovah and the covenant path.

15 ¶ But **thou didst trust in thine own beauty, and playedst the harlot** [*became a prostitute; symbolic of "stepping out on God," in other words, infidelity, and becoming involved with other gods, idols, etc.*] because of thy renown, and **pouredst out thy fornications** [*sexual involvement*] **on every one that passed by**; his it was [*your beauty became his*].

16 And of thy garments thou didst take, and deckedst thy high places with divers colours, **and playedst the harlot** thereupon: *the like things* shall not come, neither shall it be *so* [*you should not have done these things*].

17 Thou hast also taken thy fair jewels of my gold and of my silver, which I had given thee, and madest to thyself images of men, **and didst commit whoredom** [*sexual immorality*] **with them**,

Verses 18–19 show how those involved in sexual immorality entrapped others to join them in their sexual exploits, symbolic of how the Lord's covenant people have deserted Him and used the prosperity He blessed them with to enhance their opportunities for their sexual exploits.

18 And **tookest thy broidered garments, and coveredst them** [*decorated your lairs for sexual encounters*]: and thou hast set mine oil and mine incense before them.

19 **My meat** [*food*] **also which I gave thee**, fine flour, and oil, and honey, *wherewith* I fed thee, **thou hast even set it before them** [*your lovers*] for a sweet savour [*to entice them*]: and *thus* it was, saith the Lord GOD.

Next, in verses 20–21, Ezekiel points out the practice of sacrificing their children to idols, a common practice among the pagans around them.

20 Moreover [*in addition*] **thou hast taken thy sons and thy daughters**, whom thou hast borne unto me [*who were supposed to be dedicated to Me*], **and these hast thou sacrificed unto them** [*your idols*] to be devoured. *Is this* of thy whoredoms a small matter [*isn't this even worse than your sexual immorality?*],

21 That **thou hast slain my children**, and delivered them to cause them to pass through *the fire* for them [*a pagan fire god used for burning children in his fire-pit stomach as*

sacrifices—see "Molech," in the Bible Dictionary]?

22 And in all thine abominations and thy whoredoms **thou hast not remembered the days of thy youth**, when thou wast naked and bare, *and* wast polluted in thy blood [*you haven't remembered what I, the Lord, did for you when you were so needy*].

Starting with verse 23, the Lord basically says, "As if your past wickedness weren't enough, you went right on with more and more of it!!!

23 And it came to pass **after all thy wickedness**, (woe, woe unto thee! saith the Lord GOD [*a warning that great trouble is coming*];)

24 *That* **thou hast also built unto thee an eminent place, and hast made thee an high place** [*a place for worshiping idols*] **in every street** [*you have made idol worship shrines in every street*].

25 **Thou hast built thy high place at every head of the way** [*street*], and **hast made thy beauty to be abhorred** [*abused your beauty*], and **hast opened thy feet to every one that passed by** [*invited every passerby to commit adultery with you*], and multiplied thy whoredoms.

26 **Thou hast also committed fornication with the Egyptians** thy neighbours [*you have adopted the false religions of Egypt*], great of flesh [*who love the sins of the flesh*]; and hast increased [*added to*] thy whoredoms, **to provoke me to anger**.

In verse 27, Ezekiel prophesies of coming famine and subjection to enemies.

Remember that these verses contain much of dual meaning. First, symbolism pointing out that Israel has broken their covenants with Jehovah and embraced the false religions and practices of pagan nations far and near. And second, literal depiction of the debauchery and wickedness of the vast majority of the Jews of the time as they have given themselves over to idol worship, rampant sexual immorality, and human sacrifice, especially their own children.

27 Behold, therefore **I have stretched out my hand over thee, and have diminished thine ordinary** *food* [*caused famine*], **and delivered thee unto** the will of them that hate thee, **the daughters of the Philistines, which are ashamed of thy lewd way** [*embarrassed by your open sexual immorality*].

28 **Thou hast played the whore also with the Assyrians, because thou wast unsatiable** [*your physical appetites could not be satisfied*]; yea, thou hast played the harlot with them, and yet **couldest not be satisfied**.

29 **Thou hast moreover multiplied thy fornication in the land of Canaan unto Chaldea** [*all the way from Jerusalem (in the original land of Canaan)] to Babylon*]; and **yet thou wast not satisfied herewith.**

30 **How weak is thine heart** [*how weak-willed you are*], saith the Lord GOD, **seeing thou doest all these** *things,* the work of an imperious [*brazen*] whorish woman;

31 **In that thou buildest thine eminent place** in the head of every way, and makest **thine high place in every street** [*places for worshiping idols*]; **and hast not been as an harlot, in that thou scornest hire** [*in that you were not like a normal prostitute, refusing payment for your acts*];

It helps to know that prostitution and sexual immorality was often part of idol worship. It was common to use groves of trees for such involvements. Thus, they often made mounds or hills where trees could be planted to afford some privacy. The "high place" in verse 31, above, reflects this.

32 ***But as*** **a wife that committeth adultery** [*the covenant "wife," is being unfaithful to her "Husband," the Lord*], *which* **taketh strangers** [*idols*] **instead of her husband!**

33 **They give gifts to all whores** [*pay for the prostitutes' services*]: **but thou** [*Jerusalem, Israel*] **givest thy gifts to all thy lovers** [*the idols, false gods*], **and hirest them** [*you give gifts to your idols, which is just backwards from normal prostitution*], that they may come unto thee on every side for thy whoredom [*infidelity to God*].

Verse 34 basically repeats what was said in verses 32–33, above.

34 And **the contrary is in thee from** *other* **women in thy whoredoms** [*you are different from other prostitutes*],

whereas none followeth thee to commit whoredoms [*your idols do not chase after you for your favors*]: **and in that thou givest a reward, and no reward is given unto thee, therefore thou art contrary** [*you are just the opposite*].

In verses 35–43, the basic message is that the people of Judah, Israel, have sunk so far into idol worship and accompanying sexual immorality, along with child sacrifice, that their coming punishments from the Lord should be no surprise to them. And, the Lord details what these punishments will be.

35 ¶ **Wherefore, O harlot, hear the word of the LORD:**

36 Thus saith the Lord GOD; **Because thy filthiness was poured out, and thy nakedness discovered through thy whoredoms with thy lovers**, and with all **the idols** of thy abominations, **and by the blood of thy children**, which thou didst give unto them [*sacrificing children to idols*];

37 Behold, **therefore I will gather all thy lovers** [*both idols and actual partners in sexual immorality*], with whom thou hast taken pleasure, and all *them* that thou hast loved, with all *them* that thou hast hated; **I will even gather them round about against thee**, and will discover [*expose*] thy nakedness unto them, that they may see all thy nakedness [*you and your wickedness will be completely exposed to all around you*].

38 And **I will judge thee, as women that break wedlock** [*who are unfaithful to their husbands*] **and shed blood** [*and who commit murder*] **are judged**; and I will give thee blood in fury and jealousy.

Next, in verses 39–41, Ezekiel prophesies that the non-Israelite nations, whom the unfaithful Jews joined in pagan idol worship, etc., will turn against these wicked covenant people of the Lord and devastate them.

39 And **I will also give thee into their hand**, and they shall throw down thine eminent place, and shall break down thy high places: they shall strip thee also of thy clothes, and shall take thy fair jewels, **and leave thee naked and bare**.

40 **They shall also bring up a company against thee**, and they shall stone thee with stones, and thrust thee through with their swords.

41 And **they shall burn thine houses with fire**, and execute judgments upon thee in the sight of many women: and **I will cause thee to cease from playing the harlot**, and thou also shalt give no hire any more.

In verse 42, next, Jehovah explains that the above-prophesied punishments will finally come to an end and a more peaceful and calm time will follow.

42 **So will I make my fury toward thee to rest**, and **my jealousy** [*My anger against you for turning to idols instead of Me*] **shall depart from thee,**

and **I will be quiet, and will be no more angry**.

In verse 43, the Lord provides a very brief review of why He must punish apostate Israel.

43 **Because thou hast not remembered the days of thy youth** [*you have forgotten the covenants you made with Me when you first became My covenant people*], **but hast fretted me** [*vexed Me; caused Me much worry and concern*] **in all these** *things* [*with all your abominations and covenant breaking*]; behold, **therefore I also will recompense** [*pay back*] **thy way upon** *thine* **head, saith the Lord GOD**: and thou shalt not commit this lewdness above all thine abominations.

We mentioned earlier that there is much repetition in this chapter. It will be used to make the point that these rebellious people have left their "Husband," the Lord and His "family," covenant Israel and instead, adopted the religions and practices of the very people who preceded them in the Land of Canaan (who were driven out by Joshua and the children of Israel as they entered the promised land.)

44 ¶ **Behold, every one that useth proverbs** [*comes up with slogans, sayings, clever depictions of others*] **shall use** *this* **proverb against thee**, saying, **As** *is* **the mother, so is** her **daughter**.

45 **Thou** *art* **thy mother's daughter, that lotheth her husband and her children**; and thou *art* the sister of thy sisters, which lothed their husbands and their children: **your mother** *was* **an Hittite, and your father an Amorite** [*you Israelites are just like the Canaanites you drove out of the land so you could worship your God, Jehovah and keep His commandments*].

46 And **thine elder sister** *is* **Samaria, she and her daughters** [*you are just like the Samaritans*] **that dwell at thy left hand** [*who live to the north*]: and **thy younger sister**, that dwelleth at thy right hand [*to the south*], *is* **Sodom and her daughters**.

47 **Yet hast thou not walked after their ways, nor done after their abominations** [*you have not only walked in their wicked ways*]: **but, as** *if that were* **a very little** *thing* [*as if that were not enough*], **thou wast corrupted more than they in all thy ways** [*you exceeded their wickedness in all things*].

48 *As* **I live** [*the most solemn expression of fact in Jewish culture of the day*], **saith the Lord** GOD, **Sodom thy sister hath not done, she nor her daughters, as thou hast done**, thou and thy daughters [*you, Jerusalem and her people, have done far worse than the people of Sodom*].

49 **Behold, this was the iniquity of thy sister Sodom** [*here are some of the major sins of Sodom*], **pride, fulness of bread** [*materialism*], **and abundance of idleness** was in her and in her daughters, **neither did she strengthen the hand of the poor and needy**.

50 And they were **haughty** [*full of pride*], and **committed abomination** [*extreme wickedness*] before me: **therefore I took them away** as I saw *good* [*destroyed them—see Genesis 19:24–29*].

51 **Neither hath Samaria committed half of thy sins; but thou hast multiplied thine abominations more than they**, and hast justified thy sisters in all thine abominations which thou hast done [*the heathen nations around you look righteous compared to you and your wickedness*].

52 Thou also, which hast judged thy sisters, bear thine own shame [*disgrace*] for **thy sins that thou hast committed more abominable than they: they are more righteous than thou**: yea, be thou confounded also, and **bear thy shame, in that thou hast justified thy sisters** [*you have made your neighbors look righteous, in comparison to you*].

> Verses 53–55 seem to show that all of these wicked nations will someday have to face up to their wickedness, and when they do, they will be given a chance to repent and come back to Jehovah, see especially verse 55.

> The Martin Luther translation of the German Bible supplies the translations I use in verse 53.

53 **When I shall bring again** [*reverse, change*] their captivity, **the captivity of Sodom and her daughters, and the captivity of Samaria and her daughters**, then *will I*

bring again [*change; turn around*] **the captivity of thy captives** [*the Jews*] in the midst of them [*among them*]:

54 **That thou mayest bear thine own shame**, and mayest be confounded [*stopped*] in all that thou hast done, in that **thou art a comfort unto them** [*you make them not feel so wicked*].

55 **When** thy sisters, **Sodom and her daughters, shall return to their former estate**, and **Samaria and her daughters shall return to their former estate, then thou and thy daughters shall return to your former estate**.

56 For **thy sister Sodom was not mentioned by thy mouth in the day of thy pride** [*you looked down upon Sodom as a wicked city when you were prospering in your own wickedness and wouldn't even lower yourself to mention her name*],

57 **Before thy wickedness was discovered** [*uncovered and exposed by the Lord*], as at the time of *thy* reproach of the daughters of Syria, and **all** *that are* **round about her**, the daughters of the Philistines, which **despise thee** round about.

58 **Thou hast borne thy lewdness** [*sexual immorality and pervisions*] **and thine abominations** [*you will have to take the consequences of your wickedness*], saith the LORD.

59 For thus saith the Lord GOD; **I will even deal with thee as thou hast done, which hast despised the**

oath in breaking the covenant [*they have despised Jehovah by breaking their covenants with Him*].

Finally, the repeatedly-forgiving Lord still holds out hope to His rebellious covenant people, foretelling the far-distant day when Israel and others will repent and return to Him. We are watching and participating in the long-prophesied gathering of Israel now, on both sides of the veil.

60 ¶ **Nevertheless I will remember** [*fulfill*] **my covenant with thee** in the days of thy youth, and **I will establish unto thee an everlasting covenant**.

61 **Then thou shalt remember thy ways, and be ashamed** [*you will repent*], when thou shalt receive thy sisters, thine elder and thy younger: and I will give them unto thee for daughters, **but not by thy covenant** [*we don't know what this phrase means; we do know that anyone who does not have any of the blood of Israel in them becomes the "seed" of Abraham through baptism—see Abraham 2:10*] .

62 And **I will establish my covenant with thee**; and **thou shalt know that I** *am* **the LORD**:

63 **That thou mayest** remember, and be confounded, and **never open thy mouth any more because of thy shame** [*the Atonement of Jesus Christ allows us to completely leave past sins behind and go forward with a "perfect brightness of hope"—see 2 Nephi 31:20*], **when I am pacified toward thee** [*when I have forgiven you*]

for all that thou hast done, saith the Lord GOD.

EZEKIEL 17

Selection: all verses

In this chapter, Jehovah has Ezekiel give a prophetic parable (the Parable of the Cedar Tree) foretelling various waves of Babylonian captivity for the rebellious Jews and other members of the house of Israel (see the introduction to Ezekiel in this study guide.)

One of the most interesting parts of this parable for us as members of the Church is the part that prophesies that one of King Zedekiah's sons (we know from the Book of Mormon that his name was Mulek) will be brought to America by the hand of the Lord (see verse 22, footnote a.) The Bible mentions the killing of Zedekiah's sons in 2 Kings 25:7 but doesn't provide any separate information about Mulek.

Ezekiel shows in a parable how Israel, while subject to Babylon, wrongfully sought help from Egypt—Yet the Lord will bring forth, in the last days, a goodly tree from the cedars of Lebanon.

1 AND **the word of the LORD came unto me, saying**,

2 Son of man [*Ezekiel*], **put forth a riddle** [*a parable*], and **speak a parable unto the house of Israel**;

Verses 3–6, next, basically prophesy that the King of Babylon will come to Jerusalem and take the king of Judah captive back to Babylon. This was fulfilled when King Jehoiachin of Jerusalem was taken captive by King Nebuchadnezzar of Babylon about 597 BC.

3 And say, Thus saith the Lord GOD; **A great** *eagle* [*the powerful king of Babylon*] **with great wings, long-winged, full of feathers, which had divers colours** [*a description of the power and glory of King Nebuchadnezzar*], **came unto Lebanon** [*the Holy Land*], **and took the highest branch** [*the King of Judah*] **of the cedar** [*of the Jews—trees often represent people in ancient biblical symbolism*]:

4 **He cropped off the top of his young twigs** [*took captive many of the most promising and capable young Jews*], **and carried it into a land of traffick** [*where much trading took place*]; **he set it in a city of merchants.**

5 **He took also of the seed of the land** [*the Jews*], **and planted it in a fruitful field**; he placed *it* by great waters, *and* set it *as* a willow tree.

One possible interpretation of verse 6, next, is that the Jews who were exiled to Babylon actually prospered and grew in numbers.

6 **And it grew,** and became a spreading vine **of low stature** [*although they were still captives and subject to the King of Babylon*], whose branches turned toward him, and the roots thereof were under him: so it became a vine, and brought forth branches, and shot forth sprigs.

Verses 7–20 prophesy of another attack against Israel, a few years later, in which another king of Judah, this time Zedekiah, is captured by Nebuchadnezzar and taken captive to Babylon, with many of his people. Zedekiah was king of Judah when Lehi and his family fled Jerusalem.

7 **There was also another great eagle** [*King Nebuchadnezzar of Babylon, again*] **with great wings and many feathers** [*glorious and powerful*]: and, behold, this vine did bend her roots toward him, and shot forth her branches toward him, that he might water it by the furrows of her plantation.

8 It was planted in a good soil by great waters, that it might bring forth branches, and that it might bear fruit, that it might be a goodly vine.

9 Say thou, Thus saith the Lord GOD **Shall it prosper?** shall he not pull up the roots thereof [*they will be uprooted and taken to Babylon*], and cut off the fruit thereof, that it wither? **it shall wither** in all the leaves of her spring, even without great power or many people to pluck it up by the roots thereof.

10 Yea, behold, *being* planted, **shall it prosper?** shall it not utterly wither, when the east wind toucheth it? **it shall wither** in the furrows where it grew.

11 ¶ Moreover the word of the LORD came unto me, saying,

Starting with verse 12, next, we are given the over-all interpretation of the above verses. It is a prophecy of the near future for these rebellious members of the house of Israel.

12 Say now to the rebellious house [the Jews, house of Israel], Know ye not what these *things mean?* tell *them,* Behold, the king of Babylon is come to Jerusalem, and hath taken the king thereof, and the princes [the leaders] thereof, and led them with him to Babylon;

13 And hath taken of the king's seed, and made a covenant with him, and hath taken an oath of him [Nebuchadnezzar made a treaty with Zedekiah under which Babylon would protect Judah in return for tribute goods]: he hath also taken the mighty of the land [the highly skilled and capable, like Daniel and Ezekiel]:

14 That the kingdom might be base [subject to Babylon], that it might not lift itself up [not rebel against Babylon], but that by keeping of his covenant it might stand [be at peace with Babylon].

Starting with verse 15, we see that the king of Judah was breaking his treaty with Babylon and had turned instead to Egypt for help and protection against Babylon. It won't work.

15 But he [the king of Judah] rebelled against him [the king of Babylon] in sending his ambassadors into Egypt [sent to Egypt to negotiate a treaty with them for help and protection], that they [the Egyptians] might give him [Judah] horses [military help] and much people [many soldiers]. Shall

he prosper [will it work]? shall he escape that doeth such *things?* or shall he break the covenant, and be delivered [if he breaks the treaty with Babylon, will the Jews be saved from Babylon]?

We see the answer in verses 16–21.

16 *As* I live, saith the Lord GOD, surely in the place *where* the king dwelleth [Babylon] that made him king [the king of Babylon had set up the King of Judah to be a puppet king in Jerusalem], whose oath he despised, and whose covenant he brake [the King of Judah broke the treaty he made with the King of Babylon], *even* with him [the King of Babylon] in the midst of Babylon he [the King of Judah, Zedekiah] shall die [Zedekiah was captured, blinded, and carried in chains to Babylon where he died].

Next, in verses 17–18, Ezekiel prophesies that no help from Egypt will come.

17 Neither shall Pharaoh [King of Egypt] with *his* mighty army and great company make for him in the war [help the Jews in their war against Babylon], by casting up mounts, and building forts, to cut off many persons:

18 Seeing he despised the oath [broke his treaty with Babylon] by breaking the covenant, when, lo, he had given his hand [had given his pledge to honor the treaty], and hath done all these *things,* he shall not escape.

In verse 19, next, the Lord points out that the Jews and house of Israel have, in fact, broken their covenant with the Lord and departed from His commandments, just as they and the King of Judah have broken their treaty for protection with the King of Babylon. Severe consequences result from both instances of covenant-breaking.

19 Therefore thus saith the Lord GOD; *As* I live, surely **mine oath that he hath despised** [*broken*]**, and my covenant that he hath broken**, even it **will I recompense** [*pay back*] **upon his own head** [*this is the law of justice in action, for those who do not choose to repent*].

20 And **I will spread my net** [*like a net used to trap animals*] upon him [*punish him*]**, and he shall be taken in my snare, and I will bring him to Babylon**, and **will plead with him there** [*bring him to judgment, to face his wickedness*] **for his trespass** [*breaking of My commandments*] **that he hath trespassed against me.**

21 **And all his fugitives** with all his bands [*troops, soldiers*] **shall fall by the sword**, and they that remain **shall be scattered toward all winds** [*a remnant of Israel will be scattered throughout the earth*]: and **ye shall know that I the LORD have spoken** *it.*

We see verses 22–24 as a dual prophecy, in other words, there are two different prophecies involved.

As a general prophecy, we see the latter-day gathering of Israel when

we follow footnote 22c in our Latter-day Saint English Bible. We are seeing this happening now.

As a very specific prophecy, we follow footnote 22b, likewise in our Latter-day Saint Bible, and see a prophecy about Mulek, son of King Zedekiah, being brought to America by the hand of the Lord. His emigration to America resulted in the establishing of the Mulekites, who became known as the people of Zarahemla (Omni 1:15; Mosiah 25:2; Helaman 6:10; 8:21.) We will include a helpful quote from the Old Testament Student Manual, used by the Institutes of Religion, quoting Elder Orson Pratt:

"When Zedekiah, king of Judah, was carried away captive into Babylon, the Lord took one of his sons, whose name was Mulok [*Mulek*] with a company of those who would hearken unto His words, and brought them over the ocean, and planted them in America. This was done in fulfillment of the 22nd and 23rd verses of the seventeenth chapter of Ezekiel, which read thus: [Ezekiel 17:22–23.] By reading this chapter [17], it will be seen that the Jews were the 'high cedar,' that Zedekiah the king was the 'highest branch,' that the 'tender one' cropped off from the top of his young twigs, was one of his sons, whom the Lord brought out and planted him and his company upon the choice land of America, which He had given unto a remnant of the tribe of Joseph for an inheritance, in fulfillment of the blessing of Jacob and Moses upon the head of that tribe [*Genesis 48–49; Deuteronomy 43*]." (Orson Pratt's Works on the

Doctrines of the Gospel, pp. 280–81.)

22 ¶ Thus saith the Lord GOD; **I will also take of the highest branch** [*King Zedekiah*] of the **high cedar** [*the Jews*], and will set *it;* **I will crop off** from the top of his young twigs **a tender one** [*Mulek*], and **will plant** *it* **upon an high mountain and eminent** [*America*]:

23 **In the mountain of the height of Israel will I plant it** [*I, the Lord, will plant this branch of the house of Israel in America*]: **and it shall bring forth boughs, and bear fruit, and be a goodly cedar** [*it will grow*]: and under it shall dwell all fowl of every wing; in the shadow of the branches thereof shall they dwell [*a way of saying, symbolically, that Mulek's people will grow to be a significant group*].

24 **And all the trees of the field** [*all people*] **shall know that I the LORD** have brought down the high tree, have exalted the low tree, have dried up the green tree, and have made the dry tree to flourish: I the LORD **have spoken and have done** *it.*

EZEKIEL 18

Selection: all verses

The revelation given by the Lord here, through Ezekiel, corrects a misunderstanding that arose among the Israelites from Exodus 20:5. We will quote this verse, then continue.

"Thou shalt not bow down thyself to them, nor serve them: for I the LORD thy God *am* a jealous God, **visiting the iniquity of the fathers upon the children unto the third and fourth** *generation* of them that hate me;"

The misunderstanding is that the children are held accountable for and are punished for the sins of their parents down to the third and fourth generation. This is false. This chapter clearly gives us the correct doctrine that each accountable person is responsible for his or her own sins.

As you know, the second Article of Faith also clearly states this: "We believe that men will be punished for their own sins, and not for Adam's transgression [*or their parents' or anyone else's transgressions*]."

Watch now as Ezekiel thoroughly corrects this misunderstanding among his people.

1 **THE word of the LORD came unto me again, saying,**

2 **What mean ye** [*what have you got to say for yourselves*], **that ye use this proverb** [*saying*] **concerning the land of Israel, saying** [*in that you keep using this saying*], **The fathers have eaten sour grapes, and the children's teeth are set on edge** [*the children are held accountable for the sins of their fathers*]?

3 *As* I live, saith the Lord GOD, **ye shall not have** *occasion* **any more to use this proverb in Israel** [*stop teaching this*].

4 Behold, all souls are mine; as the soul of the father, so also the soul of the son is mine: **the soul that sinneth, it shall die** [*only the sinners are held accountable for their sins*].

By the way, we all know that the sins of the parents can affect the children into the third and fourth generation. For example, alcoholism, drug abuse, child abuse, and so forth. Some children are able to break the chain, so to speak, but others continue to struggle because of the bad example of parents. That is not what this chapter is about. It is about accountability for personal sins.

5 ¶ **But if a man be just** [*righteous*], **and do that which is lawful and right,**

Starting with verse 6, Ezekiel points out several examples of sins being committed by the Jews at the time.

6 *And* **hath not eaten upon the mountains** [*has not eaten food offerings as part of idol worship*], **neither hath lifted up his eyes to the idols of the house of Israel** [*has not worshiped idols*], **neither hath defiled his neighbour's wife** [*committed adultery*], **neither hath come near to** [*had sexual relations with*] **a menstruous woman,**

7 And **hath not oppressed any,** *but* **hath restored to the debtor his pledge** [*has been honest in his dealings with others*], **hath spoiled none by violence** [*has not bullied others*], **hath given his bread to the hungry, and hath covered the naked**

with a garment [*has taken care of the poor and the needy*];

It helps in understanding verse 8, next, to know that "usury" was forbidden by the Law of Moses (Exodus 22:25.) Usury was the practice of charging interest on loans to fellow Jews and other members of the house of Israel. It was generally permitted to charge interest to Gentiles.

8 **He** *that* **hath not given forth upon usury, neither hath taken any increase** [*has practiced usury*], *that* **hath withdrawn his hand from iniquity** [*has repented*], **hath executed true judgment between man and man** [*has been honest with others*],

9 **Hath walked in my statutes, and hath kept my judgments** [*has kept My commandments*], **to deal truly** [*to be honest*]; **he** *is* **just** [*righteous*], **he shall surely live** [*spiritually; will ultimately live with God*], saith the Lord GOD.

Next, in verses 10–13, Ezekiel explains what the situation is in the case of a wicked son of a righteous father.

10 ¶ **If he** [*a righteous father*] **beget a son** [*has a son*] *that is* **a robber,** a **shedder of blood,** and *that* **doeth the like to** *any* **one of these** *things* [*does anything like it*],

11 And **that doeth not any of those** *duties* [*the righteous things his father does*], **but even hath eaten upon the mountains** [*worshiped idols*], **and defiled his neighbour's wife** [*committed adultery*],

12 **Hath oppressed the poor and needy**, hath **spoiled by violence, hath not restored the pledge, and hath lifted up his eyes to the idols** [*see verses 6 and 7*], **hath committed abomination** [*all kinds of wickedness*],

13 Hath given forth upon **usury**, and hath taken increase: **shall he then live** [*be saved in heaven*]**? he shall not live**: he hath done all these abominations; **he shall surely die**; **his blood** [*sins*] **shall be upon him** [*he will be held accountable*].

Next, what if the wicked man, described above, has a son who sees all the wicked things his father does?

(Have you noticed that the Lord and Ezekiel are excellent teachers?)

14 ¶ **Now, lo** [*think about it*], *if* **he beget a son, that seeth all his father's sins** which he hath done, **and considereth** [*thinks carefully about it*], and **doeth not such like**,

15 *That* **hath not eaten upon the mountains, neither hath lifted up his eyes to the idols of the house of Israel, hath not defiled his neighbour's wife**,

16 **Neither hath oppressed** any, hath not **withholden the pledge**, neither hath **spoiled by violence**, *but* **hath given his bread to the hungry, and hath covered the naked with a garment**,

17 *That* **hath taken off his hand from the poor** [*does not oppress the poor*], *that* **hath not received usury nor increase** [*interest*], **hath executed my judgments, hath walked in my statutes** [*has kept the Lord's commandments*]; **he shall not die for the iniquity of his father** [*he will not be held accountable for his father's sins*], **he shall surely live**.

18 *As for* **his father**, because he cruelly oppressed, spoiled his brother by violence, and did *that* which *is* not good among his people, lo, **even he shall die in his iniquity** [*his wickedness will kill his spirituality*].

The question posed in verse 19, next, goes back to the original question posed in verse 2, namely, "What about the proverb or saying we've always heard that the children are punished for the sins of their parents, into the third and forth generation?" Watch as the Lord emphatically answers the question in the last half of the verse

19 ¶ **Yet say ye, Why? doth not the son bear the iniquity of the father** [*is it not true that the children bear the sins and wickedness of the parents, like we've always heard*]**? When the son hath done that which is lawful and right,** *and* **hath kept all my statutes**, and hath done them, **he shall surely live**.

Next, a brief summary of the whole message.

20 **The soul that sinneth, it shall die. The son shall not bear the iniquity of the father, neither shall the father bear the iniquity of the**

son: **the righteousness of the righteous shall be upon him**, and **the wickedness of the wicked shall be upon him**.

Next, in verses 21–23, a very important question: What if a wicked person truly repents?

21 But **if the wicked will turn from all his sins** that he hath committed, **and keep all my statutes**, and do that which is lawful and right, **he shall surely live, he shall not die**.

22 **All his transgressions** that he hath committed, **they shall not be mentioned unto him** [*the Atonement of Christ washes them away completely; (they won't even be mentioned on Judgment Day; the same message as in D&C 58: 42)*]: in his righteousness that he hath done **he shall live**.

23 **Have I any pleasure at all that the wicked should die** [*do I like it at all when people are wicked and I can't bring them to My Father in Heaven with Me*]? saith the Lord GOD: ***and* not that he should return from his ways, and live** [*don't you think that I far prefer that they repent*]?

Next question: What about the person who has lived a righteous life, but then leaves the Church and the true gospel and indulges in the wickedness of the world? In other words, will past righteous deeds and covenant keeping help a person on Judgment Day, who leaves the covenant path and adopts a sinful lifestyle? Answer: verse 24.

24 ¶ But **when the righteous turneth away** from his righteousness, **and committeth iniquity**, *and* doeth according to all the abominations that the wicked *man* doeth, **shall he live? All his righteousness that he hath done shall not be mentioned**: in his trespass that he hath trespassed, and in his sin that he hath sinned, **in them shall he die** [*his past righteousness will not help him at all*].

Next, in verses 25–30, the Great Jehovah answers the criticism that He is not fair.

25 ¶ **Yet ye say, The way of the Lord is not equal** [*not fair; He doesn't treat everyone fairly*]. **Hear now, O house of Israel; Is not my way equal? are not your ways unequal?**

26 **When a righteous *man*** [*a once-righteous man*] **turneth away from his righteousness, and committeth iniquity, and dieth in them** [*does not ultimately repent*]; **for his iniquity** that he hath done **shall he die**.

27 Again, **when the wicked *man* turneth away from his wickedness** that he hath committed, **and doeth that which is lawful and right, he shall save his soul alive** [*the Atonement of Christ will cleanse him completely and he will attain celestial glory*].

28 **Because he considereth** [*thinks it over*], **and turneth away** [*truly repents*] **from all his transgressions** that he hath committed, **he shall surely live, he shall not die** [*spiritually*].

29 **Yet saith the house of Israel, The way of the Lord is not equal**. O house of Israel, **are not my ways equal? are not your ways unequal?**

30 **Therefore** [*because of your warped, unrighteous thinking against Me*] **I will judge you**, O house of Israel, **every one according to his ways** [*everyone will be judged for his or her own sins, not for the sins of others*], saith the Lord GOD. Repent, and turn *yourselves* from all your transgressions; so iniquity shall not be your ruin.

A very important scripture for us to understand in regards to the bad example given by some parents to their children, that, basically, does not give the children a fair chance in this life, is found in D&C 50:7. It is:

"Behold, verily I say unto you, there are hypocrites among you, who have deceived some, which has given the adversary power; but behold such **shall be reclaimed**;"

Did you notice that those whose opportunities to understand and embrace the full gospel are hampered by the bad examples of others will "be reclaimed"? In other words, they will be given a completely fair opportunity, either in this life or the post-mortal spirit world, to hear the gospel, understand it, have the Holy Ghost bear witness to them that the gospel is true, and then accept or reject the gospel, using their individual agency, before final judgment.

Finally, in the last two verses, the Lord gives a tender and wonderful invitation to these people to repent and live, spiritually.

31 ¶ **Cast away from you all your transgressions** [*repent*], **whereby ye have transgressed**; and **make you a new heart and a new spirit**: for **why will ye die, O house of Israel?**

32 For **I have no pleasure in the death** [*spiritual death*] **of him that dieth**, saith the Lord GOD: wherefore **turn *yourselves*** [*turn around, repent*], **and live ye**.

EZEKIEL 19

Selection: all verses

This chapter is given in what can be called "future prophetic mode." In other words, it speaks of the future as if it has already taken place or is taking place. It is a "lamentation" for Israel, in other words, a formal mourning for Israel and all that her people have lost because of wickedness.

By the way, the Prophet, Jeremiah, gave a "lamentation" that was five chapters long (see "The Lamentations of Jeremiah" right after Jeremiah in the Bible.)

The *Old Testament Student Manual* used by the Institutes of Religion provides help for understanding verses 1–9. We will quote from it:

Ezekiel 19:1–9. The Allegory of the Lioness and the Whelps

"The interpretation of this allegory seems fairly clear. The lioness, if not the doomed country [Judah], is Hamutal, the mother of Zedekiah. (2 Kings 24:18) The first of her whelps would then be Jehoahaz, who after reigning for a short time was taken prisoner to Egypt by Pharaoh-nechoh. (2 Kings 23:31–33) Jehoahaz was in turn succeeded by Jehoiakim, a son of Josiah by a wife other than Hamutal. Jehoiakim was succeeded by his son Jehoiachin. When the last-named was taken captive by the Babylonians, Hamutal's second son, Zedekiah, was appointed king in his stead. He must, therefore, be the other 'whelp' of the allegory. When taken captive by Nebuchadrezzar and carried to Babylon, Zedekiah fulfilled the requirements of the last two verses." (Sperry, Voice of Israel's Prophets, p. 211.)

Notice that, as before, Ezekiel uses the terms "Judah," "the Jews," "Jerusalem," and "Israel," pretty much interchangeably.

Remember also, that the real solution for Israel and Judah is to repent and be worthy of the help and protection of the Lord rather than continuing in their wicked ways and depending on treaties with foreign powers for protection.

1 MOREOVER **take thou up a lamentation for the princes of Israel** [*make a prophecy of mourning for the leaders of the kingdom of Judah, meaning the Jews, and all of Israel*],

2 And say, **What** *is* **thy mother? A lioness** [*symbolic of Judah and Jerusalem in better days*]: **she lay down among lions** [*she was an important nation*], she nourished her whelps [*cubs*] among young lions.

3 And **she brought up one of her whelps** [*Jehoahaz*]**: it became a young lion** [*a king of Judah*]**, and it learned to catch the prey; it devoured men** [*this king of Judah was once powerful*].

4 The nations also heard of him; **he was taken in their pit** [*captured*]**, and they brought him with chains unto the land of Egypt**.

5 Now when she saw that she had waited, *and* her hope was lost, then **she took another of her whelps,** *and* **made him a young lion** [*king; probably referring to Zedekiah*].

6 And he went up and down among the lions, **he became a young lion** [*powerful*]**, and learned to catch the prey,** *and* **devoured men** [*he had great power*].

7 And he knew their desolate palaces, and **he laid waste their cities**; and the land was desolate, and the fulness thereof, by the noise of his roaring.

8 **Then the nations set against him** on every side from the provinces, **and spread their net over him: he was taken in their pit** [*caught him and took him prisoner*].

9 **And they put him** [*Zedekiah*] **in ward** [*under arrest*] **in chains, and brought him to the king of Babylon**: they brought him into holds [*prisons*], that his voice should no more be heard upon the mountains of Israel.

In verses 10–14, we see another allegory used in Ezekiel's lamentation. Again, we will quote from the *Old Testament Student Manual*:

The Allegory of the Vine and Its Branches

The allegory in Ezekiel 19:10–14 deals with the conditions in Israel at the time of Ezekiel: "Israel resembled a vine planted by the water. … This vine sent out strong shoots for rulers' sceptres; that is to say, it brought forth powerful kings, and grew up to a great height, … It was torn up in fury by the wrath of God, cast down to the ground, so that its fruit withered. … The uprooting ends in the transplanting of the vine into a waste, dry, unwatered land,— in other words, in the transplanting of the people, Israel, into exile. The dry land is Babylon, so described as being a barren soil in which the kingdom of God could not flourish." (Keil and Delitzsch, Commentary, 9:1:261–62.)

With the destruction of Judah by Nebuchadnezzar and the killing of Zedekiah's sons [*we know that Mulek survived this*], "she hath no strong rod to be a sceptre to rule" (Ezekiel 19:14). Clarke summarized: "None of the blood-royal of Judah [was] left. And from that time not one of her own royal race ever sat upon the throne of Israel." (Commentary, 4:474.)

10 ¶ **Thy mother** [*Israel, in her glory days*] *is* **like a vine in thy blood** [*in your likeness—see footnote 10b in your Bible*], planted by the waters: **she was fruitful and full of branches**

by reason of many waters [*she was nourished by the Lord originally*].

11 And **she had strong rods for the sceptres of them that bare rule** [*she had many powerful kings*], and **her stature was exalted among the thick branches** [*she was a strong nation among nations*], and she appeared in her height with the multitude of her branches.

Next, in verse 12, we see that the Lord destroyed Israel because of the wickedness and rebellion of her people. This reflects the law of justice in action.

12 But **she was plucked up in fury** [*by the Lord*], she was cast down to the ground, and **the east wind** [*symbolic of devastation and destruction*] **dried up her fruit: her strong rods** [*kings*] **were broken and withered**; **the fire** [*the wrath of God*] **consumed them**.

13 **And now she** *is* **planted in the wilderness** [*Babylon*], **in a dry and thirsty ground**.

14 And fire is gone out of a rod of her branches, *which* hath devoured her fruit, so that **she hath no strong rod** *to be* **a sceptre to rule** [*all of Zedekiah's sons, heirs to the throne, were killed, except Mulek, and he was taken to America by the Lord, thus, there were no heirs to the throne*]. **This** *is* **a lamentation, and shall be for a lamentation** [*this is, indeed, cause for great lamentation*].

EZEKIEL 20

Selection: all verses

In verse 1, the elders or leaders of the Jewish exiles in Babylon come to Ezekiel to ask him to ask the Lord some questions. In verse 3, Jehovah refuses to talk to them and the rest of the chapter explains why. This is similar to what we saw in chapter 14.

Note that, as is typical with many Old Testament prophets, Ezekiel uses much repetition for emphasis. Because of this, I will define terms and phrases when you first come to them, but afterwards, for the most part, will merely **bold** them.

1 AND it came to pass **in the seventh year, in the fifth** *month,* **the tenth** *day* **of the month** [*August 14, 591 BC, according to some Bible scholars*], *that* **certain of the elders** [*leaders*] **of Israel came to enquire of the LORD,** and sat before me [*Ezekiel*].

2 **Then came the word of the LORD unto me, saying,**

3 Son of man [*Ezekiel*], speak unto the elders of Israel, and **say unto them,** Thus saith the Lord GOD; Are ye come to enquire of me? *As* I live, saith the Lord GOD, **I will not be enquired of by you.**

As a prophet, Ezekiel is also a judge of his people, as is the case with all prophets, including ours. They will all assist in judging their people on Judgment Day (1 Nephi 12:9.) Next, in verse 4, Ezekiel is instructed, as a judge, to explain to these leaders why the Lord refuses to speak to them.

4 Wilt thou judge them, son of man, wilt thou judge *them*? **cause them to know the abominations of their fathers:**

5 ¶ And **say unto them,** Thus saith the Lord GOD; **In the day when I chose Israel** [*way back when I made Abraham's descendants My covenant people (Abraham 2:9–11)*], **and lifted up mine hand** [*made a covenant with them*] **unto the seed of the house of Jacob** [*the twelve tribes of Israel*], and **made myself known unto them in the land of Egypt** [*I revealed Myself to them while they were in Egyptian bondage, through Moses*], **when I lifted up mine hand unto them, saying, I** *am* **the LORD your God;**

6 In the day *that* I lifted up mine hand unto them [*when I covenanted with them*], **to bring them forth of the land of Egypt into a land that I had espied** [*picked out*] **for them,** flowing with milk and honey [*a land where you could prosper*], which *is* the glory of all lands:

7 **Then said I unto them** [*gave them some requirements to receive My blessings*], **Cast ye away** [*get rid of*] **every man the abominations of his eyes** [*get rid of your sins; repent*]**, and defile not yourselves with the idols of Egypt**: I *am* the LORD your God.

8 **But they rebelled against me**, and would not hearken unto me: **they did not every man cast away the**

abominations of their eyes, neither did they forsake the idols of Egypt: **then I said, I will pour out my fury upon them**, to accomplish my anger against them in the midst of the land of Egypt.

9 **But I wrought** [*acted*] **for my name's sake, that it** [*My name*] **should not be polluted before the heathen**, among whom they *were,* in whose sight I made myself known unto them, in bringing them forth out of the land of Egypt [*the Egyptians saw the miracles I did to bring My covenant people out of bondage in Egypt*].

10 ¶ Wherefore **I caused them** [*the children of Israel*] **to go forth out of the land of Egypt**, and brought them into the wilderness.

> Verse 11, next, is basically a very brief thumbnail sketch of the plan of salvation.

11 And **I gave them my statutes** [*commandments and laws*], **and shewed** [*pronounced "showed"*] **them my judgments** [*the rules for receiving My blessings and help*], **which** *if* a **man do, he shall even live** [*prosper, physically and spiritually*] **in them**.

> Pay close attention to the purpose of the Sabbath Day, as stated by the Lord, the premortal Christ, in verse 12.

12 Moreover also **I gave them my sabbaths, to be a sign between me and them**, that they might know that I *am* the LORD that sanctify them

[*whose Atonement will, if they strive to keep My commandments, ultimately cleanse them and make them pure, clean, and fit to be in the presence of the Father—the definition of "sanctify"*].

13 **But the house of Israel rebelled against me in the wilderness:** they **walked not in my statutes**, and they **despised my judgments**, which *if* a man do, he shall even live [*spiritually, and ultimately get to heaven*] in them; and **my sabbaths they greatly polluted**: then I said, I would pour out my fury upon them in the wilderness, to consume them.

14 **But I wrought** [*acted*] **for my name's sake, that it** [*My name*] **should not be polluted** [*brought into disrespect*] **before the heathen**, in whose sight I brought them out.

15 Yet **also I lifted up my hand unto them in the wilderness, that I would not bring them into the land** which I had given *them,* flowing with milk and honey, which *is* the glory of all lands;

16 **Because** they despised my judgments, and walked not in my statutes, but polluted my sabbaths: for their heart went after their idols.

17 **Nevertheless mine eye spared them from destroying them**, neither did I make an end of them in the wilderness [*for 40 years, until the rebellious older generation had pretty-much died off*].

18 **But I said unto their children** in the wilderness, **Walk ye not in the**

statutes of your fathers, neither observe their judgments, nor defile yourselves with their idols [*do not follow the bad example of your parents and ancestors*]:

19 I *am* the LORD your God; **walk in my statutes, and keep my judgments, and do them**;

20 And **hallow my sabbaths; and they shall be a sign between me and you, that ye may know that I** *am* **the LORD your God**.

21 **Notwithstanding** [*in spite of My warnings and invitations to repent*] **the children rebelled against me**: they **walked not in my statutes, neither kept my judgments** to do them, **which** *if* **a man do, he shall even live in them** [*which, if a person does, he or she will be blessed and ultimately gain salvation*]; **they polluted my sabbaths**: then **I said, I would pour out my fury upon them, to accomplish my anger** [*punishments*] **against them in the wilderness** [*during the 40 years of wandering in the wilderness*].

22 Nevertheless **I withdrew mine hand** [*I withdrew My blessings*], and wrought for my name's sake, that it should not be polluted in the sight of the heathen, in whose sight I brought them forth.

23 I lifted up mine hand unto them also in the wilderness, **that I would scatter them among the heathen, and disperse them through the countries** [*the scattering of Israel*];

24 **Because they had not executed my judgments, but had despised my statutes, and had polluted my sabbaths**, and their eyes were after their fathers' idols [*they worshiped idols, like their ancestors before them did*].

25 Wherefore **I gave them also statutes** *that were* **not good, and judgments whereby they should not live** [*I, the Lord, allowed them their agency to live wickedly*];

In order to understand the depths of sin and depravity to which these rebellious Israelites had fallen, to which Ezekiel refers in verse 26, next, you need to know that a part of idol worship involved being with prostitutes. The illegitimate babies born as a result were burned as a sacrifice to Molech, the fire god (see Bible Dictionary, under "Molech.")

26 And I polluted them in their own gifts, in that **they caused to pass through** *the fire* [*burned as sacrifices*] **all that openeth the womb** [*all the babies born to prostitutes involved in idol worship*]**, that I might make them desolate** [*thus, I, the Lord, was justified in allowing them to be devastated by enemy armies and scattered to all nations*]**, to the end that they might know that I** *am* **the LORD**.

27 ¶ Therefore, **son of man, speak unto the house of Israel, and say unto them**, Thus saith the Lord GOD; Yet **in this your fathers have blasphemed me** [*completely disregarded sacred covenants*]**, in that**

they have committed a trespass against me.

28 *For* when I had brought them into the land, *for* the which I lifted up mine hand [*made a covenant*] to give it to them, **then they saw every high hill, and all the thick trees** [*as ideal places for idol worship and the sexual immorality that went along with it*], and they offered there their sacrifices, and there they presented the provocation of their offering: there also they made their sweet savour, and poured out there their drink offerings [*all parts of idol worship*].

29 Then I said unto them, **What** *is* **the high place whereunto ye go** [*what are you doing going to these high places*]? And the name thereof is called Bamah [*"high place"—see NIV, footnote 29e*] unto this day.

30 Wherefore say unto the house of Israel, Thus saith the Lord GOD; **Are ye polluted after the manner of your fathers** [*just like your parents and ancestors*]? **and commit ye whoredom** [*sexual sins*] **after their abominations** [*just like they did*]?

31 **For when ye offer your gifts** [*to your idols*], **when ye make your sons to pass through the fire** [*child sacrifices to fire gods*], **ye pollute yourselves with all your idols, even unto this day** [*you have been doing such things ever since Egyptian bondage and up to Ezekiel's day*]: **and shall I be enquired of by you**, **O house of Israel** [*and you dare to come to Ezekiel's house to have him enquire of Me*

for you]? *As* **I live, saith the Lord GOD, I will not be enquired of by you**.

32 **And that which cometh into your mind shall not be at all** [*what you have in mind will not work at all*], **that ye say, We will be as the heathen, as the families of the countries, to serve wood and stone** [*you want to ask Me for permission to live like other nations and worship their gods, their idols*].

> Verses 33–44 refer to the eventual, successful, gathering of Israel in the last days before the second coming of Christ.

33 ¶ *As* I live, saith the Lord GOD, **surely with a mighty hand, and with a stretched out arm, and with fury poured out, will I rule over you** [*I will punish you as needed and will eventually gather you and be your God again*]:

34 And **I will** bring you out from the people, and will **gather you out of the countries wherein ye are scattered**, with a mighty hand [*great power*], and with a stretched out arm, and with fury poured out.

35 And I will bring you into the wilderness of the people, and **there will I plead with you face to face** [*there will be much revelation and manifestation of the Lord's power as He gathers Israel*].

36 **Like as I pleaded with your fathers** [*ancestors*] in the wilderness [*spiritual wilderness*] of the land

of Egypt, **so will I plead with you,** saith the Lord GOD.

37 And **I will cause you to pass under the rod** [see note, next], and I will bring you into the bond of the covenant:

> Passing under the rod (see Ezekiel 20:37) is a figure of speech that "alludes to the custom of tithing the sheep . ... The sheep were all penned; and ... only one sheep could come out at once. ... [The shepherd] counted ... and as the tenth came out, he marked it with the rod [*dipped in vermilion*], and said, 'This is ... set apart for the Lord.'" (Clarke, Commentary, 4:477.) Thus, the converted Israelites will be the Lord's, just as tithing is. (*Old Testament Student Manual Kings-Malachi*, p 274.)

38 And **I will purge out from among you the rebels, and them that transgress against me**: I will bring them forth out of the country where they sojourn [*where they live temporarily*], and they shall not enter into the land of Israel: and ye shall know that I *am* the LORD.

39 **As for you, O house of Israel**, thus saith the Lord GOD; Go ye [*go ahead*], serve ye every one his idols, and hereafter *also,* if ye will not hearken unto me: but pollute ye my holy name no more with your gifts, and with your idols.

The NIV (New International Version of the Holy Bible) gives verse 39, above, as follows:

"As for you, people of Israel, this is what the Sovereign Lᴏʀᴅ says: Go and serve your idols, every one of you! **But afterward** [*in the last days*] **you will surely listen to me and no longer profane my holy name with your gifts and idols.**"

In this translation, you can see that the last half of the verse is a prophecy that the day will come that Israel will be loyal and faithful to the Lord. Thus, starting with the last half of verse 39 and continuing through verse 44, we see a prophecy of the restoration and gathering of Israel as the Lord's covenant people in the last days.

40 For in mine holy mountain, in the mountain of the height of Israel, saith the Lord GOD, **there shall all the house of Israel, all of them in the land, serve me: there will I accept them**, and there will I require your offerings, and the firstfruits of your oblations, with all your holy things.

41 **I will accept you** with your sweet savour, **when I** bring you out from the people, and **gather you out of the countries wherein ye have been scattered**; and I will be sanctified in you before the heathen.

42 And ye shall know that I *am* the LORD, **when I shall bring you into the land of Israel, into the country *for* the which I lifted up mine hand** [*I covenanted*] **to give it to your fathers**.

43 And **there shall ye remember your ways, and all your doings,**

wherein ye have been defiled [*you will think back on your sins and rebellion*]; **and ye shall lothe yourselves in your own sight for all your evils that ye have committed** [*you will have true godly sorrow—2 Corinthians 7:10—for your sins and rebellion, and thus, will be able to truly repent*].

44 **And ye shall know that I** *am* **the LORD, when I have wrought** [*worked*] **with you for my name's sake** [*according to My plan of salvation; there is no other name under which you can be saved; 2Nephi 25:20*], **not according to your wicked ways, nor according to your corrupt doings**, O ye house of Israel, saith the Lord GOD.

Next, in verses 45–48, Jehovah has Ezekiel repeat once more the prophecy that rebellious Judah and her people will be destroyed.

45 ¶ **Moreover** [*in addition*] the word of the LORD came unto me, saying,

46 **Son of man, set thy face toward the south** [*the kingdom of Judah, located in the southern portion of the land of Israel*], and drop *thy word* [*speak*] toward the south, and **prophesy against the forest** [*trees represent people in Biblical symbolism*] **of the south field** [*the people in Judah*];

47 And **say to the forest of the south**, Hear the word of the LORD; Thus saith the Lord GOD; **Behold, I will kindle a fire in thee, and it shall devour every green tree in thee, and every dry tree**: the flaming flame shall not be quenched,

and all faces from the south to the north shall be burned therein [*great destruction is coming to you*].

48 And **all flesh shall see that I the LORD have kindled it** [*everyone will know that the Lord did it—compare with 3 Nephi 9:3–12*]: **it shall not be quenched** [*no one can stop it*].

Sadly, almost unbelievably, we see, in verse 49, that the leaders who came to Ezekiel's house (verse 1) do not understand the message and complain that Ezekiel is speaking to them in parables that they can't understand. This reminds us that wickedness does not promote rational thought nor the ability to comprehend clear truth.

We see that Ezekiel is exasperated!

49 Then said I, **Ah Lord GOD! they say of me, Doth he not speak parables?** [*he, Ezekiel, is speaking in riddles that we cannot understand.*]

EZEKIEL 21

Selection: all verses

A sad but important message in chapter 21 is that it is often the case that the righteous suffer along with the wicked. Joseph Smith mentioned this fact when he said "that those who are innocent are compelled to suffer for the iniquities of the guilty" (Smith, Teachings, p. 34).

As you well know, for example, when the wicked take over and famines result, the righteous also suffer. In fact, they can even starve to death, along with the wicked. And, when the enemy armies attack, many good people are killed along with the intentionally rebellious and wicked. However, in the overall big picture provided by the Father's plan of salvation, there is a big difference in what happens next. The righteous, including innocent children, pass through the veil to a condition of welcome and peace. Whereas, the wicked pass through the veil to a miserable condition where they must face their sins (Alma 40:13).

In this case, it is the wicked in Jerusalem who are going to be killed and captured by the next wave of Nebuchadnezzar's armies, but the righteous, such as Daniel, Shadrach, Meshach and Abednego (Daniel 3:12), along with Ezekiel and his wife have already suffered by being taken captive along with the rebellious Jews in Jerusalem in a previous wave of attacks from Babylon.

This chapter is about the coming destruction of Jerusalem and the surrounding area. Remember, Lehi and his family escaped this in 600 BC by heeding the Lord's command to flee into the wilderness.

1 AND **the word of the LORD came unto me, saying,**

2 **Son of man** [*Ezekiel*], **set thy face toward Jerusalem** [*turn toward Jerusalem, symbolically*], **and drop** *thy word* [*prophesy*] **toward the holy places** [*such as the temple in Jerusalem*], and **prophesy against the land of Israel,**

3 And say to the land of Israel, **Thus saith the LORD; Behold, I** *am* **against thee, and will draw forth**

my sword [*in this case, the Lord will use Babylon as His "sword"*] out of his sheath, **and will cut off from thee the righteous and the wicked** [*both righteous and wicked people will be killed*].

Verses 4 and 5 are basically a repeat of verse 3. By now, you are probably getting used to such repetition for emphasis used by Ezekiel.

4 Seeing then that **I will cut off from thee the righteous and the wicked, therefore shall my sword go forth out of his sheath against all flesh from the south to the north** [*throughout the land of Israel*]:

5 **That all flesh may know that I the LORD have drawn forth my sword out of his sheath**: it shall not return any more [*the prophesied destructions will definitely come*].

Verse 6, next, has an interesting way for Ezekiel to get the people's attention.

6 **Sigh therefore**, thou son of man, with the breaking of *thy* loins [*with a broken heart*]; and **with bitterness sigh before their eyes**.

7 **And it shall be, when they say unto thee, Wherefore** [*why*] **sighest thou?** that **thou shalt answer, For the tidings** [*because of the bad news*]; because it cometh: and every heart shall melt, and all hands shall be feeble, and every spirit shall faint, and all knees shall be weak *as* water: behold, it cometh, and shall be brought to pass, saith the Lord GOD.

8 ¶ **Again the word of the LORD came unto me, saying,**

9 Son of man, **prophesy,** and say, Thus saith the LORD; **Say, A sword, a sword is sharpened, and also furbished** [*the Babylonian armies are ready and coming, indeed*]:

10 **It is sharpened to make a sore** [*huge, terrible*] **slaughter;** it is furbished that it may glitter [*it is polished bright to flash like lightening*]: **should we then make mirth** [*should we ignore it and be happy*]? **it contemneth the rod of my son** [*it despises the King of Judah*], *as* **every tree** [*and all his people*].

11 And **he hath given it to be furbished** [*prepared for the attack*], that it may be handled: this sword is sharpened, and it is furbished, **to give it into the hand of the slayer** [*the Babylonians*].

12 **Cry and howl,** son of man: **for it** [*destruction*] **shall be upon my people,** it *shall be* **upon all the princes** [*all the leaders*] of Israel: **terrors by reason of the sword shall be upon my people: smite therefore upon** *thy* **thigh** [*a cultural way, among the Jews of the day, to show great emotion, in this case, a way to show great alarm and horror at the coming calamities*].

13 Because *it is* **a trial,** and **what if** *the sword* **contemn even the rod** [*what if the Babylonians despise your king in Jerusalem*]? it shall be no *more,* saith the Lord GOD.

14 Thou therefore, son of man, prophesy, and **smite** *thine* **hands together** [*a cultural way of expressing great anguish*], and let the sword be doubled **the third time** [*three times in Biblical numerical symbolism means the worst, or best, in this case, the worst possible*], the sword of the slain: it *is* **the sword of the great** *men* [*your leaders*] *that are* slain, which entereth into their privy chambers [*private living quarters; destruction comes from every side*].

15 **I have set the point of the sword against all their gates** [*destruction will come to them everywhere*], that *their* heart may faint [*give up hope*], **and** *their* **ruins be multiplied:** ah! *it is* made bright, *it is* wrapped up for the slaughter.

16 **Go thee** [*the sword of destruction*] **one way or other,** *either* on the right hand, *or* on the left, whithersoever thy face *is* set.

17 **I will also smite mine hands together** [*such punishing causes great sorrow for the Lord, too*], **and I will cause my fury to rest** [*eventually, these punishments will cease (and the gathering of Israel will commence)*]]: I the LORD have said *it.*

18 ¶ **The word of the LORD came unto me again, saying,**

As you are seeing, Ezekiel is using much of repetition to prophesy the coming destruction from Babylon.

In verses 19 and 20, we see that the destruction will fall not only upon

Jerusalem but also upon the Ammonites (verse 20, descendants of Lot's son, Benammi, Abraham's nephew) who lived across the Jordon River to the east and northeast of Jerusalem.

19 Also, thou son of man, **appoint thee two ways, that the sword of the king of Babylon may come** [both upon Jerusalem and upon the Ammonites]: **both twain** [symbolically, swords of destruction] **shall come forth out of one land** [Babylon]: and choose thou a place, choose it at the head of the way to the city.

Symbolically, in verse 20, next, Ezekiel is told to put up a sign on the "road" that leads from Babylon to Jerusalem, and on the sign put an arrow pointing to Rabbath and one pointing to Jerusalem, so that the Babylonian armies can find both.

20 **Appoint a way, that the sword may come to Rabbath** [a major city of the Ammonites, to the northeast of Jerusalem, across the Jordon River] **of the Ammonites, and to Judah in Jerusalem** the defenced [walled city].

Starting with verse 21, Ezekiel prophesies that the King of Babylon will consult his idols and gods regarding attacking the walls of Jerusalem. Then, starting with verse 28, the prophecy shows a second front for attack, this time upon the Ammonites. Remember, this is a prophecy of soon-to-be future events.

21 For **the king of Babylon stood at the parting of the way, at the head** [intersection] **of the two ways** [one to

Jerusalem, one to Rabbath and the Ammonites], to use divination [to consult his pagan idols and charms]: he made his arrows bright, he consulted with images, he looked in the liver.

22 **At his right hand was the divination** [seeking counsel from his idols and charms] **for Jerusalem**, to appoint captains, to open the mouth in the slaughter, to lift up the voice with shouting, to appoint battering rams against the gates, to cast a mount, and to build a fort [to prepare the siege for Jerusalem].

23 And it shall be unto them as a false divination in their sight, to them that have sworn oaths: but **he will call to remembrance the iniquity, that they may be taken**.

24 Therefore thus saith the Lord GOD; Because ye have made your iniquity to be remembered, in that your transgressions are discovered, so that **in all your doings your sins do appear**; because, I say, that ye are come to remembrance, ye shall be taken with the hand.

Verses 25–27 prophesy that wicked King Zedekiah, king of Judah (who kept the Prophet Jeremiah in miserable prison conditions much of the time) will be taken captive.

25 ¶ **And thou, profane wicked prince of Israel** [King Zedekiah], **whose day is come** [whose time as king is up], when iniquity shall have an end,

26 **Thus saith the Lord GOD; Remove the diadem** [*crown, symbol of his authority and power*], and take off the crown: this *shall* not *be* the same: exalt *him that is* low, and abase *him that is* high.

27 I will **overturn, overturn, overturn, it** [*remember that repeated three times means "the ultimate" in Jewish culture*]: and it shall be no *more,* **until he come whose right it is** [*the kingdom of Judah will be overturned and her king deposed until Jesus Christ comes whose right it is to rule and reign during the Millennium*]; and I will give it *him.*

28 ¶ And thou, son of man, **prophesy** and say, Thus saith the Lord GOD **concerning the Ammonites**, and concerning their reproach; even say thou, **The sword, the sword *is* drawn: for the slaughter *it is* furbished, to consume because of the glittering** [*destruction is coming to the Ammonites too; the same glittering sword—the Babylonians—will do it*]:

> Verse 29, next, tells us that there were false prophets among the Ammonites too, telling them not to worry.

29 Whiles **they see vanity unto thee** [*speak useless things to you*]**, whiles they divine a lie unto thee**, to bring thee upon the necks of *them that are* slain, of the wicked, whose day is come, when their iniquity *shall have* an end.

30 **Shall I** [*the Lord*] **cause *it*** [*the sword of destruction, the Babylonians*]

to return into his sheath? I will judge thee in the place where thou wast created, in the land of thy nativity.

31 And **I will pour out mine indignation upon thee, I will blow against thee in the fire of my wrath, and deliver thee into the hand of brutish men,** *and* skilful to destroy [*who are skilled in killing*].

32 **Thou shalt be for fuel to the fire; thy blood shall be in the midst of the land**; thou shalt be no *more* remembered [*you will be completely destroyed*]: for I the LORD have spoken *it.*

EZEKIEL 22

Selection: all verses

Once again, Ezekiel lists and catalogues the sins of the Jews in Jerusalem. Much of this is repetition from previous chapters of Ezekiel. In fact, I will mainly just **bold** words and phrases you are already familiar with, and add minimal commentary. Hopefully, you will find that you have really learned quite a bit by studying Ezekiel up to this point in this study guide.

(By the way, have you noticed that I almost always say "we" rather than "I" when, actually, I am the one speaking. My parents taught me early on in my life to avoid "I trouble," thus, not focusing inappropriately on myself in conversations with others.)

This cataloguing of conditions in Jerusalem can be divided into three segments:

First, verses 3–12, listing all kinds of sins and evil in Jerusalem.

Second, verses 18–22, the Lord's dismay at the evil practiced by His covenant people and His plans to scatter them.

Third, verses 23–31, exposing the popular priests and false prophets as well as the general population who had also turned to robbery and oppression of others.

1 MOREOVER the word of the LORD came unto me, saying,

2 Now, thou **son of man**, wilt thou judge, wilt thou **judge the bloody city** [*Jerusalem*]? yea, thou shalt **shew her all her abominations**.

3 Then **say** thou, Thus saith the Lord GOD, **The city sheddeth blood in the midst of it** [*is completely permeated with sin*], that her time may come, and **maketh idols against herself to defile herself**.

4 **Thou art** become **guilty in thy blood that thou hast shed** [*murders*]; and **hast defiled thyself in thine idols which thou hast made**; and thou **hast caused thy days to draw near, and art come** *even* **unto thy years** [*your time is about up*]: therefore have I made thee **a reproach unto the heathen, and a mocking to all countries**.

5 *Those that be* near, and *those that be* far from thee, shall mock thee, *which art* infamous *and* much vexed.

6 Behold, **the princes of Israel**, every one were in thee to their power to **shed blood**.

7 **In thee have they set light by father and mother** [*they have treated their parents with contempt*]: in the midst of thee **have they dealt by oppression with the stranger**: in thee **have they vexed the fatherless and the widow**.

8 Thou hast **despised mine holy things** [*abused and defiled the temple*], and **hast profaned my sabbaths**.

9 **In thee** are **men** that carry tales to **shed blood**: and in thee **they eat upon the mountains** [*worship idols*]: in the midst of thee [*Jerusalem*] **they commit lewdness**.

10 **In thee have they discovered their fathers' nakedness** [*incest*]: **in thee have they humbled her that was set apart for pollution** [*have had intercourse with menstruous women (which was against the law of Moses)*].

11 And **one hath committed abomination with his neighbour's wife** [*adultery*]; and **another hath lewdly defiled his daughter in law** [*incest*]; and **another in thee hath humbled his sister, his father's daughter** [*incest*].

12 **In thee have they taken gifts to shed blood** [*bribes and payment to commit murder*]; **thou hast taken usury and increase**, and thou hast greedily **gained of thy neighbours**

by **extortion**, and **hast forgotten me, saith the Lord GOD**.

13 ¶ Behold, **therefore I have smitten mine hand at thy dishonest gain** which thou hast made, **and at thy blood which hath been in the midst of thee**.

14 **Can thine heart endure, or can thine hands be strong, in the days that I shall deal** [*punish*] **with thee?** I the LORD have spoken *it,* and will do *it.*

15 And **I will scatter thee among the heathen**, and **disperse thee in the countries**, and **will consume thy filthiness out of thee**.

16 And **thou shalt take thine inheritance in thyself in the sight of the heathen** [*you will lose your inheritance in full view of the heathen nations around you*], and **thou shalt know that I** *am* **the LORD**.

17 And **the word of the LORD came unto me, saying,**

18 Son of man, **the house of Israel is to me become dross** [*like slag, good for nothing*]: **all they** *are* **brass, and tin, and iron, and lead, in the midst of the furnace** [*the refiner's fire*]; **they are** *even* **the dross** [*the impurities at the top of the cauldron during the refining process, which are scraped off and thrown away*] **of silver**.

19 Therefore thus saith the Lord GOD; Because ye are all become dross, behold, therefore **I will gather you into the midst of Jerusalem**.

20 As they gather silver, and brass, and iron, and lead, and tin, into the midst of the furnace, **to blow the fire upon it**, to melt *it;* so will I gather *you* in mine anger and in my fury, and **I will leave** *you there,* **and melt you**.

21 Yea, **I will gather you, and blow upon you in the fire of my wrath, and ye shall be melted** in the midst thereof.

22 **As silver is melted in the midst of the furnace, so shall ye be melted in the midst** thereof; **and ye shall know that I the LORD have poured out my fury upon you**.

23 ¶ **And the word of the LORD came unto me, saying,**

24 Son of man, **say unto her, Thou** *art* **the land that is not cleansed, nor rained upon in the day of indignation** [*when your sins catch up to you*].

25 *There is* **a conspiracy of her** [*false*] **prophets** in the midst thereof, **like a roaring lion ravening the prey**; **they have devoured souls**; they **have taken the treasure and precious things**; they **have made her many widows** in the midst thereof [*in Jerusalem*].

26 Her [*false*] **priests have violated my law**, and **have profaned mine holy things**: they **have put no difference between the holy and profane** [*worldly*], **neither have they shewed** *difference* **between the unclean and the clean**, and **have hid**

their eyes from my sabbaths, and **I am profaned among them**.

27 **Her princes** [*leaders*] **in the midst thereof** *are* **like wolves ravening the prey**, to **shed blood**, *and* to **destroy souls**, to **get dishonest gain**.

28 And **her prophets have daubed them with untempered** *morter* [*symbolically, have repaired Jerusalem's spiritually crumbling walls of defense with weak, ineffective mortar*], **seeing vanity, and divining lies unto them** [*giving false counsel and prophecies from their idols and charms*], **saying, Thus saith the Lord GOD, when the LORD hath not spoken**.

29 **The people of the land have used oppression, and exercised robbery**, and have **vexed the poor and needy**: yea, they have **oppressed the stranger wrongfully**.

30 And **I sought for a** [*righteous*] **man among them**, that should make up the hedge, and stand in the gap before me for the land, that I should not destroy it: **but I found none**.

31 **Therefore have I poured out mine indignation upon them; I have consumed them with the fire of my wrath: their own way have I recompensed upon their heads, saith the Lord GOD**.

EZEKIEL 23

Selection: all verses

This chapter is similar to chapter 16. You may wish to briefly review

it in order to better understand the symbolism here. The basic message is summarized by the heading in your Latter-day Saint edition of the English-speaking Bible as follows:

Two sisters, Samaria and Jerusalem, committed whoredoms by worshipping idols—Both are destroyed for their lewdness.

We will quote from the Old Testament Student Manual:

Ezekiel 23:1–49. Allegory of the Two Sisters

Ezekiel 23 tells about the idolatry of the ten tribes (Samaria) and Judah (Jerusalem). All the references to whoredoms, to other impure sexual practices, and to various parts of the female anatomy are metaphorical. These metaphors are used in the same way as those used by Hosea, Jeremiah, Ezekiel, and others in which Jehovah is the husband and the nation Israel is the wife. Infidelity and fornication are similar, and both words have dual meanings. One meaning relates to marriage (adultery) and the other to worship (idolatry). Ezekiel plays these meanings against each other and draws out lessons on both. Dummelow summarized the relationships referred to in the allegory:

"The idolatries and foreign alliances of Jerusalem and Samaria are here described under the same strong figure which is used in c. [*chapter*] 16. Oholah (Samaria) and Oholibah (Jerusalem) were two sisters, both seduced in Egypt in their youth (v. 3), both espoused by God (v. 4), and both unfaithful to Him. Samaria took as her lovers first the Assyrians (vv. 5–7), and then the Egyptians (v. 8), and was at length slain by the former (vv. 9, 10). Jerusalem, not warned by her sister's fate, made first the Assyrians and then the Babylonians her paramours [*lovers*] (vv. 11–16). Being alienated from the latter she has turned to her early lovers of Egypt (vv. 17–21), but she will be destroyed, like her sister, by the lovers whom she has just forsaken (vv. 22–35). The sin and judgment of the two sisters are described afresh (vv. 36–49)." (Commentary, p. 507.)

In his inspired translation, Joseph Smith made small but significant changes in Ezekiel 23:17, 22, and 28. The sisters' minds were turned not from their lovers (the false gods) but from God by their lovers. (*Old Testament Student Manual Kings-Malachi*.)

We will again **bold** terms and phrases with which you are hopefully getting more familiar by now in your study of Ezekiel. Thus, my commentary will be somewhat minimal, as was the case with chapter 22.

1 **THE word of the LORD came again unto me, saying,**

2 Son of man, **there were two women, the daughters of one mother** [*two sisters, the northern ten tribes (the northern kingdom or Samaria) and Judah (the southern kingdom or Jerusalem)*]:

3 And **they committed whoredoms** [*were disloyal to the Lord*] **in Egypt** [*they adopted the false religions of their captors while in Egyptian bondage*]**;**

they committed whoredoms in their youth: there were their breasts pressed, and there they bruised the teats of their virginity.

4 **And the names of them** *were* Aholah [*Samaria*] the elder, **and Aholibah** [*Jerusalem*] **her sister**: and **they were mine** [*were My covenant people*], and they bare sons and daughters. Thus *were* their names; **Samaria** *is* **Aholah**, and **Jerusalem Aholibah**.

5 And **Aholah played the harlot when she was mine** [*she broke her "marriage" covenants with Me, the Lord*]; **and she doted on her lovers, on the Assyrians** *her* neighbours,

6 *Which were* **clothed with blue, captains and rulers, all of them desirable young men, horsemen riding upon horses** [*which were very attractive to her*].

7 **Thus she committed her whoredoms with them**, with all them *that were* the chosen **men of Assyria**, and with all on whom she doted: **with all their idols she defiled herself**.

8 **Neither left she her whoredoms** *brought* **from Egypt**: for in her youth they lay with her, and they bruised the breasts of her virginity, and poured their whoredom upon her.

9 **Wherefore I have delivered her** into the hand of her lovers, **into the hand of the Assyrians**, upon whom she doted.

10 **These discovered her naked-ness** [*committed adultery with her*]: **they took her sons and her daughters, and slew her with the sword**: and **she became famous** [*became a despised byword*] among women; for **they had executed judgment upon her.**

11 **And when her sister Aholibah saw *this*, she was more corrupt in her inordinate love than she**, and **in her whoredoms more than her sister in *her* whoredoms** [*the people of Judah did not learn a lesson from what happened to the northern kingdom when the Assyrians devastated them and took many away into captivity in about 722 BC*].

12 **She doted upon the Assyrians *her* neighbours**, captains and rulers clothed most gorgeously, horsemen riding upon horses, all of them desirable young men.

13 **Then I saw that she was defiled**, *that* they *took* both one way [*both Samaria and Jerusalem took the same path of wickedness and rebellion against the Lord*],

14 And *that* **she increased her whoredoms** [*was worse than Samaria*]: **for when she saw men** pourtrayed upon the wall, the images of the Chaldeans pourtrayed with vermilion,

15 Girded with girdles upon their loins, exceeding in dyed attire upon their heads, **all of them princes to look to**, after the manner of the Babylonians of Chaldea, the land of their nativity:

16 And as soon as she saw them with her eyes, **she doted upon them**, and sent messengers unto them into Chaldea.

Note the very important change made in the JST for the last phrase of verse 17, next.

17 And **the Babylonians came to her into the bed of love, and they defiled her with their whoredom, and she was polluted with them** [*she worshipped Babylonian idols and other false gods*], and **her mind was alienated from them** [*JST "from me by them." In other words, the sister's minds were turned not from their false gods (lovers) but were turned from God by their lovers (idols)*].

18 **So she discovered her whoredoms** [*openly participated in prostitution*], and discovered her nakedness: **then my mind** [*the Lord's mind*] **was alienated from her, like as my mind was alienated from her sister** [*Samaria*].

19 **Yet she multiplied her whoredoms** [*increased her worship of false gods*], in calling to remembrance the days of her youth, wherein **she had played the harlot in the land of Egypt**.

20 **For she doted upon their paramours** [*lovers; false gods*], whose flesh *is as* the flesh of asses, and whose issue *is like* the issue of horses.

21 **Thus thou calledst to remembrance the lewdness of thy youth**, in bruising thy teats by the Egyptians for the paps of thy youth.

22 ¶ **Therefore, O Aholibah** [*Jerusalem*], thus saith the Lord GOD; Behold, **I will raise up thy lovers** [*Babylon*] **against thee**, from whom thy mind is alienated [*JST "by whom thy mind is alienated from me." In other words, the sister's minds were turned not from their false gods (lovers) but were turned from God by their lovers (idols)*], and **I will bring them against thee on every side**;

23 **The Babylonians, and all the Chaldeans, Pekod, and Shoa, and Koa,** *and* **all the Assyrians with them**: all of them desirable young men, captains and rulers, great lords and renowned, all of them riding upon horses.

24 **And they shall come against thee** with chariots, wagons, and wheels, and with an assembly of people, *which* shall set against thee buckler and shield and helmet round about: and I will set judgment before them, and they shall judge thee according to their judgments.

25 And **I will set my jealousy against thee, and they shall deal furiously with thee**: they shall take away thy nose and thine ears; and thy remnant shall fall by the sword: they shall take thy sons and thy daughters; and thy residue shall be devoured by the fire.

26 **They shall also strip thee out of thy clothes, and take away thy fair jewels**.

27 **Thus will I make thy lewdness** [*symbolic of their idol worship and all the wicked practices that accompanied it*] **to cease from thee**, and thy whoredom *brought* from the land of Egypt: **so that thou shalt not lift up thine eyes unto them, nor remember Egypt any more** [*ultimately, Israel will be reclaimed and gathered in the last days*].

28 For thus saith the Lord GOD; Behold, **I will deliver thee into the hand** *of them* **whom thou hatest** [*the Babylonians*], into the hand *of them* from whom thy mind is alienated:

29 And **they shall deal with thee hatefully**, and shall take away all thy labour, and shall leave thee naked and bare: and **the nakedness of thy whoredoms shall be discovered** [*exposed*], both thy lewdness and thy whoredoms.

30 I [*the Lord*] **will do these** *things* **unto thee**, because thou hast gone a whoring after the heathen, *and* because thou art polluted with their idols.

31 **Thou hast walked in the way of thy sister** [*northern Israel, Samaria, the northern ten tribes*]; **therefore will I give her cup** [*her bitter cup*] **into thine hand** [*the same thing that happened to her will happen to you, Judah*].

32 Thus saith the Lord GOD; **Thou shalt drink of thy sister's cup deep and large: thou shalt be laughed to scorn and had in derision**; it containeth much.

33 **Thou shalt be filled with drunkenness and sorrow, with the cup of astonishment and desolation**, with the cup of thy sister Samaria.

34 **Thou shalt even drink it and suck** *it* **out**, and thou shalt break the sherds [*shards*] thereof, and pluck off thine own breasts: for I have spoken *it,* saith the Lord GOD.

35 Therefore thus saith the Lord GOD; **Because thou hast forgotten me, and cast me behind thy back**, therefore bear thou also thy lewdness and thy whoredoms.

By now you are no doubt used to the fact that Ezekiel and other Old Testament prophets used repetition to emphasize the points of their messages. So, it will be no surprise that verses 36–49, next, repeat the sins and coming devastation of the two sisters, Samaria and Judah, that the above verses detailed.

36 ¶ The LORD said moreover unto me; **Son of man**, wilt thou **judge Aholah** [*Samaria*] **and Aholibah** [*Judah*]? yea, **declare unto them their abominations**;

37 **That they have committed adultery, and blood** [*murder*] *is* **in their hands**, and **with their idols have they committed adultery**, and **have also caused their sons, whom they bare unto me, to pass for them through** *the fire,* to devour *them.*

38 Moreover this they have done unto me: **they have defiled my sanctuary** in the same day, and **have profaned my sabbaths**.

39 For **when they had slain their children to their idols, then they came the same day into my sanctuary to profane it**; and, lo, thus have they done in the midst of mine house.

Verses 40–44, next, describe the enticements and preparations of the Lord's people, Israel and Judah, to receive lovers from afar, symbolically representing their rejection of Jehovah and their turning to idols and other gods worshiped by their neighboring countries.

40 And furthermore, that **ye have sent for men to come from far**, unto whom a messenger *was* sent; **and, lo, they came: for whom thou didst wash thyself, paintedst thy eyes** [*put on makeup*]**, and deckedst thyself with ornaments**,

41 And satest upon a stately bed, and a table prepared before it, **whereupon thou hast set mine incense and mine oil** [*they were using incense and oil reserved for proper temple worship to make their lairs for sexual immorality more attractive for their lovers*].

42 And **a voice of a multitude being at ease** *was* **with her** [*the noise of people partying in riotous pleasures was all around*]: and with **the men of the common sort** [*rabble*] *were*

brought Sabeans from the wilderness, which **put bracelets upon their hands, and beautiful crowns upon their heads** [*the women's hands and heads—gifts to solicit their favors*].

43 **Then said I unto** *her that was* old in adulteries [*worn out by adultery*], **Will they now commit whoredoms with her, and she** *with them* [*will they still use her as a prostitute*]?

Answer, yes. In other words, will they continue "stepping out on the Lord," breaking their covenants with Him? Answer, yes.

As you have no doubt noticed, this would not be good reading for family home evening with children.

44 **Yet they went in unto her**, as they go in unto a woman that playeth the harlot: **so went they in unto Aholah and unto Aholibah**, the lewd women.

In the last verses of this chapter, we see that the righteous would call this behavior exactly what it is, namely, abhorrent and repulsive wickedness and rebellion against the Lord.

45 ¶ And **the righteous men**, they **shall judge them** [*will call it what it is*] after the manner of **adulteresses**, and after the manner of **women that shed blood; because they** *are* **adulteresses, and blood** *is* **in their hands**.

46 For thus saith the Lord GOD; **I will bring up a company** [*mob*] **upon them**, and will give them to be removed and spoiled.

47 And **the company shall stone them with stones, and dispatch them with their swords; they shall slay their sons and their daughters, and burn up their houses with fire**.

48 **Thus will I cause lewdness to cease out of the land**, that all women may be taught not to do after your lewdness.

49 And **they shall recompense your lewdness upon you** [*you will pay for your sins*], and **ye shall bear the sins of your idols**: and **ye shall know that I** *am* **the Lord GOD**.

EZEKIEL 24

Selection: all verses

This chapter continues detailing the upcoming punishments upon Jerusalem. Verses 1–14 are often referred to as "The Parable of the Boiling Pot." During an important fast among the Jews, a pot was filled with water. Choice pieces of meat, including the bones, were boiled. Then they were burned to powder and the pot was melted. As used by Ezekiel here, this is symbolic of the complete devastation and destruction coming to Jerusalem.

1 AGAIN in the ninth year, in the tenth month, in the tenth *day* of the month, **the word of the LORD came unto me, saying**,

2 Son of man, **write** thee the name of the day, *even* of this same day: **the king of Babylon set himself against Jerusalem** this same day.

3 And **utter a parable unto the rebellious house** [*the Jews in Jerusalem*], and say unto them, Thus saith the Lord GOD; **Set on a pot** [*symbolic of Jerusalem*], set *it* on, and also **pour water into it**:

4 **Gather the pieces** [*symbolic of inhabitants of Jerusalem*] **thereof into it,** *even* **every good piece** [*symbolic of the strongest and highest in importance, such as King Zedekiah and his family*], **the thigh, and the shoulder; fill** *it* **with the choice bones.**

5 **Take the choice of the flock**, and burn also the bones under it, *and* **make it boil well**, and let them seethe the bones of it therein.

6 ¶ Wherefore thus saith the Lord GOD; **Woe to the bloody city** [*Jerusalem*], **to the pot whose scum** [*symbolic of sins and impurities in the lives of the rebellious Jews*] *is* **therein, and whose scum is not gone out of it!** bring it out piece by piece; **let no lot fall upon it** [*don't have people cast lots for the pieces (because nothing will be left)*].

7 **For her blood is in the midst of her** [*Jerusalem is guilty through and through*]; **she set it upon the top of a rock; she poured it not upon the ground** [*like they were supposed to do according to Mosaic law*], to cover it with dust;

Next, in verses 8–11, the Lord says, symbolically, that He will destroy Jerusalem and its inhabitants (similar to what He said in 3 Nephi 9).

8 That it might cause fury to come up to take vengeance; **I have set her blood upon the top of a rock, that it should not be covered.**

9 Therefore thus saith the Lord GOD; **Woe to the bloody city! I will even make the pile** [*of wood*] **for fire great** [*huge*].

10 **Heap on wood, kindle the fire, consume the flesh, and spice it well, and let the bones be burned** [*let the destruction be complete*].

11 **Then set it** [*the pot*] **empty upon the coals thereof, that the brass of it may be hot, and may burn, and** *that* **the filthiness of it may be molten in it,** *that* **the scum of it may be consumed.**

Verses 12–14 are a reminder of what Judah did to deserve these punishments.

12 **She hath wearied** *herself* [*worn herself out*] with lies, and **her great scum went not forth out of her**: her scum *shall be* in the fire.

13 **In thy filthiness** *is* **lewdness** [*sexual immorality, murder, child sacrifice, idol worship*]: **because I have purged thee, and thou wast not purged,** thou shalt not be purged from thy filthiness any more, **till I have caused my fury to rest upon thee** [*NIV "until my wrath against you has subsided"*].

14 **I the LORD have spoken** *it*: **it shall come to pass, and I will do** *it;* I will not go back, neither will I

spare, **neither will I repent** [*change My mind*]; according to thy ways, and according to thy doings, shall they judge thee, saith the Lord GOD.

In verses 15–27, we see personal tragedy for Ezekiel, the loss of his dearly beloved wife, used to symbolize the loss of Jerusalem.

15 ¶ **Also the word of the LORD came unto me, saying,**

16 **Son of man, behold, I take away from thee the desire of thine eyes** [*his wife*] with a stroke: yet **neither shalt thou mourn nor weep, neither shall thy tears run down**.

Next, in verses 17–18, Ezekiel is commanded not to mourn in the traditional way of the Jews. One possible reason for this might be to show the Jews not to mourn for their losses in the coming devastation and destruction, rather, use their energy to go forward with hope to a better future. In other words, don't keep looking back and mourning your losses, but look to a brighter future by turning back to God.

17 **Forbear to cry** [, *don't cry or moan*] **make no mourning for the dead**, bind the tire of thine head upon thee [*put your turban on*], and put on thy shoes upon thy feet, and cover not *thy* lips [*don't cover the lower half of your face as a sign of mourning*] , and eat not the bread of men [*the usual food of mourners*].

18 So I spake unto the people in the morning: and **at even** [*evening*] **my** wife died; and I did in the morning as I was commanded.

19 ¶ And the people said unto me, **Wilt thou not tell us what these** *things are* **to us, that thou doest** *so* [*so, what are you trying to tell us*]*?*

20 **Then I answered them,** The word of the LORD came unto me, saying,

21 Speak unto the house of Israel, Thus saith the Lord GOD; **Behold, I will profane my sanctuary** [*your temple is no longer My temple*]**, the excellency of your strength, the desire of your eyes, and that which your soul pitieth** [*the temple that you so admire*]**; and your sons and your daughters whom ye have left shall fall by the sword.**

In verses 22–24, the Lord instructs the people to follow Ezekiel's example and to not mourn for their coming losses.

22 And ye shall do as I have done: **ye shall not cover** *your* **lips, nor eat the bread of men**.

23 And your tires *shall be* upon your heads, and your shoes upon your feet: ye shall not mourn nor weep; **but ye shall pine away for your iniquities, and mourn one toward another** [*rather than mourn for your losses, you should mourn for your sins*].

24 Thus **Ezekiel is unto you a sign: according to all that he hath done shall ye do** [*he is an example of what is going to happen to you*]: **and when**

this cometh, ye shall know that I *am* the Lord GOD.

25 Also, thou son of man, *shall it* not *be* in the day **when I take from them their strength, the joy of their glory, the desire of their eyes, and that whereupon they set their minds** [*the temple in Jerusalem*]**, their sons and their daughters,**

26 *That* **he that escapeth in that day shall come unto thee, to cause** *thee* **to hear** *it* **with** *thine* **ears** [*on that a fugitive will report it to you*]?

27 In that day shall thy mouth be opened to him which is escaped, and thou shalt speak, and be no more dumb: and **thou shalt be a sign unto them; and they shall know that I** *am* **the LORD** [*when the destruction of Jerusalem actually happens, they will know that I am indeed God*].

EZEKIEL 25

Selection: all verses

The fall of Jerusalem has now taken place. In chapters 25–32, Ezekiel prophesied mainly against foreign nations. This chapter concerns the Ammonites, Moab, Edom, and the Philistines.

1 **THE word of the LORD came again unto me, saying,**

2 **Son of man, set thy face against** [*focus on*] **the Ammonites** [*the nation across the Jordan River, north and northeast of Jerusalem*]**, and prophesy against them;**

3 And say unto the Ammonites, Hear the word of the Lord GOD; Thus saith the Lord GOD; **Because thou saidst, Aha, against my sanctuary, when it was profaned** [*because you rejoiced when the temple and Jerusalem were destroyed (and participated in looting them)*]**; and against the land of Israel,** when it was desolate; **and against the house of Judah, when they went into captivity;**

4 Behold, **therefore I will deliver thee to the men of the east** [*including the Assyrians and Babylonians*] **for a possession,** and they shall set their palaces in thee, and make their dwellings in thee: they shall eat thy fruit, and they shall drink thy milk.

5 And **I will make Rabbah** [*a major city in Ammon*] **a stable for camels,** and **the Ammonites a couching-place for flocks** [*resting place for sheep*]: and **ye shall know that I** *am* **the LORD.**

6 For thus saith the Lord GOD; **Because thou hast clapped thine hands, and stamped with the feet, and rejoiced in heart with all thy despite** [*malice*] **against the land of Israel;**

It is interesting to see how many different ways the Lord says the same thing (He will punish the Ammonites for their wickedness) in verse 7, next.

7 Behold, therefore **I will stretch out mine hand upon thee,** and **will deliver thee for a spoil to the heathen; and I will cut thee off from**

the people, and **I will cause thee to perish out of the countries: I will destroy thee**; and thou shalt know that I *am* the LORD.

Next, a prophecy of doom and punishment for the people of Moab (a heathen country east of the southern half of the Dead Sea).

8 ¶ **Thus saith the Lord GOD; Because that Moab and Seir** [*Edom— the descendants of Esau— (see their demise prophesied starting with verse 12)*] **do say, Behold, the house of Judah** *is* **like unto all the heathen** [*is like all other nations (their behaviors do not reflect that their God, Jehovah, is anything special)*];

9 **Therefore**, behold, **I will open the side** [*flank; make them vulnerable to enemy attack*] **of Moab** from the cities, **from his cities** *which are* **on his frontiers**, the glory of the country, Beth-jeshimoth, Baal-meon, and Kiriathaim [*frontier towns*],

10 **Unto the men of the east with the Ammonites** [*I will give Moab, along with the Ammonites, to the men of the east—enemies—see verse 4*], and will give them in possession, **that the Ammonites may not be remembered among the nations** [*the Ammonites will cease to exist as a nation*].

11 And **I will execute judgments** [*punishments*] **upon Moab**; and they shall know that I *am* the LORD.

Next, a prophecy of doom to Edom, a nation south of the Dead Sea.

12 ¶ Thus saith the Lord GOD; **Because that Edom hath dealt against the house of Judah** by taking vengeance, and hath greatly offended, and revenged himself upon them [*has participated in attacks and depredations upon Judah*];

13 Therefore thus saith the Lord GOD; **I will also stretch out mine hand upon Edom**, and will cut off man and beast from it; and **I will make it desolate** from Teman; and they of Dedan shall fall by the sword.

14 And **I will lay my vengeance upon Edom by the hand of my people Israel**: and **they shall do in Edom according to mine anger and according to my fury**; and **they shall know my vengeance**, saith the Lord GOD.

And finally, a prophecy of doom to the Philistines.

15 ¶ Thus saith the Lord GOD; **Because the Philistines have dealt by revenge, and have taken vengeance with a despiteful heart, to destroy** *it* [*Judah*] for the old hatred;

16 Therefore thus saith the Lord GOD; Behold, **I will stretch out mine hand upon the Philistines, and I will cut off the Cherethims** [*better translated "Cretans," a sub group among the Philistines*], **and destroy the remnant of the sea coast** [*the people living on the coast southwest of Jerusalem*].

17 And **I will execute great vengeance** [*punishment*] **upon them**

with furious rebukes; and **they shall know that I *am* the LORD** [*the true God*]**, when I shall lay my vengeance upon them.**

EZEKIEL 26

Selection: all verses

This prophecy of destruction is leveled against Tyre, about 90 miles north of Jerusalem, on the coast of Palestine, half way between Carmel, in Israel, and Beirut, Lebanon.

Do you remember Korihor, in the Book of Mormon, the one who said that no one can know the future (Alma 30:13)? These incredible prophecies of Ezekiel prove over and over that Korihor or any likeminded people are completely wrong!

1 AND it came to pass in the eleventh year, in the first *day* of the month, *that* **the word of the LORD came unto me, saying,**

2 Son of man, **because that Tyrus** [*Tyre*] **hath said against Jerusalem, Aha** [*see 25:3*]**, she is broken *that was* the gates of the people** [*that used to flourish*]: she is turned unto me: **I shall be replenished, *now* she is laid waste** [*I will prosper now that Jerusalem has been laid waste*]:

3 Therefore thus saith the Lord GOD; Behold, **I *am* against thee, O Tyrus**, and **will cause many nations to come up against thee,** as the sea causeth his waves to come up.

4 And **they shall destroy** the walls of **Tyrus**, and break down her towers: I will also scrape her dust from her, and make her like the top of a rock [*completely devastate her*].

5 **It shall be *a place for* the spreading of nets in the midst of the sea** [*a lonely place where fishermen can fish*]: for I have spoken *it,* saith the Lord GOD: and **it shall become a spoil to the nations.**

6 And **her daughters which *are* in the field shall be slain by the sword**; and they shall know that I *am* the LORD.

7 ¶ For thus saith the Lord GOD; Behold, **I will bring upon Tyrus Nebuchadrezzar king of Babylon, a king of kings, from the north** [*Nebuchadnezzar's armies came west from Babylon, then south to Palestine*], **with horses, and with chariots, and with horsemen, and companies, and much people.**

8 **He shall slay** with the sword **thy daughters in the field**: and he **shall make a fort against thee**, and **cast a mount against thee** [*lay siege*], and **lift up the buckler** [*shield*] **against thee.**

9 And **he shall set engines of war** [*battering rams*] **against thy walls,** and with his axes **he shall break down thy towers.**

10 **By reason of the abundance of his horses** [*he will have so many horses that*] **their dust shall cover thee: thy walls shall shake at the noise of the horsemen, and of the wheels, and of the chariots, when he shall**

enter into thy gates, as men enter into a city wherein is made a breach.

11 With the hoofs of his horses shall he tread down all thy streets: he shall slay thy people by the sword, and thy strong garrisons shall go down to the ground.

12 And they shall make a spoil of thy riches, and make a prey of thy merchandise: and they shall break down thy walls, and destroy thy pleasant houses: and they shall lay thy stones and thy timber and thy dust in the midst of the water.

13 And I will cause the noise of thy songs to cease; and the sound of thy harps shall be no more heard [*all your pleasant music will be gone*].

14 And I will make thee like the top of a rock [*I will strip you bare*]: thou shalt be *a place* to spread nets upon; thou shalt be built no more: for I the LORD have spoken *it,* saith the Lord GOD.

Verses 15–18 prophesy that the nations around Tyre will be shocked, appalled and astonished at her downfall.

15 ¶ Thus saith the Lord GOD to Tyrus; Shall not the isles shake at the sound of thy fall, when the wounded cry, when the slaughter is made in the midst of thee?

16 Then all the princes of the sea [*leaders of seafaring nations around you*] shall come down from their thrones, and lay away their robes, and put off their broidered garments: they shall clothe themselves with trembling; they shall sit upon the ground [*in mourning and shock*], and shall tremble at *every* moment, and be astonished at thee.

17 And they shall take up a lamentation [*a formal mourning*] for thee, and say to thee, How art thou destroyed, *that wast* inhabited of seafaring men, the renowned city, which wast strong in the sea, she and her inhabitants, which cause their terror *to be* on all that haunt [*lived in*] it [*who was so powerful and well known that all feared her*]!

18 Now shall the isles tremble in the day of thy fall; yea, the isles that *are* in the sea shall be troubled at thy departure.

19 For thus saith the Lord GOD; When I shall make thee a desolate city, like the cities that are not inhabited; when I shall bring up the deep upon thee, and great waters shall cover thee;

20 When I shall bring thee down with them that descend into the pit [*with those who end up in hell*], with the people of old time [*the other wicked people from the past*], and shall set thee in the low parts of the earth, in places desolate of old, with them that go down to the pit, that thou be not inhabited; and I shall set glory in the land of the living [*NIV "you will not return to take your place in the land of the living"*];

21 **I will make thee a terror** [*I will bring you to a horrible end*], and **thou shalt be** no *more:* though thou be sought [*even though people look for you*] for, **yet shalt thou never be found again**, saith the Lord GOD.

EZEKIEL 27

Selection: all verses

In this chapter, Ezekiel laments (mourns) for Tyre and the economic losses her downfall causes for other nations.

1 **THE word of the LORD came again unto me, saying,**

2 Now, thou son of man, **take up a lamentation for Tyrus** [*Tyre*];

3 And say unto Tyrus, **O thou that art situate at the entry of the sea** [*situated in a strategic business location as a gateway to the sea*], *which art* a **merchant of the people for many isles** [*your economic pursuits affect many nations*], Thus saith the Lord GOD; O Tyrus, **thou hast said, I** *am* **of perfect beauty** [*prideful*].

4 **Thy borders** *are* **in the midst of the seas** [*you dominated the high seas*], **thy builders have perfected thy beauty** [*with merchandise from many nations*].

5 **They have made all thy** *ship* **boards of fir trees** [*pine trees*] of Senir [*from Mt. Hermon*]: they have taken **cedars from Lebanon to make masts for thee.**

6 *Of* **the oaks of Bashan have they made thine oars**; the company of **the Ashurites have made thy benches** *of* **ivory, brought out of the isles of Chittim** [*Cyprus*].

7 **Fine linen** with broidered work **from Egypt** was that which thou spreadest forth **to be thy sail** [*to make sails for your ships*]; blue and purple **from the isles of Elishah** was that which covered thee [*for your awnings*].

8 **The inhabitants of Zidon** [*the men of Sidon*] **and Arvad were thy mariners** [*oarsmen*]: **thy wise** *men* [*skilled men*], O Tyrus, *that* were in thee, **were thy pilots.**

9 **The ancients** [*veteran craftsmen*] of Gebal [*Byblos*] and the wise *men* thereof **were** in thee **thy calkers** [*sealed the seams in your ships*]: **all the ships of the sea with their mariners were in thee to occupy thy merchandise** [*came along side to trade merchandise with you*].

10 **They of Persia** and of **Lud** and of **Phut** [*Libia*] **were in thine army,** thy men of war: **they hanged the shield and helmet in thee** [*were in your armies*]; **they set forth thy comeliness** [*brought splendor and fame to you*].

11 **The men of Arvad with thine army** *were* **upon thy walls** [*were in your armies*] round about, and the **Gammadims were in thy towers:** they hanged their shields upon thy

walls round about; they have made thy beauty perfect.

12 **Tarshish** *was* **thy merchant** by reason of the multitude of all *kind of* riches; with silver, iron, tin, and lead, **they traded in thy fairs**.

13 **Javan** [*Greece*], **Tubal, and Meshech, they** *were* **thy merchants**: **they traded** the persons of men and vessels of brass **in thy market**.

14 **They of the house of Togarmah** [*Armenia*] **traded in thy fairs** with horses and horsemen and mules.

15 **The men of Dedan** [*Rhodes*] *were* **thy merchants**; many isles [*islands and nations*] *were* the merchandise of thine hand: **they brought thee** *for* **a present horns of ivory and ebony**.

16 **Syria** *was* **thy merchant** by reason of the multitude of the wares of thy making: they occupied in thy fairs with emeralds, purple, and broidered work, and fine linen, and coral, and agate.

17 **Judah, and the land of Israel, they** *were* **thy merchants**: they traded in thy market wheat of Minnith, and Pannag, and honey, and oil, and balm.

18 **Damascus** *was* **thy merchant** in the multitude of the wares of thy making, for the multitude of all riches; in the wine of Helbon, and white wool.

19 **Dan also and Javan** [*Greece*] going to and fro occupied in thy fairs:

bright iron, cassia, and calamus, were in thy market.

20 **Dedan** *was* **thy merchant** in precious clothes for chariots.

21 **Arabia, and all the princes of Kedar**, they occupied with thee in lambs, and rams, and goats: in these *were they* thy merchants.

22 **The merchants of Sheba and Raamah**, they *were* **thy merchants**: they occupied in thy fairs with chief of all spices, and with all precious stones, and gold.

23 **Haran**, and **Canneh**, and **Eden**, the merchants of **Sheba**, **Asshu**r, *and* **Chilmad,** *were* **thy merchants**.

24 **These** *were* **thy merchants in all sorts** *of things,* in blue clothes, and broidered work, and in chests of rich apparel, bound with cords, and made of cedar, among thy merchandise.

25 The ships of Tarshish did sing of thee in thy market: and **thou wast replenished, and made very glorious in the midst of the seas** [*you prospered greatly in your trade with all these trading partners*].

Next, Ezekiel switches from detailing the great merchandizing accomplishments and prosperity of Tyre and her multiple business partners (first part of verse 26) to her coming downfall and demise (the last phrase of verse 26). The "east wind" symbolizes destruction, in Biblical symbolism. (Think of the devastation and drying up caused to crops in Palestine by the dreaded east winds coming off of the hot, barren sands of Arabia.)

26 ¶ **Thy rowers** [*oarsmen*] **have brought thee into great waters** [*have taken you far out to sea*]: **the east wind hath broken thee in the midst of the seas** [*in the middle of your prosperity, you will be destroyed*].

27 **Thy riches**, and thy fairs, thy merchandise, thy mariners, and thy pilots, thy calkers, and the occupiers of thy merchandise, and all thy men of war, that *are* in thee, and in all thy company which *is* in the midst of thee, **shall fall into the midst of the seas in the day of thy ruin.**

28 **The suburbs shall shake at the sound of the cry of thy pilots.**

29 **And all that handle the oar**, the **mariners**, *and* all the **pilots** of the sea, shall come down from their ships, they **shall stand upon the land;**

Verses 30–32 depict deep mourning in Biblical cultures.

30 **And shall cause their voice to be heard against thee, and shall cry bitterly**, and **shall cast up dust upon their heads**, they shall **wallow themselves in the ashes:**

31 And **they shall make themselves utterly bald** [*will shave their heads*] for thee, **and gird them with** [*will dress themselves in*] **sackcloth** [*a burlap-like fabric*], and they **shall weep for thee** with bitterness of heart *and* bitter wailing.

32 And in their wailing **they shall take up a lamentation for thee, and lament over thee,** *saying,* **What** *city is* **like Tyrus, like the destroyed in the midst of the sea** [*how could a city like Tyre be destroyed*]?

33 **When thy wares went forth out of the seas** [*your merchandise went everywhere*], **thou filledst many people; thou didst enrich the kings of the earth** with the multitude of thy riches and of thy merchandise.

34 In the time *when* thou shalt be broken by the seas in the depths of the waters **thy merchandise and all thy company in the midst of thee shall fall** [*you and all your business partners will be devastated*].

35 **All the inhabitants of the isles shall be astonished at thee**, and their kings shall be sore afraid, they shall be troubled in *their* countenance.

36 **The merchants among the people shall hiss at thee** [*will whistle in amazement*]; thou shalt be **a terror**, and **never** *shalt be* **any more** [*you will no more be powerful and feared*].

EZEKIEL 28

Selection: all verses

Tyre (starting with verse 2) and Zidon, or Sidon, (starting with verse 20) were sister cities, about 25 miles apart on the Palestinian coast of the Mediterranean Sea. Sidon was north of Tyre. Both cities had caused much trouble for Israel.

This chapter continues with prophecies of the downfall of these two cities. You will see a familiar pattern in Ezekiel's prophecy of doom for Tyre, first a prophecy of destruction, then a lament. However, starting with verse 24, you will see that all is not ultimately lost because Israel will be gathered in the last days and will become the Lord's people again.

1 THE word of the LORD came again unto me, saying,

2 Son of man [*Ezekiel*], say unto the prince of Tyrus [*the leader of Tyre*], Thus saith the Lord GOD; Because thine heart *is* lifted up [*you are full of pride*], and thou hast said, I *am* a God, I sit *in* the seat of God, in the midst of the seas [*I am like a god over a large empire*]; yet thou *art* a man, and not God, though thou set thine heart as the heart of God [*although you act like one*]:

3 Behold, thou *art* wiser than Daniel [*you act like you think you are wiser than Daniel*]; there is no secret that they can hide from thee:

4 With thy wisdom and with thine understanding thou hast gotten thee riches, and hast gotten gold and silver into thy treasures:

5 By thy great wisdom *and* by thy traffick [*with your great skill in trading and business dealings*] hast thou increased thy riches, and thine heart is lifted up because of thy riches [*you have become very prideful*]:

6 Therefore thus saith the Lord GOD; Because thou hast set thine heart as the heart of God [*Because you think you are God*];

7 Behold, **therefore I will bring strangers** [*foreigners*] **upon thee**, the terrible of the nations: and they shall draw their swords against the beauty of thy wisdom, and they shall defile thy brightness.

8 They shall bring thee down to the pit [*to the depths of hell*], and thou shalt die the deaths of *them that are* slain in the midst of the seas [*you will die just like any other mortal*].

9 Wilt thou yet say before him [*the true God, Jehovah*] that slayeth thee, I *am* God? but thou *shalt be* a man, and no God, in the hand of him that slayeth thee.

10 Thou shalt die the deaths of the uncircumcised [*Gentiles, heathen*] by the hand of strangers: for I have spoken it, saith the Lord GOD.

11 ¶ Moreover the word of the LORD came unto me, saying,

Next comes the lamentation or formal mourning for Tyre.

12 Son of man, take up a lamentation upon the king of Tyrus, and say unto him, Thus saith the Lord GOD; Thou sealest up the sum, full of wisdom, and perfect in beauty.

13 Thou hast been in Eden the garden of God [*you have lived in a paradise, like the Garden of Eden*]; every precious stone *was* thy covering, the sardius, topaz, and the diamond, the beryl, the onyx, and the jasper,

the sapphire, the emerald, and the carbuncle [*a precious gem stone*], and gold: the workmanship of thy tabrets and of thy pipes was prepared in thee in the day that thou wast created.

14 Thou *art* the anointed cherub that covereth; and I have set thee *so* [*you had the potential to be good*]*:* thou wast upon the holy mountain of God; thou hast walked up and down in the midst of the stones of fire.

15 Thou *wast* perfect in thy ways from the day that thou wast created [*you started out innocent*]**, till iniquity was found in thee** [*but you became wicked*].

16 By the multitude of thy merchandise they have filled the midst of thee with violence, and **thou hast sinned**: therefore I will cast thee as profane out of the mountain of God: and **I will destroy thee**, O covering cherub, from the midst of the stones of fire.

17 Thine heart was lifted up because of thy beauty, thou hast corrupted thy wisdom by reason of thy brightness [*you became corrupt because of your material success*]**: I will cast thee to the ground**, I will lay thee before kings, that they may behold thee.

> Remember that all people are born with a conscience and, thus, have a sense of right and wrong. We see this in the accountability to which this mighty leader of Tyre (and the other leaders of heathen cities and

nations) is being held in this section of Ezekiel.

18 Thou hast defiled thy sanctuaries by the multitude of thine iniquities [*by your gross wickedness*]**, by** the iniquity of thy traffick; **therefore will I bring forth a fire from the midst of thee, it shall devour thee, and I will bring thee to ashes upon the earth** in the sight of all them that behold thee.

19 All they that know thee among the people shall be astonished at thee: thou shalt be a terror [*you will come to a terrible end*]**, and never *shalt* thou *be* any more**.

Next, a prophecy of doom to Sidon.

20 ¶ Again the word of the LORD came unto me, saying,

21 Son of man, **set thy face against Zidon, and prophesy against it,**

22 And say, Thus saith the Lord GOD; Behold, **I *am* against thee, O Zidon**; and **I will be glorified in the midst of thee** [*My power will be seen in your midst*]**: and they shall know that I *am* the LORD**, when I shall have executed judgments in her, and shall be sanctified in her.

23 For **I will send into her pestilence, and blood into her streets**; and the wounded shall be judged in the midst of her by the sword upon her on every side; and they shall know that I *am* the LORD.

24 ¶ And **there shall be no more a pricking brier unto the house of Israel** [*these nations, Tyre and Sidon, will no longer trouble Israel*], **nor *any* grieving thorn of all *that are* round about them** [*likewise, other nations*], that despised them; and they shall know that I *am* the Lord GOD.

25 Thus saith the Lord GOD; **When I shall have gathered the house of Israel from the people among whom they are scattered** [*this is taking place now, in our day*], **and shall be sanctified in them in the sight of the heathen** [*other nations will notice the Lord's covenant people in the last days*], **then shall they dwell in their land that I have given to my servant Jacob** [*the Jews will return to Jerusalem*].

The prophecy given in verse 26, next, would seem to yet be for a future day.

26 And **they shall dwell safely therein, and shall build houses, and plant vineyards**; yea, **they shall dwell with confidence, when I have executed judgments upon all those that despise them round about them**; and they shall know that I *am* the LORD their God.

EZEKIEL 29

Selection: all verses

Chapters 29–32 go together. They are messages of doom and lamentation against Egypt. With the things you have learned about "the manner of prophesying among the Jews" (2 Nephi 25:1–2), you just might find that you do quite well in understanding many of the **bolded** words and phrases in these four chapters. Again, there will be considerable repetition. With this in mind, I will add a minimal of commentary.

Remember that the Egyptians considered their pharaohs to be gods.

1 IN the tenth year, in the tenth *month,* in the twelfth *day* of the month, **the word of the LORD came unto me, saying,**

2 Son of man, **set thy face against Pharaoh king of Egypt, and prophesy against him, and against all Egypt**:

3 Speak, and **say, Thus saith the Lord GOD; Behold, I *am* against thee, Pharaoh king of Egypt**, the great dragon that lieth in the midst of his rivers, which hath said, **My river** [*the Nile*] **is mine own**, and **I have made it for myself** [*I created it*].

Verses 4–5, next, have interesting imagery as to how the true God will destroy Pharoah and his kingdom. Remember that the crocodile symbolized Pharaoh (see Facsimile No. 1, figure 9, in the Pearl of Great Price, Abraham.)

4 But **I will put hooks in thy jaws** [*bring you into captivity*], and **I will cause the fish of thy rivers to stick unto thy scales, and I will bring thee up out of the midst of thy rivers** [*I will bring you up out of your comfortable kingdom*], and all the fish of thy rivers shall stick unto thy scales.

5 **And I will leave thee** *thrown* **into the wilderness, thee and all the fish of thy rivers** [*your kingdom*]: thou shalt fall upon the open fields; thou shalt not be brought together, nor gathered: **I have given thee for meat to the beasts of the field and to the fowls of the heaven.**

6 And **all the inhabitants of Egypt shall know that I** *am* **the LORD** [*the only true God*], because they have been a staff of reed to the house of Israel [*Israel made treaties with Egypt (the flimsy "staff of reed)" for protection from Babylon, rather than repenting and relying on Jehovah—see Isaiah 30:1–5*].

7 When they took hold of thee by thy hand, **thou didst break**, and rend all their shoulder: and when they leaned upon thee, thou brakest, and madest all their loins to be at a stand.

8 ¶ Therefore thus saith the Lord GOD; Behold, **I will bring a sword upon thee**, and cut off man and beast out of thee.

9 And **the land of Egypt shall be desolate and waste;** and they shall know that I *am* the LORD: because he hath said, The river *is* mine, and I have made *it*.

10 Behold, therefore **I** *am* **against thee, and against thy rivers, and I will make the land of Egypt utterly waste** *and* **desolate**, from the tower of Syene [*in southern Egypt*] even unto the border of Ethiopia.

11 No foot of man shall pass through it, nor foot of beast shall pass through it, **neither shall it be inhabited forty years** [*"forty years" can mean "40 years" or it can mean "a very long time" in Biblical numerical symbolism*].

12 And **I will make the land of Egypt desolate** in the midst of the countries *that are* desolate, and her cities among the cities *that are* laid waste shall be desolate forty years: and **I will scatter the Egyptians among the nations, and will disperse them through the countries.**

13 ¶ **Yet thus saith the Lord GOD; At the end of forty years will I gather the Egyptians** from the people whither they were scattered:

14 And **I will** bring again the captivity of Egypt, and will **cause them to return** *into* **the land of Pathros** [*upper Egypt*], into the land of their habitation; **and they shall be there a base** [*less powerful*] **kingdom.**

15 It shall be the basest of the kingdoms; **neither shall it exalt itself any more above the nations**: for I will diminish them, that **they shall no more rule over the nations** [*they will no longer be a world-class power*].

16 **And it shall be no more the confidence of the house of Israel** [*Israel will no longer rely on them for protection*], which bringeth *their* iniquity to remembrance, when they shall look after them: but they shall know that I *am* the Lord GOD.

17 ¶ And it came to pass in the seven and twentieth year, in the first *month,* in the first *day* of the month, **the word of the LORD came unto me, saying,**

In verse 18, next, Ezekiel prophesies that the King of Babylon will not be successful in completely conquering Tyre and looting her great treasures. In fact, many merchants of Tyre loaded their rich treasures into their ships and escaped to Carthage.

18 Son of man, **Nebuchadrezzar king of Babylon caused his army to serve a great service against Tyrus**: every head *was* made bald, and every shoulder *was* peeled: **yet had he no wages, nor his army** [*they will not get much loot*], for Tyrus, for the service that he had served against it:

19 Therefore thus saith the Lord GOD; Behold, **I will give the land of Egypt unto Nebuchadrezzar king of Babylon**; and he shall take her multitude, and take her spoil, and take her prey; and **it shall be the wages for his army.**

20 **I have given him the land of Egypt** *for* his labour wherewith he served against it, because they wrought for me, saith the Lord GOD.

And finally, a prophecy that Israel will one day wield great power in that region.

21 ¶ **In that day will I cause the horn** [*symbol of power*] **of the house of Israel to bud forth**, and **I will give thee the opening of the mouth** [*power to speak and be heard*] **in the midst of them**; and they shall know that I *am* the LORD.

EZEKIEL 30

Selection: all verses

See heading to chapter 29.

1 **THE word of the LORD came again unto me, saying,**

2 Son of man, prophesy and say, Thus saith the Lord GOD; **Howl ye, Woe worth the day** [*dread the coming of that day*]!

3 For **the day** *is* **near**, even the day of the LORD *is* near, a cloudy day; it shall be the time of the heathen.

4 And **the sword shall come upon Egypt**, and great pain shall be in Ethiopia, when the slain shall fall in Egypt, and **they shall take away her multitude, and her foundations shall be broken down.**

5 **Ethiopia, and Libya, and Lydia, and all the mingled people, and Chub, and the men of the land that is in league** [*with whom they have a treaty*], **shall fall with them by the sword.**

6 Thus saith the LORD; **They also that uphold Egypt shall fall**; and **the pride of her power shall come down**: from the tower of Syene shall they fall in it by the sword, saith the Lord GOD.

7 **And they shall be desolate in the midst of the countries** *that are* **desolate**, and her cities shall be in the midst of the cities *that are* wasted.

8 And **they shall know that I** *am* **the LORD, when I have set a fire in Egypt, and** *when* **all her helpers shall be destroyed.**

9 **In that day shall messengers go forth from me in ships to make the careless** [*complacent*] **Ethiopians afraid**, and great pain shall come upon them, as in the day of Egypt: for, lo, it cometh.

10 Thus saith the Lord GOD; **I will also make the multitude of Egypt to cease by the hand of Nebuchadrezzar king of Babylon.**

11 **He and his people with him, the terrible of the nations, shall be brought to destroy the land**: and **they shall draw their swords against Egypt, and fill the land with the slain.**

12 And **I will make the rivers dry**, and **sell the land into the hand of the wicked**: and I will **make the land waste**, and all that is therein, **by the hand of strangers** [*foreigners; foreign enemies*]: I the LORD have spoken *it.*

13 Thus saith the Lord GOD; **I will also destroy the idols, and I will cause** *their* **images to cease out of Noph** [*the city of Memphis in lower Egypt*]; and **there shall be no more a prince** [*a central leader*] **of the land of Egypt: and I will put a fear in the land of Egypt.**

14 And **I will make Pathros** [*upper Egypt*] **desolate**, and **will set fire in Zoan** [*the city of Rameses in the Nile River delta*], and **will execute judgments in No** [*the city of Thebes in upper Egypt*].

15 And **I will pour my fury upon Sin**, the strength of Egypt; and **I will cut off the multitude of No.**

16 And **I will set fire in Egypt**: Sin shall have great pain, and No shall be rent asunder, and Noph *shall have* distresses daily.

17 **The young men of Aven** [*the sacred city of Heliopolis in lower Egypt*] **and of Pi-beseth shall fall by the sword**: and **these** *cities* **shall go into captivity.**

18 At Tehaphnehes also **the day shall be darkened, when I shall break there the yokes** [*power*] of Egypt: and **the pomp of her strength shall cease** in her: as for her, a cloud shall cover her, and **her daughters shall go into captivity.**

19 **Thus will I execute judgments** [*punishments for wickedness*] **in Egypt**: and they shall know that I *am* the LORD.

20 ¶ And it came to pass in the eleventh year, in the first *month,* in the seventh *day* of the month, *that* **the word of the LORD came unto me, saying,**

Remember, Ezekiel is prophesying of the future as if it had already taken place.

21 Son of man, **I have broken the arm** [power] **of Pharaoh king of Egypt**; and, lo, **it shall not be bound up to be healed**, to put a roller [splint] to bind it, **to make it strong to hold the sword** [Egypt will not regain its former power and status].

22 Therefore **thus saith the Lord GOD; Behold, I** am **against Pharaoh king of Egypt**, and will break his arms, the strong, and that which was broken; and I will cause the sword to fall out of his hand.

23 And **I will scatter the Egyptians among the nations**, and will disperse them through the countries.

24 And **I will strengthen the arms of the king of Babylon, and put my sword in his hand: but I will break Pharaoh's arms** [power], and he shall groan before him with the groanings of a deadly wounded man.

25 But **I will strengthen the arms of the king of Babylon, and the arms of Pharaoh shall fall down; and they shall know that I** am **the LORD** [the true God, Jehovah], **when I shall put my sword into the hand of the king of Babylon** [when I, the Lord, use Babylon to be My sword of destruction upon the wicked heathen nations], and **he shall stretch it out upon the land of Egypt.**

26 And **I will scatter the Egyptians among the nations, and dis-**perse them among the countries; and they shall know that I am the LORD.

EZEKIEL 31

Selection: all verses

See heading to chapter 29.

The heading to your Bible summarizes this chapter.

Pharaoh's glory and fall compared to that of the Assyrians.

1 AND it came to pass in the eleventh year, in the third *month,* in the first *day* of the month, *that* **the word of the LORD came unto me, saying,**

2 Son of man, **speak unto Pharaoh king of Egypt, and to his multitude** [peope]**; Whom art thou like in thy greatness?**

3 ¶ **Behold, the Assyrian** [King Sennacherib—see Isaiah 36–37] *was* **a cedar in Lebanon** [a truly powerful king] with fair branches [lots of subjects], and with a shadowing shroud, and of an high stature; and his top was among the thick boughs [the King of Assyria was truly powerful with a widespread domain].

4 **The waters made him great**, the deep set him up on high with her rivers running round about his plants, **and sent out her little rivers unto all the trees of the field.**

5 Therefore **his height was exalted above all the trees of the field,** and

his boughs were multiplied, and his branches became long because of the multitude of waters, when he shot forth.

6 **All the fowls of heaven** [*many nations*] **made their nests in his boughs** [*were under his rule*], and under his branches did all the beasts of the field bring forth their young, and **under his shadow** [*protection*] **dwelt all great nations**.

7 **Thus was he fair in his greatness**, in the length of his branches: for his root was by great waters.

8 **The cedars in the garden of God could not hide** [*eclipse*] **him**: the fir trees were not like his boughs, and the chesnut trees were not like his branches; nor any tree in the garden of God was like unto him in his beauty.

9 I have made him fair by the multitude of his branches: **so that all the trees of Eden**, that *were* in the garden of God, **envied him**.

Remember, this is all symbolism and comparison to put across the point that the King of Assyria was truly a powerful ruler. Starting with verse 10, Ezekiel prophesies the pride, fall, and death of Sennacherib, King of Assyria. Pharoah is heading for the same downfall.

10 ¶ Therefore thus saith the Lord GOD; Because thou hast lifted up thyself in height, and he hath shot up his top among the thick boughs, and his heart is lifted up in his height;

11 **I have therefore delivered him into the hand of the mighty one of the heathen** [*enemy heathen nations*]; he shall surely deal with him: **I have driven him out for his wickedness**.

Next, in verses 12–16, Ezekiel prophesies of the repercussions on other nations when Assyria falls.

12 And strangers, **the terrible** [*tyrants*] **of the nations, have cut him off, and have left him**: upon the mountains and in all the valleys his branches are fallen, and his boughs are broken by all the rivers of the land; and **all the people of the earth are gone down from his shadow** [*protection*], **and have left him**.

13 **Upon his ruin shall all the fowls of the heaven remain, and all the beasts of the field shall be upon his branches** [*nations formerly under his protection shall try, unsuccessfully, to find protection in the ruins of his kingdom—see verse 14*]:

14 **To the end that none of all the trees by the waters exalt themselves** for their height, neither shoot up their top among the thick boughs, neither their trees stand up in their height, all that drink water: for **they are all delivered unto death**, to the nether parts of the earth, in the midst of the children of men, **with them that go down to the pit** [*hell—see verse 17*].

15 Thus saith the Lord GOD; In the day when he went down to the grave I caused a mourning: I covered the deep for him, and I restrained the

floods thereof, and the great waters were stayed: and **I caused Lebanon to mourn for him, and all the trees of the field fainted** [*were devastated and weakened*] **for him**.

16 **I made the nations to shake at the sound of his fall**, when **I cast him down to hell with them that descend into the pit** [*with other wicked people*]: and all the trees of Eden, the choice and best of Lebanon, all that drink water [*all mortals*], shall be comforted in the nether [*farthest out*] parts of the earth.

17 **They also went down into hell with him** unto *them that be* slain with the sword; and *they that were* his arm, *that* dwelt under his shadow in the midst of the heathen.

Lastly, in verse 18, next, Pharoah, who thought he was really something, is asked (symbolically, in this prophecy) if he can see any similarities between himself and the King of Assyria, as far as his final state is concerned.

18 ¶ **To whom art thou thus like** in glory and in greatness among the trees of Eden? **yet shalt thou** [*Pharoah and his people*] **be brought down** with the trees of Eden **unto the nether parts of the earth: thou shalt lie in the midst of the uncircumcised** [*the heathen, those who have not successfully made and kept covenants with the Lord*] with *them that be* slain by the sword. **This** *is* **Pharaoh and all his multitude**, saith the Lord GOD.

EZEKIEL 32

Selection: all verses

See heading to chapter 29.

In this chapter, we see a prophetic lament (formal mourning) for the frightening downfall of Pharaoh and Egypt. Remember, Ezekiel is prophesying of things yet to come as though they had already taken place.

1 AND it came to pass in the twelfth year, in the twelfth month, in the first *day* of the month, *that* **the word of the LORD came unto me, saying**,

2 **Son of man** [*Ezekiel*], **take up a lamentation for Pharaoh king of Egypt, and say unto him, Thou art like a young lion of the nations, and thou** *art* **as a whale in the seas** [*you think of yourself as a powerful, admirable, young lion, but, in reality, you are a monster of the sea*]: and **thou camest forth with thy rivers, and troubledst the waters with thy feet, and fouledst their rivers** [*you made your stewardship to stink*].

3 Thus saith the Lord GOD; **I will therefore spread out my net** [*fishing net*] **over thee** with a company of many people; and **they shall bring thee up in my net**.

4 Then will I leave thee upon the land [*destroy you*], **I will cast thee forth upon the open field, and will cause all the fowls of the heaven to remain upon thee** [*you will become carrion for birds of prey*], **and I will fill**

the beasts of the whole earth with thee [*beasts will eat your carcass*].

5 And **I will lay thy flesh upon the mountains, and fill the valleys with thy height** [*NIV "remains"*].

6 **I will also water with thy blood the land wherein thou swimmest**, *even* to the mountains; and the rivers shall be full of thee.

7 And **when I shall put thee out** [*destroy you*], I will cover the heaven, and make the stars thereof dark; I will cover the sun with a cloud, and the moon shall not give her light.

8 **All the bright lights of heaven** [*your once-powerful leaders*] **will I make dark over thee** [*because of your demise*], and set darkness upon thy land, saith the Lord GOD.

9 **I will also vex the hearts of many people** [*many people will be troubled because of your destruction*], when I shall bring thy destruction among the nations, into the countries which thou hast not known [*this will affect nations you don't even know of*].

10 Yea, **I will make many people amazed** [*appalled*] **at thee**, and **their kings shall be horribly afraid for thee** [*will shudder in horror because of what happen to you*], when I shall brandish my sword before them; and **they shall tremble at *every* moment, every man for his own life** [*they will shudder because of their loss of security caused by your downfall*], **in the day of thy fall**.

11 ¶ For thus saith the Lord GOD; The sword of **the king of Babylon shall come upon thee**.

12 **By the swords of the mighty will I cause thy multitude to fall**, the terrible of the nations, all of them: and **they shall spoil the pomp of Egypt, and all the multitude thereof shall be destroyed**.

Next, in verses 13–16, we see the economy of Egypt destroyed.

13 **I will destroy also all the beasts thereof** from beside the great waters; neither shall the foot of man trouble them any more, nor the hoofs of beasts trouble them.

14 **Then will I make their waters deep** [*perhaps meaning unseasonal floods*], and cause their rivers to run like oil, saith the Lord GOD.

15 **When I shall make the land of Egypt desolate**, and **the country shall be destitute of that whereof it was full**, when I shall smite all them that dwell therein, then shall they know that I *am* the LORD.

16 **This *is* the lamentation wherewith they shall lament her**: the daughters of the nations shall lament her: they shall lament for her, *even* for Egypt, and for all her multitude, saith the Lord GOD.

Next, in verses 17–32, Ezekiel is told to mourn the final relegation of Egypt and her wicked people to hell, where other wicked nations already there would greet her and even mock her for being there too.

17 ¶ It came to pass also in the twelfth year, in the fifteenth *day* of the month, *that* the word of **the LORD came unto me, saying**,

18 Son of man, **wail for the multitude of Egypt, and cast them down** [*and, in your prophecy, portray them*], *even* her, **and the daughters of the famous nations, unto the nether parts of the earth** [*the underworld, hell*], **with them that go down into the pit** [*hell*].

19 Whom dost thou pass in beauty? **go down, and be thou laid with the uncircumcised** [*you are going to end up with the unrighteous in hell*].

20 **They shall fall in the midst of** *them that are* **slain by the sword** [*great slaughter is coming to Egypt*]: she is delivered to the sword: **draw her and all her multitudes** [*picture this happening to all the wicked in Egypt*].

21 **The strong among the mighty** [*the mighty and famous among the dead in hell*] **shall speak to him** [*greet him*] **out of the midst of hell** with them that help him: they are gone down, they lie uncircumcised, slain by the sword.

22 **Asshur** [*Assyria*] *is* **there and all her company**: his graves *are* about him: all of them slain, fallen by the sword:

23 **Whose graves are set in the sides of the pit** [*the deepest part of hell*], and her company is round about her grave: **all of** them slain, fallen by the sword, **which caused terror in the land of the living** [*all of whom caused terror among mortals while they were alive*].

24 **There** [*also in hell*] *is* **Elam** [*a mountainous country to the east of Babylon*] **and all her multitude round about her grave** [*who have also died*], all of them slain, fallen by the sword, which are gone down uncircumcised into the nether parts of the earth, **which caused their terror in the land of the living; yet have they borne their shame with them that go down to the pit**.

25 **They have set her a bed in the midst of the slain with all her multitude** [*they have prepared a place for her right in the middle of hell*] : her graves *are* round about him: all of them uncircumcised, slain by the sword: though their terror was caused in the land of the living, yet have **they borne their shame with them that go down to the pit** [*they have carried their sins with them into hell*]: he is put in the midst of *them that be* slain.

26 **There** *is* **Meshech, Tubal** [*two more wicked nations*], and all her multitude: her graves *are* round about him: **all of them uncircumcised, slain by the sword, though they caused their terror in the land of the living**.

27 **And they shall not lie** [*shall they not also lie*] with the mighty *that are* **fallen** [*have died*] **of the uncircumcised** [*the heathen*], **which are gone**

down to hell with their weapons of war: and they have laid their swords under their heads [*their weapons were buried with them*], but their iniquities shall be upon their bones, though *they were* the terror of the mighty in the land of the living.

28 **Yea, thou** [*Egypt*] **shalt be broken in the midst of the uncircumcised, and shalt lie with *them that are* slain with the sword.**

29 **There *is* Edom, her kings, and all her princes**, which with their might are laid by *them that were* slain by the sword: **they shall lie with the uncircumcised, and with them that go down to the pit.**

30 **There *be* the princes of the north, all of them, and all the Zidonians**, which are gone down with the slain; with their terror they are ashamed of their might; **and they lie uncircumcised with *them that be* slain by the sword, and bear their shame with them that go down to the pit**.

31 **Pharaoh shall see them** [*in hell*], and shall be comforted over all his multitude [*will be "comforted" by all these (not a very "comforting" thought)*], *even* **Pharaoh and all his army slain by the sword, saith the Lord GOD.**

32 For I have caused my terror in the land of the living: and **he shall be laid in the midst of the uncircumcised** with *them that are* slain with

the sword, *even* **Pharaoh and all his multitude**, saith the Lord GOD.

EZEKIEL 33

Selection: all verses

After eight chapters of Ezekiel's prophesying the downfall of neighboring wicked nations, this chapter turns back to the Lord's messages to Israel.

Verses 1–10 detail Ezekiel's responsibilities as a "watchman" for Israel and compare him to a "lookout" or watchman posted by a city to warn them of approaching dangers.

1 AGAIN **the word of the LORD came unto me, saying,**

2 **Son of man** [*Ezekiel*], **speak to the children of thy people** [*Israel*], and say unto them, **When I bring the sword upon a land** [*when danger is approaching*], **if the people of the land take a man of their coasts** [*one of their own people*]**, and set him for their watchman** [*post a lookout*]**:**

3 **If when he seeth the sword come** upon the land, **he blow the trumpet, and warn the people;**

4 **Then whosoever heareth the sound of the trumpet, and taketh not warning** [*ignores the warning*]**; if the sword come, and take him away, his blood shall be upon his own head** [*the responsibility is his*].

5 **He heard the sound of the trumpet, and took not warning; his blood shall be upon him** [*he carries full blame for what happens to him*].

But he that taketh warning shall deliver his soul [*whoever heeds the warning will save himself*].

> Verse 6, next, has very serious doctrine regarding the accountability of leaders, teachers, parents and others who have stewardships for the spiritual well-being of those under their care.

6 **But if the watchman see the sword come, and blow not the trumpet** [*if the lookout sees the danger coming but does not sound the warning*], **and the people be not warned; if the sword come, and take** *any* **person from among them, he is taken away in his iniquity** [*he dies in his wickedness without repenting*]; **but his blood will I require at the watchman's hand** [*but the watchman will be held accountable for his sins*].

7 **So thou, O son of man** [*Ezekiel*], **I have set thee a watchman unto the house of Israel**; therefore **thou shalt hear the word at my mouth, and warn them from me.**

8 **When I say unto the wicked, O wicked** *man,* **thou shalt surely die; if thou dost not speak to warn the wicked from his way**, that wicked *man* shall die in his iniquity; but **his blood will I require at thine hand.**

9 **Nevertheless, if thou warn the wicked of his way to turn from it**; if he do not turn from his way, he shall die in his iniquity; but **thou hast delivered thy soul** [*you will not be held accountable for his sins*].

10 **Therefore**, O thou son of man, **speak unto the house of Israel; Thus ye speak, saying** [*this is what I hear you asking*], **If our transgressions and our sins** *be* **upon us** [*if we are to be held accountable for our sins*], **and we pine away in them** [*and we are burdened down by our sins*], **how should we then live** [*what can we do to repent and be alive spiritually*]?

11 **Say unto them,** *As* I live, saith the Lord GOD, **I have no pleasure in the death of the wicked; but that the wicked turn from his way and live** [*I have no pleasure in destroying the wicked but have great joy when they repent*]: **turn ye** [*repent*], **turn ye from your evil ways**; for why will ye die, O house of Israel?

> Next, in verses 12–16, we are clearly taught that if we live righteously and strive to stay on the covenant path for part of our lives, but then start breaking the commandments and breaking our covenants, our former righteousness will not save us. On the other hand, if a person truly repents and turns away from sin, the former sins will not get in the way of salvation for him or her.

12 Therefore, thou son of man, say unto the children of thy people, **The righteousness of the righteous shall not deliver** [*save him*] **him in the day of his transgression** [*if he turns to sin*]: **as for the wickedness of the wicked, he shall not fall thereby in the day that he turneth** [*repents*] **from his wickedness**; neither shall the righteous be able to

live for his *righteousness* in the day that he sinneth.

13 **When I shall say to the righteous,** *that* **he shall surely live** [*he is on the covenant path leading to exaltation*]; **if he trust to his own righteousness** [*makes his own rules*], **and commit iniquity** [*turns to wickedness*], **all his righteousnesses shall not be remembered** [*on Judgment Day*]; but for his iniquity that he hath committed, he shall die [*spiritually*] for it.

14 **Again, when I say unto the wicked, Thou shalt surely die** [*you are heading for spiritual death, hell*]; **if he turn from his sin** [*repents*], **and do that which is lawful and right**;

15 *If* **the wicked restore the pledge** [*if he gives back what he took in collateral for a loan*], **give again that he had robbed, walk in the statutes of life** [*keeps the commandments that lead to eternal life*], **without committing iniquity; he shall surely live, he shall not die**.

16 **None of his sins that he hath committed shall be mentioned unto him** [*on Judgment Day—see D&C 58:42*]: **he hath done that which is lawful and right; he shall surely live**.

17 ¶ **Yet the children of thy people** [*your countrymen*] **say, The way of the Lord is not equal** [*not just, not fair*]: **but as for them, their way is not equal**.

Verses 18–20, next, provide a beautifully simple summary of the above doctrines.

18 **When the righteous turneth from his righteousness, and committeth iniquity, he shall even die thereby**.

19 **But if the wicked turn from his wickedness, and do that which is lawful and right, he shall live thereby**.

20 ¶ Yet ye say, The way of the Lord is not equal. O ye house of Israel, **I will judge you every one after his ways**.

Verse 21, next, was given three years after the final siege against Jerusalem began. Verses 21–29 deal with Jerusalem's downfall.

21 ¶ And it came to pass in the twelfth year of our captivity, in the tenth *month,* in the fifth *day* of the month, *that* **one that had escaped out of Jerusalem** [*a refugee*] **came unto me, saying, The city is smitten** [*Jerusalem is under siege*].

22 **Now the hand of the LORD was upon me in the evening, afore he that was escaped came** [*the evening before the refugee came*]; **and had opened my mouth**, until he [*the refugee*] came to me in the morning; and my mouth was opened, and **I was no more dumb** [*see Ezekiel 3:26–27, 24:26–27*].

23 Then **the word of the LORD came unto me, saying,**

Next, in verse 24, the exiled Jews in Babylon are complaining that the land of Israel was given to Abraham, and that, as Abraham's rightful heirs, they should still be living in Israel, not as exiles in Babylon. The Lord has an answer for them, in verses 25–29.

24 Son of man, they that inhabit those wastes of the land of Israel speak, saying, **Abraham was one, and he inherited the land** [*was given the land of Israel by the Lord as an inheritance*]: **but we** *are* **many; the land is given us for inheritance.**

25 **Wherefore say unto them** [*answer their complaint*], Thus saith the Lord GOD; **Ye eat with the blood, and lift up your eyes toward your idols** [*you are worshiping idols instead of Me*], **and shed blood** [*you are murderers*]: **and shall ye possess the land** [*what makes you think you deserve to possess the land of Israel*]?

26 **Ye stand upon your sword** [*you rely upon your military might instead of Me*], **ye work abomination, and ye defile every one his neighbour's wife** [*you are constantly committing adultery*]: **and shall ye possess the land?**

27 Say thou thus unto them, Thus saith the Lord GOD; *As* I live, surely **they that** *are* **in the wastes shall fall by the sword, and him that** *is* **in the open field will I give to the beasts to be devoured, and they that** *be* **in the forts and in the caves shall die of the pestilence.**

28 For **I will lay the land most desolate,** and the pomp of her strength shall cease; and **the mountains of Israel shall be desolate,** that none shall pass through.

29 Then shall they know that I *am* the LORD, when I have laid the land most desolate **because of all their abominations which they have committed.**

Finally, in verses 30–33, the Lord consoles and reassures Ezekiel, telling him that He knows what a challenge he is facing, being a prophet to such rebellious Israelites.

30 ¶ Also, thou son of man, the children of **thy people still are talking** [*gossiping and complaining*] **against thee** by the walls and in the doors of the houses, and speak one to another, every one to his brother, **saying, Come, I pray you, and hear what is the word that cometh forth from the LORD** [*let's go see what else Ezekiel is saying*].

31 And **they come unto thee as the people cometh** [*like people typically do*], and they sit before thee *as* my people, and **they hear thy words, but they will not do them**: for **with their mouth they shew much love,** *but* **their heart goeth after their covetousness** [*they are hypocrites*].

32 And, lo, thou *art* unto them as a very lovely song of one that hath a pleasant voice, and can play well on an instrument: for **they hear thy words, but they do them not.**

33 **And when this cometh to pass** [*Ezekiel's prophecies*], (lo, it will come,) **then shall they know that a prophet hath been among them.**

EZEKIEL 34

Selection: all verses

In this chapter, the Lord scolds and condemns the "shepherds of Israel," the priests and religious leaders of Israel in Ezekiel's day who were supposed to nourish them in the word of the Lord and help them avoid wickedness. But, instead, these leaders profited from their positions and failed to strive to keep the people worthy of the Lord's protection (verses 2–10).

Verses 11–19, prophesy the gathering of Israel in the last days by the Good Shepherd, in other words, the Lord.

Verses 20–24 show that in the last-days gathering of scattered Israel, the bad shepherds will be replaced by true shepherds, servants of the Lord who will truly minister to the "sheep" and nourish them in the word of God. These verses also prophecy that Christ will rule and reign during the Millennium.

Verses 25–31 remind us that the Savior is the Good Shepherd and that, ultimately, everything belongs to Him.

1 AND **the word of the LORD came unto me, saying,**

2 Son of man, **prophesy against the shepherds of Israel**, prophesy, and **say unto them,** Thus saith the Lord GOD unto the shepherds; **Woe** *be* to the shepherds of Israel that do feed themselves! should not the shepherds feed the flocks [*who profit from their position rather than serving their people*]?

3 **Ye** eat the fat, and **ye** clothe **you** with the wool, **ye** kill them that are fed: *but* **ye feed not the flock.**

4 **The diseased have ye not strengthened, neither have ye healed that which was sick** [*you have not taken care of the poor and the needy*], neither have ye bound up *that which was* broken, neither have ye brought again that which was driven away, neither have ye sought that which was lost; **but with force and with cruelty have ye ruled them.**

5 And **they were scattered, because** *there is* **no shepherd**: and they became meat [*food, prey*] to all the beasts of the field, when they were scattered.

6 **My sheep wandered** through all the mountains, and upon every high hill: yea, **my flock was scattered upon all the face of the earth,** and **none did search or seek** *after them.*

7 ¶ **Therefore, ye shepherds, hear the word of the LORD;**

8 *As* I live [*the absolute, highest promise in Biblical culture*], saith the Lord GOD, surely **because my flock became a prey, and my flock became meat** [*food, prey*] **to every beast of the field** [*enemy of Israel*], **because** *there was* **no shepherd** [*because you failed so miserably in*

your responsibilities], **neither did my shepherds search for my flock, but the shepherds fed themselves, and fed not my flock**;

9 **Therefore, O ye shepherds, hear the word of the LORD**;

10 Thus saith the Lord GOD; **Behold, I** *am* **against the shepherds**; and **I will require my flock at their hand** [*hold them accountable*], and cause them to cease from feeding the flock; neither shall the shepherds feed themselves any more; for **I will deliver my flock from their mouth** [*I will eventually gather Israel back into the fold*], that they may not be meat for them.

11 ¶ For thus saith the Lord GOD; Behold, I, *even* **I, will both search my sheep, and seek them out**.

12 **As a shepherd seeketh out his flock** in the day that he is among his sheep *that are* scattered; **so will I seek out my sheep, and will deliver them out of all places where they have been scattered** in the cloudy and dark day.

13 And **I will bring them out from the people, and gather them from the countries**, and **will bring them to their own land**, and feed them upon the mountains of Israel by the rivers, and in all the inhabited places of the country.

14 **I will feed them in a good pasture** [*the true gospel*], and **upon the high mountains of Israel** shall their fold be: there shall they lie in a good

fold, and *in* **a fat pasture shall they feed upon the mountains of Israel**.

15 **I will feed my flock**, and I will cause them to lie down, saith the Lord GOD.

16 **I will seek that which was lost**, and bring again that which was driven away, and will bind up *that which was* broken, and will strengthen that which was sick: **but I will destroy the fat and the strong** [*the wicked leaders of Israel*]; **I will feed them with judgment** [*I will hold them accountable*].

17 **And** *as for* **you, O my flock**, thus saith the Lord GOD; Behold, **I judge between cattle and cattle** [*I will judge you individually*], between the rams and the he goats.

18 ***Seemeth it* a small thing unto you** [*does it seem like just a small sin to you bad shepherds*] **to have eaten up the good pasture,** but ye must tread down with your feet the residue of your pastures? and to have drunk of the deep waters, **but ye must foul the residue with your fee**t [*you have polluted everything you touched*]?

19 And *as for* my flock [*Israel*], **they eat that which ye have trodden with your feet**; and they drink that which ye have fouled with your feet [*they have been swallowing your polluted false teachings, idol worship, etc.*].

20 ¶ **Therefore** thus saith the Lord GOD unto them; Behold, **I,** *even* **I, will judge between the fat cattle and between the lean cattle** [*I will*

take over and gather My sheep with fairness].

21 **Because ye have** thrust with side and with shoulder, and **pushed all the diseased with your horns** [*you pushed all the poor and needy away*], **till ye have scattered them abroad** [*you led them astray so thoroughly that you have brought about the scattering of Israel*];

Verse 22 repeats the prophetic fact that the Lord will gather Israel in the last days and that Christ will rule and reign during the Millennium (see *Old Testament Student Manual, 1 Kings to Malachi*, section 13–57, Isaiah 11:1, starting with page 147).

22 **Therefore will I save my flock,** and they shall no more be a prey; and I will judge between cattle and cattle.

23 And **I will set up one shepherd** [*Christ*] **over them, and he shall feed them,** *even* my servant David [*Christ; David was an ancestor of Jesus and often symbolizes Jesus Christ in Biblical symbolism*]; **he shall feed them, and he shall be their shepherd.**

24 And **I the LORD will be their God,** and **my servant David a prince among them**; I the LORD have spoken *it.*

25 And **I will make with them a covenant of peace,** and **will cause the evil beasts to cease out of the land**: and **they shall dwell safely in the wilderness, and sleep in the woods** [*among other things, this sym-*

bolizes the peace that will exist during the Millennium].

26 And **I will make them and the places round about my hill a blessing**; and I will cause the shower to come down in his season; **there shall be showers of blessing.**

27 **And the tree of the field shall yield her fruit, and the earth shall yield her increase, and they shall be safe in their land**, and **shall know that I** *am* **the LORD**, when I have broken the bands of their yoke [*delivered them from literal physical bondage and spiritual bondage*], **and delivered them out of the hand of those** [*the "bad shepherds"*] **that served themselves of them.**

28 And **they shall no more be a prey to the heathen, neither shall the beast of the land devour them; but they shall dwell safely, and none shall make *them* afraid.**

29 And **I will raise up for them a plant of renown** [*Isaiah 61:3 suggests that this means receiving "beauty for ashes, "in other words, receiving bounteous blessings after all they have gone through*], and **they shall be no more consumed with hunger** in the land, neither bear the shame of the heathen any more.

30 **Thus shall they know that I the LORD their God** *am* **with them, and *that* they, *even* the house of Israel, *are* my people**, saith the Lord GOD.

31 And ye my flock, the flock of my pasture, *are* men, **and I *am* your God**, saith the Lord GOD.

EZEKIEL 35

Selection: all verses

Chronologically, this chapter goes with chapters 25–32, which contain Ezekiel's prophecies of doom to Israel's wicked neighbor nations. The background for Seir (also known as Edom and, later, Idumea), a nation (Esau's descendants) south of the Dead Sea, is that the people of Edom had long been a relentless enemy of Israel. And, after the Babylonian siege, they had hoped to take over portions of Israel ·and otherwise benefit from their destruction.

1 MOREOVER **the word of the LORD came unto me, saying,**

2 Son of man, **set thy face against mount Seir** [*Edom*] **prophesy against it,**

3 And say unto it, Thus saith the Lord GOD; Behold, **O mount Seir, I *am* against thee**, and I will stretch out mine hand against thee, and **I will make thee most desolate.**

4 **I will lay thy cities waste, and thou shalt be desolate, and thou shalt know that I *am* the LORD.**

5 **Because thou hast had a perpetual hatred, and hast shed** *the blood of* **the children of Israel** by the force of the sword **in the time of** their calamity, in the time *that their* iniquity *had* an end:

6 **Therefore** [*this is the reason why*], *as* I live, saith the Lord GOD, **I will prepare thee unto blood, and blood shall pursue thee: sith** [*since*] **thou hast not hated blood** [*since you did not hesitate to kill and harm Israelites*], even **blood shall pursue thee.**

7 **Thus will I make mount Seir most desolate** [*a desolate waste*], **and cut off from it him that passeth out and him that returneth** [*to the point that no one will ever come and go from it again*].

8 And **I will fill his mountains with his slain *men:* in thy hills, and in thy valleys, and in all thy rivers, shall they fall that are slain with the sword.**

9 **I will make thee perpetual desolations, and thy cities shall not return**: and ye shall know that I *am* the LORD.

10 **Because thou hast said, These two nations** [*Israel and Judah*] **and these two countries shall be mine, and we will possess it**; whereas the LORD was there:

11 Therefore, *as* I live, saith the Lord GOD, **I will even do according to thine anger, and according to thine envy which thou hast used out of thy hatred against them**; and I will make myself known among them, when I have judged thee.

12 And **thou shalt know that I** *am* **the LORD, *and that* I have heard all thy blasphemies** which thou hast spoken **against** the mountains of **Israel**, saying, **They are laid desolate, they are given us to consume** [*we can profit from their destruction*].

13 **Thus with your mouth ye have boasted against me**, and have multiplied your words against me [*have said many things against Me*]: **I have heard** *them*.

14 Thus saith the Lord GOD; When the whole earth rejoiceth, **I will make thee desolate.**

15 **As thou didst rejoice at** the inheritance of the house of **Israel, because it was desolate, so will I do unto thee: thou shalt be desolate,** O mount Seir, and all Idumea, *even* all of it: and **they shall know that I** *am* **the LORD** [*the real God*].

EZEKIEL 36

Selection: all verses

This chapter is mainly a pleasant and upbeat one, prophesying the last-days gathering of Israel. It is a sequel to chapters 33–34. We are living in the times about which it prophesies. Be aware, though, that verses 16–22 do remind us why the Lord scattered Israel in the first place. None of the prophesied events in this chapter have been fully fulfilled, although they are now underway.

Verses 1–7 basically say that, because Israel has had trouble long enough, because they have been held in

contempt and derided by their enemies long enough, because they have been prey to mocking and despising by other nations long enough, the Lord will bless them in the latter-days.

1 ALSO, thou son of man, **prophesy unto the mountains of Israel** [*another way of saying "Israel"*], and say, Ye mountains of Israel, **hear the word of the LORD:**

2 Thus saith the Lord GOD; **Because the enemy hath said against you, Aha** [*because they have rejoiced about your troubles—see 25:3*], **even the ancient high places** [*Israel*] **are ours in possession** [*they have gladly taken over your land*]:

3 **Therefore prophesy** and say, Thus saith the Lord GOD; **Because they have made** *you* **desolate, and swallowed you up on every side, that ye might be a possession unto the residue of the heathen** [*unbelievers*]**, and ye are taken up in the lips of talkers** [*you have been much gossiped about*]**, and** *are* **an infamy of the people** [*have been slandered by the heathen*]:

4 **Therefore, ye mountains of Israel, hear the word of the Lord GOD; Thus saith the Lord GOD to** [*Israel*] the mountains, and to the hills, to the rivers, and to the valleys, to the desolate wastes, and to the cities that are forsaken, **which became a prey and derision to the residue of the heathen that** *are* **round about;**

5 Therefore thus saith the Lord GOD; **Surely in the fire of my jeal-**

ousy have I spoken against the residue of the heathen, and against all Idumea [the wicked unbelievers], which have appointed my land into their possession with the joy of all *their* heart, with despiteful minds, to cast it out for a prey.

6 **Prophesy therefore concerning the land of Israel**, and say unto the mountains, and to the hills, to the rivers, and to the valleys, **Thus saith the Lord GOD; Behold, I have spoken in my jealousy and in my fury, because ye have borne the shame of the heathen** [you have suffered ridicule long enough]:

Remember, this is a prophecy of the future.

7 **Therefore** thus saith the Lord GOD; **I have lifted up mine hand** [I will exercise My power in your behalf], **Surely the heathen that** *are* **about you, they shall bear their shame** [will suffer the consequences of their actions against you].

Verses 8–15, next, prophesy that Israel will prosper in the latter-days.

8 ¶ **But ye, O mountains of Israel, ye shall shoot forth your branches** [grow and prosper], **and yield your fruit to my people of Israel; for they are at hand to come** [they will soon come home].

9 For, behold, **I** *am* **for you**, and **I will turn unto you**, and ye shall be tilled and sown [your land will be productive for you]:

10 And **I will multiply men upon you, all the house of Israel,** *even* **all of it** [people from all the tribes of Israel will come to the land of Israel, not just the Jews]: and **the cities shall be inhabited, and the wastes shall be builded:**

11 And **I will multiply upon you man and beast**; and they shall increase and bring fruit: and **I will settle you after your old estates** [like you were before], **and will do better** *unto you* **than at your beginnings** [I will bless you even more abundantly than I did originally]: and ye shall know that I *am* the LORD.

Verses 12–14, next, prophecy, in several ways, that Israel will prosper in the latter-days.

12 Yea, **I will cause men** [Israelites] **to walk upon you** [the land of Israel], *even* **my people Israel**; and they shall possess thee, and thou shalt be their inheritance, and **thou shalt no more henceforth bereave them** *of men* [deprive them of posterity].

13 Thus saith the Lord GOD; **Because they say unto you, Thou** *land* **devourest up men, and hast bereaved thy nations** [because people talk about you and say you are not a good place to live];

14 **Therefore thou shalt devour men no more, neither bereave thy nations any more, saith the Lord GOD.**

Hopefully, you are well-adjusted to the fact that Ezekiel and other Old Testament prophets used repetition to emphasize and explain their teachings. You are seeing much of it here in the next several verses.

15 **Neither will I cause** *men* **to hear in thee the shame of the heathen any more** [*you will no longer hear the taunts of other nations in your land*], **neither shalt thou bear the reproach of** [*scorn*] **the people any more, neither shalt thou** *cause* **thy nations to fall any more** [*NIV or fall as a nation*], saith the Lord GOD.

As mentioned above, verses 16–22 remind the people of Israel why they lost their land before.

16 ¶ Moreover **the word of the LORD came unto me, saying,**

17 Son of man, **when the house of Israel dwelt in their own land, they defiled it** by their own way and by their doings: their way was before me as the uncleanness of a removed woman [*was like the ritual uncleanness—according to the law of Moses—of a women during her time of the month*].

18 **Wherefore I poured my fury upon them for** [*because of*] **the blood that they had shed upon the land, and for their idols** *wherewith* **they had polluted it:**

19 And **I scattered them among the heathen**, and they were dispersed through the countries: according to their way and according to their doings I judged [*punished*] them.

20 And when they entered unto the heathen, whither they went, **they profaned my holy name**, when they [*heathen nations*] said to them, These *are* the people of the LORD, and are gone forth out of his land [*they were a terrible example to others of what Jehovah's followers should be like*].

21 ¶ **But I had pity for mine holy name** [*I had concern for My reputation*], which the house of Israel had profaned among the heathen, whither they went.

22 Therefore say unto the house of Israel, Thus saith the Lord GOD; **I do not** *this* **for your sakes, O house of Israel, but for mine holy name's sake,** which ye have profaned among the heathen, whither ye went.

Verses 23–24 prophesy of the gathering of Israel in the last days.

23 And **I will sanctify my great name**, which was profaned among the heathen, which ye have profaned in the midst of them; **and the heathen shall know that I** *am* **the LORD**, saith the Lord GOD, when I shall be sanctified in you before their eyes.

24 For **I will take you from among the heathen, and gather you out of all countries, and will bring you into your own land**.

Verses 25–38 foretell that, in the last days, Israel will be cleansed from their filthiness and have a change of heart and return to being the Lord's covenant people. Throughout these verses, we see that this last days' gathering of Israel will be quite miraculous!

25 ¶ **Then will I sprinkle clean water upon you** [*can symbolize baptism*], **and ye shall be clean**: from all your filthiness, and from all your idols, will I cleanse you.

26 **A new heart** [*attitude about the gospel*] also will I give you, and **a new spirit** [*can symbolize the gift of the Holy Ghost*] will I put within you: and **I will take away the stony heart out of your flesh, and I will give you an heart of flesh** [*one that is sensitive to the Spirit*].

27 And **I will put my spirit within you, and cause you to walk in my statutes** [*keep My commandments*], and ye shall keep my judgments, and do *them*.

28 And **ye shall dwell in the land that I gave to your fathers**; and **ye shall be my people, and I will be your God**.

29 **I will also save you from all your uncleannesses** [*the net result of repentance, baptism and the gift of the Holy Ghost*]: and **I will call for the corn** [*all types of grain*], **and will increase it, and lay no famine upon you** [*you will have prosperity*].

30 And **I will multiply the fruit of the tree, and the increase of the field**, that ye shall receive no more reproach of famine among the heathen.

31 **Then shall ye remember your own evil ways, and your doings** that *were* not good, and **shall lothe yourselves in your own sight** [*have godly sorrow for your sins—see 2 Corinthians 7:10*] **for your iniquities and for your abominations** [*you will truly repent*].

32 **Not for your sakes do I** *this*, **saith the Lord GOD** [*not because you have fully earned it; none of us can do this on our own*], be it known unto you: **be ashamed and confounded for your own ways, O house of Israel** [*when you stop making excuses and accept full responsibility for your own sins, then forgiveness can come*].

33 Thus saith the Lord GOD; **In the day that I shall have cleansed you from all your iniquities I will also cause** *you* **to dwell in the cities, and the wastes shall be builded** [*you will be restored to your own land*].

34 And **the desolate land shall be tilled**, whereas it lay desolate in the sight of all that passed by.

35 And **they shall say, This land that was desolate is become like the garden of Eden**; and the waste and desolate and ruined cities *are* become fenced, *and* are inhabited.

36 **Then the heathen that are left round about you shall know that I the LORD build the ruined** *places*, *and* **plant that that was desolate**: I the LORD have spoken *it*, and **I will do** *it*.

37 Thus saith the Lord GOD; **I will** yet *for* this be enquired of by the house of Israel, to **do** *it* **for them**; I

will increase them with men like a flock.

38 As the holy flock, as the flock of Jerusalem in her solemn feasts; **so shall the waste cities be filled with flocks of men: and they shall know that I *am* the LORD.**

EZEKIEL 37

Selection: all verses

The first 14 verses of this chapter are quite well known to Christians in general as well as most members of the Church. Songs have been written and sung in many church and school choirs about the "dry bones" that come together in the resurrection of the dead.

Verses 1–14 are what we often call a "dual" prophecy. First, they prophesy of the literal resurrection wherein the physical body is restored to the spirit. Second, they prophecy the latter-day gathering of Israel with the accompanying restoration of "spiritually dead," spiritually bankrupt Israel, back to being spiritually alive as the Lord's covenant people in the last days. We will quote from the *Old Testament Student Manual*:

> The symbolic meaning of this prophecy as it relates to the gathering of Israel is apparent: The bones represent Israel in its lost and scattered state; the graves indicate where Israel is as well as its condition of spiritual death. The spirit, or *ruach* in Hebrew (see Ezekiel 37:9), means the new spirit of righteousness the people will have when they have been resurrected, that is, restored from their fallen state. The source of

this new life will be the Holy Ghost. (*Old Testament Student Manual, I Kings-Malachi,* p. 283.)

We will say more about verses 15–28 when we get to them. Suffice it to say here that they prophesy of the day when the Bible ("the stick of Judah") and the Book of Mormon ("the stick of Joseph") will come together as "one in mine hand." This has already taken place and continues to be fulfilled in our day.

1 **THE hand of the LORD** was upon me, and **carried me out** in the spirit of the LORD, **and set me down in the midst of the valley** which *was* **full of bones,**

2 **And caused me to pass by them round about** [*to view them from many angles*]: and, behold, *there were* very many in the open valley; and, lo, *they were* very dry.

3 And **he said unto me, Son of man, can these bones live** [*is it possible for these bones to come back alive, literally; also, is it possible for Israel to come back to the Lord and be His people again*]? **And I answered, O Lord GOD, thou knowest** [*I don't know, but You do*].

> Next, in verses 4–14, the Lord answers His own question. Yes, resurrection is literal, and yes, Israel can repent and come alive spiritually and thus become the Lord's people again, and, once again, possess their land of inheritance.

4 Again he said unto me, **Prophesy upon these bones**, and say unto

them, **O ye dry bones, hear the word of the LORD**.

5 Thus saith the Lord GOD unto these bones; Behold, **I will cause breath to enter into you, and ye shall live** [*you will be resurrected, literally, and, you will be restored as the Lord's covenant people*]:

> Next, Ezekiel sees the literal resurrection. This must have been quite a sight for him!

6 And **I will lay sinews upon you, and will bring up flesh upon you, and cover you with skin, and put breath in you, and ye shall live**; and ye shall know that I *am* the LORD [*you will know for sure that I am the true God*].

7 **So I prophesied as I was commanded**: and as I prophesied, **there was a noise, and behold a shaking, and the bones came together, bone to his bone**.

8 And when I beheld, lo, **the sinews and the flesh came up upon them, and the skin covered them above: but** *there was* **no breath in them**.

> Can you feel the drama in Ezekiel's heart and the curiosity in Ezekiel's mind as almost everything has been done, but they are still not alive? Truly, the Lord is *the* Master Teacher! He knows how to get His students to focus and really want to learn.

9 Then said he unto me, **Prophesy unto the wind, prophesy, son of man, and say to the wind**, Thus saith the Lord GOD; **Come from the four winds, O breath, and breathe upon these slain, that they may live**.

10 **So I prophesied as he commanded me, and the breath came into them, and they lived**, and stood up upon their feet, an exceeding great army.

> Next, the premortal Savior explains the meaning of what Ezekiel has seen.

11 ¶ Then he said unto me, Son of man, **these bones are the whole house of Israel**: behold, **they say, Our bones are dried, and our hope is lost** [*we have lost hope of ever being the Lord's covenant people again*]: **we are cut off for our parts** [*German Bible* [*"it is over for us."*]].

> With the background of extreme discouragement and loss of hope, in verse 11, above, feel the bright hope given by the Lord in verse 12, next.

12 Therefore prophesy and say unto them, **Thus saith the Lord GOD; Behold, O my people, I will open your graves, and cause you to come up out of your graves, and bring you into the land of Israel**.

13 And **ye shall know that I** *am* **the LORD, when I have opened your graves, O my people, and brought you up out of your graves**,

14 **And shall put my spirit in you, and ye shall live, and I shall place you in your own land**: then shall ye know that I the LORD have spoken *it,* and performed *it,* saith the LORD.

Verses 15–28 are quite well known among members of the Church. This part of Ezekiel's prophecy foretells the coming together of the "stick of Judah (the Bible) and the stick of Joseph (the Book of Mormon).

According to footnote 16a, for Ezekiel, chapter 37 in your Bible, the Hebrew word for "stick," in this context, is "wood," meaning a wooden writing tablet of the type commonly used in Babylon in the days of Ezekiel. We will quote from a fascinating article in the September 1977 Ensign, pages 24–26, which sheds additional light on the subject of such wooden writing tablets:

"Recent exciting discoveries now confirm the correctness of Joseph Smith's interpretation in a way impossible in 1830. But before discussing these new discoveries, let's take quick look at some linguistic points. Both stick, in the English King James Version, and rod, in the Greek Septuagint Version, are very unusual translations of the Hebrew word etz . . . whose basic meaning is wood. . . .

"The modern nation of Iraq includes almost all of Mesopotamia, the homeland of the ancient kingdoms of Assyria and Babylonia. In 593 BC, when Ezekiel was called to be a prophet, he was living in exile in Babylonia. . . . As he walked its streets, he would have seen the typical scribe pressing a wedge-shaped stylus into moist clay tablets to make the complex writings familiar to us as cuneiform (wedge-shaped). But scholars today know that other kinds of records were being made in Mesopotamia: papyrus, parchment, and wooden tablets.

Though only the clay tablets have survived the millennia, writers referred to the other writing materials on their clay tablets. [*One such writing style was called "wood tablets."*]

"Modern archaeologists knew what papyrus and parchment were, but what were these wood tablets? How could cuneiform be written on wood? . . .

". . . Some years ago . . . San Nicolo [*an archaeologist*] remembered that Romans and Greeks both made wooden wax tablets for record-keeping purposes out of boards whose surfaces had been cut below the edges in order to hold a thin coating of wax. Scribes wrote on the wax. The raised edges protected the inscribed surfaces when two tablets were put together.

"Could the Babylonians have done the same thing? . . . But five years later, . . . a discovery made in the territory that had been ancient Assyria confirmed his theory to the letter.

"The discovery, directed by archaeologist Max Mallowan, was made in a layer of sludge deep in a well in Nimrod, a city known as Calah in the Bible. . . . By the end of the day workmen had found . . . fragments of two complete sets of tablets, one of ivory and the other of walnut, each composed of sixteen boards. . . .

"All of the surfaces of the boards were cut down a tenth of an inch, leaving a half-inch-wide raised edge all around. The lowered surfaces provided a bed for wax filling, of which some thin biscuit-like fragments were found either still adhering to the boards or mixed in the sludge nearby. . . .

"The cover boards . . . had hinge marks on both sides, making it evident that all sixteen in each set had once been joined together like a Japanese folding screen. The whole work made such an extensive record that Mallowan could announce his discovery as the oldest known example of a book. . . .

"With these things in mind, we can see how we might translate Ezekiel 37:15–17 in this way:

"'These were the words of the Lord to me: Man, take one leaf of a wooden tablet and write on it, "Judah and his associates of Israel." Then take another leaf and write on it, "Joseph, the leaf [*wooden tablet*] of Ephraim and all his associates of Israel."

"'Now bring the two together to form one tablet; then they will be a folding tablet in your hand.'

"This translation is faithful to what we now know of Ezekiel's language and culture" (Keith H. Meservy, "Ezekiel's 'Sticks,'" Ensign, September 1977, pages 24–26, as quoted in the Old Testament Student Manual, I Kings to Malachi, page 283–284).

We will now go ahead and read the relevant verses in Ezekiel. As mentioned previously, you will see that this is a dual prophecy, meaning that it has two different meanings. First, it foretells the coming together of the Bible and the Book of Mormon in the last days. Second, it predicts the latter-day reuniting of the kingdoms of Judah (the Jews) and Joseph (Israel).

15 ¶ The word of the LORD came again unto me, saying,

16 Moreover, thou son of man, **take thee one stick, and write upon it, For Judah** [*the Bible*], and for the children of Israel his companions: **then take another stick, and write upon it, For Joseph** [*the Book of Mormon*], the stick of Ephraim, and *for* all the house of Israel his companions [*all of Israel will benefit from these two books*]:

17 **And join them one to another** into one stick; **and they shall become one in thine hand**.

Have you noticed that there are several ways in which this prophecy has been fulfilled in our day? One way is the literal fact that both the Bible and the Book of Mormon are part of our Latter-day Saint "standard works." We literally hold them together as we pick up our scriptures. They are "one in [*our*] hand."

Another literal fulfillment is that the Bible and the Book of Mormon are cross-referenced in our Topical Guide, Bible Dictionary, and Index. Yet another fulfillment is that both books of scripture have come together in our hearts.

Another very important fulfillment is that the Book of Mormon bears witness of the truthfulness of the Bible. This is vital in our day, when so many Christians and others are discounting the Bible's importance and interpreting it to condone sin in our day.

You can no doubt think of other ways in which the Bible and the Book of Mormon have been "joined" together in our day.

18 ¶ And when the children of thy people shall speak unto thee, saying, Wilt thou not shew us what thou *meanest* by these [*would you please explain what you mean by this prophecy*]?

19 Say unto them, Thus saith the Lord GOD; Behold, **I will take the stick of Joseph**, which *is* in the hand of Ephraim, and the tribes of Israel his fellows, **and will put them with him,** *even* **with the stick of Judah**, and make them one stick, and they shall be one in mine hand.

20 ¶ And the sticks whereon thou writest shall be in thine hand before their eyes [*in other words, this is a literal prophecy; there will literally be two books, and they will come together such that you can see them together with your eyes*].

Next, we see the second meaning of this prophecy explained. The kingdoms of Judah and Israel will be reunited in the last days. Remember that the twelve tribes of Israel split into two nations after the death of King Solomon (I Kings 12:16–20). They became the Northern Kingdom (the ten tribes), often referred to as Ephraim or Israel, with headquarters in Samaria; and the Southern Kingdom (Judah), consisting of the tribes of Judah and Benjamin, with headquarters in Jerusalem. These next verses are a major prophecy concerning the gathering

of Israel. Remember that the most important aspect of the gathering of Israel is gathering them to Jesus Christ, who brings them onto the covenant path and, ultimately, to the Father to dwell in celestial glory.

21 And say unto them, **Thus saith the Lord** GOD; Behold, **I will take the children of Israel from among the heathen, whither they be gone, and will gather them on every side, and bring them into their own land**:

22 **And I will make them one nation** in the land upon the mountains of Israel; **and one king** [*Christ*] **shall be king to them all**: and they shall be no more two nations, neither shall they be divided into two kingdoms any more at all:

In verse 23, next, we see the Atonement of Jesus Christ in action.

23 **Neither shall they defile themselves any more with their idols, nor with their detestable things, nor with any of their transgressions:** but **I will save them out of all their dwellingplaces, wherein they have sinned, and will cleanse them: so shall they be my people, and I will be their God.**

24 **And David** [*symbolic of Christ in this context*] **my servant** *shall be* **king over them;** and they all shall have one shepherd [*Jesus Christ*]: **they shall also walk in my judgments, and observe my statutes, and do them** [*in other words, they will

understand and keep the command-ments].

25 And they shall dwell in the land that I have given unto Jacob my servant, wherein your fathers have dwelt; and they shall dwell therein, *even* they, and their children, and their children's children for ever [*the righteous will inherit the earth, which will ultimately become the celestial kingdom—see Doctrine and Covenants 130:9–11*]: and my servant David *shall be* their prince for ever.

A quote from the Old Testament institute manual helps us understand verses 26–28, next, wherein Ezekiel prophesies that a temple will be built in Jerusalem in the last days. this temple will be described in Ezekiel, chapters 40–48.

26 Moreover **I will make** a covenant of peace with them; it shall be **an everlasting covenant with them**: and I will place them, and multiply them, and will set my sanctuary [*a temple, yet to be built*] in the midst of them for evermore.

27 My tabernacle [*NIV "My dwelling place;" see also D&C 124:37–40 referring to ordinances performed in temples*] also shall be with them: yea, **I will be their God, and they shall be my people**.

28 And the heathen shall know that I the LORD do sanctify Israel [*make Israel a holy people*], when my sanctuary shall be in the midst of them for evermore.

EZEKIEL 38

Selection: all verses

Chapters 38 and 39 go together and give many prophetic details concerning the battle of Armageddon.

Many people have heard of two great battles mentioned in the scriptures. They are:

1. The battle of Armageddon.
2. The battle of Gog and Magog.

The battle of Armageddon is yet future and will take place shortly before the Second Coming of Christ. All nations will be involved, most against Israel, some for Israel. The central battlefield for this great conflict will include Jerusalem and will reach northward to southern Galilee, in Israel, to a beautiful valley known as "Megiddo." In Hebrew, this valley is called "Har-Megiddo," in English, "Armageddon" (See Revelation 16:16.)

The battle of Gog and Magog will take place after the Millennium is over (after Jesus Christ has ruled and reigned on earth for a thousand years—see Revelation 20:1–4). This will be the final battle between the forces of good and evil on this earth. At that time, Satan will gather all his evil forces to fight against Michael (Adam) and all the forces of righteousness. Righteousness will win and Satan and his followers will be permanently cast out (D&C 88:111–114.)

Going back to the battle of Armageddon, there is some confusion generated by the name of this huge battle. Ezekiel is the only prophet who refers to it as the "battle of Gog and Magog" (Ezekiel 38:2.) The other prophets call it the "battle of Armageddon." (See Joel 3;

Zechariah 11–14; Revelation 16:16; and D&C 45.) In Ezekiel's case, the terms "Gog" and "Magog" are somewhat general terms referring to the combination of nations who are combined together in the last days to overthrow and destroy Israel. We will quote from Elder Bruce R. McConkie to help explain this:

> "The prophecies do not name the modern nations which will be fighting for and against Israel, but the designation Gog and Magog is given to the combination of nations which are seeking to overthrow and destroy the remnant of the Lord's chosen seed." (*Mormon Doctrine*, pp. 324–325.)

Remember that this will take place after the Jews (Israel) have been gathered back to Palestine, the Holy Land.

1 AND **the word of the LORD came unto me, saying,**

> You will see, in verses 2–6, that these avowed enemies of Israel will come from all directions, north, east, south, and west to engage in the battle of Armageddon.

2 **Son of man** [*Ezekiel*], **set thy face against** [*German Bible, "turn against"*] **Gog, the land of Magog, the chief prince of Meshech and Tubal** [*Lands in northern Asia Minor (to the north of Israel)*]**, and prophesy against him** [*symbolic of an alliance of great evil power throughout the world in the last days who seek to destroy Israel*]**,**

3 And say, **Thus saith the Lord GOD; Behold, I** *am* **against thee,**

O Gog, the chief prince of Meshech and Tubal:

4 And **I will turn thee back,** and put hooks into thy jaws [*stop you in your tracks*], and I will bring thee forth, and all thine army, horses and horsemen [*symbolic of vast military might*], **all of them clothed with all sorts** *of* **armour** [*all kinds of weapons*]*, even* a great company *with* bucklers and shields, all of them handling swords:

5 **Persia** [*east of Israel*]**, Ethiopia, and Libya** [*south of Israel (northern Africa)*] with them; **all of them with shield and helmet** [*all of these nations will have great military capabilities*]:

6 **Gomer,** and all his bands; the house of **Togarmah** of the north quarters [*associated with peoples in Asia Minor and Europe, in other words, coming from the north and the west*]*,* and all his bands: *and* many people with thee.

7 **Be thou prepared,** and prepare for thyself, thou, **and all thy company** that are assembled unto thee, and be thou a guard unto them [*get ready to be stopped when the battle is well underway*].

8 ¶ **After many days thou** [*Gog and all the other nations against Israel*] **shalt be visited** [*meet with destruction by the Lord*]**: in the latter years** [*the last days*] **thou shalt come into the land** [*Israel*] *that is* **brought back from the sword** [*destructions, such as the Assyrians and Babylonians and*

Romans and modern anti-Israel nations], **and is gathered out of many people, against** [to] **the mountains of Israel,** which have been always waste: but it is **brought forth out of the nations,** and **they shall dwell safely all of them** [Israel will have been gathered out of many nations and restored to their land in Palestine by the hand of the Lord].

Next, in verses 9–11, we see that there will be extremely large numbers of soldiers attacking Israel (see verse 15) in the battle of Armageddon. They will be like a large storm cloud over the whole land.

9 **Thou** [Gog and his allies] **shalt ascend and come like a storm, thou shalt be like a cloud to cover the land,** thou, and all thy bands [troops], and many people with thee.

10 Thus saith the Lord GOD; **It shall also come to pass, that** at the same time [about the time of the battle of Armageddon] shall things come into thy mind, and **thou shalt think an evil thought** [you will decide to invade Israel]:

Verses 11–12, next describe the thought prophesied to come into Gog's mind (verse 10.)

11 And thou shalt say, **I will go up to the land of unwalled villages; I will go to them that are at rest, that dwell safely, all of them dwelling without walls, and having neither bars nor gates** [Israel will appear very vulnerable to attack],

12 **To take a spoil, and to take a prey**; to turn thine hand upon the desolate places that are now inhabited, and **upon the people that are gathered out of the nations,** which have gotten cattle and goods [who are now prospering], **that dwell in the midst of the land.**

13 **Sheba** [in Ethiopia], **and Dedan** [northwestern Arabia], **and the merchants of Tarshish** [at the far western end of the Mediterranean Sea; these merchant nations will be interested in getting some of the spoils of this war], **with all the young lions thereof** [with powerful, aggressive merchants], **shall say unto thee,** Art thou come to take a spoil? hast thou gathered thy company to take a prey? to carry away silver and gold, to take away cattle and goods, to take a great spoil?

Watch now as Ezekiel creates a dialogue, as it were, between Gog and the Lord in which this prophecy of the battle of Armageddon is repeated.

14 ¶ Therefore, son of man, **prophesy and say unto Gog,** Thus saith the Lord GOD; **In that day when my people of Israel dwelleth safely** [when Israel is well-established as a nation], **shalt thou not know it** [will you not notice it]?

15 And **thou shalt come from thy place out of the north** parts, thou, and **many people with thee,** all of them riding upon horses, **a great company, and a mighty army:**

16 And **thou shalt come up against my people of Israel**, as a cloud to cover the land; **it shall be in the latter days**, and I will bring thee against my land, that the heathen [*unbelievers*] may know me, when **I shall be sanctified in thee, O Gog, before their eyes** [*the Lord will be magnified in the eyes of unbelievers when He saves Israel from Gog and his allies*].

Verse 17, next, emphasizes that this prophecy about the battle of Armageddon was given long before it will be fulfilled (about 600 BC). The Lord does indeed, know the future!

17 Thus saith the Lord GOD; *Art thou he* [*are you the one*] **of whom I have spoken in old time by my servants the prophets** of Israel, **which prophesied** in those days *many* years **that I would bring thee against them?**

18 And it shall come to pass **at the same time** [*when the battle of Armageddon is raging*] **when Gog shall come against the land of Israel**, saith the Lord GOD, *that* **my fury shall come up** in my face [*I, the Lord, will step in and stop it*].

19 For in my jealousy [*fervor*] *and* in the fire of my wrath have I spoken, Surely **in that day there shall be a great shaking** [*a great earthquake*] **in the land of Israel**;

It would seem that the great earthquake spoken of in verse 19, above, would be caused by the splitting of the Mount of Olives in two, as the Savior descends upon it to save His people. We are told that the whole earth will shake (see verse 20) when this takes place (D&C 45:48–53.) Thus, if we are still alive at this time, we, too, will feel it.

20 So that the fishes of the sea, and the fowls of the heaven, and the beasts of the field, and all creeping things that creep upon the earth, and **all the men that** *are* **upon the face of the earth, shall shake at my presence**, and the mountains shall be thrown down, and the steep places shall fall, and every wall shall fall to the ground.

21 And I will call for a sword against him throughout all my mountains, saith the Lord GOD: **every man's sword shall be against his brother**.

22 And **I will plead against him** [*Gog and his armies*] **with pestilence and with blood; and I will rain upon him, and upon his bands, and upon the many people that** *are* **with him**, an overflowing rain, and great **hailstones, fire, and brimstone**.

John, the Revelator, also prophesied about these "great hailstones" spoken of by Ezekiel in verse 22, above, that the Lord would rain down upon the vast armies of Gog during the battle of Armageddon (Revelation 16:21.) Each hailstone was prophesied to weigh about one talent. Some Bible scholars suggest that this would be about 75.6 pounds (see Bible Dictionary under "Weights and Measures.")

23 Thus will I magnify myself, and sanctify myself; and **I will be known in the eyes of many nations, and they shall know that I** *am* **the LORD.**

EZEKIEL 39

Selection: all verses

This chapter continues with the battle of Armageddon, including its aftermath. You will see that the left-over weaponry of the battle will provide seven years of fuel for the remaining Israelites. This prophecy also informs us that it will take seven months to bury all of the dead resulting from the battle. After all this, the gathering of Israel will continue.

First, verses 1–7 review the destruction of Gog and his allies as the Savior intervenes to stop the slaughter of His people in the land of Israel.

1 THEREFORE, thou son of man, **prophesy against Gog**, and say, **Thus saith the Lord GOD; Behold, I** *am* **against thee, O Gog**, the chief prince of Meshech and Tubal:

2 And **I will turn thee back, and leave but the sixth part of thee**, and will cause thee to come up from the north parts, and will bring thee upon the mountains of Israel [*you will be allowed to attack Israel*]:

3 And **I will smite thy bow out of thy left hand, and will cause thine arrows to fall out of thy right hand** [*I will stop your military capabilities*].

4 **Thou shalt fall upon the mountains of Israel**, thou, and all thy bands, and the people that *is* with thee: **I will give thee unto the ravenous birds of every sort** [*you will become carrion for birds of prey*], and *to* the beasts of the field to be devoured.

5 **Thou shalt fall upon the open field**: for I have spoken *it,* saith the Lord GOD.

6 And **I will send a fire on Magog, and among them that dwell carelessly** [*at ease*] **in the isles** [*I will send destruction upon your homelands*]: **and they shall know that I** *am* **the LORD** [*the true God*].

7 So will **I make my holy name known in the midst of my people Israel; and I will not** *let them* **pollute my holy name any more: and the heathen** [*unbelievers*] **shall know that I** *am* **the LORD, the Holy One in Israel** [*all people will know that it doesn't pay to go against the true God of heaven*].

8 ¶ Behold, **it is come, and it is done**, saith the Lord GOD; **this** *is* **the day whereof I have spoken** [*in prophecy*].

Next, in verses 9–16, you will see that it will take a long time to clean up after the battle.

9 And **they that dwell in the cities of Israel shall go forth, and shall set on fire and burn the weapons**, both the shields and the bucklers, the

bows and the arrows, and the handstaves, and the spears, and **they shall burn them with fire seven years** [*the citizens of Israel will have sufficient fuel for seven years as they burn the weaponry left over from the war*]:

10 **So that they shall take no wood out of the field, neither cut down** *any* **out of the forests**; for they shall burn the weapons with fire: and **they shall spoil those that spoiled them, and rob those that robbed them,** saith the Lord GOD.

Next, in verses 11–16, it will take seven months to bury the dead bodies of the enemy soldiers and the stench of rotting bodies will be horrible.

11 ¶ And it shall come to pass in that day, *that* **I will give unto Gog a place there of graves in Israel** [*Gog and his allies' dead soldiers will not be buried in their homelands, rather, in Israel*], the valley of the passengers on the east of the sea: **and it shall stop the** *noses* [*it will stink terribly*] of the passengers: and there shall they bury Gog and all his multitude: and **they shall call** *it* **The valley of Hamon-gog** [*"Hamongog" means the "multitude of Gog"*].

12 And **seven months shall the house of Israel be burying of them**, that they may cleanse the land.

13 Yea, **all the people of the land shall bury** *them* [*everyone will have to help bury these dead bodies*]*;* and it shall be to them a renown the day

that I shall be glorified, saith the Lord GOD.

Next, the government of Israel will have to hire burial crews to help get the job done.

14 And **they shall sever out men of continual employment, passing through the land to bury** with the passengers those that remain upon the face of the earth, to cleanse it: **after the end of seven months shall they search** [*they will still have to keep searching for remains*].

15 **And the passengers** [*the passersby*] *that* **pass through the land, when** *any* **seeth a man's bone, then shall he set up a sign by it** [*will be required to set up a sign to notify the burial crews where the remains are*], **till the buriers have buried it in the valley of Hamon-gog**.

16 And **also the name of the city shall be** Hamonah [*NIV, they will establish a city named "*horde*" there*]]. Thus shall they cleanse the land.

Next, Ezekiel prophesies that the blood and carnage of the battle will provide a great feast for birds and beasts that feed on carrion (dead bodies.) As you well-know by now, from your studies of Ezekiel so far, repetition and use of symbolism are major aspects of Ezekiel's style of prophesying.

17 ¶ And, thou son of man, thus saith the Lord GOD; **Speak unto every feathered fowl, and to every beast of the field,** Assemble yourselves, and **come; gather yourselves on**

every side to my sacrifice that I do sacrifice for you, *even* a great sacrifice upon the mountains of Israel, that ye may eat flesh, and drink blood.

18 Ye shall eat the flesh of the **mighty** [*those powerful people who attacked Israel in this battle*], **and drink the blood of the princes** [*leaders*] of the earth, of rams, of lambs, and of goats, of bullocks, **all of them fatlings** [*the best*] of Bashan [*located north of Israel, known today as Syria*].

19 And **ye shall eat fat till ye be full, and drink blood till ye be drunken**, of my sacrifice which I have sacrificed for you.

20 **Thus ye shall be filled at my table with horses and chariots, with mighty men, and with all men of war**, saith the Lord GOD.

21 And I will set my glory among the heathen, and **all the heathen shall see my judgment that I have executed, and my hand that I have laid upon them**.

22 **So the house of Israel shall know that I** *am* **the LORD their God from that day and forward** [*there will be a mass conversion to the Savior among the people of Israel as a result of being saved by Him—see D&C 45:48–53*].

23 ¶ **And the heathen shall know that the house of Israel went into captivity for their iniquity** [*because of their wickedness*]: because **they trespassed against me, therefore** hid I my face from them [*stopped blessing them*], **and gave them into the hand of their enemies: so fell they all by the sword**.

24 **According to their uncleanness and according to their transgressions have I done unto them** [*the law of justice*], and hid my face from them.

25 Therefore thus saith the Lord GOD; **Now will I** bring again the captivity of Jacob, and **have mercy upon the whole house of Israel**, and will be jealous for my holy name;

26 **After that they have borne their shame, and all their trespasses whereby they have trespassed against me** [*after they have repented*], when they dwelt safely in their land, and none made *them* afraid.

27 **When I have** brought them again from the people, and **gathered them out of their enemies' lands**, and am sanctified in them in the sight of many nations;

28 **Then shall they know that I** *am* **the LORD their God**, which cause them to be led into captivity among the heathen: but **I have gathered them unto their own land**, and have left none of them any more there.

Remember, this is prophecy of the future, as if it had already taken place.

29 **Neither will I hide my face any more from them: for I have poured**

out my spirit upon the house of Israel, saith the Lord GOD.

EZEKIEL 40

Selection: all verses

Chapters 40–48 go together and include Ezekiel's vision of the great latter-day temple to be built in Jerusalem, before the Savior's Second Coming. Some details of the millennial reign of Christ and land distribution to the twelve tribes of Israel are also included.

In chapter 1, we see that Ezekiel was taken by the Spirit (similar to Nephi—1 Nephi 11:1) to a high mountain in the future land of Israel where he was shown the future temple to be built there.

Verse 1 informs us that this vision came to him in the 25th year of his living as an exile in Babylonia and 14 years after Jerusalem was conquered and the temple destroyed by the armies of King Nebuchadnezzar of Babylon.

1 **IN the five and twentieth year of our captivity**, in the beginning of the year, in the tenth *day* of the month, **in the fourteenth year after that the city** [*Jerusalem*] **was smitten**, in the selfsame day **the hand of the LORD was upon me, and brought me thither** [*brought me to the future land of Israel*].

2 **In the visions of God brought he me into the land of Israel, and set me upon a very high mountain**, by which *was* as the frame of a city on the south.

3 And **he brought me thither** [*here*], **and, behold,** *there was* **a man** [*a guide was provided for Ezekiel to show him around in this vision*], whose appearance *was* like the appearance of brass, **with a line of flax** [*a linen cord*] **in his hand, and a measuring reed** [*kind of like a measuring tape in our day*]; and he stood in the gate.

Next, in verse 4, his guide instructs him to pass the details of this vision on to the house of Israel.

4 And the man said unto me, Son of man, **behold** [*look*] with thine eyes, and **hear** with thine ears, and **set thine heart** [*internalize*] **upon all that I shall shew thee**; for to the intent that I might shew *them* unto thee *art* thou brought hither: **declare all that thou seest to the house of Israel**.

5 And behold a wall on the outside of the house round about, and in the man's hand a measuring reed of six cubits *long* by the cubit [*a cubit was the length from the elbow to the tip of the fingers for an average man, about 17 ½ inches (see Bible Dictionary under "Weights and Measures")*] and an hand breadth: so **he measured the breadth of the building**, one reed; and the height, one reed.

Unless you are an architect and are fascinated by measurements and such details, verses 6–49 hold but casual interest. Therefore, I will do comparatively little by way of commentary with them. But it is easy to see that this will be a magnificent temple with magnificent temple grounds and auxiliary buildings around it. I will include a quote by Apostle James E. Talmage here in which he described some of the features of this temple:

"In the twenty-fifth year of the Babylonian captivity, while yet the people of Israel were in exile in a strange land, the word of the Lord came to the prophet Ezekiel; the power of God rested upon him; and he saw in vision a glorious Temple, the plan of which he minutely described. As to whether the prophet himself considered the design so shown as one to be subsequently realized, or as but a grand yet unattainable ideal, is not declared. Certain it is that the Temple of the vision has not yet been builded.

"In most of its essential features Ezekiel's ideal followed closely the plan of Solomon's Temple; so close, indeed, is the resemblance, that many of the details specified by Ezekiel have been accepted as those of the splendid edifice destroyed by Nebuchadnezzar. A predominant characteristic of the Temple described by Ezekiel was the spaciousness of its premises and the symmetry of both the Holy House and its associated buildings. The area was to be a square of five hundred cubits, walled about and provided with a gateway and arches on each of three sides; on the west side the wall was to be unbroken by arch or portal. At each of the gateways were little chambers regarded as lodges, and provided with porches. In the outer court were other chambers. The entire area was to be elevated, and a flight of steps led to each gateway. In the inner court was seen the great altar, standing before the House, and occupying the center of a square of one hundred cubits. Ample provision was made for every variety of sacrifice and offering, and for the accommodation of the priests, the singers, and all engaged in the holy ritual. The main structure comprised a Porch, a Holy Place, and an inner sanctuary or Most Holy Place, the last named elevated above the rest and reached by steps. The plan provided for even greater exclusiveness than had characterized the sacred area of the Temple of Solomon; the double courts contributed to this end. The service of the Temple was prescribed in detail; the ordinances of the altar, the duties of the priests, the ministry of the Levites, the regulations governing oblations and feasts were all set forth.

"The immediate purpose of this revelation through the vision of the prophet appears to have been that of awakening the people of Israel to a realization of their fallen state and a conception of their departed glory." (*The House of the Lord*, by James E. Talmage, Published by the Church of Jesus Christ of Latter-day Saints, 1912, pp. 37–38.) Did you notice that Elder Talmage, in the first paragraph of the quote, above, suggested that we do not know whether or not the temple Ezekiel saw in this vision will actually be built as shown or if it represented, in ways Ezekiel could relate to, that a beautiful temple will be built in the future. Elder Joseph Fielding Smith, who later became President of the Church, taught that this temple will be used for ordinance work. (*Doctrines of Salvation*, Vol. II, p. 244.)

6 ¶ Then came he unto **the gate which looketh** [*faces*] **toward the east**, and went up the stairs thereof, and measured the threshold of the gate, *which was* one reed broad; and the other threshold *of the gate, which was* one reed broad.

7 And *every* little chamber *was* one reed long, and one reed broad; and between the little chambers *were* five cubits; and the threshold of the gate by the porch of the gate within *was* one reed.

8 He measured also the porch of the gate within, one reed.

9 Then measured he the porch of the gate, eight cubits; and the posts thereof, two cubits; and the porch of the gate *was* inward.

10 And the little chambers of the gate eastward *were* three on this side, and three on that side; they three *were* of one measure: and the posts had one measure on this side and on that side.

11 And he measured the breadth of the entry of the gate, ten cubits; *and* the length of the gate, thirteen cubits.

12 The space also before the little chambers *was* one cubit *on this side,* and the space *was* one cubit on that side: and the little chambers *were* six cubits on this side, and six cubits on that side.

13 He measured then the gate from the roof of *one* little chamber to the roof of another: the breadth *was* five and twenty cubits, door against door.

14 He made also posts of threescore cubits, even unto the post of the court round about the gate.

15 And from the face of the gate of the entrance unto the face of the porch of the inner gate *were* fifty cubits.

16 And *there were* narrow windows to the little chambers, and to their posts within the gate round about, and likewise to the arches: and windows *were* round about inward: and upon *each* post *were* palm trees.

> Verses 17–19, next, give details of the outer court, perhaps the equivalent of our temple grounds.

17 **Then brought he me into the outward court**, and, lo, *there were* chambers, and a pavement made for the court round about: thirty chambers [*rooms*] *were* upon the pavement.

18 And the pavement by the side of the gates over against the length of the gates *was* the lower pavement.

19 Then he measured the breadth from the forefront of the lower gate unto the forefront of the inner court without, an **hundred cubits** [*about 146 feet*] eastward and northward.

> Verses 20–23 give details regarding the north gate. These gates are obviously rather large and have several large alcoves that could

possibly be a station for officiators in the temple.

20 ¶ And the gate of the outward court that looked toward the north, he measured the length thereof, and the breadth thereof.

21 And the little chambers thereof *were* three on this side and three on that side; and the posts thereof and the arches thereof were after the measure of the first gate: the length thereof *was* **fifty cubits** [*about 73 feet*], and the breadth **five and twenty cubits** [*about 36 feet*].

22 And their windows, and their arches, and their palm trees, *were* after the measure of the gate that looketh toward the east; and they went up unto it by **seven steps** [*in Biblical number symbolism, "seven" represents perfection; can symbolize becoming like God*]; and the arches thereof *were* before them.

23 And the gate of the inner court *was* over against the gate toward the north, and toward the east; and he measured from gate to gate an hundred cubits.

Verses 24–27 describe the south gate.

24 ¶ After that he brought me toward the south, and behold **a gate toward the south**: and he measured the posts thereof and the arches thereof according to these measures.

25 And *there were* windows in it and in the arches thereof round about,

like those windows: the length *was* **fifty cubits**, and the breadth **five and twenty cubits**.

26 And *there were* **seven steps** to go up to it, and the arches thereof *were* before them: and it had palm trees, one on this side, and another on that side, upon the posts thereof.

27 And *there was* a gate in the inner court toward the south: and he measured from gate to gate toward the south an hundred cubits.

Verses 28–34 give details about gates to the inner court.

28 And **he brought me to the inner court by the south gate**: and he measured the south gate according to these measures;

29 And the little chambers thereof, and the posts thereof, and the arches thereof, according to these measures: and *there were* windows in it and in the arches thereof round about: it *was* **fifty cubits long**, and **five and twenty cubits broad**.

30 And the arches round about *were* five and twenty cubits long, and five cubits broad.

31 And the arches thereof *were* toward the utter court; and palm trees *were* upon the posts thereof: and the going up to it *had* **eight steps**.

32 ¶ And he brought me into the inner court toward the east: and he measured the gate according to these measures.

33 And the little chambers thereof, and the posts thereof, and the arches thereof, *were* according to these measures: and *there were* windows therein and in the arches thereof round about: *it was* **fifty cubits long, and five and twenty cubits broad**.

34 And the arches thereof *were* toward the outward court; and palm trees *were* upon the posts thereof, on this side, and on that side: and the going up to it *had* **eight steps.**

Verses 35–43 describe rooms for preparing sacrifices.

35 ¶ And **he brought me to the north gate**, and measured *it* according to these measures;

36 The little chambers thereof, the posts thereof, and the arches thereof, and the windows to it round about: the **length *was* fifty cubits**, and the **breadth five and twenty cubits**.

37 And the posts thereof *were* toward the utter court; and palm trees *were* upon the posts thereof, on this side, and on that side: and the going up to it *had* **eight steps.**

38 And the chambers and the entries thereof *were* by the posts of the gates, **where they washed the burnt offering.**

39 ¶ And in the porch of the gate *were* **two tables on this side, and two tables on that side, to slay thereon the burnt offering and the sin offering and the trespass offering** [*various offerings conducted*

by Aaronic priests as part of the law of Moses*].

40 And **at the side without** [*outside*], as one goeth up to the entry of the north gate, *were* **two tables**; and on the other side, which *was* at the porch of the gate, *were* **two tables.**

41 **Four tables *were* on this side, and four tables on that side**, by the side of the gate; eight tables, **whereupon they slew *their sacrifices*.**

42 And **the four tables *were* of hewn stone for the burnt offering**, of a cubit and an half long, and a cubit and an half broad, and one cubit high: **whereupon also they laid the instruments wherewith they slew the burnt offering and the sacrifice.**

43 And **within *were* hooks** [*these would be double-pronged hooks*], an hand broad [*a hand-breadth long*], fastened round about: and **upon the tables *was* the flesh of the offering.**

Verses 44–47 describe rooms for the priests.

44 ¶ **And without** [*outside of*] the inner gate *were* **the chambers of the singers in the inner court**, which *was* at the side of the north gate; and **their prospect *was*** [*they were facing*] toward the south: one at the side of the east gate *having* the prospect toward the north.

45 **And he** [*Ezekiel's guide*] **said unto me, This chamber**, whose prospect *is* toward the south, *is* **for the**

priests, the keepers of the charge of the house.

46 And the chamber whose prospect *is* toward the north *is* for the priests, the keepers of the charge of the altar: these *are* the sons of [*descendants of*] Zadok among the sons of Levi [*Zadok was a faithful Aaronic high priest, the first to officiate in Solomon's temple (1 Kings 2:26–27, 35)*], which come near to the LORD to minister unto him.

47 So he measured the court, an hundred cubits long, and an hundred cubits broad, foursquare; and the altar *that was* before the house.

Verses 48–49 refer to the temple.

48 ¶ And he brought me to the porch of the house [*the roof supported by columns over the entrance to the temple*], and measured *each* post of the porch, five cubits on this side, and five cubits on that side: and the breadth of the gate *was* three cubits on this side, and three cubits on that side.

49 The length of the porch *was* twenty cubits, and the breadth eleven cubits; and he brought me by the steps whereby they went up to it: and *there were* pillars by the posts, one on this side, and another on that side.

EZEKIEL 41

Selection: all verses

In this chapter, the vision of the future temple continues as Ezekiel sees additional details of the inner temple and the Holy of Holies. As mentioned in the introduction to chapter 40, it mainly consists of architectural details. Consequently, my commentary will be minimal.

1 AFTERWARD he [*Ezekiel's guide*] brought me to the temple, and measured the posts, six cubits broad on the one side, and six cubits broad on the other side, *which was* the breadth of the tabernacle.

2 And the breadth of the door *was* ten cubits; and the sides of the door *were* five cubits on the one side, and five cubits on the other side: and he measured the length thereof, forty cubits: and the breadth, twenty cubits.

3 Then went he inward, and measured the post of the door, two cubits; and the door, six cubits; and the breadth of the door, seven cubits.

4 So he measured the length thereof, twenty cubits; and the breadth, twenty cubits, before the temple: and he said unto me, This *is* the most holy place [*the holy of holies*].

By the way, the Holy of Holies in the Jerusalem Temple was in the westernmost end of the temple building and was a perfect cube, 20 cubits by 20 cubits by 20 cubits high, in other words, about 30 feet by 30 feet by 30 feet. The Ark of the Covenant was kept inside it.

5 After he measured the wall of the house, six cubits; and the breadth of *every* side chamber, four cubits, round about the house on every side.

6 And the side chambers *were* three, one over another, and thirty in order; and they entered into the wall which *was* of the house for the side chambers round about, that they might have hold, but they had not hold in the wall of the house.

7 And *there was* an enlarging, and a winding about still upward to the side chambers: for the winding about of the house went still upward round about the house: therefore the breadth of the house *was still* upward, and so increased *from* the lowest *chamber* to the highest by the midst.

8 I saw also the height of the house round about: the foundations of the side chambers *were* a full reed of six great cubits.

9 The thickness of the wall, which *was* for the side chamber without [*on the outside*], *was* five cubits: and *that* which *was* left *was* the place of the side chambers that *were* within.

10 And between the chambers *was* the wideness of twenty cubits round about the house on every side.

11 And the doors of the side chambers *were* toward *the place that was* left, one door toward the north, and another door toward the south: and the breadth of the place that was left *was* five cubits round about.

12 Now the building that *was* before the separate place at the end toward the west *was* seventy cubits broad; and the wall of the building *was* five cubits thick round about, and the length thereof ninety cubits.

13 So he measured the house, an hundred cubits long; and the separate place, and the building, with the walls thereof, an hundred cubits long;

14 Also the breadth of the face of the house, and of the separate place toward the east, an hundred cubits.

15 And he measured the length of the building over against the separate place which *was* behind it, and the galleries thereof on the one side and on the other side, an hundred cubits, with the inner temple, and the porches of the court;

16 The door posts, and the narrow windows, and the galleries round about on their three stories, over against the door, cieled with wood round about, and from the ground up to the windows, and the windows *were* covered;

17 To that above the door, even unto the inner house, and without, and by all the wall round about within and without, by measure.

You can see that the temple Ezekiel saw in this vision was beautifully adorned. An example is seen in verses 18–20 and 25, next.

18 And *it was* **made with cherubims and palm trees, so that a palm tree *was* between a cherub and a cherub; and *every* cherub had two faces;**

19 **So that the face of a man** *was* **toward the palm tree on the one side, and the face of a young lion toward the palm tree on the other side:** *it was* **made through all the house round about**.

20 **From the ground unto above the door** *were* **cherubims and palm trees made, and** *on* **the wall of the temple**.

21 The posts of the temple *were* squared, *and* the face of the sanctuary; the appearance *of the one* as the appearance *of the other.*

22 The altar of wood *was* three cubits high, and the length thereof two cubits; and the corners thereof, and the length thereof, and the walls thereof, *were* of wood: and he said unto me, This *is* the table that *is* before the LORD.

23 And the temple and the sanctuary had two doors.

24 And the doors had two leaves *apiece,* two turning leaves; two *leaves* for the one door, and two leaves for the other *door.*

25 And **there were** **made on them**, on the doors of the temple, **cherubims and palm trees**, like as *were* made upon the walls; and *there were* thick planks upon the face of the porch without.

26 And *there were* narrow windows and palm trees on the one side and on the other side, on the sides of the

porch, and *upon* the side chambers of the house, and thick planks.

EZEKIEL 42

Selection: all verses

In this chapter, Ezekiel is shown the rooms in the temple for the priests.

1 THEN he brought me forth into the utter court, the way toward the north: and he brought me into the chamber that *was* over against the separate place, and which *was* before the building toward the north.

2 Before the length of an hundred cubits *was* the north door, and the breadth *was* fifty cubits.

3 Over against the twenty *cubits* which *were* for the inner court, and over against the pavement which *was* for the utter court, *was* gallery against gallery in three *stories.*

4 And before the chambers *was* a walk of ten cubits breadth inward, a way of one cubit; and their doors toward the north.

5 Now the upper chambers *were* shorter: for the galleries were higher than these, than the lower, and than the middlemost of the building.

6 For they *were* in three *stories,* but had not pillars as the pillars of the courts: therefore *the building* was straitened more than the lowest and the middlemost from the ground.

7 And the wall that *was* without over against the chambers, toward

the utter court on the forepart of the chambers, the length thereof *was* fifty cubits.

8 For the length of the chambers that *were* in the utter court *was* fifty cubits: and, lo, before the temple *were* an hundred cubits.

9 And from under these chambers *was* the entry on the east side, as one goeth into them from the utter court.

10 The chambers *were* in the thickness of the wall of the court toward the east, over against the separate place, and over against the building.

11 And the way before them *was* like the appearance of the chambers which *were* toward the north, as long as they, *and* as broad as they: and all their goings out *were* both according to their fashions, and according to their doors.

12 And according to the doors of the chambers that *were* toward the south *was* a door in the head of the way, *even* the way directly before the wall toward the east, as one entereth into them.

13 ¶ Then said he unto me, **The north chambers *and* the south chambers**, which *are* before the separate place, **they *be* holy chambers, where the priests that approach unto the LORD shall eat the most holy things**: there shall they lay the most holy things, and the meat offering, and the sin offering, and the trespass offering; for the place *is* holy.

Verse 13, above, reminds us that the priests who officiated in the Tabernacle and Temple in Old Testament times were allowed to take a portion of the offerings people brought to the temple for their own food.

Verse 14, next, is a reminder that special clothing was used in temple worship then as is the case for our temple worship now. And, from verse 14, we see that it will be the case in the future temple in Jerusalem.

14 When the priests enter therein, then shall they not go out of the holy *place* into the utter court, but there they shall lay **their garments wherein they minister; for they** *are* **holy**; and shall put on other garments, and shall approach to *those things* which *are* for the people.

15 Now when he had made an end of measuring the inner house, he brought me forth toward the gate **whose prospect *is*** [*which faces*] toward the east, and measured it round about.

16 He measured the east side with the measuring reed, five hundred reeds, with the measuring reed round about.

17 He measured the north side, five hundred reeds, with the measuring reed round about.

18 He measured the south side, five hundred reeds, with the measuring reed.

19 ¶ He turned about to the west side, *and* measured five hundred reeds with the measuring reed.

20 He measured it by the four sides: it had a wall round about, five hundred *reeds* long, and five hundred broad, to make a separation between the sanctuary and the **profane** [*common*] place.

EZEKIEL 43

Selection: all verses

In this chapter, Ezekiel is shown in vision that the glory of the Lord will fill this future temple in Jerusalem. We will see many parallels between this future temple and our temples today, including the requirement for patrons to be worthy to enter and do ordinance work.

1 AFTERWARD he [*Ezekiel's "guide"*] **brought me to the gate**, *even* the gate **that looketh toward the east** [*faces east*]:

2 And, behold, **the glory of the God of Israel came from the way of the east** [*"east" seems to symbolically represent the Lord; for example, He will come from the east at the Second Coming (Matthew 24:27—see also Ezekiel 43:4)*]: and his **voice *was* like a noise of many waters** [*same as in the Kirtland Temple, D&C 110:3*]: and **the earth shined with his glory**.

3 And *it was* according to the appearance of the vision which I saw, *even* according to the vision that I saw when I came to destroy the city: and **the visions *were* like the vision that I saw by the river Chebar** [*the first vision he saw—see Ezekiel 1:1*]; and I fell upon my face.

4 And the **glory of the LORD came into the house** [*temple*] by the way of the gate whose prospect *is* [*that faces*] toward the east [*in other words, the glory of the Lord came to the temple from the east*].

5 So the spirit took me up, and brought me into the inner court; and, behold, **the glory of the LORD filled the house** [*the temple*].

6 **And I heard *him*** [*the Lord*] **speaking unto me out of the house; and the man** [*guide*] **stood by me**.

> Next, in verse 7, the premortal Savior tells Ezekiel that He often walks in His temples. Also, in this verse and verse 8, He prophesies that no one will defile this future Jerusalem temple like the Israelites of old did the olden-days temple in Jerusalem by bringing their idol worship, prostitution, and other wicked acts into the former temple.

7 ¶ And he said unto me, Son of man, the place of my throne, and **the place of the soles of my feet** [*the place where I walk*], where I will dwell in the midst of the children of Israel for ever, **and my holy name, shall the house of Israel no more defile, *neither*** they, nor their kings, by their whoredom, nor by the carcases of their kings in their high places.

8 **In their setting of their threshold by my thresholds, and their post by my posts, and the wall between

me and them [*by bringing their idol worship and accompanying wickedness into the temple*], **they have even defiled my holy name** by their abominations that they have committed: **wherefore I have consumed them in mine anger** [*this is why I, the Lord, destroyed them*].

9 **Now let them put away their whoredom, and the carcases of their kings, far from me, and I will dwell in the midst of them for ever.**

In verses 10–11, next, Jehovah has Ezekiel tell the house of Israel what they must do to qualify to enter this future temple and be the Lord's covenant people once again, in the last days.

10 ¶ Thou son of man, **shew the house to the house of Israel, that they may be ashamed of their iniquities** [*in order that they may have true sorrow for their past sins and truly repent*]: **and let them measure the pattern** [*understand the plan of salvation—see Ezekiel 43:10, footnote b, in our English Bible*].

11 **And if they be ashamed of all that they have done**, shew them the form of the house [*the design of the temple*], and the fashion thereof, and the goings out thereof, and the comings in thereof, and all the forms thereof [*everything that goes on in it*], **and all the ordinances thereof**, and all the forms thereof, **and all the laws thereof**: and write *it* in their sight [*teach it to them*], **that they may keep the whole form thereof, and all the ordinances thereof, and do them**.

12 **This *is* the law of the house** [*these are the laws upon which the future temple will operate*]; Upon the top of the mountain **the whole limit thereof round about *shall be* most holy** [*everything about the temple, including the temple grounds and associated buildings will be sacred*]. Behold, this *is* the law of the house.

Verses 13–27 provide details about the altar and the sacrifices to be offered upon it.

Remember, the altar symbolizes sacrifice, and, ultimately, the greatest sacrifice of all, namely the sacrifice of the Lamb of God, the Savior Jesus Christ, who was sacrificed for the sins of all (2 Nephi 9:21) that all might, if they so choose, come unto Christ and be brought by Him unto the Father in exaltation.

13 ¶ And these *are* the measures of the altar after the cubits: The cubit *is* a cubit and an hand breadth; even the bottom *shall be* a cubit, and the breadth a cubit, and the border thereof by the edge thereof round about *shall be* a span: and this *shall be* the higher place of the altar.

14 And from the bottom *upon* the ground *even* to the lower settle *shall be* two cubits, and the breadth one cubit; and from the lesser settle *even* to the greater settle *shall be* four cubits, and the breadth *one* cubit.

15 So the altar *shall be* four cubits; and from the altar and upward *shall be* four horns.

16 And the altar *shall be* twelve *cubits* long, twelve broad, square in the four squares thereof.

17 And the settle [*NIV, "the four corners of the upper ledge"*] *shall be* fourteen *cubits* long and fourteen broad in the four squares thereof; and the border about it *shall be* half a cubit; and the bottom thereof *shall be* a cubit about; and his stairs shall look toward the east.

18 ¶ And he said unto me, Son of man, thus saith the Lord GOD; **These** *are* **the ordinances of the altar** in the day when they shall make it, to offer burnt offerings thereon, and to sprinkle blood thereon.

19 And thou shalt give to the priests the Levites that be of the seed of Zadok, which approach unto me, to minister unto me, saith the Lord GOD, a young bullock for a **sin offering**.

20 And thou shalt **take of the blood thereof, and put** *it* **on the four horns of it** [*symbolic of safety provided by the Lord—see 1 Kings 1:50*], and on the four corners of the settle, and upon the border round about: thus shalt thou cleanse and purge it.

21 Thou shalt take the bullock also of the **sin offering**, and he shall burn it in the appointed place of the house, without the sanctuary.

22 And on the second day thou shalt offer a kid of the goats **without blemish** [*symbolic of the Savior's sacrifice for us*] for a sin offering; and they shall cleanse the altar, as they did cleanse *it* with the bullock.

23 When thou hast made an end of cleansing *it,* thou shalt offer a young bullock **without blemish**, and a ram out of the flock **without blemish**.

24 And thou shalt offer them before the LORD, and the priests shall cast salt upon them, and they shall offer them up *for* a burnt offering unto the LORD.

25 **Seven days** [*symbolic of perfection, completeness; available to us eventually as we strive to stay on the covenant path and become like the Savior and the Father*] shalt thou prepare every day a goat *for* a **sin offering**: they shall also prepare a young bullock, and a ram out of the flock, **without blemish**.

26 **Seven days** shall they purge the altar and purify it; and they shall consecrate themselves.

27 And when these days are expired, it shall be, *that* upon the eighth day, and *so* forward, the priests shall make your **burnt offerings** upon the altar, and your **peace offerings**; and I will accept you, saith the Lord GOD.

EZEKIEL 44

Selection: all verses

This chapter contains continued instructions pertaining to the future temple to be built in Jerusalem in the last days, before the Second Coming of Christ.

Remember that Ezekiel is speaking of the future as if it had already taken place. This type of prophesying is sometimes referred to as "future perfect tense," in other words, "already completed."

In verses 1–3, we see that the east gate was to be kept shut because it was reserved only for use by the Lord.

1 **THEN he brought me back the way of the gate of the outward sanctuary which looketh toward** [faces] **the east**; and **it** *was* **shut.**

2 **Then said the LORD unto me; This gate shall be shut**, it shall not be opened, and **no man shall enter in by it; because the LORD, the God of Israel, hath entered in by it**, therefore it shall be shut.

3 *It is* **for the prince** [while we don't know for sure who this prince is, Ezekiel, chapters 45–46 lead us to believe that this prince could possibly be the leader of the government of Israel at the time these prophecies are fulfilled]; the prince, **he shall sit in it to eat bread before the LORD**; he shall enter by the way of the porch of *that* gate, and shall go out by the way of the same.

In verses 4–10, Ezekiel is instructed that no one is to be permitted to enter the temple except those covenant people who are striving to keep the commandments.

4 ¶ **Then brought he** [Ezekiel's guide] **me the way of the north gate before the house**: and I looked, and, behold, **the glory of the LORD filled the house of the LORD: and I fell upon my face** [a demonstration of deep respect, in Ezekiel's culture].

5 And the LORD said unto me, **Son of man, mark well** [pay very close attention], and behold with thine eyes, and hear with thine ears **all that I say unto thee concerning all the ordinances of the house of the LORD, and all the laws thereof**; and **mark well the entering in of the house** [pay close attention to who is allowed to enter the temple], with every going forth of the sanctuary.

In verses 6–10, Ezekiel is instructed to remind the future Israelites about the past wicked ways of Israel and to avoid such sinful living now, in order to be worthy to enter the temple now.

6 And thou shalt say to the rebellious, *even* to the house of Israel, Thus saith the Lord GOD; O ye house of Israel, **let it suffice you of all your abominations** [there has been enough of your terrible wickedness in the past],

7 **In that ye have brought** *into my* *sanctuary* **strangers** [foreigners, unbelievers], uncircumcised in heart, and uncircumcised in flesh, to be in my sanctuary, to pollute it, *even*

my house, when ye offer my bread, the fat and the blood, and **they have broken my covenant because of all your abominations.**

8 And **ye have not kept the charge of mine holy things** [*you defiled and polluted the holy things of My temple in past times*]: but ye have set keepers of my charge in my sanctuary for yourselves.

9 ¶ Thus saith the Lord GOD; **No stranger, uncircumcised in heart, nor uncircumcised in flesh, shall enter into my sanctuary**, of any stranger [*unbelievers; the equivalent of non-members in our day*] that *is* among the children of Israel.

10 And **the Levites that are gone away far from me** [*the Aaronic priests had apostatized*], **when Israel went astray, which went astray away from me after their idols**; they shall even bear their iniquity.

Verses 11–16 are a mixture of encouragement for the future officiators in the Jerusalem temple and warnings not to repeat the sins and rebellions of past generations of Israel.

11 **Yet they shall be ministers in my sanctuary** [*the Jerusalem temple*], *having* charge at the gates of the house, and ministering to the house: they shall slay the burnt offering and the sacrifice for the people, and they shall stand before them to minister unto them.

12 **Because they ministered unto them before their idols, and caused the house of Israel to fall into iniquity** [*the sins of past generations of Israel*]; **therefore have I lifted up mine hand against them** [*this is why I punished them*], saith the Lord GOD, and they shall bear their iniquity.

13 And they [*such people as these past generations of Israel*] **shall not come near unto me, to do the office of a priest** unto me, nor to come near to any of my holy things, in the most holy *place:* but they shall bear their shame, and their abominations which they have committed.

14 But **I will make them** [*future righteous covenant Israel*] **keepers of the charge of the house, for all the service thereof**, and for all that shall be done therein.

15 ¶ **But the priests the Levites, the sons of Zadok, that kept the charge of my sanctuary when the children of Israel went astray** from me, **they** [*the descendants of the former, wicked priests who helped lead Israel astray*] **shall come near to me to minister unto me** [*in the temple*], and they shall stand before me to offer unto me the fat and the blood, saith the Lord GOD:

Have you noticed that there is a consistent and wonderful theme in these verses, namely, that the Atonement of Jesus Christ can and does make people clean from past sins and allows them to serve the Lord now in their present lives, including in the temple? We have a strong reminder of this fact in D&C 60:7 where the Savior says "I am able to make you holy."

16 **They shall enter into my sanctuary** [*temple*]**, and they shall come near to my table** [*will officiate in ordinances of the temple*], to minister unto me, and they shall keep my charge.

Next, in verses 17–19, we see references to special clothing used in temple service.

17 ¶ And it shall come to pass, *that* **when they enter in at the gates** of the inner court, **they shall be clothed with linen garments**; and no wool shall come upon them, whiles they minister in the gates of the inner court, and within.

18 They shall have **linen bonnets upon their heads**, and shall have **linen breeches** [*NIV, "linen undergarments"*] upon their loins; they shall not gird *themselves* with any thing that causeth sweat.

19 And **when they go forth into the utter court**, *even* **into the utter court to the people** [*the outer court where non-temple patrons are*]**, they shall put off their garments wherein they ministered, and lay them in the holy chambers** [*rooms in the temple*]**, and they shall put on other garments** [*basically, regular street clothes*]; and they shall not sanctify the people with their garments.

20 **Neither shall they shave their heads**, nor suffer their locks to grow long; **they shall only poll** [*trim, cut*] **their heads**.

21 **Neither shall any priest drink wine, when they enter into the inner court.**

22 Neither shall they take for their wives a widow, **nor her that is put away** [*divorced*]: but **they shall take maidens** [*virgins*] **of the seed of the house of Israel, or a widow that had a priest before** [*a widow of a priest who has passed away*].

Next, in verse 23, we see that the officiators in the future Jerusalem temple will have a role in teaching.

23 And **they shall teach my people** *the difference* **between the holy and profane** [*common, worldly*]**, and** cause them **to discern between the unclean and the clean.**

Next, in verse 24, we see that these priests will serve as judges among the people, much the same as bishops in our day serve as "judges in Israel," including judging as to whether or not we are worthy of a temple recommend.

24 And **in controversy they shall stand in judgment**; *and* they shall judge it according to my judgments: and they shall keep my laws and my statutes in all mine assemblies; and they shall hallow my sabbaths.

It helps us in understanding verse 25, next, if we know that Leviticus 21:1–3 and 7:24 forbade contact with dead persons. No doubt this was a law for maintaining health and not spreading disease among the children of Israel. (They did not know about germs, but the Lord did.)

25 **And they shall come at no dead person to defile themselves: but for father,** or for **mother,** or for **son,** or for **daughter,** for **brother,** or for **sister** that hath had no husband, **they may defile themselves** [*a kind exception for helping in certain family circumstances*].

26 And **after he is cleansed, they shall reckon unto him seven days** [*he must wait seven days before he resumes his temple service*].

27 **And in the day that he goeth into the sanctuary** [*the temple*], unto the inner court, **to minister** in the sanctuary, **he shall offer his sin offering,** saith the Lord GOD.

28 **And it** [*the temple service—see footnote 28a in your Bible)*] **shall be unto them for an inheritance: I *am* their inheritance: and ye shall give them no possession in Israel:** I *am* their possession [*the Levites or priests were not given a certain section of Palestine for a place to settle on, as was the case with all the other tribes of Israel*].

29 **They shall eat the meat offering,** and **the sin offering,** and **the trespass offering;** and **every dedicated thing in Israel shall be theirs** [*the priests were provided food and upkeep by being allocated a certain portion of the meat that was brought by patrons for offerings as well as having*

access, as needed, to other things in the temple].

Likewise, in verse 30, the priests were given fruit, vegetables, bread, etc., for their maintenance, allocated from other offerings brought to the temple.

30 And **the first of all the firstfruits of all *things,* and every oblation** [*offering*] **of all, of every *sort* of your oblations, shall be the priest's:** ye shall also **give unto the priest the first of your dough, that he may cause the blessing to rest in thine house** [*in order for him to be able to officiate in the work of the Lord in the temple*].

Verse 31 is a reminder that the priests were to follow the same rules as all other Israelites when it came to animals that died on their own or were killed and left as carrion (Leviticus 22:8.).

31 **The priests shall not eat of any thing that is dead of itself, or torn,** whether it be fowl or beast.

EZEKIEL 45

Selection: all verses

Verses 1–8 provide instructions for dividing up the Holy Land of the future. First, a very large rectangle is specified, in the midst of which is a square to be set aside for the temple. Land within the large rectangle was also allocated for the priests and Levites and other Israelites involved with the temple. We will be told more about this in chapters 47 and 48.

1 MOREOVER, when ye shall divide by lot the land for inheritance [*when you divide the land among the tribes of Israel by casting lots*], ye shall offer an oblation unto the LORD, an holy portion of the land [*you are to set aside, as an offering to the Lord, a portion of the land for the temple and temple grounds*]: the length *shall be* the length of five and twenty thousand *reeds,* and the breadth *shall be* ten thousand. This *shall be* holy in all the borders thereof round about [*the whole area will be considered holy*].

2 Of this there shall be for the sanctuary [*the temple*] five hundred *in length,* with five hundred *in breadth,* square round about; and fifty cubits round about for the suburbs thereof.

3 And of this measure shalt thou measure the length of five and twenty thousand, and the breadth of ten thousand: and in it shall be the sanctuary *and* the most holy *place.*

4 The holy *portion* of the land shall be for the priests the ministers of the sanctuary, which shall come near to minister unto the LORD: and it shall be a place for their houses, and an holy place for the sanctuary.

Next, in verse 5, we see that an area 25,000 cubits long and 10,000 cubits wide will belong to the Levites for towns to live in.

5 And the five and twenty thousand of length, and the ten thousand of breadth, shall also the Levites, the ministers of the house, have for themselves, for a possession for twenty chambers [*rooms*].

6 ¶ And ye shall appoint the possession of the city five thousand broad, and five and twenty thousand long [*NIV, about 7 miles*], over against the oblation of the holy *portion:* it shall be for the whole house of Israel.

7 ¶ And *a portion shall be* for the prince [*see note in 44:3*] on the one side and on the other side of the oblation of the holy *portion,* and of the possession of the city, before the oblation of the holy *portion,* and before the possession of the city, from the west side westward, and from the east side eastward: and the length *shall be* over against one of the portions, from the west border unto the east border.

8 In the land shall be his possession in Israel: and my princes [*leaders*] shall no more oppress my people [*like they did in times past, including wicked King Zedekiah (at the time Lehi and his family fled Jerusalem)*]; and the rest of the land shall they give to the house of Israel according to their tribes.

We will quote from the institute of religion student manual to explain the last phrase in verse 8, above concerning the dividing up of the land among the tribes of Israel:

According to Ezekiel's vision of the future, the Holy Land will be divided in strips running between the Mediterranean Sea on the west and the Dead Sea and the Jordan River on the east. Each of the twelve tribes will be given a strip of land with a strip out of the middle for the prince, the city, and the Levites, that is, the priests. Joseph will receive a double portion (Ezekiel 47:13) since Ephraim and Manasseh, Joseph's sons, both became tribes in Israel. The city will have twelve gates, one for each tribe (including Levi and one for Joseph). On the north will be the tribes of Reuben, Judah, and Levi; on the east will be Joseph, Benjamin, and Dan; on the south will be Simeon, Issachar, and Zebulun; on the west will be Gad, Asher, and Naphtali. (Old Testament Student Manual Kings-Malachi, p. 287.)

Next, inverses 9–12, the Lord emphasizes that the future leaders of Israel must be absolutely honest in their dealings.

9 ¶ Thus saith the Lord GOD; Let it suffice you, **O princes** [*leaders*] **of Israel: remove violence and spoil**, and **execute judgment** [*fairness*] **and justice, take away your exactions** [*expropriations; illegal taking away of property or possessions—see Ezekiel; 45:9, footnote b, in your Bible*] from my people, saith the Lord GOD.

10 Ye shall have **just balances** [*honest scales*], and a **just ephah**, and a **just bath** [*units of weights and measures*].

11 **The ephah** [*a dry measure*] **and the bath** [*a liquid measure*] **shall be of one measure** [*NIV, "the same size"*],

that the bath may contain the tenth part of an homer, and the ephah the tenth part of an homer: the measure thereof shall be after the homer.

12 And **the shekel** *shall be* **twenty gerahs**: twenty shekels, five and twenty shekels, fifteen shekels, shall be your maneh.

> Verses 13–25 give instructions for the various sacrifices and offerings to be officiated in by the priests in this Jerusalem temple of the future.
>
> By the way, we don't know if these Aaronic Priesthood ordinances are part of the "restitution of all things" spoken of in the scriptures (Acts 3:20–21), or if they are symbolic of the ordinances in our temples today, or both. We would be wise to wait for further revelation on this question.

13 **This** *is* **the oblation that ye shall offer**; the sixth part of an ephah of an homer of wheat, and ye shall give the sixth part of an ephah of an homer of barley:

14 Concerning **the ordinance of oil**, the bath of oil, *ye shall offer* the tenth part of a bath out of the cor, *which is* an homer of ten baths; for ten baths *are* an homer:

15 And **one lamb out of the flock**, out of two hundred, out of the fat [*the best*] pastures of Israel; for a **meat offering**, and for a **burnt offering**, and for **peace offerings, to make reconciliation** [*symbolic of the Atonement of Christ for us*] for them, saith the Lord GOD.

16 All the people of the land shall give **this oblation** for the prince in Israel.

17 And **it shall be the prince's part** *to give* **burnt offerings, and meat offerings, and drink offerings**, in the feasts, and in the new moons [*special sacrifices were offered in conjunction with the new moons—see Bible Dictionary under "New Moon"*], and **in the sabbaths, in all solemnities of the house of Israel**: he shall prepare the sin offering, and the meat offering, and the burnt offering, and the peace offerings, to make reconciliation for the house of Israel.

18 Thus saith the Lord GOD; In the first *month,* in the first *day* of the month, thou shalt take a young bullock **without blemish** [*symbolic of Jesus Christ*], and cleanse the sanctuary:

19 And **the priest shall take of the blood** [*symbolic of being cleansed of sin by the blood of Christ*] of the sin offering, and put *it* upon the posts of the house, and upon the four corners of the settle of the altar, and upon the posts of the gate of the inner court.

20 And so thou shalt do the seventh *day* of the month **for every one that erreth** [*NIV, "sins unintentionally"*], **and for** *him that is* **simple** [*sins in ignorance of the laws and commandments*]: so shall ye reconcile the house.

21 In the first *month,* in the fourteenth day of the month, ye shall have **the passover, a feast of seven days**; unleavened bread shall be eaten.

22 And upon that day shall the prince prepare for himself and for all the people of the land **a bullock** *for* **a sin offering**.

23 And seven days of the feast he shall prepare a burnt offering to the LORD, seven bullocks and seven rams **without blemish** daily the seven days; and a kid of the goats daily *for* **a sin offering**.

24 And he shall prepare **a meat offering** of an ephah for a bullock, and an ephah for a ram, and an hin [*NIV, "about four quarts"*] of oil for an ephah.

25 In the seventh *month,* in the fifteenth day of the month, shall he do the like in the feast of the seven days, according to the **sin offering**, according to the **burnt offering**, and according to the **meat offering**, and **according to the oil**.

EZEKIEL 46

Selection: all verses

In this chapter, Ezekiel is given more information about the flow of traffic in the temple as well as additional information about sacrifices and offerings.

1 THUS saith the Lord GOD; **The gate of the inner court that looketh toward the east shall be shut the six working days; but on the sabbath it shall be opened**, and **in the day of the new moon** [*special*

offerings and rites held in conjunction with new moons—see Bible Dictionary under "New Moon"] it shall be opened.

2 And the prince shall enter by the way of the porch of *that* gate without [*outside*], and shall stand by the post of the gate, and the priests shall prepare his **burnt offering** and his **peace offerings**, and he shall worship at the threshold of the gate: then he shall go forth; but the gate shall not be shut until the evening.

3 Likewise **the people of the land shall worship at the door of this gate** before the LORD in the sabbaths and in the new moons.

4 And the **burnt offering** that the prince shall offer unto the LORD in the sabbath day *shall be* **six lambs without blemish** [*symbolic of Jesus Christ's being perfect, without blemish*] **, and a ram without blemish.**

5 And the **meat offering** *shall be* an ephah for a ram, and the meat offering for the lambs as he shall be able to give, and an hin of oil to an ephah.

6 And **in the day of the new moon** *it shall be* **a young bullock without blemish, and six lambs, and a ram**: they shall be **without blemish.**

7 And he shall prepare a **meat offering**, an ephah for a bullock, and an ephah for a ram, and for the lambs according as his hand shall attain unto, and an hin of oil to an ephah.

In verse 8, next, you will see another example of the repetition typically

used by Ezekiel to emphasize a point he is making.

8 And **when the prince shall enter, he shall go in by the way of the porch of *that* gate,** and he shall go forth by the way thereof [*NIV, "he is to come out the same way"*].

9 ¶ But when the people of the land shall come before the LORD in the solemn feasts, **he that entereth in by the way of the north gate to worship shall go out by the way of the south gate**; and he that entereth by the way of the south gate shall go forth by the way of the north gate: **he shall not return by the way of the gate whereby he came in, but shall go forth over against it** [*they are to go out the opposite gate*].

10 And **the prince in the midst of them, when they go in, shall go in**; and when they go forth, shall go forth.

11 And in the feast and in the solemnities the **meat offering** shall be an ephah to a bullock, and ephah to a ram, and to the lambs as he is able to give, and an hin of oil to an ephah.

12 Now **when the prince shall prepare a voluntary burnt offering or peace offerings** voluntarily unto the LORD, *one* **shall then open him the gate that looketh toward the east,** and he shall prepare his burnt offering and his peace offerings, as he did on the sabbath day: then he shall go forth; and **after his going forth** *one* **shall shut the gate.**

13 Thou shalt daily prepare a burnt offering unto the LORD *of* a lamb of the first year **without blemish**: thou shalt **prepare it every morning.**

14 And thou shalt **prepare a meat offering for it every morning**, the sixth part of an ephah, and the third part of an hin of oil, to temper with the fine flour; a meat offering continually by a perpetual ordinance unto the LORD.

15 Thus shall they **prepare the lamb, and the meat offering, and the oil, every morning** *for* **a continual burnt offering.**

16 ¶ Thus saith the Lord GOD; **If the prince give a gift unto any of his sons, the inheritance thereof shall be his sons'**; it *shall be* their possession by inheritance.

17 **But if he give a gift of his inheritance to one of his servants, then it shall be his to the year of liberty; after it shall return to the prince:** but his inheritance shall be his sons' for them.

18 Moreover **the prince shall not take of the people's inheritance by oppression, to thrust them out of their possession;** *but* **he shall give his sons inheritance out of his own possession**: that my people be not scattered every man from his possession.

Did you notice the strict requirement for the governor or prince (as we suppose), in verse 18, above, to be absolutely fair with his people?

This implies that at this point in time, when the temple is built in Jerusalem, that the governor and people will be living a high gospel standard of behavior.

Next, in verses 19–24, Ezekiel's guide shows him through the priests' chambers.

19 ¶ **After he** [*Ezekiel's heavenly guide*] **brought me through the entry,** which *was* at the side of the gate, **into the holy chambers of the priests**, which looked toward the north [*faced north*]: and, behold, there *was* a place on the two sides westward.

20 **Then said he unto me, This** *is* **the place where the priests shall boil the trespass offering and the sin offering, where they shall bake the meat offering**; that they bear *them* not out into the utter [*outer*] court, to sanctify the people.

21 **Then he brought me forth into the utter court**, and caused me to pass by the four corners of the court; and, behold, in every corner of the court *there was* a court.

22 **In the four corners of the court** *there were* **courts** joined of forty *cubits* long and thirty broad: these four corners *were* of one measure.

23 **And** *there was* **a row** *of building* [*NIV, "a ledge of stone"*] round about in them, round about them four, and *it was* **made with boiling places under the rows round about** [*NIV,*

"with places for fire built all around under the ledge"].

24 **Then said he unto me, These** *are* the places of them that boil, **where the ministers of the house shall boil the sacrifice of the people.**

EZEKIEL 47

Selection: all verses

This new scene in the vision is an extra fascinating one because it shows Ezekiel that water will come out from under the temple in Jerusalem and will, among other things, heal the waters of the Dead Sea. Joseph Smith prophesied of this as follows: "Judah must return, Jerusalem must be rebuilt, and the temple, and water come out from under the temple, and the waters of the Dead Sea be healed. It will take some time to rebuild the walls of the city and the temple, &c; and all this must be done before the Son of Man will make His appearance." (Teachings of the Prophet Joseph Smith, p. 286.)

From the above quote, we learn that what we will be reading about in verses 1–12, next, will take place before the Second Coming. There is much symbolism in this chapter.

1 AFTERWARD **he brought me again unto the door of the house** [*the entrance of the temple*]; and, behold, **waters issued out from under the threshold of the house eastward** [*water came out from under the temple and flowed eastward, toward the Dead Sea*]: for **the forefront of the house** *stood toward* **the east** [*the temple faced east*], and the waters

came down from under from **the right side** [*in Biblical symbolism, "right" often represents the covenant hand of the Lord, covenant blessings, and so forth*] of the house, at the south *side* of the altar.

It is interesting to note from Zechariah 14:8, that not only will water flow out from under the temple and heal the Dead Sea, but they will also flow out to the west and heal the Mediterranean Sea.

Note also that the healing of the Dead Sea can be symbolic, on a grand scale, of the healing of the whole world of bitterness and stagnation as far as spirituality is concerned.

2 Then brought he me out of the way of the gate northward, and led me about the way without unto the utter gate by the way that looketh eastward; and, **behold, there ran out waters on the right side.**

Notice, in verses 3–5, that as the guide takes Ezekiel into the water gushing out from under the temple, it gets deeper and deeper, from ankle deep to knee deep to waist deep, to too deep, as they continue eastward. Among other things, this could symbolize the unfathomable power of the Savior's Atonement to heal and cleanse from sin.

3 And **when the man that had the line** [*a tape measure, so to speak—see Ezekiel 40:3*] in his hand went forth eastward, he measured a thousand cubits [*they went about 1500 feet*], and **he brought me through the waters; the waters** *were* **to the ankles.**

4 **Again he measured a thousand** [*another 1500 feet*], and brought me through the waters; **the waters *were* to the knees.** Again he measured a thousand, and brought me through; **the waters *were* to the loins** [*the waist*].

5 Afterward he measured a thousand; *and **it was** a river that I could not pass over:* for the waters were risen, **waters to swim in, a river that could not be passed over.**

6 ¶ And he said unto me, Son of man, hast thou seen *this*? **Then he** brought me, and caused me to return to the brink [*bank*] **of the river.**

We know from the scriptures that Christ is the "living water" (John 4:10.) by partaking of His "living water," His gospel, Atonement, covenants and commandments, we can flourish and prosper. We see this represented symbolically in verses 7–12, next.

7 **Now when I had returned** [*to the shore*], behold, **at the bank of the river *were* very many trees** [*"trees" often represent people, in the scriptures*] **on the one side and on the** other.

8 Then said he unto me, **These waters issue out toward the east country, and go down into the desert** [*often symbolic of apostasy*], and go into the sea [*the Dead Sea, often symbolic of those who take but do not give*]: *which being* brought forth into the sea, **the waters shall be healed** [*can be symbolic of the prophetic fact*

that Israel will be healed by the living waters of Christ].

9 And it shall come to pass, *that* **every thing that liveth, which moveth, whithersoever the rivers shall come, shall live:** and **there shall be a very great multitude of fish** [*great prosperity*], **because these waters shall come thither: for they shall be healed; and every thing shall live whither the river cometh.**

10 And it shall come to pass, *that* **the fishers** [*fishermen*] **shall stand upon it** [*by it—see Ezekiel 47:10, footnote a*] **from En-gedi even unto En-eglaim** [*towns located near the Dead Sea*]; **they shall be a *place* to spread forth nets;** their fish shall be according to their kinds, as the fish of the great sea, exceeding many.

In verse 11, next, we see that even during this extraordinary and marvelous time in the future, people will still have their agency to reject the Lord and His gospel.

11 But the **miry places thereof and the marshes thereof** [*symbolic of people who will be unreceptive to the gospel*] **shall not be healed;** they shall be given to salt [*will be like salt in which nothing can grow*].

12 And by **the river** upon the bank thereof, **on this side and on that side, shall grow all trees for meat** [*food, fruit*], whose leaf shall not fade, **neither shall the fruit thereof be consumed** [*it will not run out, will continue to produce*]: it shall bring forth new fruit according to his months

all [*year-round*], because their waters they issued out of the sanctuary [*the temple*]: and **the fruit thereof shall be for meat** [*food*], and **the leaf thereof for medicine** [*the leaves will be used for medicinal purposes*].

Verses 13–23 specify what the borders of the Holy Land are to be and how the land is to be divided up among the 12 tribes of Israel at the time of the Jerusalem temple.

13 ¶ Thus saith the Lord GOD; **This** *shall be* **the border, whereby ye shall inherit the land according to the twelve tribes of Israel**: Joseph *shall have two* portions [*one for the tribe of Ephraim and one for the tribe of Manasseh*].

14 And **ye shall inherit it, one as well as another** [*equally*]: *concerning* the which **I lifted up mine hand** [*made a covenant*] to give it unto your fathers: and this land shall fall unto you for inheritance.

15 And this *shall be* the border of the land toward **the north side**, from the great sea, the way of Hethlon, as men go to Zedad;

16 Hamath, Berothah, Sibraim, which *is* between the border of Damascus and the border of Hamath; Hazar-hatticon, which *is* by the coast of Hauran.

17 And the border from the sea shall be Hazar-enan, the border of Damascus, and the north northward, and the border of Hamath. And *this is* the north side.

18 And **the east side** ye shall measure from Hauran, and from Damascus, and from Gilead, and from the land of Israel *by* Jordan, from the border unto the east sea. And *this is* **the east side.**

19 And **the south side** southward, from Tamar *even* to the waters of strife *in* Kadesh, the river to the great sea. And *this is* **the south side southward.**

20 **The west side** also *shall be* the great sea from the border, till a man come over against Hamath. **This** *is* **the west side.**

21 So shall **ye divide this land unto you according to the tribes of Israel.**

22 ¶ And it shall come to pass, *that* **ye shall divide it by lot** [*draw lots (to keep it completely fair)*] for an inheritance unto you, **and to the strangers** [*foreigners, non-Israelites*] that sojourn [*live*] among you, which shall beget children among you [*who settle permanently among you*]: and **they shall be unto you as born in the country among the children of Israel; they shall have inheritance with you among the tribes of Israel.**

23 And it shall come to pass, *that* **in what tribe the stranger sojourneth, there shall ye give** *him* **his inheritance, saith the Lord GOD** [*you are to treat non-Israelites among you as equals as far as land and inheritance are concerned*].

EZEKIEL 48

Selection: all verses

In this final vision, Ezekiel is given more details regarding the division of the future Holy Land among the twelve tribes of Israel (remember, Joseph receives a double portion, one for his son, Ephraim, and one for his son, Manasseh; therefore, you will see 13 tribes mentioned, but remember, the Levites—the tribe of Levi—do not get a major land inheritance like the other tribes, rather, will serve in the cities with smaller portions of land in each for housing, gardens, etc. We understand that these land inheritances will be in place at the time of the Savior's Second Coming.) More information is provided about the gates of Jerusalem and the city receives another name.

First, in verses 1–7 (compare with 47:13–21,) the north border of the Holy Land is again defined and then equal portions of the land are described for seven of the tribes.

1 NOW **these** *are* **the names of the tribes**. From the north end to the coast of the way of Hethlon, as one goeth to Hamath, Hazar-enan, the border of Damascus northward, to the coast of Hamath; for these are his sides east *and* west; **a** *portion for* **Dan**.

2 And by the border of Dan, from the east side unto the west side, **a** *portion for* **Asher**.

3 And by the border of Asher, from the east side even unto the west side, **a** *portion for* **Naphtali**.

4 And by the border of Naphtali, from the east side unto the west side, **a** *portion for* **Manasseh**.

5 And by the border of Manasseh, from the east side unto the west side, **a** *portion for* **Ephraim**.

6 And by the border of Ephraim, from the east side even unto the west side, **a** *portion for* **Reuben**.

7 And by the border of Reuben, from the east side unto the west side, **a** *portion for* **Judah**.

Next, in verses 8–22, additional details are given regarding the large tracts of land for the temple, the priests, the Levites, and the "prince" as well as specifications for the area where the common people will live.

8 ¶ **And by the border of Judah** [*bordering the portion of land allocated to the tribe of Judah*], from the east side unto the west side, **shall be the offering** [*tract of land*] which ye shall offer of five and twenty thousand *reeds* [*NIV, "cubits"*] *in* breadth, and *in* length as one of the *other* parts, from the east side unto the west side: and **the sanctuary** [*temple*] **shall be in the midst of it**.

9 **The oblation** [*offering of land*] **that ye shall offer unto the LORD** *shall be* of five and twenty thousand in length, and of ten thousand in breadth.

Next, we see that the priests will receive a large rectangle of land for their needs and that the temple will be in the middle of it.

10 And for them, *even* **for the priests**, shall be *this* holy oblation; toward the north **five and twenty thousand** *in length*, and toward the west **ten thousand in breadth**, and toward the east **ten thousand in breadth**, and toward the south **five and twenty thousand in length**: and **the sanctuary** [*Jerusalem temple*] **of the LORD shall be in the midst thereof**.

> Verse 11, next, reminds us that, in Old Testament times, the sons of Zadok (descendants of Levi who served in Solomon's Temple) remained faithful when the rest of the people of Israel were going astray.

11 *It shall be* **for the priests** that are sanctified of **the sons of Zadok; which have kept my charge** [*who served in the temple, anciently*], **which went not astray when the children of Israel went astray**, as the **Levites went astray** [*along with the Levite priests who helped lead the people into idol worship, defiling the temple, and rebelling against the true God*].

12 And *this* oblation of **the land** that is offered **shall be unto them a thing most holy** by the border of the Levites.

> Next, the Levites, a subset of the priests, will get their own portion of land.

13 And over against the border of the priests **the Levites** *shall have* five and twenty thousand in length, and ten thousand in breadth: all the length *shall be* five and twenty thousand, and the breadth ten thousand.

14 And **they shall not sell of it, neither exchange**, nor alienate the firstfruits of the land: for *it is* holy unto the LORD.

15 ¶ And **the five thousand, that are left** in the breadth over against the five and twenty thousand, **shall be a profane** *place* **for the city**, for dwelling, and for suburbs [*a place where the common people can live*]: and the city shall be in the midst thereof.

16 And **these** *shall be* **the measures** [*the specifications*] **thereof**; the north side four thousand and five hundred, and the south side four thousand and five hundred, and on the east side four thousand and five hundred, and the west side four thousand and five hundred.

17 And **the suburbs of the city** [*NIV, "the pastureland for the city"*] shall be toward the north two hundred and fifty, and toward the south two hundred and fifty, and toward the east two hundred and fifty, and toward the west two hundred and fifty.

18 And **the residue** [*what remains*] in length over against the oblation of the holy *portion shall be* ten thousand eastward, and ten thousand westward: and it shall be over against the oblation of the holy *portion;* and the increase thereof **shall be for food** [*used to raise crops*] **unto them that serve the city**.

19 And **they that serve the city shall serve it out of all the tribes of Israel**.

20 All the oblation *shall be* five and twenty thousand by five and twenty thousand: **ye shall offer the holy oblation foursquare** [*allocate a square of land*], with the possession of the city.

21 ¶ And **the residue *shall be* for the prince**, on the one side and on the other of the holy oblation, and of the possession of the city, over against the five and twenty thousand of the oblation toward the east border, and westward over against the five and twenty thousand toward the west border, over against the portions for the prince: and it shall be the holy oblation; and **the sanctuary** of the house *shall be* **in the midst thereof**.

Next, in verses 22–29, we see the portions of the future Holy Land that will be allocated to the tribe of Levi as well as to the other 5 tribes of Israel.

22 Moreover from **the possession of the Levites**, and from the possession of the city, *being* in the midst *of that* which is the prince's, between the border of Judah and the border of Benjamin, shall be for the prince.

23 **As for the rest of the tribes**, from the east side unto the west side, **Benjamin *shall have* a *portion*.**

24 And by the border of Benjamin, from the east side unto the west side, **Simeon *shall have* a *portion*.**

25 And by the border of Simeon, from the east side unto the west side, **Issachar a *portion*.**

26 And by the border of Issachar, from the east side unto the west side, **Zebulun a *portion*.**

27 And by the border of Zebulun, from the east side unto the west side, **Gad a *portion*.**

Verse 28 defines the southern border of the future Holy Land.

28 And by the border of Gad, at the south side southward, **the border shall be even from Tamar *unto* the waters of strife *in* Kadesh, *and* to the river toward the great sea**.

29 **This *is* the land which ye shall divide by lot unto the tribes of Israel for inheritance**, and these *are* their portions, saith the Lord GOD.

In verses 30–35, Ezekiel sees that there will be three gates in each of the four walls of the future city of Jerusalem. (You may wish to compare these descriptive verses with those of Revelation 21:12–27.) These gates will be named after each of the tribes of Israel.

30 ¶ And **these *are* the goings out of the city** [*the exits or gates of the city*] on the north side, four thousand and five hundred measures.

31 And **the gates of the city *shall be* after** [*named after*] **the names of the tribes of Israel**: three gates northward [*on the north wall*]; **one gate of Reuben, one gate of Judah, one gate of Levi**.

32 And **at the east side** four thousand and five hundred: and three gates; and **one gate of Joseph, one gate of Benjamin, one gate of Dan**.

33 And **at the south side** four thousand and five hundred measures: and three gates; **one gate of Simeon, one gate of Issachar, one gate of Zebulun**.

34 **At the west side** four thousand and five hundred, *with* their three gates; **one gate of Gad, one gate of Asher, one gate of Naphtali**.

At the end of verse 35, next, we see that the city will be given another name. Such re-naming is common in Biblical symbolism. It is used to describe a new function or state of being for the city. In this case, the JST renders a clarification for the name, as seen in the note at the end of the verse.

35 *It* [*the city*] *was* **round about eighteen thousand** *measures* [*NIV, "The distance around will be 18,000 cubits" (a little over 5 miles around)*]*:* and **the name of the city from** *that* **day** *shall be,* **The LORD** *is* **there** [*JST, "And the name of the city from that day shall be called, Holy; for the Lord shall be there*]."

DANIEL

Daniel was taken captive to Babylon with other Jews by Nebuchadnezzar (perhaps the crown prince of Babylon at this time—according to some Bible scholars, his father was still alive), in about 606 BC, not quite twenty years before the fall of Jerusalem in 587 BC. It appears that he was among one of the first waves of captives, which included skilled craftsmen and likely candidates for being educated in Babylon. It was customary for the king of Babylon to take the cream of the crop among those he captured and treat them well, educating them and giving them responsibilities in his government. Daniel and three other Hebrew young men, Shadrach, Meshach, and Abednego, were among the promising young men chosen for privilege by Nebuchadnezzar.

The Book of Daniel can be divided into two general categories. Chapters 1–6 are accounts of Daniel and his three young friends in Babylon. Chapters 7–12 consist of prophetic visions that Daniel saw while in Babylon. As you know, some of our favorite Bible stories come from the Book of Daniel, including Daniel in the lions' den (Daniel 6:16).

In a way, Daniel might be considered to be the "Joseph" in Babylonian captivity since his story and values closely parallel those of Joseph who was sold into Egypt.

There are several major messages in Daniel, including:

1. The value of living a healthy lifestyle and living according to the Lord's laws of health (1:5–15).

2. Being strictly loyal to God; having "no other gods" before Him (chapter 3).

3. The power of prayer (chapters 2, 6, and 9).

4. The value of a good reputation (4:8; 5:11–14; 6:14).

5. The value of showing gratitude (chapter 4).

6. The value of gifts of the Spirit (chapters 2, 4, 5, 7–12).

Due to space limitations, we will study Daniel, chapters 1–6, plus parts of chapter 7 for purposes of this study guide.

DANIEL 1

Selection: all verses

In this introductory chapter to the book of Daniel, we see that King Nebuchadnezzar of Babylon has laid siege to Jerusalem. Daniel and his young friends are among the Jews who are taken captive to Babylon, which is some 500 miles east of Jerusalem as the crow flies, but closer to 800–1000 miles of travel by the normal trade routes of the day.

1 IN the third year of the reign of Jehoiakim king of Judah [*about 606 BC*] **came Nebuchadnezzar king of Babylon unto Jerusalem, and besieged it**.

The gross wickedness of the Jews at this time made them weak and unable to defend themselves. Likewise, their lifestyles had separated them from the Lord and His help.

2 And **the Lord gave Jehoiakim king of Judah into his hand**, with part of the vessels of the house of God: which he carried into the land of Shinar to the house of his god; and he brought the vessels into the treasure house of his god.

3 ¶ And **the king** [*Nebuchadnezzar*] **spake** unto Ashpenaz the master of his eunuchs [*the chief of his palace officers*], that he should **bring certain of the children of Israel**, and of the king's seed, and of the princes;

4 Children **in whom** *was* **no blemish, but well favoured, and skilful in all wisdom, and cunning in knowledge, and understanding science**, and such as *had* ability in them to stand in the king's palace, and **whom they might teach the learning and the tongue of the Chaldeans** [*Babylonians*].

According to verse 5, next, the plan was to feed them the same sumptuous food eaten by the king, and to educate them for three years, at which time they would be presented to the king to enter into his service. Remember that the word "meat" in our Bible means "food." When Old Testament writers mean beef or lamb or whatever, they usually use the word "flesh."

It is almost certain that the "king's meat" included the meat of several different kinds of animals, many of which would have been against the Jews' "word of wisdom" (see Leviticus 11)—the Law of Moses regarding what a faithful Israelite could and could not eat. For example, the king's food could have included pork and meat that had not been bled before cooking. All of these would have violated the commitments of Daniel and his friends to the Lord, just as smoking and drinking would violate our covenants with the Lord.

Major Message

Living according to the Lord's law of health provides both physical and spiritual blessings.

5 And **the king appointed them a daily provision of the king's meat** [*had them eat the same food that the king ate*], **and** of the **wine** which he drank: so nourishing them three years, **that at the end thereof they might stand before the king** [*be given responsible positions in the king's service*].

6 **Now among these were** of the children of Judah [*from among the Jewish captives*], **Daniel, Hananiah** [*Shadrach*]**, Mishael** [*Meshach*]**, and Azariah** [*Abednego*]:

7 **Unto whom the prince of the eunuchs gave names**: for he gave unto **Daniel** *the name* of **Belteshazzar**; and to Hananiah, of Shadrach; and to Mishael, of Meshach; and to Azariah, of Abed-nego.

8 ¶ **But Daniel** purposed in his heart that he **would not defile himself** [*break the covenants he had made with the Lord*] **with** the portion of **the king's meat, nor with the wine** which he drank: **therefore he requested of the prince of the eunuchs that he might not defile himself.**

The "prince of the eunuchs"—in other words, the chief servant in charge of these young men—was put in a dangerous position by Daniel's request. If he granted Daniel's request, and it did not work out, he could be imprisoned or executed.

9 **Now God had brought Daniel into favour and tender love with the prince of the eunuchs.**

10 And **the prince of the eunuchs said unto Daniel, I fear my lord the king**, who hath appointed your meat [*food*] and your drink: **for why should he see** [*if he sees*] **your faces worse** liking than the children which are of your sort [*what if you look less healthy than others in your class*]? **then shall ye make** *me* **endanger my head to the king.**

11 **Then said Daniel to Melzar**, whom the prince of the eunuchs had set over Daniel, Hananiah, Mishael, and Azariah,

12 **Prove thy servants, I beseech thee, ten days**; and let them give us pulse [*seeds, grains—see footnote 12a in your Bible; NIV: "vegetables"*] to eat, and water to drink [*just try our Hebrew diet out on us for ten days*].

13 **Then let our countenances** [*faces*] **be looked upon before thee, and the countenance of the children that eat of the portion of the king's meat: and as thou seest, deal with thy servants** [*then see how healthy we look compared to others in our group of trainees, and then you make a decision*].

14 **So he consented** to them in this matter, and proved them ten days.

15 **And at the end of ten days their countenances appeared fairer and fatter** in flesh than all the children which did eat the portion of the king's meat.

16 **Thus Melzar took away** the portion of **their meat, and the wine** that they should drink; **and gave them pulse**.

17 ¶ As **for these four children, God gave them knowledge and skill in all learning and wisdom: and Daniel had understanding in all visions and dreams**.

> Let's see what happened when the three years ended.

18 Now at the end of the days that the king had said he should bring them [*the group of trainees*] in, then **the prince of the eunuchs brought them in before Nebuchadnezzar**.

19 **And the king communed with them; and among them all was found none like Daniel, Hananiah, Mishael, and Azariah**: therefore stood they before the king [*they were chosen to take responsible positions in the government*].

20 **And in all matters of wisdom** *and* **understanding**, that the king enquired of them, **he found them ten times better** than all the magicians *and* astrologers that *were* in all his realm.

21 And Daniel continued *even* unto the first year of king Cyrus.

DANIEL 2

Selection: all verses

This chapter contains the great prophecy that, in the latter days, the kingdom of God will be restored and taken to the whole earth. The stone cut out of the mountain without hands will roll forth to fill the whole earth.

King Nebuchadnezzar had a troubling dream and demanded that his wise men, astrologers, magicians, and so forth interpret the dream for him but refused to tell them what the dream was.

1 And in the second year of the reign of Nebuchadnezzar **Nebuchadnezzar dreamed dreams**, wherewith **his spirit was troubled, and his sleep brake from him** [*he could not sleep*].

2 **Then the king commanded to call the magicians**, and the **astrologers**, and the **sorcerers**, and the **Chaldeans** [*NIV: "astrologers"*], for **to shew** [*interpret*] **the** king his **dreams**. So they came and stood before the king.

3 **And the king said** unto them, **I have dreamed a dream, and my spirit was troubled to know the dream** [*the interpretation of the dream*].

4 **Then spake the Chaldeans** to the king in Syriack [*Aramaic, a language related to Hebrew*], O king, live for ever: **tell thy servants the dream,**

and we will shew the interpretation,

5 The king answered and said to the Chaldeans, The thing is gone from me [*he actually remembered the dream but was testing the astrologers—see footnote 5a in your Bible*]: if ye will not make known unto me the dream, with the interpretation thereof, ye shall be cut in pieces, and your houses shall be made a dunghill.

6 But if ye shew the dream [*tell me what the dream was*], and the interpretation thereof, ye shall receive of me gifts and rewards and great honour: therefore shew me the dream, and the interpretation thereof.

7 They answered again and said, Let the king tell his servants the dream, and we will shew the interpretation of it.

8 The king answered and said, I know of certainty that ye would gain the time [*you are stalling for time*], because ye see the thing is gone from me.

9 But if ye will not make known unto me the dream, *there is but* one decree for you [*as stated in verse 5*]: for ye have prepared lying and corrupt words to speak before me, till the time be changed [*hoping the situation will change*]: therefore tell me the dream, and I shall know that ye can shew me the interpretation thereof.

10 ¶ The Chaldeans answered before the king, and said, There is not a man upon the earth that can shew the king's matter: therefore *there is* no king, lord, nor ruler, *that* asked such things at any magician, or astrologer, or Chaldean.

11 And *it is* a rare thing that the king requireth, and there is none other that can shew it before the king, except the gods, whose dwelling is not with flesh.

12 For this cause the king was angry and very furious, and commanded to destroy all the wise *men* of Babylon.

13 And the decree went forth that the wise *men* should be slain; and they sought Daniel and his fellows to be slain.

14 ¶ Then Daniel answered [*responded*] with counsel and wisdom to Arioch the captain of the king's guard, which was gone forth to slay the wise *men* of Babylon:

15 He answered and said to Arioch the king's captain, Why *is* the decree *so* hasty from the king [*why is the king in such a hurry to kill us all*]? Then Arioch made the thing known [*explained the situation*] to Daniel.

16 Then Daniel went in, and desired of the king that he would give him time, and that he would shew the king the interpretation.

17 Then Daniel went to his house, and made the thing known

to Hananiah, Mishael, and Azariah [*to Shadrach, Meshach, and Abednego*], his companions:

18 **That they would desire mercies of the God of heaven concerning this secret** [*so that they would join him in praying to God for help*]; that Daniel and his fellows should not perish with the rest of the wise *men* of Babylon.

19 ¶ **Then was the secret revealed unto Daniel in a night vision.** Then Daniel blessed [*praised and thanked*] the God of heaven.

20 Daniel answered and said, Blessed be the name of God for ever and ever: for wisdom and might are his:

21 And he changeth the times and the seasons: he removeth kings, and setteth up kings: he giveth wisdom unto the wise, and knowledge to them that know understanding:

22 He revealeth the deep and secret things: he knoweth what *is* in the darkness, and the light dwelleth with him.

23 **I thank thee, and praise thee, O thou God of my fathers, who hast given me wisdom and might, and hast made known unto me now what we desired of thee**: for thou hast *now* made known unto us the king's matter.

24 ¶ **Therefore Daniel went in unto Arioch**, whom the king had ordained [*assigned*] to destroy the wise

men of Babylon: he went **and said** thus unto him; **Destroy not the wise *men* of Babylon: bring me in before the king, and I will shew unto the king the interpretation**.

25 Then **Arioch brought in Daniel before the king in haste**, and said thus unto him, I have found a man of the captives of Judah, that will make known unto the king the interpretation.

26 **The king answered** [*responded*] **and said to Daniel**, whose name *was* Belteshazzar, **Art thou able to make known unto me the dream which I have seen, and the interpretation thereof?**

This is a "missionary moment" for Daniel. Watch as he gives credit to the Lord.

27 **Daniel answered** in the presence of the king, and said, **The secret** which the king hath demanded cannot the wise *men,* the astrologers, the magicians, the soothsayers, **shew unto the king**;

28 **But there is a God in heaven that revealeth secrets**, and maketh known to the king Nebuchadnezzar what shall be in the latter days. **Thy dream, and the visions of thy head upon thy bed, are these**;

29 As for thee, O king, **thy thoughts came *into thy mind* upon thy bed, what should come to pass hereafter** [*you were shown the future*]: **and he** [*the Lord*] **that revealeth secrets**

maketh known to thee what shall come to pass.

Next, in verse 30, Daniel humbly tells the king that he, himself, is nothing special and that the Lord revealed the dream to him in order to save the advisers the king had ordered to be executed.

30 **But as for me, this secret is not revealed to me for** *any* **wisdom that I have** more than any living, but for *their* sakes that shall make known the interpretation to the king, and that thou mightest know the thoughts of thy heart.

Next, because of what the Lord had shown him, Daniel tells the king what he saw in his dream.

31 ¶ **Thou, O king, sawest**, and behold **a great image**. This great image, whose brightness *was* excellent [*dazzling*], stood before thee; and the form thereof *was* terrible [*awe inspiring*].

32 **This image's head** *was* **of fine gold**, his **breast and his arms of silver**, his **belly and his thighs of brass**,

33 His **legs of iron**, his **feet part of iron and part of clay**.

President Spencer W. Kimball gave the interpretation of the above images. He taught that:

a. The head of gold represented King Nebuchadnezzar and the kingdom of Babylon.

b. The breast and arms of silver symbolized Cyrus the Persian, whose armies would conquer Babylon.

c. The brass represented Philip and Alexander and the Greek or Macedonian kingdom.

d. The Roman Empire was represented by the legs of iron.

e. The feet of iron and clay symbolized a group of European nations.

("The Stone Cut Without Hands," *Ensign*, May 1976, page 8.)

Next, in verses 34–35, the stone, representing The Church of Jesus Christ of Latter-day Saints, goes forth into the whole earth, destroying all earthly kingdoms (D&C 65:2; D&C 87:6), until it fills the earth.

34 **Thou sawest** till that **a stone** was **cut out without hands** [*the stone is not man-made; in other words, it is the work of God, the true Church*], **which smote the image upon his feet** *that were* **of iron and clay, and brake them to pieces**.

One other consideration about the stone or rock, in verse 34, above, is that Jesus Christ is often referred to in scripture as the "Rock of our salvation," the sure Foundation. He and His gospel will ultimately overcome all obstacles and enemies and fill the earth with truth and light.

35 **Then was the iron, the clay, the brass, the silver, and the gold, broken to pieces** together, and became like the chaff of the summer threshingfloors; and the wind carried them away, that no place was found for

them: **and the stone that smote the image became a great mountain, and filled the whole earth.**

36 ¶ **This** *is* **the dream; and we will tell the interpretation thereof** before the king.

37 **Thou, O king,** *art* **a king of kings**: for the God of heaven hath given thee a kingdom, power, and strength, and glory.

38 And wheresoever the children of men dwell, the beasts of the field and the fowls of the heaven hath he given into thine hand, and hath made thee ruler over them all. **Thou** *art* **this head of gold.**

39 And **after thee shall arise another kingdom inferior to thee,** and **another third kingdom of brass,** which shall bear rule over all the earth.

40 And **the fourth kingdom shall be strong as iron**: forasmuch as iron breaketh in pieces and subdueth all *things:* and as iron that breaketh all these, shall it break in pieces and bruise.

41 And whereas thou sawest **the feet and toes, part of potters' clay, and part of iron, the kingdom shall be divided**; but there shall be in it of the strength of the iron, forasmuch as thou sawest the iron mixed with miry clay.

42 And *as* **the toes of the feet** *were* **part of iron, and part of clay**, *so* the kingdom shall be **partly strong, and partly broken**.

43 And whereas thou sawest iron mixed with miry clay, **they shall mingle themselves with the seed of men: but they shall not cleave one to another,** even as iron is not mixed with clay [*the nations of Europe will have a difficult time forming a solid union*].

44 And **in the days of these kings** [*in the last days, when the nations of Europe have been formed*] **shall the God of heaven set up a kingdom** [*The Church of Jesus Christ of Latter-day Saints*], **which shall never be destroyed**: and **the kingdom shall not be left to other people** [*it will never go into apostasy and thus need to be saved by others*], *but* it shall break in pieces and consume all these kingdoms, **and it shall stand for ever.**

Do you realize how important the phrase "shall not be left to other people" is? Over many years, especially while serving as a stake president, people occasionally approached me to say that the First Presidency of the Church had gone astray and that the apostles were not doing as they should. In several cases, I asked them if they still believed the Bible. They said they did. I then asked them to turn to Daniel 2:44 and tell me what it means when it says, "the kingdom shall not be left to other people." In one case in particular, the people said, "We have never noticed that verse before. It has to mean that the First Presidency will never lead us astray. The Church will never be turned over to someone else who will have to straighten it out and save it." With that realization, they returned to full activity and commitment in the Church.

45 Forasmuch as thou sawest that the stone was cut out of the mountain without hands, and that it brake in pieces the iron, the brass, the clay, the silver, and the gold; the great God hath made known to the king what shall come to pass hereafter [what will happen in the future]: and **the dream is certain, and the interpretation thereof sure.**

In other words, the Church will never go into apostasy again. It will continue strong and vibrant, ever increasing and expanding, until it fills the whole earth during the Millennium.

Next, we see that the king was so impressed and overwhelmed— even humbled—by Daniel's interpretation of this dream that he did something unheard of. He bowed down to Daniel. He fell on his face before Daniel and worshiped him.

46 ¶ **Then the king Nebuchadnezzar fell upon his face, and worshipped Daniel,** and commanded that they should offer an oblation and sweet odours unto him.

47 **The king answered** [responded] unto **Daniel, and said, Of a truth it is, that your God is a God of gods, and a Lord of kings, and a revealer of secrets**, seeing thou couldest reveal this secret.

48 Then **the king made Daniel** a great man, and gave him many great gifts, and made him **ruler over the whole province of Babylon, and chief of the governors over all the wise men of Babylon.**

49 Then **Daniel requested of the king, and he set Shadrach, Meshach, and Abed-nego, over the affairs of the province of Babylon**: but Daniel sat in the gate of the king [Daniel remained close to the king in the royal court].

DANIEL 3

Selection: all verses

In Daniel, chapter 3, King Nebuchadnezzar has a huge, about 90 foot tall, image made and commands all the people to fall down and worship it whenever a signal is given. Daniel's friends, Shadrach, Meshach, and Abednego put their lives on the line as they disobey Nebuchadnezzar in order to keep their covenants to God.

1 **Nedbuchadnezzar the king made an image of gold**, whose height was threescore cubits [about ninety feet high—"score" means twenty, and a cubit was about eighteen inches], and the breadth thereof six cubits [about nine feet]: he set it up in the plain of Dura, in the province of Babylon.

Next, the king invites leaders and dignitaries from throughout the kingdom to attend the dedication of the statue.

2 **Then Nebuchadnezzar the king sent to gather together the princes,** the **governors,** and the **captains,** the **judges,** the **treasurers,** the **counsellors,** the **sheriffs,** and all the **rulers** of the provinces, **to come to the dedication of the image** which Nebuchadnezzar the king had set up.

3 Then the princes, the governors, and captains, the judges, the treasurers, the counsellors, the sheriffs, and **all** the rulers of the provinces, **were gathered together unto the dedication** of the image that Nebuchadnezzar the king had set up; and they stood before the image that Nebuchadnezzar had set up.

4 Then an herald cried aloud, **To you it is commanded,** O people, nations, and languages,

5 *That* **at what time ye hear the sound** of the cornet, flute, harp, sackbut, psaltery, dulcimer, and all kinds of musick, **ye fall down and worship the golden image** that Nebuchadnezzar the king hath set up:

6 And **whoso falleth not down and worshippeth shall the same hour be cast into the midst of a burning fiery furnace.**

7 Therefore **at that time, when all the people heard the sound** of the cornet, flute, harp, sackbut, psaltery, and all kinds of musick, **all the people,** the nations, and the languages, **fell down** *and* **worshipped the golden image** that Nebuchadnezzar the king had set up.

8 ¶ Wherefore **at that time certain Chaldeans** [*Babylonians who lived in a major section of Babylon*] came near, and **accused the Jews.**

9 They spake **and said to the king** Nebuchadnezzar, O king, live for ever.

10 **Thou, O king, hast made a decree, that every man that shall hear the sound** of the cornet, flute, harp, sackbut, psaltery, and dulcimer, and all kinds of musick, **shall fall down and worship the golden image:**

11 And **whoso falleth not down and worshippeth,** *that* he **should be cast into the midst of a burning fiery furnace.**

12 **There are certain Jews** whom thou hast set over the affairs of the province of Babylon, **Shadrach, Meshach, and Abed-nego;** these men, O king, have not regarded thee: **they serve not thy gods, nor worship the golden image** which thou hast set up.

13 ¶ **Then Nebuchadnezzar in** *his* **rage and fury commanded to bring Shadrach, Meshach, and Abed-nego.** Then they brought these men before the king.

14 Nebuchadnezzar spake **and said unto them,** *Is it* **true, O Shadrach, Meshach, and Abed-nego, do not ye serve my gods, nor worship the golden image which I have set up?**

Next, Nebuchadnezzar gives the three young men another chance.

15 **Now if** ye be ready that at what time **ye hear the sound** of the cornet, flute, harp, sackbut, psaltery, and dulcimer, and all kinds of musick, ye **fall down and worship the image** which I have made; *well* [*I am willing to forgive you*]*:* **but if ye worship not, ye shall be cast the same hour into the midst of a burning fiery furnace**; and **who** *is* **that God that shall deliver you out of my hands** [*what god do you worship who you think has power to save you from the furnace*]?

These young Jewish men are wonderful examples of what it means to keep commitments to God at all costs. Abraham was likewise such an example, as you can see by looking at Facsimile No. 1 in the Pearl of Great Price and reading Abraham, chapter 1.

16 **Shadrach, Meshach, and Abednego, answered** and said to the king, O Nebuchadnezzar, **we** *are* **not careful to answer thee in this matter** [*we will give you a straight answer*].

17 **If it be** *so,* **our God whom we serve is able** to deliver us from the burning fiery furnace, **and** he **will** [*and it is His will to save us*] deliver *us* out of thine hand, O king.

18 **But if not, be it known unto thee, O king, that we will not serve thy gods, nor worship the golden image which thou hast set up.**

19 ¶ **Then was Nebuchadnezzar full of fury**, and the form of his visage was changed against Shadrach, Meshach, and Abed-nego: *therefore* he spake, and **commanded that they should heat the furnace one seven times more than it was wont to be heated.**

20 And **he commanded the most mighty men that** *were* in his army **to bind Shadrach, Meshach, and Abed-nego,** *and* **to cast** *them* into the burning fiery furnace.

21 **Then these men were bound** in their coats, their hosen [*pants, trousers*], and their hats, and their *other* garments, **and were cast into the midst of the burning fiery furnace.**

22 Therefore because the king's commandment was urgent, and the furnace exceeding hot, **the flame of the fire slew those men that took up Shadrach, Meshach, and Abed-nego.**

23 **And these three men, Shadrach, Meshach, and Abed-nego, fell down bound into the midst of the burning fiery furnace.**

24 Then Nebuchadnezzar the king **was astonied, and rose up in haste,** *and* **spake**, and said unto his counsellors, **Did not we cast three men** bound **into the midst of the fire?** They answered and said unto the king, True, O king.

25 He answered and said, Lo, **I see four men loose, walking in the midst of the fire**, and they have no

hurt; and the form of the fourth **is like the Son of God.**

Look closely at the wording in verse 25, above. The point of our looking especially at verse 25 is the phrase "like the Son of God." This is a reference to Jesus Christ, or Jehovah, who is the God of the Old Testament and is the Son of God.

We see a similar phrase in Daniel 7:13 and another in Abraham 3:24, where it says "there stood one among them that was like unto God." Footnote 24a for Abraham 3 informs us that it is a reference to Jesus Christ. We see yet another such reference in 1 Nephi 1:8, where Lehi sees the Father, but as Nephi records it, he says concerning his father, "he thought he saw God sitting upon his throne."

The answer is simple. In Old Testament culture, people were careful not to take the name of the Lord in vain, as commanded in the Ten Commandments. They became so cautious that they avoided almost any chance of inappropriately using the sacred name and thus often used an indirect reference rather than directly stating it.

Verses 26–27, next, are thrilling verses, especially for children as this Bible story is read to them.

26 ¶ Then Nebuchadnezzar came near to the mouth of the burning fiery furnace, *and* spake, and said, Shadrach, Meshach, and Abed-nego, ye servants of the most high God, come forth, and come *hither.* Then Shadrach, Meshach, and Abed-nego, came forth of the midst of the fire.

27 And the princes, governors, and captains, and the king's counsellors, being gathered together, saw these men, upon whose bodies the fire had no power, **nor was an hair of their head singed, neither were their coats changed, nor the smell of fire had passed on them** [*they didn't even smell like smoke*].

28 *Then* Nebuchadnezzar spake, and **said, Blessed** *be* **the God of Shadrach, Meshach, and Abed-nego,** who hath sent his angel, and delivered his servants that trusted in him, and have changed the king's word, and yielded their bodies, that they might not serve nor worship any god, except their own God.

29 **Therefore I make a decree, That every people, nation, and language, which speak any thing amiss against the God of Shadrach, Meshach, and Abed-nego, shall be cut in pieces**, and their houses shall be made a dunghill [*a pile of rubble*]: because there is no other God that can deliver after this sort [*there is no other god; in other words, no idol or image that can rescue like the god of these Jews*].

30 **Then the king promoted Shadrach, Meshach, and Abed-nego, in the province of Babylon**.

DANIEL 4

Selection: all verses

In this chapter, among other things, King Nebuchadnezzar has another dream, and Daniel interprets it. In verses 1–5, the king writes a letter in which he describes the dream, which terrified him.

1 NEBUCHADNEZZAR the king, unto all people, nations, and languages, that dwell in all the earth; Peace be multiplied unto you.

2 I thought it good to shew the signs and wonders that the high God hath wrought [done] toward me.

3 How great *are* his signs! and how mighty *are* his wonders! his kingdom *is* an everlasting kingdom, and his dominion *is* from generation to generation.

4 ¶ I Nebuchadnezzar was at rest in mine house, and flourishing in my palace:

5 I saw a dream which made me afraid, and the thoughts upon my bed and the visions of my head troubled me.

He called his wise men to interpret the dream but they could not.

6 Therefore made I a decree to bring in all the wise *men* of Babylon before me, that they might make known unto me the interpretation of the dream.

7 Then came in the magicians, the astrologers, the Chaldeans, and the soothsayers: and I told the dream before them; but they did not make known unto me the interpretation thereof.

8 ¶ But at the last Daniel came in before me, whose name *was* Belteshazzar, according to the name of my god, and in whom *is* the spirit of the holy gods [*the king knew that Daniel was an inspired man*]: and before him I told the dream, *saying,*

9 O Belteshazzar [*another name for Daniel*], master of the magicians, because I know that the spirit of the holy gods *is* in thee, and no secret troubleth thee, tell me the visions of my dream that I have seen, and the interpretation thereof.

Next, in verses 10–17, the king retells his dream to Daniel.

10 Thus *were* the visions of mine head in my bed; I saw, and behold a tree in the midst of the earth, and the height thereof *was* great.

11 The tree grew, and was strong, and the height thereof reached unto heaven, and the sight thereof to the end of all the earth:

12 The leaves thereof *were* fair, and the fruit thereof much, and in it *was* meat for all: the beasts of the field had shadow under it, and the fowls of the heaven dwelt in the boughs thereof, and all flesh was fed of it.

13 I saw in the visions of my head upon my bed, and, behold, a watcher and an holy one came down from heaven;

14 He cried aloud, and said thus, Hew down the tree, and cut off his branches, shake off his leaves, and

scatter his fruit: let the beasts get away from under it, and the fowls from his branches:

15 Nevertheless leave the stump of his roots in the earth, even with a band of iron and brass, in the tender grass of the field; and let it be wet with the dew of heaven, and *let* his portion *be* with the beasts in the grass of the earth:

16 Let his heart be changed from man's, and let a beast's heart be given unto him; and let seven times pass over him.

17 This matter *is* by the decree of the watchers, and the demand by the word of the holy ones: to the intent that the living may know that the most High ruleth in the kingdom of men, and giveth it to whomsoever he will, and setteth up over it the basest of men.

18 **This dream I king Nebuchadnezzar have seen. Now thou, O Belteshazzar, declare the interpretation** thereof, forasmuch as all the wise *men* of my kingdom are not able to make known unto me the interpretation: but **thou** *art* **able; for the spirit of the holy gods** *is* **in thee**.

In verse 19, next, we are told that Daniel was very concerned, because the dream was not a good one for the king and it was a problem to know how to go about telling him.

19 ¶ **Then Daniel,** whose name *was* Belteshazzar, **was astonied** [*very concerned; bewildered*] for one hour, and his thoughts troubled him. **The king spake, and said, Belteshazzar, let not the dream, or the interpretation thereof, trouble thee** [*don't worry, just tell me straight*]. Belteshazzar answered and said, My lord, the dream *be* to them that hate thee, and the interpretation thereof to thine enemies [*may the dream refer to your enemies*].

The basic content of the dream was that the judgments of God were going to come upon Nebuchadnezzar, the king.

20 **The tree that thou sawest**, which grew, and was strong, **whose height reached unto the heaven**, and the sight thereof to all the earth;

21 **Whose leaves** *were* **fair, and the fruit thereof much, and in it** *was* **meat** [*provided food*] **for all**; under which the beasts of the field dwelt, and upon whose branches the fowls of the heaven had their habitation:

22 **It** *is* **thou, O king**, that art grown and become strong: for thy greatness is grown, and reacheth unto heaven, and thy dominion to the end of the earth.

23 And **whereas the king saw a watcher and an holy one coming down from heaven, and saying, Hew the tree down, and destroy it; yet leave the stump of the roots thereof in the earth, even with**

a band of iron and brass, in the tender grass of the field; and let it be wet with the dew of heaven, and *let* his portion *be* with the beasts of the field, till seven times pass over him;

24 **This** *is* **the interpretation**, O king, and **this** *is* **the decree of the most High**, which is come upon my lord the king:

Next, in the dream, the king is told that he will be severely humbled.

25 That **they shall drive thee from men**, and **thy dwelling shall be with the beasts of the field**, and **they shall make thee to eat grass as oxen**, and **they shall wet thee with the dew of heaven**, and **seven times shall pass over thee, till thou know that the most High ruleth in the kingdom of men, and giveth it to whomsoever he will**.

26 And **whereas they command-ed to leave the stump of the tree roots; thy kingdom shall be sure unto thee**, after that **thou shalt have known that the heavens do rule**.

Next, Daniel tells the king that he should repent, and, among other things, be merciful to the poor.

27 Wherefore, O king, let my coun-sel be acceptable unto thee, and **break off thy sins by righteous-ness, and thine iniquities by shew-ing mercy to the poor**; if it may be a lengthening of thy tranquillity.

28 ¶ **All this came upon the king Nebuchadnezzar** [*all this eventually happened to King Nebuchadnezzar*].

29 **At the end of twelve months he walked in the palace** of the king-dom of Babylon.

At this point, he is anything but humble.

30 The king spake, and said, **Is not this great Babylon, that I have built** for the house of the kingdom **by the might of my power, and for the honour of my majesty?**

31 **While the word** *was* **in the king's mouth, there fell a voice from heaven,** *saying,* O king Nebu-chadnezzar, to thee it is spoken; **The kingdom is departed from thee.**

32 And **they shall drive thee from men, and thy dwelling** *shall be* **with the beasts of the field: they shall make thee to eat grass as oxen, and seven times shall pass over thee, until thou know that the most High** [*the true God, the Lord*] **ruleth in the kingdom of men, and giveth it to whomsoever he will.**

33 **The same hour was the thing fulfilled** upon Nebuchadnezzar: and he was driven from men, and did eat grass as oxen, and his body was wet with the dew of heaven, till his hairs were grown like eagles' *feathers,* and his nails like birds' *claws.*

Finally, after a long time, Nebu-chadnezzar humbles himself and repents and acknowledges the Lord (verses 34–37).

34 **And at the end of the days I Nebuchadnezzar lifted up mine eyes unto heaven, and mine**

understanding returned unto me, and **I blessed the most High, and I praised and honoured him** that liveth for ever, whose dominion *is* an everlasting dominion, and his kingdom *is* from generation to generation:

35 And **all the inhabitants of the earth** *are* **reputed as nothing**: and he doeth according to his will in the army of heaven, and *among* the inhabitants of the earth: and **none can stay his hand, or say unto him, What doest thou?**

36 **At the same time my reason returned unto me**; and for the glory of my kingdom, mine honour and brightness returned unto me; and my counsellors and my lords sought unto me; and **I was established in my kingdom, and excellent majesty was added unto me**.

37 **Now I Nebuchadnezzar praise and extol and honour the King of heaven**, all whose works *are* truth, and his ways judgment: and those that walk in pride he is able to abase [*humble*].

DANIEL 5

Selection: all verses

The Bible Dictionary, at the back of your Bible, under "Belshazzar," informs us that Belshazzar, in verse 1, was Nebuchadnezzar's son and successor, and was king at the time this chapter begins. Daniel is still serving in the king's court.

1 **BELSHAZZAR the king made a great feast** to a thousand of his lords, **and drank wine** before the thousand.

During this feast, the king commands that the gold and silver cups that the Babylonian armies had looted from the Jerusalem temple be brought in for the revelers to drink out of. This would be disrespectful and mocking of the God of the Jews.

2 **Belshazzar**, whiles he tasted the wine, **commanded to bring the golden and silver vessels which his father Nebuchadnezzar had taken out of the temple which** *was* **in Jerusalem**; that the king, and his princes, his wives, and his concubines, might drink therein.

3 Then **they brought the golden vessels** that were taken out of the temple of the house of God which *was* at Jerusalem; **and the king, and his princes, his wives, and his concubines, drank in them**.

4 **They drank wine, and praised the gods of gold, and of silver, of brass, of iron, of wood, and of stone**.

Next, writing on the wall appears, much to the dismay of the somewhat drunken revelers.

5 ¶ **In the same hour came forth fingers of a man's hand, and wrote** over against the candlestick **upon** the plaister of the **wall of the king's palace: and the king saw the part of the hand that wrote**.

6 Then the king's countenance was changed [*his face turned pale and looked shocked*], **and his thoughts troubled him**, so that the joints of his loins were loosed, and his knees smote one against another [*NIV, "his knees knocked together and his legs gave way"*].

The king promises great rewards and high position for whoever can interpret the writing on the wall.

7 **The king cried aloud to bring in the astrologers, the Chaldeans, and the soothsayers.** *And* the king spake, **and said** to the wise *men* of Babylon, **Whosoever shall read this writing, and shew me the interpretation thereof, shall be clothed with scarlet, and** *have* **a chain of gold about his neck, and shall be the third ruler in the kingdom**.

8 Then came in **all the king's wise** *men:* but they **could not read the writing, nor make known to the king the interpretation thereof**.

9 **Then was king Belshazzar greatly troubled**, and his countenance [*face*] was changed in him, and **his lords were astonied** [*baffled*].

Next, the queen hears the commotion and comes in and reminds him that his father, King Nebuchadnezzar, relied much on Daniel for interpretation of such things.

10 ¶ *Now* **the queen**, by reason of the words of the king and his lords, **came into the banquet house:** *and* the queen spake **and said, O king,**

live for ever: let not thy thoughts trouble thee, nor let thy countenance be changed [*please don't be mad at me for coming in uninvited*]:

11 **There is a man in thy kingdom, in whom** *is* **the spirit of the holy gods; and in the days of thy father light and understanding and wisdom, like the wisdom of the gods, was found in him**; whom the king Nebuchadnezzar thy father, the king, *I say,* thy father, made master of the magicians, astrologers, Chaldeans, *and* soothsayers;

12 Forasmuch as **an excellent spirit, and knowledge, and understanding, interpreting of dreams, and shewing of hard sentences, and dissolving of doubts, were found in the same Daniel**, whom the king named Belteshazzar: **now let Daniel be called, and he will shew the interpretation**.

The king has Daniel brought in and asks him if he is the Jew that came with the Jews his father had brought as captives to Babylon from Jerusalem.

13 **Then was Daniel brought in before the king.** *And* **the king** spake and **said** unto Daniel, *Art* **thou that Daniel, which** *art* **of the children of the captivity of Judah, whom the king my father brought out of Jewry?**

14 **I have even heard of thee, that the spirit of the gods** *is* **in thee**, and *that* **light and understanding and excellent wisdom is found in thee**.

15 And **now the wise *men*, the astrologers, have been brought in before me**, that they should read this writing, and make known unto me the interpretation thereof: **but they could not shew the interpretation of the thing** [*the writing on the wall*]:

16 And **I have heard of thee**, that thou canst make interpretations, and dissolve doubts: now **if thou canst read the writing, and make known to me the interpretation** thereof, **thou shalt be clothed with scarlet, and *have* a chain of gold about thy neck, and shalt be the third ruler in the kingdom**.

Next, Daniel says, in effect, that as a prophet of the true God, Jehovah, he cannot accept pay for functioning in his office. This is basically the same as Melchizedek Priesthood holders today not accepting pay for administering to the sick, etc.

17 ¶ Then **Daniel answered** and said before the king, **Let thy gifts be to thyself** [*keep your gifts*], and give thy rewards to another; yet **I will read the writing unto the king, and make known to him the interpretation**.

Next, Daniel reviews the earthly power that an earthly king has.

18 O thou king, **the most high God gave Nebuchadnezzar thy father a kingdom**, and **majesty**, and **glory**, and **honour**:

19 And **for the majesty that he gave him, all people, nations, and languages, trembled and feared before him**: whom he would he slew; and whom he would he kept alive; and whom he would he set up; and whom he would he put down.

20 **But when his heart was lifted up** [*when he became prideful*], and his mind hardened **in pride, he was deposed from his kingly throne, and they took his glory from him**:

21 And he was driven from the sons of men; and his heart was made like the beasts, and his dwelling *was* with the wild asses: they fed him with grass like oxen, and his body was wet with the dew of heaven; **till he knew that the most high God ruled in the kingdom of men**, and *that* he appointeth over it whomsoever he will.

Next, Daniel severely chastises Belshazzar for not keeping himself humble when he knows very well what happened to his father to humble him.

22 And **thou his son, O Belshazzar, hast not humbled thine heart**, though thou knewest all this;

23 **But hast lifted up thyself against the Lord of heaven**; and they have **brought the vessels of his house** before thee, and thou, and thy lords, thy wives, and thy concubines, have **drunk wine in them**; and thou hast **praised the gods** of silver, and gold, of brass, iron, wood, and stone, **which see not, nor hear, nor know**: and **the God in whose hand thy breath *is*, and whose *are* all thy ways, hast thou not glorified**:

24 Then was the part of the hand sent from him [*the Lord*]; and this writing was written.

25 ¶ And this *is* the writing that was written, MENE, MENE, TEKEL, UPHARSIN.

26 This *is* the interpretation of the thing: MENE; **God hath numbered thy kingdom, and finished it** [*your time as a king is about up*].

27 TEKEL; **Thou art weighed in the balances, and art found wanting**.

28 PERES; **Thy kingdom is divided** [*will be divided*], **and given to the Medes and Persians** [*who conquered Babylon easily, without a battle, in 538 BC*].

29 **Then commanded Belshazzar,** and **they clothed Daniel with scarlet, and** *put* **a chain of gold about his neck, and made a proclamation concerning him, that he should be the third ruler in the kingdom.**

30 ¶ In **that night was Belshazzar** the king of the Chaldeans **slain**.

31 And **Darius the Median took the kingdom,** *being* about threescore and two years old [*when he was about 62 years old*].

DANIEL 6

Selection: all verses

After Nebuchadnezzar died (about 561 BC), his son, Belshazzar, succeeded him as king of Babylon. Belshazzar was later killed (Daniel 5:30), and Darius the Mede took over the kingdom (Daniel 5:31). Darius is the king who was tricked by jealous advisers to have Daniel thrown to the lions. Since Daniel, as a young man, was taken along with many other Jews of higher social status into Babylonian captivity about 606 BC (see chronology chart in the Bible Dictionary, where it says "Daniel carried captive," 606), he would now be getting along in years. He could easily be between seventy and eighty years old at the time he was cast into the lions' den. He is an example of one who is willing to place it all on the altar—in other words, he was willing to be loyal to his commitment to God at all costs.

As we look at this chapter, we see that Daniel was highly thought of by King Darius, who was considering putting him in charge of all things in the kingdom, under himself (much the same as Joseph was when he became second in command in Egypt). This prompted jealousy among the king's top officers.

1 IT **pleased Darius to set over the kingdom an hundred and twenty princes,** which should be over the whole kingdom;

2 And **over these three presidents; of whom Daniel** *was* **first**: that the princes might give accounts unto them, and the king should have no damage [*would not suffer losses*].

3 Then this **Daniel was preferred above the presidents and princes,** because an excellent spirit was in him; and the king thought to set him over the whole realm.

4 ¶ **Then the presidents and princes sought to find occasion against**

Daniel concerning the kingdom; but they could find none occasion nor fault; forasmuch as he was faithful, neither was there any error or fault found in him.

5 **Then said these men, We shall not find any occasion** [*any way to get him in trouble with the king*] against this Daniel, **except we find** *it* **against him concerning the law of his God.**

The plot: If anyone prays to any god or person other than King Darius during the next thirty days (verses 6–9) . . .

6 **Then these presidents and princes assembled together to the king,** and said thus unto him, King Darius, live for ever.

7 All the presidents of the kingdom, the governors, and the princes, the counsellors, and the captains, have consulted together to establish a royal statute, and to **make a firm decree, that whosoever shall ask a petition of any God or man for thirty days, save of thee, O king, he shall be cast into the den of lions.**

8 **Now, O king**, establish the decree, and **sign the writing**, that it be not changed, according to the law of the Medes and Persians, which altereth not [*according to their laws, once the king puts it in writing, even he cannot change it*].

9 **Wherefore king Darius signed the writing and the decree.**

Despite the decree, Daniel continued his personal habit of praying formally, three times a day. He preferred to pray facing the direction of Jerusalem and the temple there.

10 ¶ **Now when Daniel knew that the writing was signed**, he went into his house; and his windows being open in his chamber toward Jerusalem, **he kneeled upon his knees three times a day, and prayed**, and gave thanks before his God, **as he did aforetime** [*just like he had been doing before the decree*].

11 **Then these men assembled, and found Daniel praying** and making supplication before his God.

12 **Then they** came near, and **spake before the king concerning the king's decree**; Hast thou not signed a decree, that every man that shall ask *a petition* of any God or man within thirty days, save of thee, O king, shall be cast into the den of lions? The king answered and said, The thing *is* true, according to the law of the Medes and Persians, which altereth not.

Next, they smoothly tattle on Daniel, as if they were just doing their duty and expressing their loyalty to the king and the laws of the kingdom.

13 **Then answered** [*responded*] **they** and said before the king, **That Daniel, which** *is* **of the children of the captivity of Judah, regardeth not thee, O king, nor the decree** that thou hast signed, but maketh his petition three times a day.

The king immediately realizes that he has been caught in a vicious trap by these jealous, self-serving advisers.

14 Then the king, when he heard *these* words, was sore displeased with himself, and set *his* heart on Daniel to deliver him [*and immediately began trying to figure out a way to save Daniel*]: and he laboured till the going down of the sun to deliver him.

Can you picture the faces of these men as they continue to pressure King Darius to carry out the law of the land?

15 Then these men assembled unto the king, and said unto the king, Know, O king, that the law of the Medes and Persians *is,* That no decree nor statute which the king establisheth may be changed.

Next, in verse 16, we feel the anxiety of Darius for Daniel, and we sense that he and Daniel must have had previous discussions about the Lord and the role of faith and prayer.

16 Then the king commanded, and they brought Daniel, and cast *him* into the den of lions. *Now* the king spake and said unto Daniel, Thy God whom thou servest continually, he will deliver thee.

17 And a stone was brought, and laid upon the mouth of the den; and the king sealed it with his own signet [*signet ring*], and with the signet of his lords; that the purpose might not be changed concerning Daniel.

18 ¶ Then the king went to his palace, and passed the night fasting: neither were instruments of musick brought before him: and his sleep went from him [*he couldn't sleep*].

19 Then the king arose very early in the morning, and went in haste unto the den of lions.

20 And when he came to the den, he cried with a lamentable [*worried*] voice unto Daniel: *and* the king spake and said to Daniel, O Daniel, servant of the living God [*in contrast to all the "dead" or inanimate idols and false gods*], is thy God, whom thou servest continually, able to deliver thee from the lions?

21 Then said Daniel unto the king, O king, live for ever.

22 My God hath sent his angel, and hath shut the lions' mouths, that they have not hurt me: forasmuch as before him innocency was found in me; and also before thee, O king, have I done no hurt [*I have done nothing wrong*].

23 Then was the king exceeding glad for him [*an understatement!*], and commanded that they should take Daniel up out of the den. So Daniel was taken up out of the den, and no manner of hurt was found upon him, because he believed in his God.

24 ¶ **And the king commanded, and they brought those men which had accused Daniel, and they cast** *them* **into the den of lions,** them, their children, and their wives; and the lions had the mastery of them, and brake all their bones in pieces or ever they came at the bottom of the den.

25 ¶ **Then king Darius wrote unto all people,** nations, and languages, that dwell in all the earth; Peace be multiplied unto you.

26 **I make a decree, That in every dominion of my kingdom men tremble and fear before the God of Daniel**: for he *is* the living God, and stedfast for ever, and his kingdom *that* which shall not be destroyed, and his dominion *shall be even* unto the end.

27 He delivereth and rescueth, and he worketh signs and wonders in heaven and in earth, **who hath delivered Daniel from the power of the lions.**

28 **So this Daniel prospered in the reign of Darius, and in the reign of Cyrus the Persian.**

DANIEL 7

Selection: verses 9–10, 13–14

In chapter 7, Daniel sees in vision the meeting at Adam-ondi-Ahman, to be held in the last days before the Second Coming of the Savior.

We will take a minute to discuss background to this vision that Daniel was given. About seventy miles, northeast of Independence, Missouri, is a sacred place called Adam-ondi-Ahman. "It is the place where Adam shall come to visit his people, or the Ancient of Days [Adam] shall sit, as spoken of by Daniel the prophet" (D&C 116:1).

In the Doctrine and Covenants we are taught that a great conference of Adam and Eve's righteous posterity was held at Adam-ondi-Ahman three years prior to Adam's death. We read:

Doctrine & Covenants 107:53–56

53 **Three years previous to the death of Adam, he called Seth, Enos, Cainan, Mahalaleel, Jared, Enoch, and Methuselah,** who were all high priests, **with the residue of his posterity who were righteous, into the valley of Adam-ondi-Ahman,** and there bestowed upon them his last blessing.

54 And **the Lord appeared unto them,** and **they rose up and blessed Adam,** and called him Michael, the prince, the archangel.

55 And **the Lord administered comfort unto Adam,** and said unto him: I have set thee to be at the head; a multitude of nations shall come of thee, and thou art a prince over them forever.

56 **And Adam stood up** in the midst of the congregation; **and,** notwithstanding he was bowed down with age, **being full of the Holy Ghost, predicted whatsoever should befall**

his posterity unto the latest generation.

Shortly before the Second Coming of Christ, another great council will be held at Adam-ondi-Ahman. We read of this in Daniel. He had a vision in which he saw that millions of righteous people will attend this great meeting.

9 I beheld till the thrones were cast down [*Daniel saw the future, including the downfall of governments in the last days, as spoken of in D&C 87:6*], and **the Ancient of days** [*Adam*] **did sit**, whose garment *was* **white as snow**, and the hair of his head like the **pure wool** [*see Isaiah 1:18, where "white as snow" and "pure wool" are associated with one's being completely cleansed by the Atonement of Christ*]: **his throne** [*Adam is in a position of great power and authority*] *was like* **the fiery flame**, *and* his wheels *as* burning fire.

10 A fiery stream issued and came forth from before him: **thousand thousands** [*millions*] **ministered unto him, and ten thousand times ten thousand** [*a hundred million*] **stood before him** [*this will be a large meeting*]: the judgment was set, and the books were opened.

13 I [*Daniel*] **saw in the night visions,** and, behold, *one* **like the Son of man** [*a biblically respectful way of saying Jehovah—in other words, Christ*] came with the clouds of heaven, and **came to the Ancient of days** [*Adam*], and they brought him [*Christ*] near before him [*Adam—see*

Teachings of the Prophet Joseph Smith, page 157].

Next, we see in Daniel's vision that the keys of leadership are given back to Christ during this grand council in preparation for His ruling and reigning as "Lord of lords, and King of kings" (Revelation 17:14) during the Millennium.

14 And **there was given him** [*Christ*] **dominion**, and **glory**, and **a kingdom, that all people, nations, and languages, should serve him** [*during the Millennium*]: his dominion *is* an everlasting dominion, which shall not pass away, and his kingdom *that* which shall not be destroyed.

Joseph Fielding Smith taught about this meeting at Adam-ondi-Ahman before the Second Coming. He said that "all who have held keys will make their reports and deliver their stewardships, as they shall be required. Adam will . . . then . . . make his report, as the one holding the keys for this earth, to his Superior Officer, Jesus Christ. Our Lord will then assume the reins of government; directions will be given to the Priesthood; and He, whose right it is to rule, will be installed officially by the voice of the Priesthood there assembled. This grand council of Priesthood will be composed, not only of those who are faithful who now dwell on this earth, but also of the prophets and apostles of old, who have had directing authority. Others may also be there, but if so they will be there by appointment, for this is to be an official council called to attend to the most momentous matters concerning the destiny of this earth" (Way to Perfection, pages 290–91).

Among other things, Bruce R. McConkie taught the following about this council at Adam-ondi-Ahman (bold added for emphasis):

"But Daniel has yet more to say about the great events soon to transpire at Adam-ondi-Ahman. And we need not suppose that all these things shall happen in one single meeting or at one single hour in time. It is proper to hold numerous meetings at a general conference, some for the instruction of leaders, others for edification of all the Saints. In some, business is transacted; others are for worship and spiritual refreshment. And so Daniel says: 'I saw in the night visions, and, behold, one like the Son of man came with the clouds of heaven, and came to the Ancient of days, and they brought him near before him.' Christ comes to Adam, who is sitting in glory. He comes to conform to his own priestal order. He comes to hear the report of Adam for his stewardship. He comes to take back the keys of the earthly kingdom. He comes to be invested with glory and dominion so that he can reign personally upon the earth" (The Millennial Messiah: The Second Coming of the Son of Man, page 585).

You may wish to read more about this meeting at Adam-ondi-Ahman in Millennial Messiah, pages 578–88.

Elder McConkie also taught:

"At this council, all who have held keys of authority will give an accounting of their stewardship to Adam. Christ will then come, receive back the keys, and thus take one of the final steps preparatory to reigning personally upon the earth. (Dan. 7:9–14; Teachings, p. 157.)" (Mormon Doctrine, page 21).

Before we leave Daniel, we will consider one other insight. It is interesting to note that the Garden of Eden was located in what is now Jackson County, Missouri. Joseph Fielding Smith taught this:

"In accord with the revelations given to the Prophet Joseph Smith, we teach that the Garden of Eden was on the American continent located where the City Zion [in Jackson County, Missouri], or the New Jerusalem, will be built. . . . When Adam and Eve were driven out of the Garden, they eventually dwelt at a place called Adam-ondi-Ahman, situated in what is now Daviess County, Missouri" (Doctrines of Salvation, vol. 3, page 74).

Thus, when Adam and Eve were cast out of the Garden of Eden, they went to the area of Adam-ondi-Ahman to dwell. In other words, things got started in Missouri, in the Garden of Eden, as far as mortal life on this earth is concerned, and things will have gone full circle back to Missouri and the council at Adam-ondi-Ahman as the time for the Millennium nears.

HOSEA

Hosea was a contemporary of Isaiah, Amos, and Micah. His ministry as a prophet went from about 755 BC to 725 BC. If you read Hosea 1:1 and Isaiah 1:1, you will see that they both served as prophets during the reign of the same kings of Judah.

In 2 Nephi 25:1, Nephi said that in order to understand the writings of Isaiah, one has to understand "the manner of prophesying among the Jews." This applies likewise to the writings of Hosea. To understand his writings, you must be aware that he makes extensive use of metaphors and symbolism. A metaphor involves the use of one thing to represent another. For example, "sheep" are often used to represent Israel. The Savior is the "Shepherd." When Israel goes into apostasy and gets lost spiritually, we say "the sheep are lost," and the Shepherd goes into the wilderness to find them and bring them back to the "fold," which is symbolic of the Church and the celestial kingdom.

Hosea's writings and prophecies contain marvelous examples of the power of the Atonement of Jesus Christ to cleanse and heal.

For purposes of this study guide, we will study Hosea chapters 1–6 and 10–14.

HOSEA 1

Selection: all verses

Hosea uses the marriage of a husband and wife in this chapter to represent the covenant relationship between Israel and the Lord. The Lord (the husband) and Israel (the wife) have the potential to have a beautiful and tender relationship. But the wife commits adultery (symbolic of going into apostasy and worshiping false gods, materialism, and so forth). Despite the wickedness and infidelity of his wife, the husband invites her back and promises to forgive her and take good care of her and her children. It is the story of Israel (including Judah) and the Lord's willingness to take His covenant people back after they have continually broken their covenants ("marriage vows") with Him by choosing other "lovers" (false gods, materialism, and wickedness).

1 **The word of the LORD that came unto Hosea**, the son of Beeri, **in the days of Uzziah, Jotham, Ahaz,** *and* **Hezekiah, kings of Judah** [*the same kings as ruled Judah during Isaiah's ministry—see Isaiah 1:1*], and in the days of Jeroboam the son of Joash, king of Israel.

2 The beginning of the word of the LORD by Hosea. And **the LORD said to Hosea, Go, take unto thee a wife of whoredoms** [*in other words, marry a harlot, a prostitute*] and children of whoredoms: **for the land** [*the people of Israel, including Judah*] **hath committed great whoredom** [*spiritual adultery; breaking covenants made with the Lord*], *departing* **from the LORD**.

There has been much debate among Bible scholars as to whether verse 2, above, is literal or symbolic, or a combination of both. We will use a quote from Latter-day Saint Bible scholar Sidney B. Sperry, as quoted in the Old Testament Student Manual 1 Kings—Malachi, page 104, to answer this question.

"Sperry said that Hosea never did actually contract such a marriage. He defends his viewpoint with an argument that seems authoritative to the Latter-day Saint: 'The Lord's call to Hosea to take a harlotrous woman to wife represents the prophet's call to the ministry— a ministry to an apostate and covenant-breaking people. The evil children of this apparent union represent the coming of the judgments of the Lord upon Israel, warning of which was to be carried to the people by the prophet. The figure of the harlotrous wife and children would, I believe, be readily understood at the time by the Hebrew people without reflecting on Hosea's own wife, or, if he was unmarried, on himself.' (Voice of Israel's Prophets, p. 281.)"

3 **So he went and took Gomer** the daughter of Diblaim; **which conceived, and bare him a son.**

4 And the LORD said unto him, **Call his name Jezreel** [*the name of a valley in Israel*]; for yet a little *while,* and I will avenge the blood of Jezreel upon the house of Jehu, and will cause to cease the kingdom of the house of Israel.

5 And it shall come to pass at that day, that **I will break the bow** [*power; ability to defend*] **of Israel in the valley of Jezreel.**

6 ¶ **And she conceived again, and bare a daughter.** And *God* said unto him, **Call her name Lo-ruhamah** [*didn't obtain mercy—see footnote 6a in your Bible*]: **for I will no more have mercy upon the house of Israel** [*the northern ten tribes (in this context), with headquarters in Samaria—they will be conquered by Assyria in about 722 BC and taken away*]; **but I will utterly take them away** [*scatter them*].

7 **But I will have mercy upon the house of Judah** [*the Southern Kingdom, consisting of the tribes of Judah and Benjamin, with headquarters in Jerusalem*], and will save them by the LORD their God, and will not save them by bow, nor by sword, nor by battle, by horses, nor by horsemen [*they will be protected from the Assyrians by the power of the Lord, as recorded in 2 Kings 19:32–37, when 185,000 Assyrian soldiers died in one night*].

8 ¶ Now **when she had weaned Lo-ruhamah, she conceived, and bare a son.**

9 **Then said** *God,* **Call his name Lo-ammi** [*meaning they are not My people anymore*]: **for ye** *are* **not my people, and I will not be your** *God.*

Verses 10–11, next, are a prophecy of the gathering of Israel in the last days, when the righteous are gathered unto Christ by making and keeping covenants in His name. The implications of these verses continue into the Millennium and beyond that into celestial exaltation.

10 ¶ Yet the number of the children of Israel shall be as the sand of the sea, which cannot be measured nor numbered; and it shall come to pass, *that* in the place where it was said unto them, Ye *are* not my people, *there* it shall be said unto them, *Ye are* the sons of the living God.

11 Then shall the children of Judah and the children of Israel be gathered together, and appoint themselves one head [*perhaps meaning that they will come unto Christ and be loyal to Him as their King*], and they shall come up out of the land: for great *shall be* the day of Jezreel.

HOSEA 2

Selection: all verses

This chapter prophesies of the punishments that will come upon the people because of apostasy. It also foretells the restoration of the gospel in the last days and eventual millennial peace.

1 Say ye unto your brethren, Ammi [*my people—see footnote 1a in your Bible*]; and to your sisters, Ruhamah [*Having obtained mercy—see footnote 1b in your Bible*].

2 Plead with your mother [*apostate Israel*], plead: for she *is* not my wife, neither *am* I her husband [*she has broken our marriage covenant*]: let her therefore put away her whoredoms out of her sight [*try to convince her to repent*], and her adulteries from between her breasts;

3 Lest I strip her naked [*leave her with no excuses, expose her sins— compare with 2 Nephi 9:14*], and set her as in the day that she was born [*without any cover up*], and make her as a wilderness, and set her like a dry land, and slay her with thirst [*famine*].

4 And I will not have mercy upon her children [*because they too have grown up and chosen wickedness*]; for they *be* the children of whoredoms.

5 For their mother hath played the harlot [*has broken her covenants with Me, the Lord*]: she that conceived them hath done shamefully: for she said, I will go after my lovers [*false gods, idols, all kinds of wickedness*], that give *me* my bread and my water, my wool and my flax, mine oil and my drink [*covenant Israel credits her false gods as being the power behind her prosperity; in other words, wicked people attribute their prosperity to their evil pursuits*].

6 ¶ Therefore, behold, I will hedge up thy way with thorns, and make a wall, that she shall not find her paths [*she will not prosper*].

In verses 7–8, next, we are taught that troubles can sometimes bring wicked people back to the Lord.

7 And she shall follow after her lovers [*false gods and so forth*], but she shall not overtake them; and she shall seek them, but shall not find *them:* then shall she say, I will go and return to my first husband [*l*

will repent and return to the Lord]; **for then** *was it* **better with me than now**.

8 For she did not know [*realize*] that I gave her corn, and wine, and oil, and multiplied her silver and gold, *which* they prepared for Baal [*a major false god adopted by the Israelites from neighboring nations*].

9 **Therefore will I return, and take away** my corn in the time thereof, and my wine in the season thereof, and will recover my wool and my flax *given* to cover her nakedness [*the Lord will take away the blessings of prosperity*].

10 **And now will I discover** [*uncover*] **her lewdness** [*symbolic of sins in this metaphor*] in the sight of her lovers, and **none shall deliver her out of mine hand** [*no one, including her false gods, will be able to stop the punishments of God upon her*].

11 **I will also cause all her mirth** [*partying*] **to cease**, her feast days, her new moons, and her sabbaths, and all her solemn feasts [*elements of their religious worship*].

12 And **I will destroy her vines and her fig trees, whereof she hath said, These** *are* **my rewards that my lovers have given me**: and I will make them a forest [*no longer cultivated*], and the beasts of the field shall eat them.

13 **And I will visit upon her the days of** [*I will punish her for the days when she worshiped*] **Baalim** [*plural for Baal, a false god whose worship included sexual immorality and sometimes child sacrifice*], wherein she burned incense to them, and she decked herself with her earrings and her jewels, and she went after her lovers [*false gods*], and forgat me, saith the LORD.

Next, beginning with verse 14, the Lord prophesies, through Hosea, that He will restore Israel, after her apostasy.

14 ¶ **Therefore, behold, I will allure her** [*attract her back to Me*], and bring her into the wilderness, **and speak comfortably unto her**.

15 And **I will give her her vineyards** [*she will once again prosper*] from thence, and the valley of Achor for a door of **hope**: and **she shall sing there, as in the days of her youth, and as in the day when she came up out of the land of Egypt**.

16 And it shall be at that day, saith the LORD, *that* **thou shalt call me Ishi** [*husband; a sweet, intimate relationship*]; and shalt call me **no more Baali** [*master, symbolizing a harsh servant-to-master relationship*].

17 For **I will take away the names of Baalim out of her mouth** [*the tribulation I send her through will purge the sins out of her*], and they shall no more be remembered by their name.

Verse 18, next, can depict many things, including Millennial peace, eternal life, the peace in one's soul that comes from doing right and keeping covenants, and so forth.

18 **And in that day will I make a covenant for them with the beasts of the field, and with the fowls of heaven, and** *with* **the creeping things of the ground** [*Millennial peace*]: and I will break the bow and the sword and the battle out of the earth [*there will be no fighting during the Millennium*], **and will make them to lie down safely.**

19 **And I will betroth thee unto me for ever** [*you will be My wife—my people— forever*]; yea, I will betroth thee unto me **in righteousness, and in judgment, and in lovingkindness, and in mercies.**

20 **I will even betroth thee unto me in faithfulness: and thou shalt know the LORD.**

21 And it shall come to pass **in that day** [*during the Millennium*], **I will hear** [*respond to your needs*], saith the LORD, I will hear the heavens, and they shall hear the earth;

22 And **the earth shall hear the corn, and the wine, and the oil**; and **they shall hear Jezreel** [*means "the Lord plants," in other words, the Lord will bless crops*].

23 And I will sow her unto me in the earth; and **I will have mercy upon her that had not obtained mercy; and I will say to** *them which were* not my people, Thou *art* my people; and they shall say, *Thou art* my God.

Israel will go through a time of apostasy, during which time they will be far from God, but they will be brought back in the latter days.

HOSEA 3

Selection: all verses

In this chapter, we see the gathering of Israel in the last days. We are a part of this. It is comforting to know that even though Israel will go through a time of apostasy, during which time they will be far from God, they will be brought back in the latter days.

1 **THEN said the LORD unto me, Go yet, love a woman** [*probably the same symbolism of being married to an adulterous wife—Israel, in this time of history—see commentary for Hosea 1:1–3 in this study guide*] beloved of *her* friend, yet **an adulteress**, according to the love of the LORD toward **the children of Israel**, who **look to other gods** [*worship idols*], and love flagons of wine.

2 **So I bought her to me for fifteen** *pieces* **of silver, and** *for* **an homer of barley, and an half homer of barley** [*NIV, "about 10 bushels"*]:

Verse 2, above, symbolizes the fact that our Father in Heaven is willing to purchase us from our slavery to sin, with the blood of his Only Begotten Son.

3 And I said unto her, Thou shalt abide for me many days; **thou shalt not play the harlot, and thou shalt not be for** *another* **man: so** *will* **I also** *be* **for thee** [*I will accept you back*].

4 For the children of Israel shall abide many days without a king [*without the Lord; in other words, in apostasy*], and without a prince, and without a sacrifice, and without an image [*perhaps a reference to the revelations, images, seen through the Urim and Thummim—see Exodus 28:30*], and without an ephod [*part of the dress of the Aaronic Priesthood high priest, to which the Urim and Thummim was attached*], and *without* teraphim [*in other words, without the ordinances of the priesthood*]:

5 Afterward shall the children of Israel return, and seek the LORD their God, and David [*Christ*] their king; and shall fear [*respect*] the LORD and his goodness in the latter days.

HOSEA 4

Selection: all verses

This chapter gives many details of how apostate Israel was breaking their "marriage" covenant with Jehovah. In other words, in the symbolism used by Hosea, how the wife, Israel, was "stepping out" on the husband, Jehovah, through various forms of wickedness.

1 HEAR the word of the LORD, ye children of Israel: for the LORD hath a controversy with the inhabitants of the land, because *there is* no truth, nor mercy, nor knowledge of God in the land.

2 By **swearing**, and **lying**, and **killing**, and **stealing**, and committing adultery, they break

out [*breaking all boundaries of sin*], and blood toucheth blood [*murder after murder*].

3 Therefore [*this is the reason why*] shall the land mourn [*because of your wickedness, the land will not support you well—there is a relationship between righteousness and prosperity*], and every one that dwelleth therein shall languish, with the beasts of the field, and with the fowls of heaven; yea, the fishes of the sea also shall be taken away.

4 Yet let no man strive, nor reprove another: for **thy people** *are* **as they that strive with the priest** [*your people are always fighting against righteousness*].

5 **Therefore shalt thou fall** in the day, and the prophet [*false prophets*] also shall fall with thee in the night, and I will destroy thy mother [*Israel will be destroyed*].

6 ¶ **My people are destroyed for lack of knowledge** [*of the true God*]: **because thou hast rejected knowledge, I will also reject thee**, that thou shalt be no priest to me: seeing **thou hast forgotten the law of thy God, I will also forget thy children**.

7 As they were increased, so **they sinned against me:** *therefore* **will I change their glory into shame**.

Verse 8, next, means basically that the apostate priests are encouraging the people to sin more so they can get more sin offering meat to eat themselves.

8 **They eat up the sin of my people, and they set their heart on their iniquity.**

9 And there shall be, **like people, like priest**: and I will punish them for their ways, and reward them their doings.

10 For they shall eat, and not have enough: they shall commit whoredom, and shall not increase: **because they have left off to take heed to the LORD** [because they have quit obeying the Lord].

11 **Whoredom and wine** and new wine take away the heart.

12 ¶ **My people ask counsel at their stocks** [their wooden idols], **and their staff** [divining rods] **declareth unto them** [they seek revelation from their idols and seances, and so forth]: for **the spirit of whoredoms hath caused *them* to err**, and **they have gone a whoring from under their God** [they have chased after other gods].

Next, we see that their idol worship encourages sexual immorality.

13 They sacrifice upon the tops of the mountains, and burn incense upon the hills, under oaks and poplars and elms, because the shadow thereof *is* good: **therefore your daughters shall commit whoredom, and your spouses shall commit adultery** [this is why your people are so involved in sexual immorality].

14 **I will not punish your daughters when they commit whoredom, nor your spouses when they commit adultery**: for themselves are separated with whores [because the men, themselves, are bad examples because they consort with prostitutes], **and they sacrifice with harlots** [their idol worship involves being with prostitutes]: **therefore the people *that* doth not understand** [don't know right from wrong anymore] **shall fall.**

15 ¶ **Though thou, Israel** [the northern ten tribes, with headquarters in Samaria], **play the harlot, *yet* let not Judah** [the Jews and half of the tribe of Benjamin, headquartered in Jerusalem] **offend** [a warning to Judah not to follow Israel's bad example]; and come not ye unto Gilgal, neither go ye up to Beth-aven, nor swear, The LORD liveth.

16 For **Israel slideth back** as a **backsliding** heifer: now the LORD will feed them **as a lamb in a large place** [out in an open place with no protection, perhaps foreshadowing the scattering of Israel].

17 **Ephraim** [the nation of Israel, to the north] *is* **joined to idols**: let him alone [stay away from them; don't follow their bad example].

18 Their drink is sour: **they have committed whoredom continually**: her rulers *with* shame do love, Give ye.

19 **The wind hath bound her up in her wings** [*NIV, "a whirlwind will sweep them away"*], and they shall be ashamed because of their sacrifices [*to idols*].

HOSEA 5

Selection: all verses

As you have no doubt noticed, these chapters of Hosea are not particularly pleasant to read. So also, wickedness is ugly and disgusting for those who are striving to be righteous. Perhaps you have also noticed that the sins of Israel and Judah are very much like the sins in our modern world as we get closer to the Second Coming of the Savior. Satan uses the same sins in various settings to pull God's children away from Him!

Verses 1 and 2, next, refer to false priests and leaders who are like hunters who herd animals into a pit or net where they are trapped and become prey. Mizpah and Tabor are mountains in the Holy Land, famous for hunting.

1 **HEAR ye this, O priests**; **and** hearken, ye house of Israel; and give ye ear, **O house of the king**; **for judgment** *is* **toward you** [*God will catch up with you*], because ye have been a snare on Mizpah, and a net spread upon Tabor.

2 And **the revolters** [*those who herd animals into traps*] are profound to **make slaughter, though I** *have been* **a rebuker of them all** [*the Lord will punish them*].

3 I know **Ephraim, and Israel** [*both words refer to the northern ten tribes*]

is not hid from me: for now, O **Ephraim**, thou. **committest whoredom,** *and* **Israel is defiled**

4 They will not frame their doings to turn unto their God: for **the spirit of whoredoms** *is* **in the midst of them**, and they have not known the LORD.

5 And the pride of Israel doth testify to his face: **therefore shall Israel and Ephraim fall in their iniquity; Judah also shall fall with them.**

6 **They shall go with their flocks and with their herds to seek the LORD; but they shall not find** *him;* **he hath withdrawn himself from them.**

7 **They have dealt treacherously against the LORD**: for **they have begotten strange children** [*have raised their children to be sinners like they are*]: now shall a month devour them with their portions.

8 **Blow ye the cornet in Gibeah** [*sound the alarm*], *and* the trumpet in Ramah: cry aloud *at* Beth-aven, after thee, O Benjamin.

9 **Ephraim shall be desolate in the day of rebuke** [*will be severely punished*]: among the tribes of Israel have I made known that which shall surely be.

10 **The princes** [*leaders*] **of Judah were like them that remove the bound** [*who have removed all the boundaries against sin*]: *therefore* **I will pour out my wrath upon them like water.**

11 **Ephraim** *is* **oppressed** [*punished*] **and broken** in judgment, **because he willingly walked after the commandment** [*filth—see footnote 11a in your Bible*].

12 **Therefore** *will* **I** *be* **unto Ephraim as a moth, and to the house of Judah as rottenness.**

Verses 13–14, next, depict these wicked people going to other countries for help rather than repenting and turning to the Lord, who certainly can help them get out of their miseries and woes.

13 **When Ephraim saw his sickness, and Judah** *saw* **his wound, then went Ephraim to the Assyrian**, and sent to king Jareb: **yet could he not heal you, nor cure you of your wound.**

14 **For I** [*the Lord*] *will be* unto Ephraim as a lion, and as a young lion to the house of Judah: I, *even* I, will tear and go away; I will take away, and none shall rescue *him*.

15 ¶ **I will go** *and* **return to my place** [*heaven*], **till they acknowledge their offence, and seek my face** [*until they repent*]: **in their affliction they will seek me early.**

HOSEA 6

Selection: all verses

In this chapter we see that the Lord is still willing to forgive, despite the gross wickedness of His people. This is a beautiful and marvelous message for His children every-

where. It reminds us of Jacob 6:4–5, in the Book of Mormon, where the Savior assures us that His arms of mercy are always stretched out toward us to receive us back.

1 **COME, and let us return unto the LORD**: for **he hath torn** [*punished*], and **he will heal us**; he hath **smitten**, and **he will bind us up.**

We don't know what the "days" are in verse 2, next. We do know from 1 Peter 3:8 that one day for the Lord is a thousand days on earth. And so, we might conjecture that verse 2 is prophesying that in roughly 3,000 years, Israel will be gathered back to the Savior, in other words, in our day, the gathering of Israel will be a major emphasis in the Lord's true Church.

2 After **two days** will he revive us: in the **third day** he will raise us up [*gather us again*], and we shall live in his sight.

3 **Then shall we know,** *if* we follow on to know **the LORD**: his going forth is prepared as the morning; and **he shall come unto** us as the rain, **as the latter** *and* **former rain unto the earth** [*in Israel, there were two critical seasons of rain; the first softened the soil for plowing and planting, the second watered the crops for growth and a good harvest—see also Joel 2:23*].

Next, the Lord bemoans the fleeting love and loyalty of His covenant people.

4 ¶ **O Ephraim, what shall I do unto thee? O Judah, what shall I do unto thee? for your goodness** *is*

as a morning cloud, and **as the early dew it goeth away** [*your righteousness is short-lived*].

5 **Therefore have I hewed** *them* by the prophets; I have **slain them** by the words of my mouth: and thy judgments *are as* the light *that* goeth forth.

6 For **I desired mercy** [*I wanted you to be merciful and kind, like the gospel teaches*], **and not sacrifice** [*and not just going through the empty motions of offering sacrifices*]; and **the knowledge of God more than burnt offerings**.

7 **But they** like men **have transgressed the covenant**: there have **they dealt treacherously against me**.

8 **Gilead** *is* **a city of them that work iniquity,** *and is* **polluted with blood**.

9 And as troops of **robbers wait for a man**, *so* the company of **priests murder** in the way by consent: for **they commit lewdness**.

10 **I have seen an horrible thing in the house of Israel**: there *is* **the whoredom of Ephraim, Israel is defiled** [*has broken their covenants with Me*].

11 **Also**, O **Judah**, he hath set an harvest for thee, when I returned the captivity of my people.

HOSEA 10

Selection: all verses

In this chapter, Hosea reviews Israel's wickedness and prophesies that they will be carried captive by the Assyrians (see verse 6.) This Assyrian captivity will take place in about 722–721 BC. Remember that Hosea's mission as a prophet was from about 755 to 725 BC. Thus, he was a contemporary of Isaiah. In this chapter, the Lord will invite Israel (the northern kingdom) to repent again.

In verses 1–2, Hosea describes Israel as a nonproductive vine, self-centered, and deeply involved in apostasy, including idol worship.

1 **ISRAEL** *is* **an empty vine**, he bringeth forth fruit unto himself: according to the multitude of his fruit **he hath increased the altars** [*idol worship*]; according to the goodness of his land **they have made goodly images** [*magnificent idols*].

2 **Their heart is divided**; now shall they be found faulty: **he shall break down their altars, he shall spoil their images**.

Next, Israel boasts that not worshiping the Lord has not hurt them, because no foreign king has conquered them. They are still a free nation.

3 For now they shall say, **We have no king, because we feared not the LORD; what then should a king do to us?**

4 **They have spoken words, swearing falsely in making a covenant** [*they have not kept their covenants with God*]: thus judgment springeth up as hemlock [*a poisonous plant*] in the furrows of the field.

5 **The inhabitants of Samaria** [*northern Israel*] **shall fear** because of the calves of Beth-aven: for the people thereof shall mourn over it, and the priests thereof *that* rejoiced on it, for the glory thereof, because it is departed from it.

6 **It shall be also carried unto Assyria** *for* a present to king Jareb: Ephraim shall receive shame, and **Israel shall be ashamed** of his own counsel.

7 *As for* **Samaria, her king is cut off** as the foam upon the water.

8 **The high places** [*shrines for worshiping idols*] also of Aven, the sin of Israel, **shall be destroyed**: the thorn and the thistle shall come up on their altars; and **they shall say to the mountains, Cover us; and to the hills, Fall on us**.

9 **O Israel, thou hast sinned** from the days of Gibeah: there they stood: the battle in Gibeah against the children of iniquity did not overtake them.

In verse 10, next, the Lord says that He will have to punish them.

10 *It is* **in my desire that I should chastise them**; and the people [*enemy nations will come against them*] shall be gathered against them, when they shall bind themselves in their two furrows.

Verses 11–12, next, are another invitation to repent.

11 And Ephraim *is as* an heifer *that is* taught, *and* loveth to tread out *the corn;* but I passed over upon her fair neck: I will make Ephraim to ride; Judah shall plow, *and* Jacob shall break his clods.

12 **Sow to yourselves in righteousness, reap in mercy**; break up your fallow ground: for *it is* **time to seek the LORD, till he come and rain righteousness upon you**.

Verses 13–15, next, are a prophecy of destruction, including that Israel will cease to be a nation. This was fulfilled when the ten tribes were carried away into Assyrian captivity and became the lost ten tribes.

13 **Ye have plowed wickedness, ye have reaped iniquity**; ye have eaten the fruit of lies: because thou didst trust in thy way, in the multitude of thy mighty men.

14 **Therefore shall a tumult arise among thy people, and all thy fortresses shall be spoiled**, as Shalman spoiled Beth-arbel in the day of battle: **the mother was dashed in pieces upon** *her* **children**.

15 **So shall Beth-el do unto you because of your great wickedness: in a morning shall the king of Israel utterly be cut off**.

HOSEA 11

Selection: all verses

Hosea continues his use of imagery to describe Israel at the time they were brought by the Lord out of Egypt and their current deep wickedness. In spite of Israel's wickedness, you will see many statements of God's love for them. This can be encouraging for all of us.

1 **WHEN Israel** *was* **a child, then I loved him, and called my son out of Egypt**.

2 *As* they called them, so they went from them: **they sacrificed unto Baalim** [*a major false god*], **and burned incense to graven images**.

3 **I taught Ephraim also to go, taking them by their arms; but they knew not** [*refused to acknowledge*] **that I healed them**.

4 **I drew them with cords of a man** [*with tender cords of kindness*], **with bands of love**: and I was to them as they that take off the yoke on their jaws [*I freed them from bondage*], and **I laid meat unto them** [*I fed them*].

5 ¶ He shall not return into the land of Egypt, but **the Assyrian shall be his king, because they refused to return** [*repent*].

6 And **the sword shall abide on his cities, and shall consume his branches, and devour** *them,* **because of their own counsels** [*because of their wickedness*].

7 And **my people are** bent to **backsliding from me** [*are going backward, away from the Lord*]: **though they called them to the most High, none at all would exalt** *him* [*even though they pretended to worship Him, they refused to worship Him in reality*].

Admah and Zeboim, in verse 8, next, were sister cities of Sodom and Gomorrah, which God destroyed (see Deuteronomy 29:23).

8 **How shall I give thee up, Ephraim?** *how* **shall I deliver thee, Israel?** how shall I make thee as Admah? *how* shall I set thee as Zeboim? **mine heart is turned within me, my repentings are kindled together.**

The JST (Joseph Smith Translation of the Bible) makes significant changes to the last line of verse 8 as follows:

JST Hosea 11:8

8 How shall I give thee up, Ephraim? how shall I deliver thee, Israel? how shall I make thee as Admah? how shall I set thee as Zeboim? **My heart is turned toward thee, and my mercies are extended to gather thee**.

9 I will not execute the fierceness of mine anger, I will not return to destroy Ephraim: for **I** *am* **God, and not man; the Holy One in the midst of thee**: and I will not enter into the city.

10 **They shall walk after the LORD**: he shall roar like a lion:

when he shall roar, then the children shall tremble from the west.

In verse 11, next, Hosea indicates that throughout the years Egypt and Assyria were nations to whom Israel and Judah turned for protection, rather than repenting and turning to God.

11 They shall tremble as a bird out of **Egypt**, and as a dove out of the land of **Assyria**: and I will place them in their houses, saith the LORD.

12 **Ephraim** [*another name for northern Israel*] **compasseth** [*surrounds*] **me about with lies, and the house of Israel with deceit**: but **Judah yet ruleth with God, and is faithful with the saints** [*at this point, Israel, to the north, is more wicked than Judah, to the south*].

HOSEA 12

Selection: all verses

By way of review, remember that Hosea was called to be a prophet to the northern kingdom, consisting of the ten tribes of Israel headquartered in Samaria. Often referred to as Israel, this nation was somewhat ahead of the southern kingdom, Judah, in wickedness and consequently will be carried away captive in 722–721 BC by the Assyrians. Judah will finally be taken away to Babylon in several waves of captivity, ending in about 588–587 BC, about twelve to thirteen years after Lehi and his family fled Jerusalem in 600 BC.

As a prophet to Israel in the northern kingdom, Hosea witnessed their gross

wickedness and described it prophetically. However, he also reminded these apostate covenant people of the love Jehovah has for them, despite their wickedness. We see both of these themes here in chapter 12.

Also, in this chapter and elsewhere in Hosea's writings, you will see a lot of back-and-forth; namely, a verse or a few verses will talk about Israel's wickedness. Then a verse or two will mention that they can repent or that the Lord will someday bring them back. Then another describes their wickedness, followed by another prophesying that they will return to the Lord, and so on.

1   **EPHRAIM** [*northern Israel*] **feedeth on wind** [*believes on things that have no substance or truth*], **and followeth after the east wind** [*symbolic of destruction and devastation*]: **he daily increaseth lies** and desolation; and **they do make a covenant with the Assyrians** [*they make alliances with Assyria for protection rather than repenting and turning to God for protection*], and **oil is carried into Egypt** [*they make an alliance with Egypt and pay tribute to them for protection*].

2 **The LORD hath also a controversy with Judah** [*Judah is also being wicked*], **and will punish Jacob** [*the twelve tribes of Israel, all of whom are being wicked at this time*] **according to his ways; according to his doings** [*Jacob's wickedness*] **will he recompense him** [*punish Jacob*].

Verses 3–5 are a brief review of Isaac and Rebekah's twin sons, Jacob and Esau. Remember, Esau, the firstborn of the twins, was not interested in living the gospel and sold his birthright for a mess of pottage (a bowl of stew) to Jacob, who did live the gospel. See Genesis 25:29–34.

3 ¶ He took his brother by the heel in the womb [**Genesis 25:26**], and by his strength **he had power with God** [*was righteous*]:

4 Yea, he had power over the angel, and prevailed: he wept, and **made supplication unto him** [*the Lord— see Genesis 28:13, footnote 13c, in your Bible*]: he found him *in* Beth-el, and there he [*Jacob*] spake with us [*the Lord—see footnote 4d in your Bible*];

5 Even the LORD God of hosts; **the LORD *is* his memorial**.

Next, another invitation to repent.

6 Therefore **turn thou to thy God: keep mercy and judgment, and wait on thy God** [*live the gospel*] **continually**.

Next, back to the wickedness among the people of Israel.

7 ¶ *He is* a merchant, the balances of deceit *are* in his hand [*he cheats constantly in his business dealings*]: **he loveth to oppress**.

8 And **Ephraim** [*northern Israel*] **said, Yet I am become rich, I have found me out substance** [*boasting that he has become rich (even though he has broken his covenants with God)*]: *in* all my labours **they shall find none iniquity in me that** *were*

sin [*you won't find me committing any sins, because God is obviously blessing me*].

Next, in verses 9–10, Hosea prophesies that someday the Lord will bring Israel back to Him.

9 **And I** *that am* **the LORD** thy God from the land of Egypt [*who brought you out of Egyptian bondage*] **will yet make thee to dwell in tabernacles** [*symbolic of peace and protection of God*], **as in the days of the solemn feast** [*symbolic of the rites and ordinances of the true gospel*].

10 **I have** also **spoken by the prophets**, and I have multiplied visions, and used similitudes, by the ministry of the prophets.

Next, back again to the wickedness among the people of Israel and a prophecy of their coming destruction.

11 *Is there* iniquity *in* Gilead [*the area east of the Jordan River by the southern end of the Sea of Galilee, in what is now modern Jordan*]? **surely they are vanity** [*wicked*]: they sacrifice bullocks in Gilgal; yea, their altars *are* as heaps in the furrows of the fields [*will be piles of stones in a plowed field—a prophecy of coming destruction*].

Verse 12, next, is a one-sentence summary of how Jacob went to Syria/southern Turkey on a quest to find a wife. He found Rachel, served her father, Laban, a total of fourteen years raising sheep—see Genesis 29.

12 And Jacob fled into the country of Syria, and Israel served for a wife, and for a wife he kept *sheep*.

13 And **by a prophet the LORD brought Israel out of Egypt, and by a prophet was he preserved**.

14 **Ephraim provoked *him* to anger most bitterly**: therefore shall he leave his blood upon him, and his reproach shall his Lord return unto him.

HOSEA 13

Selection: all verses

The heading to chapter 12 in this study guide serves also as background for this chapter. In addition, this chapter has more about the Atonement of Jesus Christ and what it can do for us and all people. Remember, "Ephraim" in these chapters means the northern ten tribes; in other words, Israel, head-quartered in Samaria (the nation north of Judah and Jerusalem in Palestine).

In verse 1, next, you see a prophecy that once-powerful Israel will be reduced to weakness because of idol worship and the attendant wickedness.

1 **WHEN Ephraim spake trembling** [*Israel was once a powerful nation, people trembled when he spoke*], **he exalted himself in Israel** [*he became prideful*]; **but when he offended in Baal** [*when Israel started worshiping Baal*], **he died**.

2 And **now they sin more and more, and have made them molten images** [*idols*] **of their silver**, *and* idols according to their own understanding, all of it the work of the craftsmen: they say of them, Let the men that sacrifice kiss the calves.

Next, in verse 3, Hosea prophesies that these wicked Israelites will soon be gone like the morning mists when the sun comes up.

3 **Therefore they shall be as the morning cloud**, and as the early dew that passeth away, as the chaff *that* is driven with the whirlwind out of the floor, and as the smoke out of the chimney.

4 Yet **I *am* the LORD thy God** from the land of Egypt, and thou shalt know no god but me: for ***there is* no saviour beside me**.

Next, in verses 5–8, we see a brief review of the "cycle of apostasy." (People turn to God, are blessed, things go well, they get prideful, leave God, reap punishment, get humbled, turn again to God.)

5 ¶ **I did know thee in the wilderness, in the land of great drought** [*I helped you in the wilderness when you needed water and food (manna)*].

6 According to their pasture, so were they filled; **they were filled, and their heart was exalted** [*they became full of pride*]; **therefore have they forgotten me**.

7 **Therefore I will be unto them as a lion** [*I will destroy them*]: **as a leopard by the way will I observe *them*** [*I will lurk for them along the path as a leopard does watching for prey*]:

8 **I will meet them as a bear** *that is* bereaved *of her whelps,* **and will rend the caul of their heart** [*tears them wide open*], and there will I devour them like a lion: the wild beast shall tear them.

9 ¶ **O Israel, thou hast destroyed thyself; but in me** *is* **thine help** [*you can still repent*].

10 **I will be thy king**: where *is any other* that may save thee in all thy cities [*who else can save you*]? and thy judges of whom thou saidst, Give me a king and princes?

11 **I gave thee a king** [*Saul—1 Samuel 11:15*] **in mine anger** [*1 Samuel 8:7*], and took *him* away in my wrath.

In verses 12–13, next, Hosea prophesies that Israel's wickedness will bring destruction, and they will not be able to avoid it any more than a woman in hard labor can get out of having a baby with its attendant pain and suffering.

12 The iniquity of Ephraim *is* bound up; his sin *is* hid.

13 **The sorrows of a travailing woman shall come upon him: he** *is* **an unwise son**; for he should not stay long in *the place of* the breaking forth of children.

The resurrection, prophesied in verse 14, next, is also prophetic symbolism of the gathering and restoration of Israel in the last days.

14 **I will ransom them from the power of the grave; I will redeem them from death**: O death, I will be thy plagues; **O grave, I will be thy destruction: repentance shall be hid from mine eyes** [*perhaps referring to the time when the opportunity of repentance has passed for those who refuse to repent; see Alma 34:33–35*].

Verses 15–16, next, are the Lord's prophecy, through Hosea, that wicked, rebellious, prideful Israel will be destroyed. This will take place when the Assyrians (in other words, Ephraim) conquer the northern ten tribes and take most of them away as captives in 722–721 BC.

15 ¶ Though he be fruitful among *his* brethren, **an east wind** [*terrible destruction*] **shall come, the wind of the LORD shall come** up from the wilderness, and his spring shall become dry, and his fountain shall be dried up: he shall spoil the treasure of all pleasant vessels.

16 **Samaria** [*where the ten tribes lived*] **shall become desolate; for she hath rebelled against her God: they shall fall by the sword: their infants shall be dashed in pieces, and their women with child shall be ripped up.**

HOSEA 14

Selection: all verses

This is a chapter of prophetic hope for Israel, foreseeing the last days' gathering of Israel. It is a message of hope and encouragement for all of us, a reminder that the Atonement works and that we can stand spotless (2 Nephi 33:7) and clean (2 Nephi 9:14, last half of the verse) before our merciful Savior on judgment day.

1 O ISRAEL, return unto the LORD thy God; for thou hast fallen by thine iniquity.

2 Take with you words, and turn to the LORD: say unto him, Take away all iniquity, and receive *us* graciously: so will we render the calves of our lips [the *"offerings"* of our lips; a reference to offerings for sins, of young oxen or bullocks, under the law of Moses; *"lips"* symbolize the sincere and humble prayers for forgiveness that pass through our lips to God as we invoke the Atonement to make us free from sin].

3 Asshur [Assyria—see footnote 3a in your Bible] shall not save us; we will not ride upon horses [we will not depend on military power]: neither will we say any more to the work of our hands, Ye are our gods [we will not pray to our idols, which we made with our own hands, anymore]: for in thee the fatherless findeth mercy.

4 ¶ I [the Lord] will heal their backsliding, I will love them freely: for mine anger is turned away from him.

5 I will be as the dew unto Israel: he shall grow as the lily, and cast forth his roots as Lebanon [like a tall, stately, prosperous cedar tree in Lebanon].

6 His branches shall spread, and his beauty shall be as the olive tree, and his smell as Lebanon [the pleasant fragrance of the cedars of Lebanon].

Next, another prophecy of the return of Israel, the gathering of Israel in the last days.

7 They that dwell under his shadow [the protection of God] shall return; they shall revive *as* the corn, and grow as the vine: the scent thereof *shall be* as the wine of Lebanon.

8 Ephraim *shall say,* What have I to do any more with idols? [*I am through with idols.*] I have heard *him* [the Lord], and observed him: I *am* like a green fir tree. From me is thy fruit found [*I have the fruits of the gospel in my life*].

9 Who *is* wise, and he shall understand these *things?* prudent, and he shall know them? for the ways of the LORD *are* right, and the just [truly righteous] shall walk in them: but the transgressors shall fall therein.

JOEL

Bible scholars have not been able to determine with any degree of reliable accuracy when Joel lived. It could have been as early as 850 BC or as late as the return of the Jews from Babylon, in 537 BC. He was a prophet who ministered to Judah, the southern kingdom, headquartered in Jerusalem. The background for his prophecy here is that of a severe drought and plague of locusts. Among other things, he assures the people that if they repent, the Lord will bless them again. You may find it helpful as you study the book of Joel to keep in mind that pretty much the whole book is referring to the last days before the Second Coming of the Savior and on into the Millennium. In fact, as Moroni introduced Joseph Smith to the work he would be doing, he quoted Joel, chapter 2, from verse 28 to verse 32 (see Joseph Smith—History 1:41).

JOEL 1

Selection: all verses

Chapter 1 is basically a call to repentance; a call for the people, who are deeply involved in gross wickedness, to open their eyes to the drastic need for them to repent.

1 **THE word of the LORD that came to Joel** the son of Pethuel.

2 **Hear this, ye old men** [*the elders, leaders of the people*], **and give ear, all ye inhabitants of the land**. Hath this been in your days, or even in the days of your fathers [*have you ever seen things as bad as they are now*]?

3 **Tell ye your children of it, and** *let* **your children** *tell* **their children, and their children another generation.**

In verse 4, next, Joel prophesies that things are going to go from bad to worse, and from worse to even more worse, as conquering armies invade because of the wickedness of the people. A footnote in our Bible helps us understand what "palmerworm" means. It says, "The invading or conquering armies are compared to four varieties (or stages of growth) of locusts." (See footnote 4a in your Bible.

4 **That which the palmerworm hath left hath the locust eaten**; and **that which the locust hath left hath the cankerworm eaten**; and **that which the cankerworm hath left hath the caterpiller eaten.**

5 **Awake, ye drunkards** [*drunk, out of control with wickedness*], and **weep; and howl,** all ye drinkers of wine, because of the new wine; for it is cut off from your mouth [*terrible conditions are coming*].

Next, in verses 6–13, Joel prophesies of invading armies and their power to destroy. This can apply to the Assyrians and Babylonians, as well as to enemies in our day as they attack other nations. It can apply also to Internet filth, movie and entertainment filth, social media attacks on morality, and so forth.

6 **For a nation is come up upon my land**, strong, and without number, whose teeth *are* the teeth of a lion, and he hath the cheek teeth of a great lion [*has great power to destroy*].

7 **He hath laid my vine waste, and barked my fig tree: he hath made it clean bare, and cast** *it* **away; the branches thereof are made white.**

8 ¶ **Lament** [*mourn*] **like a virgin girded with sackcloth** [*symbolic of a nation and people in mourning for past prosperity*] **for the husband of her youth.**

9 **The meat offering and the drink offering is cut off from the house of the LORD** [*the Lord's true religion has been taken away*]; the priests, the LORD's ministers, mourn.

10 **The field is wasted, the land mourneth**; for the corn is wasted: the new wine is dried up, the oil languisheth.

11 **Be ye ashamed**, O ye husbandmen; howl, O ye vinedressers, for the wheat and for the barley; because the harvest of the field is perished.

12 The vine is dried up, and the fig tree languisheth; the pomegranate tree, the palm tree also, and the apple tree, *even* **all the trees** [*trees are often symbolic of people in Bible language*] **of the field, are withered:** because **joy is withered away** from the sons of men.

13 Gird yourselves, and **lament**, ye priests: **howl**, ye ministers of the al-tar: come, **lie all night in sackcloth** [*coarse, burlap-type fabric worn when mourning, in this culture*], ye ministers of my God: for **the meat offering and the drink offering is withholden from the house of your God**.

Next, in verse 14, is an invitation to repent. The good news is that they can still repent! This can apply to any of us who need such encouragement.

14 ¶ Sanctify ye a fast, call a solemn assembly, gather the elders *and* all the inhabitants of the land *into* the house of the LORD your God, and **cry unto the LORD,**

Verses 15–20, next, depict how bad conditions can get because people refuse to repent. These conditions were fulfilled by the Assyrian attacks on Israel and the Babylonian attacks on Judah and will be fulfilled in the last days leading up to the Second Coming.

15 Alas for the day! for **the day of the LORD** *is* **at hand** [*in the scriptures, this phrase often refers to the time shortly before the Second Coming*], **and as a destruction from the Almighty shall it come.**

16 **Is not the meat** [*food*] **cut off before our eyes** [*in other words, famine*], *yea,* **joy and gladness from the house of our God** [*loss of temple worship under the laws of Moses*]?

17 **The seed is rotten under their clods** [*doesn't grow when planted*], **the garners are laid desolate**

[*storehouses are empty*], **the barns are broken down**; for the corn is withered [*prophecies of famine*].

18 How do the beasts groan! the herds of **cattle** are perplexed, because they **have no pasture**; yea, the flocks of sheep are made desolate.

19 **O LORD, to thee will I cry**: for the fire hath devoured the pastures of the wilderness, and the flame hath burned all the trees of the field .

20 **The beasts of the field cry also unto thee**: for the rivers of waters are dried up, and the fire hath devoured the pastures of the wilderness.

JOEL 2

Selection: all verses

Chapters 2 and 3 refer to the final days before the Second Coming of the Savior; in other words, to our day.

The word "Zion" can have many meanings in the scriptures (see Bible Dictionary, under "Zion"). In verse 1, next, the words "Zion" and "holy mountain" mean, among other things, the headquarters of the Church as well as stakes, wards, districts, and branches wherever members of the Church are gathered. The sense of this verse is to alert members of the Church and everyone else who will listen to our prophets that we are getting close to the Second Coming.

1 **BLOW ye the trumpet in Zion, and sound an alarm in my holy mountain**: let all the inhabitants of the land tremble: **for the day of the LORD** [*the Second Coming*] **cometh, for it is nigh** [*near*] **at hand**;

Verses 2–11 contain a vivid description of the battle of Armageddon as enemies of Israel in great numbers descend in battle upon the land of Israel in the latter days. We see much posturing of nations and much dialogue of hatred and threatenings toward the Jews and their nation of Israel in our news today as preparations for this prophesied battle continue.

2 **A day of darkness and of gloominess**, a day of clouds and of thick darkness, as the morning spread upon the mountains: **a great people and a strong** [*most nations (not "all" nations) of the earth combine to attack Israel in their land*]; there hath not been ever the like, neither shall be any more after it, *even* to the years of many generations.

3 A fire devoureth before them; and behind them a flame burneth: **the land *is* as the garden of Eden before them, and behind them a desolate wilderness; yea, and nothing shall escape them**.

4 **The appearance of them *is* as the appearance of horses** [*"horses" are symbolic of military power in biblical symbolism*]; and as horsemen, so shall they run.

5 Like **the noise of chariots** [*also symbolic of military power in biblical symbolism*] on the tops of mountains shall they leap, like the noise of a flame of fire that devoureth the

stubble, **as a strong people set in battle array**.

6 Before their face **the people shall be much pained**: all faces shall gather blackness [*NIV, "every face turns pale"*].

7 **They** [*the enemies*] **shall run like mighty men; they shall climb the wall like men of war**; and they shall march every one on his ways, and they shall not break their ranks:

8 **Neither shall one thrust another** [*the enemies will not hurt each other, even though they are in close ranks*]; **they shall walk every one in his path** [*they will march straight ahead*]: and ***when* they fall upon the sword, they shall not be wounded** [*weapons against them will be ineffective*].

9 **They** [*the enemies of Israel*] **shall run to and fro in the city** [*Jerusalem and other cities in Israel*]; **they shall run upon the wall, they shall climb up upon the houses; they shall enter in at the windows like a thief**.

10 **The earth shall quake before them** [*there will be so many enemy soldiers that the earth will shake as they come*]; **the heavens shall tremble: the sun and the moon shall be dark, and the stars shall withdraw their shining** [*this can have dual meaning by also referring to the signs of the times mentioned in Matthew 24:29*]:

Verse 11 refers to when the Savior will appear on the Mount of Olives, which is just outside of Jerusalem, and stop this terrible destruction of His people (see D&C 45:47–53). His unseen army, so-to-speak, is more powerful than any earthly army, and the powers of heaven can stop any earthly forces.

11 **And the LORD shall utter his voice before his army: for his camp *is* very great: for *he is* strong that executeth his word**: for the day of the LORD *is* great and very terrible; and who can abide it?

In verses 12–22, Joel prophesies that the Lord will ultimately redeem His people as they repent and turn to Him.

12 ¶ Therefore also now, saith the LORD, **turn ye *even* to me with all your heart**, and with fasting, and with weeping, and with mourning:

The JST makes significant changes to verses 13 and 14, next.

13 And **rend your heart, and not your garments** [*tearing one's clothing was a sign of sorrow and mourning in the biblical culture of the day*], and **turn unto the LORD** your God: for **he *is* gracious and merciful, slow to anger, and of great kindness**, and repenteth him of the evil.

JST Joel 2:13

13 And rend your **hearts**, and not your garments, and repent, and turn unto the Lord your God; for he is gracious and merciful, slow to anger, and of great kindness, and he will turn away the evil from you.

14 Who knoweth *if* he will return and repent, and leave a blessing behind him; *even* a meat offering and a drink offering unto the LORD your God?

JST Joel 2:14

Therefore repent, and who knoweth but he will return and leave a blessing behind him; that you may offer a meat offering, and a drink offering, unto the Lord your God?

A "solemn assembly" is mentioned in verse 15, next. Solemn assemblies are sacred meetings of priesthood leaders and members to consider sacred matters. A general conference session where a new prophet and president of the Church is sustained is a solemn assembly.

15 ¶ Blow the trumpet in Zion [*sound the call for the Saints to rally to the Lord's cause*], sanctify a fast, **call a solemn assembly**:

Verse 16, next, is a reminder that Israel can repent and will be gathered in the last days.

16 **Gather the people**, sanctify [*cleanse and make holy through the Atonement*] **the congregation**, assemble the elders, gather the children, and those that suck the breasts: **let the bridegroom** [*Christ*] **go forth of his chamber, and the bride** [*faithful members of the Church; in other words, Israel*] **out of her closet.** [*See the parable of the ten virgins in Matthew 25:1–13.*]

17 **Let the priests**, the ministers of the LORD, weep between the porch and the altar, and let them **say, Spare thy people, O LORD**, and give not thine heritage to reproach, that the heathen should rule over them: wherefore should they say among the people, Where *is* their God?

Among other things, verse 18 can refer to the return of the Jews to the land of Israel.

18 ¶ **Then will the LORD be jealous** [*zealous—see footnote 18a in your Bible*] **for his land** [*the Holy Land*], **and pity** [*have compassion for—see footnote 18b in your Bible*] **his people** [*the Jews will return to Israel*].

Verses 19–20, next, prophesy that the Savior will bless the Jews to prosper in the Holy Land after He drives the invading armies in the battle of Armageddon out of their land.

19 Yea, **the LORD will** answer and say unto his people, Behold, I will **send** you **corn** [*grain*], and **wine**, and **oil**, and **ye shall be satisfied therewith** [*you will prosper*]: and **I will no more make you a reproach among the heathen** [*NIV, "an object of scorn among the nations"*]:

20 But **I will remove far off from you the northern** *army* [*the invading Armageddon armies*], and will drive him into a land barren and desolate, with his face toward the east sea, and his hinder part toward the utmost sea, and his stink shall come up, and his ill savour shall come up,

because he hath done great things [*horrible things against the Jews in the Holy Land*].

21 ¶ **Fear not, O land** [*of Israel*]; **be glad and rejoice: for the LORD will do great things.**

22 **Be not afraid**, ye beasts of the field: for the pastures of the wilderness do spring, for the tree beareth her fruit, the fig tree and the vine do yield their strength.

23 **Be glad then, ye children of Zion, and rejoice in the LORD your God**: for he hath given you the former rain moderately, and he will cause to come down for you the rain, **the former rain, and the latter rain** [*symbolic of revelation*] in the first *month*.

24 And **the floors** [*threshing floors*] **shall be full of wheat** [*symbolic of Christ, who is the "bread of life"—see John 6:35*], and **the fats** [*vats, containers*] **shall overflow with wine and oil**.

Next, Joel prophesies of the restoration in the last days after so many years of apostasy and accompanying plagues, wars, and devastation.

25 And **I will restore to you** the years that the locust hath eaten, the cankerworm, and the caterpiller, and the palmerworm [*see Joel 1:4*], my great army which I sent among you.

26 And **ye shall eat in plenty, and be satisfied, and praise the name** of the LORD your God, that hath dealt wondrously with you: and **my people shall never be ashamed** [*disappointed*].

27 And ye **shall know that I** *am* in the midst of Israel, and *that* I *am* the LORD your God, and none else: and **my people shall never be ashamed**.

President Gordon B. Hinckley taught that one of Joel's best-known prophecies has been fulfilled. We will quote the prophecy and then quote President Hinckley's statement about it. It is a prophecy about the last days, and some signs of the times that will be fulfilled before the Second Coming of the Savior.

28 ¶ And it shall come to pass afterward [*in the last days*], *that* **I will pour out my spirit upon all flesh**; and your sons and your daughters shall prophesy, your old men shall dream dreams, your young men shall see visions:

29 And also upon the servants and upon the handmaids **in those days will I pour out my spirit**.

30 **And I will shew wonders** [*signs of the times*] **in the heavens and in the earth**, blood, and fire, and pillars of smoke [*wars and natural disasters will be everywhere*].

31 **The sun shall be turned into darkness, and the moon into blood**, before the great and the terrible day of the LORD [*the Second Coming*] come.

32 And it shall come to pass, *that* **whosoever shall call on the name of the LORD shall be delivered**: for **in mount Zion and in Jerusalem shall be deliverance** [*the gospel of Jesus Christ will once again be available on earth*], as the LORD hath said, and in the remnant whom the LORD shall call.

We will focus our attention on verse 31, above. One of the signs of the times spoken of several times in the scriptures is that the sun will be darkened and the moon will become as blood. As I lectured on the signs of the times over the course of many years at BYU Campus Education Week, Know Your Religion lectures, and in my classes in seminary and institute of religion, I told my students that we don't know what this means and we don't know whether it has been fulfilled.

However, in the October 2001 general conference of the Church, during the Saturday morning session, President Hinckley said something that changed my mind on this prophecy. He said (bold added for emphasis):

"The era in which we live is the fulness of times spoken of in the scriptures, when God has brought together all of the elements of previous dispensations. From the day that He and His Beloved Son manifested themselves to the boy Joseph, there has been a tremendous cascade of enlightenment poured out upon the world. The hearts of men have turned to their fathers in fulfillment of the words of Malachi. The vision of Joel has been fulfilled

wherein he declared:" ("Living in the Fulness of Times," Ensign, November 2001, page 4).

He then quoted Joel 2:28–32. As soon as President Hinckley said that these words of Joel had been fulfilled, quoting them exactly as written, I accepted it on faith. We are now left to wonder exactly what "the sun shall be turned into darkness, and the moon into blood" means and how it has been fulfilled. We will not speculate but will wait for additional revelation from the Lord's living prophet, when the time is right.

JOEL 3

Selection: all verses

As was the case with chapter 2, chapter 3 deals mainly with conditions in the last days leading up to the Second Coming of the Savior. We are living in these times now when virtually all nations are at war. You will no doubt notice that these Old Testament prophets did not put things in chronological order, which is typical of their time and culture. If you are not aware of this, you will likely become confused as Joel switches back an forth between the future and past.

Verses 1–2, next, refer to the final days before the Second Coming when most nations of the earth join forces against the Jews in the nation of Israel.

1 FOR, behold, **in those days**, and in that time, when **I shall bring again the captivity of Judah and Jerusalem** [*severe troubles upon the Jews and the nation of Israel*],

Verse 2, next, contains a reminder that Israel was scattered throughout the world because of their wickedness and rebellion against the Lord.

2 I will also gather all nations, and will bring them down into the valley of Jehoshaphat [*probably the Kidron Valley, between Jerusalem and the Mount of Olives*]**, and will plead with them there for my people and** *for* **my heritage Israel** [*my people, Israel, covenant Israel*]**, whom they have scattered among the nations**, and parted my land.

Verse 3 is a reminder of the terrible treatment Israel has received through being scattered into all the world by enemies.

3 And **they have cast lots for my people**; and have **given a boy for an harlot**, and **sold a girl for wine, that they might drink**.

In verses 4–6, next, the Lord chastises enemy nations west of Israel and Judah, along the east coast of the Mediterranean Sea, for their brutal treatment of the Lord's people in times past.

4 Yea, and what have ye to do with me, O **Tyre**, and **Zidon**, and **all the coasts of Palestine**? will ye render me a recompence? and if ye recompense me, swiftly *and* **speedily will I return your recompence upon your own head** [*I will pay you back for what you did to My people*];

5 **Because ye have taken my silver and my gold, and have carried into your temples** [*shrines to idols*] my goodly pleasant things:

6 **The children** [*people*] also **of Judah** and the children of **Jerusalem** have **ye sold unto the Grecians, that ye might remove them far from their border**.

Next, in verses 7–8, we see that the Lord will gather scattered Israel in the last days, and the tables will be turned such that the Jews will have power over their former enemies.

7 Behold, **I will raise them out of the place whither ye have sold them**, and will return your recompence upon your own head:

8 And **I will sell your sons and your daughters into the hand of the children of Judah**, and they shall sell them to the Sabeans, to a people far off: for the LORD hath spoken *it*.

Verses 9–15 appear to be a summary of many things associated with the battle of Armageddon described in chapter 2. You can read more in Ezekiel, chapters 38–39.

9 ¶ **Proclaim ye this among the Gentiles; Prepare war, wake up the mighty men, let all the men of war draw near**; let them come up:

10 **Beat your plowshares into swords, and your pruninghooks into spears**: let the weak say, I *am* strong.

11 **Assemble yourselves, and come, all ye heathen, and gather**

yourselves together round about: thither cause thy mighty ones to come down, O LORD.

12 **Let the heathen** be wakened, and **come up to the valley of Jehoshaphat**: for there will I sit to judge all the heathen round about.

13 Put ye in the sickle, for the harvest is ripe: **come,** get you down; for the press is full, the fats overflow; **for their wickedness** *is* **great.**

14 **Multitudes** [*soldiers in the battle of Armageddon*], **multitudes in the valley of decision** [*valley of Jehoshaphat*]: for the day of the LORD *is* near in the valley of decision.

15 **The sun and the moon shall be darkened, and the stars shall withdraw their shining.**

Verses 16–21 appear to describe conditions during the Millennium.

16 **The LORD also shall roar out of Zion, and utter his voice from Jerusalem**; and the heavens and the earth shall shake: **but the LORD** *will be* **the hope of his people, and the strength of the children of Israel.**

17 **So shall ye know that I** *am* **the LORD your God** dwelling in Zion, my holy mountain: **then shall Jerusalem be holy,** and there shall no strangers [*enemies*] pass through her any more.

18 ¶ And it shall come to pass in that day, *that* the mountains shall drop down new wine, and the hills shall flow with milk, and all the rivers of Judah shall flow with waters, and a fountain shall come forth of the house of the LORD, and shall water the valley of Shittim.

It is helpful to know that "Egypt" and "Edom," as used in verse 19, next, often symbolize wickedness and the wicked people of the world.

19 **Egypt shall be a desolation, and Edom shall be a desolate wilderness, for the violence** *against* **the children of Judah,** because they have shed innocent blood in their land.

20 But **Judah shall dwell for ever, and Jerusalem from generation to generation.**

21 **For I will cleanse their blood** *that* **I have not cleansed: for the LORD dwelleth in Zion** [*this can include New Jerusalem, in Missouri, before the Millennium, and also during the Millennium, when the Savior will have two headquarters; namely, Old Jerusalem and New Jerusalem*].

AMOS

Amos was a contemporary of Isaiah and Hosea. He was a shepherd from Tekoa, a small town in the Judean hills about six miles south of Bethlehem and twelve miles south of Jerusalem. He was assigned by the Lord to prophesy to the Northern Kingdom, the ten tribes, often referred to as Israel, with headquarters in Samaria. His ministry was about 750 BC. His major emphasis was on the perfect moral character of Jehovah, and the fact that the sacrifice He desires most from His covenant people is that of a righteous life. Consequently, Amos's message also includes invitations to repent and gain eternal life, which is exaltation, as well as stern warnings that unrepented of wickedness blocks the gate to eternal life.

AMOS 1

Selection: all verses

This chapter contains warnings of coming judgments of God to several Gentile nations surrounding Israel and Judah, including Syria to the north, the Philistines to the southwest, Tyre on the seacoast northwest of the Sea of Galilee, Edom to the south of the Dead Sea, and Ammon, across the Jordon River, east of the northern part of the Dead Sea.

1 **THE words of Amos**, who was among the herdmen of Tekoa, **which he saw concerning Israel** [*the northern ten tribes*] in the days of Uzziah king of Judah, and **in the days of Jeroboam the** son of Joash **king of Israel**, two years before the earthquake [*we don't know anything about this earthquake, except that it was men-*

tioned again by Zechariah 2½ centuries later—see Zechariah 14:5].

2 And he said, **The LORD will roar from Zion, and utter his voice from Jerusalem**; and the habitations of the shepherds shall mourn, and **the top of Carmel shall wither** [*a reference to the nation of northern Israel, where Mt. Carmel is located*].

The phrase "for three transgressions and for four," in verse 3 and other verses, next, is an idiomatic phrase meaning "many, many." As you read the bolded words and phrases in the rest of this chapter, you will no doubt get the picture; namely, that the Lord is angry and that wickedness does not pay. Unrepentant sinners eventually get caught up with.

3 **Thus saith the LORD; For** three **transgressions of Damascus** [*Syria*], and for four, **I will not turn away** *the punishment* thereof; **because they have threshed Gilead** [*the land east of the Jordan River, settled by the tribes of Gad, Reuben, and Manasseh*] **with threshing instruments of iron** [*cruelly crushed their captives under heavy iron threshing sleds*]:

4 But **I will send a fire** into the house of Hazael, which shall devour the palaces of Ben-hadad.

5 **I will break also the bar of Damascus**, and **cut off the inhabitant from the plain of Aven**, and **him that holdeth the sceptre** [*the king*]

from the house of Eden: and **the people of Syria shall go into captivity** unto Kir, **saith the LORD.**

6 ¶ **Thus saith the LORD**; For three transgressions of Gaza, and for four, **I will not turn away** *the punishment* thereof; because they carried away captive the whole captivity, to deliver *them* up to Edom:

7 But **I will send a fire** on the wall of Gaza, which shall devour the palaces thereof:

8 And **I will cut off the inhabitant from Ashdod, and him that holdeth the sceptre** from Ashkelon, and I will turn mine hand against Ekron: and the remnant of the Philistines shall perish, saith the Lord GOD.

9 ¶ Thus saith the LORD; For three transgressions of Tyrus, and for four, **I will not turn away** *the punishment* **thereof**; because they delivered up the whole captivity to Edom, and remembered not the brotherly covenant:

10 But **I will send a fire on the wall** of Tyrus, which shall **devour the palaces** thereof.

11 ¶ Thus saith the LORD; For three transgressions of Edom, and for four, **I will not turn away** *the punishment* thereof; because he did pursue his brother with the sword, and did cast off all pity, and his anger did tear perpetually, and he kept his wrath for ever:

12 But **I will send a fire** upon Teman, which shall devour the palaces of Bozrah.

13 ¶ Thus saith the LORD; **For three transgressions of the children of Ammon,** and for four, **I will not turn away** *the punishment* thereof; **because they have ripped up the women with child** of Gilead, that they might enlarge their border:

14 But **I will kindle a fire** in the wall of Rabbah, and it shall devour the palaces thereof, with shouting in the day of battle, with a tempest in the day of the whirlwind:

15 And **their king shall go into captivity, he and his princes** together, saith the LORD.

AMOS 2

Selection: all verses

This chapter continues the theme for chapter 1; namely, that the unrepentant wicked will eventually be punished by the Lord when it is time for the law of justice to take over from mercy.

1 **THUS saith the LORD; For three transgressions of Moab** [*an enemy nation east of the southern half of the Dead Sea*]**, and for four** [*see note after Amos 1:2 for an explanation of this phrase*]**, I will not turn away** *the punishment* thereof; because he burned the bones of the king of Edom into lime:

2 But **I will send a fire upon Moab**, and it shall devour the palaces of

Kirioth: and Moab shall die with tumult, with shouting, *and* with the sound of the trumpet [*enemies will destroy Moab*]:

Next, Moab will lose its wise men and leaders.

3 And **I will cut off the judge from the midst thereof, and will slay all the princes** [*leaders*] thereof with him, saith the LORD.

4 ¶ **Thus saith the LORD; For** three **transgressions of Judah**, and for four, **I will not turn away** *the punishment* thereof; **because they have despised the law of the LORD, and have not kept his commandments**, and their lies caused them to err, after the which their fathers have walked:

5 But **I will send a fire upon Judah, and it shall devour the palaces of Jerusalem**.

Next, Amos turns attention to the nation of Israel in the north.

6 ¶ Thus saith the LORD; For three **transgressions of Israel**, and for four, I will not turn away *the punishment* thereof; **because they sold the righteous for silver, and the poor for a pair of shoes**;

Next, you will see rampant sexual immorality.

7 **That pant after the dust of the earth on the head of the poor** [*enjoy seeing the poor miserable*], and turn aside the way of the meek: and **a man and his father will go in unto**

the *same* **maid** [*commit adultery with the same girl*], to profane [*mock*] my holy name [*thus, breaking My commandment*]:

8 And **they lay** *themselves* **down** [*as they worship their idols*] **upon clothes laid to pledge** [*donated*] by every altar, and they drink the wine of the condemned *in* the house of their god.

Next, Amos prophetically warns the people of Israel that, even if they think they are so strong that no enemy nation can successfully attack them, they'd better think again.

9 ¶ **Yet destroyed I the Amorite** before them, whose height *was* like the height of the cedars, and he *was* strong as the oaks; **yet I destroyed his fruit from above, and his roots from beneath** [*I, the Lord, destroyed them completely*].

In verses 10–11, the Lord reminds these wicked and rebellious Israelites of past blessings from Him.

10 Also **I brought you up from the land of Egypt, and led you forty years through the wilderness, to possess the land of the Amorite**.

11 And I **raised up of your sons for prophets,** and of your young men for Nazarites. *Is it* **not even thus, O ye children of Israel?** saith the LORD.

12 **But ye gave the Nazarites** [*men who dedicated themselves to serve the Lord, which vow included not drinking wine and not cutting their hair*] **wine to drink**; and **commanded the prophets, saying, Prophesy not**

[*you commanded My prophets not to prophesy and teach you*].

13 Behold, I am pressed under you, as a cart is pressed *that is* **full of sheaves** [*NIV, "Now then, I will crush you as a cart crushes when loaded with grain"*].

Next, in verses 14–16, Amos prophesies that none will be able to successfully get away from these prophesied destructions.

14 Therefore the flight shall perish from the swift [*the fastest runners will not be able to run fast enough to get away*], **and the strong shall not strengthen his force, neither shall the mighty deliver himself:**

15 Neither shall he stand that handleth the bow [*even good archers will not survive*]; **and** *he that is* **swift of foot shall not deliver** *himself:* **neither shall he that rideth the horse deliver himself.**

16 And *he that is* **courageous among the mighty shall flee away naked in that day, saith the LORD.**

AMOS 3

Selection: all verses

In this chapter, the Lord speaks to both houses of Israel—all twelve tribes—Judah and Israel (see verse 1). You will likely recognize verse 7, which is an oft-quoted verse of scripture in the Church, especially in missionary work. This chapter contains stern warnings to covenant Israel because they are more accountable than other nations.

1 HEAR this word that the LORD hath spoken against you, O children of Israel, against the whole family [*all tribes of Israel*] **which I** brought up from the land of Egypt, saying,

2 You only have I known of all the families of the earth [*you are My covenant people*]: **therefore I will punish you for all your iniquities** [*wickedness*].

3 Can two walk together, except they be agreed? [*A reminder that Israel needs to walk with the Lord along the covenant path*]

Verses 4–6 lead up to verse 7 and warn and remind all Israel that the Lord knows of coming destruction (if people don't repent) and will always warn in advance. Amos asks if the Lord would warn if no trouble were coming.

4 Will a lion roar in the forest, when he hath no prey [*would the Lord warn you if no trouble were coming*]? **will a young lion cry out of his den, if he have taken nothing?**

5 Can a bird fall in a snare upon the earth, where no gin [*trap, snare*] *is* **for him?** shall *one* take up a snare from the earth, and have taken nothing at all?

6 Shall a trumpet be blown in the city, and the people not be afraid? shall there be evil in a city, and the LORD hath not done *it* [*has not warned in advance*]*?*

7 Surely the Lord GOD will do nothing, but he revealeth his secret unto his servants the prophets.

In verses 8–15, next, Amos says that the Lord has indeed warned and is warning, because trouble is indeed coming!

8 The lion hath roared, who will not fear? the Lord GOD hath spoken, who can but prophesy?

In verses 9–10, Amos proclaims that even the heathen nations, with all their wickedness, who have not been taught God's laws in order to know better, stand astonished at the wickedness they see among the Israelites.

9 ¶ Publish in the palaces at **Ashdod** [*a Philistine capital west of Jerusalem on the coast of the Mediterranean Sea*], and in the palaces in the land **of Egypt**, and say, Assemble yourselves upon the mountains of **Samaria**, and **behold the great tumults in the midst thereof**, and the oppressed in the midst thereof.

10 For **they know not to do right**, saith the LORD, who store up violence and robbery in their palaces.

11 **Therefore thus saith the Lord GOD; An adversary** *there shall be* even round about the land; and **he shall bring down thy strength** from thee, and **thy palaces shall be spoiled**.

12 Thus saith the LORD; **As the shepherd taketh out of the mouth of the lion two legs, or a piece of an**

ear [*Israel will not escape the terrible destruction that is coming to her*]; **so shall the children of Israel be taken out that dwell in Samaria** [*The Assyrians will conquer the ten tribes and take most of them away into captivity in 722–721 BC. (They will become the lost ten tribes.)*] in the corner of a bed, and in Damascus *in* a couch.

13 **Hear ye, and testify in the house of Jacob** [*the house of Israel*], **saith the Lord GOD, the God of hosts,**

14 **That in the day that I shall visit** [*punish*] **the transgressions of Israel upon him** I will also visit the altars of Beth-el [*used for idol worship and other wicked practices by Israel*]: and **the horns of the altar** [*symbolic of protection*] **shall be cut off, and fall to the ground** [*the Lord will not protect rebellious Israel from coming destruction and captivity*].

15 And **I will smite the winter house with the summer house; and the houses of ivory shall perish, and the great houses** [*in other words, all your wealth and prosperity*] **shall have an end, saith the LORD.**

AMOS 4

Selection: all verses

In chapter 4, the Lord punishes rebellious Israel by withholding rain, which causes famine. Still, the people do not repent and turn back to Jehovah. In verse 1, Amos compares the women of Samaria (Israel) with the fat cows that feed in the rich, green pastures in the mountains of Samaria without doing any other work except eat and take care of themselves. His point is that the women of Israel are not taking proper care of their children and are not raising them to know and keep the commandments of the Lord. The lesson is that as the mothers go, so go the children, and so goes the nation. Furthermore, these women are pressing their husbands to squeeze money out of the poorer citizens in order to bring their lazy wives better drink and richer food.

1 **HEAR this word, ye kine** [*"cows,"* *meaning the women*] **of Bashan**, that *are* in the mountain of Samaria, **which oppress the poor, which crush the needy, which say to their masters** [*husbands*], **Bring, and let us drink**.

In verse 2, Amos prophesies that these women will be torn away from their affluence and wicked lifestyles.

2 **The Lord GOD hath sworn** by his holiness, **that, lo, the days shall come upon you, that he will take you away with hooks, and your posterity with fishhooks** [*you will be taken into slavery*].

3 **And ye shall go out at the breaches** [*your protective fences (walls, defenses) will break down*], every cow at that which is before her; and ye shall cast *them* into the palace, saith the LORD.

Next, in verses 4–5, we see that these Israelites are going through the motions of their religion but are not living it in their hearts and lives. In other words, their worship is empty.

4 ¶ **Come to Beth-el** [*a center for their religious worship*], **and transgress; at Gilgal multiply transgression** [*sin more at Gilgal, another center for worship*]; and **bring your sacrifices every morning,** *and* **your tithes** after three years:

5 **And offer a sacrifice** of thanksgiving with leaven, and **proclaim** *and* **publish the free offerings**: for **this liketh you** [*this is what you like to do*], O ye children of Israel, saith the Lord GOD.

Next, in verses 6–11, the Lord says that despite the fact that He is punishing them, they still do not repent.

6 ¶ And **I also have given you cleanness of teeth** [*they have nothing to eat so their teeth are clean*] in all your cities, **and want** [*lack*] **of bread** in all your places: **yet have ye not returned unto me, saith the LORD**.

7 And **also I have withholden the rain from you, when** *there were* **yet three months to the harvest**: and **I caused it to rain upon one city, and caused it not to rain upon another city**: one piece was rained upon, and the piece whereupon it rained not withered.

8 **So two** *or* **three cities wandered unto one city, to drink water; but they were not satisfied** [*but there was not enough to go around*]: **yet have ye not returned unto me, saith the LORD.**

9 **I have smitten you** with blasting [*blight*] and mildew: when your

gardens and your vineyards and your fig trees and your olive trees increased, the palmerworm devoured *them:* **yet have ye not returned unto me, saith the LORD.**

10 **I have sent among you the pestilence** after the manner of Egypt: **your young men have I slain with the sword,** and **have taken away your horses**; and I have made the stink of your camps to come up unto your nostrils: **yet have ye not returned unto me, saith the LORD.**

11 **I have overthrown** *some* **of you,** as God overthrew Sodom and Gomorrah, and ye were as a firebrand plucked out of the burning: **yet have ye not returned unto me, saith the LORD.**

12 **Therefore thus will I do unto thee, O Israel**: *and* because I will do this unto thee, **prepare to meet thy God, O Israel** [*prepare to be destroyed*].

Finally, Jehovah reminds them that He is the Creator and their God, implying that He has not lost His power and that they would be wise to repent and return to Him because He still has power to save them.

13 For, lo, he that formeth the mountains, and createth the wind, and declareth unto man what *is* his thought, that maketh the morning darkness, and treadeth upon the high places of the earth, **The LORD, The God of hosts,** *is* **his name** [*in other words, He is Jehovah, the premortal Jesus Christ*].

AMOS 5

Selection: all verses

Here we see the Lord invite fallen Israel to repent and return to Him. It is still not too late.

1 **HEAR ye this word which I take up against you,** *even* **a lamentation** [*a formal mourning, weeping, and howling because of great loss*], **O house of Israel.**

2 **The virgin of Israel is fallen; she shall no more rise: she is forsaken upon her land;** *there is* **none to raise her up.**

Next, Amos prophesies that the population of Israel will be greatly reduced.

3 For thus saith the Lord GOD; **The city that went out** *by* **a thousand shall leave an hundred,** and **that which went forth** *by* **an hundred shall leave ten,** to the house of Israel.

Next, an invitation to repent, still.

4 ¶ For **thus saith the LORD unto the house of Israel, Seek ye me, and ye shall live:**

5 **But seek not Beth-el, nor enter into Gilgal, and pass not to Beersheba** [*where empty worship is still being performed*]: for **Gilgal shall surely go into captivity, and Beth-el shall come to nought** [*nothing*].

6 **Seek the LORD, and ye shall live;** lest he break out like fire in the

house of Joseph, and devour *it,* and *there be* none to quench *it* in Beth-el.

7 **Ye who turn judgment** [*fairness and kindness*] **to wormwood** [*bitterness*], **and leave off righteousness** in the earth,

8 *Seek him* [*your all-powerful God*] that maketh the seven stars and Orion, and turneth the shadow of death into the morning, and maketh the day dark with night: that calleth for the waters of the sea, and poureth them out upon the face of the earth: **The LORD** [*Jehovah*] *is* **his name:**

9 **That strengtheneth the spoiled against the strong, so that the spoiled shall come against the fortress** [*who can provide protection for you*].

10 **They** [*the wicked people in Israel*] **hate him that rebuketh in the gate** [*the prophets who rebuke them in the public gate alcoves in the wall of the city*], **and they abhor him that speaketh uprightly** [*is honest*].

11 **Forasmuch therefore as your treading** *is* **upon the poor, and ye take from him burdens of wheat** [*since you have stolen from the poor*]: **ye have built houses of hewn stone, but ye shall not dwell in them; ye have planted pleasant vineyards, but ye shall not drink wine of them** [*destruction is coming*].

12 **For I know your manifold** [*many*] **transgressions and your mighty sins: they afflict the just,** they **take a bribe,** and they **turn**

aside **the poor in the gate** *from their right* [*they use their knowledge of the legal system to cheat the poor*].

13 Therefore the prudent shall keep silence in that time; for **it** *is* **an evil time.**

Next, another invitation to repent.

14 **Seek good, and not evil, that ye may live: and so the LORD, the God of hosts, shall be with you,** as ye have spoken.

15 **Hate the evil, and love the good, and establish judgment in the gate:** it may be that the LORD God of hosts will be gracious unto the remnant of Joseph.

But if you still choose not to repent . . .

16 Therefore the LORD, the God of hosts, the Lord, saith thus; **Wailing** *shall be* **in all streets; and they shall say in all the highways, Alas! alas!** and they shall call the husbandman [*farmer*] to mourning, and such as are skilful of lamentation [*the paid mourners*] to wailing.

17 And in **all vineyards** *shall be* **wailing: for I will pass through thee, saith the LORD.**

18 **Woe unto you that desire the day of the LORD** [*who want the Lord to come*]! to what end *is* it for you? **the day of the LORD** *is* **darkness, and not light** [*you will be disappointed*].

Next, Amos says that if Israel does not repent, punishment will come. It will be hopeless, like running from a lion, only to run into a bear.

19 **As if a man did flee from a lion, and a bear met him; or went into the house, and leaned his hand on the wall** [*thinking he has escaped*], and a serpent bit him.

20 ***Shall*** **not the day of the LORD** [*in which He comes to punish rather than to bless*] **be darkness, and not light? even very dark, and no brightness in it?**

Next, Jehovah says what He thinks about their empty, hypocritical worship rites and services.

21 ¶ **I hate, I despise your feast days, and I will not smell in your solemn assemblies.**

22 **Though ye offer me burnt offerings and your meat offerings, I will not accept** ***them:*** **neither will I regard the peace offerings of your fat beasts.**

23 **Take thou away from me the noise of thy songs; for I will not hear the melody of thy viols** [*musical instruments used in proper law of Moses worship*].

24 **But let judgment** [*righteousness, kindness, honesty, and fairness*] **run down as waters, and righteousness as a mighty stream.**

25 **Have ye offered unto me sacrifices and offerings in the wilderness forty years, O house of Israel** [*remember when you offered Me proper sacrifices*]?

26 **But ye have borne the tabernacle** [*carried the shrines of your idols*] **of your Moloch and Chiun your images** [*heathen gods that the women of Israel had adopted*], **the star of your god, which ye made to yourselves** [*they made miniature replicas of these gods or idols and carried them with them*].

27 **Therefore will I cause you to go into captivity beyond Damascus** [*a prophecy of coming Assyrian captivity, in about 721 BC*], **saith the LORD, whose name** *is* **The God of hosts.**

AMOS 6

Selection: all verses

In this chapter we see more of the warnings and prophecies of Amos of coming captivity and destruction for rebellious Israel, the nation consisting of the northern ten tribes of Israel with headquarters in Samaria, north of Judah and Jerusalem.

Remember that, over two hundred years ago, in about 975 BC, when the twelve tribes of Israel split into two nations or kingdoms, Jeroboam took ten tribes and established them in Samaria with him as king. Rehoboam became king in Jerusalem over the southern kingdom consisting of the tribe of Judah and about half of the tribe of Benjamin (which by that time was a very small tribe) plus some Levites and various others from the other tribes of Israel. Jeroboam refused to allow his subjects to worship in Jerusalem. Instead, he established a center for worship in Samaria, with apostate priests to officiate in the rites, sacrifices, and offerings of the law of Moses. He also set up two calves to worship, as well as other images.

Verses 1–2 are another prophetic warning to Israel, whose citizens trust in the false gods and rites established by Jeroboam in Samaria.

1 **WOE to them** *that are* **at ease in Zion, and trust in the mountain of Samaria** [*the false worship established long ago by King Jeroboam*], **which** *are* named chief of the nations, to whom the house of Israel came!

In verse 2, next, the Lord invites these wicked Israelites to visit other nations who have already reaped punishment and destruction for their wickedness. It's a hint of what is coming to them if they don't repent.

2 **Pass ye unto** [*go visit*] **Calneh** [*in Mesopotamia*], **and see**; and from thence **go ye to Hamath** [*in Syria*] the great: **then go down to Gath of the Philistines**: *be they* better than these kingdoms? or their border greater than your border?

3 **Ye that put far away the evil day** [*in your minds, you don't think that day will come to you*], and cause the seat of violence to come near [*your continued wickedness is bringing your destruction closer and closer*];

Next, in verses 4–6, Amos addresses the wealthy in Israel who live lives of luxury and decadence.

4 **That lie upon beds of ivory, and stretch themselves upon their couches**, and eat the lambs out of the flock, and the calves out of the midst of the stall;

5 **That chant to the sound of the viol,** *and* **invent to themselves instruments of musick, like David;**

6 **That drink wine in bowls, and anoint themselves with the chief ointments**: but **they are not grieved for the affliction of Joseph** [*but they are not worried about what is coming*].

7 ¶ **Therefore now shall they go captive with the first that go captive**, and the banquet of them that stretched themselves shall be removed.

8 The Lord GOD hath sworn by himself, **saith the LORD the God of hosts, I abhor the excellency** [*those high in social status*] of Jacob [*Israel*], **and hate his palaces: therefore will I deliver up the city with all that is therein.**

9 And it shall come to pass, **if there remain ten men in one house**, that **they shall die.**

10 And a man's uncle shall take him up, and he that burneth him, to bring out the bones out of the house, and shall say unto him that *is* by the sides of the house, *Is there* yet *any* **with thee** [*are there any other dead inside*]? and he shall say, No. **Then shall he say, Hold thy tongue: for we may not make mention of the name of the LORD** [*they are trying to hide from the Lord and don't want Him to hear them*].

11 For, behold, **the LORD** comman-deth, and he **will smite the great house** with breaches, **and the little house** with clefts [*the destruction will be complete*].

Next, Amos again uses imagery to teach the lesson. Israel has brought about their own destruction. They have tried to do the impossible by continuing in wickedness and think-ing that the Lord will not catch up to them. In effect, Amos says that they are like horses trying to run on rock without falling down, or like oxen try-ing to plow through rock in order to plant crops. It just doesn't work!

12 ¶ **Shall horses run upon the rock? will** *one* **plow** *there* **with oxen?** for **ye have turned judgment** [*fairness*] **into gall** [*bitterness*], **and the fruit** [*results*] **of righteousness into hemlock** [*poison*]:

13 **Ye which rejoice in a thing of nought** [*that is worthless, such as your decadent lifestyle and terrible treatment of the poor*], **which say, Have we not taken to us horns** [*protection*] by our own strength? [*In other words, we don't need God. We can protect our-selves.*]

14 **But, behold, I will raise up against you a nation** [*the Assyrians*], **O house of Israel, saith the LORD the God of hosts; and they shall afflict you** from the entering in of Hemath unto the river of the wilder-ness.

What Amos prophesied in verse 14, above, will happen within thirty years.

AMOS 7

Selection: all verses

Amos relates how he was called of God to be a prophet—He prophesies the captivity of Israel.

Chapters 7, 8, and 9 tell us about five visions that Amos had. They all proph-esy of the downfall and destruction of Israel, and the fifth includes the de-struction of the wicked at the Second Coming. We will list the visions here.

1. **Amos 7:1–3**, a plague of grasshop-pers (locusts).

2. **Amos 7:4–6**, devouring fire.

3. **Amos 7:7–9**, the Lord measures Israel with a plumbline (a builder's tool) to see how they measure up. They don't.

4. **Amos 8:1–9**, Israel is compared to a basket of ripe summer fruit, symbolizing that Israel is ripe for destruction.

5. **Amos 9:1–6**, at the Second Com-ing, the Savior will destroy all the wicked. None will escape.

The first four visions begin with some-thing like, "the Lord shewed unto me," and the fifth vision begins with, "I saw the Lord."

1 **THUS hath the Lord GOD shewed unto me**; and, behold, **he formed grasshoppers in the beginning of the shooting up of the latter growth** [*the grasshoppers came at the beginning of the second crop of grain's growth; in other words, destroyed the crop*]; and, lo, *it was*

the latter growth after the king's mowings.

2 And it came to pass, *that* **when they had made an end of eating the grass** of the land, **then I said, O Lord GOD, forgive, I beseech thee: by whom shall Jacob arise?** for he *is* small. [*How will Israel survive? There are so few of them left.*]

The JST provides important correction for verses 3 and 6.

3 The LORD repented for this: It shall not be, saith the LORD.

JST Amos 7:3

3 And the Lord said, concerning Jacob, Jacob shall repent for this, therefore I will not utterly destroy him, saith the Lord.

4 ¶ **Thus hath the Lord GOD shewed unto me**: and, behold, **the Lord GOD called to contend by fire**, and it devoured the great deep, and did eat up a part.

5 **Then said I, O Lord GOD, cease, I beseech thee: by whom shall Jacob arise?** for he *is* small.

6 The LORD repented for this: This also shall not be, saith the Lord GOD.

JST Amos 7:6

3 And the Lord said, concerning Jacob, Jacob shall repent of his wickedness, therefore I will not utterly destroy him, saith the Lord God.

7 ¶ **Thus he shewed me**: and, behold, **the Lord stood upon a wall** *made*

by a plumbline, **with a plumbline in his hand**.

8 And **the LORD said unto me, Amos, what seest thou? And I said, A plumbline**. Then said the Lord, Behold, I will set a plumbline in the midst of my people Israel [*I will see how they measure up to the standards of My commandments*]: **I will not again pass by them any more** [*the time has come to destroy them*]:

9 And **the high places of Isaac** [*Israel*] **shall be desolate**, and the sanctuaries of Israel shall be **laid waste**; and **I will rise against the house of Jeroboam** [*Israel's first king when they split from Judah*] **with the sword**.

10 ¶ **Then Amaziah the priest of Beth-el** [*a center for worship, including idol worship set up by King Jeroboam*] **sent to Jeroboam king of Israel, saying, Amos hath conspired against thee** in the midst of the house of Israel: **the land is not able to bear all his words** [*we can't stand to keep hearing his negative prophecies about us and you*].

11 For **thus Amos saith, Jeroboam shall die by the sword, and Israel shall surely be led away captive out of their own land**.

Verses 10–11, above, remind us of the complaints of wicked King Noah's priests to him about the negative prophecies of Abinadi (see Mosiah 12:9–10).

12 Also **Amaziah said unto Amos, O thou seer, go, flee thee away into**

the land of Judah [*go back to your home in Judah*], and there eat bread, and prophesy there:

13 **But prophesy not again any more at Beth-el: for it** *is* **the king's chapel, and it** *is* **the king's court.**

Next, Amos will briefly review his call as a prophet as he responds to Amaziah's demand that he get out of the country and go home.

14 ¶ **Then answered Amos, and said to Amaziah,** I *was* no prophet, neither *was* I a prophet's son; but I *was* an herdman, and a gatherer of sycomore fruit:

15 **And the LORD took me** [*called me*] as I followed the flock, **and the LORD said unto me, Go, prophesy unto my people Israel.**

16 ¶ Now therefore **hear thou the word of the LORD: Thou sayest, Prophesy not against Israel,** and drop not *thy word* against the house of Isaac [*the descendants of Isaac*].

17 **Therefore thus saith the LORD; Thy wife shall be an harlot in the city** [*Israel (the "wife") will continue to step out on her "husband" (the Lord) and thus bring on the prophesied destruction*], and **thy sons and thy daughters shall fall by the sword,** and thy land shall be divided by line [*measured and divided up by the conquering armies*]; and **thou shalt die in a polluted land** [*in a foreign, non-Israelite land (Assyrian captivity)*]: and **Israel shall surely go into captivity** forth of his land [*away from Palestine*].

AMOS 8

Selection: all verses

See heading to chapter 7 for information about this chapter. You may have heard verses 11 and 12, which are often used by our missionaries as they teach the need for the restoration of the gospel.

1 **THUS hath the Lord GOD shewed unto me:** and **behold a basket of summer fruit.**

2 And **he said, Amos, what seest thou?** And **I said, A basket of summer fruit.** Then **said the LORD unto me, The end is come upon my people of Israel;** I will not again pass by them any more [*I won't be able to forgive them any more*].

3 And **the songs** [*pleasant music*] **of the temple shall be** [*will be turned into*] **howlings in that day,** saith the Lord GOD: **there shall be many dead bodies in every place;** they shall cast *them* forth with silence.

4 ¶ **Hear this, O ye that swallow up the needy** [*who oppress the poor and the needy*], even to make the poor of the land to fail,

Verses 5–6, next, detail some of Israel's wickedness.

5 Saying, **When will the new moon be gone** [*a time of offering special sacrifices under the law of Moses—see Bible Dictionary, under "New Moon"*], that we may sell corn? and the sabbath, that we may set forth wheat, making the ephah small [*cheating our*

customers], and the shekel great, **and falsifying the balances** by deceit?

6 **That we may buy the poor for silver, and the needy for a pair of shoes**; *yea,* **and sell the refuse of the wheat** [*mixing the dust and sweepings with the wheat we sell*]?

7 **The LORD hath sworn** by the excellency of Jacob, Surely **I will never forget any of their works** [*the Lord knows everything you are doing*].

8 **Shall not the land tremble for this, and every one mourn that dwelleth therein?** and it shall rise up wholly as a flood; and it shall be cast out and drowned, as *by* the flood of Egypt.

Next, Amos prophesies that the destruction of the northern ten tribes, Israel, will come at the height of their prosperity.

9 And it shall come to pass in that day, saith the Lord GOD, **that I will cause the sun to go down at noon, and I will darken the earth in the clear day**:

10 And **I will turn your feasts into mourning, and all your songs into lamentation**; and I will bring up **sackcloth** upon all loins, and **baldness** [*symbolic of slavery in biblical symbolism*] upon every head; and I will make it as the mourning of an only *son,* and the end thereof as **a bitter day**.

Verses 11–12, next, prophesy of the coming loss of the gospel through wide-spread apostasy. This would include the lack of prophets and the word of the Lord during the period from about 400 BC to the ministry of Christ as well as the well over 1,000 years during the great apostasy and the dark ages until the time of the Restoration through Joseph Smith.

11 ¶ Behold, the days come, saith the Lord GOD, that **I will send a famine** in the land, not a famine of bread, nor a thirst for water, but **of hearing the words of the LORD**:

12 And they shall wander from sea to sea, and from the north even to the east, **they shall run to and fro to seek the word of the LORD, and shall not find** *it.*

13 In that day shall the fair virgins and young men faint for thirst.

14 They that swear by the sin of Samaria, and say, Thy god, O Dan, liveth; and, The manner of Beer-sheba liveth; even they shall fall, and never rise up again.

AMOS 9

Selection: all verses

See heading to chapter 7 for information about this chapter. Chapter 9 also includes prophecy of the scattering of Israel as well as prophecy of the gathering of Israel in the last days, including the gathering of the Jews to their own land.

First, verses 1–6, as a dual prophecy, depicts the terrible destruction coming upon Israel shortly after Amos's ministry, as well as the complete destruction of the wicked at the time of the Second Coming.

1 **I SAW the Lord** standing upon the altar [*symbolic of heaven*]: and he said, Smite the lintel of the door, that the posts may shake: and cut them in the head, all of them; **and I will slay the last of them** [*the wicked*] **with the sword: he that fleeth of them shall not flee away, and he that escapeth of them shall not be delivered** [*nobody will get away*].

2 **Though they dig into hell, thence shall mine hand take them; though they climb up to heaven, thence will I bring them down**:

3 And **though they hide themselves** in the top of Carmel, **I will search and take them out** thence; and **though they be hid from my sight** in the bottom of the sea, thence will **I command the serpent, and he shall bite them**:

4 And **though they go into captivity before their enemies**, thence will **I command the sword, and it shall slay them**: and **I will set mine eyes upon them for evil, and not for good**.

5 And the Lord GOD of hosts *is* he that toucheth **the land**, and it **shall melt** [*with the heat of the burning at the Second Coming*], and **all that dwell therein shall mourn**: and **it shall rise up wholly like a flood; and shall be drowned**, as *by* the flood of Egypt [*like the Egyptian armies drowned in the Red Sea*].

Next, no one among the wicked can escape, because it is the Lord Who is after them!

6 *It is* he [*the Lord*] **that buildeth his stories in the heaven** [*Who lives in heaven*], and hath founded his troop in the earth; **he that calleth for the waters of the sea, and poureth them out upon the face of the earth: The LORD** *is* **his name**.

7 *Are* **ye not as children of the Ethiopians unto me, O children of Israel** [*are you not wicked just like other nations*]? **saith the LORD**. Have not I brought up Israel out of the land of Egypt? and the Philistines from Caphtor, and the Syrians from Kir?

8 Behold, **the eyes of the Lord GOD** *are* **upon the sinful kingdom, and I will destroy it from off the face of the earth**; saving that **I will not utterly destroy the house of Jacob** [*Israel*], saith the LORD [*except that I will save a remnant*].

Verse 9, next, refers to the gathering of Israel from among all nations.

9 For, lo, I will command, and **I will sift** [*gather*] **the house of Israel among all nations**, like as *corn* [*grain, flour*] is sifted in a sieve, **yet shall not the least grain fall upon the earth** [*not one worthy member of covenant Israel will be missed*].

Back to the destruction of the wicked.

10 **All the sinners of my people shall die** by the sword, which say,

The evil shall not overtake nor prevent us.

Next, a prophecy of the gathering of Israel in the last days, including the return of the Jews to Jerusalem and Judah.

11 ¶ **In that day will I raise up the tabernacle of David that is fallen** [*Jerusalem will be rebuilt*], **and close up the breaches thereof** [*repair the walls*]; **and I will raise up his ruins, and I will build it as in the days of old:**

Next, Amos prophesies that the gospel will go to all the world in the last days such that all people who so desire can join with covenant Israel.

12 **That they** [*the Lord's people*] **may possess** [*may include*] **the remnant of Edom** [*a heathen nation to the south of the Dead Sea*], **and of all the heathen, which are called by my name** [*who have joined the Church*], **saith the LORD that doeth this.**

Verses 13–15, next, refer to prosperity that comes through righteousness. Such words and phrases are also used in the scriptures to refer to conditions during the Millennium.

13 Behold, **the days come, saith the LORD, that the plowman shall overtake the reaper** [*one good crop after another*], **and the treader of grapes him that soweth seed; and the mountains shall drop sweet wine, and all the hills shall melt** [*flow with wine*].

14 And **I will bring again the captivity of my people of Israel** [*I will bring My people in from their captivity*], **and they shall build the waste cities, and inhabit** *them;* **and they shall plant vineyards, and drink the wine thereof; they shall also make gardens, and eat the fruit of them** [*prosperity and the blessings of the Lord; also often refers to the Millennium*].

15 And **I will plant them upon their land,** and **they shall no more be pulled up out of their land which I have given them,** saith the LORD thy God.

OBADIAH

Very little is known about Obadiah. Some Bible scholars suspect that he may have lived around the Babylonian conquest of Jerusalem about 587–586 BC. (See Bible Dictionary under "Obadiah.") He prophesied against the nation of Edom (directly south of the Dead Sea), a long-time enemy of Judah and the Jews in Jerusalem.

Edom was settled by the descendants of Esau, Jacob's twin brother, who sold his birthright to Jacob for a mess of pottage. Residents of Edom jeered at the Jews as they were led away captive by the Babylonians and looted their belongings after they were gone. In the scriptures, "Edom" also became known as "Idumea" or the "world," and the "wicked worldly."

OBADIAH 1

Selection: all verses

1 **THE vision of Obadiah. Thus saith the Lord GOD concerning Edom**; We have heard a rumour from the LORD, and an ambassador is sent among the heathen, Arise ye, and let us rise up against her in battle.

> Next, bad times are coming for Edom.

2 **Behold, I** [*the Lord*] **have made thee small** among the heathen [*among your fellow heathen nations*]: **thou art greatly despised**.

3 ¶ **The pride of thine heart hath deceived thee**, thou that dwellest in the clefts of the rock, whose habitation *is* high; that saith in his heart, **Who shall bring me down** to the ground? [*You think you are safe in your rugged, mountainous land*]

4 Though thou exalt *thyself* as the eagle, and though thou set thy nest among the stars, thence **will I bring thee down, saith the LORD**.

5 **If thieves came to thee, if robbers by night, (how art thou cut off!) would they not have stolen till they had enough?** if the grapegatherers came to thee, would they not leave *some* grapes?

6 **How are *the things* of Esau** [*Edom*] **searched out!** *how* **are his hidden things sought up** [*you are not safe*]!

7 All the men of thy confederacy have brought thee *even* to the border: **the men that were at peace with thee have deceived thee, *and* prevailed against thee**; *they that eat* **thy bread** have laid a wound under thee: *there is* none understanding in him.

8 **Shall I not in that day, saith the LORD, even destroy the wise *men* out of Edom**, and understanding out of the mount of Esau?

9 And **thy mighty *men*, O Teman, shall be dismayed**, to the end that **every one** of the mount of Esau **may be cut off by slaughter**.

> Obadiah next gives one of the reasons for the coming destruction of Edom. It is because of their actions against the Jews.

10 ¶ **For *thy* violence against thy brother Jacob** [*the house of Israel*] **shame shall cover thee, and thou shalt be cut off for ever**.

11 **In the day that thou stoodest on the other side, in the day that the strangers** [*foreigners, Babylonians*] **carried away captive his forces**, and foreigners entered into his gates, and cast lots upon Jerusalem, even **thou *wast* as one of them** [*you joined with the Babylonians in looting Jerusalem and Judah*] .

12 But thou shouldest not have looked on the day of thy brother in the day that he became a stranger; **neither shouldest thou have rejoiced over the children of Judah**

in the day of their destruction; neither shouldest thou have spoken proudly in the day of distress.

13 **Thou shouldest not have entered into the gate of my people** [*the Jews*] **in the day of their calamity**; yea, thou shouldest not have looked on their affliction in the day of their calamity, **nor have laid** *hands* **on their substance** [*looted, plundered*] **in the day of their calamity;**

14 **Neither shouldest thou have stood in the crossway, to cut off those of his that did escape** [*you shouldn't have cut off the Jews who were escaping the Babylonian armies*]; **neither shouldest thou have delivered up those of his that did remain in the day of distress** [*and turned them over to the Babylonians*].

15 For the day of the LORD *is* near upon all the heathen: **as thou hast done, it shall be done unto thee: thy reward shall return upon thine own head.**

Verse 16, next, basically says that just as the people of Edom have profited from the downfall and destruction of the Jews, so also will their wicked lifestyle ultimately lead to their own destruction.

16 **For as ye have drunk upon my holy mountain** [*Jerusalem*], *so* shall all the heathen drink continually, yea, they shall drink, and they shall swallow down, and **they shall be as though they had not been** [*will cease to exist*].

Verses 17–21 refer mainly to the gathering and restoration of Israel in the last days.

17 ¶ **But upon mount Zion shall be deliverance** [*Jerusalem will be restored*], and there shall be holiness [*Israel will become the righteous, covenant people of the Lord*]; **and the house of Jacob** [*Israel*] shall possess their possessions [*will be restored*].

18 And **the house of Jacob shall be a fire** [*a light to the world*], and the house of Joseph a flame, **and the house of Esau** [*Idumea*] **for stubble** [*the wicked will be destroyed (at the Second Coming)*], and they shall kindle in them, and devour them; and **there shall not be** *any* **remaining of the house of Esau**; for the LORD hath spoken *it*.

19 And *they of* **the south shall possess the mount of Esau**; and *they of* the plain the Philistines: and they shall possess the fields of Ephraim, and the fields of Samaria: and Benjamin *shall possess* Gilead.

Among other things, verse 20, next, can prophesy that the righteous will inherit the earth during the Millennium.

20 And the captivity of **this host of the children of Israel** *shall possess* **that of the Canaanites**, *even* unto Zarephath; and the captivity of Jerusalem, which *is* in Sepharad, shall possess the cities of the south.

21 And **saviours shall come up on mount Zion** to judge the mount of

Esau; and **the kingdom shall be the LORD's.**

President Gordon B. Hinckley gave one possible interpretation of the phrase "saviours on mount Zion," connecting the phrase to temple and family history work: "[*In the temple*] we literally become saviors on Mount Zion. What does this mean? Just as our Redeemer gave His life as a vicarious sacrifice for all men, and in so doing became our Savior, even so we, in a small measure, when we engage in proxy work in the temple, become as saviors to those on the other side who have no means of advancing unless something is done in their behalf by those on earth" ("Closing Remarks," *Ensign* or *Liahona*, Nov. 2004, 105).

JONAH

Jonah lived somewhere around 800 BC and was called to preach in Nineveh, a terribly wicked city known for torturing and killing outsiders. The book of Jonah was not written by Jonah himself but by a later, unidentified writer. Jonah is, of course, one of the best-known Bible stories and is a favorite of Christians everywhere.

A major message of Jonah is that the Lord wants to save the wicked. He loves them also and wants them to repent and come to live with Him eternally.

We will quote from Nahum to give you an idea as to why Jonah was reluctant to accept a mission call to preach to Nineveh. While we are not suggesting that it was at all proper for Jonah to run the other way when the call came, we may be a bit less critical when we realize the terrors of Nineveh to outsiders. A brief description of Nineveh, a prominent city in Assyria about five hundred miles northeast of Jerusalem, is given by the prophet Nahum as he prophesied against their wickedness.

Nahum 3:1–5

1 **Woe to the bloody city** [*Nineveh*]! it *is* **all full of lies** *and* **robbery**; the prey departeth not [*NIV: "never without victims"*];

2 **The noise of a whip**, and the noise of the rattling of the wheels, and of the pransing **horses**, and of the jumping **chariots** [*in other words, a mighty military power*].

3 The horseman lifteth up both the bright **sword** and the glittering **spear**: and *there is* **a multitude of slain**, and **a great number of carcases**; and *there is* **none end of *their* corpses**; they stumble upon their corpses [*there are so many dead bodies that the people in Nineveh are constantly tripping over them*]:

4 Because of the multitude of the **whoredoms** of the wellfavoured **harlot**, the mistress of **witchcrafts**, that selleth nations through her whoredoms, and families through her witchcrafts.

5 Behold, **I** *am* **against thee, saith the LORD of hosts**; and I will discover thy skirts upon thy face, and I will shew the nations thy nakedness,

and the kingdoms thy shame [*your wickedness will be exposed by the Lord*].

JONAH 1

<u>Selection: all verses</u>

In this chapter, Jonah receives his call from the Lord to go to Nineveh and preach repentance. Instead of accepting the call, he flees the other direction and ends up being swallowed by a whale.

1 NOW **the word of the LORD came unto Jonah** the son of Amittai, saying,

2 **Arise, go to Nineveh** [*a city located in modern-day Iraq*], that great city, **and cry against it** [*preach repentance to it*]; for their wickedness is come up before me.

3 **But Jonah rose up to flee unto Tarshish** [*probably somewhere in modern Spain, near the Straits of Gibraltar*] **from the presence of the LORD**, and **went down to Joppa** [*a sea port city on the coast of the Mediterranean Sea, northwest of Jerusalem*]; and he found a ship going to Tarshish: so he paid the fare thereof, and went down into it, to go with them unto Tarshish **from the presence of the LORD.**

4 ¶ **But the LORD sent out a great wind** into the sea, and **there was a mighty tempest in the sea, so that the ship was like to be broken** [*the ship was about to be broken up*].

5 Then **the mariners** [*sailors*] **were afraid, and cried every man unto his god** [*every sailor prayed to his god*], and **cast forth the wares that** *were* **in the ship into the sea, to lighten** *it* of them. **But Jonah** was gone down into the sides of the ship; and he lay, and **was fast asleep**.

Next, the ship's captain found Jonah sleeping and angrily awakened him and told him to pray to his god.

6 **So the shipmaster came to him**, and said unto him, **What meanest thou, O sleeper? arise, call upon thy God**, if so be that God will think upon us, **that we perish not.**

Next, the sailors superstitiously assume that someone among them is the cause of the storm. They cast lots to determine who he is.

7 And they said every one to his fellow, **Come, and let us cast lots, that we may know for whose cause this evil** *is* **upon us**. So they cast lots, and **the lot fell upon Jonah.**

8 **Then said they unto him, Tell us, we pray thee, for whose cause this evil** *is* **upon us** [*who is the guilty one who is the cause of this storm?*]; What *is* thine occupation? and **whence comest thou?** what *is* thy country? and of what people *art* thou?

9 And **he said unto them, I** *am* **an Hebrew; and I fear the LORD, the God of heaven** [*my god is Jehovah*], which hath made the sea and the dry land.

10 Then were the men exceedingly afraid, and said unto him, **Why hast thou done this?** For **the men knew that he fled from the presence of the LORD, because he had told them.**

11 ¶ Then said they unto him, **What shall we do unto thee, that the sea may be calm** unto us? for the sea wrought, and was tempestuous.

12 And **he said unto them, Take me up, and cast me forth into the sea; so shall the sea be calm** unto you: for **I know that for my sake this great tempest** *is* **upon you** [*I know that I am the cause of this storm*].

The men were not willing at first to throw Jonah overboard.

13 **Nevertheless the men rowed hard to bring** *it* **to the land; but they could not**: for the sea wrought, and was tempestuous against them.

Next, the sailors pray to God not to hold it against them when they throw Jonah overboard.

14 Wherefore **they cried** [*prayed*] **unto the LORD**, and said, **We beseech thee, O LORD**, we beseech thee, **let us not perish for this man's life** [*because Jonah has offended Thee*], and **lay not upon us innocent blood**: for thou, O LORD, hast done as it pleased thee.

15 **So they took up Jonah, and cast him forth into the sea: and the sea ceased from her raging.**

When the storm stops, the men offer thanks to God in several ways, including a sacrifice and making promises to God.

16 Then the men feared the LORD exceedingly, and **offered a sacrifice** unto the LORD, and **made vows**.

Finally, the huge fish swallows Jonah and he has been in its belly for three days.

17 ¶ Now **the LORD had prepared a great fish to swallow up Jonah. And Jonah was in the belly of the fish three days and three nights.**

There is Atonement symbolism in verse 17, above. Just as Jonah was in the belly of the fish for three days and nights, so also was the Savior in the tomb for three days and three nights and then resurrected.

JONAH 2

Selection: all verses

Chapter 2 is the prayer that a very repentant Jonah offers during the time he is inside of the big fish. It can be symbolic of our prayers during times of extremity when we find that Heavenly Father is the only one who can help us out of our dire circumstances, including, sometimes, our sins.

1 **THEN Jonah prayed unto the LORD** his God out of the fish's belly,

2 And said, **I cried by reason of mine affliction unto the LORD, and he heard me**; out of the belly

of hell cried I, *and* thou heardest my voice.

3 For **thou hadst cast me into the deep**, in the midst of the seas; and the floods compassed me about: all thy billows and thy waves passed over me.

4 **Then I said, I am cast out of thy sight** [*I am taking the consequences of running from Thee*]; **yet I will look again toward thy holy temple** [*I will turn around toward Jerusalem and come back to Thee*].

Verses, 5–9, next, continue to describe Jonah's thoughts during his time inside the fish. It can be symbolic of our thoughts as we determine to repent.

5 The waters compassed me about, *even* to the soul: **the depth** [*symbolic of spiritual darkness*] **closed me round about**, the weeds were wrapped about my head.

6 **I went down to the bottoms of the mountains** [*can be symbolic of the depths of despair—see Alma 36:11–18*]; the earth with her bars *was* about me for ever: **yet hast thou brought up my life from corruption, O LORD my God** [*yet, Thou hast redeemed me*].

7 **When my soul fainted within me I remembered the LORD**: and my prayer came in unto thee, into thine holy temple.

8 **They that observe lying vanities forsake their own mercy** [*those who cling to their sins miss out on the*

mercy *that is available through the Atonement*].

9 **But I will sacrifice unto thee with the voice of thanksgiving**; I will pay *that* that I have vowed. Salvation *is* of the LORD.

10 ¶ **And the LORD spake unto the fish, and it vomited out Jonah upon the dry *land.***

JONAH 3

Selection: all verses

In this chapter, Jonah gets a second chance. He goes to Nineveh. He preaches, and, surprisingly, the people repent. By the way, Nineveh was a huge city for that day, with about sixty miles of walls required to go all the way around it. The walls were wide enough on top for two chariots to drive side by side along it.

1 AND **the word of the LORD came unto Jonah the second time, saying,**

2 **Arise, go unto Nineveh**, that great city, **and preach unto it** the preaching **that I bid thee** [*saying what I inspire you to say*].

3 **So Jonah arose, and went unto Nineveh**, according to the word of the LORD. Now Nineveh was an exceeding great city of three days' journey.

4 And **Jonah began to enter into the city a day's journey** [*was a day's journey into the city*], **and he cried** [*preached*], and said, **Yet forty days,**

and **Nineveh shall be overthrown** [*you have forty days until your city is destroyed (because of your wickedness)*].

Next, the people repent!

5 ¶ So **the people of Nineveh believed God**, and **proclaimed a fast**, and **put on sackcloth** [*course burlap-type fabric, symbolic of mourning for their sins*], **from the greatest of them even to the least of them** [*all of them*].

6 For **word came unto the king of Nineveh, and he arose from his throne, and he laid his robe from him, and covered *him* with sackcloth, and sat in ashes** [*symbolic of mourning in that culture, including mourning for sins*].

The king commands everyone to repent in sackcloth and ashes and to fast, even their animals, to ask the Lord for forgiveness.

7 And he caused *it* to be proclaimed and published through Nineveh **by the decree of the king and his nobles**, saying, **Let neither man nor beast, herd nor flock, taste any thing: let them not feed, nor drink water:**

8 But **let man and beast be covered with sackcloth, and cry mightily unto God**: yea, **let them turn every one from his evil way, and from the violence that *is* in their hands.**

9 **Who can tell *if* God will** turn and repent, and **turn away from his fierce anger, that we perish not?**

JST Jonah 3:9

9 Who can tell, **if we will repent**, and turn unto God, but he will turn away from us his fierce anger, that we perish not?

10 ¶ **And God saw their works, that they turned from their evil way**; and God repented of the evil, that he had said that he would do unto them; **and he did *it* not** [*did not destroy them*].

JST Jonah 3:10

10 And God saw their works that they turned from their evil way and repented; and **God turned away the evil that he had said he would bring upon them.**

JONAH 4

Selection: all verses

Chapter 4 is a bit disheartening, because Jonah is angry when the city repents and is not destroyed. He feels that now nobody will believe him because his prophecy was not fulfilled. You will see that the Lord chastises him for not being happy that the people repented so Jehovah could extend mercy to them.

1 **BUT it** [*the fact that Nineveh was not destroyed*] **displeased Jonah exceedingly, and he was very angry.**

2 And **he prayed unto the LORD**, and said, I pray thee, O LORD, *was* **not this my saying, when I was yet in my country?** [*this is what I was afraid of when the call was first issued to me*] **Therefore** [*this is why*] **I fled**

before unto Tarshish: for **I knew that thou** *art* **a gracious God, and merciful, slow to anger, and of great kindness, and repentest thee of the evil** [*this is why I fled toward Tarshish in the first place, because I was afraid if I prophesied destruction for Nineveh, You wouldn't do it*].

3 **Therefore** now, O LORD, **take, I beseech thee, my life from me**; for *it is* better for me to die than to live [*I can't bear to face these people (or those at home)*].

Next, the Lord calls Jonah to repentance for being angry and self-centered rather than rejoicing in the saving of souls. A major lesson here is that God loves all His children.

4 ¶ **Then said the LORD, Doest thou well to be angry?**

5 So **Jonah went out of the city, and sat on the east side of the city,** and there made him a booth [*a small shelter*], **and sat under it in the shadow, till he might see what would become of the city** [*to still see what might happen*].

6 And **the LORD God prepared a gourd, and made** *it* **to come up over Jonah, that it might be a shadow over his head,** to deliver him from his grief [*to make him happy*]. So **Jonah was exceeding glad of the gourd**.

7 **But God prepared a worm when the morning rose the next day, and it smote the gourd that it withered.**

8 And it came to pass, **when the sun did arise, that God prepared a vehement** [*strong*] **east wind**; and **the sun beat upon the head of Jonah, that he fainted, and wished in himself to die**, and said, *It is* better for me to die than to live.

In verses 9–11, next, the Lord teaches His wayward prophet a lesson. It is a reminder that the Savior is patient and merciful, even when we know better and slip up. Jonah is a bit stubborn about being taught a lesson.

9 And **God said to Jonah, Doest thou well to be angry for the gourd?** And he said, **I do well to be angry,** *even* **unto death** [*yes, I will stay angry, even if it kills me*].

10 **Then said the LORD, Thou hast had pity on the gourd**, for the which thou hast not laboured, neither madest it grow; which came up in a night, and perished in a night:

11 **And should not I spare Nineveh, that great city, wherein are more than sixscore thousand** [*120,000*] **persons that cannot discern between their right hand and their left hand** [*who don't yet really understand the gospel; in other words, have not yet been spiritually reborn—see Jonah 4:11 footnote c*]; and *also* much cattle?

MICAH

Micah was another prophet who served in Isaiah's day (740–701 BC). He was a native of Moresheth Gath in the lower plain country of Judah. Among other things, he prophesied the downfall of the nation of Judah. He also gave many prophecies about the mission of Israel in the last days. It appears that he served somewhere around 725 BC.

It is insightful to note that the Savior quoted Micah several times. Some of his major themes and messages concern the gathering of Israel, the covenant people of the Lord, and their role and mission in the last days.

MICAH 1

Selection: all verses

In this chapter, Micah prophesies the downfall of both Samaria (the northern ten tribes with headquarters in Samaria—the Assyrians will conquer them and carry them away about 722–721 BC) and Judah (with headquarters in Jerusalem—the Babylonians will conquer them and carry them away to Babylon in several waves, beginning in 605 BC and ending in 587 BC). You will also see some references to the burning at the time of the Second Coming.

1 THE word of the LORD that came to Micah the Morasthite in the days of Jotham, Ahaz, *and* Hezekiah, kings of Judah, which he saw concerning Samaria and Jerusalem.

2 Hear, all ye people; hearken, O earth, and all that therein is: and let the Lord GOD be witness against you [*because of your wickedness*], the Lord from his holy temple [*heaven*].

3 For, behold, the LORD cometh forth out of his place, and will come down, and tread upon the high places [*see verse 5*] of the earth [*punish you for your wickedness; also a reference to the burning of the wicked at the Second Coming*].

4 And the mountains shall be molten under him [*a reference to the Second Coming—see D&C 101:23–25*], and the valleys shall be cleft, as wax before the fire, *and* as the waters *that are* poured down a steep place.

Next, Micah gives reasons for the destruction for these covenant people of the Lord.

5 For the transgression of Jacob [*Israel*] *is* all this, and for the sins of the house of Israel. What *is* the transgression of Jacob? *is it* not Samaria? and what *are* the high places of Judah? *are they* not Jerusalem?

6 Therefore I will make Samaria as an heap of the field, *and* as plantings of a vineyard: and I will pour down the stone [*stones for altars for idol worship*] thereof into the valley, and I will discover [*lay bare—see footnote 6b in your Bible*] the foundations thereof.

7 And **all the graven images** [*idols used in idol worship*] **thereof shall be beaten to pieces**, and **all the hires** [*the equipment used for idolatry*] thereof **shall be burned** with the fire, and **all the idols thereof will I lay desolate**: for she gathered *it* of the hire of an harlot, and they shall return to the hire of an harlot. [*"Harlot" is symbolic of Israel and Judah, who have left their covenant "marriage" with Jehovah and stepped out with other gods, idols, and so on.*]

In verses 8–16, we see the mourning of Israel and Judah when the punishments of God finally catch up to them.

8 Therefore **I will wail and howl**, I will go **stripped and naked** [*stripped of pride*]: I will make a wailing like the dragons [*hyenas*], and mourning as the owls.

9 For **her wound** *is* **incurable** [*it is too late for Israel to repent*]; for **it is come unto Judah** [*Israel's sins have spread to Judah*]; he is come unto the gate of my people, *even* to Jerusalem.

Each of the cities mentioned in verses 10–16 will meet a similar fate—see footnote 10b in your Bible.

10 ¶ Declare ye *it* not at Gath, weep ye not at all: in the house of Aphrah roll thyself in the dust.

11 Pass ye away, thou inhabitant of Saphir, having thy shame naked [*having had your wickedness exposed*]: the inhabitant of Zaanan came not forth in the mourning of Beth-ezel; he shall receive of you his standing.

12 For the inhabitant of Maroth waited carefully for good: **but evil came down from the LORD unto the gate of Jerusalem**.

13 O thou inhabitant of Lachish, bind the chariot to the swift beast: she *is* the beginning of the sin to the daughter of Zion: for **the transgressions of Israel were found in thee**.

14 Therefore shalt thou give presents to Moresheth-gath: the houses of Achzib *shall be* a lie to the kings of Israel.

15 **Yet will I bring an heir** [*NIV, "a conquerer"*] unto thee, O inhabitant of Mareshah: he shall come unto Adullam the glory of Israel.

It helps to understand verse 16, next, if you know that "baldness" symbolizes slavery in this culture. When enemies conquered a people, those whom they made slaves were shaved bald to identify them as slaves as well as to humiliate them and keep them more sanitary.

16 **Make thee bald** [*prepare to be made slaves*], and **poll thee** [*shave your heads*] for thy delicate children; **enlarge thy baldness** as the eagle [*make yourselves bald like the eagle, or vulture*]; for **they are gone into captivity** from thee.

MICAH 2

Selection: all verses

This chapter deals with the last days' gathering of Israel, of which we are a part. But first, in verses 1–11, Micah prophesies against the wicked who constantly devise ways to cheat others, especially the poor, in order to make themselves richer and acquire more wealth.

1 **WOE to them that devise iniquity, and work evil upon their beds** [*stay awake most of the night thinking up new ways to cheat others*]! **when the morning is light, they practise it** [*put their evil schemes into practice*], because it is in the power of their hand.

2 And **they covet fields, and take** *them* **by violence; and houses, and take** *them* **away**: so they oppress a man and his house, even a man and his heritage.

3 **Therefore thus saith the LORD; Behold, against this family** [*people who cheat others*] **do I devise an evil**, from which ye shall not remove your necks [*you won't get out of being punished*]; neither shall ye go haughtily: for this time *is* evil.

In verse 4, next, Micah pointedly lodges a complaint against those who cheat the poor out of their property and homes and lands.

4 ¶ **In that day shall** *one* **take up a parable** [*register a formal complaint*] **against you**, and lament with a doleful lamentation, *and* say, We be utterly spoiled [*you have ruined us (the poor)*]: he hath changed the portion of my people: **how hath he removed** *it* **from me!** turning away **he hath divided our fields** [*such cheats take our land fraudulently and then divide it and sell each piece to make even more profit*].

5 Therefore thou shalt have none that shall cast a cord by lot in the congregation of the LORD [*you will not get blessings from the Lord*].

Next, the wealthy who are making money by oppressing the poor strongly ask Micah and other prophets such as Isaiah, Hosea, and Amos to stop prophesying against them. This tactic caused Micah to prophesy even stronger against them.

6 **Prophesy ye not**, *say they to them that* **prophesy: they shall not prophesy** to them, *that* they shall not take shame [*don't try to embarrass us any more in public*].

7 ¶ **O** *thou that art* **named** the house of Jacob [*you are the guilty ones in Israel who are being called out for your wickedness*], is the spirit of the LORD straitened? *are* these his doings? **do not my words do good to him that walketh uprightly** [*do the righteous take offense at my words*]?

8 **Even of late my people is risen up as an enemy** [*the wicked of Israel are turning up everywhere*]: **ye pull off the robe with the garment** [*you are taking the shirt from the backs of the*

poor] from them that pass by securely as men averse from war.

9 **The women of my people have ye cast out from their pleasant houses; from their children have ye taken away my glory for ever** [*you are ruining the chances for prosperity among the children of the poor Israel*].

10 Arise ye, and depart; for this *is* not *your* rest: because it is polluted, **it shall destroy *you*,** even with a sore destruction.

In next, Micah says, in effect, that these wicked Israelites gladly accept false prophets.

11 **If a man** [*a false prophet*] **walking in the spirit and falsehood do lie,** *saying,* **I will prophesy unto thee** of wine and of strong drink; **he shall even be the prophet of this people**.

In verses 12–13, next, Micah prophesies of the future gathering of Israel.

12 ¶ **I will surely assemble** [*gather*], O **Jacob** [*another name for Israel*], **all of thee; I will surely gather the remnant of Israel**; I will put [*gather*] them together [*bring them into the fold*] as the sheep of Bozrah [*a city southeast of the Dead Sea, famous for its large flocks of sheep*], as the flock in the midst of their fold: **they shall make great noise by reason of *the multitude of* men** [*there will be large numbers of Israel gathered in the last days; the Church will grow rapidly and flourish*].

13 The breaker [*one who breaks open the way for others, leads them*] is come up before them: they have broken up, and have passed through the gate, and are gone out by it: **and their king** [*Christ*] **shall pass before them** [*will go in front of them*], and **the LORD on the head of them** [*they will follow the Lord*].

MICAH 3

Selection: all verses

Here in chapter 3, you will see Micah return to prophesying against the wicked leaders and false prophets of Israel who are causing so much wickedness among the people.

1 AND I said, **Hear,** I pray you, **O heads of Jacob, and ye princes** [*leaders*] **of the house of Israel;** *Is it* **not for you to know judgment** [*how long do you think you can get away with leading the people astray*]?

In verses 2–3, Micah compares these leaders to cannibals who eat their own people.

2 **Who hate the good, and love the evil**; who pluck off their skin from off them, and their flesh from off their bones;

3 **Who also eat the flesh of my people, and flay their skin from off them; and they break their bones, and chop them in pieces, as for the pot, and as flesh within the caldron.**

4 Then shall they cry unto the LORD, but he will not hear them: he will even hide his face from them at that time, as they have behaved themselves ill in their doings.

5 ¶ Thus saith the LORD concerning the prophets [false prophets] that make my people err, that bite with their teeth, and cry, Peace; and he that putteth not into their mouths [whoever won't donate to them], they even prepare war against him.

6 Therefore night *shall be* unto you [you will continue to live in spiritual darkness], that ye shall not have a vision; and it shall be dark unto you, that ye shall not divine; and the sun shall go down over the prophets, and the day shall be dark over them.

7 Then shall the seers be ashamed, and the diviners confounded: yea, they shall all cover their lips; for *there is* no answer of God [God does not work through false prophets and fortune tellers].

Next, Micah exclaims that he is a true prophet.

8 ¶ But truly I am full of power by the spirit of the LORD, and of judgment, and of might, to declare unto Jacob his transgression, and to Israel his sin.

Micah speaks again against the wicked leaders and false prophets.

9 Hear this, I pray you, ye heads of the house of Jacob, and princes of the house of Israel, that abhor judgment [fairness and righteousness], and pervert all equity.

10 They build up Zion with blood, and Jerusalem with iniquity.

11 The heads thereof judge for reward [take bribes], and the priests thereof teach for hire [teach what people want to hear so the people give them more money (in other words, priestcraft—2 Nephi 26:29)], and the prophets thereof divine for money: yet will they lean upon the LORD, and say, *Is* not the LORD among us? none evil can come upon us [they will claim that the Lord is with them and thus, they are teaching true religion].

12 Therefore shall Zion for your sake [because of what you are doing] be plowed *as* a field, and Jerusalem shall become heaps [piles of rubble], and the mountain of the house as the high places of the forest [this is why Israel and Judah are going to be destroyed].

MICAH 4

Selection: all verses

This contains a marvelous prophecy of the gathering of the Lord's covenant people to the top of the mountains in the last days. It is both symbolic and literal. In it, Micah prophesies that temples will be built in the last days, and Israel will be gathered to them. He speaks of the Millennium and that the Savior will strengthen His church and people.

1 But **in the last days** it shall come to pass, *that* **the mountain of the house of the LORD** [*the restored Church, the temple*] **shall be established in the top of the mountains** [*one meaning of this is in the Rocky Mountains (especially Salt Lake City)— compare with Isaiah 2:2*], and it shall be exalted above the hills; **and people shall flow unto it.**

2 **And many nations shall come** [*many converts from many nations will come into the Church*], **and say, Come, and let us go up to the mountain of the LORD** [*let us look to the living prophets at Church headquarters*], **and to the house of the God of Jacob** [*and let us learn in the temples of God*]; and **he will teach us of his ways** [*the Savior will reveal much to us and teach us much*], **and we will walk in his paths** [*we will keep the commandments*]: for the **law shall go forth of Zion, and the word of the LORD from Jerusalem** [*"law" and "word of the Lord" are synonyms; in other words, there will be two headquarters of the Church during the Millennium; Zion, in Jackson County, Missouri—the New Jerusalem, and Old Jerusalem—see Ether 13:3–5; compare with Isaiah 2:3—from which people will be taught the gospel*].

3 ¶ **And he** [*Christ*] **shall judge among many people, and rebuke strong nations afar off** [*the wicked will be destroyed at the Second Coming, thus paving the way for peace*]; **and they shall beat their swords into plowshares, and their spears into pruninghooks** [*there will be peace during the Millennium*]: **nation shall not lift up a sword against nation, neither shall they learn war any more.**

4 But they shall sit every man under his vine and under his fig tree; and **none shall make** *them* **afraid** [*there will be peace during the Millennium*] for the mouth of the LORD of hosts hath spoken *it* [*the Lord has prophesied this and it will happen*].

5 For all people will walk every one in the name of his god, and **we will walk in the name of the LORD our God** for ever and ever.

6 In that day, saith the LORD, will I assemble her that halteth, and I will gather her that is driven out, and her that I have afflicted [*Israel will be gathered again*];

7 **And I will make her that halted** [*was lame; perhaps symbolizing one who is spiritually lame, unable to move ahead on the strait and narrow path—1 Nephi 8:20*] **a remnant** [*a part of covenant Israel*], **and her that was cast far off** [*Israel, who was rejected because of apostasy*] **a strong nation:** and **the LORD shall reign over them** in mount Zion [*usually refers to Jerusalem—1 Kings 8:1*] from henceforth, even **for ever.**

Verses 8–10 contain a prophecy that the Jews and Jerusalem will be conquered and taken away to Babylon. We have a strong example and testimony here of the fact that God does have true prophets. At the time

Micah gave this prophecy, Babylon was merely a somewhat weak province of the mighty nation of Assyria. (So it was an unlikely prophecy.) But Micah was a true prophet of the living God, and about 130 years later, after Babylon had emerged as a powerful nation, they indeed conquered Jerusalem.

8 ¶ And thou, O tower of the flock, the strong hold of the daughter of Zion [*Jerusalem; also, the people of the Lord*], **unto thee shall it come**, even the first dominion; the kingdom shall come to the daughter of Jerusalem.

9 Now why dost thou cry out aloud? *is there* **no king in thee?** is thy counsellor perished? for **pangs have taken thee as a woman in travail** [*you can't stop the coming destruction any more than a woman in hard labor can stop it*].

10 Be in pain, and labour to bring forth, O daughter of Zion, like a woman in travail: for now shalt thou go forth out of the city, and thou shalt dwell in the field [*a foreign country*], and **thou shalt go** *even* **to Babylon**; there shalt thou be delivered; **there the LORD shall redeem thee from the hand of thine enemies** [*the Lord will eventually free you from Babylonian exile*].

Verses 11–13 prophesy of the gathering of Israel in the last days.

11 ¶ Now also **many nations are gathered against thee** [*Israel*], that say, Let her be defiled, and let our eye look upon Zion.

12 **But they know not the thoughts of the LORD, neither understand they his counsel** [*plans*]: for **he shall gather them** as the sheaves into the floor [*in the last days, the Lord will gather Israel to the Church like farmers gather the harvest of grain to their barns*].

13 **Arise and thresh** [*win the battle against your enemies, spiritually and physically*], **O daughter of Zion** [*people of the Lord*]: for I will make thine horn iron, and I will make thy hoofs brass: and **thou shalt beat in pieces many people** [*righteous Israel will finally triumph over all her enemies*]: and **I will consecrate their gain unto the LORD**, and their substance unto the Lord of the whole earth.

MICAH 5

Selection: all verses

This chapter contains a prophecy that Christ will be born in Bethlehem. It also deals with the great spreading of the gospel in the last days and the fact that the Church, which was once severely persecuted, will become strong and a powerful influence for good throughout the earth.

1 **NOW gather thyself in troops, O daughter of troops** [*the day will come that Israel will be gathered in large numbers*]: he [*enemies of righteousness*] hath laid siege against us: **they shall smite the judge of Israel** [*Christ*] with a rod **upon the cheek.**

2 But **thou, Beth-lehem** Ephratah, *though* thou be little among the thousands of Judah, *yet* **out of thee shall he** [*Jesus Christ*] **come forth unto me** *that is* **to be ruler in Israel;** whose goings forth *have been* from of old, from everlasting [*Jesus Christ will be born in Bethlehem*].

3 **Therefore will he give them up** [*the Lord will reject Israel for a time because of apostasy*], **until the time** *that* **she which travaileth hath brought forth** [*until the restoration of the gospel in the last days—see JST Revelation 12:7*]: **then the remnant of his brethren shall return unto the children of Israel**.

4 ¶ **And he** [*Israel*] **shall stand and feed in the strength of the LORD, in the majesty of the name of the LORD his God; and they shall abide: for now shall he be great unto the ends of the earth** [*the Church will spread throughout the earth*].

> In verses 5–11, next, Micah prophesies that the Lord will strengthen and protect Israel in the last days. This can literally be the nation of Israel and also that no one will stop the gathering of Israel out of all nations.

5 And this *man* shall be the peace, **when the Assyrian shall come into our land**: and when he shall tread in our palaces, **then shall we raise against him** seven shepherds, and eight principal men.

6 And they shall waste the land of Assyria with the sword, and the land of Nimrod in the entrances thereof:

thus shall he deliver *us* **from the Assyrian, when he cometh into our land, and when he treadeth within our borders**.

7 **And the remnant of Jacob** [*the members of the Church in the last days*] **shall be in the midst of many people as a dew from the LORD, as the showers upon the grass** [*will be as dew and refreshing rain among the spiritually parched inhabitants of the earth*], that tarrieth not for man, nor waiteth for the sons of men.

8 ¶ And **the remnant of Jacob shall be among the Gentiles in the midst of many people as a lion among the beasts of the forest** [*the members of the Church will become a strong influence throughout the earth*], as a young lion among the flocks of sheep: who, if he go through, both treadeth down, and teareth in pieces, and **none can deliver** [*none will stop the growth of the Church after it is restored in the last days*].

9 **Thine hand shall be lifted up upon thine adversaries, and all thine enemies shall be cut off.**

10 And it shall come to pass in that day, saith the LORD, that **I will cut off thy horses** out of the midst of thee, **and I will destroy thy chariots** [*"horses" and "chariots" are symbolic of armies and military might in biblical symbolism*]:

11 And **I will cut off the cities of thy land, and throw down all thy strong holds:**

Verses 12–14 prophesy, among other things, that as Israel is gathered in to the Church in the last days, as they are converted and baptized into the Church, they will turn away from their involvement with the occult, fortune tellers, idol worship, and so forth, as the gift of the Holy Ghost purges these sins out of them and they become new people, "born again."

12 And **I will cut off witchcrafts** out of thine hand [*out of your belief systems and practices*]; and **thou shalt have no** *more* **soothsayers** [*fortune tellers, astrology, etc.*]:

13 **Thy graven images** [*idols*] **also will I cut off, and thy standing images out of the midst of thee**; and **thou shalt no more worship the work of thine hands** [*idols that you have made with your own hands*].

14 And **I will pluck up thy groves** [*shrines with groves of trees, set up for idol worship*] out of the midst of thee: so will I destroy thy cities.

15 And **I will execute vengeance in anger and fury upon the heathen** [*wicked nations and people*], such as they have not heard.

MICAH 6

Selection: all verses

In effect, this chapter starts out by inviting the people to debate with the Lord, to "contend" with Him. The issue is this: after all the blessings He has given you and all the good He has done for you,

why are you not keeping His commandments? Why are you going through empty rituals and rites of the law of Moses but have not internalized the gospel? Why are you "outward Saints" but "inward sinners and hypocrites?" Verses 6–8 summarize this great concern the Lord has about His people, Israel. These verses provide one of the clearest views of what kind of sacrifice the Lord desires from his people, the kind that will do them the most good.

1 **HEAR ye now what the LORD saith; Arise, contend thou** before the mountains, and let the hills hear thy voice.

2 **Hear ye**, O mountains, **the LORD's controversy** [*what the Lord has against you*], and ye strong foundations of the earth: for **the LORD hath a controversy with his people, and he will plead** [*debate, as in a court of law*] **with Israel.**

3 **O my people, what have I done unto thee** [*where did I go wrong*]**? and wherein have I wearied thee? testify against me.**

4 **For I brought thee up out of the land of Egypt, and redeemed thee out of the house of servants; and I sent before thee Moses, Aaron, and Miriam** [*look at everything I have done for you*].

5 O my people, **remember now what Balak king of Moab consulted, and what Balaam** the son of Beor answered him from Shittim unto Gilgal [*Numbers 22–24; remember the story of Balaam and his talking*

donkey]; that ye may know the righteousness of the LORD.

6 ¶ **Wherewith shall** [*what kind of offering shall I bring when*] **I come before the LORD**, *and* bow myself before the high God? **shall I come before him with burnt offerings, with calves of a year old?**

7 **Will the LORD be pleased with thousands of rams,** *or* **with ten thousands of rivers of oil?** shall I give **my firstborn** *for* my transgression, the fruit of my body *for* the sin of my soul?

8 He hath shewed thee, O man, what *is* good; and **what doth the LORD require of thee**, but to **do justly**, and to **love mercy, and** to **walk humbly with thy God**?

Verses 9–16 are another review of Israel's wickedness and sins, the things they are doing wrong, such that the Lord invites them to debate with Him, above.

9 **The LORD's voice crieth unto the city** [*Israel*], and *the man of* wisdom shall see thy name: **hear ye the rod** [*the "Ruler," Christ*], and who hath appointed it.

10 ¶ **Are there yet the treasures of wickedness in the house of the wicked** [*the wicked in Israel are causing much sin and violence*], and **the scant measure** [*the wicked are using weighted scales to cheat people they sell to*] *that is* abominable?

11 **Shall I count** *them* **pure with the wicked balances, and with the bag of deceitful weights** [*can I consider them righteous when they are not*]?

12 For **the rich men thereof are full of violence, and the inhabitants thereof have spoken lies, and their tongue** *is* **deceitful in their mouth.**

13 **Therefore also will I make** *thee* sick in smiting thee, in making *thee* **desolate because of thy sins.**

14 **Thou shalt eat, but not be satisfied**; and thy casting down *shall be* in the midst of thee; and **thou shalt take hold, but shalt not deliver**; and *that* which thou deliverest will I give up to the sword [*your possessions will be taken away from you by enemies*].

15 **Thou shalt sow** [*plant crops*], **but thou shalt not reap** [*harvest*]; thou shalt tread the olives, but thou shalt not anoint thee with oil; and sweet wine, but shalt not drink wine.

16 ¶ For **the statutes of Omri** [*the corrupt laws of wicked King Ahab's wicked father*] **are kept**, and **all the works of the house of Ahab, and ye walk in their counsels**; that I should make thee a desolation [*you are causing Me to have to destroy you*], **and the inhabitants thereof an hissing** [*the Jews will become objects of scorn throughout all nations*]: **therefore ye shall bear the reproach of my people** [*you, the rich in Israel, are the main cause of the sins of My people*].

MICAH 7

Selection: all verses

In this chapter, Micah continues to describe Israel's wickedness as the cause of coming punishments and destruction. You will no doubt see similarities between his day and our day. You will also see the gathering of Israel in the last days in this chapter. First, in verse 1, he describes famine.

1 WOE is me! for **I am as when they have gathered the summer fruits**, as the grapegleanings of the vintage: *there is* **no cluster to eat** [*basically, after the fall harvest of grapes, there is only one grape to eat*]: my soul desired the firstripe fruit.

2 The good *man* is perished out of the earth: and *there is* **none upright among men: they all lie in wait for blood; they hunt every man his brother with a net** [*a net was sometimes used in hand-to-hand combat to tangle up the opponent*].

3 ¶ That **they** may **do evil with both hands** [*they do evil right and left*] earnestly, **the prince asketh, and the judge** *asketh* **for a reward** [*bribe*]; and the great *man,* he uttereth his mischievous desire: so they wrap it up.

4 **The best of them** *is* **as a brier** [*useless, does only damage to others*]: the most upright *is sharper* than a thorn hedge: **the day of thy watchmen** *and* **thy visitation cometh** [*the day of your punishment is coming*]; now shall be their perplexity.

5 ¶ **Trust ye not in a friend** [*no one can trust anybody*], **put ye not confidence in a guide**: keep the doors of thy mouth from her that lieth in thy bosom.

6 For **the son dishonoureth the father**, the **daughter riseth up against her mother, the daughter in law against her mother in law**; **a man's enemies** *are* **the men of his own house**.

> In verses 7–20, Micah looks forward to the future day when Israel will turn to the Lord.

7 **Therefore I will look unto the LORD; I will wait for the God of my salvation**: my God will hear me.

8 ¶ Rejoice not against me, O mine enemy: **when I fall, I shall arise; when I sit in darkness, the LORD** *shall be* **a light unto me**.

9 I will bear the indignation of the LORD, because I have sinned against him, until he plead my cause, and execute judgment for me [*Israel will have to bear their punishment and face the law of justice*]: **he will bring me forth to the light,** *and* **I shall behold his righteousness** [*eventually, Israel will repent and come to Christ*].

10 **Then** *she that is* **mine enemy shall see** *it,* **and shame shall cover her** which said unto me, Where is the LORD thy God? mine eyes shall behold her: **now shall she be trodden down as the mire of the streets** [*the enemies of Israel will eventually be caught up with*].

Verses 11–12 specifically prophesy of the last days' gathering and restoration of Israel.

11 *In* the day that thy walls are to be built [*Israel's cities will be rebuilt*], *in* that day shall the decree be far removed [*the "decree" to gather Israel will extend to all the world*].

12 *In* that day [*the last days*] *also* he shall come even to thee from Assyria, and *from* the fortified cities, and from the fortress even to the river, and from sea to sea, and *from* mountain to mountain [*Israel will be gathered out of the whole world*].

13 Notwithstanding the land shall be desolate because of them that dwell therein, for the fruit of their doings [*even though, in times past, Israel was much conquered and destroyed because of her wickedness*].

14 ¶ Feed thy people with thy rod, the flock of thine heritage, which dwell solitarily *in* the wood, in the midst of Carmel: let them feed *in* Bashan and Gilead, as in the days of old.

15 According to [*just like in*] the days of thy coming out of the land of Egypt will I shew unto him marvellous *things* [*the Lord will do great miracles in gathering Israel*].

16 ¶ The nations shall see and be confounded at all their might [*people will be amazed at the gathering of Israel*]: they shall lay *their* hand upon *their* mouth [*in astonishment*], their ears shall be deaf.

17 They shall lick the dust like a serpent, they shall move out of their holes like worms of the earth: they shall be afraid of the LORD our God, and shall fear because of thee [*the wicked will not be able to stop the last-days' gathering of Israel*].

18 Who *is* a God like unto thee [*who can compare to Jehovah, Jesus Christ*], that pardoneth iniquity, and passeth by [*forgives*] the transgression of the remnant of his heritage [*in other words, Israel; those who wish to become His covenant people*]? he retaineth not his anger for ever, because he delighteth *in* mercy.

19 He will turn again [*He will turn toward us, with outstretched arms, welcoming us back*], he will have compassion upon us; he will subdue our iniquities [*He will pay the price of our sins—compare with 2 Nephi 9:21*]; and thou wilt cast all their sins into the depths of the sea.

20 Thou wilt perform the truth [*keep the covenant made*] to Jacob, *and* the mercy to Abraham, which thou hast sworn [*promised, covenanted*] unto our fathers [*ancestors*] from the days of old [*from the beginning*].

NAHUM

Based on clues within Nahum's prophecies, it appears that he served as a prophet somewhere between 663 BC and 612 BC. His prophecies were directed mainly at Nineveh, the capital city of Assyria. Perhaps you remember that Jonah was called to preach repentance to the people of Nineveh, and they repented. By Nahum's time, they had fallen back into extreme wickedness and, thus, needed to be called to repentance again. This in itself is a reminder to us that Heavenly Father loves all His children and is willing to call prophets to give them a chance to return to Him. We are reminded that we are greatly loved and blessed to have living prophets in our day.

NAHUM 1

Selection: all verses

In this chapter we are reminded of the Lord's matchless power, His anger at wickedness, and His matchless mercy and willingness to forgive. Nahum also prophesies the Second Coming. You will see that he shifts back and forth, sometimes in the same verse, between the anger of the Lord and His mercy.

1 **THE burden of** [*message of doom to*] **Nineveh. The book of the vision of Nahum** the Elkoshite.

2 **God** *is* **jealous, and the LORD revengeth; the LORD revengeth, and** *is* **furious**; the LORD will take vengeance on his adversaries, and he reserveth *wrath* for his enemies.

3 **The LORD** *is* **slow to anger**, and great in power, and **will not at all acquit** *the wicked* [*will not let the wicked get away*]: the LORD *hath* his way in the whirlwind and in the storm, and the clouds *are* the dust of his feet.

4 **He rebuketh the sea, and maketh it dry, and drieth up all the rivers**: Bashan languisheth, and Carmel, and the flower of Lebanon languisheth.

The power of the Lord is preached next.

5 **The mountains quake at him**, and the hills melt, and **the earth is burned at his presence, yea, the world, and all that dwell therein** [*a reference to the Second Coming*].

6 **Who can stand before his indignation** [*righteous anger*]? and **who can abide** [*survive*] **in the fierceness of his anger?** his fury is poured out like fire, and the rocks are thrown down by him.

7 **The LORD** *is* **good, a strong hold in the day of trouble; and he knoweth them that trust in him** [*the righteous can rely on Him*].

8 But with an overrunning flood **he will make an utter end of the place**[*the wicked (like Niniveh)*] thereof, and darkness shall pursue his enemies.

9 What do ye imagine against the LORD? **he will make an utter end: affliction shall not rise up the second time**.

10 For while *they be* folden together *as* thorns, and while they are drunken *as* drunkards, **they shall be devoured as stubble fully dry**.

11 There is *one* [*possibly the king of Nineveh*] come out of thee, that imagineth evil against the LORD, a wicked counsellor.

12 Thus saith the LORD: Though *they be* quiet, and likewise many, yet **thus shall they be cut down**, when he shall pass through. Though I have afflicted thee, I will afflict thee no more.

13 For **now will I break his yoke from off thee**, and will burst thy bonds in sunder.

14 And the LORD hath given a commandment concerning thee, *that* **no more of thy name be sown** [*your line of posterity will be cut off*]: out of the house of thy gods will I cut off the graven image and the molten image: **I will make thy grave**; for thou art vile.

15 **Behold upon the mountains the feet of him** [*the Savior at the Second Coming; can also refer to prophets and missionaries*] **that bringeth good tidings, that publisheth peace! O Judah, keep thy solemn feasts, perform thy vows: for the wicked shall no more pass through thee**; he is utterly cut off.

NAHUM 2

Selection: all verses

In this chapter, Nahum prophesies the destruction of Nineveh. Nineveh is a "type" of the destruction of the wicked in the last days and, finally, at the Second Coming of Christ. A "type" is something that symbolizes something else.

1 **HE** [*Nineveh's enemies*] **that dasheth in pieces is come up before thy** [*dual: Nineveh and the wicked at the Second Coming*] **face**: keep the munition, watch the way, make *thy* loins strong, fortify *thy* power mightily [*you won't be able to get away from the coming destruction*].

> Next, just as the Lord destroyed Israel because of wickedness, Nineveh will also be destroyed.

2 For **the LORD hath turned away** the excellency of Jacob [*Israel*], as the excellency of **Israel**: for **the emptiers** [*enemies*] **have emptied them out**, and marred their vine branches.

3 **The shield of his mighty men is made re**d [*with blood*], the valiant men *are* in scarlet: the chariots *shall be* with flaming torches in the day of his preparation, and **the fir trees** [*people*] **shall be terribly shaken**.

4 **The chariots** [*enemy armies*] **shall rage in the streets**, they shall justle one against another in the broad ways: they shall seem like torches, they shall run like the lightnings.

5 He shall recount **his worthies** [*nobles, leaders*]: they **shall stumble**

in their walk; they shall make haste to the wall thereof, and the defence shall be prepared.

6 **The gates** of the rivers **shall be opened** [*enemies will enter the city*], and **the palace shall be dissolved**.

7 **And Huzzab** [*the queen*] **shall be led away captive**, she shall be brought up, and her maids shall lead *her* as with the voice of doves [*mourning*], tabering [*beating*] upon their breasts.

8 But **Nineveh** *is* **of old like a pool of water: yet they shall flee away** [*they shall be taken away*]. Stand, stand, *shall they cry;* but none shall look back.

9 **Take ye** [*the enemies of Nineveh*] **the spoil** of silver, take the spoil of gold: for *there is* none end of the store *and* glory out of all the pleasant furniture.

10 **She** [*Nineveh*] **is empty, and void, and waste**: and the heart melteth, and the knees smite together, and much pain *is* in all loins, and the faces of them all gather blackness [*their faces are all pale*].

Next, Nahum says, in effect, "Look at Nineveh now."

11 **Where** *is* **the dwelling of the lions, and the feedingplace of the young lions**, where the lion, *even* the old lion, walked, *and* the lion's whelp, and **none made** *them* **afraid**?

12 **The lion did tear in pieces enough for his whelps** [*cubs; in other*

words, before this destruction, the king of Nineveh provided well for his family]*, and strangled for his lionesses, and filled his holes with prey, and his dens with ravin [*torn pieces of meat*].

13 Behold, **I** *am* **against thee, saith the LORD of hosts**, and I will burn her chariots in the smoke, and the sword shall devour thy young lions: and I will cut off thy prey from the earth, and the voice of thy messengers shall no more be heard.

NAHUM 3

Selection: all verses

Having read so many prophecies of gloom and doom to the wicked in these books of the Bible, it will come as no surprise that this chapter continues that theme as Nahum details their sins and abominations that result from their apostasy from the Lord. But don't forget the wonderfully important messages of mercy and forgiveness that also accompany the teachings of these mighty prophets.

1 **WOE to the bloody city** [*Nineveh*]! it *is* all full of lies *and* robbery; the prey departeth not;

Next, we see misuse of military might, pride, killing, murder, sexual immorality, the occult, dishonesty.

2 The noise of a whip, and **the noise of the rattling of the wheels, and of the pransing horses, and of the jumping chariots**.

3 The horseman lifteth up both the bright sword and the glittering

spear: and *there is* a multitude of slain, and a great number of carcases; and *there is* none end of *their* corpses; they stumble upon their corpses:

4 Because of the multitude of the **whoredoms** of the wellfavoured **harlot**, the mistress of **witchcrafts**, that selleth nations through her **whoredoms**, and families through her **witchcrafts**.

5 Behold, **I** *am* **against thee, saith the LORD** of hosts; and **I will discover thy skirts upon thy face** [*I will expose your sins and abominations*], and I will shew the nations thy nakedness, and the kingdoms thy shame.

6 And **I will cast abominable filth upon thee**, and make thee vile, **and will set thee as a gazingstock** [*people will look upon you in horror because of what I do to you*].

7 And it shall come to pass, *that* **all they that look upon thee shall flee from thee**, and say, **Nineveh is laid waste**: who will bemoan her [*who will feel sorry for her*]? whence shall I seek comforters for thee?

8 **Art thou better than populous No** [*densely populated Thebes, in Egypt*], that was situate among the rivers, *that had* the waters round about it, whose rampart *was* the sea, *and* her wall *was* from the sea?

9 **Ethiopia and Egypt** *were* **her strength**, and *it was* infinite; Put and Lubim were thy helpers.

10 **Yet** *was* **she carried away, she went into captivity**: her young children also were dashed in pieces at the top of all the streets: and **they cast lots for her honourable men, and all her great men were bound in chains** [*were made slaves*].

11 **Thou also shalt be drunken** [*out of control with wickedness*]: thou shalt be hid, thou also shalt seek strength because of the enemy.

12 **All thy strong holds** *shall be like* **fig trees with the firstripe figs: if they be shaken, they shall even fall into the mouth of the eater** [*you will be just like fig trees at the peak of your productivity; when you are shaken by your enemies, you will be devoured by them*].

13 Behold, **thy people in the midst of thee** *are* **women** [*weak as far as military defense is concerned*]: the gates of thy land shall be set wide open unto thine enemies: **the fire shall devour thy bars**.

14 Draw thee waters for the siege, fortify thy strong holds: go into clay, and tread the morter, make strong the brickkiln.

15 **There shall the fire devour thee; the sword shall cut thee off**, it shall eat thee up like the cankerworm: make thyself many as the cankerworm, make thyself many as the locusts.

16 **Thou hast multiplied thy merchants above the stars of heaven** [*you have become prosperous in your*

wickedness]: the cankerworm [*locust larvae*] spoileth, and flieth away.

Next, Nahum prophesies that they will be left without leadership.

17 **Thy crowned** *are* as the locusts, and **thy captains** as the great grasshoppers, which camp in the hedges in the cold day, *but* when the sun ariseth they **flee away**, and their place is not known where they *are*.

18 **Thy shepherds slumber, O king of Assyria**: thy nobles shall dwell *in the dust:* **thy people is scattered upon the mountains, and no man gathereth** *them*.

19 *There is* **no healing of thy bruise**; thy wound is grievous: all that hear the bruit of thee shall clap the hands over thee: for **upon whom hath not thy wickedness passed continually** [*is there anyone you have not brutalized*]?

HABAKKUK

Almost all we know about Habakkuk is that he was a prophet who was sent to preach to Judah (the southern kingdom with headquarters in Jerusalem) perhaps somewhere around 600 BC. It is possible that he was one of the "many prophets" (1 Nephi 1:4) sent by the Lord to warn the Jews in Jerusalem and Judah about the impending Babylonian captivity.

HABAKKUK 1

Selection: all verses

Habakkuk asks a question that many people would like to ask but don't dare. In effect, he asks the Lord why the wicked prosper and the righteous always have it rough. We will look at the question and how he poses it to the Lord in chapter 1, and then we'll look at the Lord's answer to him at the beginning of chapter 2. It is basically a question-and-answer session between Habakkuk and the Lord. We will have a bit of fun with it.

Question

2 **O LORD, how long shall I cry** [*pray*], **and thou wilt not hear** [*why don't you hear the prayers of the righteous?*]! *even* **cry out unto thee** *of* **violence, and thou wilt not save** [*you are not doing a very good job of saving the righteous*]!

3 **Why dost thou shew me iniquity, and cause** *me* **to behold grievance** [*why don't you get rid of the wickedness I have to see all the time*]? for **spoiling and violence** *are* **before me** [*are all around me*]: and there are *that* raise up strife and contention [*everyone is always fighting and arguing*].

4 Therefore **the law** *is* **slacked** [*Your laws that say the wicked will be punished are never enforced*], **and judgment doth never go forth** [*I don't like the way You are running things*]:

for **the wicked doth compass about the righteous** [*the righteous are surrounded with the wicked*]; **therefore wrong judgment proceedeth** [*You are making a mistake by ignoring it*].

Answer

5 ¶ **Behold** [*look*] ye [*Habakkuk*] **among the heathen, and regard** [*pay close attention to what you see*], **and wonder marvelously** [*prepare to be surprised*]: for *I* **will work a work in your days,** *which* **ye will not believe,** though it be told *you* [*I will do something that you won't believe, even if I tell you in advance*].

Next, the Lord tells Habakkuk that He is going to use the coming Babylonian army (the Chaldeans) to punish and hammer the wicked in heathen nations as well as in Judah and Jerusalem.

6 For, **lo, I raise up the Chaldeans,** *that* **bitter and hasty nation, which shall march through the breadth of the land,** to possess the dwelling-places *that are* not theirs [*they will occupy Judah*].

7 **They** *are* **terrible and dreadful**: their judgment and their dignity shall proceed of themselves.

8 **Their horses also are swifter than the leopards, and are more fierce than the evening wolves**: and their horsemen shall spread themselves, and their horsemen shall come from far; they shall fly as the eagle *that* hasteth to eat [*eager to gobble up the wicked among you, Habakkuk*].

9 **They shall come all for violence**: their faces shall sup up *as* the east wind [*devastating destruction*], and they shall gather the captivity as the sand.

10 And **they shall scoff at the kings**, and the princes shall be a scorn unto them: **they shall deride every strong hold**; for they shall heap dust, and take it.

11 **Then shall** *his* **mind change, and he shall pass over, and offend,** *imputing* **this his power unto his god** [*the Babylonians will give credit to their false god, Bel, rather than realizing that the Lord has allowed them to do this*].

Next, Habakkuk is not satisfied with the Lord's answer and so he continues with his questions.

Question

12 ¶ *Art* **thou not from everlasting** [*don't You have power to smite them*], O LORD my God, mine Holy One? **we shall not die** [*nobody seems to get zapped anymore*]. O LORD, thou hast ordained them for judgment; and, O mighty God, thou hast established them for correction [*You say they are headed for punishment, but nothing seems to happen to them*].

Next, Habakkuk changes his approach and comes at the Lord from another direction.

13 *Thou art* **of purer eyes than to behold evil** [*You shouldn't have to be watching all this wickedness with Your pure eyes*], **and canst not look on**

iniquity [*You are not supposed to be able to look upon iniquity "with the least degree of allowance"—D&C 1:31*]: wherefore [*so, why*] **lookest thou upon them that deal treacherously** [*the wicked*], **and holdest thy tongue** [*and never command them to be smitten*] when the wicked devoureth *the man that is* more righteous than he [*while the wicked are destroying the righteous; in other words, why do You just keep watching and never take any action*]?

14 **And makest men as the fishes of the sea, as the creeping things,** *that have* **no ruler over them?** [*It appears that we are no more important to You than fish or bugs, with no one to protect us. It is like we don't even have a God.*]

15 They [*the wicked*] take up all of them with the angle, they catch them in their net, and gather them in their drag: therefore they rejoice and are glad [*the wicked prosper in their business pursuits*].

16 **Therefore** [*because they are so successful*] **they sacrifice unto their net, and burn incense unto their drag** [*they worship their fishing equipment*]; **because by them their portion** *is* **fat, and their meat plenteous** [*because their false gods are blessing them bounteously*].

17 **Shall they therefore empty their net, and not spare continually to slay the nations** [*is there any good reason for them to stop plundering and pillaging*]?

HABAKKUK 2

Selection: all verses

Habakkuk is nervous about what he has just said to the Lord in chapter 1, so he stands by to see what the Lord will say when He scolds him. He begins to try to come up with an answer to defend himself.

1 **I will** stand upon my watch, and set me upon the tower, and will **watch to see what he** [*the Lord*] **will say unto me, and what I shall answer when I am reproved** [*chastised*].

Answer

2 **And the LORD answered me, and said, Write the vision, and make** *it* **plain upon tables** [*get this straight and write it down*], that he may run that readeth it [*so that the herald or messenger can take it throughout the city for others to read*].

3 **For the vision** [*the punishment of the wicked*] *is* **yet for an appointed time** [*will take place when I am ready—in other words, "in mine own due time"*], **but at the end it shall speak** [*but it will happen*], and not lie [*not be a false prophecy*]: **though it tarry** [*even if it takes longer than you think for the wicked to be punished*], **wait for it; because it will surely come,** it will not tarry.

4 **Behold, his soul** *which* **is lifted up is not upright in him** [*the person who pridefully complains to the Lord is not righteous*]: but **the just shall live by his faith** [*hint, hint, Habakkuk, you need to have more faith*].

One of the major messages we learn through the above dialogue between the Lord and Habakkuk is that the Lord is not eager to destroy the wicked. Indeed, He gives them chance after chance after chance to repent. He wants to save them, not destroy them. This should be encouraging for each of us!

After finishing verse 4, above, with a major message for the righteous, namely that the future belongs to those who live by faith, Habakkuk warns against many sins of his day.

5 ¶ Yea also, because **he transgresseth by wine** [*drunkenness*], *he is* a **proud man** [*pride*], **neither keepeth at home** [*doesn't take care of things at home*], **who enlargeth his desire as hell** [*loves wickedness*], and *is* as death, and **cannot be satisfied**, but gathereth unto him all nations, and heapeth unto him all people:

6 Shall not all these take up a parable against him, and a taunting proverb against him, and say, **Woe to him that increaseth** *that which is* **not his!** how long? and to him that ladeth himself with thick clay!

7 Shall they not rise up suddenly that shall bite thee, and awake that shall vex thee, and **thou shalt be for booties** [*booty, loot, plunder*] unto them? [*You will be plundered by the people you stole from*]

8 **Because thou hast spoiled many nations, all the remnant of the people shall spoil thee;** because of men's blood, and *for* the violence of

the land, of the city, and of all that dwell therein.

9 ¶ **Woe to him that coveteth an evil covetousness** to his house, that **he may set his nest on high, that he may be delivered from the power of evil** [*you can't permanently escape from your wickedness*]!

10 **Thou hast** consulted shame to thy house by cutting off many people, and hast **sinned** *against* **thy soul.**

11 For the stone shall cry out of the wall, and the beam out of the timber shall answer it.

12 ¶ **Woe to him that buildeth a town with blood, and stablisheth a city by iniquity!**

Next, Habakkuk prophesies that the law of justice will eventually catch up with the wicked.

13 Behold, *is it* not of the LORD of hosts that **the people shall labour in the very fire**, and the people shall weary themselves for very vanity?

Verse 14, next, foretells that, during the Millennium, the gospel will fill the whole earth—see Isaiah 11:9.

14 For **the earth shall be filled with the knowledge of the glory of the LORD**, as the waters cover the sea.

Next, in verses 15–16, Habakkuk warns against getting someone drunk in order to become involved sexually with them.

15 ¶ **Woe unto him that giveth his neighbour drink**, that puttest

thy bottle to *him*, and makest *him* drunken also, **that thou mayest look on their nakedness!**

16 **Thou art filled with shame** for glory: drink thou also, and let thy foreskin be uncovered [*let them see your nakedness*]: **the cup of the LORD's right hand** [*covenant hand; in other words, you are breaking the commandment against adultery*] **shall be turned unto thee, and shameful spewing** *shall be* **on thy glory.**

17 **For the violence of Lebanon shall cover thee** [*the violence you have done to others will come back upon your own head*], and the spoil of beasts, *which* made them afraid, because of men's blood, and for the violence of the land, of the city, and of all that dwell therein.

Next, a strong warning against idol worship (and pointing out how absolutely foolish it is.)

18 ¶ **What profiteth the graven image that the maker thereof hath graven it**; the molten image, and a teacher of lies, **that the maker of his work trusteth therein,** to make dumb idols?

19 **Woe unto him that saith to the wood** [*idol*], **Awake; to the dumb stone** [*carved idol of stone that cannot hear or speak*], **Arise, it shall teach!** Behold, it *is* laid over with gold and silver, and *there is* **no breath at all in** the midst of **it.**

20 **But the LORD** *is* **in his holy temple** [*the Lord is in heaven and*

available to you]: **let all the earth keep silence before him** [*all the idols in the world are nothing compared to God*].

HABAKKUK 3

Selection: all verses

In this chapter, Habakkuk offers a prayer in which he expresses awe at the power of God.

1 **A PRAYER of Habakkuk the prophet upon Shigionoth** [*probably a musical instrument used to accompany the reading of this prayer*].

2 **O LORD, I have heard thy speech**, *and* was afraid: O LORD, revive thy work in the midst of the years, in the midst of the years make known; **in wrath remember mercy.**

3 God came from Teman, and the Holy One from mount Paran. **Se-lah** [*a musical term, probably giving direction to musicians accompanying the reading of this prayer—see Bible Dictionary, under "Selah"*]. **His glory covered the heavens, and the earth was full of his praise.**

4 And *his* **brightness was as the light**; he had **horns** [*symbolic of power to protect and save*] *coming* **out of his hand**: and **there** *was* **the hiding of his power** [*He can withhold His power to save when people are wicked*].

5 **Before him went the pestilence** [*He has power to send pestilence*], and burning coals went forth at his feet.

6 **He stood, and measured** [*judged*] **the earth**: he beheld, and drove asunder the nations; and the ever-lasting mountains were scattered, the perpetual hills did bow: his ways *are* everlasting.

Next, Habakkuk gives historical examples of occasions when the power of the Lord was manifested, similar to in verse 3, above.

7 I saw the tents of **Cushan** in afflic-tion: *and* the curtains of the land of **Midian** did tremble.

8 Was the LORD displeased against the rivers? *was* thine anger against the rivers? *was* thy wrath against the sea, that thou didst ride upon thine horses *and* thy chariots of salvation?

9 Thy bow was made quite naked, *according* to the oaths of the tribes, *even thy* word. **Selah**. Thou didst cleave the earth with rivers.

10 **The mountains saw thee, *and* they trembled**: the overflowing of the water passed by: the deep uttered his voice, *and* lifted up his hands on high.

11 **The sun *and* moon stood still in their habitation** [*Joshua 10:12*]: at the light of thine arrows they went, *and* at the shining of thy glittering spear.

12 Thou didst march through the land in indignation, **thou didst thresh the heathen in anger**.

13 **Thou wentest forth** [*exercised Thy power*] **for the salvation of thy** **people**, *even* for salvation with thine anointed; **thou woundedst the head out of the house of the wicked**, by discovering the foundation unto the neck. **Selah**.

14 Thou didst strike through with his staves the head of his villages: they came out as a whirlwind to scatter me: **their** [*the wicked*] **rejoicing** *was* **as to devour the poor secretly**.

15 **Thou didst walk through the sea with thine horses, *through* the heap of great waters** [*God has power over the elements; example, when the waters of the Red Sea were parted*].

16 **When I heard** [*that enemies were coming against us*], **my belly trem-bled; my lips quivered at the voice**: rottenness entered into my bones [*my frame was weak*], and **I trembled** in myself, that I might rest in the day of trouble: when he cometh up unto the people, he will invade them with his troops.

Next, in his prayer, Habakkuk says, in effect, that no matter how bad conditions get, he will still trust in the Lord.

17 ¶ Although the fig tree shall not blossom, neither *shall* fruit *be* in the vines; the labour of the olive shall fail, and the fields shall yield no meat; the flock shall be cut off from the fold, and *there shall be* no herd in the stalls:

18 **Yet I will rejoice in the LORD, I will joy in the God of my salva-tion.**

19 **The LORD God** *is* **my strength**, and he will make my feet like hinds' *feet,* and he will make me to walk upon mine high places. **To the chief singer on my stringed instruments** [*a note to the chief musician*].

ZEPHANIAH

Zephaniah was a prophet to Judah about 639–608 BC. He would likely have been a contemporary of (preaching the gospel at the same time as) Jeremiah, Lehi, Nahum, and perhaps Habakkuk. He preached to the Jews during the reign of Josiah, righteous king of Judah (see verse 1), who ruled from 641–610 BC. No doubt, his preaching helped King Josiah accomplish a reformation among the wicked inhabitants of Judah at this time. His message was straight to the point: unless the Jews successfully repented, they would be destroyed as a nation.

ZEPHANIAH 1

Selection: all verses

In chapter 1, we see the destruction of Judah as a "type" of the destruction of the wicked that will accompany the Second Coming. Thus, you will see many verses that have dual meaning, referring to both Jerusalem's downfall and the destruction of the wicked at the time of the Second Coming.

1 **THE word of the LORD which came unto Zephaniah** the son of Cushi, the son of Gedaliah, the son of Amariah, the son of **Hizkiah** [*righteous King Hezekiah*], **in the days of Josiah** the son of Amon, king of Judah.

You will see typical repetition for emphasis in verses 2–6 as Zephaniah details many of the sins of the people of Judah.

2 **I will utterly consume all** *things* **from off the land, saith the LORD.**

3 **I will consume man and beast; I will consume the fowls of the heaven, and the fishes of the sea** [*the economy of the Jews will be devastated*], and the stumblingblocks with the wicked; and **I will cut off man from off the land, saith the LORD.**

4 **I will also stretch out mine hand upon Judah, and upon all the inhabitants of Jerusalem**; and **I will cut off the remnant of Baal** [*idol worship*] **from this place,** *and* **the** name of the **Chemarims** [*priests who officiated in idol worship*] **with the priests;**

5 **And them that worship the host of heaven** [*the sun, moon, and stars*] upon the housetops; and them that worship *and* that swear by the LORD, **and that swear by Malcham** [*a heathen god*];

6 And **them that are turned back from the LORD; and** *those* **that have not sought the LORD, nor enquired for him.**

7 Hold thy peace at the presence of the Lord GOD: **for the day of the LORD** *is* at hand [*usually a reference to the Second Coming*]: for the LORD hath prepared a sacrifice, he hath bid his guests.

8 And it shall come to pass in the day of the LORD's sacrifice, that **I will punish the princes, and the king's children, and all such as are clothed with strange apparel** [*special clothing signaling loyalty to certain idols*].

9 **In the same day also will I punish all those** that leap on the threshold, **which fill their masters' houses with violence and deceit** [*dishonesty*].

10 And it shall come to pass in that day, saith the LORD, *that **there shall be** the noise of a cry from the fish gate* [*the gate on the north wall of Jerusalem from which people would first see enemy armies approaching from the north*], and **an howling from the second** [*the fish gate opened into the part of Jerusalem known as the "second quarter"*], **and a great crashing from the hills** [*the noise of an approaching army*].

11 **Howl, ye inhabitants of Maktesh** [*the merchants' quarter of Jerusalem*], for **all the merchant people are cut down**; all **they** [*the merchants*] **that bear silver are cut off**.

12 And it shall come to pass at that time, *that* **I will search Jerusalem with candles, and punish the men** that are settled on their lees: **that say in their heart, The LORD will not do good, neither will he do evil** [*they are apathetic about God and religion*].

13 **Therefore their goods shall become a booty** [*plunder, loot, for invading armies*], and **their houses a desolation**: they shall also build houses, but not inhabit *them;* and they shall plant vineyards, but not drink the wine thereof.

14 **The great day of the LORD** *is* **near**, *it is* near, **and hasteth greatly**, *even* the voice of the day of the LORD: the mighty man shall cry there bitterly.

15 **That day** *is* **a day of wrath**, a day of **trouble** and **distress**, a day of **wasteness** [*German Bible, "weather," implying devastating storms*] and **desolation**, a day of **darkness** and **gloominess**, a day of clouds and thick darkness,

16 A day of the **trumpet and alarm** [*sounds of destruction*] against the fenced cities, and against the high towers.

17 And **I will bring distress upon men**, that **they shall walk like blind** [*spiritually blind*] **men, because they have sinned against the LORD**: and **their blood shall be poured out as dust, and their flesh as the dung**.

18 **Neither their silver nor their gold shall be able to deliver them in the day of the LORD's wrath;**

but **the whole land shall be devoured by** the fire of his jealousy: for **he shall make even a speedy riddance** [*destruction*] **of all them that dwell in the land**.

ZEPHANIAH 2

Selection: all verses

This chapter offers a ray of hope for those who will reconsider their ways, repent, and return to the Lord.

1 **GATHER yourselves together, yea, gather together, O nation not desired** [*rethink your ways and repent*];

2 Before the decree bring forth, *before* the day pass as the chaff, **before the fierce anger of the LORD come upon you, before the day of the LORD's anger come upon you**.

3 **Seek ye the LORD, all ye meek of the earth**, which have wrought his judgment; <u>**seek righteousness, seek meekness**</u>: it **may be ye shall be hid in the day of the LORD's anger** [*it just may be that you can repent in time to escape the righteous anger of the Lord*].

Other wicked cities besides Jerusalem will also be destroyed.

4 ¶ For **Gaza** [*a Philistine city*] **shall be forsaken**, and **Ashkelon** [*a Philistine city*] **a desolation: they shall drive out Ashdod** [*a Philistine city*] at the noon day, and **Ekron** [*a Philistine city*] **shall be rooted up**.

5 **Woe unto the inhabitants of the sea coast**, the nation of the Cherethites! **the word of the LORD** *is* **against you; O Canaan, the land of the Philistines**, I will even destroy thee, that there shall be no inhabitant.

The land where wicked cities once flourished will revert back to pastureland and agriculture.

6 And **the sea coast shall be dwellings** *and* **cottages for shepherds, and folds for flocks**.

When the Lord gathers the Jews in the last days, He will open the doors for them return to the Holy Land.

7 And **the coast** [*Holy Land*] **shall be for the remnant of the house of Judah**; they shall feed thereupon: in the houses of Ashkelon shall they lie down in the evening: for **the LORD their God shall visit them, and turn away their captivity**.

Next, Zephaniah prophesies against nations and peoples who have treated the Jews badly.

8 ¶ **I have heard the reproach of Moab, and the revilings of the children of Ammon, whereby they have reproached my people, and magnified** *themselves* **against their border**.

9 Therefore *as* I live, saith the LORD of hosts, the God of Israel, **Surely Moab shall be as Sodom, and the children of Ammon as Gomorrah**, *even* the breeding of nettles, and saltpits, and **a perpetual desolation: the residue of my people** [*the remnant of Judah, Israel*] **shall spoil**

them, and the remnant of my people shall possess them.

10 **This shall they have for their pride** [*because of their arrogance against the Jews*], **because they have reproached and magnified** *themselves* **against the people of the LORD of hosts**.

Next, we see another prophetic reference to the destruction at the time of the Second Coming, along with a prophecy that Christ will rule and reign on earth during the Millennium.

11 **The LORD** *will be* **terrible unto them**: for **he will famish all the gods of the earth**; and *men* **shall worship him, every one from his place**, *even* **all the isles of the heathen**.

12 ¶ **Ye Ethiopians also, ye** *shall be* **slain by my sword**.

13 And **he will** stretch out his hand against the north, and **destroy Assyria**; and **will make Nineveh** [*the capitol of Assyria*] **a desolation,** *and* **dry** like a wilderness [*it will become pastureland and agricultural land*].

14 And **flocks shall lie down in the midst of her**, all the beasts of the nations: **both the cormorant and the bittern shall lodge in the upper lintels of it** [*birds that like solitude will like to live there*]; *their* voice shall sing in the windows; **desolation** *shall be* **in the thresholds** [*the buildings will be in ruins*]: for he shall uncover the cedar work.

15 **This** *is* **the rejoicing city that dwelt carelessly** [*that lived wickedly*], that said in her heart, I *am,* and *there is* none beside me: **how is she become a desolation, a place for beasts to lie down in**! every one that passeth by her shall hiss, *and* wag his hand [*will shake their heads and wonder what happened here*].

ZEPHANIAH 3

Selection: all verses

One of the exciting things we learn from this chapter is that those who live during the Millennium will all speak a pure language (verse 9). This will obviously simplify communication. We do not know what this language will be, but it will be a "pure language."

We know that one of the signs of the times is that there will constantly be "wars and rumors of war" in the last days (Matthew 24:6; see also the heading to this chapter in the Bible). In verses 1–7, Zephaniah points out to us the things that will lead to the wars that will be going on when the Savior comes.

1 **WOE to her that is filthy and polluted, to the oppressing city!**

2 She obeyed not the voice; she received not correction; **she trusted not in the LORD; she drew not near to her God**.

3 **Her princes** [*political leaders, rulers*] **within her** *are* **roaring lions;** **her judges** *are* **evening wolves;** they gnaw not the bones till the morrow.

4 **Her prophets** [*false prophets*] *are* **light** *and* **treacherous persons: her priests** [*apostate priests*] **have polluted the sanctuary** [*temple*]**, they have done violence to the law** [*have corrupted the law*].

5 **The just** [*completely righteous*] **LORD** *is* **in the midst thereof** [*knows everything that is going on*]; he will not do iniquity: every morning doth he bring his judgment to light, he faileth not; but **the unjust knoweth no shame.**

6 **I have cut off the nations: their towers are desolate; I made their streets waste** [*empty*]**,** that none passeth by: **their cities are destroyed, so that there is no man, that there is none inhabitant.**

7 **I said, Surely thou wilt fear me, thou wilt receive instruction**; so their dwelling should not be cut off, **howsoever I punished them** [*because they did not listen to Me*]: but **they rose early,** *and* **corrupted all their doings.**

Next, Zephaniah prophesies the burning of the wicked at the Second Coming. It helps to be aware that all the righteous will already be taken up before the burning of the wicked takes place (D&C 88:96). By the way, all those good and honorable (D&C 76:75) people on earth who are living a terrestrial lifestyle will somehow be spared this burning too. We just have not been told how. So, it is the truly, intentionally wicked who will be burned. They will be burned by the brightness of the Savior's glory when He comes

(D&C 5:19, 2 Nephi 12:10, 19, and 21).

8 ¶ Therefore wait ye upon me, saith the LORD, until the day that I rise up to the prey: for my determination *is* to gather the nations, that I may assemble the kingdoms, to pour upon them mine indignation, *even* all my fierce anger: for **all the earth shall be devoured with the fire of my jealousy** [*Hebrew, "zeal"*].

9 **For then** [*during the Millennium*] **will I turn to the people a pure language,** that they may all call upon the name of the LORD, to serve him with one consent.

Next, in verse 10, Zephaniah returns to the gathering of Israel before the Second Coming.

10 **From beyond the rivers of Ethiopia my suppliants** [*worshipers*]**,** *even* **the daughter of my dispersed** [*the descendants of scattered Israel*]**,** shall bring mine offering [*will worship Me*].

11 **In that day shalt thou not be ashamed for all thy doings, wherein thou hast transgressed against me** [*because you will have repented*]: for **then I will take away out of the midst of thee them that rejoice in thy** [*NIV, "their"*] **pride, and thou shalt no more be haughty because of my holy mountain** [*because you will follow the true gospel*].

12 I will also leave in the midst of thee an afflicted and poor people [*meek people, a truly humbled people*],

and **they shall trust in the name of the LORD.**

13 The remnant of Israel shall not do iniquity, nor speak lies; neither shall a deceitful tongue be found in their mouth: for they shall feed and lie down, and none shall make *them* **afraid.**

14 ¶ Sing, O daughter of Zion; shout, O Israel; be glad and rejoice with all the heart, O daughter of Jerusalem.

15 The LORD hath taken away thy judgments [*His punishments*], he hath cast out thine enemy: **the king of Israel,** *even* **the LORD,** *is* **in the midst of thee: thou shalt not see evil any more** [*millennial conditions*].

Verse 16, next, mentions the two headquarters of the Savior during the Millennium.

16 In that day it shall be said to **Jerusalem** [*Old Jerusalem*], Fear thou not: *and to* **Zion** [*New Jerusalem,* *in Independence, Missouri*], Let not thine hands be slack.

17 **The LORD thy God in the midst of thee** *is* mighty; he will save, he **will rejoice over thee with joy**; he will rest in his love, he will joy over thee with singing.

18 **I will gather** *them that are* sorrowful for the solemn assembly [*we don't know what this solemn assembly is*], *who* are of thee, *to whom* the reproach of it *was* a burden.

19 Behold, **at that time I will undo all that afflict thee**: and I will save her that halteth, and gather her that was driven out; and I will get them praise and fame in every land where they have been put to shame.

20 **At that time will I bring you** *again*, even in the time that I gather you: **for I will make you a name and a praise among all people of the earth**, when I turn back your captivity before your eyes, saith the LORD.

HAGGAI

Haggai (a contemporary of Zechariah) was a prophet to Judah and Jerusalem. He served about 520 BC, which was about 65–70 years after the final wave of Babylonian armies carried the Jews into Babylonian exile. Cyrus the Persian conquered Babylon easily in about 538 BC. One of his first moves as king over the Persian Empire was to allow the Jewish exiles who so desired to return to their homeland and rebuild the temple in Jerusalem. By the time Haggai arrived in Jerusalem from Babylon, work on the temple had stalled. Thus, in chapter 1, you will see Haggai urging his fellow Jews to resume work on the temple.

HAGGAI 1

Selection: all verses

1 **IN the second year of Darius the king** [*of the Persian Empire, now including Babylon*], in the sixth month, in the first day of the month, **came the word of the LORD by Haggai** the prophet **unto Zerubbabel** the son of Shealtiel, **governor of Judah, and to Joshua** the son of Josedech, **the high priest**, saying,

> You can see in verse 2, next, that the Jews who have returned to Jerusalem are saying that it is not time yet to resume work on rebuilding the temple. You will also see in verses 4–8 that the Lord disagrees.

2 **Thus speaketh the LORD of hosts**, saying, **This people say, The time is not come**, the time **that the LORD's house should be built**.

3 **Then came the word of the LORD by Haggai the prophet, saying**,

4 *Is it* **time for you, O ye, to dwell in your ceiled** [*finished*] **houses, and this house** [*the temple*] *lie* **waste** [*unfinished*]?

5 Now therefore thus saith the LORD of hosts; **Consider your ways**.

> In verse 6, next, the Lord reminds these people that they are not prospering. The implied message is that if they will prioritize on the Lord's

work (in this case rebuilding the temple), they will prosper. The same message applies to us today.

6 **Ye have sown** [*planted*] **much, and bring in little** [*harvest little*]; ye eat, but ye have not enough; ye drink, but ye are not filled with drink; ye clothe you, but there is none warm; and he that earneth wages earneth wages *to put it* into a bag with holes.

7 ¶ Thus saith the LORD of hosts; **Consider your ways**.

8 Go up to the mountain, and bring wood, and **build the house** [*temple*]; and I will take pleasure in it, and I will be glorified, saith the LORD.

> The setting for the message in verse 9, next, is that of the threshing of grain on the threshing floor. The grain stalks are put on the threshing floor and then walked on or run over by cart wheels to separate the grain from the stalks and the chaff. Then, when the wind is blowing hard enough, the mix is tossed into the air. The wind separates the grain from the chaff and stalks and the kernels of grain drop back to the floor.

9 Ye looked for much [*a big harvest*], and, lo, *it came* to little [*you didn't get much*]; and when ye brought *it* home, I did blow upon it [*the Lord blew away what little you brought home*]. **Why?** saith the LORD of hosts. **Because of mine house that** *is* **waste, and ye run every man unto his own house** [*you are prioritizing on your own needs and putting the Lord's work in second place*].

10 **Therefore the heaven** over you **is stayed from dew, and the earth is stayed** *from* **her fruit** [*that's why you are not prospering*].

11 And **I called for a drought upon the land**, and upon the mountains, and upon the corn, and upon the new wine, and upon the oil, and upon *that* which the ground bringeth forth, and upon men, and upon cattle, and upon all the labour of the hands.

12 ¶ **Then Zerubbabel** the son of Shealtiel, **and Joshua** the son of Josedech, the high priest, **with all the remnant of the people, obeyed the voice of the LORD their God, and the words of Haggai the prophet**, as the LORD their God had sent him, and the people did fear before the LORD.

13 **Then spake Haggai** the LORD's messenger in **the LORD's message unto the people, saying, I** *am* **with you, saith the LORD**.

14 And the LORD stirred up the spirit of Zerubbabel the son of Shealtiel, governor of Judah, and the spirit of Joshua the son of Josedech, the high priest, and the spirit of all the remnant of the people; **and they came and did work in the house of the LORD of hosts, their God**,

15 In the four and twentieth day of the sixth month, in the second year of Darius the king.

HAGGAI 2

Selection: all verses

In chapter 2, the Lord first speaks to those Jews who were old enough to have seen the Jerusalem Temple before it was destroyed (verse 3). They are now back from their captivity in Babylon and apparently are comparing the magnificence of Solomon's Temple to the one they are rebuilding with their meager resources.

1 IN the seventh *month,* in the one and twentieth *day* of the month, came **the word of the LORD by the prophet Haggai**, saying,

2 **Speak now to Zerubbabel** the son of Shealtiel, **governor of Judah**, and to **Joshua** the son of Josedech, **the high priest, and to the residue of the people**, saying,

3 **Who** *is* **left among you that saw this house** [*temple*] **in her first glory** [*Solomon's Temple*]? and **how do ye see it now?** *is it* **not in your eyes in comparison of it as nothing?**

4 Yet now be strong, O Zerubbabel, saith the LORD; and be strong, O Joshua, son of Josedech, the high priest; and be strong, all ye people of the land, saith the LORD, and work: for **I** *am* **with you, saith the LORD of hosts**:

5 *According to* the word that I covenanted with you when ye came out of Egypt, so **my spirit remaineth among you: fear ye not**.

Verses 6–7 foretell that people of all nations will come to the temple that is to be built in Jerusalem in the last days.

6 For thus saith the LORD of hosts; Yet once, **it** *is* **a little while**, and I will shake the heavens, and the earth, and the sea, and the dry *land;*

7 And I will shake all nations, and the desire of **all nations shall come**: and **I will fill this house with glory**, saith the LORD of hosts.

8 **The silver** *is* **mine, and the gold** *is* **mine**, saith the LORD of hosts [*the Lord will provide the needed resources to build this temple*].

In verse 9, next, Haggai prophesies that, in the future, there will be a temple in Jerusalem that will surpass Solomon's Temple in splendor and glory. It refers to the temple that will yet be built in Jerusalem in our day before the Second Coming (see Ezekiel, chapter 44, in this study guide).

9 **The glory of this latter house shall be greater than of the former**, saith the LORD of hosts: and **in this place will I give peace**, saith the LORD of hosts.

Verses 10–19, next, address the fact that the Jews, who are complaining that it is not yet time to resume the work of rebuilding the temple, are themselves unclean and still need to repent. Everything they touch is "unclean." They are compared to a man who has touched a dead body and is thus unclean according to the law of Moses. Everything he touches becomes unclean. These Jews are invited to repent.

10 ¶ In the four and twentieth *day* of the ninth *month,* in the second year of Darius, came **the word of the LORD by Haggai** the prophet, saying,

Next, the Lord basically asks the question that if someone who is ritually unclean touches other items, will that make them clean? The answer is no. The point is that these Jews are not clean before the Lord. They need to repent and get to work on the temple.

11 Thus saith the LORD of hosts; **Ask now the priests** *concerning* **the law** [*of Moses*], saying,

12 **If one bear holy flesh** [*flesh donated as part of the sacrifices in the temple*] in the skirt of his garment, **and with his skirt do touch bread, or pottage, or wine, or oil, or any meat, shall it be holy? And the priests answered and said, No**.

13 Then said Haggai, **If** *one that is* **unclean by a dead body touch any of these, shall it be unclean?** And the priests **answer**ed and said, **It shall be unclean**.

14 Then answered Haggai, and said, **So** *is* **this people, and so** *is* **this nation before me**, saith the LORD; and **so** *is* **every work of their hands; and that which they offer there** *is* **unclean**.

Next, the Lord reminds them that they are not prospering. They still need to turn to Him with all their hearts.

15 And now, I pray you, **consider from this day and upward** [*starting right now, reconsider your ways*], from before a stone was laid upon a stone in the temple of the LORD:

Next, they are reminded that they are always coming up short.

16 Since those *days* were, **when *one* came to an heap of twenty *measures*, there were *but* ten**: when *one* came to the pressfat [*wine vat*] for **to draw out fifty *vessels*** out of the press, **there were *but* twenty**.

17 **I smote you with blasting and with mildew and with hail** in all the labours of your hands; **yet ye *turned* not to me** [*you still did not repent*], saith the LORD.

18 **Consider now from this day and upward**, from the four and twentieth day of the ninth *month, even* **from the day that the foundation of the LORD's temple was laid**, consider *it*.

19 **Is the seed yet in the barn?** yea, as yet the vine, and the fig tree, and the pomegranate, and the olive tree, hath not brought forth: **from this day will I bless *you*.**

20 ¶ **And again the word of the LORD came unto Haggai** in the four and twentieth *day* of the month, saying,

Finally, Haggai prophesies that the day will yet come that the Jews will prosper.

21 Speak to Zerubbabel, governor of Judah, saying, **I will shake the heavens and the earth;**

22 And **I will overthrow the throne of kingdoms, and I will destroy the strength of the kingdoms of the heathen**; and I will overthrow the chariots [*symbolic of military might*], and those that ride in them; and the horses and their riders shall come down, **every one by the sword of his brother** [*many nations who fight against the Jews in the last days will also fight against each other*].

23 **In that day** [*the last days*], saith the LORD of hosts, will **I take** [*rescue*] **thee, O Zerubbabel** [*symbolically representing the Jews*], my servant, the son of Shealtiel, saith the LORD, **and will make thee as a signet** [*a signet ring, symbolically saying that, in the last days, the Jews, and all Israel, who come unto Christ, will be the Lord's people—possibly a reference also to the Millennium*], for **I have chosen thee, saith the LORD of hosts**.

ZECHARIAH

Zechariah prophesied and taught from about 520 BC to 518 BC. He was a contemporary of the prophet Haggai (see Ezra 5:1). At the time Zechariah and Haggai arrived back in Jerusalem from their Babylonian captivity (remember, Cyrus, the Persian, conquered Babylon and encouraged Jews to return to Jerusalem and rebuild their temple), the Jews who had arrived earlier and had started rebuilding the temple had become discouraged. Consequently, they had stopped work on the temple and had concentrated on building their own homes (Haggai, chapter 1).

ZECHARIAH 1

Selection: all verses

In this chapter, Zechariah calls the Jews to repent and return to work on the temple. He will have visions that will give encouragement to these Jews that their cities and temple will indeed be built.

1 IN the eighth month, in the second year of Darius [*king of the Persian Empire*], came **the word of the LORD unto Zechariah**, the son of Berechiah, the son of Iddo the prophet, saying,

2 **The LORD hath been sore** [*very*] **displeased with your fathers**.

In verse 3, next, we see a statement of true doctrine that applies today as well.

3 Therefore say thou unto them, Thus saith the LORD of hosts; **Turn ye** unto me, saith the LORD of hosts, and I will turn unto you, saith the LORD of hosts.

4 **Be ye not as your fathers** [*ancestors*], **unto whom the former prophets have cried, saying**, Thus saith the LORD of hosts; **Turn ye now from your evil ways**, and *from* your evil doings: **but they did not** hear, nor hearken unto me, saith the LORD.

5 **Your fathers, where** *are* **they** [*what is their condition now*]? and the prophets, do they live for ever?

In verse 6, next, we are reminded that the words of the Lord are always fulfilled!

6 **But my words and my statutes** [*laws and commandments*], which I commanded my servants the prophets, **did they not take hold of your fathers?** and they returned and said, Like as the LORD of hosts thought to do unto us, according to our ways, and according to our doings, **so hath he dealt with us** [*sure enough, we were punished*].

7 ¶ Upon the four and twentieth day of the eleventh month, which *is* the month Sebat, in the second year of Darius, came the word of the LORD unto Zechariah, the son of Berechiah, the son of Iddo the prophet, saying,

In verses 8–17, you will see the first vision that Zechariah had at this time.

8 **I saw by night**, and behold a man riding upon a red horse, and he stood among the myrtle trees that *were* in the bottom; and behind him *were there* red horses, speckled, and white.

9 **Then said I, O my lord, what** *are* **these?** And **the angel** that talked with me **said** unto me, **I will shew thee** what these *be*.

10 And the man that stood among the myrtle trees answered and said, **These** *are they* **whom the LORD hath sent to walk to and fro through the earth**.

11 And **they answered the angel** of the LORD that stood among the myrtle trees, and said, **We have walked to and fro through the earth, and, behold, all the earth sitteth still, and is at rest** [*there is considerable peace at this time; no nations are threatening Judah at present*].

12 ¶ **Then the angel of the LORD answered** [*asked the Lord a question*] and said, O LORD of hosts, **how long wilt thou not have mercy on Jerusalem and on the cities of Judah** [*how long will it be before Thou canst bless the Jews*], **against which thou hast had indignation these threescore and ten years** [*a reference to the seventy years between the time the Jews were conquered and taken to Babylon and the present time when they were allowed to return to Jerusalem*]?

13 And **the LORD answered** the angel that talked with me *with* good words *and* comfortable words [*with pleasant prophecies about the future of Jerusalem*].

14 So the angel that communed with me said unto me, Cry thou, saying, **Thus saith the LORD of hosts; I am jealous for** [*zealous, strongly interested in and involved with*] **Jerusalem** and for Zion with a great jealousy.

15 And **I am very sore displeased with the heathen** *that are* at ease: for I was but a little displeased, and they helped forward the affliction [*helped persecute the Jews*].

16 Therefore thus saith the LORD; **I am returned to Jerusalem with mercies: my house shall be built in it** [*a temple will be built in Jerusalem in the last days*], saith the LORD of hosts, and a line [*a measuring device*] shall be stretched forth upon Jerusalem [*Jerusalem will finally measure up*].

17 Cry yet, saying, Thus saith the LORD of hosts; My cities through prosperity shall yet be spread abroad; and **the LORD shall yet comfort Zion, and shall yet choose** [*bless*] **Jerusalem**.

18 ¶ **Then lifted I up mine eyes, and saw**, and behold **four horns** [*influential powers*].

19 **And I said unto the angel** that talked with me, **What** *be* **these?** And **he answered me, These** *are*

the horns which have scattered Judah, Israel, and Jerusalem.

20 And **the LORD shewed me four carpenters.**

Verse 21 prophesies that in the last days all the powers, nations, and people who have persecuted and scattered the Jews will ultimately be stopped by the Lord from disturbing them.

21 **Then said I, What come these to do?** And he spake, saying, **These** *are* **the horns which have scattered Judah**, so that no man did lift up his head: but **these are come to fray them, to cast out the horns** [*power*] **of the Gentiles, which lifted up** *their* **horn over the land of Judah to scatter it.**

ZECHARIAH 2

Selection: all verses

In this chapter, we get a few prophetic details of the return of the Jews to Jerusalem in the last days. By the way, Israel became a nation in 1948 with the help of the United Nations.

1 I LIFTED up mine eyes again, and looked, and behold **a man with a measuring line in his hand.**

2 Then said I, **Whither goest thou?** And **he said** unto me, **To measure Jerusalem**, to see what *is* the breadth thereof, and what *is* the length thereof [*to see how Jerusalem measures up for the fulfillment of these prophecies*].

3 And, behold, **the angel that talked with me went forth, and another angel went out to meet him,**

Next, a prophecy that in the future Jerusalem will expand beyond her walls and be protected by the Lord.

4 And said unto him, Run, speak to this young man, saying, **Jerusalem shall be inhabited** *as* **towns without walls for the multitude of men and cattle therein:**

5 **For I, saith the LORD, will be unto her a wall of fire round about, and will be the glory in the midst of her** [*this includes the Millennium, when the Savior will have two headquarters, one in Jerusalem and one in the New Jerusalem in Jackson County, Missouri*].

Next, we see that many of the Jews will come from the north as they return.

6 ¶ Ho, ho, *come forth,* **and flee from the land of the north,** saith the LORD: for **I have spread you abroad as the four winds** of the heaven [*you have been scattered throughout the world*], saith the LORD.

7 **Deliver thyself, O Zion, that dwellest** *with* **the daughter of Babylon** [*repent and deliver yourself from the wicked ways of the world*].

8 For **thus saith the LORD** of hosts; After the glory hath he sent me unto the nations which spoiled you: for **he that toucheth you toucheth the apple of his eye** [*the Jews are very dear*

to the Lord, and anyone who hurts them will be in big trouble with Him].

9 For, behold, **I will shake mine hand upon them**, and **they shall be a spoil to their servants** [the tables will be turned such that the Jews will be the masters over their former persecutors]: and **ye shall know that the LORD of hosts hath sent me**.

10 ¶ **Sing and rejoice, O daughter of Zion** [Jerusalem]: **for, lo, I come, and I will dwell in the midst of thee, saith the LORD** [the Millennium].

11 And **many nations shall be joined to the LORD in that day** [the Millennium]**, and shall be my people: and I will dwell in the midst of thee**, and thou shalt know that the LORD of hosts hath sent me unto thee.

12 And **the LORD shall inherit Judah his portion in the holy land** [the Jews will return to their former lands in Palestine], and shall choose Jerusalem again.

13 Be silent, O all flesh, before the LORD: for he is raised up out of his holy habitation [you will be watching the Lord keep His word to the Jews].

ZECHARIAH 3

Selection: all verses

The main message of this chapter is that the wicked will be completely destroyed at the time of the Second Coming (see verse 9).

1 AND **he shewed me Joshua the high priest standing before the angel** of the LORD, **and Satan standing at his right hand** [covenant hand, implying that we are safe when we keep our covenants, but when we break them, we fall into Satan's hands] **to resist him**.

2 And **the LORD said unto Satan, The LORD rebuke thee, O Satan; even the LORD that hath chosen Jerusalem** rebuke thee: is not this a brand plucked out of the fire?

Next, "filthy garments" symbolize wickedness and evil lifestyles.

3 Now Joshua was clothed **with filthy garments**, and stood before the angel.

In verses 4–10, we see the marvelous cleansing provided by the Atonement of Christ. Christ is the "Branch" spoken of in verse 8.

4 And he answered and spake unto those that stood before him, saying, **Take away the filthy garments from him**. And unto him he said, Behold, **I have caused thine iniquity to pass from thee, and I will clothe thee with change of raiment** [cleansed and "born again"].

Verse 5 can refer to our temple worship, including temple clothing.

5 And I said, **Let them set a fair mitre** [cap—see Exodus 28] upon his head. So they set a fair mitre upon his head, and **clothed him with garments**. And the angel of the LORD stood by.

temple clothing?

6 And the angel of the LORD protested [*said*] unto Joshua, saying,

Next, we see an "if . . . then" clause.

7 Thus saith the LORD of hosts; **If** thou wilt walk in my ways, and **if** thou wilt keep my charge, **then** thou shalt also judge my house, and shalt also keep my courts, and I will give thee places to walk among these that stand by.

8 Hear now, O Joshua the high priest, thou, and thy fellows that sit before thee: for they *are* men wondered at [*admired*]: for, behold, **I will bring forth my servant the BRANCH** [*Christ*].

9 For behold the stone that I have laid before Joshua; upon one stone *shall be* seven eyes [*facets*]: behold, I will engrave the graving thereof, saith the LORD of hosts, and **I will remove the iniquity of that land in one day.**

10 **In that day, saith the LORD of hosts, shall ye call every man his neighbour** [*there will be peace*] under the vine and under the fig tree [*millennial conditions*].

ZECHARIAH 7

Selection: all verses

Living the gospel outwardly but not inwardly is a major topic in this chapter.

1 AND it came to pass in the fourth year of king Darius, *that* **the word of the LORD came unto Zechariah** in the fourth *day* of the ninth month, *even* in Chisleu;

2 When they had sent unto the house of God Sherezer and Regem-melech, and their men, to pray before the LORD,

3 *And* to speak unto the priests which *were* in the house of the LORD of hosts, and to the prophets, saying, **Should I weep in the fifth month, separating myself, as I have done these so many years** [*should we continue our fasts and worship that we used while we were in exile in Babylon all those years*]?

4 ¶ **Then came the word of the LORD** of hosts unto me, saying,

5 Speak unto all the people of the land, and to the priests, saying, **When ye fasted and mourned in the fifth and seventh *month*, even those seventy years, did ye at all fast unto me, *even* to me** [*during those fasts, were you thinking of Me, the Lord, at all or were you just going through the motions*]?

6 And **when ye did eat, and when ye did drink, did not ye eat *for yourselves*, and drink *for yourselves*** [*weren't you just eating and drinking, without your mind on God*]?

7 *Should ye* not *hear* [*shouldn't you have paid attention to*] **the words which the LORD hath cried by the former prophets, when Jerusalem was inhabited** [*before the Babylonian exile*] **and in prosperity**, and the cities thereof round about her, when

men inhabited the south and the plain?

8 ¶ And **the word of the LORD came unto Zechariah**, saying,

Next, Zechariah repeats some of the messages the Jews were ignoring before the Babylonian captivity.

9 Thus speaketh the LORD of hosts, saying, **Execute true judgment** [*fairness*], **and shew mercy and compassions every man to his brother**:

10 And **oppress not the widow, nor the fatherless, the stranger, nor the poor; and let none of you imagine evil against his brother in your heart.**

11 **But they refused to hearken**, and **pulled away the shoulder** [*turned their backs*], and **stopped their ears**, that they should not hear.

12 Yea, **they made their hearts** *as* an adamant **stone, lest they should hear the law, and the words which the LORD of hosts hath sent in his spirit by the former prophets**: therefore [*this is why*] came a great wrath from the LORD of hosts.

13 Therefore it is come to pass, *that* **as he cried, and they would not hear; so they cried, and I would not hear**, saith the LORD of hosts:

14 **But I scattered them** with a whirlwind **among all the nations** whom they knew not. **Thus the land was desolate after them**, that no man passed through nor returned:

for they laid the pleasant land desolate.

ZECHARIAH 8

Selection: all verses

This chapter is an amazing chapter of prophecy about the last days when the Jews are gathered back to their homeland in Palestine. It includes prophecies of prosperity and blessings far beyond any in their previous history. Relatively speaking, it is a pleasant and upbeat chapter.

1 AGAIN **the word of the LORD of hosts came** *to me*, saying,

2 **Thus saith the LORD** of hosts; **I was jealous for Zion with great jealousy** [*including that you were worshiping other gods, idols, and false religions*], and **I was jealous for her with great fury** [*In the past, I, the Lord, was angry with you*].

Next, Zechariah sees in vision a future day when the inhabitants of Jerusalem are righteous ("a city of truth") and the last days' temple in Jerusalem has been built.

3 Thus saith the LORD; **I am returned unto Zion, and will dwell in the midst of Jerusalem**: and **Jerusalem shall be called a city of truth**; and **the mountain of the LORD of hosts the holy mountain** [*the temple*].

4 Thus saith the LORD of hosts; **There shall yet old men and old women dwell in the streets of Jerusalem** [*because of peace, people*

will *live to be old*], and every man with his staff in his hand for very age.

5 And the streets of the city shall be full of boys and girls playing in the streets thereof.

6 Thus saith the LORD of hosts; If it be marvellous in the eyes of the remnant of this people in these days, should it also be marvellous in mine eyes? saith the LORD of hosts.

7 Thus saith the LORD of hosts; Behold, **I will save my people from the east country, and from the west country** [*the Jews will be gathered to Jerusalem from all over the world*];

8 And **I will bring them, and they shall dwell in the midst of Jerusalem: and they shall be my people, and I will be their God, in truth and in righteousness.**

Next, the Lord speaks to the Jews who have been commanded to rebuild the temple.

9 ¶ Thus saith the LORD of hosts; **Let your hands be strong** [*in rebuilding the temple*], ye that hear in these days these words by the mouth of the prophets, which *were* in the day *that* the foundation of the house of the LORD of hosts was laid, that the temple might be built.

10 For **before these days** [*before now*] **there was no hire for man, nor any hire for beast** [*there were no jobs for man or beast*]; **neither *was* there any peace** to him that went out or came in because of the affliction:

for I set **all men every one against his neighbour.**

11 But now I *will* not *be* unto the residue of this people as in the former days, saith the LORD of hosts [*now, I will be able to bless you*].

12 For **the seed *shall be* prosperous; the vine shall give her fruit, and the ground shall give her increase, and the heavens shall give their dew**; and I will cause the remnant [*the remnant of the Jews of this people to possess all these things*].

13 And it shall come to pass, *that* **as ye were a curse among the heathen, O house of Judah, and house of Israel; so will I save you, and ye shall be a blessing**: fear not, *but* let your hands be strong.

14 For thus saith the LORD of hosts; As **I thought to punish you, when your fathers provoked me to wrath**, saith the LORD of hosts, **and I repented** [*Hebrew, "relented"*] **not** [*the law of justice had to come into play*]:

15 So again have **I thought in these days to do well unto Jerusalem and to the house of Judah: fear ye not.**

16 ¶ **These *are* the things that ye shall do; Speak ye every man the truth** to his neighbour; **execute the judgment of truth and peace in your gates**:

17 And **let none of you imagine evil in your hearts against his**

neighbour; and **love no false oath**: for all these *are things* that I hate, saith the LORD.

18 ¶ And **the word of the LORD of hosts came unto me, saying,**

Next, the Lord speaks of various fasts observed under the law of Moses.

19 Thus saith the LORD of hosts; The fast of the fourth *month,* and the fast of the fifth, and the fast of the seventh, and the fast of the tenth, shall be to the house of Judah joy and gladness [*true righteousness brings joy*], and cheerful feasts; therefore **love the truth and peace.**

The friendship and enjoyment of righteousness together is prophesied in verses 20–21, next.

20 Thus saith the LORD of hosts; *It shall* yet *come to pass,* that there shall come people, and the inhabitants of many cities:

21 And the inhabitants of one *city* shall go to another, saying, Let us go speedily to pray before the LORD, and to seek the LORD of hosts: I will go also.

22 Yea, **many people and strong nations shall come to seek the LORD of hosts in Jerusalem, and to pray before the LORD.**

Verse 23, next, is a delightful prophecy that the Jews will be highly respected in the latter part of the last days.

23 Thus saith the LORD of hosts; **In those days** *it shall come to pass,* that ten **men shall take hold out of all languages of the nations, even shall take hold of the skirt of him that is a Jew, saying, We will go with you: for we have heard** *that* **God** *is* **with you.**

ZECHARIAH 9

Selection: all verses

One of the best-known prophecies about the Savior is found in this chapter. It is found in verse 9 and prophesies that Christ will enter Jerusalem riding on an ass to begin the final week of His mortal mission. It was, among other things, symbolic of His humility and complete submission to the will of the Father as He carried out the Atonement. Verses 1–8 use specific, powerful, heathen cities to represent the enemies of the Lord's work and of the Jews, representing the covenant people of the Lord.

1 THE burden of the word of the LORD in the land of **Hadrach**, and **Damascus** *shall be* the rest thereof: when **the eyes of man, as of all the tribes of Israel,** *shall be* **toward the LORD.**

2 And **Hamath** also shall border thereby; **Tyrus**, and **Zidon**, though it be very wise.

Next, Zechariah describes materialism as a threat to righteousness and a cause of wickedness.

3 And **Tyrus did build herself a strong hold, and heaped up silver**

as the dust, **and fine gold** as the mire of the streets.

4 Behold, **the Lord will cast her out, and he will smite her power in the sea; and she shall be devoured with fire**.

5 **Ashkelon shall** see *it,* and **fear**; **Gaza also** *shall see it,* and be very sorrowful, and **Ekron**; for her expectation **shall be ashamed**; and **the king shall perish from Gaza, and Ashkelon shall not be inhabited**.

6 And **a bastard shall dwell in Ashdod** [*NIV, "Foreigners shall occupy Ashdod"*], and **I will cut off the pride of the Philistines**.

7 And **I will take away his blood out of his mouth, and his abominations from between his teeth** [*the Lord will destroy them because of their wickedness*]: but **he that remaineth, even he,** *shall be* **for our God**, and he shall be as a governor in Judah, and Ekron as a Jebusite.

8 And I will encamp about mine house because of the army, because of him that passeth by, and because of him that returneth: and **no oppressor shall pass through them any more**: for now have I seen with mine eyes.

9 ¶ **Rejoice greatly, O daughter of Zion** [*Jerusalem*]; shout, O daughter of Jerusalem: behold, **thy King cometh unto thee: he** *is* **just, and having salvation** [*He comes, bringing salvation to all who will follow the gospel*]; **lowly** [*humble*], **and riding**

upon an ass, and upon a colt the foal of an ass.

We will mention two things in conjunction with verse 9, above. First, in the Jewish culture of the day, donkeys symbolized submission and humility. Horses symbolized military triumph and victory. The Savior rode into Jerusalem on a donkey, symbolizing His submission to the will of the Father, and to the Jewish leaders and Roman soldiers who would crucify Him.

Second, did you know that the donkey on which Jesus rode into Jerusalem had never been ridden? Mark tells us that the donkey that Jesus rode was "a colt . . . whereon never man sat" (Mark 11:2). This is a reminder of the Savior's power and mastery over all things, including the animal kingdom.

Among the many prophecies of Zechariah, some of the most fascinating deal with the last days. Verses 10–11 are two of them.

10 And **I will cut off the chariot from Ephraim, and the horse from Jerusalem** [*I will protect Ephraim and Judah from their enemies—this would be in the final days of the last days*], and the battle bow shall be cut off: and **he shall speak peace unto the heathen**: and his dominion *shall be* from sea *even* to sea, and from the river *even* to the ends of the earth.

Verses 11–12, next, have much symbolism. Without understanding it, these verses would make no sense at all. With understanding, we see the doctrine of baptism for the dead. Those in the postmortal spirit prison can accept the gospel from the missionaries, but they cannot be baptized themselves because there is no baptism in the "pit," meaning spirit world prison—see 1 Peter 3:19. Therefore, mortals are baptized for them in our temples.

11 As for thee also, **by the blood of thy covenant** [through the Atonement of Jesus Christ] **I have sent forth thy prisoners** [I, the Lord, have brought them out of spirit prison] **out of the pit wherein is no water** [no baptism].

12 ¶ Turn you to the strong hold, **ye prisoners of hope: even to day do I declare** that **I will render double unto thee** [the Lord will greatly bless them];

13 **When I have bent** [humbled] **Judah** for me, **filled the bow with Ephraim** [brought prosperity to Israel], and **raised up thy sons, O Zion, against thy sons, O Greece** [symbolic of the enemies of the Lord's covenant people], and made thee as the sword of a mighty man.

14 And **the LORD shall be seen over them** [the Lord's covenant people], and his arrow shall go forth as the lightning: and the Lord GOD shall blow the trumpet, and shall go with whirlwinds of the south.

15 **The LORD of hosts shall defend them**; and they shall devour, and subdue with sling stones; and they shall drink, *and* make a noise as through wine; and they shall be filled like bowls, *and* as the corners of the altar.

16 And **the LORD their God shall save them** in that day as the flock of his people: for *they shall be as* the stones of a crown, lifted up as an ensign upon his land.

17 For **how great** *is* **his goodness**, and how great *is* his beauty! corn shall make the young men cheerful, and new wine the maids.

ZECHARIAH 10

Selection: all verses

In this chapter, we see more prophecies of the gathering of Israel. Verse 1, next, tells of the blessings of the Lord to covenant Israel in the last days. Jesus Christ is the True Shepherd.

1 ASK ye of the LORD rain in the time of the latter rain; *so* **the LORD shall make bright clouds, and give them showers of rain, to every one grass in the field**.

Verses 2–3 condemn the wicked leaders, idol worship, fortune tellers, and so forth among the Lord's covenant people throughout history by which Israel and Judah have been led astray.

2 For the **idols have spoken vanity**, and the **diviners** [fortune tellers, the occult] **have seen a lie, and have told false dreams**; they comfort in vain: therefore they went their way as a flock, **they were troubled, because** *there was* **no shepherd** [they had no righteous leaders].

3 Mine anger was kindled against the shepherds, and I punished the goats: for the LORD of hosts hath visited his flock the house of Judah, and hath made them as his goodly horse in the battle.

4 Out of him came forth the corner [Jesus Christ is the cornerstone], out of him the nail [He is the nail in the sure place—Isaiah 22:23], out of him the battle bow, out of him every oppressor together [He will ultimately destroy all our enemies].

5 ¶ And they shall be as mighty men, which tread down their enemies in the mire of the streets in the battle: and they shall fight, because the LORD is with them, and the riders on horses shall be confounded.

6 And I will strengthen the house of Judah, and I will save the house of Joseph [Ephraim and Manasseh], and I will bring them again [gather them again] to place them; for I have mercy upon them: and they shall be as though I had not cast them off: for I am the LORD their God, and will hear them.

7 And they of Ephraim shall be like a mighty man, and their heart shall rejoice as through wine: yea, their children shall see it, and be glad; their heart shall rejoice in the LORD.

8 I will hiss [call] for them, and gather them; for I have redeemed them: and they shall increase as they have increased.

9 And I will sow them among the people [send them out to all the world]: and they shall remember [worship] me in far countries; and they shall live with their children, and turn again [return to Me].

The Lord will bring them out of the wickedness of the world.

10 I will bring them again also out of the land of Egypt [often used to represent wickedness in biblical symbolism], and gather them out of Assyria; and I will bring them into the land of Gilead and Lebanon [symbolic of Palestine, the Holy Land]; and place shall not be found for them [they will be gathered in great numbers].

Next, at the Second Coming, the wicked will be destroyed.

11 And he shall pass through the sea with affliction, and shall smite the waves in the sea, and all the deeps of the river shall dry up: and the pride of Assyria shall be brought down, and the sceptre of Egypt shall depart away.

Verse 12 prophesies that during the Millennium almost all people will eventually join the Church and worship the Savior.

12 And I will strengthen them in the LORD; and they shall walk up and down in his name, saith the LORD.

ZECHARIAH 11

Selection: all verses

You most likely remember that Judas Iscariot betrayed the Savior for thirty pieces of silver (Matthew 27:3). In this chapter, you will see the prophecy by Zechariah that this would take place (verse 12). Verses 1–3 foretell the downfall of the political kingdom of Judah.

1 **OPEN thy doors, O Lebanon** [*the land of Israel, Judah*] **that the fire may devour thy cedars** [*your lofty leaders, stately cities, and so forth*].

2 **Howl, fir tree** [*people*]; for the cedar is fallen; because the mighty are spoiled: howl, **O ye oaks of Bashan** [*same as cedars in verse 1, above*]; for the forest of the vintage is come down.

3 ¶ *There is* a voice of the howling of the shepherds [*false prophets, false priests, corrupt leaders*]; for **their glory is spoiled**: a voice of the roaring of young lions; for **the pride of Jordan is spoiled**.

In verses 4–14, we see the Lord punishing the wicked nations who have been punishing His covenant people because of their sins. This is an answer to those who say that they are justified in sinning in order to help the Lord with the need for opposition for the righteous.

4 Thus saith the LORD my God; Feed the flock of the slaughter;

5 Whose possessors slay them, and hold themselves not guilty: and **they** that sell them say, Blessed *be* the LORD; for I am rich: and their own shepherds pity them not.

6 For I will no more pity the inhabitants of the land, saith the LORD: but, lo, **I will deliver the men every one into his neighbour's hand**, and into the hand of his king: and **they shall smite the land, and out of their hand I will not deliver** *them* [*wars with each other are often the way the wicked are punished*].

7 And **I will feed the flock of slaughter** [*the flocks who are destined to be slaughtered are fed and fattened up so the shepherd can make more money*], *even* you, O poor of the flock. And I took unto me two staves; the one I called Beauty, and the other I called Bands; and I fed the flock.

8 **Three shepherds** [*enemies to the flock, symbolic of enemies to the Lord's covenant people*] **also I cut off in one month; and my soul lothed them, and their soul also abhorred me.**

Verse 9, next, refers to wicked people who fight each other and kill each other off.

9 Then said I, I will not feed you: that that dieth, let it die; and that that is to be cut off, let it be cut off; and **let the rest eat every one the flesh of another**.

10 ¶ And **I took my staff,** *even* Beauty, and cut it assunder, **that I might break my covenant which I had made with all the people**

[*I could no longer hold back from punishing the wicked heathen nations*].

11 **And it was broken** in that day: and so the poor of the flock that waited upon me knew that it *was* the word of the LORD.

12 And I said unto them, If ye think good, give *me* my price; and if not, forbear. **So they weighed for my price thirty** *pieces* **of silver.**

13 And the LORD said unto me, Cast it unto the potter: a goodly price that I was prised at of them. **And I took the thirty** *pieces* **of silver, and cast them to the potter** [*the Jewish leaders took the thirty pieces of silver that Judas brought back to them and bought a potters field—Matthew 27:7*] in the house of the LORD.

There is no reliable interpretation for verses 14–16, next.

14 Then I cut asunder mine other staff, *even* Bands, that I might break the brotherhood between Judah and Israel.

15 ¶ And the LORD said unto me, Take unto thee yet the instruments of a foolish shepherd.

16 For, lo, I will raise up a shepherd in the land, *which* shall not visit those that be cut off, neither shall seek the young one, nor heal that that is broken, nor feed that that standeth still: but he shall eat the flesh of the fat, and tear their claws in pieces.

17 **Woe to the idol shepherd that leaveth the flock! the sword** *shall* *be* **upon his arm**, and upon his right eye: his arm shall be clean dried up, and his right eye shall be utterly darkened.

ZECHARIAH 12

Selection: all verses

In this chapter, you will read about the Jews, who, in previous centuries, were walked on by pretty much any nation that wanted to wipe its feet on them. But in the last days, the Jews will be a fearsome people for anyone who tries to attack them. They will be a "cup of trembling" to all potential enemies (verses 2–3). We are seeing this fulfilled in our day.

1 THE **burden of the word of the LORD for Israel**, saith the LORD, which stretcheth forth the heavens, and layeth the foundation of the earth, and formeth the spirit of man within him.

2 **Behold, I will make Jerusalem** [*the Jews*] **a cup of trembling unto all the people round about** [*the Jews will become a fearsome enemy to their adversaries*], **when they shall be in the siege both against Judah** *and* **against Jerusalem** [*when many nations are fighting against the Jews in the Holy Land*].

3 ¶ And in that day will I make Jerusalem a burdensome stone for all people: **all that burden themselves with it shall be cut in pieces**, though all the people of the earth be gathered together against it [*even if every nation*

on earth joins together to fight against the Jews].

4 **In that day, saith the LORD, I will smite every horse** [*military power*] **with astonishment, and his** rider with madness: and I will open mine eyes upon the house of Judah, **and will smite every horse of the people** [*the enemies of Judah*] with blindness.

5 And **the governors of Judah shall say in their heart, The inhabitants of Jerusalem** *shall be* **my strength in the LORD of hosts their God**.

6 ¶ **In that day will I make the governors of Judah like an hearth of fire among the wood, and like a torch of fire in a sheaf** [*like a torch in a bundle of dry grain stalks*]; **and they shall devour all the people round about, on the right hand and on the left: and Jerusalem shall be inhabited again in her own place,** *even* **in Jerusalem.**

7 The **LORD also shall save the tents of Judah** first, that the glory of the house of David and the glory of the inhabitants of Jerusalem do not magnify *themselves* against Judah.

8 **In that day shall the LORD defend the inhabitants of Jerusalem**; and he that is feeble among them at that day shall be as David; and the house of David *shall be* as God, as the angel of the LORD before them.

9 ¶ And it shall come to pass **in that day,** *that* **I will seek to destroy all**

the nations that come against Jerusalem.

10 And **I will pour upon the house of David, and upon the inhabitants of Jerusalem, the spirit of grace** [*help from heaven*] and of supplications: **and they shall look upon me whom they have pierced** [*crucified*], and they shall mourn for him, as one mourneth for *his* only *son,* and shall be in bitterness for him, as one that is in bitterness for *his* firstborn.

In verses 11–14, we see that after the Jews have accepted Jesus Christ as the savior for whom they have waited so long, they will go into deep mourning because of their past behavior toward Him. This will be part of their repentance.

11 **In that day shall there be a great mourning in Jerusalem**, as the mourning of Hadadrimmon in the valley of Megiddon.

12 **And the land shall mourn**, every family apart; the family of the house of David apart, and their wives apart; the family of the house of Nathan apart, and their wives apart;

13 The family of the house of Levi apart, and their wives apart; the family of Shimei apart, and their wives apart;

14 All the families that remain, every family apart, and their wives apart.

ZECHARIAH 13

Selection: all verses

In this chapter, Zechariah is seeing more, in vision, about the last great battle against the Jews, most commonly referred to as the battle of Armageddon (see Revelation 16:16). During the height of this battle, the Savior will appear on the Mount of Olives (see Zechariah 14:4) and save the Jews from further destruction. When they see Him and see the wounds in His hands and realize who He is, they will ask Him what happened to Him. You will read His answer in verse 6.

First, in verse 1, Zechariah prophesies that baptism will be made available to the inhabitants of Jerusalem in the last days for remission of their sins.

1 IN that day there shall be a fountain [*baptism, see footnote 1a in your Bible*] opened to the house of David and to the inhabitants of Jerusalem for sin and for uncleanness.

Verse 2 prophesies that Idol worship and false prophets, etc., will be done away with among the Jews in the Holy Land.

2 ¶ And it shall come to pass **in that day**, saith the LORD of hosts, *that* **I will cut off the names of the idols out of the land**, and they shall no more be remembered: and **also I will cause the prophets and the unclean spirit to pass out of the land.**

Next, In verse 3, Zechariah foresees that if any false prophets attempt to deceive people by pretending to prophesy (or by preaching Informa-

tion they get from Satan), their own family will stop them.

3 And **it shall come to pass,** *that* **when any** [*false prophets*] **shall yet prophesy, then his father and his mother that begat him shall say unto him, Thou shalt not live; for thou speakest lies in the name of the LORD**: and his father and his mother that begat him shall thrust him through when he prophesieth.

4 And **it shall come to pass in that day,** *that* **the prophets** [*false prophets*] **shall be ashamed every one of his vision** [*of his false visions*], when he hath prophesied; **neither shall they wear a rough garment to deceive** [*they won't wear clothing designed to make themselves look like prophets*]:

5 **But he shall say** [*admit*], **I** *am* **no prophet**, I *am* an husbandman [*farmer*]; for man taught me to keep cattle from my youth.

Next, Zechariah jumps to the appearance of the Savior on the Mount of Olives, after it has split open, when the Jews fleeing from the battle of Armageddon have seen Him, including the wounds in His hands from crucifixion, and are asking questions. (By the way, as mentioned previously In this study guide, in the culture of prophets like Zechariah, they don't worry about keeping things In chronological order, and thus they jump around, like Zechariah did here in verse 6.)

6 And *one* **shall say unto him, What** *are* **these wounds in thine hands?** Then **he shall answer,** *Those* **with**

which I was wounded *in* the house of my friends.

In verse 7, among other things, we see an allusion to the crucifixion of the Savior and the scattering of His disciples at that time.

7 ¶ Awake, O sword, against my shepherd, and against the man *that is* my fellow, saith the LORD of hosts: **smite the shepherd, and the sheep shall be scattered**: and I will turn mine hand upon the little ones.

Next, he prophesies that a remnant of the Jews will be left after the devastation and slaughter of the Jews throughout the centuries.

8 And it shall come to pass, *that* in all the land, saith the LORD, **two parts therein** [*remnant of the Jews*], **shall be cut off *and* die; but the third shall be left** therein.

9 And **I will bring the third part through the fire** [*the refiner's fire*], and will refine them as silver is refined, and will try them as gold is tried: **they shall call on my name, and I will hear them: I will say, It** *is* **my people: and they shall say, The LORD** *is* **my God.**

ZECHARIAH 14

Selection: all verses

In this part of his vision, Zechariah sees more of the battle of Armageddon and parts of the Second Coming. You will have to pay close attention to keep these two events separate as you study.

1 BEHOLD, the day of the LORD cometh, and thy spoil shall be divided in the midst of thee [*the wicked will be cut off from the righteous; see D&C 1:14*].

2 For **I will gather all nations against Jerusalem to battle;** and **the city shall be taken,** and **the houses rifled,** and the **women ravished**; and half of the city shall go forth into captivity, and the residue of the people shall not be cut off from the city.

Many people misinterpret verse 2, above, to mean that every nation in the world will be joined together in this battle of Armageddon against Israel. That is not true. While all nations will be involved, and most will be aligned against Israel, some will support Israel. We will quote from the *Old Testament Student Manual*, Enrichment I. "The prophets agreed that all nations should be joined in this alliance In one way or another (see Jeremiah 25:26; Joel 3:1; Zechariah 14:2; Revelation 16:14)."

This prophecy of Zechariah is one of the signs of the times that is yet to be fulfilled. The Savior will appear on the Mount of Olives, and it will split in two.

3 **Then shall the LORD go forth, and fight against those nations**, as when he fought in the day of battle [*the Savior will stop the Invading armies*].

4 ¶ **And his feet shall stand in that day upon the mount of Olives,** which *is* before Jerusalem [*just outside of Jerusalem*] on the east, **and**

the mount of Olives shall cleave [*split*] in the midst thereof toward the east and toward the west, ***and there shall be* a very great valley**; and half of the mountain shall remove toward the north, and half of it toward the south.

We will turn to the Doctrine and Covenants for additional information about this marvelous event.

Doctrine & Covenants 45:48, 51–52

48 And then shall the Lord set his foot upon this mount, and it shall cleave in twain, and the earth shall tremble, and reel to and fro, and the heavens also shall shake.

51 And **then shall the Jews look upon me and say: What are these wounds in thine hands and in thy feet?**

52 **Then shall they know that I am the Lord** [*many of them will be converted*]; for I will say unto them: These wounds are the wounds with which I was wounded in the house of my friends. I am he who was lifted up. I am Jesus that was crucified. I am the Son of God.

Next, the surviving Jews from the battle of Armageddon will flee into the earthquake-created valley, caused by the splitting of the Mount of Olives. It is there that they will see the Savior.

5 And **ye shall flee *to* the valley of the mountains**; for the valley of the mountains shall reach unto Azal: yea, ye shall flee, like as ye fled from before the earthquake in the days of Uzziah king of Judah: and the LORD my God shall come, *and* all the saints with thee.

6 And it shall come to pass in that day, *that* the light shall not be clear, *nor* dark:

7 But it shall be one day which shall be known to the LORD, not day, nor night: but it shall come to pass, *that* at evening time it shall be light.

Verse 8, next, shows us that, at some point in the last days, a large spring of water will flow from Jerusalem, part of the water flowing west and part east, which will heal the waters of the Dead Sea and turn the shores around it into lush foliage. Fish will abound in its waters (Ezekiel 47:6–12).

8 And it shall be in that day, *that* **living waters shall go out from Jerusalem; half of them toward the former sea, and half of them toward the hinder sea**: in summer and in winter shall it be [*it will flow year round*].

Next, more about the Millennium.

9 And **the LORD shall be king over all the earth** [*Christ will rule during the Millennium; see Revelation 17:14*]: in that day shall there be one LORD, and his name one.

10 **All the land shall be turned as a plain** from Geba to Rimmon south of Jerusalem: **and it** [*Jerusalem*] **shall be lifted up, and inhabited in her place**, from Benjamin's gate

unto the place of the first gate, unto the corner gate, and *from* the tower of Hananeel unto the king's winepresses.

11 And *men* shall dwell in it, and **there shall be no more utter destruction; but Jerusalem shall be safely inhabited**.

Next, back to the destruction of the Jews' enemies.

12 ¶ And this shall be the plague wherewith **the LORD will smite all the people that have fought against Jerusalem**; Their flesh shall consume away while they stand upon their feet, and their eyes shall consume away in their holes, and their tongue shall consume away in their mouth [*likely a reference to the destruction of the wicked at the Second Coming*].

Next, in verses 13–15, we see a reference to conditions before the Second Coming.

13 And it shall come to pass in that day, *that* a great tumult from the LORD shall be among them; and **they shall lay hold every one on the hand of his neighbour, and his hand shall rise up against the hand of his neighbour**.

14 And **Judah also shall fight at Jerusalem**; and the wealth of all the heathen round about shall be gathered together, gold, and silver, and apparel, in great abundance.

15 And **so shall be the plague** of the horse, of the mule, of the camel, and of the ass, and of all the beasts that shall be in these tents, as this plague.

Verses 16–19, next, are a bit of a surprise to most people. It is that there will be some wicked people on earth, as time goes on, during the Millennium. Joseph Smith taught this. He said, "There will be wicked men on the earth during the thousand years. The heathen nations who will not come up to worship will be visited with the judgments of God, and must eventually be destroyed from the earth (*Teachings of the Prophet Joseph Smith*, pages 268–69.)

16 ¶ And it shall come to pass, *that* **every one that is left of all the nations** which came against Jerusalem **shall even go up from year to year to worship the King, the LORD of hosts**, and **to keep the feast of tabernacles** [*symbolic of worshiping the Lord*].

17 And it shall be, *that* **whoso will not come up** of *all* the families of the earth unto Jerusalem **to worship the King**, the LORD of hosts, **even upon them shall be no rain**.

18 And **if the family of Egypt** [*symbolic of the wicked*] **go not up, and come not**, that *have* no *rain;* **there shall be the plague, wherewith the LORD will smite the heathen that come not up to keep the feast of tabernacles**.

19 **This shall be the punishment of Egypt, and the punishment of all nations that come not up to keep the feast of tabernacles** [*who refuse*

to worship the Lord during the Millennium].

Finally, In verses 20–21, Zechariah beautifully symbolizes that there will be peace and harmony and worshiping of the Lord even in the little things (like writing "Holiness to the Lord" on the little bells attached to harnesses on horses) during the Millennium.

20 ¶ **In that day** [the Millennium] **shall there be upon the bells of the horses, HOLINESS UNTO THE LORD**; and the pots in the LORD's house shall be like the bowls before the altar.

Have you noticed that our temples have "Holiness to the Lord" written on them?

21 Yea, **every pot in Jerusalem and in Judah shall be holiness unto the LORD of hosts**: and all they that sacrifice shall come and take of them, and seethe [cook] therein: and **in that day there shall be no more the Canaanite in the house of the LORD of hosts** [possibly referring to the time during the Millennium when there will be no apostates, false priests, or even Gentiles in the temple of the Lord like there were before the destruction of the wicked at the Second Coming].

MALACHI

The book of Malachi was given about 430 BC (see Bible Dictionary, under "Malachi"). It is the last book of the Old Testament. After Malachi, there is about a 430 year gap in the Bible, until the New Testament.

The Savior quoted Malachi, chapters 3 and 4, to the Nephites (see 3 Nephi, chapters 24 and 25), and requested that they write them down. Also, Moroni quoted chapters 3 and 4 to Joseph Smith on the evening of September 21, 1823 (Joseph Smith—History 1:36–39).

MALACHI 1

Selection: all verses

In this chapter, Malachi addresses many types of wickedness among the Jews of his day. Among other things,

they were using polluted bread for their offerings and sacrificing animals with blemishes. Remember that in order to truly symbolize the Savior's sacrifice for us, the animals used for sacrifices had to be without blemish. So the Jews were probably saving money by using their blemished animals for sacrifices.

In this chapter, we also see a prophecy that the gospel will spread throughout the Gentiles (non-Jews) in the last days. We are seeing this now.

1 **THE burden** [message of warning] **of the word of the LORD to Israel by Malachi**.

2 **I have loved you, saith the LORD**. Yet ye say, Wherein hast thou loved us? *Was* not Esau Jacob's brother? saith the LORD: **yet I loved Jacob** [the Abrahamic covenant comes

through the descendants of Jacob (the twelves tribes of Israel)],

3 And **I hated Esau** [could not bless Esau and his descendants], and laid his mountains and his heritage waste for the dragons [Jackals] of the wilderness.

4 **Whereas Edom** [the descendants of Esau] **saith, We are impoverished** [we don't get the blessings of Jacob; or, in other words, the blessings of covenant Israel], **but we will return and build the desolate places** [but we will do it on our own terms; we don't want to make and keep covenants with Jehovah]; **thus saith the LORD of hosts, They shall build, but I will throw down** [because they don't make and keep covenants with Me]; and **they shall call them, The border** [the neighboring country] **of wickedness, and, The people against whom the LORD hath indignation for ever.**

5 And **your eyes shall see, and ye shall say, The LORD will be magnified from the border of Israel** [they, Edom, will see that the Lord does bless His covenant people (when they are righteous)].

Next, in verses 6–7, we see that the apostate Jews of Malachi's day were offering polluted bread as part of their offerings under the law of Moses.

6 ¶ A son honoureth *his* father, and a servant his master: if then I *be* a father, where *is* mine honour? and if I *be* a master, where *is* my fear? saith the LORD of hosts unto you, **O priests, that despise my name.**

And ye say, Wherein have we despised thy name?

7 **Ye offer polluted bread upon mine altar**; and ye say, Wherein have we polluted thee? In that ye say, The table of the LORD *is* contemptible.

8 **And if ye offer the blind** [your blind and blemished animals] **for sacrifice, is it not evil? and if ye offer the lame and sick** [animals], *is it* **not evil? offer it now unto thy governor** [why don't you give it to your corrupt leaders instead of Me]; **will he be pleased with thee, or accept thy person** [would he accept your reject animals for a gift]? **saith the LORD of hosts.** [Answer: not a chance!]

9 **And now, I pray you** [false priests], **beseech God that he will be gracious unto us: this hath been by your means** [you corrupt priests and leaders are the ones who have led us away from the Lord]: **will he regard your persons** [will He listen to you]? saith the LORD of hosts.

10 Who *is there* even among you that would shut the doors *for nought*? neither do ye kindle *fire* on mine altar for nought. **I have no pleasure in you, saith the LORD of hosts, neither will I accept an offering at your hand.**

Next, we see a prophecy that the gospel will be taken first to the Gentiles (everyone but the Jews) in the last days. It is called "the times of the Gentiles," and we are in it now. After It goes to the Gentiles, then It will go to the Jews. This is what is meant by the phrase "the first shall be last and the last shall be first" (Matthew 19:30). The Jews got the gospel "first" when the Savior preached it to them and the Gentiles got it "last" after Jesus Instructed His disciples to preach it to them after He was gone. In the last days, the Gentiles get it "first," and, when the time is right, the Jews, in large numbers, will get it "last."

11 For from the rising of the sun even unto the going down of the same **my name** *shall be* **great among the Gentiles**; and in every place incense *shall be* offered unto my name, and a pure offering: for **my name** *shall be* **great among the heathen, saith the LORD of hosts**.

12 ¶ But **ye have profaned it** [*treated the law of sacrifices with disrespect and contempt*], in that ye say, The table of the LORD *is* **polluted**; and the fruit thereof, even his meat, is **contemptible**.

13 **Ye said also, Behold, what a weariness is it!** [*we are getting tired of giving our best for the sacrifices*] and **ye have snuffed** [*thumbed your noses*] **at it, saith the LORD** of hosts; and **ye brought** *that which* **was torn, and the lame, and the sick**; thus ye brought an offering: **should I accept this of your hand?** saith the LORD.

14 But **cursed** *be* **the deceiver, which hath in his flock a male, and voweth, and sacrificeth unto the Lord a corrupt thing: for I** *am* **a great King** [*you would never give your reject animals to your earthly kings*], saith the LORD of hosts, and my name *is* dreadful among the heathen.

MALACHI 2

Selection: all verses

In this chapter the Lord condemns the actions of the wicked priests among the Jews who have led the Lord's covenant people astray.

1 AND now, **O ye priests, this commandment is for you**.

2 **If ye will not hear, and if ye will not lay it to heart, to give glory unto my name, saith the LORD of hosts, I will even send a curse upon you, and I will curse your blessings: yea, I have cursed them already, because ye do not lay** *it* **to heart** [*because you are not keeping My commandments*].

3 Behold, **I will corrupt** [*rebuke*] **your seed, and spread dung upon your faces** [*your corrupt deeds will come back to harm you*], *even* **the dung of your solemn feasts;** and *one* shall take you away with it.

4 And **ye shall know that I have sent this commandment unto you**, that my covenant might be with Levi [*the authorized, true priests of the Aaronic Priesthood*], **saith the LORD of hosts** [*Jehovah*].

5 **My covenant was with him of life and peace;** and **I gave them to him** *for* **the fear** [*because of the respect and honor he gave Me*] **wherewith he feared me, and was afraid before my name.**

6 **The law of truth was in his mouth, and iniquity was not found in his lips: he walked with me in peace and equity, and did turn many away**

from iniquity [*and helped many others keep the commandments*].

7 **For the priest's lips should keep knowledge** [*should teach truth*], and **they should seek the law** at his mouth: for **he** *is* **the messenger of the LORD** of hosts.

8 **But ye are departed out of the way; ye have caused many to stumble at the law; ye have corrupted the covenant of Levi, saith the LORD of hosts**.

9 **Therefore have I also made you contemptible and base before all the people**, according as **ye have not kept my ways, but have been partial in the law** [*you have not treated people equally in your office as priests*].

10 **Have we not all one father? hath not one God created us? why do we deal treacherously every man against his brother, by profaning the covenant of our fathers?**

11 ¶ **Judah** [*the Jews*] **hath dealt treacherously** [*have become wicked*], and **an abomination is committed in Israel** [*all of the Lord's covenant people*] **and in Jerusalem**; for **Judah hath profaned the holiness of the LORD** which he loved, **and hath married the daughter of a strange god** [*have married outside of the covenant people*].

12 **The LORD will cut off the man that doeth this**, the master and the scholar, out of the tabernacles of Jacob, and him that offereth an offering unto the LORD of hosts.

13 **And this have ye done** again, **covering the altar of the LORD with tears, with weeping, and with crying out** [*acting like you are worshiping the Lord*], **insomuch that he regardeth not the offering any more, or receiveth** *it* **with good will at your hand** [*this is why the Lord no longer accepts your offerings*].

14 ¶ **Yet ye say, Wherefore** [*why not*]? **Because the LORD hath been witness between thee and the wife of thy youth** [*the covenant people you used to be*], **against whom thou hast dealt treacherously: yet** *is* **she thy companion, and the wife of thy covenant**.

15 And **did not he make one**? Yet had he the residue of the spirit [*back then, you were keeping the covenants*]. And wherefore one? That he might seek a godly seed. **Therefore take heed to your spirit, and let none deal treacherously against the wife of his youth**.

16 **For the LORD, the God of Israel, saith that he hateth putting away** [*the Lord hates your trying to cover up your wickedness with pretended righteousness*]: for one covereth violence with his garment, saith the LORD of hosts: therefore **take heed to your spirit, that ye deal not treacherously**.

17 ¶ **Ye have wearied the LORD with your words.** Yet ye say, Wherein have we wearied him? When **ye say, Every one that doeth evil is good in the sight of the LORD, and he delighteth in them;** or, Where is the God of judgment?

MALACHI 3

Selection: all verses

More prophecies of the future, especially the last days and the Second Coming are found in this chapter.

1 BEHOLD, I will send my messenger [John the Baptist in the meridian of time, and Joseph Smith in the last days], and he shall prepare the way before me: and the Lord, whom ye seek, shall suddenly come to his temple [the Second Coming], even the messenger of the covenant [Christ], whom ye delight in: behold, he shall come, saith the LORD of hosts."

In this chapter, a very important question is asked in two different ways. It deals with the Second Coming. The answer is vital to us.

2 But who may abide the day of his coming [who will survive the Second Coming]? and who shall stand when he appeareth? for he is like a refiner's fire, and like fullers' soap [powerful soap; in other words, He will cleanse the earth when He comes again]:

The answer to the question is those whose lifestyles would fit in with the standards of terrestrial glory (Doctrine & Covenants 76:71–79) or with the standards of celestial glory (Doctrine & Covenants 76:50–53). All others will be burned by the Savior's glory when He comes (see 2 Nephi 12:10).

3 And he [Jesus Christ] shall sit as a refiner and purifer of silver: and he shall purify the sons of Levi [righteous, worthy priesthood holders in our

day], and purge them as gold and silver, that they may offer unto the LORD an offering in righteousness.

4 Then [in the last days, after the restoration of the gospel and during the Millennium] shall the offering of Judah and Jerusalem be pleasant unto the LORD, as in the days of old, and as in former years.

5 And I will come near to you to judgment [destruction of the wicked at the Second Coming]; and I will be a swift witness against the sorcerers, and against the adulterers, and against false swearers, and against those that oppress the hireling in his wages, the widow, and the fatherless, and that turn aside the stranger from his right, and fear not me, saith the LORD of hosts.

6 For I am the LORD, I change not; therefore ye sons of Jacob [those who are now righteous] are not consumed.

7 ¶ Even from the days of your fathers ye [unrighteous priests and covenant people in past times] are gone away from mine ordinances, and have not kept them. Return unto me [please repent], and I will return unto you, saith the LORD of hosts. But ye said, Wherein shall we return [what do we need to do to repent]?

Next, we see the importance of paying our tithing. First, in verses 8–9, the Lord's covenant people are severely chastised for not paying tithing. Then, in a marvelous teaching approach (verses 10–12), we are all reminded of the tender blessings that attend honest and willing payment of tithing.

8 ¶ Will a man rob God? Yet ye have robbed me. But ye say, Wherein have we robbed thee? In tithes and offerings.

9 Ye *are* cursed with a curse: for ye have robbed me, *even* this whole nation.

10 Bring ye all the tithes into the storehouse, that there may be meat [*food for the poor*] in mine house, and prove [*test*] me now herewith, saith the LORD of hosts, if I will not open you the windows of heaven, and pour you out a blessing, that *there shall* not *be room* enough *to receive it.*

11 And I will rebuke the devourer for your sakes, and he shall not destroy the fruits of your ground; neither shall your vine cast her fruit before the time in the field, saith the LORD of hosts.

12 And all nations shall call you blessed: for ye shall be a delight-some land, saith the LORD of hosts.

13 ¶ Your words have been stout against me, saith the LORD. Yet ye say, What have we spoken so *much* against thee?

14 Ye have said, It *is* vain [*useless*] to serve God: and what profit *is it* that we have kept his ordinance, and that we have walked mournfully before the LORD of hosts?

15 And now we call the proud happy; yea, they that work wickedness are set up [*prosper*]; yea, *they that* tempt God are even delivered [*nothing bad happens to them when they are wicked*].

16 ¶ Then they that feared the LORD spake often one to another: and the LORD hearkened, and heard *it*, and a book of remembrance was written before him for them that feared the LORD, and that thought upon his name.

17 And they shall be mine, saith the LORD of hosts, in that day when I make up my jewels; and I will spare them, as a man spareth his own son that serveth him.

18 Then shall ye return, and discern between the righteous and the wicked, between him that serveth God and him that serveth him not.

MALACHI 4

Selection: all verses

One of the most significant events in the last days is the coming of Elijah the prophet to the Kirtland Temple on April 3, 1836. He there restored the keys of sealing and work for the dead to Joseph Smith and Oliver Cowdery.

First, in verse 1, we find a direct and dire warning to the wicked who are on the earth at the time of the Second Coming.

1 For, behold, the day cometh [*the Second Coming*], that shall burn as

an oven; and **all the proud**, yea, **and all that do wickedly, shall be stubble** [*dried grain stalks, which burn easily*]: and **the day that cometh shall burn them up**, saith the LORD of hosts, that **it shall leave them neither root nor branch** [*in effect, they will not have families, or "family trees," with roots and branches, in the next life; in other words, they will not inherit exaltation in the celestial kingdom where the family unit will continue—see Doctrine & Covenants 132:19–20*].

Next, the Lord tells us what will happen to the righteous at His coming.

2 ¶ **But unto you that fear** [*respect and honor*] **my name shall the Sun of righteousness** [*"Son of Righteousness"—see 3 Nephi 25:2*] **arise with healing in his wings** [*you will be blessed by the full powers of the Atonement*]; and ye shall go forth, and grow up as calves of the stall [*you will be protected from evil just as calves are protected from the elements by their stalls in the barn*].

3 **And ye shall tread down the wicked** [*you will triumph over all your former enemies, physical and spiritual*]; for **they shall be ashes under the soles of your feet** in the day that I shall do *this*, saith the LORD of hosts.

4 ¶ **Remember ye** [*keep, obey*] **the law of Moses my servant**, which I commanded unto him in Horeb [*another name for Sinai—see Bible Dictionary, under "Horeb"*] for all Israel, *with* the statutes and judgments.

Verses 5–6, next, are perhaps some of the most meaningful verses in the scriptures for Latter-day Saints because Elijah restored the keys of sealing families together when he came to Joseph Smith and Oliver Cowdery in the Kirtland Temple—see Doctrine & Covenants 110:13–16. These keys are the basis for the tremendous family history and temple work of the Church.

5 ¶ Behold, **I will send you Elijah the prophet before the coming of the great and dreadful day of the LORD** [*before the Second Coming*]:

6 **And he shall turn the heart of the fathers to the children, and the heart of the children to their fathers** [*families will desire to be sealed together for time and all eternity; also, people's hearts will yearn to seek out their ancestors in order to seal them to their families*], **lest I come and smite the earth with a curse** [*lest the main purpose of the earth, to bring exaltation to our Father's children, not be fulfilled*].

SOURCES

Book of Mormon Student Manual. Salt Lake City: The Church of Jesus Christ of Latter-day Saints, 1982.

Bryant, T. Alton. *The New Compact Bible Dictionary.* Grand Rapids, Mich.: Zondervan, 1981.

Clark, James R., comp. *Messages of the First Presidency of The Church of Jesus Christ of Latter-day Saints.* 6 vols. Salt Lake City: Bookcraft, 1965–75.

Conference Reports of The Church of Jesus Christ of Latter-day Saints. Salt Lake City: The Church of Jesus Christ of Latter-day Saints, 1898 to present.

Doctrines of the Gospel Student Manual. Salt Lake City: The Church of Jesus Christ of Latter-day Saints (Institutes of Religion), 2000.

Dummelow, J. R. *A Commentary on the Holy Bible.* New York: Macmillan, 1937.

Encyclopedia of Mormonism. Edited by Daniel H. Ludlow. 5 vols. New York: Macmillan, 1992.

German Bible, The Martin Luther Edition of. Wien (Vienna), Austria, 1960.

Hymns of The Church of Jesus Christ of Latter-day Saints. Salt Lake City: The Church of Jesus Christ of Latter-day Saints, 1985.

NIV. International Bible Society. *The Holy Bible: New International Version (NIV).* Grand Rapids, Mich.: Zondervan, 1984.

Josephus. *Antiquities of the Jews.* Philadelphia: John C. Winston Co., n.d.

Journal of Discourses. 26 vols. London: Latter-day Saints' Book Depot, 1854–86.

Kiel, C. F., and F. Delitzsch. *Commentary on the Old Testament.* 10 vols. Grand Rapids, Mich.: William B. Eerdmans Publishing, 1991.

Kimball, Spencer W. *Faith Precedes the Miracle.* Salt Lake City: Deseret Book, 1972.

Ludlow, Victor L. Isaiah: Prophet, Seer, and Poet. Salt Lake City: Deseret Book, 1982.

Maxwell, Neal A. *Deposition of a Disciple.* Salt Lake City: Deseret Book, 1976.

McConkie, Bruce R. *A New Witness for the Articles of Faith.* Salt Lake City: Deseret Book, 1985.

————. Doctrinal New Testament Commentary. 3 vols. Salt Lake City: Deseret Book, 1972.

————. *Mormon Doctrine.* 2d ed. Salt Lake City: Bookcraft, 1966.

————. *The Millennial Messiah.* Salt Lake City: Deseret Book, 1982.

————. *The Promised Messiah—The First Coming of Christ.* Salt Lake City: Deseret Book, 1978.

Nyman, Monte S. *Great Are the Words of Isaiah.* Salt Lake City: Bookcraft, 1980.

Ogden, Kelly D., and Andrew C. Skinner. *Verse by Verse—The Old Testament*, Volume 2, 1 Kings through Malachi. Salt Lake City, Deseret Book, 2013.

Old Testament Gospel Doctrine Teacher's Manual. Salt Lake City: The Church of Jesus Christ of Latter-day Saints (Institutes of Religion), 2001.

Old Testament Student Manual: Genesis–2 Samuel. Salt Lake City: The Church of Jesus Christ of Latter-day Saints (Institutes of Religion), 1981.

Old Testament Student Manual, I Kings–Malachi (Religion 302). Salt Lake City: The Church of Jesus Christ of Latter-day Saints, 1981.

Petersen, Mark E. *Moses, Man of Miracles.* Salt Lake City: Deseret Book, 1977.

Rasmussen, Ellis T. *An Introduction to the Old Testament and its Teachings.* 2d ed. 2 vols. Provo, Utah: BYU Press, 1972–74.

———. *A Latter-day Saint Commentary on the Old Testament.* Salt Lake City: Deseret Book, 1993.

Richards, LeGrand. *Israel! Do You Know?* Salt Lake City: Deseret Book, 1954.

Smith, Joseph. *History of The Church of Jesus Christ of Latter-day Saints.* Edited by B. H. Roberts. 2d ed. rev., 7 vols. Salt Lake City: The Church of Jesus Christ of Latter-day Saints, 1932–1951.

———. Joseph Smith's "New Translation" of the Bible. Independence, Missouri: Herald Publishing House, 1970.

———. *Teachings of the Prophet Joseph Smith.* Selected by Joseph Fielding Smith. Salt Lake City: Deseret Book, 1977.

NOTES

NOTES

ABOUT THE AUTHOR

David J. Ridges taught for the Church Educational System for thirty-five years and taught for several years at BYU Campus Education Week. He taught adult religion classes and Know Your Religion classes for BYU Continuing Education for many years. He has also served as a curriculum writer for Sunday School, seminary, and institute of religion manuals.

He has served in many callings in the Church, including Gospel Doctrine teacher, bishop, stake president, and patriarch. He and Sister Ridges have served two full-time CES missions together. They are the parents of six children and grandparents of sixteen grandchildren so far. They make their home in Springville, Utah.

Scan to visit

www.davidjridges.com